Building New Currency Unions

Building New Currency Unions

Building New Currency Unions:
Lessons from the European Monetary Union

With a chapter on The Digital Euro

Russell Krueger

2022

ISBN: 978-0-578-26686-2

Dedications

To Sherlene, Elise, and Anna

For their support throughout the project and keeping everything in proper perspective

and thanks to…

the many talented and dedicated people who put together the European Monetary Union

Special Thanks…

are owed to Sherlene Lum, Gregg Forte, and Andy Fegan for their careful reading of the text and making many suggestions and improvements. We have all benefitted from their work.

Preface – Monetary Unions in 20-20 Hindsight

This volume is a history of the creation of the European Monetary Union (EMU). It looks at the inspirations and political forces that propelled Europe to create an entirely new model of central banking. Politicians and technicians put together a complex multi-country organization involving many coordinated actions and institutions.

This book draws a number of conclusions about how the European experience could guide similar experiments elsewhere in the world. After the EMU was launched, other regions enthusiastically investigated whether they could also create monetary unions. In hindsight, many judgements can be made about the original process and the current state of affairs. Among the milestones;

- The EMU is an undoubted success and stands one of the two most important central banking institutions in the world. The union and the euro have global importance.
- The EMU was built on deep financial, policy, and staff resources of the European central banks - resources in short supply in many other regions of the world.
- The EMU has survived multiple crises largely unforeseen when it was created, evolving significantly to deal with financial crises, political tensions, fiscal distress, and market innovations.
- The European Central Bank (ECB) led in introducing best international financial and disclosure standards and practices. (Likewise, other regional financial institutions have promoted introduction of such standards.)
- The original ECB architecture left responsibility for prudential supervision of financial institutions with national authorities, which proved unworkable during financial crises and led to numerous significant alterations of the model.
- The Global Financial Crisis was a major reformative event that .....
  - Pushed financial stability to the forefront of priorities – at the ECB, the financial stability wing is now larger than the monetary policy wing, and ....
  - Led to aggressive new policy actions – often coordinated with international organizations and other central banks – in directions never before envisioned.
- When the Covid19 financial crisis hit, the Eurosystem quickly and effectively applied the toolkit built during the GFC with a willingness to do whatever was necessary to address the unparalleled financial and economic threats.
- The lack of a fiscal mechanism in the original EMU architecture would prove to be a continuing headache. New fiscal actions to address national fiscal crises and provide fiscal support during the Covid19 crisis needed to be coordinated with monetary policy.
- Outside Europe, existing monetary unions and nascent monetary and economic union initiatives are playing important policy, supervisory, and developmental roles within their respective regions and have seats at the table in many contexts.
- Finally, the expected introduction of a digital euro as a central bank digital currency (CBDC) will change European monetary and financial soundness conditions in many ways.

Looking forward globally, the current covid crisis and subsequent inflationary spike are just the start of at least a decade of economic, financial, and social turmoil with unemployment, massive structural change, and developmental challenges. This is not a time for regional financial institutions to be timid, but to step forward into leadership positions and innovate within the bounds of their mandates. The challenges are large and when people look back a decade or two in the future, it is to be hoped that the institutions will have shown they were up to the challenges and helped build strong foundations for recovery, financial stability, and growth.

As a volume on history, readers are also directed to excellent studies of the period by some of the founders of the system such as Hanspeter Scheller (2006), Otmar Issing (2008), or Peter Bull (2004). Readers should always reference the excellent products of the ECB itself, which has led the way in transparency regarding central bank matters. And we should also look forward to guidance within any future volumes by Erwin Nierop (when his schedule permits) – a former ECB insider and the leading global practitioner in monetary integration projects over the past two decades (and also my mentor).

This volume is now offered to help document part of the history of the EMU and perhaps provide some insights that might help move regional financial initiatives forward. Best of luck to all facing the challenges ahead!

Background

I was part of a three person IMF team led by Edgar Ayales along with Jaroslav Kucera (and sometimes Randall Merris and others) that investigated how the new European monetary statistics program would affect the IMF's monetary statistics. In Frankfurt and throughout Europe we found extraordinary teams working to exhaustion and beyond, dedicated to putting together what they knew would be revolutionary. The head of the union's statistics section, Peter Bull, welcomed our team as providing an opportunity for a rigorous review of the planned system by qualified outsiders. He allowed us to see how statistical arrangements were integrated into the core functions of the union. The collaboration led to complete overhaul of the IMF's monetary statistics for all EMU countries and a new set of statistics for the union as a whole.

Later, during a year-long sabbatical to study the overall building of the EMU, I worked closely with Erwin Nierop of the ECB legal department, who educated me about the legal foundations and structure of the union and the complex interactions of the many parts of a union program. The legal perspectives he provided synergistically melded with the statistical perspective into a fuller understanding of the union-building process.

Later, I was a visiting scholar at the Asian Bank Development Institute in Tokyo during its investigations into how the European experience could inform financial integration projects in Asia – an experience that opened perspectives on other currency union projects. Later, I was part of a joint ECB/IMF conference in Frankfurt with existing and possible new currency unions on practical guidance that could be offered to them.

I was fortunate – as a privileged observer and sometime participant – to be involved in the EMU and several other regional initiatives. The greatest privilege was to have met and worked alongside many dedicated and inventive pioneers, many of whom are still friends. Some still lead within their regions or make continuing intellectual contributions. My thanks to all – and to many who I will thank personally.

Note to union-builders

Much is expected of those laboring to create or strengthen monetary unions. This volume is intended to help by providing union builders an overview of the broad scope of a regional monetary project, specific tasks ahead and how they interact, and examples of how the issues were addressed in Europe. Each region must filter the information to address its particular needs, resources, and political and social priorities.

As this volume will demonstrate, most regions face greater challenges creating their unions than experienced in Europe. A legitimate alternative to full monetary union is to map out an evolutionary path toward union. In several regions, this process is already partially underway with financial sector integration projects gradually being implemented based on their priorities and feasibility. Many new standards, financial practices, and technologies could be the primary focus of early efforts with limited resources, but should be integrated within a broad vision of how they ultimately can all fit together to create a complete regional entity. Polishing that vision, building trust and cooperative structures, participating in financial sector policy and legislative debates, and influencing outcomes are all part of the process. The union-builders' technical and political skills will be critical in achieving the end result.

Russell Krueger
May 2022

Names and Acronyms

It is hopelessly confusing – don't feel bad – it is impossible to keep all the names, acronyms, and entities straight. The Europeans themselves acknowledge this.

It seems to be regular practice to create new institutions, laws, directives, programs, etc. that the public can scarcely follow. Moreover, they can evolve over time – ERM becomes ERM II.

The specific titles and descriptions in this volume are unimportant to many future regional financial integration and currency union projects. What is important is to realize that the European solutions address important financial integration features or problems and thus can provide insights that might guide local initiatives. The Europeans have created one model, which despite being very complex and confusing has proven successful – the model cannot be ignored and can provide lessons for others. Learning those lessons and applying them to diverse local settings and problems will not be easy, but this volume views the process as part of the evolution of the international financial system in the XXIst Century.

Acronym	Description
AAOIFI	Accounting and Auditing Organization of Islamic Financial Institutions
ACH	Automated Clearing House
ACU	Asian Currency Unit
ADB	African Development Bank
AICU	Asian Infrastructure Currency Unit
AML	Anti-Money Laundering
ASEAN	Association of South East Asian Nations
ATM	Automated Teller Machines
BCBS	Basel Committee for Banking Supervision
BIC	Bank Identification Code
BIS	Bank for International Settlements
BNWG	Banknote Working Group
BRF	Banknote Recycling Framework
BSC	Banking Supervision Committee
CABEI	Central American Bank for Economic Integration
CAC	Counterfeit Analysis Center
CAMC	Central American Monetary Council
Caricom	Caribbean Community
CBCDG	Central Bank Counterfeit Deterence Group
CBDC	Central Bank Digital Currency
CCBM	Correspondent Central Banking Model
CCEG	Counterfeit Coin Experts Group
CCP	Central Counterparty Facilities
CD	Certificate of Deposit
CDS	Credit Default Swap
CEMAC	Economic and Monetary Community of Central Africa
CFA	Communauté Financière Africaine/African Financial Community
CFT	Countering Financing of Terrorism
CGER	Consultive Group on Exchange Rates
CLS	Continuous Linked Settlement
CMA	Common Monetary Area
CMFB	Committee on Monetary, Financial, and Balance of Payment Statistics
CMI	Chiang Mai Initiative
CMIM	Chiang Mai Initiative Multilateralized
COG	Committee of Governors

CPSS	Committee on Payments and Settlement Systems
CRT	Credit Risk Transfer
CSD	Central Securities Depositories
DCash	ECCU's CBDC
DCS	Depository Corporations Survey
DeFi	Decentralized Finance
DGD	Deposit Guarantee Directive
DLT	Distributed Ledger Technology
DM	Deutsche Mark
DORA	Digital Operational Resilience Act
D-SIB	Domestic - Systemically Important Bank
DvP	Delivery versus Payment
EAC	East African Community
EBA	1. ECU Banking Association; later Euro Banking Association
EBA	2. European Banking Authority
EC	European Community
EC$	ECCU Dollar
ECB	European Central Bank
ECCB	Eastern Caribbean Central Bank
ECCU	Eastern Caribbean Currency Union
ECI	Extended Custodial Inventory
ECJ	European Court of Justice
e-CNY	Electronic Chinese Yuan
ECOFIN	Economic and Financial Committee
ECU	European Currency Unit
EDP	Excessive Deficit Procedure
EEA	European Economic Area
EEC	European Economic Community
EFC	Economic and Financial Committee
EFSB	European Financial Stability Board
EFSF	European Financial Stability Facility
EIOPA	European Insurance and Occupational Pensions Authority
ELMI	Electronic Money Institutions
ELRIC	**E**xternal audit mechanism, **L**egal structure and independence, financial **R**eporting, **I**nternal audit, and internal **C**ontrols
EMDE	Emerging Market and Developing Economies
EMI	European Monetary Institute
EMS	European Monetary System
EMU	European Monetary Union
EREER	Equilibrium Real Effective Exchange Rate6.
ERER	Equilibrium Real Exchange Rate
ERM	Exchange Rate Mechanism
ERMII	Exchange Rate Mechanism II
ES2	Europa Series 2 euro banknotes
ESA	1. European Supervisory Authorities
ESA	2. European System of Accounts
ESCB	European System of Central Banks
ESFS	European System of Financial Supervision
ESMA	European Securities and Market Authority
ESRB	European Systemic Risk Board
ESS	1. European Supervisory System
ESS	2. Eurosystem Strategic Stock

EU	European Union
EUA	European Unit of Account
Euro1	Bank-sponsored euro settlement system
EWS	Early Warning System
FAS	Financial Access Survey
FATF	Financial Action Task Force
FFIEC	Federal Financial Institutions Examination Council
FSA	Financial Stability Assessments
FSAP	Financial Soundness Assessment Program
FSB	Financial Stability Board
FSF	Financial Stability Forum
GCC	Gulf Cooperation Council
GCC-Stat	Gulf Cooperation Council Statistical Office
GDP	Gross Domestic Product
GFC	Global Financial Crisis
GFSR	Global Financial Stability Review
G-SIB	Global Systemically Important Bank
GSP	Growth and Stability Pact
HCI	Harmonized Competitiveness Indices
HICP	Harmonized Index of Consumer Prices
IADI	International Association of Deposit Insurers
IAIS	International Association of Insurance Supervisors
IAS	International Accounting Standards
IASB	International Accounting Standards Board
ICD	Investor Compensation Directive
ICP	International Comparison Project
ICT	Information and Communications Technology
IFAC	International Financial Auditing Council
IFI	Islamic Financial Institution
IFRS	International Financial Reporting Standards
IFSB	Islamic Financial Services Board
IFTS	Interbank Funds Transfer System
IILM	International Islamic Liquidity Mechanism
IMF	International Monetary Fund
IO	International Organization
IOSCO	International Organization of Securities Commissions
ISA	International Standard on Auditing
KKC	Krueger/Kamar/Carlotti
KYC	Know Your Customer
LOLR	Lender of Last Resort
M1	Narrow money
M2	M1 plus short- or medium-term instruments
M3	Broad measure of money – M2 plus long-term instruments
m-CBDC	Multi-CBDC
MESA	Mutual ECU Settlement Accounts
MFI	Monetary Financial Institutions
MiCA	Markets in CryptoAssets
MiFID	Markets in Financial Instruments Directive
MOU	Memorandum of Understanding
MUFA	Monetary Union Financial Accounts
MUMS	Monetary Union Member States
NBFI	Nonbank Financial Institution

NCB	National Central Banks
NER	Nominal Exchange Rate
NFA	Net Foreign Assets
NPISH	NonProfit Institutions Serving Households
OCA	Optimum Currency Area
OECD	Organization for Economic Cooperation and Development
OMFI	Other Monetary Financial Institutions
OTC	Over-the-Counter Securities or Derivatives
PEACH	Pan-European Automated Clearing House
PEPP	Pandemic Emergency Purchase Programme
PPP	Purchasing Power Parity
PRGF	IMF Poverty Reduction and Growth Facility
PSIFI	Prudential and Structural Indicators for Islamic Financial Institutions
PSSC	Payment and Settlement Systems Committee
PvP	Payment versus Payment
QR	Quick Response [Code]
RBW	Registered-Based Wallet
REER	Real Effective Exchange Rate
ROSC	Reports on Observance of Standards and Codes
RTGS	Real-time Gross Settlement
SADC	South African Development Community
SDMX	Statistical Data and Metadata Exchange
SDR	"Special Drawing Right"
SEPA	Single Euro Payment Area
SFD	Settlement Finality Directive
SGP	Stability and Growth Pact
SIPS	Systemically Important Payments Systems
SNA	System of National Accounts
SOV	Marshall Islands' CBDC
SPV	Special Purpose Vehicle
SSS	Securities Settlement System
STC	Statistics Committee
STEP2	Euro Banking Association sponsored PEACH
SWF	Sovereign Wealth Funds
SWIFT	Society for Worldwide Interbank Financial Telecommunication
T2S	TARGET2-Securities
TARGET	**T**rans-European **A**utomated **R**eal-time **G**ross settlement **E**xpress **T**ransfer System
TARGET2	TARGET successor introduced in 2008
TIPS	TARGET Instant Payments System
UAE	United Arab Emirates
UNCTAD	U.N. Conference on Trade and Development
VBW	Value-Based Wallet
VSCA	Voluntary Specific Cooperation Agreement
VSFM	Very Short Financing Mechanism
WAEMU	West African Economic and Monetary Union
WAMZ	West African Monetary Zone
WEO	World Economic Outlook
WGLE	Working Group of Legal Experts
WGS	Working Group on Statistics
XBRL	Extensible Bank Reporting Language

Corrections and updates.

This volume was put together in stages – in the field, during sabbatical research, and with continuing updating to reflect significant changes in policy, institutions, and economic events. As work progressed, it became apparent that new material needed to be introduced to reflect new conditions – and especially the expected introduction of a digital euro (which has earned the honor of a separate chapter).

Also, a broad range of material is covered – further apologies for gaps in coverage or misinterpretations about happenings in Europe or other regions. Important events in the regions have certainly been missed. Anything in this volume might be overtaken by new events and policies in a broad and rapidly evolving field – readers must be aware of the possibilities.

On many topics, the following pages will be read by some far more experienced or expert than I am. I am happy to receive comments, corrections, updates, hints, or suggestions. Any revision of this volume can only benefit from readers' contributions. Comments are welcome at kruegerstatistics@gmail.com. Please be explicit if anything should be treated as sensitive or confidential.

But better than focusing on this volume, readers' experience and expertise can make important contributions to future work on currency unions and other regional financial integration projects. Thank you in advance for considering how you might contribute to this global phenomenon.

Topical Guidance for Readers

Few readers will read this volume front to back. The table below highlights chapters for readers interested in several major topics. Key chapters are in **bold**.

Topic	Chapter
History of the Euroarea	**1, 2, 3**
Future of global financial system	**1, 19**, 7, 9D
Euroarea policy framework	**4, 5, 6, 7**
Optimum currency areas; Convergence criteria	***4**, 12*
Monetary policy	***5***
Exchange rate; International reserves	***6, 9***
Macroeconomic policy; Growth and Stability Pact	*7*
International economic relations of currency unions	**8**, 16
Financial integration	**10**
Financial crises	7, 13
Currency	**3, 9, 9D**, 18
Currency baskets	***3***
Currency (Cash and coins)	***9, 9D**, 3, 18*
Central Bank Digital Currency (CBDC); Cryptoassets	***9D**, 18*
Currency Union Operations	**11, 12, 13, 14, 15, 16, 17**
Payments systems	***11, 9D***
Financial supervision	***13***
Statistics	***12***
Accounting and finances	***14, 15**, 9*
Legal framework	***16**, 3, 9, 11*
Communications	***17***
Blueprints for future unions; Partial regional financial integration	**1, 19**, 3, 11, 16
Transition into a new union	**9, 18, 19**

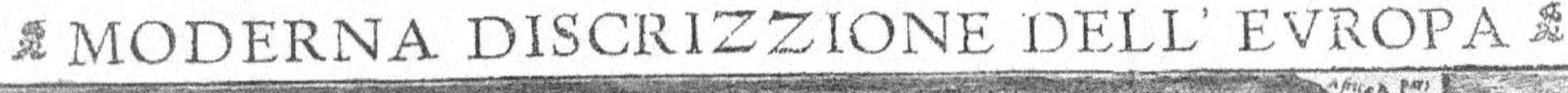

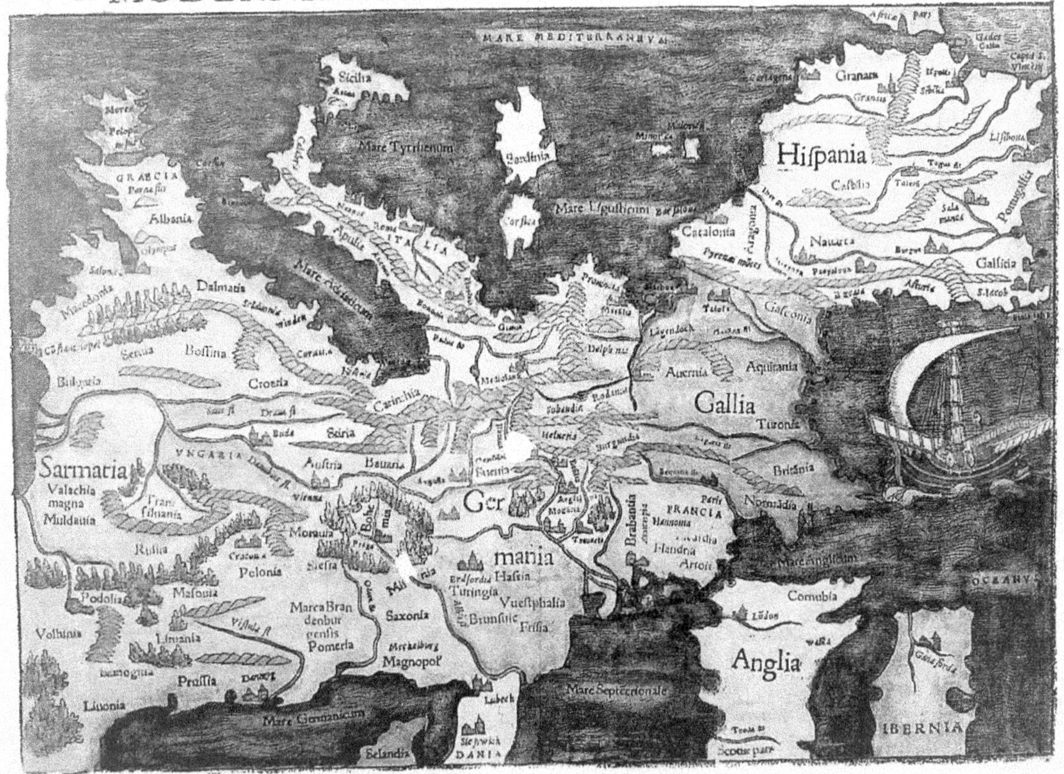

SEBASTIAN MÜNSTER 1544

Black and white image from ECB Holiday Card sent to author

Color original is in ECB Art Collection

Woodcutting. First modern map of the European continent. Hand-colored versions of this map were widely circulated throughout Europe.

BUILDING NEW CURRENCY UNIONS: LESSONS FROM THE EUROPEAN MONETARY UNION

RUSSELL KRUEGER

CHAPTERS

BUILDING NEW CURRENCY UNIONS: LESSONS FROM THE EUROPEAN MONETARY UNION

CHAPTER 1 – UNIONS: A GLOBAL MOVEMENT

An introduction to past, present, and possible future currency unions. Variations in types of unions and near unions. Descriptions of key decisions that all unions must make.

A. Introduction

1.1. This study examines the process of building currency unions. The successful launch of the euro trigger[1]ed global interest in currency unions. At the time of writing in 2021, about half of the countries of the world are in a currency union, or are building new unions. And in regions where an union is not an official goal, many countries act through regional surveillance schemes that have some of the features and benefits of an union without actually creating one. Currency unions are now at the very heart of the global monetary system, and will become even more important over time.

1.2. This study examines the experience of the European Monetary Union (EMU, or Euroarea) to draw lessons for use in building unions in other regions. Every union being planned will look to the experiences in Europe for guidance. It will be shown that the EMU was created at the end of a long and challenging process, despite having the large benefits of high incomes, well-developed financial systems, and an overarching legal framework. Most other regions lack such advantages and face greater challenges than Europe in building their unions. On the other hand, making changes to simpler and less sophisticated systems might prove more direct than was the case in Europe, where the process was quite complex.

1.3. Each union is different. Every union will have different histories, institutions, policy perspectives, and political paths to follow. Rarely can the lessons of one union be replanted without change in other unions.

1.4. With considerations such as those above, this study examines the lessons of the EMU in terms of the broad and flexible principles that can be applied in other regions customized to local history, institutions, and goals. Planners for future unions will always need to review whether each principle applies, and if so, how it should be implemented given the specific institutions, goals, markets, and politics of their specific union.

1.5. In each major task area of building a union, a broad timeline is drawn to demonstrate the sequencing of tasks and the time that must be allotted. This study concludes that the minimum time needed to create a successful union often is longer than stated in official pronouncements about the start of an union.

1.6. Although flexibility in arrangements exists to adapt future unions to local situations, union planners should not assume that everything is flexible and that a local adaptation will always be possible. Certain tasks must be accomplished, often in a certain sequence or by a certain time. For example, the security features of the new currency must be selected years before the union starts so that currency can be printed, banks and vendors can adjust their machines, machines can be physically tested with currency samples, and a public campaign can explain the features of the currency. This is a long process and steps cannot be skipped. Union planners must ensure that all minimum requirements are successfully achieved, in proper order, and coordinated between countries.

1.7. There are many individual tasks involved in creating a union – well over one hundred. There will be many decision points where this study cannot – *and should not* – make the decisions for the union planners. Will monetary policy follow an inflation targeting regime, or an exchange rate peg? Will monetary policy operations be centralized or handled at the national level? Will the union central bank be responsible for bank supervision? Such decisions, and many others, can only be decided locally in light of local conditions and goals, but always with cognizance of international standards and best practices. This study can describe some of the consequences of each branch of a decision, including how in some cases other decisions might be affected, but the responsibility must rest with local authorities.

1.8. The ability to make such decisions will be an important test of whether the planned union will ultimately succeed. The process can be long and complex, with multiple tasks that must function well individually and in conjunction with other tasks. Decisions must be effectively enacted, and impacts on other task areas need to be worked out. This requires extensive oversight and coordination. The skills learned in this process of building the union will greatly benefit the union in its operations, economic oversight, policy making, dialog with member countries and the public, and interactions with global financial markets and international financial institutions.

1.9. A final point is that failure is possible. It took decades of effort, including notable failures, in Europe before the successful creation of the EMU. The reasons for failure might not be local – for example, in Europe the first oil price crisis contributed heavily to the failure of an earlier union scheme, the "Werner Plan". But failure can also stem locally from factors such as lack of political commitment, poor planning, lack of coordination between countries, etc. *The public and private costs and political consequences of attempting to create an union and failing can be severe.* This study seeks to contribute information that will allow planners the best realistic prospects of succeeding in creating an union.

1.10. But – equally importantly – *conditions in some regions might not be suitable to create an union and therefore it should not be pursued.* All are better off bolstering individual countries with strong and effective monetary and external economic policies instead of constructing a poorly designed union that ineffectively reflects the economic conditions of its member countries, has weak institutions, and fails to build a credible policy regime. If the proper choice is not to create an union, this study also succeeds if it helps lead to that negative decision.

B. Unions as a global phenomenon

Global urge to build unions

1.11. In nearly every region of the globe, countries are now in a currency union, seeking to join an existing union, or working to build a new union. Joining into a currency union is a major step that alters the international financial relationships of a country. National sovereignty over the currency, the exchange rate, and international reserves is given up, and new, interactive modes of financial and economic policy are introduced that link the member economies.

1.12. In contrast to creating a full-fledged currency union, many countries are setting up cooperative arrangements or regional surveillance schemes to deal with monetary and financial issues on a regional basis. These arrangements might be seen as seeking to achieve some of the advantages of unions without actually creating an union. In regional schemes, countries agree among themselves to cooperate in specific ways that might limit their scope of activity and policy leeway, but the limitations are not absolute or irrevocable. Some schemes are designed to be precursors to currency unions, but in other cases there is no intention to go in that direction.

1.13. The Global Financial Crisis (GFC) and the need to address some major global imbalances led to a proposal by China that the SDR become a more important component of international reserves, be used for denominating securities, and have an international settlement system. The 2016 inclusion of the yuan in the SDR basket makes it a much more comprehensive measure of global money. The proposal did not include an effort to make the SDR into a currency that could be widely used, but hypothetically it lays a foundation for eventual development of SDR-based currencies, if future decisions of the international community go that way, and thus has elements relevant to the discussion of currency unions.[2]

[2] If there ever will be a single global currency, it might be based on the SDR, or whatever the next generation SDR might be. However, the SDR is based on exchange rates between major currencies; alternatively, a global currency might be based on purchasing power

(continued)

1.14. Taken together, the movement to create unions and strengthen regional schemes is a major transformative process that will dominate the international financial relationships of many countries during the next 15 to 20 years, especially in Eastern Europe, the Middle East, Africa, and East and South East Asia. Currently, more than 60 countries are now working to join or create currency unions. If we include regional schemes, well over half of humanity is involved in changing their national financial systems in order to build a currency union or integrated monetary, exchange rate, and financial market arrangements.

1.15. As the 21st Century progresses, the urge to join a currency union, or regional cooperative or reserves arrangements that capture various characteristics of a currency union, is a global phenomenon that will change the nature and operation of the international financial system. During the past three decades, there have been predictions that by around 2050 there will be only a few currencies or major blocks of currencies. Only a few effectively independent national currencies will exist. If that prediction is to hold true, on average each year about three currencies will disappear or become firmly linked to one of the major blocks.[3]

1.16. The process of merging currencies of individual countries into currency unions has paused during the second decade of the 21st Century under pressure first from the GFC and then the covid pandemic. Conversely, as discussed *in Chapter 9D – The Digital Euro*, on central bank digital currencies (CBDCs) pressures from financial digitalization might tend to push countries into regional arrangements.

1.17. As we look forward, will the formal currency union process accelerate or will the emphasis shift toward strengthening regional cooperative nonunion arrangements to deal with new global strains? My suspicions are that both types of arrangements will continue to develop, but specifically that the union urge is strong enough in Africa, the Gulf, and central Asia that the union process will continue despite the decade and half setback – maybe the predictions for 2050 might still have some validity.

---

parity (PPP) as measured in the global International Comparison Project described in Chapters 9 and 12. The ICP has shown that exchange rates can exhibit significant and sustained differences from PPP.

[3] Indeed, in this scenario, by 2050 the term "inter*national* financial system" may be antiquated, and a new term such as "global financial system" may need to be used. Or perhaps the term "inter*regional*" will apply.

Table 1.1 – Current and planned currency unions *as of 2021*

Common Monetary Area (CMA) – South Africa and several neighboring states[4]

East African Community (EAC) – Six East African countries (future)

Eastern Caribbean Currency Union (ECCU) – Small Caribbean island countries

Economic and Monetary Community of Central Africa (CEMAC) – Mostly French-speaking countries in Central Africa

Eurasian Monetary Union (future)[5]

European Monetary Union (EMU or Euroarea) – Nineteen European countries.

Gulf Cooperation Council (GCC) – Arabian Gulf countries (future)

Antilles Guilder Area – Former Netherlands Antilles Islands that continue use of the Antilles guilder

Singapore-Brunei Currency Interchangeability Agreement

Pacific Financial Community – Three jurisdictions in the Pacific related to France

West African Economic and Monetary Union[6] (WAEMU) - Mostly francophone countries in West Africa

West African Monetary Zone[5] (WAMZ) – Six West African countries, mostly English speaking (future)

Table 1.2 – Regional Monetary and Exchange Rate Cooperation Arrangements *as of 2021*

Central American Monetary Council

ASEAN Economic Research and Policy Discussion Group

Commission of Andean Nations

South African Development Community (SADC) (which will encompass the CMA)[7]

Caricom (Caribbean Community, which will encompass the ECCU)

Chiang Mai Initiative Multilaterized (CMIM)/East Asian Community

South East Asian Central Banks (19 member central banks)

---

[4] Botswana, Lesotho, Namibia, Swaziland, and South Africa. In the CMA, national currencies are retained but are fixed 1-to-1 to the South African rand. Each currency is legal tender throughout the area. The rand commonly cocirculates with the other national currencies.

[5] Creation of an Eurasian Central Bank by 2025 is envisioned within the five-country Eurasian Economic Union.

[6] Plans are under development to merge WAEMU and WAMZ to create a single monetary union for ECOWAS – Economic Union of West African States, which would have about 15 members.

[7] The SADC comprises the four countries of the CMA and an additional ten countries in southern Africa. Members have signed a Memorandum of Understanding on macroeconomic convergence that seeks to create a framework for coordination of macroeconomic stability in the region.

1.18. The potential rise of numerous large regional currencies or currency blocs raises questions about how they will operate within the global financial system and their relationship with international financial institutions (the International Monetary Fund, World Bank, Bank for International Settlements, Organization for Economic Cooperation and Development, Financial Stability Board, and G-20, among others). Will such institutions remain strong? Will new institutions attuned to the new environment absorb them? Will globalization and the requirements of international financial stability result in powerful institutions at the center of the global financial system, or will regional bodies and major countries consort to run the system and acquire surveillance and infrastructure development functions and thus cause current international institutions to wither? Will there be "soft convergence" of countries to international codes and standards that will foster *de facto* linkages between economies? The answers to many of these questions are ultimately beyond the scope of this book, but the questions naturally arise and must be seriously addressed in coming decades. Some of the issues are discussed in Chapter 8 on the International Relations of Unions.

Currency unions as instruments for economic, social, and political development

1.19. Currency unions can have a major transformative role by fostering economic, social, and political development.

The currency union

1.20. As will be described in this volume, a currency union changes many economic conditions in the union. Forging an union is viewed in many developing regions as a means to promote economic development, attack poverty by opening new opportunities, create larger and more competitive markets, reduce exchange rate volatility, etc..

Financial integration

1.21. Currency unions also promote financial market integration by turning multiple small financial systems into a single large system. This aspect usually receives little notice, but the EMU believed that the transformation of Europe into a single, integrated economy without economic and financial borders would help harvest the full potential benefits of the currency union. An integrated economy is larger and more competitive, less volatile, financially more robust, provides better price signals, and lacks many frictions between countries that increase costs and inhibit growth. Old vested national financial interests are opened to new competition and must improve the quality of their services to survive. Moreover, monetary policy should operate seamlessly throughout the union in order to be effective and achieve policy goals, which is possible only with a fully integrated single economy. Also, financial integration of the economies will often involve adoption of internationally recognized financial sector standards and best practices, which will modernize the economies and make the union more competitive globally.

1.22. In Europe, the ECB and the EU aggressively pursued many ambitious programs to promote integration, as listed in *Chapter 10 – Financial Markets*. Future unions (and other regional schemes) will be heavily involved in creating new institutions and harmonizing practices and legal rules in order to support the smooth operation of the currency union and bring about the benefits of financial integration.

Cooperation and better governance

1.23. A third major transformation from currency unions is promoting cooperation between the member states and better governance. A currency union joins individual states into a cooperative venture for common benefit. All countries must feel that they participate fairly in decision making and that the distribution of income and costs is equitable.

1.24. Also, an union has huge financial assets and transactions that must be handled prudently and honestly for the benefit of the entire union. All union funds and their expenditure must be fully accounted for, with careful controls and audits.

Political influence over expenditures cannot be permitted because it violates the rights of the other member states. Funds are the property of the union and cannot be raided by national authorities, nor can national fiscal deficits be monetized under pressure from political leaders.

1.25. Similarly, policy must be developed for the benefit of the union and all member states. The union central bank must be independent of political influence in decision making and the distribution of assets and income. A currency union must build policy and operational capacity and be able to participate in international financial policy discussions and standards setting bodies.

1.26. Much of the complexity of setting up a currency union comes from devising institutions and procedures that provide for common oversight, a fair distribution of costs and income, and legitimate participation by all parties in decision-making. Countries suffering from poorly operating or corrupt institutions can experience important improvements in overall governance by becoming part of an union. In some regions, the cooperative oversight of the union central bank can transform it into one of the best governed governmental bodies in a region, with major positive benefits.

1.27. It can also be speculated that a new reason to join an union is to participate in the advantages and avoiding the risks associated with central bank digital currencies (CBDCs). CBDCs require significant market and technical infrastructure and oversight that are beyond many countries, but might be available within regional arrangements.

1.28. Being part of a currency union is not a passive activity. Each country must build its capacity to contribute to the joint effort in a prudent and professional manner in order to defend its own interests and contribute to the common effort. At the union level, analytical, policy, and operational expertise must be built to be able operate the union for common benefit. Large improvements in overall governance can result from these efforts.

C. The decision to join an union

Reasons to join an union

1.29. Among reasons to join an union were emulate the newly created European Monetary Union, which until recently was widely regarded as a major success and now in recent years is seen as demonstrating dogged survivability in tough times. In the years following creation of the EMU, nearly every country had a prominent economist, banker, or politician proposing an union. The number of serious efforts launched was much less.

1.30. The costs of exchanging currencies within the union are erased.

1.31. Interest in a common currency is strong within regional customs and trade unions to eliminate uncertainty about exchange rate changes between trading partners and eliminate exchange costs. The example of the EMU was particular interesting to such unions.

1.32. The need for harmonized or common accounting, statistics, financial access, and policy instruments across a union will tend to reduce frictions in cross-border commerce and effectively expand market access.

1.33. Overcoming monetary and exchange policy failures in individual countries. Countries with a history of monetary or exchange rate policy failures may look to a union as a way to obtain financial stability that has eluded them. Within a union, a system of mutual support and policy oversight might allow authorities to accomplish things impossible as single countries. Moreover, countries lacking resources to sustain their currency, or are judged as not credible by markets, may achieve financial stability by joining an union.

1.34. For small countries, an union may be seen as a way to create larger markets and bring about economic growth. A larger market may permit larger and more competitive banks and corporations to develop.[8]

1.35. For poor countries, an union may be viewed as a path out of poverty, to be able to have part of what the Europeans enjoy.

1.36. An union may permit some countries greater ability to design their monetary and exchange rate policies. Countries with exchange rates pegged to an external currency import the monetary and exchange policies of the country of the external currency, which will often not be appropriate for local conditions. Joining a union permits the possibility of adopting other policies that may be more appropriate for the region.

1.37. Small countries on the peripheral of a larger union can be so linked to the currency of the union currency through trade, services, production links, and tourism that formal linkage with the union is the only practical step. Some small countries physically surrounded by EMU countries are effectively absorbed into the union although they are not formal members.

1.38. A currency union is seen as the culmination of a process of other regional integration programs, such as creating regional customs unions (South Africa, East African Community), or political agreements (Gulf Cooperation Council). The absence of a single currency can contribute to strains within alliances of various sorts that can lead to proposals to create a currency union. The EMU was widely viewed as the logical final step in the continuing process of trade, social, and political integration in Europe – the capstone on the integration process.

1.39. Some countries join unions to have some voice in the international financial system. Individual countries may be economically too small to have any influence on international financial policies, but an union may have opportunities to participate in the global financial system. The ability of an union to speak for a region can make it an important voice in international financial deliberations.[9]

1.40. Economic and financial oversight by an union over its members may partly supplant surveillance by the International Monetary Fund (IMF). Some union member countries may prefer local oversight. (The non-union Chiang Mai Initiative (CMI) collaboration in Southeast Asia seeks to minimize reliance on the IMF.)

1.41. In regions with extensive cross-border trade, travel, labor migration, or intraregional remittances, a single union currency can cut costs.

1.42. An union is seen as a tool to promote integration in trade and services, integration of financial markets, and to help alleviate poverty. Increasingly, views are that greater economic and financial integration endogenously follow from joining an union.

1.43. Integration of financial markets between union member countries promotes competition that can reduce costs, create more competitive financial institutions, promote capital flows into productive investments throughout the union, build more liquid and resilient markets, etc. Stronger financial institutions in larger markets may contribute to greater financial stability.

1.44. A territory or other jurisdiction may be under the effective control of a union member. For

[8] For example, the EAC explicitly cites the importance of moving from being marginal individual countries to become a larger market of about 180 million people that can have some influence in international markets.

[9] For example, in East Africa where six countries of the EAC are working towards a common currency; M. Mukaruliza stated "Rwandans and others cannot reap the benefits of globalization as long as economies in individual countries are still small and vulnerable; and J. Mutuboba stated "integration is no longer a question of choice. It is a *sine qua non* for survival of weak entities such as our five sister states in this region. Fast-tracking and deepening integration is the only way forward for the bloc to avoid further marginalization in the global economy'". (Karuhanga 2008).

example, the euro is used in French overseas territories.

1.45. In post-conflict situations, it might be easier to join an existing union rather than attempt to establish an independent monetary and exchange system.

Reasons to not join an union

1.46. In contrast, there are reasons for not joining an union. Some are economic and technical in nature, but many are related to fears about consequences of joining an union. In designing the program to build an union, it will often be necessary to address such fears in order to create a political climate in which the union can succeed.

1.47. National control over money, exchange rates, and international reserves is lost and ceded to the union. The ability to respond to shocks affecting individual economies is lost or compromised. (This issue has acquired new prominence during the financial crisis because some EMU experienced very severe imbalances that had to be addressed without the option of changing exchange rates or running an independent monetary policy.)

1.48. Union policies suitable for the region could be inappropriate or harmful for individual countries.

1.49. The national currency, which is symbolic of the country and which may be beloved by the population, will be replaced by a union currency.

1.50. Political commitment to the union may not be strong. Without such commitment, efforts to create an union can be a waste of resources.

1.51. National political influence in financial matters is reduced or lost. This may create feelings of resentment or loss of control.

1.52. There can be fear of domination by bigger or more powerful neighbors and their businesses. Domestic industries may seek protection from competition from other union countries.

1.53. Often, there is fear that the changeover to the new currency will bring inflation or a spike in prices. As discussed in Chapter 18, *this is a common concern that planners should address*.

1.54. There is fear that free capital inflows under an union will result in spikes in real estate prices, takeovers of local businesses, etc.

1.55. Joining a union will bring about movement toward equalization of prices. The movement of local prices up to union levels could be inflationary or could harm segments of the population.

1.56. Seigniorage from producing money is affected or may be lost.[10] Joining an union will mean that the union gains control over total monetary production and the distribution of seigniorage.

1.57. Substantial professional and technical resources are needed that some potential member countries may not have. The process of setting up an union involves all central banking tasks plus additional tasks of harmonization and coordination and the full professional and technical resources of the central banks of potential members - some central banks might not be able to afford this commitment or key resources needed may be absent or not up to the tasks.

1.58. Setting up an union may involve setting up harmonized, regional financial infrastructure, such as payments systems or a financial communications structure. If key components of the financial infrastructure are missing or inadequate, a long and costly process may be involved in setting up a system for the union.

1.59. Creating an union will fundamentally change the economic conditions prevailing in each of the member countries. Thus there will be great

---

[10] Seigniorage is the value of the currency to the government over its costs of production. It can be an important source of income (equal to several percent of GDP) for some economies.

uncertainty about new conditions and the appropriate policies to follow. Moreover, economic conditions in new unions could change rapidly for several years, further increasing uncertainties.

1.60. Creating an union is costly. Substantial direct and often unrecoverable costs could affect union institutions, national governments, banks, businesses, and the public throughout the union. Some regions may not be able to handle the costs of setting up a fully configured union and may choose a more limited regional monetary arrangement instead.

1.61. Countries need to weigh the pros and cons of joining or creating an union. There are legitimate reasons to go either way. Globally, at the present time, there appears to be more interest in joining unions than remaining outside. This study suspects that the prime reason is the sense that joining an union is a necessary part of integrating into the global economy and that individual countries often are not powerful enough economically to do well in isolation. Dutta (2008) argues that nearly all countries are too small to compete effectively in global markets and inevitably a system of continent-wide monetary unions will develop over the coming decades. Conversely, the strains on the EMU from the Greek crisis, the GFC, and the COVID19 and other crises might have prompted some second thoughts about the desirability of joining unions.

D. Definitions and variations

True currency and monetary unions

1.62. A true currency union involves a formal agreement by countries to create centralized monetary and exchange rate arrangements. A treaty or some other formal agreement lists the powers and structure of the union, its central organization, and the rights, obligations, and financial status of the member countries. Typically, a treaty or agreement will start a process running for several years that will set up the union. The treaty will also establish goals, policies, or conditions that will affect the future union. As the process of setting up the union continues, new structures or policies might be introduced, which will be formally adopted through new treaties, agreements, or regulations. At the end of the process an union is created with a central organization as a separate supranational entity that executes the currency, monetary, and/or exchange rate policies of the member countries.

1.63. The EMU is an example of a true union. This volume describes the key aspects of the creation of the union beginning before the Maastricht Treaty that set up the process, through the many steps to create the union, to the formal start of the union in 1999 and the circulation of union banknotes and coins in 2002. The union-building process continued after 2002, as new countries enter, union competencies expand (such as centralizing bank supervisory standards during the GFC), and new tasks are undertaken.

Regional surveillance and integration schemes

1.64. In contrast to a true, full-fledged union, many partial arrangements exist that have some but not all elements of a union, or which may permit the national members to have greater flexibility in some areas than in a full union. The goal is to capture many of the benefits of a union, but without necessarily creating a formal union.

1.65. One important example of such regional arrangements is a *currency bloc*, in which a group of countries voluntarily link and hold constant the relative configuration of their currencies against each other. A good example is the CMI in Southeast Asia, later strengthened during the GFC into the CMIM (Chiang Mai Initiative Multilaterization). Following the Asian Crisis of the late 1990's, there was concern over the danger of renewed attacks on national currencies, and a desire to defend the existing relative configuration of exchange rates – defining a currency bloc – to avoid disruption to the highly integrated regional production arrangements.

The ten ASEAN countries[11] created a reserves swap arrangement that could be drawn on to defend currencies. A policy review and dialog arrangement was also set up to provide oversight of national economic situations and policies to help build the foundations for stable currency arrangements. The arrangement proved inadequate during the GFC as countries also drew on US, Chinese, and Japanese resources. The regional arrangement was strengthened in 2008 and again in 2009, with new participation of China, Japan, and South Korea, to create the CMIM with a larger swap pool with a legally binding contract for management of the pool. This ASEAN+3 group sought greater exchange rate stability and the policy oversight functions similar to those of a true currency union and enhanced resources, but without creating a union. The strength of the oversight arrangements and the ability of the central entity to independently initiate action is an important variation in such arrangements. Thus, the region moved from bilateral swap arrangements into a common swap arrangement with expanded resources, in effect transforming from an umbrella for bilateral arrangements toward becoming a genuine supranational entity.

1.66. There are many such arrangements. One important area of activity is development of harmonized financial statistics to support regional oversight. For example, with support of the IMF, the Central American Monetary Council (CAMC) instituted a program of harmonized data collection to support reviews of country conditions. Also, the IMF is contributing to regional statistical harmonization programs in several different regions of Africa that encompass about half of the African countries. There seems to be great interest in developing regional arrangements that can support regional economic and policy oversight, some of which might ultimately evolve into currency unions.

1.67. A key aspect of regional arrangements is whether central institutions exist and have a decision-making process and powers that can promote union.[12] In a regional arrangement, the key task is not planning for a future union, but carrying out effective, current oversight of conditions and engaging in deliberations that can be implemented to address weaknesses and promote suitable policies. The regional body might also act as an honest broker or agent to coordinate national actions or to undertake agreed common actions. To do this, oversight must be frequent, based on access to good current information, with a vigorous process of review of economic conditions in the region, and with a frank decision-making process to propose policy initiatives for individual countries or for the group. The method of implementation can vary, relying on individual initiative, peer pressure or public pressure, or binding rules, but it needs to be effective and appropriate for the regional setting. This is likely to require regular statistics and information gathering, continuing oversight and analysis, and secretarial support for analytical or policy sessions. This may only be possible by setting up a continuing body (secretariat or council) with a permanent professional and technical staff.

1.68. For purposes of this study, many of the principles that apply to the building of currency unions might also apply to regional cooperative arrangements. The collection of harmonized monetary and financial statistics needed for currency unions is already mentioned above, but other types of programs, such as regular economic dialog, regional interbank clearing arrangements, cross-border securities

[11] Association of Southeast Asian Nations, comprised of countries; Brunei, Cambodia, Indonesia, Laos, Malaysia, Myanmar, Philippines, Singapore, Thailand, and Vietnam.

[12] For example, the ASEAN has a loose structure that relies mostly on twice yearly meetings of heads of state and finance ministers in which decisions are by full consensus. There is a small secretariat, a regular process for review of economic situations – the Economic Research and Policy Dialog process, and the CMIM for mutual swap lines for defense of currencies – but relationships are driven by provisions of the 2007 ASEAN Charter that support full sovereign decision making and noninterference in internal affairs (and do not call for a currency union).

markets, harmonization of accounting standards, etc., also contribute importantly to support regional arrangements. Such programs can be steps toward development of currency unions, but they are fully justified in themselves. For example, the discussion in Chapter 9 of European financial sector integration programs, such as the Single Euro Payment Area (SEPA) that seeks to erase cross-border impediments affecting retail financial markets, can provide useful information to countries seeking to create unions, but it can also provide information to countries only wishing to improve and integrate their financial markets for the benefit of their public.

1.69. However, important conditions that existed in Europe that supported building the union do not exist elsewhere and the lessons of Europe can go only so far. As discussed in Chapter 2 on the EMU, the differences mean that the European experience cannot be completely replicated elsewhere and thus different structures, institutions, and policies will be followed. Each planned union will look toward the EMU for guidance, but must be prepared to go in new directions – sometimes frequently. The same economic functions will need to be performed in new unions and executed equally effectively, but the ways in which they are done will often differ.

1.70. An important reason to set up a regional arrangement is to promote greater stability between exchange rates in the region, or perhaps defend a specific configuration of rates. This can support increased trade within a region because of greater price transparency, reduction in exchange conversion costs over time, and reducing price shifts between suppliers and customers within vertically integrated direct investments. Regional schemes with exchange stability as a goal will need to have reserves available to defend the arrangement, as discussed in Chapter 3.

Text Box: Financial integration taxonomy

In considering levels of integration short of a fully integrated monetary union, it is useful to have a taxonomy of different levels of integration. The Euroarea has a very high level of integration with a single monetary and exchange rate policy. But other regional arrangements might only involve partial integration. Countries might wish to move to one of the intermediate phases short nd not create a full monetary union; or could pass through several stages of integration along the path to full monetary union.

Levels of financial integration are described below.

<u>Independent national financial market development</u>

This describes a situation in which each country, acting independently, seeks to create financial sector infrastructure and effective markets. International or regional standards and best practices can be followed, but this is done on a national basis.

<u>Coordinated policy research and decision-making</u>

In this stage, countries continue to act independently, but have procedures for regular consultations and agreements over policy and standards. Decisions are made through multi-country consultations in which each country participates. Agreements can have degrees of strictness, from agreement to adhere to voluntary codes, memos of understanding, to full treaties. Implementation is the responsibility of the individual countries. Examples include the initial Chiang Mai Initiative, in which Asian countries agreed amongst themselves to behave in certain ways, including carrying out regular consultations and making reserves swap lines available.[13] *Establishing macroeconomic convergence criteria, but leaving the implementation to individual national initiatives, such as in the GCC or Andean Community, is at this level. The CAMC is also at this level of integration.*

[13] Positions within this hierarchy are not fixed. For example, the strengthening of the Chiang Mai Initiative into the Chiang Mai Initiative Multilaterization moved it towards the third stage above.

Transnational oversight

Countries agree by treaty or other mechanism to set up a transnational entity with specified powers over the participating states. Powers could be broad or tightly defined. The International Monetary Fund is an example – it holds resources provided by the members, carries out regular overview of country situations and policies, and can extend resources with conditions and sanctions. The aborted Asian Monetary Fund would also have been an example. In some cases, the authority might be limited to a specific area, such as being a standard setter for clearing systems operations, a regional transportation authority, or monitor implementation of agreements or technical standards. The supranational legal arrangements of the Andean Community are an example. A country could be a member of multiple such entities.

Monetary and financial union

In a full currency union, countries cede substantial sovereignty to a transnational entity and integrate activities so that a single standard prevails or national differences are reduced or disappear. In Europe, such powers reside in the Eurosystem, which is a single system operating in all countries using the euro, and which controls many policies as if national markets no longer exist. At this level of integration, important binding decisions can be made at the transnational level.

Special purpose unions

1.71. Most unions are comprised of geographically contiguous countries, or are within the same general region even though some countries might not physically abut with other union countries (for example, Finland is distant from the rest of the Euro Area.) However, proposals are sometimes made for special purpose unions that would draw widely separated countries into an union.

1.72. *Islamic currency union.* Proposals have been made to create a currency union for the Ummah – the scattered community of Muslims throughout the world. For example, Malaysia made such a proposal in 2003. Given the extreme diversity and spread of countries that might be included, this proposal could only reasonably be interpreted as an arrangement in which Muslims remain within their existing national monetary and financial markets frameworks, but have access to some Shari'a-compliant financial instruments (sukuk securities, Haj-savings instruments, takaful insurance instruments, etc.) *issued by some central authority*. An example is the International Islamic Liquidity Mechanism (IILM) created in 2010 that issues Shariah-compliant bonds in international markets that promote overall market development and address a critical need for high quality liquid assets for bank regulatory purposes. A challenge of such proposals is how to allow unfettered cross-border access to such instruments without undermining national monetary policy.[14]

1.73. More ambitious schemes are working to create a fully functional Shariah compatible monetary policy framework covering multiple countries. Investigations have looked at how a fully Shari'a compliant monetary policy might work, but there are large challenges such as the lack of short-term monetary policy securities, or absence of interest-rate based financial instruments. Considerably more conceptual work remains before this option is feasible.

1.74. *Latin American leftist currency zone.* Several Latin American countries with left-leaning governments have discussed the possibility of creating a monetary zone to coordinate their monetary and exchange policies independently of the IMF or the influence of the United States. One proposal included widely separated and diverse countries as Cuba, Venezuela, Bolivia, and Nicaragua. It is unclear whether these are operational proposals to work toward an union-like entity or whether they are only

[14] The IILM created in 2010 as an international organization has tackled some of these issues, including issuance of short-term Shariah-compliant money market paper supported by a new cross-border market trading network with compatible regulatory treatment across borders.

expressions of disappointment with other arrangements.

Unilateral linking of currencies

1.75. Currencies can unilaterally be linked to another currency. Five situations are common;

1.76. *Link to a larger economy.* A smaller currency could link to a larger one out of convenience and to minimize costs because of large trade, tourism, or remittances links between the economies. The costs for transactions between the economies is reduced and possibilities of disruptions stemming from exchange rate movements are minimized. Investment links between the economies can also be strengthened, especially because the interest rates are linked to the larger economy. The smaller economy necessarily adopts the monetary policy of its larger neighbor in lieu of exercising its own monetary policy, but for many smaller economies there might be little realistic option to have an independent policy.[15]

1.77. *Future union membership.* Countries can link to an union currency in anticipation of joining the union in the future. This allows the pricing structure of the economy to adjust to prices in the union, and can facilitate financial integration with the union. This can also be a political signal of firm intentions to join the union.

1.78. *Monetary and Exchange Rate Credibility.* Countries can link to another economy to gain credibility in monetary and exchange policy by adopting the policy of a strong currency economy. A country with a poor policy history might gain credibility by announcing its links to another currency then taking steps to maintain the links.[16] This type of linkage is sometimes part of stabilization programs, and can take the form of a "currency board" in which a country holds foreign currency assets equal to or more than its monetary liabilities and can exchange the liabilities for foreign exchange at a fixed price.[17]

1.79. *Cross-border investment.* Linking to another currency can facilitate cross-border investment between the economies by making pricing transparent, reducing exchange rate uncertainty, linking to the interest rates of the larger economy, and providing price signals through a larger area as a guide for investment decisions. This might partly reflect recognition that capital markets are becoming globalized and by linking currencies it will be possible to more easily tap into larger, more liquid markets.

1.80. *Post-conflict situations.* After wars or internal conflicts, the conditions, abilities, and resources to carry out independent exchange rate policies might be missing. A simple link to a stable international currency could be the best option. The link might be to the currency of the country providing most recovery assistance.

---

[15] The linkage can be between a national currency and a foreign currency, or could involve replacement of the national currency and legal (*de jure*) use of the foreign currency. The latter arrangement has some important disadvantages including having to use foreign currency assets to purchase the physical foreign currency at a cost of giving up the interest income on the foreign currency assets, an inability to switch easily from a fixed to flexible exchange rate regime or use a currency basket, and extensive preparations and costs to re-introduce a national currency if desired.

[16] McKinnon (2000) implied that linking to the leadership of the U.S. dollar helped stabilize individual European currencies up until 1970 prior to the delinking of the dollar to gold in 1971. During the following floating years, exchange rate pressures within Europe contributed to urges to create more stable currency arrangements, beginning with the European Unit of Account (EUA), and progressing through the European Currency Unit (ECU) and resulting in the euro.

[17] A currency board is considered a very restrictive arrangement that countries adopt only when needed to demonstrate credibility. A country with a currency board gives up its independent monetary policy, and because it cannot purchase domestic assets with the proceeds of its monetary liabilities it cannot act as a lender of last resort in crisis situations, nor can it sterilize the monetary effects of its foreign currency transactions.

1.81. *Crisis links to a monetary union.* As discussed above, countries on the periphery of larger unions might unilaterally adopt the union currency to benefit from the stability of the union currency during the crisis.

1.82. Unilateral linkage is not rare and is a policy option in several types of situations. A large body of theoretical work related to unilateral linkage has been developed in the theory of the Optimum Currency Area (OCA). OCA theory is commonly used to analyze currency unions, but it was originally developed to cover the economics of countries that irrevocably link their currencies to another currency. Thus, much of what will be said in this volume related to currency unions might also be applicable to countries that have linked their currencies.

Cocirculation

1.83. Cocirculation is the simultaneous use of two or more currencies in an economy. It is not rare, as shown by the wide use of the U.S. dollar and euro outside their home areas. Other currencies also cocirculate, such as the Russian ruble or the South African rand. Cocirculation can exist even if not formally recognized or is actively suppressed by authorities. Cocirculation is a form of *de facto* currency integration relevant for understanding currency unions. Cocirculation can apply to countries who maintain flexible exchange rate policies, but also can exist in countries that have linked their currencies to the cocirculating currency.

> Numerous economists have proposed introducing new union currencies as a cocirculating parallel currency that will compete with the national currencies[18] and ultimately replace them;
>
> Countries seeking to join unions might encourage cocirculation of the union currency as a step in linking with the union and helping the public become familiar with their future legal currency.

1.84. Although in some cases cocirculation appears to have little impact on domestic policy, a cocirculating currency might significantly alter or impair monetary policy to the point that countries might no longer be able to operate independent monetary or exchange rate policies.

1.85. A cocirculation economy can import aspects of the monetary policy of another country, including interest rates, means of clearing, inflation, etc. The public in cocirculation economies might have an effective option to switch between the domestic and the cocirculation currencies whichever is most favorable under different market conditions, or could be effectively limited to use of the cocirculating currency.

1.86. As of 2008, nineteen countries used currency of another country as their legal currency, or almost 10 percent of all countries. The three largest are Latin American countries (Ecuador, El Salvador, and Panama) that had long had heavy cocirculation of dollars before legally switching over to official use of the dollar. (Kenen and Meade 2008, p. 145). Cocirculation is discussed in several sections of the main text, as relevant.

E. Six big decisions

1.87. This section describes six major decisions that future monetary unions must make. This volume focuses on the EMU answers to the questions, which can provide some guidance to future unions, but it must be emphasized that multiple crises during the past two decades have spurred major innovations in central banking practice and policy. Future unions face the dual tasks of learning from the experiences in Europe and also reflecting current practices and standards.

[18] For example, the European Currency Unit (ECU) had some characteristics of a cocirculating monetary instrument; Eichengreen (2003) proposed an Asian Currency Unit as a parallel currency for Asia, and DiVanna (2010) proposed an 'Islamic currency union' in which Shariah-compliant financial instruments cocirculate with national currencies. Chapter 3 has a discussion of parallel currency approaches.

1.88. Papadia (2020) argues that all the standard tenets of central banking were ejected in the course of international coordinated actions by central banks and international financial organizations to address the GFC, and that consequently the aggressive actions undertaken at that time cleared the way for similar quick action during the Covid crisis. This creates a quandary for future unions because much of the policy model embedded in the foundations of the EMU has sharply changed. Future unions must rigorously evaluate how the early EMU practice applies to current conditions and adapt as needed.

1.89. The six decisions affect the goals, structure, and operations of a currency union. Planners should address the questions early so that institutions, rules and regulations, operations, and governance of the union can be designed accordingly. These decisions will be affected by the political environment of the new union because they affect the nature of the relationships between the member countries.

"Big Bang"; Gradual introduction of the currency; Virtual currency

1.90. Should the new currency be introduced in all countries and the old currencies withdrawn quickly or simultaneously? This has been described as a "Big Bang", which was the EMU approach. Alternatively, the new currency could be introduced gradually, either as a "virtual" currency that exists only as an accounting entity, or as a physical currency that cocirculates alongside the existing national currencies for an extended period.

1.91. The Big Bang requires extensive preparations so that all systems are operational on the first day of the union, which this study will refer to as "Union Day". The big bang involves two simultaneous complex operations – introducing the new currency and retiring the old national currencies.

1.92. Gradual approaches are designed to permit time for the public and the operations of the union to prepare and even experiment with features of the union. Gradual approaches might be more appropriate in countries with large or remote populations, where machine handling of currency is not common, where capacity is insufficient to simultaneously issue and retire currency, or where there is uncertainty about the commitment to adopt the union currency. Three variants of the gradual approach are possible;

1.93. *"Virtual" currency, sometimes called a "synthetic" currency*, in which a currency-like accounting identity is created to denominate transactions or stocks of financial assets as if a real currency existed, but no physical currency exists. In Europe, a virtual currency called the European Currency Unit (ECU) existed prior to creation of the euro, and during the first three years of its life the euro was a virtual currency.

1.94. *Central bank digital currencies (CBDCs)* are a new type of instrument that might be introduced along with virtual currencies, but they could have unprecedented impacts on monetary markets and financial soundness that must be thoroughly researched, and thus might be introduced independently from the schedules for virtual currencies or cash.

1.95. *Replacement approach*, in which at a given date the national currencies are no longer produced but continue in use until they wear out and are replaced by the union currency, and

1.96. *Parallel currency approach*, in which national currencies and the union currency are both issued and cocirculate as legal tender for extended periods.

"Big Bang"	
Advantages	**Disadvantages**
Suitable for smaller economies with good communications	Complete currency stock must be printed before Union Day
Better in economies with many ATM and cash handling machines	Crush of tasks to simultaneously introduce and withdraw currencies.
Accounting change-over on Union-day	Difficulty in reaching remote regions
Speed of introduction same or nearly the same in all countries	Difficult to reach all populations where communications or education is poor
Concentrated period for public education	Large security demands
Minimizes period of double money stock	All goods and services must be repriced at once
Lesser danger of counterfeiting	Little time to recover if problems occur
Minimizes period for handling two currencies	

Gradual Introduction of the Union Currency	
Advantages	**Disadvantages**
Appropriate for very large countries, remote regions, poor communications, low educational levels	Multiple currencies in circulation
Better where hand processing is used	Problems for cash-handling machines
Gradual printing of currency is possible	Indefinite period for public education
Speed of introduction can vary between countries.	Greater chance of counterfeiting
More time to adjust if problems occur.	Greater danger of fraud
Experimentation might be possible.	Accounting issues are complex
Countries can move at different speeds	Danger of holding off the complete changeover
	Political issues can develop

The degree of centralization

1.97. A key issue is which functions will be handled by a single authority at the center of the union and which functions will be retained by national authorities. Centralization might make decision making easier and result in more common practices, but might require more substantial preparations, might limit national contributions, and might not reflect local practices or customs, etc. Political factors will often be decisive in decisions about which aspects of the union will be centralized and which will remain under national control. The Euroarea followed a rather complex mixed approach, called "subsidiarity", in which NCBs implement monetary policy actions and national central bank governors contribute to monetary policy decisions, but in which a strong union central bank makes decisions that apply across the union. The history of the U.S. Federal Reserve System could also be relevant – over its history, the system has moved from a relative loose system with fairly strong regional banks (especially the New York bank) and a relatively weak Board in Washington into a strongly centralized system in which the regional banks have relatively weak powers.

1.98. Centralization is necessary in several areas, such as monetary and interest rate policy, and setting the exchange rate. In other areas, either centralized or decentralized approaches can be followed – in the Euroarea for example, monetary policy implementation is primarily at the national level, as was supervision of the banking system when the union started. There could be a dozen or so areas in which decisions will be needed on whether or not to centralize operations. The institutional and operational arrangements for the union will depend upon such decisions, and planners will need to have a sense of the centralization/decentralization decisions in multiple areas in order to design the union.

Centralized Approach	
Advantages	**Disadvantages**
Decisions are based on union-wide evidence Reflects financial integration of the union Policy applies equally to all countries Rapid action is possible Staff and decision-makers are together Less resource intensive Finances can be less complex More political independence	Resentment by countries Complex governance arrangements Lack of knowledge of local conditions Possible poor fit to local practice and law Need a strong legal framework Possible arrogance of power

Decentralized Approach	
Advantages	**Disadvantages**
Uses local resources and expertise Knowledge of local markets Oversight of local banks and markets More participatory Fits local practice and laws Might be politically necessary Suitable for gradual building of union New centralized institutions unneeded Flexibility to react to local emergencies More resources might be available	Unequal distribution of political power Difficulty in applying common policies to local situations Different legal frameworks Possible political interference Possible lack of resources Financing is complex Need strong judicial oversight

The policy regime

1.99. Unions can choose different policy regimes. Each has different institutional and operations implications. There might be historical or institutional preferences about which regime to follow and how it should be implemented. Among possible policy regimes are monetary base or monetary aggregate targets, credit targets, exchange rate pegs, and inflation targeting. Chapter 5 covers monetary policy regimes and chapter 6 deals with external policy regimes.

1.100. In addition to the specific policies and targets for monetary and exchange policy, a broader range of macroeconomic goals (sometimes specifically related to convergence between the union countries) might also be formally introduced into the union policy arrangements. These are sometimes intended to bring about macroeconomic convergence between the countries of an union in terms of growth, inflation, government deficit, and internal and external debt. *Chapter 5 – Monetary Policy* discusses convergence criteria in their role in bringing about macroeconomic convergence; *Chapter 12 – Statistics* discusses the criteria as statistical indicators.

1.101. Also, broader targets or goals, such as diversification of economies, economic development, employment, social justice, environmental protection, preserving resources for future generations or passing the benefits of growth to future generations, might also be established as goals of a union. Sometimes, such goals are part of a larger framework in which the monetary union operates and thus establish policy for the union – for example, all Euroarea countries are also EU members, which has a comprehensive set of political, social, and economic goals, such as integration of the economies of Europe and reduced economic disparities. Consequently, the monetary union incorporates such goals in its programs to integrate financial markets under the Single Euro Payments Area (SEPA) program. Similarly, the GCC covers many issues broader than the currency union, and includes some countries that have chosen to stay outside the union.

1.102. Planning for the union will need to create a process to review the policy regime options and decide on the framework, and then create instruments to make the regime operable. The institutions, rules, and modes of operation of the union must take into consideration the chosen policy regimes, the narrow monetary and exchange policies as well as broader goals. Activities in all functional areas must be adjusted to support implementation of the chosen policies, such as defining accounting standards that identify policy variables, or creating rules for acceptable collateral for monetary policy operations.

Fiscal redistribution

1.103. A key question for future unions is whether the union or its member countries can aid other member countries facing fiscal difficulties or provide assistance to equalize fiscal conditions. The Maastricht Treaty setting up the EMU strictly prohibited the union or its members from aiding other countries, as well as prohibiting monetization of fiscal deficits. Moreover, strict rules with penalties were put in place to punish countries that exceed fiscal limits, in order to prevent countries from engaging in irresponsible behavior that can affect the union as a whole. The principle of fiscal responsibility was fundamental to the EMU system during its first decade.

1.104. Crisis conditions during the EMU's second decade forced changes to this view. During the GFC several economies with weaker credit ratings and higher fiscal borrowing costs sought issuance of bonds with union-side backing which would lower borrowing costs for those countries and pass default risk to the union as a whole. These proposals were not adopted, in large part due to opposition from Germany. Subsequently, in 2014 the ECB gradually introduced a negative interest rate policy to stimulate the economy and counter potential price deflation. This action spread across the yield spectrum lowering borrowing costs including on sovereign debt. (Schnabel 2020). The recent COVID19 crisis saw large issuance of community-backed bonds, a large portion of which were picked up by the ECB in its asset purchase program.

1.105. This interaction between fiscal support and monetary support or hesitance is likely to be a continuing issues – future unions might permit fiscal assistance between countries. For example, countries with large resource endowments might provide assistance to poorer members, or come to the aid of countries that experience severe deficits during a recession. The experience of Greece, which reported a large deficit in 2010 several times the permitted limit, and the difficulties of the EU and EMU to find ways to provide assistance despite legal restrictions has shown the importance of this issue.

1.106. New unions will need to develop rules covering fiscal distributions. The rules could forbid the practice, such as initially done in Europe, or carefully define the conditions under which redistributions can occur and the amounts involved. Care must be taken that redistributions are not abused or allow countries to avoid making necessary adjustments. An important factor is that international markets could view fiscal redistributions as threats to the credibility of the currency, and therefore any redistributions must be done cautiously and transparently.

Financial soundness and bank supervision

1.107. In many countries, the central bank is responsible both for monetary policy and supervision of the banking system because monetary policy and the commercial banking system of the country involve the same set of institutions. The central bank might execute open market operations with a bank that it also supervises and regulates to ensure its soundness. That is, the central bank has responsibility for both monetary policy and financial sector soundness. In one fundamental sense, this is logical because a weak banking system cannot support strong growth and inhibits the execution of monetary policy.[19]

1.108. In contrast, the functions can be treated as separate, to avoid possible conflicts of interest between executing monetary policy and making regulatory decisions that decide the fate of individual banks, and to separate possible large costs of lender of last resort (LOLR) actions from affecting the condition of the union central bank's balance sheet. In the EMU, the Maastricht Treaty strictly separated the central banking and supervisory function, but as a result of the financial crisis new more centralized arrangements were put in place.

1.109. Following the GFC, the view has grown that macroprudential tools – policies aimed at strengthening the resilience of the financial system – are needed alongside traditional monetary policy tools to address a range of financial sector stability issues. By early 2010, a fundamental change in central banking was taking place in which macroprudential policy became nearly coequal with monetary policy. The crisis marked the transition from inflation targeting as the dominant framework to a new regime in which interest rate policy actions are supplemented by a potentially wide range of macroprudential tools designed to tackle specific financial sector conditions. This describes a multi-policy environment in which macroprudential policy comes to the fore. Monetary policy can no longer be premised on existence of a smoothly operating financial system; rather, monitoring of the financial system and intervention in a variety of ways might be needed to bolster the effectiveness of monetary policy; Conversely, monetary policy actions can affect financial stability.

[19] A 1996 IMF Study, *Bank Soundness and Macroeconomic Policy*, described how banking crises have affected many countries and impaired monetary policy (IMF 1996).

Original EMU Case: Separate monetary and supervision functions	
Advantages	**Disadvantages**
Monetary policy and supervision policy independence Central bank balance sheet not threatened Countries want to retain supervisory powers; political necessity Complex supervision rules need specialists	Supervisors lack relevant information for monetary policy and macrofinancial surveillance Central bank isolated from emergency actions Banking and fiscal postures might clash Monetary policy is union oriented; Supervision has global perspective Lender of last resort responsibilities are unclear Supervisory overlaps and gaps Lack of cooperation

Integrated monetary and supervision functions	
Advantages	**Disadvantages**
More appropriate for cross-border banking Better information exchange Quicker responses Better macrofinancial surveillance Coverage gaps can be closed Conserves resources Necessary in small countries	Central bank balance sheet under threat Ambiguous monetary policy situations possible Rivalry between monetary and supervisory wings

Crisis resolution

1.110. The Greek crisis created massive unforeseen strains within the system and in the view of some threatened the existence of the union. The crisis demanded actions that violated the spirit of the Maastricht Treaty and which were politically unpopular, including involving the IMF in EMU matters.

1.111. The Greek crisis demonstrated that unforeseen events will require flexible and innovative methods to resolve crises. Future unions will need to consider how they will respond to crises, who will make decisions, and who will bear the costs. This is very difficult because each future crisis will have different causes and effects, and there are likely to be political sensitivities, but the long drawn-out process in Europe showed that crisis situations will be faced and that there can be severe problems and dangers if means of crisis resolution regimes are not in place.

Summary

1.112. The six major decisions described above will affect many aspects of the design and operation of the currency union. They are interrelated, and thus a decision in one area can affect what can be done in other areas.

1.113. These decisions must be made by each union, and there is no simple template that this study can provide in how to put them all together. The decisions must often be made early in the union planning process, or flexibility must be built into the plans to permit decisions to be made at later times. For example, in the EMU, it was unclear what policy instruments would be used until late in the process, and thus statistical and accounting programs had to remain flexible late into the process to be able to deal with several options. This redundancy in planning creates expenses, but might be unavoidable.

F. Structure of the study

1.114. This study comprises 20 chapters that discuss the nature of the tasks involved in all major areas in setting up an union. For example, *Chapter 9 – Currency* covers a range of issues related to the design and use of the union currency. Many individual tasks are involved, such as overall design, security features, printing, standards for cash handling machines and vending machines, counterfeiting, currency usage patterns and demand, electronic currency, and plastic banknotes, among other items. Other chapters go into discussions of other specific topics, monetary policy options, or financial accounting for a currency union, for examples.

1.115. A wide range of major topics will be discussed. Creating a monetary union involves replicating all major central bank functions, but with greater complexity because of the need to harmonize and coordinate work of multiple countries. Thus, each chapter will discuss a major topic – legal foundations, finances, policy, communications, etc – but will emphasize the aspects that are unique to unions. The intent of all the chapters taken as a whole is to provide a good overview of the process of building a currency union. The chapters are also intended to be useful to various committees or working groups that authorities might set up to plan for future unions and all the numerous tasks involved.

1.116. Within each major area, there are numerous specific tasks, such as those listed for currency. The European Central Bank has identified about 200 unique tasks involved in setting up a union. Moreover, the list tends to expand over time reflecting new situations, ranging for example from creation of CBDCs, greater concern over financial sector stability, or policy shifts resulting from global financial crises.

1.117. Another major area of complexity is that European conditions were quite favorable to development of an union, but other regions lack such advantages. Some special discussions are included on how general principles drawn from the European situation need modification when used in different environments.

Timelines

1.118. Most chapters end with a timeline of tasks and actions to prepare for a currency union. The framework is presented below.

1.119. The first line covers preparatory steps, which cover actions prior to the actual process of creating the union. This includes negotiations involved to make the agreement to create an union and the drafting and ratification of the agreement.

1.120. Subsequent lines refer to tasks or actions that should be undertaken in or completed by that time period. Unless otherwise indicated, entries mean that the action should be completed during that period.

1.121. For example, in *Chapter 9 – Currency*, the timeline says "Select security features" three years prior to the union start up. This means final decisions on the anti-counterfeiting features of the currency should be made at least three years prior to issuing the currency. A long lead time is needed to set up the printing process, create and implement standards for ATMs and cash handling machines to reflect the security features, to train tellers and law enforcement officials, to inform the public, and print the currency, among other tasks. If the decision on security features is delayed, all the subsequent steps will be delayed and the start-up date of the union is in jeopardy.

1.122. Completion of steps earlier than shown in the timeline might be useful or necessary.

1.123. The timelines are intended to cover small or regional unions of around five to eight members. Large or continent-wide unions should move all steps at least one year earlier.

1.124. The overall timeline and the timelines for individual tasks indicate that at least four years should be allotted to set up a currency union, and five or six years is more comfortable. There are many complex processes, some require specific sequencing of steps, activities in different areas need to be coordinated, technical and policy research is needed, approvals and possible changes of course are needed at several points in the process, consultations with the public and market participants are needed, institutions built, technical processes changed, and a thorough process to introduce the new currency to the public and withdraw the old currencies must be set up. All these steps can easily take up four years of concentrated effort.

1.125. Some of the individual tasks are critical and failure to complete one task in the four-year period can delay the launch of the union. Building in extra time to allow for changes of policy or to correct errors is very useful. Although it might be possible to build an union in four years, there is little room for laxity, error, or indecision. A five-or-six year period would be more comfortable, but even that is less time than used to set up the EMU, which had resources that exceed those of most future unions. The time period might be compressed somewhat because lessons and principles can be drawn from the European experience, and future unions are likely to have less complex structures or fewer countries or a more direct decision-making process.

Timeline

Time	Tasks/Actions
Preparatory period	Ratification of a decision to create an union, including name, provisional goals, provisional membership, start-up date, and institutions and methods to prepare for the union.
Early actions (four years prior) Large unions and unions needing extensive capacity building should budget more than 4 years.	Create Monetary Council or Institute to design the union. Establish financing rules for Council or Institute Agree on allocation of union expenses and responsibilities. Gather information on national practices. Consultations with public, financial markets, authorities, and international financial institutions. Set up working group structure. Agree on convergence criteria and publication of first convergence report

Three years prior	Complete and ratify master plan for implementation of the union
	Committee work, with progress reports
	Key projects launched
	   Policy framework
	   Currency design
	   Central bank digital currency
	   Payments and settlements systems
	   Supervisory framework
	   Accounting and statistics frameworks
	   Legal framework
	Clarify responsibilities of countries, banks, and businesses.
	Begin adoption of legal standards.
	Begin implementation of policy operations framework.
	Publish convergence report, listing specific deficiencies

24 months prior	Preparation of operations systems. National ratification of legal standards. Design of public information campaign Negotiations with IMF, BIS, etc. on status of union
18 Months Prior	Currency production begins. Public information campaign partially begins
Final 12 months	Set membership of union. Final report on convergence and preparations. Establish policy framework Finish changes to legal systems.
Final 6 months	Permanent bodies of the union, such as union central bank or financial stability authority, are founded. Key systems tested and ready. Currency stock in place. Public communications campaign Exchange rate policy for new currency Union central bank begins relations with IMF and BIS

Run-up to union	Final actions to implement Public involvement. Currency distributed to money handlers and businesses On last day, national financial accounts are finalized.
Union day	***Union officially established.*** ***New currency is officially launched*** ***Policy control passes to union; policy operations begin*** ***All internal systems are operational.*** ***Payment and settlement systems are operational.***
Early union period	New currency circulates. National currencies withdrawn from circulation First policy actions taken. Close monitoring of experiences; Corrections as needed. Formal evaluations of results and key systems. Auditing of finances
Union steady state	Analysis of economic and financial results of the union. Review of all systems and introduce structural changes.

Chapter 2 – The European Monetary Union (EMU)

An introduction to its membership, institutions, and policies of the European Monetary Union. The historical development of the EMU is explained through descriptions of its predecessor organizations, the Committee of Governors of the Central Banks of the European Union and the European Monetary Institute.

A. European Monetary Union (EMU)

2.1. This chapter describes the EMU institutions and policy framework.[20] It describes steps leading up to the union, the union institutions, the monetary and external policy frameworks, policy instruments, criteria for joining the union and the process of accepting members. Descriptions of specific operations of the union, including lessons from the European experience for other planned union, follow in other chapters.

History

2.2. The EMU (or Euroarea) was created on January 1, 1999, when eleven countries entered. The event followed a long process that began shortly after World War II. Following the war, a vision of a continent in which wars could not recur led to programs for increased economic and political integration, including creating a common currency. Difficulties faced in early attempts to create a common currency or a coordinated monetary system for Europe ultimately led to the conclusion that a staged process was needed in which a predecessor agency would set up the institutions and operations and create the policy framework for the union. This view was presented in the Delors Committee report in 1988, which ultimately became the basic model for creating the EMU.

2.3. The *Treaty establishing the European Community*, better known as the Maastricht Treaty, (Maastricht) was ratified in 1991. It advanced the program for political, trade, and financial integration in Europe, and included the legal provisions that enabled the creation of the monetary union. The provisions were included in the main treaty, but were also attached in a more detailed form to the Treaty as a protocol called the *Statute of the European System of Central Banks and of the European Central Bank*. (Statute)

2.4. The system is built around the European System of Central Banks (ESCB), which encompasses all the national central banks (NCBs) of the European Union (EU) and the European Central Bank (ECB). All banks within the ESCB have specified duties within the monetary union. However, each NCB retains its own identity within the system, has its own financing, and can undertake activities in its national context not described in the Statute.

2.5. All EU central banks are members of the ESCB, but each country must meet certain criteria before it can adopt the euro as its currency and join what is called the "Eurosystem". Some members of the ESCB did not immediately adopt the euro. This was thus a split system in which countries that have adopted the euro are in the "Eurosystem" with rights to participate in monetary policy decision-making and implementation; the countries retaining their own currencies were referred to as "Pre-ins" and participate in some activities but not all.

2.6. The split is reflected in the governance structure. The "General Council" comprising the members of the ECB Executive Board and all ESCB central banks deals with issues related to all ESCB members. In contrast, the "Governing Council" includes the Executive Board and only countries that have adopted the euro. Euroarea monetary policy matters are discussed only in the Governing Council

2.7. Countries meeting the entry criteria and who choose to adopt the euro move into the Eurosystem when they adopt the euro. In 2002, Greece was the first country to make the transition, and a number of countries have done so since. They also enter the Governing Council and participate in monetary policy deliberations.

2.8. Major expansion of the EU in May 2004 brought in ten new members from Eastern European and the Mediterranean. It led to some changes in the governing structure of the ESCB in anticipation of an awkwardly large group of voting countries. A weighted voting system for the Governing Council was introduced, in which medium and small countries vote on a rotating base during different years.

2.9. The union was built on a methodical plan involving three distinct stages;

June 1988 – A committee chaired by Jacques Delors proposes a plan for monetary union involving three

[20] This chapter draws heavily on the ECB's excellent review of its policy framework, The Monetary Policy of the ECB, 2nd Edition. 2004. The third edition (2011) extends descriptions to cover innovations in response to the GFC.

stages. A year later, the European Council adopted the scheme and set the date for Stage 1 for July 1990.

July 1990 – Stage 1 began. It included abolition of all restrictions on capital movements between member countries. The *Committee of Governors of the Central Banks of the Member States*[21] (COG) was given responsibility to hold consultations to coordinate the monetary policies of the member countries with the goal of achieving price stability. The COG was also tasked to identify all issues for union preparation that should be addressed at an early stage, to establish a work program by the end of 1993, and create mandates for committees and working groups.

February 1992 – The Maastricht Treaty was signed. It incorporated plans for the monetary union and institutional changes needed for the union. It created the legal structure of the ESCB and ECB. It also took an important step in political integration through the founding of the European Community (EC).

January 1994 – Stage 2 began with the founding of the European Monetary Institute (EMI). The EMI absorbed the work of the COG in strengthening monetary policy coordination, and made preparations for the operations of the ESCB and ECB, execution of a single monetary policy, and creation of the euro.

December 1995 – The EMI published a schedule in which Stage 3 begins on January 1, 1999 with the creation of the euro.

June 1997 – The Growth and Stability Pact (GSP) was adopted to ensure government budgetary discipline in the Euroarea to support smooth operation of monetary policy.

May 1998 – Based on a review of the degree of convergence of EU countries, an announcement was made of the eleven initial Euroarea member states, and the irrevocable rates for translation of national currencies into the euro were set. Three EU countries remained outside the Eurosystem.

June 1998 – The ECB was established as the successor to the EMI.

January 1, 1999 – Stage 3 began. A single monetary and exchange rate policy applied for the union and all member countries. The euro was created as an accounting identity, with the exchange rate of each currency irrevocably linked to the euro. National currencies remained in circulation as "subcomponents" of the euro. At this point, the euro was a virtual currency used in the accounts of European governments, the ESCB, and the banking system, and over time in private financial markets.

January 2002 – Euro banknotes and coins were circulated and national currencies withdrawn from circulation.

Euroarea policy goals and tasks

2.10. The Maastricht Treaty established the hierarchy of policy goals for the Euroarea. It stated "the primary objective of the ESCB[22] shall be to maintain price stability" (Article 105), which was viewed as the most important contribution that a central bank could make in promoting growth and employment.

2.11. Other broad goals were also promoted, "without prejudice to the objective of price stability, the ESCB shall support the general economic policies of the [European] Community with a view of contributing to the objectives of the Community...The ESCB shall act in accordance with the principle of an open market economy with free competition, favoring an efficient allocation of resources..."

2.12. The list of other goals was lengthy, including a high level of employment, sustainable and noninflationary growth, balanced and sustainable economic development, a high degree of competitiveness, and convergence in economic performance. Even broader goals included promoting equality between men and women, protecting the quality of the environment, raising the standard of living and quality of life, and

[21] The COG is described later in this chapter.

[22] At the time the Maastricht Treaty was prepared, no distinction was envisioned between countries adopting the euro and other ESCB members. Therefore, its provisions referred to all members of the ESCB.

promoting social cohesion and solidarity between countries.

2.13. The point of the long list of secondary goals was not that the ESCB devotes considerable energy in pursuing them, but that the monetary union exists within the overarching EC framework, in which all official entities are mandated to respect, and to contribute as appropriate to the common goals. The EC does the heavy lifting in establishing goals and standards and implementing them, thus permitting the ECB to focus on its primary goal. The EC tasks covered numerous areas such as establishing accounting standards, creating legal standards and a dispute settlement system, setting up a bank supervisory system, creating mechanisms for economic oversight of countries, etc. These important contributions to building the monetary union considerably eased the process.

2.14. Maastricht Articles 105 and 106 set out specific tasks for the Eurosystem, as paraphrased below;

Define and implement the monetary policy of the Community

Have the exclusive right to issue banknotes

Approve and harmonize the issuance of coins by the member states

Conduct foreign exchange operations

Hold and manage the official foreign reserves of the Member States (although members can hold and manage working balances)

Promote the smooth operation of payment systems

Be consulted on and comment on any EC act within its competence, and

Contribute to the smooth conduct of policies pursued by competent authorities relating to supervision of financial institutions and stability of the financial system.

Structure and governance

2.15. The Maastricht Treaty Articles 107 through 115 and a Protocol annexed to the Treaty set up the structure and governance system of the ESCB and ECB and their associated powers and obligations, as paraphrased below. Many of the specific steps required reporting to, consultation with, or assent by the European Commission or European Parliament.

The ESCB is composed of the national central banks and the ECB

The ESCB is governed by the decision-making bodies of the ECB

The ECB is governed by a Governing Council and an Executive Board.

The independence of the ESCB is ensured by requiring that it will neither seek or take instructions from the member states.

Member states are required to adjust national legislation and statutes of their central banks to be compatible with the Treaty and the Statute

The ECB has powers to issue regulations necessary to implement defined tasks that are binding on all member states

The ECB has powers to make binding decisions affecting specific parties necessary for it to carry out its tasks

The ECB can impose fines or periodic penalty payments on firms for failure to comply with their obligations under the regulations and decisions.

The ECB can formulate the general orientation for exchange rate policy vis-à-vis currencies outside the EC, or make formal arrangements on an exchange rate system in relation to such currencies.

The ECB has authority to conduct negotiations with other countries or international organizations on monetary or exchange rate issues, and ensure that a single position is expressed. Agreements made are binding on the EC, the ECB, and the member countries.

However, without prejudice to Community agreements regarding the union, the member states may negotiate with international bodies and make agreements.

2.16. The Governing authorities of the ESCB are the Executive Board of the ECB, the General Council, and the Governing Council.[23]

The *Executive Board* consists of the President and Vice President of the ECB and four other members appointed after an extended approval process. The terms in office are eight years and may not be renewed.

The *General Council* comprises the Executive Board and governors of the central banks of all EU countries.

The *Governing Council* comprises the Executive Board and the Governors of countries that have adopted the euro. The Governing Council takes decisions to ensure that the Eurosystem's tasks are performed and formulates the monetary policy of the euro area, including making decisions on intermediate monetary objectives, interest rates, and reserves.

2.17. The *Executive Board* prepares the meetings of the Governing Council, implements monetary policy in line with guidance from the Governing Council, gives instructions on policy implementation to the NCBs, handles current business of the ECB, and assumes some regulatory powers granted by the Governing Council.

2.18. Some Governing Council decisions on important issues call for a "qualified majority". (Statute. Article 10.3). Greater than simple majorities are required for some major issues so that changes are possible only if there is a strong preference for the change. Votes are weighted according to the NCB's subscribed capital in the ECB; the weights of members of the Executive Board on the Council are zero. Decisions requiring a qualified majority must represent 2/3^{rds} of the ECB's subscribed capital and at least half of the countries.

2.19. The ECB regularly reports the ESCB's activities to the European Community and European Parliament, which may hold debates on the reports. It also makes many types of reports to the public, which enhances the public's oversight of the ECB and the results of its policies.

2.20. Prior to the start of the union, an advisory committee was created that evolved into the Economic and Financial Committee (EFC) at the start of the union. The EFC helped coordinate policies of the member countries and review the general monetary and financial situations and payments systems. Following the start of the union, it also reviewed the economic situations of countries that have not yet adopted the euro.

2.21. Within the ECB, numerous technical committees were set up to coordinate and implement actions in particular fields, such as banknotes, statistics, payments systems, etc. The committees have important roles in making general regulations and guidelines operational and for harmonizing practices in the member countries. Member countries participate in the committees and thus provide national inputs into the specific practices of the ESCB.

Subsidiarity

2.22. Under this doctrine, the implementation of ESCB policies is left to the extent possible with the NCBs, unless there are compelling reasons for their centralization. The concept of subsidiarity strongly influences the operational arrangements between the ECB and the NCBs. This important doctrine is laid out in very simple language in the Statute,

> "To the extent deemed possible and appropriate and without prejudice to the provisions of this article, the ECB shall have recourse to the national banks to carry out operations which form part of the tasks of the ECB." (Statute, Article 12)

2.23. Subsidiarity respects the traditions, closeness to markets, and expertise of national authorities in regulating their own economy and its institutions. It takes advantage of the resources and expertise of national staff. On-going national programs can be incorporated into the union-building effort. The NCBs maintain an active input in the process, thereby sustaining good policy and institutional development. Importantly, many costs are borne by the national central banks, but projects are instituted for the general operation of the

[23] The ESCB is divided into the Euroarea countries and the others. The others have a complex set of rights and obligations, including participating in some governance work (in the General Council) but not in the Governing Council, which is restricted to Euroarea members. For much of the public, the system is hopelessly confusing.

union. Subsidiarity was also important for political reasons because countries were not yet ready to give up some functions – such as currency printing – to a central authority.

Two pillars of EMU monetary policy

2.24. The Maastricht Treaty established the goal of the ESCB to ensure price stability in the union, but the policy framework was unspecified. A framework of a large monetary union had never been developed previously, and the potential member countries had followed a range of policies. A research program reviewed empirical research and theories about how to achieve price stability and constructed a framework consisting of two "pillars" – (1) the role of money and (2) comprehensive review of economic conditions that contribute to price stability and growth.

2.25. Faced with substantial uncertainties about the transmission mechanism and policy models, the EMU choose a strategy based on two pillars – A prominent role for money and comprehensive analysis of a wide range of economic and financial indicators.

2.26. In the first pillar, a broad measure of money (M3) is used as a reference value, but not as a specific target.[24] Euroarea monetary policy does not respond automatically to movements of M3 outside of its band. Instead, information about M3 is closely analyzed along with other information to gain comprehensive information on prospects for price stability in the union. However, the ECB said that "it has proven extremely difficult to give money a prominent role in conventional real economy models, despite the consensus that money and prices are related and the empirical evidence that monetary aggregates may be a leading indicator of price development." (ECB 2004, p. 54)

2.27. The second pillar consists of comprehensive examination of a wide range of indicators about the real economy and financial markets and variables and asset prices. The exchange rate and external factors are explicitly considered. This analysis seeks to determine the current condition of the economy as a whole and its many subsectors, the factors affecting the sectors, subsectors, and markets, and the effect of prior policy actions on the indicators.[25]

2.28. Information from both pillars is cross checked for consistency and evaluated by the Governing Council. The full range of information is used to set the monetary policy of the Euroarea.

2.29. Given the uncertainties, the ECB provides specific advice that might apply in future unions. "Given the uncertainties they face, central banks should always cross-check and compare the signals given by different indicators and evaluate the available information and the consequences of their actions in the light of a range of plausible models of the economy. In this context, policy choices which perform reasonably well under many plausible models and in a range of possible circumstances are often the best choice over the medium term." (ECB 2004, p. 55)

Price Stability

2.30. The ECB strongly defended its primary objective of price stability as a lesson built on long practical experience and intense research that it is the best method to achieve economic health and growth.

> "A central bank which maintains price stability makes a substantial contribution to the achievement of broader economic goals, such as a higher standard of living, high levels of economic activity, and better employment prospects. This conclusion is supported by economic evidence which – for a wide variety of countries, methodologies, and periods – demonstrates that economies with lower inflation appear, on average, to grow more rapidly in real terms in the long run." (ECB 2001; p. 38)

2.31. Reasons supporting this conclusion included;

> Price stability makes changes in relative prices transparent, which can provide signals to consumers and producers so that they can allocate resources efficiently. This raises the productive potential of the economy.

[24] See Chapter 5 – Policy, section "EMU policy on monetary aggregates."

[25] Chapter 5 has a more detailed discussion of indicators used in the second pillar.

Assurance of low inflation reduces the inflation risk premium in interest rates, which allows capital markets to allocate capital more productively.

Price stability limits diversion of resources into nonproductive investments (gold, land, commodities, etc.) held for possible speculative capital gains. The hoarding of real resources for possible future gain is not viewed as a productive use that supports economic growth.

Inflation can distort tax and welfare systems.

Inflation contributes to substantial redistribution of wealth, which can be damaging to social cohesion and stability. Poorer segments of the population are often less able to hedge against the costs of inflation.

2.32. The Governing Council of the ECB announced just before the start of the union that it sought to achieve price stability over the medium term because short-term changes can be affected by random or unanticipated disturbances and because monetary policy cannot be fine-tuned to ensure short-term stability given uncertainties about the strength and lag of the effects of monetary policy changes.

2.33. The Council defined price stability as annual increases of 2 percent or less in the Euroarea's Harmonized Index of Consumer Prices (HICP). Although not stated as obviously, price *deflation* was viewed as unhealthy and should be avoided.[26] Thus, the target range was an increase in prices between 0.1 % and 2.0 % per annum. The announcement of a quantitative goal was designed to make the policy transparent and to provide the public with a yardstick to measure the performance of the ECB. The announcement was also intended to affect expectations about future inflation by making clear the ECB's intentions to achieve the announced low level of inflation. Markets are expected to adjust to the commitment to price stability, which can contribute to moderation in price increases, wage demands, and demanded investment returns, all of which will help sustain the low inflation environment.

Transmission Mechanism

2.34. The ECB was interested in understanding the channels and mechanisms by which changes in monetary policy actions affect the real economy and prices. This knowledge is needed to understand the strength and speed by which policy actions affect the economy. The characteristics of the transmission mechanism can affect the ability of the central bank to act. One concern is whether the transmission mechanism in a union differs from the situation in individual countries; for example, in ensuring that monetary policy impulses are spread equally throughout the entire union. Also, knowledge of the mechanism helps understand how disruptions to policy effectiveness could occur and how they might be remedied.

2.35. Underlying the ECB view of the transmission mechanism was the view that monetary actions could affect real variables in the short term, but in the long run monetary actions have no effect on real output, unemployment, or real interest rates. Long-run real income, for example, is viewed as determined by supply-side factors, including technology, population growth, flexibility of markets, and the institutional framework of the economy. (ECB 2004, p. 41) Given the unchanged underlying real economy, changes in the amount of money in the system will only result in differences in the price level.

2.36. The ECB described a multistage monetary policy transmission mechanism and its effect on prices with a long chain of causes and effects.[27] In simplified terms;

The process begins with a change in monetary policy affecting official interest rates.

The change in interest rates affects rates offered by banks and market interest rates.

The policy change also affects expectations about future conditions.

[26] The need to avoid price deflation became policy imperatives during the GFC and Covid19 crises.

[27] ECB 2004, pages 44 through 49, describes the interactions in more detail.

The changes in interest rates and expectations affect the stock of money in the system, the flow of credit to businesses and households, the exchange rate, and asset prices.

These effects in turn have interactions with the real economy and the demand and supply of goods and labor. The changes in activity, in conjunction with changed expectations, affect the setting of prices of goods and services and wages.

Domestic prices are changed, as are import prices because of changes in demand and exchange rate changes. Overall prices are affected.

2.37. The ECB model provides a useful summary picture of the transmission process.[28] It is a complex process in which a range of effects result from a policy action. It is interesting to note that in the short-term the role of money *per se* is only one element in the process, and is closely linked with how credit is provided in total and to whom. Given the transmission process, with its mix of real, money and credit, and price effects, policy officials could adjust policy to have short-term effects on variables other than money (for example, raising interest rates to influence exchange rates) and thus there might be short term varying relationships between policy actions and monetary aggregates.

"The transmission process of monetary policy is thus a complex web of economic interactions. Despite the best efforts of economists' work in academia, in research institutes and central banks, it remains imperfectly understood. Indeed, the level of uncertainty facing the ECB may even be somewhat greater than faced by other central banks, since the ECB is responsible for an entirely new currency area. Moreover, institutional and behavioral changes following the introduction of the single currency at the beginning of 1999 may have changed the relationships between different economic variables" (ECB 2001; pp. 44-45)

B. Predecessors: Committee of Governors (COG) and the European Monetary Institute (EMI)

2.38. Two institutions that preceded the ESCB and ECB directed some of the early stages in the development of the Euroarea. The EMI in particular undertook many activities and roles that future unions will undertake.[29]

Three stages in building the Monetary Union

2.39. Two institutions played important roles in the preparations for the EMU. The first was the preexisting *Committee of Governors of the Central Banks of the Member States of the European Economic Community* followed by a new institution, the *European Monetary Institute* that made the specific preparations for the monetary union. The Delors Committee report in 1988 reflected a view that a more disciplined, multi-stage process of preparing for the union was needed than had attempted previously, such as in the Werner Plan of 1970.[30] The Delors Plan envisioned a three-

[28] The description above leaves out some elements of the model, such as export price effects, savings and investment changes, induced capital flows, or effects from changes in the economic cycle.

[29] This section, and other discussions about the EMI, benefitted from a day-long interview with Hanspeter Scheller, former Secretary General of the EMI, on November 30, 2007. See Scheller 2007.

[30] The Werner Report in 1970 sought to create monetary union by 1980. However, it was not specific about actions needed for preparation and organizational structure. It simply advocated creating a body to examine the purpose and institutions of the union. The effort lacked both political agreement and means of technical preparation. For example, Germany was not enthusiastic and viewed the proposed entity as a possible constraint on Bundesbank policy. Other central banks were split in their support. Also, during that period there was insufficient convergence between the European economies and generally unsettled economic conditions prevailed. The Bretton Woods system broke down and the onset of the first oil crisis put an end to the effort as different countries took divergent actions to either adjust to or monetize the effects of the oil price shock.

However, some recommendations of the Werner Report were later put into effect. In April 1972, the central banks of the EEC agreed to narrow the margins for exchange rate fluctuations between the member currencies, which

(continued)

stage process, which was an original idea of the Committee. It was endorsed by the European Council in 1989, with introduction of Stage 1 set for in July 1990.

> **Stage 1** – July 1990 to end 1993. It involved abolition of all restrictions on capital movements between member countries and beginning preparations for the union. The COG was in charge during this stage.
>
> **Stage 2** – January 1, 1994 to end 1998. The European Monetary Institute was created to take over planning duties from the COG.
>
> **Stage 3** – beginning January 1, 1999. The European Monetary Union would be launched with the euro as the single currency for the union and all member countries.

Committee of Governors Era (Stage 1)

2.40. The early preparations for the union during Stage 1 were entrusted to the COG which had been established in 1964 as a forum for coordinating monetary and exchange rate policies between countries in the European Economic Community (EEC).[31] Stage 1 included two tracks - abolition of all restrictions on capital movements between member countries and beginning preparations for the union.

2.41. The COG was asked to identify all issues for union preparation that needed to be addressed at an early stage, establish a work program for union preparations by the end of 1993, and create mandates for various committees and working groups. It was given increased responsibility to hold consultations to coordinate the monetary policies of the member countries with the goal of achieving price stability. Increased economic convergence as a result of consultations was also seen as contributing to the eventual successful operation of the union.

2.42. The Maastricht Treaty, signed in February 1992, was largely based on drafts prepared by the COG. It incorporated plans for the monetary union and the legal structure of the ESCB and ECB, In April 1992, COG published its first Annual Report (COG 1992), covering the period from the beginning of Stage 1 in July 1990 through December 1991.

2.43. As early as the first Annual Report, price stability was cited as the primary goal in guiding monetary policy of the eventual monetary union. The Annual Report states that although responsibility for execution of monetary policy would remain with countries through Stages 1 and 2, there was a heightened need to coordinate national policies and bring about convergence in economic situations to contribute to the smooth introduction of the monetary union. The report recognized that the interdependence of economies had increased as a result of liberalization of capital flows, greater financial integration, and operation of the Exchange Rate Mechanism (ERM) that created greater stability between national exchange rates. In this environment, it was felt that coordination of central bank monetary policies was increasingly necessary and room for national monetary policy independence was becoming restricted. (ibid pp. 1-3)

2.44. At this early stage, concern was also expressed over imbalances in government fiscal positions. The Report judged deficits and government borrowing requirements at the time as being too high. The high borrowing demand and interest rates were seen as possibly spilling over from national markets into the community as a whole, complicating efforts to

---

was called the "Snake". And in 1973 the European Monetary Cooperation Fund was established.

[31] The COG, comprised of the governors of the central banks, was established to assist country efforts in coordinating monetary and exchange rate policies between EEC countries. It met ten times a year.

The COG permanent secretariat was located in Basel, Switzerland at the Bank for International Settlements. Much of its work was through committees on monetary policy, foreign exchange policy, and banking supervision, with *ad hoc* groups created for special issues. It was financed by assessments on NCBs. It had a small staff, but drew on central bank staff and experts to contribute to the committee work. In 1990, an "Economic Unit" was added to undertake analytical work. In its last year, 1993, staffing increased almost 50 percent to take on duties related to preparations for the union.

enhance price stability and reducing investment and thus impairing the productive potential of the union.

Text Box: COG Oversight Functions

The early planning for the union was done by the Committee of Governors. In 1991, it acquired important new powers and oversight responsibilities of monetary and foreign exchange conditions to carry out this work;

Continue existing monthly monitoring of financial and foreign exchange markets.

Create a common framework for monitoring economic policies, including use of common and mutually consistent indicators.

Introduce annual forward-looking assessments of countries' monetary policies, based on common economic and financial assumptions.

Conduct regular reviews of outcomes relative to targets to assess whether policy stances remained appropriate.

Undertake annual reviews of public finance and implications for monetary policy.

Monitor the functioning of the European Monetary System and all factors affecting the system.

Monitor the system of short-term monetary support, which was a multilateral credit system providing short-term funds to deal with temporary balance of payments deficits.

Monitor development of the private ECU[32] *market, including monitoring of national actions affecting the market, and the state of obstacles to market development.*

Monitor conditions in payments systems.

Monitor conditions in bank supervision and regulation.

The COG was granted independence in making its assessments. The broad scope of the Committee's oversight functions anticipated the types of oversight that would ultimately be exercised by the monetary union. Moreover, convergence in national economic and financial conditions was already recognized as important for smooth operation of the union.

2.45. The COG also prepared proposals for statutes for the EMI and the subsequent ESCB and ECB. The protocols accepted in the subsequent Maastricht Treaty were quite close to the original COG proposals.

2.46. The above actions certainly anticipated much of what would later be part of the EMU. It is surprising how much seems to have already been commonly understood as necessary parts of the institutional and policy environments for the eventual union. This presumably reflected the long duration of close consultations between central banks to deal with a range of common problems. Also, part may have reflected the dominance of Germany and its policies given the size of Germany's economy and the ability at the time of Bundesbank policy to drive the monetary and financial developments in Europe.

2.47. The COG developed a list of union projects requiring long lead times. In each case, a working group was established to address the issues, in which each undertook surveys to gather information on national practices. (COG, pp. 58-64) Issues included;[33]

Conduct of a single monetary policy and harmonization of policy instruments

Printing and issuance of banknotes

Payments systems

Statistics

Accounting Principles

Information Systems

Monetary Policy and Harmonization of Policy Instruments

2.48. The COG felt that the complexity of elaborating a monetary and exchange rate strategy and setting up policy instruments in all economies required immediate work, although it was recognized that the ECB

---

[32] The ECU is described in Chapter 3.

[33] This volume includes separate chapters on each of the key topics.

would need flexibility to apply monetary policy appropriately given the situation and structural changes in markets at the time of the union. Three topics were priorities;

Concepts of the single monetary policy, including intermediate objectives, and the assessment of alternative monetary targets.

Methods of monetary policy operations, including division of responsibilities between ECB and NCBs. The practical application of subsidiarity needed to be evaluated in light of the ECB's monetary policy objectives.

Setting up harmonized monetary policy instruments, including ensuring that instruments and practices are familiar to markets prior to start-up of the union. Among instruments under review were open-market operations, standing facilities available to banks, and reserve requirements.

2.49. The third issue was a high priority. A survey was initiated of existing monetary policy instruments and procedures, covering frequency of operations, market counterparties, and terms and conditions.

Banknotes

2.50. The EMI was given responsibility for technical planning for production and distribution of banknotes, which would involve national authorities in both production and distribution. The initial survey covered legal aspects of issuing bank notes, and information on printing, circulation, issuance, handling and destruction of banknotes.[34]

2.51. The COG raised a long list of issues for review, including;

Should banknotes be universal, common with national identifiers, or national with euro area identifiers.

Security features and anti-counterfeiting.

Features for automated handling

The legal and organizational aspects of issuing and handling circulating notes.

2.52. Work was initiated on the transition to the new banknotes. The key issue was whether to suddenly introduce the notes ("Big Bang approach") or gradually introduce the currency. The options needed to be evaluated in terms of political acceptance, the credibility of the new currency, costs for businesses and the public, and practicality.

2.53. Finally, issues related to the conversion of the ECU into a circulating currency for the entire union were addressed.

Payment systems

2.54. Payment systems needed development to ensure that monetary policy impulses are transmitted effectively throughout the union. The Maastricht Treaty assigned the ESCB responsibility for smooth operation of payments systems, and this was empowered to issue regulations to ensure efficient and sound clearing of domestic and international transactions.

2.55. Key issues were seen as;

Development of commonly accepted principles for cooperative oversight of payment systems to deal with home-host country issues.

Creating minimum standards for domestic systems to ensure that they can facilitate cross-border transactions and avoid risks of scaled-down oversight because of competitive pressures.

Possibly create an union-wide large value transfer system to ensure transmission of monetary impulses through the union.

2.56. The COG recognized that payments systems are also partly run by the financial industry, which required dialog with banks and privately operated payments systems.[35]

[34] As described in *Chapter 9D – The Digital Euro*, future unions need to factor in the impacts of central bank digital currencies that could actively compete with cash money and affect overall cash demand and behavior.

[35] As also described in *Chapter 9D*, digitalization of official and private payments systems is dramatically changing payments and settlements markets, often in ways that interact with monetary conditions. In addition to creating (continued)

Statistics

2.57. The COG promoted a process to improve statistics needed for implementation and coordination of monetary policy. Statistical requirements needed to be identified and compared with available national information. Statistics should also be aligned with international standards and best practices. New methods were needed to compile statistics at the union level.

Accounting principles

2.58. The COG concluded that harmonized accounting rules were a prerequisite to operate a single monetary policy, but were also needed for internal purposes to regulate and distribute monetary income and handle foreign exchange operations. The statute calls for establishing "necessary rules for standardizing the accounting and reporting of operations undertaken by national central banks." It was expected that different national standards and legalities would make standardization a very complex task. Moreover, central bank and governmental accounts were involved, which often have special features.

Information systems

2.59. Rapid and reliable information transfer systems will be needed. In Stage 2, information exchange was expected to mainly be for statistics, but in Stage 3, all operations functions would be involved. The initial work involved stock-taking of national systems, and a preliminary review made in light of new tasks under the union.

Central bank responses during Stage 1

2.60. In general, EU central banks introduced the provisions of the Maastricht Treaty rather quickly. (COG 2003; pp. 71-89)

2.61. Several EU central banks introduced major changes in their monetary policy operations and institutional arrangements during Stage 1. Operational changes were designed to increase efficiency and flexibility in monetary policy operations. The changes often emphasized increased use of open market operations. (COG 1993; pp. 67-69) These changes may have reflected the new environment under Stage 1, when it became evident that monetary operations would need to change from a single country environment to become flexible and more competitive within a wider union context.

2.62. Numerous countries introduced provisions abolishing or phasing out central bank lending and advances to the government (as required under Maastricht), and also passed legislation guaranteeing the independence of the central bank.

2.63. Some institutional changes directly reflected the Maastricht provisions. Belgium made substantial changes, including phasing out central bank financing of the government. Spain introduced a law on central bank autonomy and to introduce all the provisions of the Treaty. Ireland introduced legislation introducing many of the Maastricht provisions. Luxembourg immediately began preparation of a bill creating a full-fledged central bank to replace its limited function monetary authority (which existed under a monetary union arrangement with Belgium). In contrast, the United Kingdom said that it would hold off making institutional changes until it made a decision to join Stage 3 (which never came).

2.64. With the founding of the EMI on January 1, 1994, the COG was dissolved. Functions and staff were transferred to the EMI, which initially was also located in Basel.

---

the types of programs in the EMU, many future unions will give high priority to digital payments systems to enhance financial inclusion of segments of the public with poor access to banking and other financial services.

European Monetary Institute Era (Stage 2)

2.65. Stage 2 began with the founding of the EMI on January 1, 1994.[36][37] The EMI was set up to advance the preparations for the union (which would be created in Stage 3), which could be as early as the end of 1996, but no later than January 1, 1999. At the beginning of Stage 3, the euro would be created and countries would transfer monetary policy to the union. The date for dissolving the EMI and founding of the European Central Bank was set for about six months before the start of Stage 3, so that the ECB could exercise continual control over the final stages of the transition into the union.

2.66. Under the Maastricht Treaty, the EMI was to specify by yearend 1996 the necessary organizational, regulatory, and logistical framework for the ESCB. This would need to include arrangements allowing selection of policy, but also all technical arrangements needed to implement the policies, whatever they prove to be. The work of the EMI would be based on the COG's preliminary work as well as its broad collection of information on national practices

2.67. It was recognized that the EMI would explore an unprecedented process and set up new types of institutions. Even given that some preparations had begun under the Committee of Governors, the EMI was given between three and five years to complete its work. This long period also permitted time for countries to enact enabling legislation and prepare the public for changes. Eventually, the full five-year span was used, which proved just barely enough time to complete preparations. (Scheller 2007)

2.68. The schedule for preparations was tight throughout the entire process. The requirement to involve national central banks in union operations to the extent possible complicated the preparations. Setting specific deadlines and reporting requirements helped push the project forward. Without an immovable deadline for the project, Scheller believes that the start of the union could have been considerably delayed. (Scheller 2007).

Duties of the EMI

2.69. The Maastricht Treaty prescribed the duties of the EMI. (EMI 2005) It inherited the COG duties and took on new responsibilities and powers that gave it greater ability to influence national policies to facilitate the creation and operation of the union. Strengthened powers included;

Strengthening monetary policy coordination to further advance the achievement of price stability.

Promoting and facilitating greater use of the ECU, including the smooth functioning of the ECU clearing system.

Taking over administration of the European Monetary System (EMS) mechanisms. This included management of foreign currency reserves as an agent at the request of national central banks (but without interfering with national monetary or foreign exchange policies).

2.70. The EMI was also to set the "regulatory, organizational, and logistical" framework for the ESCB to operate the monetary union. To do this, it set out a comprehensive plan to organize the work of the EMI and monitor and assess results. The plan included schedules for different committees and work groups, and set the chronological order for deliberations by the EMI Council.

2.71. The EMI stated that actions must be feasible and coherent. Contingency plans would also be needed, especially because of the long lead-in times

[36] A period of limbo existed followed the Maastricht Treaty agreement in February 1992 because of a German court case contesting whether the Maastricht Treaty violated the German Constitution and thus the deutsche mark could not be replaced by the new union currency. The case was resolved in favor of upholding the Maastricht Treaty only in November 1993, just before the start of Stage 2. The late start delayed for several months the move of the EMI from Basel into its new headquarters in Frankfurt.

[37] From the start of Stage 2, central banks were prohibited from extending overdrafts or credit to the public sector, and countries were required to begin the process leading to central bank independence.

for some projects. Continuous monitoring was considered necessary.

2.72. The EMI was also responsible for oversight of the development of the ECU. This primarily involved reviews of national legal systems to remove obstacles to its use. However, the EMI had to ensure that the ECU was not endowed with features of a true currency and that national monetary policy not be impinged.

2.73. The EMI also continued the function from the COG era to act as a forum for cooperation among EU central banks.

EMI Structure

2.74. The EMI was headed by a Council, including the president of the EMI and Governors of the EEC central banks.[38] A vice president was selected from among the governors. It met ten times each year. All Council meetings were confidential. Members of the Council were Governors of their national central bank, but were not to seek or take instruction from the outside, including from their governments. For certain key decisions of the Council, greater than simple majority was needed. A "qualified majority"[39] was needed for decisions related to monetary or foreign exchange policy, financial resources, or for guidelines on methods by which the ESCB would perform its tasks. This rule meant that important decisions on the future shape of the monetary union would require substantial agreement in order to be adopted.

2.75. A President was appointed based on common agreement of the Member states, at the level of Heads of State or Heads of Government. A Director General under the President handled the day-to-day management of the EMI.

2.76. The EMI had four major departments.[40] These handled responsibilities at the EMI and also provided the secretariats for the various technical committees that worked with national representatives.

General Secretariat, which had two divisions, the Policy Division and Legal Division.

Monetary, Economics, and Statistics Department. With the Department, the Stage Three Division worked on the concepts, framework, and rules for the union monetary policy.

Information and Communications, which worked on the technical strategy for the systems of the ECB and ESCB.

2.77. An important aspect of the EMI process was its committee structure. Committees were established in several major areas and were tasked to set the standards and promote implementation of the requirements of the union in their respective areas. Each committee had a permanent secretary at the EMI. Representatives of all EC countries participated. The EMI oversaw the work of each committee and coordinated activities so that the work of each committee complemented each other or did not work at cross purposes. EMI oversight was also needed to keep the contribution of each committee or working group on schedule.

2.78. Descriptions of the various EMI Sub-committees and Working Groups can give planned unions a sense of the types of activities that need to be reviewed to prepare for their union. (EMI 2005)

The *Monetary Policy Sub-committee* "assists the Council in strengthening the coordination of national economic policies in the European Union....In the framework of *ex ante* and *ex post* exercises, it contributes to the periodic consultations regarding the monitoring of monetary policies, in particular by examining the monetary policy objectives and strategies

[38] Initially, the non-EEC states Austria, Finland, Norway, and Sweden were permitted to attend many sessions as observers due to their many common interests with the EEC. In 1995, Austria, Finland, and Sweden joined as regular members, but Norway ceased participating following a negative referendum vote.

[39] A 'qualified majority' required 2/3rds majority based on a measure of capital contribution to the EMI and population, and a majority of all member countries.

[40] Legally, the EMI may act as an agent for management of NCB'' foreign exchange reserves, but no NCB exercised this option. If it had occurred, a separate Finance Department would have been created.

envisaged by the Member States and the compatibility with the aim of achieving price stability throughout the Union...the Sub-committee annually reviews developments in the budgetary field....also undertakes the necessary studies to facilitate the EMI's task of making preparations for the conduct of a single monetary policy....it studies methods and organizational aspects of the execution of the single monetary policy, with a view to the preparation of instruments and procedures necessary for fulfilling the ESCB's monetary policy tasks in Stage Three."

The *Foreign Exchange Policy Sub-committee* "assists the Council in discussion on exchange rate developments, the functioning of the EMS, and developments in the use of the private ECU. The Sub-Committee also regularly exchanges information with non-EU central banks in the framework of the "concertation procedure" involving representatives of the central banks of nineteen industrialized countries, which provides for sharing data on market development, intervention, and other official foreign exchange transactions. Furthermore, it is involved in assisting the EMI to prepare the groundwork for the ESCB's foreign exchange related functions."

The *Banking Supervision Sub-committee* "holds regular consultations on issues affecting the stability of financial institutions and markets. In the cases where the national central banks do not have legal responsibility for banking supervision, a representative of the respective national supervisory authority participates."

The *Working Group on EU Payments Systems* was responsible for coordinating central banks' activities in the field of payments systems, analyzing ways of facilitating cross-border payments within the context of the single market and as a preparation for Stage 3, preparing the EMI Council decisions concerning the oversight of the ECU Clearing and Settlement System.

The *Working Group on printing and issuing an 'European Banknote'* "assists the EMI in carrying out its task of supervising the technical preparations for the introduction of ECU banknotes. This area of work involves studying the various possible options for the design and production of European banknotes and the issuing, distribution, sorting, and handling of notes once they have been produced."

The *Working Group on Statistics* "contributes to the improvement of the statistical information needed for promoting the coordination of monetary policies in Stage 2, and also for developing the statistical base necessary for the conduct of the single monetary policy in Stage 3.

The *Working Group on Accounting Issues* developed "the accounting methodology used by the EMI. It is responsible for preparing the grounds for recommendations for the harmonization of accounting rules and standards in the ESCB with particular regard to the statutory provisions for monetary income, the paying-up of capital, and the transfer of foreign currency reserves."

The *Working Group on Information Systems* is responsible for assisting the EMI in devising and implementing a technical strategy for information and communications systems for the EMI and the ESCB.

Example: Working Group on Statistics

2.79. As an example of committee operations, the structure and functions of the EMI Statistics Committee is described below.[41] The experience of the other committees was broadly similar.

2.80. The Europeans followed a comprehensive approach beginning in the early 1990's to develop Euroarea statistical programs. It involved a range of subcommittees, numerous consultations with statistics users and national statistical officials, and interactions between compilers at the EMI and the EC Statistical Commission (Eurostat) in Luxembourg.

2.81. The early committee work resulted in broad agreement on many but not all of the many statistical aspects of the union. One problem was that statistical work has a long lead time and preparations had to begin before many policy and institutional aspects of the shape of the union were known. However, one key aspect of the work was an expectation that statistics

[41] Descriptions are drawn from Krueger and Kovarich (2006). The authoritative source on the Euroarea statistical program is Peter Bull (2004). Peter Bull directed the EMI Statistics Committee and was first Director of the ECB Statistics Department.

needed at the union level would parallel those already used by the national policy officials. The union statisticians could often draw on the range of monetary and economic statistics already compiled by national central banks as guidance for the types of statistics to collect and also for guidance on statistical standards. They could often also make use of existing statistics, but needed to address whether the methodologies were comparable across countries.

2.82. In 1991, the Committee on Monetary, Financial, and Balance of Payments Statistics (CMFB) was created by the European Council to help set the direction of statistical programs, especially regarding the allocation of responsibilities between national central banks and national statistical offices. Its oversight responsibilities from the perspective of the EC as a whole continued throughout the period of statistical development for the union.

2.83. In 1992, the Working Group on Statistics (WGS), comprised of the heads of statistics functions of the central banks, was set up. This working group was supported by a small group of statisticians—mainly seconded from central banks. Its offices were at the Secretariat of the EMI, located at the BIS in Basel, Switzerland.

2.84. The WGS began putting together statistical programs for the union, based on strategy options defined by the policy arm of the EMI. While the WGS focused on the specific needs of the union, it also needed to coordinate closely with EU statistical operations and with national statistical programs, which would be the first line data collectors and compilers.

2.85. Eurostat produced a wide range of statistics needed to support the currency union. Prior to creation of the WGS, Eurostat collected national statistics on money and interest rates, balance of payments, and financial account statistics. The monetary and interest rate statistics tasks were ultimately transferred to the ECB, and discussions were held on the boundary of responsibilities between the agencies. For example, responsibility for collection of balance of payment statistics – which includes both transactions in goods and services and in financial instruments was split between the ECB and Eurostat.

2.86. National statistical offices, either at the central bank or in national statistical institutes, also collaborated closely with the WGS and its working groups. The national offices had responsibility to collect information and carry out compilation at the national level. This often involved changing methodologies to harmonize with union practice, or introducing new data collections. National statistics offices had the responsibility to compile statistics for the country needed to evaluate economic performance and convergence between countries, and also to provide statistics needed to compile aggregate data for the union.

2.87. Eurostat and representatives of statistical offices of all EU countries contributed regularly to the statistical work of the EMI and WGS, at all relevant levels, and attended the working group meetings.

2.88. In addition, much of the EMI statistics work was coordinated with the IMF Statistics Department, which provided information on international statistical standards and methods of harmonization of statistics between countries. The IMF, and the BIS – which also contributes to international statistical work – regularly attended meetings of the WGS and other EMI statistical groups.

2.89. The WGS, which was comprised of senior statistical officials from each country, set the overall direction of statistical policy. It discussed and set standards and sent instructions down to technical groups. It also reviewed and approved the work of lower level technical groups. It was responsible for coordinating the work of technical groups in diverse areas to ensure that schedules were met and that work between groups was compatible. It also commented on developments in EU-level standards and contributed to EU reports. Many countries sent two representatives – one from the central bank and one from the national statistical office, or one each from monetary and balance of payments backgrounds. The WGS usually met once a quarter. The WGS later became the ECB Statistics Committee (STC).

2.90. In each topical area of statistics, the WGS established a working group of technical officials—in monetary, balance of payments, general statistics, and information technology. Each technical group would develop statistical practices and rules that were subject to review and approval by the WGS. Each working group had a secretary at the EMI, who maintained frequent communications with each country. Meeting as often as six to eight times a year.

2.91. The working groups created *ad hoc* task forces as needed to address specific thorny issues. Membership was voluntary and usually included about four to six people with key expertise from statistical departments in the member states. The task forces were asked to investigate issues and arrive at solutions quickly. The *ad hoc* groups were often able to arrive at a solution within several months, or were able to describe the options and implications of each option. In either case, the conclusions of the *ad hoc* groups went to the technical working group for discussion and ratification.

2.92. An important part of the committee work was collection of information on national practices. In accordance with the principle of *subsidiarity* national authorities implement the Euroarea policies whenever practicable, including the collection and compilation of statistics at the national level and transmission to the ECB for compilation of the union-wide statistics. National statistical offices were permitted some leeway to collect statistics as best suited for their own economy and institutions. It was important to collect information on the range of national practices within the union, to determine what was feasible, if proposed union standards created problems due to divergent practices, if countries followed required standards, or where standards should be modified, etc. The collection of information on national practices became a major part of the activities of the committees.

2.93. The four-level committee structure in statistics worked well, with overall direction, setting of goals, and coordination coming from the top, but with technical expertise and practical advice coming from below. It successfully gathered information on national practices and their potential harmonization.[42] One reason why the committee process was deemed successful was that inputs were received from the full membership and truly joint results were produced. (Scheller 2007)

EMI Finances

2.94. The EMI was given an endowment of resources considered sufficient to generate enough annual interest income to cover estimated normal annual expenditures, which were estimated at ECU 44 million. An allowance was also given for initial investment in equipment and to have working cash balances. The contribution came to ECU 615.6 million. Funding was supplied by central banks using a key based on each country's population and GDP. In 1994, the Bundesbank's contribution came to 24 percent of the total, down to Luxembourg's 0.15 percent.

2.95. During the first year, a total of ECU 31 million was paid, in three installments. Of that total, ECU 18.3 million went to cover current expenses, of which over a third consisted of set-up costs of various sorts. The EMI had no reserve fund and the ECU 18.3 million was made to cover income shortfalls, as permitted in the Statute for the EMI. Of the balance of contributions about half went into fixed assets and half into unearmarked working balances.

2.96. In early 1995, the EMI Council concluded that the full allotment of contributions that would be required. An additional contribution of ECU 602.5 million was paid in February 1995. The key was reallocated in 1995 to account for new members making contributions, and the 1994 contributions were reallocated according to the new key. The vast majority of the additional contribution was placed in time deposits to generate interest to cover expenses.

2.97. The accounts of the EMI were published in the Annual Report. The accounts were expressed on a going-concern basis in accordance with generally accepted accounting principles. All accounts were expressed in ECU.

2.98. The balance sheet was roughly split into two sections.

(1) Assets and liabilities related to the EMS were separately identified. The EMI's holdings of gold and foreign exchange received from EMS countries were

[42] In planned unions, the EMI's specific committee structure need not be followed, but the functions successfully executed in Europe – setting of standards, collecting information, coordination between national authorities, etc. – need to accomplished in some way in other unions.

shown on the asset side, and ECUs issued to the countries against the receipts of gold and foreign currency were shown as a liability.

> EMS assets were created by NCBs' contributions of 20 percent of their gold and U.S. dollar reserves in the form on three-month revolving swaps.
>
> EMS assets did not involve interest receipts or payments for the EMI because interest was treated as continuing to accrue to the underlying owner.
>
> EMS assets in the form of short-term discount securities was shown at cost plus accrued interest; and other securities are shown at year-end market value. This created valuation changes in assets that were carried over fully to ECU liabilities. A memorandum item also showed the ECU liabilities as "forward liability in gold and dollars" indicating a future promise to return the assets.

(2) The rest of the balance sheet overwhelmingly reflected the contributions from countries for investment in time deposits to earn income for EMI operations.

2.99. The income statement reflected the income from holdings of time deposits. By 1995, interest receipts exceeded expenses resulting in a large surplus that was carried over to balance sheet. However, by the end of the EMI, expenses considerably exceeded interest income. In 1997, expenses were over 25 percent greater than income, resulting in a deficit of €12.8 billion. The general fund covered the deficit. In the five months of 1998, the EMI ran a very large deficit of €22.0 million, which was covered partly by the remaining funds in the general reserve but mostly by additional contributions by NCBs of €17.6 million.

2.100. In the 1994 budget, 40 percent was allocated to personnel costs and 25 percent to rental and property maintenance. The balance of 35 percent was purchases of goods and services, of which one-third supported the large number of meetings needed with Member countries and with international organizations involved in the EMI's work. (EMI 1995 p. 71)

Income and Expenses of the European Monetary Institute

in millions of ECU

	Income	Expenses	*o/w staff*	*o/w other admin. costs*	Valuation and extraordinary	Net
1994	.3	18.3	*3.4*	*14.7*	--	(18.0)
1995	45.4	33.3	*15.0*	*15.8*	.4	12.5
1996	44.5	39.2	*18.2*	*18.9*	(.8)	4.6
1997	43.4	56.6	*24.9*	*28.6*	.5	(12.7)
Jan-May 1998	10.2	36.6	*14.9*	*19.0*	4.3	(22.0)
Total	143.8	184.0	*76.4*	*97.0*	4.4	(35.6)

Sources: Annual Reports of the EMI; ECB Annual Report 1998. Numbers may not add exactly due to rounding.

2.101. As can readily be seen, the costs for the EMI of setting up the union ran up quickly and greatly exceeded income accumulated during the years immediately before the start-up of the union. Many tasks were involved in setting up the operations of the union, and many coordination activities with NCBs and the public were required that could not be put off or omitted. The successful launch of the Euroarea partly reflected the availability of financial resources of the membership and preexistence of a key for contributions that allowed the necessary funds to be tapped quickly when needed.

2.102. The published accounts of the EMI do not represent the full costs of setting up the union. As stated in the Maastricht Treaty, under the subsidiarity principle the NCBs participating in the ESCB were responsible for their own expenses. No accounting has ever been made of the NCBs' costs, but they must have been substantial and probably well exceeded the costs directly borne by the EMI. The costs were multiplied by the number of countries undertaking similar actions. For example, every country developed and introduced new software to communicate data with the ECB. Moreover, the NCBs had responsibility to make up deficits of the EMI, and experienced reduced earnings because their contributions to the EMI reduced their interest earning assets. The costs of the introduction of the currency to their publics and the costs of the changeover were also borne by the NCBs and other national authorities. Thus, the costs to NCBs, and also national governments, were large, erratic, and heavily focused on the period just before the start of the union.

EMI Administration of EMS

2.103. The EMI inherited the COG tasks associated with administration of the EMS. This included automatic transfer of all assets of the European Monetary Cooperation Fund (EMCF). Initially the administrative aspects were carried out by the BIS, but the EMI took over full administration from May 1995. (EMI 2005)

2.104. The EMI carried out the creation, use, and remuneration of official ECUs. This involved swaps with central banks participating in the Exchange Rate Mechanism (ERM), or voluntary contributions of reserve assets against ECUs. ECUs are issued against the contribution of each NCBs gold and U.S. dollar reserves. The ECUs held by the participating NCBs are part of their official national reserves.[43]

2.105. Swaps were renewed every three months, which allowed adjustments to maintain the 20 percent holdings ratio, and adjust holdings for changes in the value of gold and the dollar vis-à-vis the ECU. Thus, changes can represent changed contributions, revaluation of the gold price, and exchange rate translation.

2.106. The EMI transferred ECUs resulting from transactions between NCBs' reserves accounts. Transactions occur in settlement of intervention funded through the "Very Short-Term Funding Mechanism" and voluntary transactions between central banks. The EMI also administered borrowing and lending under the Medium-Term Financial Assistance mechanism, which provided loans to countries seriously threatened with balance of payments difficulties. Under this arrangement, the EMI received funds from the European Commission that were on-lent to countries, and reversed the transactions for repayments. In practice, these types of transactions that had been created in response to earlier financial agreements were virtually unused or were being repaid during the EMI's lifetime.

2.107. The EMI itself did not pay interest on the official ECU liabilities – the earnings on the assets contributed by members to acquire ECU were considered property of the member. Interest obligations only became due if a central bank's ECU holdings exceeded its ECU liabilities. In this case, payments were covered by interest due from central banks whose forward liabilities in ECUs exceeded their holdings. That is, interest payments were handled in the EMS system on a net multilateral basis as

[43] Finland and Sweden chose not to participate in the ERM, but made voluntary contributions to the EMI in order to receive ECU. Also, Switzerland and Austria (before it joined the ERM) were recognized as other holders of official ECUs. Their ECUs were acquired in transactions with ERM-member central banks.

administered by the EMI, with no net interest flows in the consolidated accounts of the EMS.

EMI Advisory Function

2.108. The Statute for the EMI required the European Union or member states to consult with the EMI when proposing legislation in the EMI's areas of competence. This requirement allowed the EMI to influence legislation at an early stage to make it more compatible with the needs of the union. It also permitted the EMI a form of feedback on the types of issues relevant for NCBs and how they are addressing them, including;

Currency legislation

Status and powers of central banks

Instruments of monetary policy

Collection, compilation, and distribution of monetary, financial, banking, or balance of payments, statistics.

Clearing and payments systems

Rules relating to stability of financial institutions and markets.

EMI Relations with other institutions

2.109. The EMI participated in or observed various fora to advance work on preparations for the union or to collaborate with international bodies on matters of common interest. These include attending meetings of the Council of the European Union when matters related to the EMI were discussed and attending meetings of the ECOFIN Council[44] twice a year. Meetings with the European Parliament were also included.

2.110. Collaborations with EU institutions in special fields were also undertaken, including with national mint directors or Eurostat.

2.111. The EMI also interacted with international financial organizations, such as the BIS, World Bank, and IMF.

Dissolving the EMI

2.112. The EMI was dissolved in May 1998, and many of its functions and staff were absorbed into the ECB. All assets and liabilities of the EMI were converted one-to-one into euro. On January 4, 1999, the ECB repaid the NCBs' contributions to the EMI, less their shares in the final operating loss of the EMI, less amounts that the NCBs had used to make capital contributions to the ECB on June 1, 1998.

2.113. The EMI had administered the operations of the official ECU system. The ECU system was based on renewable three-month swaps. All the swaps outstanding on December 31, 1998 were reversed and the gold and U.S. dollar assets underlying the ECUs were returned to the national governments.

ECB early start-up (Stage 3)

2.114. The ECB was founded in May 1998, so it could exercise full authority during the final months before the launch of the EMU and the euro. The early start allowed time to bring staffing up to full strength and to test the full range of operations prior to start-up. Monetary policy aggregates were compiled in late 1998 so that the ECB would have a chance to examine monetary conditions at the start-up of the union. Also, some of the functions such as preloading of currency to businesses were full functions of the union even though it had not been fully set up.

2.115. The early start-up was also important because the final selection of countries for the union occurred only in May 1998. The countries needed several months to work with the new ECB and its staff and procedures to make a smooth transition into the union.

C. The European Currency Unit (ECU)

2.116. The ECU was a key part of the pre-EMU arrangements and the predecessor to the euro. The ECU was an official market-based measure of value that ultimately transitioned into the euro. The properties of the ECU are important in themselves

[44] The ECOFIN Council is comprised of national finance ministers who deliberate on a wide range of economic and financial policies and situations.

because they provide information on how a virtual currency can operate. Also, many future unions might go through periods in which they will operate with an unit of value similar to the ECU.[45] It is useful to give a brief description here, but a much fuller description is in later chapters.

2.117. The ECU was the accounting unit of the EMS, constructed as a weighted basket of EU currencies. The country weights were intended to reflect three economic factors – GDP, intraregional trade, and the share of each country in the EMS's short-term support facility as a proxy for the importance of the currency in international financial markets. Although objective factors were to be considered, changes in weights required unanimous approval and in some cases weights did not closely reflect the contributions of the three criteria. The British pound and Italian lira were underweighted, and the German mark was overweighted. By the time of the second reweighting in 1989, the economic criteria were no longer followed and some countries such as Spain were notably underweighted. (Girardin and Steinherr; p. 8-9)

2.118. As explained in Chapter 8, a basket currency will tend to harden over time because weights of appreciating currencies increase and weights of depreciating currencies decrease. Such hardening may contribute to the attractiveness of the basket currency and may support price stability, but such advantages might come at the cost of lesser export competitiveness because all currencies must have an appreciation bias to remain in line with other currencies in the basket. This loss of competitiveness and its real implications may be politically unacceptable to some countries. This hesitance can be especially strong if the strength of the basket is driven by a few strong economies while other countries lag behind. Such fears affected the ECU due to the heavy and rising weights for Germany. A policy of periodic revisions was instituted as a result. (Girardin and Steinherr; p. 8)

2.119. As covered in detail in Chapter 3, the ECU acted to regulate the exchange value of the national currencies. Each national currency was required to remain within a defined band around the "central value" of the ECU. Countries were required to intervene if necessary to remain within the band. Countries were subject to EMI oversight to ensure that they remained within the band. The ECU is likely to be an important model within the deliberations of future monetary unions.

D. Summary: Lessons and Principles

2.120. The history of the development of the EMU can convey much information for future unions.[46]

2.121. *The process was long.* A full ten years elapsed from the proposals in the Delors Report until the start of the monetary union. Importantly, the political climate to construct the union was positive at the time, and actions to start planning for the union began quickly. Thus meaningful progress for the union began early with little political wrangling or delays.

2.122. *The process built off an existing policy infrastructure.* The COG was already in place and had extensive experience in coordinating monetary and exchange rate policies in Europe. Union planning

[45] Chapter 9D suggests this option might be used in introducing central bank digital currencies in new unions.

[46] Important conditions that existed in Europe that supported the union often do not exist elsewhere and thus lessons from Europe can go only so far. Kenen and Meade (2008) argue that several conditions make impossible reproduction of the EMU elsewhere – the EMU was part of a much larger integration project in Europe that created institutional and legal foundations for the EMU; Europe was already implicitly committed to a common monetary policy; internal trade links were strong; and there were no major asymmetries in external trade. Such differences mean that the European experience cannot be completely replicated elsewhere and thus different structures, institutions, and policies must be used. Each planned union looks toward the EMU for guidance, but must be prepared to go in new directions – sometimes frequently. The same economic functions will need to be performed in new unions and executed equally effectively, but the ways that will often differ.

began as an incremental step, rather than involving creation of a new organization.

2.123. *A treaty established responsibilities, created an institutional structure, and set out phases for creating the union.* Once the framework was in place, the member countries understood the road ahead and their roles.

2.124. *A methodical, well-structured plan was needed.* The COG plan was accepted in a treaty with little change.

2.125. *The EU provided an overarching legal and operational framework that significantly eased the process.* Common rules in all countries allowed the work on the monetary union to focus on its primary goals, rather than having to introduce important legal, institutional, or operational changes in multiple countries. Important common institutions and rules included an authority to set common goals and policies, a macroeconomic oversight and policy review mechanism, a judicial arm for dispute adjudication, and common supervisory standards, etc.

2.126. The European countries were rich. Countries and their central banks could afford contributions to plan the union, pay for institutional changes and set up new systems, and pay for the changeover to the new currency. Banks and other private sector institutions and businesses were able to afford costs associated with the change.

2.127. *Costs of setting up the union were high and exceeded expectations.* Additional contributions at the end of the process were needed, which fortunately could be provided.

2.128. *Educational levels were high and communications good.* Rules and explanations could be conveyed easily to the populations and were well understood. But communications in many languages remained challenging and costly.

2.129. *Policy oversight mechanisms already existed and many policy goals had already been established.*

2.130. *Monetary policy institutions and operations were well established.* An efficient private banking system and securities market existed that could serve as counterparts to monetary policy actions and transmit monetary impulses through the economies.

2.131. A broad conclusion is that the Europeans built their union under very positive conditions. Europe had many resources unavailable elsewhere and did not face the same sorts of very serious problems that other unions will face. Despite this, building the monetary union was still a long and challenging task.

Chapter 3 – The European Currency Unit (ECU)

The European Currency Unit (ECU) is widely seen as a model for currency unions elsewhere. This chapter describes the ECU and how it operated. It also reviews the possible use of ECU-like instruments as parallel currencies during the lead up to new unions.

A. ECU – European Currency Unit

3.1. The ECU is widely seen as a model for currency unions elsewhere. This chapter describes the ECU and possible use of ECU-like instruments as parallel currencies in preparation for new currency unions.

3.2. The history of the ECU traces a process of moving from an accounting measure needed to transact official business among multiple countries, through stages including its use as a policy target, through increasing commercial uses, and ultimately its transformation into a genuine union currency. It was not a true currency, but during its 25 year-long evolution increasingly served monetary purposes. It provides a path that future unions may wish to follow.

3.3. The ECU began in 1975 as the European Unit of Account (EUA) to serve as a standardized accounting value for projects involving multiple European countries, such as the European Development Fund. Following the breakup of the Bretton Woods agreement in 1971, European countries lacked fixed exchange rates to denominate transactions between countries or for community-wide purposes. A common measure was needed to set the budget for the European Economic Community, handle settlements between countries, and administer the Common Agricultural Policy and price agricultural commodities. Moreover, a measure of value was also needed to measure investments and their future costs and returns over time. (European Communities 1984).

3.4. The EUA was defined as the weighted average of the values of the currencies of member countries of the European Economic Community. Its initial nominal value was set to equal 1 SDR. It provided a degree of stability over time in accounting despite changes in the exchange rates of the underlying currencies.[47] However, it initially suffered from use of nonstandardized values for the exchange rates, such as official values, values reported to the IMF, or market values. In 1975, this issue was resolved by following the example of the IMF's SDR (then called the Special Drawing Right) and using market-based rates in the basket. Nine currencies were included, with rates changed daily.

3.5. The initial country weights and subsequent revised rates for the ECU were intended to reflect three economic factors – GDP, intraregional trade, and a proxy for each currency's importance in international financial markets. Although objective factors were to be considered, changes in weights required unanimous approval and in some cases weights did not closely reflect the contributions of the three criteria. The British pound and Italian lire were underweighted, and the German mark was overweighted. By the time of the second reweighting in 1989, the economic criteria were no longer followed and some countries such as Spain were underweighted. (Girardin and Steinherr; p. 8-9)

3.6. When the EMS was created in 1979, the EUA – renamed as the ECU – was adopted with unchanged weights as a central element in the monetary and exchange policy of the countries. The ECU weights were reviewed every five years.

3.7. Under the EMS, countries expressed their "central exchange rates" in terms of ECU and were required to stabilize the value of their exchange rates against the ECU within a specified range (band) of 2½ percent above or below the central rate. That is, the currencies were supposed to remain nearly constant in value against the other currencies in the group, although the band permitted some flexibility. Countries were required to change their monetary policies or intervene in exchange markets in order to

[47] The need for such stability in accounting for transnational projects continues. For example, for this reason Bhattacharyay (2010) proposed a basket-based common unit for denomination of Asian investment in regional infrastructure projects. Various options for the basket weights are possible (GDP, trade, etc), but a favored measure was the weights of the inputs by currency used for infrastructure investment in Asia, or currency inputs for all transnational currency inputs within the region. This weighting ties the value of the basket currency to expected actual usage so that there is market demand from the start.

remain within the band.[48] Countries could also intervene before a currency reached the outer limits of the band, which created the possibility of an effective band tighter than the official band. Currencies acquired in the course of exchange market interventions were settled in ECU.

3.8. The composition of the ECU changed over time. Beginning in 1979, the ECU included the currencies of Belgium, Denmark, France, Germany, Great Britain, Ireland, Italy, and the Netherlands. Five years later Greece joined and all weights were recalculated. In 1989, Luxembourg, Portugal, and Spain joined, giving the final composition of twelve currencies up until the creation of the euro in 1999.

3.9. The ECU and the creation of a band for the value of currencies was designed to help stabilize currency relationships to promote economic integration. Trade and travel between the countries could expand because of more stable long-term exchange rates. Also, because countries had to make policy adjustments to remain within the band, the economies would be more likely to converge in terms of growth, inflation, etc. Countries also gained greater flexibility in the use of their international reserves because a common measure of value could be used for settlements between the countries.

3.10. The ECU also was intended to discourage speculation against exchange rates. Although currencies could move within the band in response to market conditions, if a currency moved toward the outer limits of the band a credible commitment by the central bank to intervene to move toward the central rate would convince potential speculators that movements toward the central rate were increasingly more likely. Under these circumstances, speculators themselves might buy or sell the currency in order to profit from the expected change. In effect, the speculators intervened instead of the central bank, which was a stabilizing type of speculation. This type of stabilizing speculation depended upon belief that the official commitment to remain within the band was credible – that the central bank had both the will and resources to intervene effectively.

3.11. Although the ECU was used as a measure of value and had a policy role, national currencies were still used for transactions. For example, a loan or grant to a country for investment in infrastructure denominated in ECU was still paid in the national currency, and thus its value in the national currency could change; for example, the national currency receipts and payments for loan for 1 million ECU would change as its exchange rate against the ECU changed. As long as a country remained within the band, the changes in national currency receipts and payments would be small and tolerable for market participants, but could be large if a large change occurred in exchange rates.

3.12. The ECU could be used for private commercial transactions. For example, some bank deposits were denominated in ECU, bonds were issued in ECUs, ECU derivatives were developed, and some larger companies shipping to multiple countries denominated their products in ECU. "The financial industry leaped on this standardized basket for the issuance of securities with an interesting feature of risk diversification." (Girardin and Steinherr, p.2.) ECU-denominated deposits by government spurred banks to begin providing ECU credits. The private use of the ECU gave it a greater monetary role. The Committee of Governors monitored the private use of the ECU and found that it had gained a significant amount of use for denomination of financial instruments, but had little use in nonfinancial markets. The pattern of issues reveals a mixed picture of private market use – around half of international ECU bonds were issued by national governments, and central banks held ECU 34 billion of the proceeds as reserve assets (COG 1992, pp. 43-5), which suggests that there was only a limited market for use of the proceeds. However, there was regular central bank foreign exchange intervention undertaken in private ECUs.

[48] An interesting feature of the band was that changes in other countries' exchange rates changed the limits of the band, thus forcing other countries to respond. For example, appreciation of the deutsche mark against the dollar forced other currencies to take steps to strengthen their currencies to stay within the band.

3.13. Payments and clearing arrangements for the ECU were handled by private banks. Central banks were unwilling to operate an ECU payments system. Private banks collaborated to create the ECU Banking Association (EBA) to operate an ECU payments system.[49] The role of the ECU gradually grew as more countries entered into the European Community and private market use of the ECU slowly expanded. The BIS's Triennial Survey of Exchange Markets showed that private ECU increased worldwide from .9 percent of all transactions (one side only) in April 1989 to 3.0 percent in April 1992. Within the EC, private ECU transactions comprised between 5 and 10 percent of total turnover. (COG p.33) This level of activity is not insignificant, but hardly an example of a virtual currency replacing national currencies in denominating financial transactions.

3.14. In the late 1980's, proposals were made to turn the ECU into a cocirculating currency. Britain, and later Spain, proposed a "hard ECU", that could circulate to find acceptance in markets. Such proposals were rejected in the Delors Report, and a later resubmission of the idea in preparations for the Maastricht Treaty were later ignored as a distraction from the task of setting up the union. (van den Berg 2005; p. 7)

3.15. An interesting aspect of the private use of the ECU was a slowdown in use in mid-1992 because of some threatened difficulties in ratification of the Maastricht Treaty and pressures this placed on the ERM. Increased interest rate and exchange rate volatility significantly increased the risk in ECU-denominated investments. Market participants shifted into strong currency issues or hedged ECU exposures in futures markets. (COG 1993; p. 32)

3.16. In mid-1998, in the final stages in the run-up to the monetary union, the values of each of the currencies for the countries joining were irrevocably fixed against the ECU, and the euro was created in January 1999 with a value of 1 euro equal to 1 ECU.[50] Thus, the ECU was the direct predecessor for the euro, but the process took two and one-half decades.

3.17. The experience of the ECU is potentially an important precedent for using parallel currencies in future unions. It began in a small way as a parallel means of denominating accounts, but expanded. The experiences of the EBA can provide information to planned unions considering an approach similar to the ECU. *Perhaps the key lesson is the need in planned unions for a common measure of value across countries and over time*, functions that were served by the EUA and then the ECU. With its adoption for transnational governmental accounts, the ECU had continued existence and became a commonly understood instrument, it grew to play significant roles in monetary and exchange rate policy, and had small but real commercial roles.[51] However, it took decades to develop into a true currency and experienced several notable failures before ultimately successfully serving as a transition to a new currency.

3.18. The ECU, however, was not successful as a parallel currency. It did not become a circulating paper currency that could move into general practice. It never developed as an attractive alternative to

[49] The ECU payments system converted over to become a euro payments system, and continued in competition with the official TARGET system as a result of its low transactions costs.

[50] Stage 3 of the monetary union called for adoption of "the currency rates at which their currencies would be irrevocably fixed at which irrevocably fixed rate the ECU shall be substituted for these currencies, and the ECU will become a currency in its own right. This measure shall by itself not modify the external value of the ECU." (COG 1992, p. 49)

[51] The limited success in creating a private ECU market suggests that in future unions official steps will be needed to actively promote a new parallel currency; Otherwise, the parallel currency might be limited to specific types of transactions or activities – it could be important within specific niches, but might not lead to general adoption as the single currency of the union.

national currencies and replacement for them, as was hoped when the EMS was created. (DeGrauwe 1997, p. 166). There appear to have been limited natural markets, except to serve as a cheaper and more efficient means to hedge the basket of component currencies. Girardin and Steinherr (2008, p.9) refer to the likelihood that a virtual basket currency such as the ECU or proposed Asian Currency Unit (ACU) will have a surplus of assets over liabilities. That is, uses for the basket currency will not naturally exist to provide a demand for borrowing the new asset. This appears to be an endemic problem, that can be partly addressed by mandating public use of the basket. Moreover, financial market demand could also contribute, but was not sufficient to create a critical mass in the case of the ECU. It never came close to reaching the point of collective advantage where an important reason for using the ECU was that other people were also using it (including for pricing goods and services). It never became convenient and natural to transact in ECUs.

3.19. Breaking through this barrier of common usage will, of course, be a problem for any proposed parallel currency. This will be one of the most difficult challenges for parallel currency proposals and methods must be found to address this problem if future unions elect to use the parallel currency option. One interesting aspect of this problem is that the U.S. dollar, euro, or other currencies are currently cocirculating in many countries, and thus already handle several functions that a parallel basket is meant to address (diversification, secure savings, inflation protection, ease in transactions, low interest rate, etc.). A proposed new parallel currency may well end up in direct competition with one of the cocirculating currencies and could lose that competition.[52]

3.20. The weights for the ECU were revised every five years. This was necessary to reflect changes in the economic series used for the weights, such as changes in the relative size of the GDPs of the member countries. A second reason was to deal with "hardening" of exchange rate baskets because the stronger currencies increase their weights over time and the weaker currencies become decreasingly less important. Over time, this can make the whole index too strong to be economically optimal. Hardening is discussed in more detail in the section on Properties of Basket Currencies, below.

B. Parallel Currency Approaches

3.21. One method of introducing an union currency is to cocirculate it as a parallel currency alongside national currencies. The national currencies continue to circulate, but the new union currency also circulates with legal recognition in all countries. This permits the union and the public and businesses time to set up the infrastructure for the common currency, become familiar with it, use it for transactions, build up a stock of instruments denominated in the new currency to create market depth and liquidity, set up the trading mechanisms and market infrastructure, etc. Proposals for a parallel currency are designed to not immediately restructure existing monetary arrangements and to lessen political concerns by giving new currency a chance to prove its usefulness. The use of a parallel currency also may reflect that proposed union institutions are too weak to rapidly introduce a new currency to large, poor, or isolated populations. In time, it is hoped that the new currency will be accepted and become the primary means of transactions and will replace the national currencies.

3.22. This section describes reasons why a parallel currency could be a feasible method of introducing a union currency, how it might be done, and pros and cons. There are three parts. The first looks at proposals for virtual or parallel currency in Asia as means to promote regional financial integration. The second part looks at the situation for countries moving toward joining an existing union as they increasingly begin using the union currency. This situation was widespread among the countries in Eastern Europe that looked forward to ultimately joining the

[52] Similarly, central bank digital currencies (CBDCs) floated by economically powerful countries could become liquid cocirculating threats to monetary and balance of payments conditions in developing or emerging countries or future currency unions.

EMU. The third part examines the idea of introducing currency in stages in different countries.

Asian Currency Unit (ACU)

3.23. Several proposals have been made to create an Asian Currency Unit (ACU) along the ECU model. Given the absence of strong regional institutions like in Europe, the proposals start with the proposition that a centralized program to introduce a new currency is not feasible, and therefore a new currency will have to either be a virtual (or digital) currency – essentially an accounting identity used throughout the region – or a parallel circulating currency that can cocirculate throughout the region alongside the existing national currencies. This section reviews several of the numerous proposals that have been made.

Eichengreen's parallel currency approach

3.24. Eichengreen (2003) argues that Asian countries should promote exchange rate stability between their currencies by creating a parallel currency, called ACU, to promote trade within the region, facilitate investment plans, and encourage intra-regional bond issuance and investment. (p.35) Drawing on the experience with the ECU, he proposes a multilateral currency grid in which relative exchange rates should be largely fixed, but he argues that in an environment of high capital mobility defending currency pegs can be difficult. Close convergence of policy and maintenance of confidence in the parallel currency will be necessary to sustain the grid. Alternatively, the ACU can be constructed as a parallel currency from national currency components.

3.25. The ACU would cocirculate with national currencies. Because of its construction as an average of the value of national currencies, it will be less volatile and thus might be preferred as an investment instrument or for transactions affecting numerous economies. It thus might encourage greater intraregional trade and investment. Eichengreen points out that the intraregional stability does not imply a stable relationship vis-à-vis external currencies - national currencies and the ACU currency could either be pegged to an external currency or float as a group against external currencies.[53] Intraregional rates stability would endogenously support greater trade and financial integration between the countries in the group.[54]

3.26. The ACU would be constructed by creating a basket with fixed amounts of individual country currencies. The weights are not specified but it is suggested that GDP or exports could be used.[55] [56] The contribution of each currency can vary if its exchange rate vis-à-vis the other component currencies

[53] Thus, hypothetically, Asian currencies could all appreciate as a group against the dollar in order to reduce inflationary pressures, but still retain the relative intraregional exchange rates that have been embedded into production decisions within the region.

[54] Eichengreen cites three reasons for adopting the ACU. "First, it would not be necessary to stabilize exchange rates between the currencies comprising the basket; hence fragility would be less. Second, the parallel currency would be more stable than any one national currency in terms of aggregate Asian production and exports; it would thus be a vehicle for encouraging intraregional trade and investment. Third, the decision to move to a single currency would be driven by economics rather than politics. Only when a critical mass of producers, exporters, and investors had adopted the parallel currency would it be clear that Asian economies were ready for monetary unification." (p. 36)

[55] Girardin and Steinherr (2008) give an extended discussion of possible weighting schemes for the ACU. They argue that weights depend on the purpose of the ACU. Purposes can include exchange market monitoring to measure deviation of a currency from a common value, denomination of debt instruments, a long-term store of value, or a parallel currency.

[56] Bhattacharyay (2010) argues that weights could be based on the demand for currencies for transnational uses within the region, which includes regional infrastructure and social investments, capital and operation of regional institutions, capital for settlement systems, regional assistance programs, etc.

changes. Eichengreen assumes that market arbitrage will develop between the ACU basket and the market equivalent. He argues that the ACU should be given full legal status. Although Eichengreen does not discuss it, the ACU basket would be equivalent to purchasing the full set of currencies on the market, and thus there would be an equivalent average interest rate and implicit inflation rate.

3.27. Eichengreen proposes that the ACU weights be periodically revised, as was done with the ECU. However, this feature might discourage private holdings of ACU-denominated instruments because of uncertainty over the change in value because of reweighting.

3.28. Eichengreen also proposes creating an official ACU to serve as a type of international reserve asset. Participating countries would swap part of their official reserves in exchange for ACU, which then could be used for regional settlements.[57]

3.29. Eichengreen envisions that over time a common Asian parallel currency could compete successfully in the region with the U.S. dollar as a means of valuation and trade vehicle. Over time, the market will reach a point where market depth and liquidity lower costs of trading in the new instrument and encourage accelerated use of the parallel currency. At that point, a decision can be made to move exclusively to the new currency.

3.30. The only steps described by Eichengreen to support the adoption of the new currency are issuing government debt in the parallel currency, creating a clearing and settlement system, and bolstering bank supervisory systems to ensure that banks' exposures to the parallel currency are properly handled.

3.31. Eichengreen argues that the adoption of the new currency would be the result of its economic attractiveness and not from political pressures. He believes this is compatible with the political environment in Asia where he sees little prospect of political integration as in Europe.[58] The adoption of the new currency would occur only after it had gained acceptance, at which time an Asian Central Bank would need to be created.

3.32. Eichengreen cites several potential problems with the ACU.

> First, financial fragility might be increased. For example, the banking system might face increased exposures, such as from accepting government deposits in ACU with no natural credits or liquid ACU market available. Increased supervisory oversight of such risks is suggested, but Eichengreen argues that supervision might be insufficient to contain the risks and that "an extended period when the parallel currency circulates alongside national currencies could be one of heightened financial fragility."[59] (p. 41)

[57] After Eichengreen wrote, large accumulations of international reserves in numerous Asian economies from about 2005 – 2007 suggested that another important use for the ACU could include absorbing excess foreign currency liquidity held by NCBs and serving as an emergency intervention facility to preserve the configuration of regional exchange rates, as envisioned under the CMI. Conditions changed during the financial crisis, but several countries still had very large reserves. A proposal for an ASEAN infrastructure fund to absorb excess reserves remains active – one issue is whether national holdings of infrastructure bonds qualify as official international reserve assets. (A separate but potentially important issue is that infrastructure bonds might be constructed as Shariah-compliant sukuks which could have important market development and bank regulatory roles.)

[58] Since the Eichengreen paper was written, events and programs in Asia, such as the Tokyo announcement in March 2008 of intentions to create the "World's largest business space" and increased cooperative arrangements among the ASEAN countries suggest that the atmosphere for transnational cooperation may be more auspicious than Eichengreen imagined.

[59] One possible solution not mentioned by Eichengreen is for central banks to set up ACU standing deposit facilities (perhaps on a transnational basis) to allow banks

(continued)

Second, the money stock might be hard to control with two currencies, with potentially inflationary consequences. He minimizes this danger by arguing that ACU transactions would be no different from transactions in foreign currencies, and that the central bank can use standard instruments to limit growth of bank assets and liabilities.[60]

Third, the liquidity of ACU markets is uncertain. Eichengreen says the central banks need to hold liquid ACU assets and the constituent currencies in order to maintain liquidity and avert runs. This again is a type of coordinated central bank activity, especially since illiquidity or runs in ACU are unlikely to be limited to a single country.

3.33. Numerous proposals for parallel currency regimes have been made. The review of Eichengreen proposal above yields a mixed verdict about the parallel currency approach. A parallel currency can be part of an overall plan toward creating a common union currency, and it defers addressing some thorny issues of control, ceding of national sovereignty, setting the policy regime, etc. However, it appears unlikely that a purely market-based approach will work and that some degree of government issuance, enhanced supervision, market development initiatives, and policy oversight and control are needed, both nationally and transnationally. This implies a great deal of coordination between countries in setting up and operating the parallel currency and the concept of a purely market oriented parallel currency arrangement does not seem feasible.

Bhattacharyay's Asian Infrastructure Currency Unit (AICU)

3.34. Bhattacharyay (2010) examines the relevance for Asia of the EMU-type programs to integrate European financial markets into a single market and concludes that bond market development in Asia can be promoted by creating a virtual ACU. He argues that the long tenor of bond funding based on nonAsian international reserve currencies makes them prone to exchange rate risk. A common measure of value constructed as a basket of Asian currencies reduce currency risk in bond issuance, promotes cross-border trading, supports infrastructure financing, and helps deepen regional financial markets.

3.35. Bhattacharyay's review of the European financial market development programs concluded the initiatives aggressively addressed major risks in cross-border investment, including currency risk, inflation risk, market differences, and legal uncertainties. He argues many of the initiatives could be carried over to Asia (with appropriate adaptations to local conditions) to support building of efficient, deep, and sound markets to support regional development. One of the most important elements is addressing foreign currency risk, which was resolved in Europe by creating the euro. Bhattacharyay concludes an Asian euro is not feasible for the foreseeable future, and therefore he explores using an ECU-like basket. He proposes creating a virtual unit with basket weights based on currency demand for infrastructure

---

to set off their exposures that markets do not absorb. This of course implies union-like cooperation that does not yet exist.

[60] The dangers seem greater than he suggests because the ACU can move within the region with limited control by individual NCBs. Because it is a transnational instrument, national authorities no longer control the monetary base, monetary policy instruments to control ACU flows need to be set up, and regional oversight and policy review are needed to set the policy of ACUs. All these steps would typically be the responsibility of a regional central bank (or some other active oversight mechanism), which however does not exist under the pre-union arrangements described by Eichengreen. Moreover, the ACU and individual national currencies will have different interest rates, which raises the possibility of arbitraging between instruments in ways that counter national monetary policies. These concerns could be amplified if CBDCs are involved shifts between currencies could be very rapid.

development in Asia[61] or the demands for infrastructure finance plus official cross-border transactions of Asian countries.[62] It is also possible to include non-Asian currencies in the basket because of their heavy use in procurement for infrastructure projects.

3.36. An AICU would be a more stable measure of value than individual national currencies;

Diversification into multiple currencies should incorporate counter movements between the component currencies,

Production processes are closely linked between the Asian economies and thus the economies and their currencies are likely to move in similar ways.

Policy recognition of the value of stability between Asian exchange rates can support intraregional policy analysis and dialog that are likely to preserve or strengthen that stability.

The AICU could be part of a broader program of financial market development (of which the Asian Bond Market Initiative is the prime example) that seeks to create new and deeper local financial markets. Deeper financial markets channel more investment of savings through Asian intermediaries and markets (rather than relying on the short-term recycling of savings through nonAsian financial markets) thus promoting regional internalization of investment and a shift toward regional absorption.

3.37. Thus, an AICU is an accounting device for valuation of transactions that could be a precursor to the type of parallel currency[63] but it lacks many of the features of a true currency.[64]

Pre-entry countries and the Two-tier Approach

3.38. In Europe, countries on the path for membership in the EMU are referred to as "Pre-in" countries. With expectations of joining the EMU, it can be expected that the euro will increasingly be used in pre-in countries.

3.39. Likewise, with a two-tier approach, countries may opt to delay entry until conditions are ready. In some planned unions, countries may be at different levels of institutional and market development. Some might be capable of adopting an union currency relatively quickly, but others may take longer for technical reasons, lack of political commitment, or failure to meet convergence criteria. This approach has been proposed in the GCC, SADC, ASEAN, and Caricom.

3.40. In both pre-in and two-tier situations, countries not yet in the union will continue to operate primarily in their national currency, but the union currency will exist in neighboring countries. It is likely that the union currency will increasingly penetrate the nonmember countries, resulting in a parallel currency situation. This will allow the receiving population to become familiar with the union currency, built up a stock for use in transactions, and may also result in the union currency being used for some types of transactions such as tourism, transportation, and border trade. Increased familiarity with the union currency may lead to changes in the political climate in favor of joining the union. Such conditions could ease the

[61] The investment demands for infrastructure in Asia excluding Japan are very large, with estimates of up to U.S. $450 billion equivalent. This very large demand, much of which is public or semipublic in nature, provides a large natural market for use of the basket.

[62] The second component is similar to requirements for official usage of the ECU.

[63] Such as described by Agarwala (2003).

[64] An AICU would need an institutional framework to operate the system such as provided in Europe by the EU supranational framework. The Asian Development Bank, ASEAN, or a new body might provide the framework. The organizing institution might also include arrangements to provide concessional financing for poorer borrowing countries, guarantee AICU denominated bonds issued by public entities, or provide insurance for a fee to private issuers. These types of options might be considered by new currency unions.

process of joining the union at a later date. For example, the changeover to the euro in Slovenia was aided considerably by both familiarity with the euro and by a preexisting stock of euros held by businesses and households. (Deloitte 2007, p. 4)

Legal treatment of parallel currencies

3.41. The idea of a parallel currency is that it can circulate freely within the economies in a region so that it either can serve some special purpose or so that the public can gradually increase its use until it can be adopted as a common currency replacement for national currencies. In either case, the use of the parallel currency must be permitted legally in all economies and the elements of legal protection must be similar throughout the region. Also, a cocirculating SDR currency described as a possibility in Chapter 1 would also need to be covered by appropriate legal rules. Setting up the necessary legal arrangements for all these cases may be challenging.

3.42. A parallel currency will need special legal standing.[65] It is not the national currency. The national currency is used for all transactions such as legal obligations like paying taxes, to denominate values throughout the economy, to set national monetary policy, and is internationally recognized and traded. It also has a rate of interest and has established modes for carrying out transactions and for monetary policy operations. The parallel currency has none of these properties, unless legal arrangements are made to grant them.

3.43. However, a blanket granting of domestic currency rights to the parallel currency may not be a suitable because there might be areas in which the parallel currency should be restricted. Can taxes be paid in the parallel currency? Can wages be paid in it? Is there a right to refuse the parallel currency? Can contracts denominated in the national currency be executed in the parallel currency, and what conversion rate applies?

3.44. Thus, there is a need for a legal framework that permits the parallel currency to have standing with the national currency, but perhaps with exceptions carved out for a variety of reasons. This mixed picture may be difficult to work into existing legal systems, which were not designed to handle a parallel currency and its implications. The legal process could be lengthy in order to carry out research on how the parallel currency should be treated in various situations, draft the legal standards, ratify them and put them into the national legal code, and permit time for businesses and the public to make adjustments. Also, implementation might be delayed until the beginning of a calendar or fiscal year.

3.45. In addition, secondary legislation might be needed to support the use of the parallel currency. For example, legislation might be needed to make counterfeiting of the parallel currency illegal. Or separate legislation may be needed covering allocations of costs to handle the parallel currency, or for financial accounting or statistical reporting, etc.

3.46. The parallel currency might also be a foreign currency. A foreign currency cannot be used for many domestic purposes, including taxation. It might be subject to controls. Its value changes against the domestic currency. Some countries have restrictions on use of foreign currency within the economy, or may require transactions be channeled through the central bank. Tax provisions might be different. Legislation might already be in place covering foreign currencies. It must be determined if any legislation (tax rules, accounting rules, etc.) covering foreign currencies applies to the parallel currency, and changes made if appropriate.

3.47. In some respects, the parallel currency might be similar to offshore markets that are

[65] As described in Chapter 9D, in 2021 El Salvador granted bitcoin legal currency status alongside the U.S. dollar, which is the recognized legal currency. The introduction occurred very quickly without much consideration to the legal issues described in this paragraph. El Salvador's experience might provide interesting lessons for others on operating with a parallel currency.

permitted in some countries, although these are often primarily with nonresidents. In such arrangements, the domestic financial markets are subject to one set of regulations, but different and often less restrictive regulations apply to transactions in the offshore market. Countries might wish to grant the parallel currency rights similar to those of the offshore market, but this is limited in scope and countries may want the parallel currency to have more domestic circulation than offshore market instruments are permitted.

3.48. If the virtual or parallel currency is limited to financial transactions, such as taking deposits or issuing bonds denominated in the parallel currency, relatively few changes may be needed in existing legal systems.[66] It is possible that legislation on foreign currencies can cover the parallel currency. However, such a passive approach may not allow financial markets to take advantage of special features of the parallel currency, and therefore its prospects for adoption could be limited.

3.49. In conclusion, if the parallel currency is intended for general use or to replace the national currency, it is likely that legal systems will need to define a third class of regulations for the parallel currency. The legislation will need to define the rights of and restrictions on the parallel currency and its relation with the national currency and foreign currencies.

3.50. Finally, within developing unions, because the parallel currency is intended to be useful for cross-border transactions and aid in integration of national financial systems, common rules for its treatment are needed in each country. Transactions in the parallel currency need to be handled comparably in each union member country, and must be legally enforceable in each country. To accomplish this, either a common legal code needs to be defined by some central entity, or national implementing legislation created that is scrutinized by a central entity to determine that it does what it should and is comparable across countries. The former case suffers from the possibility that a code developed by a central arm of the union will fit poorly into some national legal standards. Conversely, flexibility to allow countries to fit the requirements for the parallel currency into their own legal systems could result in loss of comparable legal treatments and a large burden may be placed on the central entity to examine all the legislation of all the countries and assess whether they are effective and comparable. In either case, a significant lapse of time will be needed for national ratification of the legislation and its implementation.

Statistical reporting of the parallel currency

3.51. Macroeconomic statistical reporting of the parallel currency will be needed. As a genuine currency used by the domestic population, it affects economic behavior and should be included in measures of the money stock, for example. It can also be a component of numerous other macroeconomic series, such as the balance of payments, central bank balance sheet, corporate balance sheets, interest rates, national accounts, etc.. The absence of information on the parallel currency can impair the analysis of economic and financial conditions. Countries and unions with an organized parallel currency system will need to take steps to measure its volume and use patterns.

3.52. Measurement of a parallel currency is likely to be quite difficult, in part because it can could be used anonymously for cross-border transactions. Techniques described in Chapter 11 – Statistics to measure cocirculating currencies might also be applied to measure parallel currencies.

Operations of a parallel currency

3.53. A parallel currency system will need an institutional framework to support its use, to gain the economic advantages it can offer, and to support its acceptance as a precursor for a full-fledged common

[66] Girardin and Steinherr (2008, p. 21) cite a limited number of special legal treatments that were created for the ECU, which was not a circulating currency and which was largely limited to financial transactions. The cases cited include creating dual foreign exchange markets in Belgium, tax exemption on ECU transactions in Italy, and special treatment related to capital controls in Ireland.

union currency. For example, a parallel currency might open up financial sector opportunities that might have otherwise not been feasible for poorer countries or countries with less credible foreign exchange positions. For example, companies in poorly governed countries or with shallow financial markets might be able to issue bonds in the parallel currency, but not in the national currency. This might also be important in money markets, where special efforts might be put into making parallel currency money markets operational, such as when national currency money markets are underdeveloped or high cost. The institutional framework to obtain such benefits of a parallel currency will need to be built as part of the union-building process.

3.54. In principle, nearly all central banking functions and nearly all functions of the union come into play when a parallel currency[67] *is launched.* The launch of a parallel currency could be a small-scale launch of the union – not all countries might be involved, only some functions might be activated, institutions and infrastructure have time to build to full operating levels, and everything can be on a smaller scale, and there might be flexibility to correct mistakes, but it would still be a complex, multi-dimensional operation. Systems will need to operate well to entice the population, businesses, and international markets to accept the parallel currency and hopefully ultimately choose it as their new union currency.[68]

C. Properties of Currency Baskets

3.55. The EUA and ECU discussed in the previous section are constructed as weighted baskets of currencies. Many proposals for new currencies, such as the ACU and AICU, are also based on weighted baskets. This section covers the construction of currency baskets and their properties. Although the concept of a basket is simple, some of the economic properties are not obvious. Adjustments over time are needed for a basket to retain its usefulness. This section draws on the demonstration of properties of baskets provided by Girardin and Steinherr (2008) and uses their numerical examples, but provides several extensions to their presentation.

Basket calculations

3.56. First, a basket is a simple weighted average of two or more currencies. The ECU had fixed weights for each currency, which were adjusted after five-year period or if a currency changed its exchange rate more than 25 percent. The currencies have fixed weights in the basket, but the exchange rates between them can change.

3.57. In a simple, two currency case with a bilateral exchange rate between the currencies:

Basket = Exchange rate A × weight $_a$ + Exchange rate B × weight $_b$

where weight $_a$ + weight $_b$ = 1

or generally in a basket of N currencies:

Basket = Σ (Exchange rate i × weight $_i$)

where i = (1,n) where i represents each of the n currencies.

3.58. For example, following Girardin and Steinherr, the basket has only two currencies, A and B with weights of 3 A's and 4 B's. That is, weight $_a$ = 3; weight $_b$ = 4. The exchange rate is 1 A = 2 B, or inversely ½ A = B. In this case, the value of the Basket is equivalent to 5 A or 10 B. Calculated either way, the contribution of A to the Basket is 60% and B's contribution is 40%.

Expressed in terms of A:

[67] Or similarly for a CBDC.

[68] The private ECU was backed up by the ECU Clearing and Settlement System, run by a consortium of private banks with the cooperation of the BIS and SWIFT. That arrangement can provide useful information about possible settlement arrangements for future parallel currencies. See Chapter 10 Appendix "The private ECU Clearing and Settlement System".

$5 = (1 \times 3) + (\frac{1}{2} \times 4) = 3 + 2$

Expressed in terms of B:

$10 = (2 \times 3) + (1 \times 4) = 6 + 4$

3.59. In such a fixed weight basket, the contribution of each currency changes if it depreciates or appreciates. The contribution of a depreciating currency decreases; the contribution of an appreciating currency increases. For example, if the B's exchange rate depreciates to 1 A = 3 B, or inversely ⅓ A = B, the value of the Basket expressed in terms of A is 4 ⅓. In this case, B's contribution to the basket falls from 40 % (= 2 / 5) to 31% (= 1 ⅓ / 4 ⅓). Conversely, the contribution for the appreciating currency A increases from 60% to 69%.

3.60. This feature is called "hardening" of the basket because stronger currencies in the basket become more important. A basket can converge asymptotically with the strongest appreciating currency in the basket.

3.61. Contributions can be adjusted without changing the value of the Basket by changing the weights. In the two-currency case above, assume that a contribution change is wanted, but the value of the Basket should remain unchanged. Assume that it is desired that the contributions change from 60/40 to 50/50, with the Basket unchanged.

3.62. That is, initially, $weight_a = 3$ and $weight_b = 4$. The exchange rate is 1 A = 2 B, or inversely ½ A = B. In this case, the value of the Basket is equivalent to 5 A or 10 B.

Expressed in terms of currency A:

Initially: $5 = (1 \times 3) + (\frac{1}{2} \times 4) = 3 + 2$

Reweighted: $5 = (1 \times 2.5) + (\frac{1}{2} \times 5) = 2.5 + 2.5$

Where $weight_a$ (2.5) is calculated as the (Basket value (5) × desired contribution (50%)) all divided by the exchange rate 1.

And $weight_b$ (2.5) is calculated as the (Basket (5) × desired contribution (50%)) all divided by the exchange rate (½).

3.63. *This flexibility means that the value of the Basket can be left unchanged, but the contribution of each currency can be changed. This is useful if currencies enter or leave the basket.*

3.64. Based on the above property, it is possible to set the initial value to be equal to any nominal value, such as the value of the U.S. dollar, euro, SDR, etc. That is, for example, the basket can be set to equal 1 SDR (like the original value of the ECU). When that value is set, it is then possible to calculate the weights. In this context, per Girardin and Steinherr, "Any resetting of the weights is nothing more than a redefinition without any financial implications."

3.65. Conversely, the calculation can estimate the value of the basket assuming the contribution of each currency is fixed. The size of the contribution of each country may have an economic reason. For example, country C may seek to construct a basket to set its exchange rate against countries A and B with contributions based the volume of external trade with A and B, which are 60 percent and 40 percent, respectively. As the exchange rates with A and B change, the value of the basket will change, and C can adjust the exchange value of its currency accordingly.

Choice of weights

3.66. The choice of weights depends on the purpose of the basket. A basket weighted broadly in accordance with its use will have a more natural demand and will not tend to wander in value away from underlying conditions. Several common weighting systems include;

Baskets constructed to reflect trends in countries' common trade in goods or goods and service. Weights based on the value of trade are relevant.

Baskets based on financial market activity. These could use weights based on the denomination of major financial instruments in key markets, such as government bonds or international bonds.

Baskets used as the basis for a parallel currency could be based on the volume of expenditures on domestic goods in the participating countries. This gives greater weight to countries that have large GDPs and have higher proportions of consumption out of domestic production.

Averages of the elements above are often considered. For example, trade, GDP, and financial market shares can each be given equal weights in the basket. This method may also be a practical necessity if the weights from the different factors are very different.[69]

3.67. The fourth choice above – the averaging of weights of likely components – can be taken as *de facto* recognition that it is difficult to identify the optimal weights to use in a basket. Rules of thumb or simple methods such as the averaging method may often be used. It must also be recognized that political influences will often affect the weights used, as was the case with the ECU. "If there is not long-term vision about the various steps and ultimate goals of regional monetary integration, then it seems best to have weighting that reflects the economic power of the participants, but avoids very large shares." (Girardin and Steinherr, p. 10)

3.68. A final point is that periodic reweighting can create breaks in the value of the basket and the implicit interest rate (see below). Because the basket might be used to denominate many types of transactions, including legal obligations, a break in series can cause serious problems, such as creating a reweighting risk premium. Girardin and Steinherr state therefore that in calculating basked interest rates for example "it might be preferable to aim in the long run at an unchanged currency unit" (p.3) However, they say that there may need to be an initial period in which reweighting could occur in order to gain experience with the initial weights to see if they are appropriate.

Weighted interest rates

3.69. Girardin and Steinherr discuss the use of basket calculations to set the interest rate for the ACU basket currency. Each currency in a basket has a different interest rate and the interest rate for the ACU is the weighted average of those rates. A weighted basket rate for interest rates will be used for economic transactions and difficulties can be created when the basket is reweighted.

3.70. An additional problem with using interest rates as weights for a basket is that countries with high interest rates are likely to depreciate because under interest rate parity conditions an exchange rate premium is built into the interest rates. The premium will be highest for long-term instruments, which will be most likely to change and have higher volatility. This premium can cause basket interest rates to differ substantially between short term and long-term instruments.

3.71. Girardin and Steinherr demonstrate this difference for overnight deposit rates, which have virtually no interest rate premium, and for one-year instruments where the premium can be significant.

Overnight deposits

3.72. In this example, there are 1.2 units of A and 1.6 units of B, with weights of .6 and .4 respectively. The overnight deposit rate for A is 2 percent and for B 10 percent. The weighted rate for ACU overnight deposits is $.6 \times 2\% + .4 \times 10\% = 1.2\% + 4\% = 5.2\%$.

[69] For example, within Asia Japan's nominal GDP weight is much higher than its weight in international trade. Similarly, Malaysia has a relatively small GDP, but its weights for trade and international debt securities issuance might be up to four times higher. In such cases, unless there is a strong reason for selecting one particular weighting scheme, an averaging process avoids the problem of potentially selecting a wrong weight out of a wide range of possibilities.

One-year rates

3.73. The difference in one-year rates taking into consideration interest rate parity implies that B is expected to depreciate by 8 percent over the year. Again, there are 1.2 units of A and 1.6 units of B, with initial weights of .6 and .4 respectively. The initial exchange rate in 1 A = 2 B, but with the expected rate after a year with 8 percent depreciation is 1 A = 2.16 B. After the depreciation, the value of the ACU in terms of A equals 1 × 1.2 + 1.6/2.16 = 1.2 + .74 = 1.94. The contribution of A is 1.2 / 1.94 = 62 percent and 38 percent for B. (.38 = [1.6/2.16] / 1.94 = .74 / 1.94).

3.74. From this calculation, the expected contributions for one-year instruments are .62 and .38 respectively. Therefore, the one-year rates are:
.62 × 2% + .38 × 10% = 1.24% + 3.80% = 5.04 %

3.75. Thus, the actual one-year rate of 5.04 % differs from the simple calculation using the overnight weights of 5.20 %. The long-term rate moves toward the lower rate in the basket. This effect will increase the longer the maturity and hence the larger the expected depreciation.

Equivalence between market value and the Basket

3.76. The market value of a currency initially derived from a basket and the current calculated value of the basket can differ unless a mechanism is in place to bring the market value back in line with the basket. During the initial period for the ECU, this was done by the EBA system which permitted payments either in ECU or in the actual basket of currencies. Under this arrangement, arbitrage ensured that differences in value did not exceed the costs of acquiring and delivering the component currencies.

3.77. However, capital controls[70] made it hard to operate this arbitrage system and it was ultimately scrapped and payments were permitted only in ECU. This broke the link between the ECU and the basket of underlying currencies. In the 1992 currency crisis, the difference between the market value of the ECU and the basket value reached 10 percent (ibid. p.5). This demonstrates that there is a need for a basket currency to have some mechanism to prevent drift of the virtual currency away from the basket. This could be done by allowing delivery in the underlying currencies, as was done by the EBA, if this is feasible; by interventions by central banks; or by a pool set up to support the virtual currency.

"Hard" baskets and the "hard ECU"

3.78. It is also possible to construct a basket with fixed contributions and variable units of each currency. In such a scheme, every change in the exchange value of a currency leads to an adjustment in the number of units of each currency to keep the weights constant. This means that the basket never changes in value against any of the component currencies. This makes the basket "harder" than any component currency because all currencies experience periods when its exchange value declines.

3.79. This type of scheme was proposed by the British during the negotiations for the Maastricht Treaty to create a "hard" ECU as a circulating currency. However, at the time it was considered a diversion from the task of creating a common currency and was never seriously deliberated.

3.80. An example is provided by Girardin and Steinherr. The initial values are the same as in the previous example, but it is given that the initial exchange values against the U.S. dollar are 1 dollar = 2 A = 4 B. If A or B change value against the dollar, their weights must be changed;

> If B devalues by 50 percent against the dollar and A, then the new rates are 1 dollar = 2 A = 6 B.

[70] Similarly, in pre-union situations, capital controls might hinder the operation of a parallel currency system. Thus, dismantling of capital controls logically should accompany programs to launch a parallel currency system.

This means that the number of units of B increase from 1.6 to 2.4 units.

After the devaluation, the dollar value of the basket is 1.2/2 + 2.4/6 = 1.

After the devaluation, the value of the basket in terms of A is 1.2/1 + 2.4/(6/2) = 2.

After the devaluation, the value of the basket in terms of B is 1.2/⅓ + 2.4/1 = 6.

That is, a "hard" basket does not decline in value against any currency, but increases in value against the depreciating currency. A "hard" basket can only increase in value. Total contributions of each currency matter, but the specific weights for number of units of currency are irrelevant for the hard basket because they will in fact constantly be changing.

Divergence from basket central rates

3.81. The ECU made special exchange policy use of basket calculations to measure whether a component currency was diverging from the central rate for the basket. Within the ECU, currencies were permitted to move in response to market pressures up to 2½ % above or below the central rate. If the currency diverged by 75 % of that band, it was required to enter consultations with other ECU countries and explain whether the divergence was caused by temporary factors or was the result of more fundamental factors. Corrective steps could follow such discussions. Countries often took actions prior to reaching the threshold for consultations. (Girardin and Steinherr, p.14) If the currency reached the 2½ % limit, countries were required to intervene to return into the band.

3.82. The movement of the basket and its central rate affect the position of every currency in the basket. It is possible that a currency with a stable exchange rate against major nonbasket currencies and which is in general macroeconomic and external balance will find that it needs to make adjustments relative to the currencies in the basket because the other currencies in the basket are appreciating or depreciating and thus the basket central rate and the divergence thresholds are moving.

3.83. Within such divergence measures, the weight of each currency matters, because it is harder for a major currency within a basket to move to the outer limits because as its exchange rate moves, it in effect drags the basket along with it. In contrast, movement of a smaller currency has less impact on the central rate.

It is possible to adjust for this effect by estimating how much a maximum permitted move in each currency will move the basket. Because the basket moves some with any currency move, the maximum permitted movement of any individual currency will always be greater than the currency's permitted divergence against the basket. For example, if the maximum permitted movement of a small currency is 3 percent, it may reach its outer limit if it moves 2.8 percent against the basket. In contrast, a major currency in the basket may reach its maximum permitted movement if it diverges only a bit more than 1 percent vis-à-vis the central rate of the basket.

To construct such divergence indicators, the value of the basket should be expressed in terms of each currency. Thus, the value of the basket expressed in currency A is

$$\text{Basket}^a = w_a + w_b R_{B/A} + w_c R_{C/A} + \quad + w_n R_{N/A}$$

Where w_i is the weight of the currency (number of units of currency i), and $R_{I/A}$ is the exchange rate of currency I relative to currency A.

The change in the value of the basket from a change in the bilateral exchange rate for A is then

$$\Delta\text{Basket}^a = w_b \Delta R_{B/A} + w_c \Delta R_{C/A} + \quad + w_n \Delta R_{N/A}$$

Then m, the maximum variation of currency A against other basket currencies, is defined, for example at 3 percent. This is represented in the above equation as Δ_m, giving the simplified expression on the right side below.

$$\Delta_m Basket^a = w_b \Delta_m R_{B/A} + w_c \Delta_m R_{C/A} + \; + w_n \Delta_m R_{N/A} = (1 - w_a)m.$$

The expression $(1 - w_a)m$ easily permits calculation of the maximum divergence of each currency against the basket. If the maximum permitted bilateral exchange change, m, is set to 3, and the currency has a weight in the basket of .4, then (1 - .4)3 = (.6)3 = 1.8 percent. Thus, if a large currency comprises 4/10[ths] of the total basket, then it reaches it maximum permitted 3 percent bilateral exchange rate changes against the other basket currencies when it diverges 1.8 percent against the central rate of the basket.

D. The ECU as a model for future unions

3.84. As already mentioned, the ECU was established as an official and market-based measure of value that ultimately transitioned into the euro. Regions planning unions might go through periods in which they will operate with an unit such as the ECU. The particular features of the ECU and its experiences are especially relevant in these cases.

3.85. As explained above, a basket currency will tend to harden over time because the weights of appreciating currencies increase and the weights of depreciating currencies decrease. Such hardening can contribute to the attractiveness of the basket currency and may support price stability, but such advantages may come at the cost of lesser export competitiveness because all countries with currencies in the basket will have an appreciation bias to remain in line with other currencies in the basket. This loss of competitiveness and its real implications may be politically unacceptable to some countries. This hesitance can be especially strong if the strength of the basket is driven by a few strong economies while other countries lag behind. The ECU was affected by such fears that stemmed in particular from the heavy and rising weights for Germany. (Girardin and Steinherr, p. 8)

3.86. The use of exchange rate divergence indicators can easily be transferred to cooperative regional arrangements where there is a desire to maintain close interrelationships between independent currencies, or where there is interest in knowing how divergence of one currency within a region might affect the other currencies. Using a preset rule based on an objective measure of exchange rate divergence from the basket can facilitate the start of discussions, and avoids political delays in initiating consultations. Importantly, within a basket, any currency can be strong or weak relative to the central rate and thus can be involved in discussions – this applies symmetrically to currencies that are too strong relative to the basket as well as those that are too weak.

3.87. The method can also be used for real exchange rate changes. This is useful if there are inflation differences between the countries that over time can cause significant differences in the relative competitiveness between the regional currencies, or to examine whether all regional currencies remain competitive against major external currencies, such as the dollar or euro.

3.88. Girardin and Steinherr argue that basket systems can admit weaker currencies. This makes the basket more representative and the operations of a basket will tend to reduce the weights of weaker currencies, unless those currencies act to strengthen their value and avoid losing weight – an implicit inducement to exercise better policy.

3.89. However, Girardin and Steinherr also argue that a basket must have some strong currencies and cannot be constructed of only weak currencies that the market does not find credible. If this argument is accepted, currencies in regions where economic conditions and governance are weak and not credible in international markets should not attempt to move toward an union by using a parallel currency approach. Potential users simply will avoid the currency. The option in this situation is to move straight to an union currency to replace all national currencies and endow it with financial backing to provide strength in markets and to exercise prudent monetary and exchange policies that help build credibility of the currency.

CHAPTER 4 – MEMBERSHIP AND CONVERGENCE

Who will be members and what are their rights and obligations within the union. The use of convergence criteria to select union member countries. Pre-union status and accepting new states.

A. Advantages and disadvantages of unions

4.1 Should a country join a currency union and share a common currency with other countries? What are the advantages or disadvantages? These are two key questions facing many countries in the world today. Countries are increasingly facing decision points about the extent to which they should establish cooperative arrangements with neighboring countries in areas such as trade, financial integration, monetary cooperation, and exchange rates. Should countries retain their independent sovereign powers to decide on policies in these areas? Or should unions be formed in which policies for multiple countries are decided jointly for the mutual benefit of the participating countries?

4.2 This chapter addresses the issue of membership in a currency union. It is divided into two parts. The first half examines the Theory of Optimum Currency Areas is see what it says and does not say about whether countries should join together in an union. The second half addresses the practical aspects of membership in an union. It looks at the European experience in selecting members, the rights and obligations of the members, and equally importantly, the handling of countries seeking future membership.

B. Optimum Currency Areas (Theory and practice)

Definition

4.3 An optimum currency area (OCA) comprises a grouping of countries that share economic characteristics that allow them to irrevocably link their exchange rates or adopt a common currency. Countries that share a certain set of characteristics can benefit from the execution of a common exchange or monetary policy, hence it can be "optimal" for them to be in an union. The elements are often called "convergence criteria." In contrast, where the characteristics differ, or are "nonconvergent", a common union policy applied to all member countries might be harmful to individual members and thus it could be prudent for nonconvergent countries to operate their own monetary and exchange rate policies rather submit to common union policies.

4.4 The idea of "optimal" implies boundaries to an OCA – some countries share properties that make it advantageous to link up, but other groups of countries do not sufficiently share the properties and thus should not forge links and should continue to operate their own monetary and exchange rate systems. The identification of OCAs has often been tried by examining the degree of common trade in goods and services between the countries, or whether the countries will respond in a similar manner to common shocks. When a grouping has sufficient common properties or behaviors, a common monetary or exchange policy for the group can make sense; if common properties are lacking, it is probably advantageous for each country to operate its policies independently. In concept, the OCA will help in drawing the boundaries between countries that should join and operate a joint policy, and those countries that should retain independent policies. An important current issue discussed below is how to define the boundaries of what constitutes convergence. (See Enoch and Krueger, 2009).

4.5 In its simplest form, OCA addresses the question of under what circumstances is it advantageous for a country to irrevocably link the exchange rate of its currency to another currency. This does not necessarily mean that a currency union – which is perhaps the purest form of an OCA - will be formed. For example, a country could unilaterally link its exchange rate to another country without creating a formal union, which is not at all uncommon. Countries in an union irrevocably surrender their monetary and exchange rate policy to a central body that makes and executes policies for the union as a whole and for the union's member countries. Countries might not wish to make that irrevocable decision, but might prefer to find other ways to cooperate with their neighbors on monetary and exchange rate issues.

4.6 OCA theory provides criteria about when countries should join into unions. Academically, the theory has held up quite well in describing key types of issues affecting the decision to form an union, but its focus and answers it gives have tended to change over time.

4.7 Numerous empirical studies have examined whether particular groups of countries constitute OCAs. More often than not they provide negative answers and thus conclude that the countries should *not* form an union.

4.8 However, initiatives to create unions have continued regardless of such empirical research and many regions still aspire to create a currency union. Indeed, it is often questioned whether the Euroarea comprised an OCA, but it has built strong linkages between the member economies and successfully executed common monetary and exchange rate policies. How does OCA theory reconcile its often negative perspective with the success of the EMU and the broad urge to create new unions? That tension has caused the focus of the theory to change over time and led to highlighting the "endogeneity" of currency unions – the idea that creating an union over time brings about convergence in the economic and financial conditions in the countries that belong to the union – in effect, over time they become more like an OCA. The endogeneity hypothesis is discussed later. .

4.9 The relevance of convergence and possible endogeneity is especially relevant for some planned unions because only loose convergence might exist before attempting to create an union. Is it prudent to attempt to create an union without first achieving a high degree of convergence? Without prior convergence, are the union experiments doomed? Conversely, can the tests of convergence be eased and by how much? Will convergence be created more easily once countries are in an union? These questions are being raised at this very instant by planned unions. A separate section on loose convergence is later in this chapter.

Evolution of OCA theory

4.10 The theory was developed by Robert Mundell in 1961, for which he was rewarded the Nobel Prize. OCA has dominated thinking about currency unions ever since and it has played an important role in developing the procedures for selecting EMU members. It continues to be used to analyze whether a group of countries should create an union. However, OCA theory has not been static but has been modified by many contributions over the years, to the point where its advice today might completely differ from the past. Today, it is common to think that countries might first create an union because they expect that over time it will help create an OCA because once in the union the countries will cooperate, harmonize legal and institutional arrangements, and become more interlinked and economically more like each other.

4.11 The evolution of OCA theory is nicely summarized by Mongelli (2002), who identifies five phases in the development of the theory;

Pioneering phase during the 1960's and early 1970's asked what constitutes an OCA and its properties, how boundaries should be drawn, and what are the benefits or costs. The macroeconomic properties of OCAs were examined and conclusions drawn about the benefits and costs.

Reconciliation phase during the 1970s examined the properties of OCA in detail and weighed their importance. A recurring theme was identifying the types of shocks that could hit an OCA and whether they hit countries in a similar or dissimilar manner.

A *reassessment phase* in the 1980s and early 1990s led to development of the "new theory of optimum currency areas", which tended to view currency unions more favorably than during the more pessimistic early assessments. The advantages of policy independence were sometimes seen as less important, and in fact some countries cannot operate credible independent monetary policies and smaller countries have little choice except to link to larger economies. In the run-up to the EMU, the focus shifted toward what should be done to implement an union once a political decision had been made to do so. OCA theory was reviewed during this process, and Mongelli concludes it did not provide clear answers, and thus the theory was extended to encompass the priorities and tasks involved in creating the EMU.[71] In doing so, it naturally tended to internalize the strict criteria for convergence amongst union member countries that were part of the Maastricht Treaty.

An *empirical phase* during the 1990's reviewed the OCA properties in detail. These reviews helped develop detailed pictures about how OCAs behave in different situations.

4.12 The final phase was not explicitly named by Mongelli, but might be called the *structural change phase.* It considers what changes occur in the macroeconomic structures of union countries and the region as a result of the creation of the union. Will countries become more specialized in their intra-union trade in goods and services, or will convergence occur as countries become more economically and financial intertwined? Views seem to be shifting towards the latter case in which creation of unions leads to endogenous convergence and interlinkages.

Elements of optimum currency areas

4.13 The OCA sets out the conditions under which a country can gain by irrevocably linking its exchange rate to the rate for another country, or by implication joining an union in which all members irrevocably link their currencies to the new union currency. By doing so, a country gives up the possibility of using changes in its exchange rate to affect its domestic economic situation or change its external competitiveness. Also, to defend the exchange rate peg, the country must also closely follow the monetary policy of the country to whose currency it is pegged. Or, in the case of an union, all member countries are bound by the single monetary policy of the union.

4.14 Thus, the OCA raises a major hurdle that must be overcome in order for linking of exchange rates (or the creation of a currency union) to be advantageous – the advantages of linking up must be sufficiently large to compensate for the loss of the ability to set one's own monetary and exchange rate policies.[72]

4.15 As mentioned above, over the years, the OCA has tended to provide pessimistic conclusions about whether conditions in various regions support creation of a currency union. However, more recent work has tended to be more supportive of joining unions because countries seem to converge economically once in an union. Böwer (2006) notes that Mundell's later work supported the idea that a currency union promotes risk sharing between the member countries. For example, cross investment within an union will tend to distribute incomes more equally throughout the union and smooth consumption. Böwer concludes that empirical analysis of the convergence process in Europe showed that "those countries with relatively asynchronous business cycles benefit most from the risk-sharing opportunities in a financially integrated currency union….the new member states may have far more to gain from euro

[71] During the 1980's work on the OCA theory was rather limited, in part reflecting the set-backs in monetary cooperation in Europe. Artis (1991) revived interest in a report that examined many theoretical and empirical aspects of the OCA theory and its relevance to the debate over setting up the EMU. It took a critical view of the relevance of the original OCA theory, and came down strongly in favor of moving toward complete monetary integration for at least some EU members. The report also analyzed what he saw as desirable features of the proposed EMU. Coming during the early days of debate over the features of the monetary union, it generated extensive new research, much of it designed to make the OCA theory operational within the European context. The experiences of the European countries, for which there was ample empirical data on the real and financial aspects, provided extensive information for testing hypotheses (using the new computing powers of desk-top computers) about the behavior of the properties of the OCA theory and how they might affect the new union.

[72] Other costs must also be incurred to create an union, including transferring international reserves to the union and paying for the maintenance of the central union operations, as well as the potential political costs. These costs, however, are not covered within the OCA framework.

adoption than previously assumed." (p.32) He also cites research by Imbs (2006) that found that financial integration within an union "improves risk-sharing opportunities in the form of cross-country consumption correlation but also boosts, to an even larger extent, business cycles synchronization across countries. (ibid) That is, the financial integration process within a currency union promotes overall convergence and the union becomes more like an OCA.[73]

4.16 Such conclusions are important to numerous regions that are now working toward creating currency unions. Moreover, the reasons cited in various planned unions might reflect different perspectives than are covered by the traditional OCA theory. For example, a common currency could be seen as a contribution toward building a free trade area by eliminating conversion costs, or as a means to rationalize the financing of regional infrastructure. Or as a means to gain greater voice in the international financial system.[74] Or as a means to create bigger, more competitive financial markets that better support long-run development. Or as a means of political solidarity. Such factors can strongly influence the urge of countries to create a currency union, but they are not directly analyzed by OCA theory.

4.17 But even where motivations to create unions lie outside the traditional scope of the OCA, its analytic framework and the insights from many contributions provide important inputs to the work of unions and other regional monetary and exchange rate policy arrangements. Quite simply, the OCA cannot be ignored. Many of its conclusions are relevant – when the OCA puts out warning signals about economic situations, it will usually be identifying a potential problem that should be addressed in order to support the effective operation of the union or even to prevent the union's collapse. The next sections review some of the key elements of the OCA – demand shifts, divergences in inflation rates, seigniorage, etc. – drawn from formulations in De Grauwe (1997).

Demand shifts in currency unions

4.18 It is clear from OCA that membership in an union greatly affects policy options. Countries might find that they are denied use of effective policy tools, and thus must find new ways to implement economic policy. An example provided by De Grauwe (1997) showing the impact of a demand shift between two countries provides a good way to see how membership in a currency union affects macroeconomic policy.

4.19 OCA as developed by Mundell was based on several Keynesian assumptions of the time – that sticky wages and prices and limited capital mobility could permit nominal exchange rate changes to affect the real exchange rate and the current-account balance. Thus, the exchange rate could act to shift expenditure, and thus it was applied to situations where a change in demand between two countries affected expenditure patterns.

4.20 Assume there are two countries (arbitrarily called Apple and Banyan), each assumed to initially have balanced domestic and external macroeconomic conditions. A change of preferences occurs in which Apple chooses to consume more goods from Banyan, as shown in Figure 1. The vertical axis represents the national levels P_a and P_b, respectively. The horizontal axis represents the output of the countries, Y_a and Y_b.

[73] Böwer further states, "In a currency union, financial market integration may develop into a powerful risk-sharing mechanism by providing income insurance across the union. Due to enhanced reserve pooling and portfolio diversification, adverse shocks to one country are shared across the union. Trade and financial integration act as income insurance since individuals across countries hold claims on each other's output and one country can draw on the resources of the other country by running down its holding of the international currency. As a result, consumption streams become smoother and more highly correlated across countries, even and particularly in the presence of idiosyncratic shocks to production."

[74] For example, even the tiny Eastern Caribbean Currency Union is invited to participate in numerous international fora where otherwise none of the individual member states would have been invited.

Figure: Aggregate Demand and Supply Curves in Apple and Banyan.

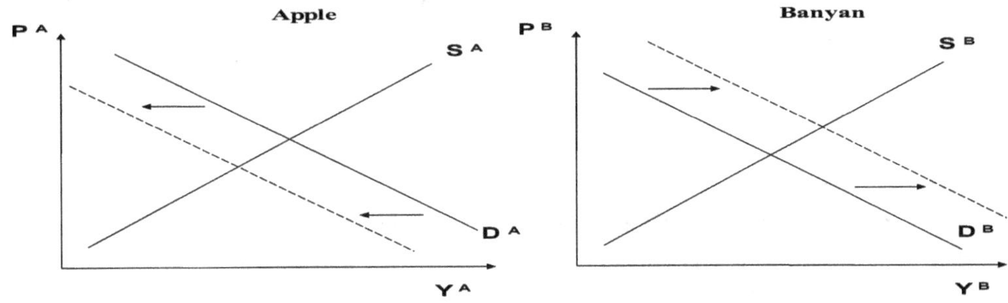

4.21 The change in demand causes production and price changes in both countries.

- In Apple, the decline in demand causes total production to fall, represented in the Figure as a leftward shift in the demand curve. $D^0_a \rightarrow D^1_a$. Output falls, unemployment increases, and aggregate prices fall from $P^0_a \rightarrow P^1_a$
- In contrast, in Banyan, the increase in demand is represented by a rightward movement in the demand curve, causing an increase in production, more employment, and a price increase, $P^0_b \rightarrow P^1_b$.
- These effects change the balance of payments of both countries, as represented by changes in their current account (flows of goods and services between the countries). The change reflects a shift in the *absorption* of the economies, defined as
Current Account =
Domestic Output - Domestic Expenditure
- For example, because of the demand shift, if Apple does not cut back on expenditures, it will absorb (consume) more goods than it produces, the difference being made up of imports from Banyan. The increase in imports is recorded as a deficit in Apple's balance of payments current account. Reasons why expenditures in Apple might remain elevated despite the demand shift and increase in unemployment could be that automatic stabilizers such as unemployment payments are activated – government fiscal expenditures increase, expenditures remain high, and the current account deficit is sustained.[75]
- Conversely, the increase in exports by Banyan (possible only because Banyan can produce more goods than it absorbs) creates a balance of payments current account surplus. For example, if production and incomes rise in Banyan, but a portion is saved and thus the value of expenditures on domestically produced goods does not rise equivalently, a portion of additional output can be used for exports to Apple.
- Conveniently, Banyan could use its new savings to make loans to Apple, which allows Apple to continue its importation from Banyan to support its absorption greater than its income. Closing the circle in this way can allow the process to continue for some time (until Apple accumulates unsustainable debt, overheating drives up Banyan's export prices, or other economic changes occur.)

4.18 Both Apple and Banyan might want to correct this situation. Apple might want to correct the rise in unemployment. Banyan might want to avoid overheating its economy and build-up of inflationary pressures.

[75] Among other reasons that a current account deficit might be sustained could include inflows that sustain levels of expenditure in Apple, such as international loans, or capital investments of Apple in Banyan that permit Apple to earn a share of the higher incomes earned in Banyan.

If they are not in a currency union, they could[76]...

Adjust their exchange rates through intervention to change the relative prices of domestic and traded goods. Depreciation of Apple's currency relative to Banyan's will increase the cost of imports relative to domestic goods, which will reduce the current-account deficit.

Or, change monetary policy. For example, Apple could raise interest rates to slow domestic activity, reduce national income, and thus cut imports. Or Banyan could allow unfettered monetary expansion to raise prices and cause its exports to Apple to be less competitive.

However, in a currency union, neither Apple nor Banyan can implement their own monetary and exchange policies. The union itself might see no reason to change its policies because it cannot play favorites between the two member countries. Thus, Apple and Banyan must rely on other means of adjustment, such as...[77]

Wage flexibility – One option is that adjustment is made through flexible wages. Workers in Apple could reduce their wages, which reduces prices in Apple, making goods more competitive, and reducing the current account deficit. In the Figure above, this is represented as a rightward shift in the supply curve in Apple. If wages are also flexible in Banyan and rise with demand increases for goods, this is reflected as a leftward shift in Banyan's supply curve.

Labor mobility – If workers can readily move between Apple and Banyan, they can move to where demand and wages are higher. In response to the demand change, movement of labor from Apple to Banyan reduces Apple's problems with unemployment and declining wages, and in Banyan eases labor shortages and eases upward pressure on wages and prices.

Mobility of other factors of production - The OCA has been extended to show that the issue is factor mobility in general, not simply labor mobility. For example, movement of physical capital from Apple to Banyan can result in higher productivity for the remaining units of capital in Apple.

4.19 However, OCA assumptions might not hold. It cannot be assumed that wages adjust flexibly, nor that labor can freely move between countries. There

[76] The GFC provided some examples of the constraints of union members in attempting to adjust to economic problems. In response to a very severe drop in GDP in Lithuania in the first quarter of 2009, Katie Martin and Joel Sherwood, writing for Dow Jones (Dow Jones 2009), wrote "With their currencies pegged to the euro, the Baltics aren't looking to devalue their way out of the crisis. Instead, economic adjustment to the downturn is coming through public spending cuts and decreasing wages and prices." Given the severity of the downturn, only very severe cuts in prices and public services were feasible.

[77] Union members might be obligated to find other ways to make adjustments. For example, unions might require member states to meet inflation targets. Banyan could be penalized if it permits inflation to rise too high, similar to a rule in Europe. Thus, Banyan might cut government expenditure to reduce stimulation to its economy.

Within an union, other adjustment methods are also foreclosed. For example, countries are forbidden to adjust tariffs or restrict capital flows between each other. Or they might be forbidden to discriminate in government procurement of goods and services from other member countries. Such prohibitions can help prevent economic distortions, but also limit options for adjustment.

In Europe during the GFC many options were considered to avoid forcing macroeconomic adjustments due to strict application of Maastricht rules. A broad range of aggressive actions were taken to bolster financial conditions and revive the economy (and which proved useful again during the COVID crisis). The story of these interventions is dramatic, complex, and beyond the scope of this volume, although some policies are referenced.

might be serious impediments to both, or the adjustment process might be politically unacceptable slow. It is sometimes proposed that policies should be changed to ease structural impediments in the economies to make the adjustment process quicker and more effective. There is certainly some truth in this, but for many economies structural rigidities are entrenched, sometimes by policy decision, and if they are malleable, they might change only through medium- or long-term effort. It is probably an empirical question how quickly (and sometimes whether) balance of payments adjustments can be affected through wage and labor adjustments, or migration of other factors of production.[78]

4.20 OCA theory indicates is that if such adjustments do not occur, the adjustment problem can persist.

> If wages in Apple do not decline (which is often politically unacceptable) or labor does not migrate, Apple can be trapped in a disequilibrium situation, with stagnation, unemployment, and a persistent current-account deficit.
>
> In Banyan, there could be continuing upward pressure on wages and prices.
>
> Ultimately, if wages and prices do not adjust downward in Apple, the adjustment might take the form of inflation in Banyan, which drives up prices and makes Banyan's products less competitive and ultimately closes the current-account surplus.
>
> However, if Banyan does not want to experience inflation and takes steps to fight it by reducing fiscal stimulus (raising taxes, cutting government expenditures, etc.) or restricting monetary policy, its prices remain low and the current-account surplus does not close and the inflationary pressures will continue.

4.21 Thus, the OCA can describe situations in which being in a currency union creates difficult policy choices. If Apple and Banyan are not in an union, a devaluation of Apple's currency against Banyan's helps resolve the dilemma above – Apple's goods become cheaper in Banyan, and Banyan's become more expensive in Apple, both effects helping to reduce the current-account imbalance and the divergent pressures on wages, production, and prices. Conversely, if Apple and Banyan are in an union, other means of adjustment must be found.

Divergent inflation rates

4.22 Economic strains can develop if countries with different inflation rates seek to join an union.

4.23 For countries outside an union, the exchange rate between two countries is affected by the purchasing power parity (PPP) condition in which the change in the bilateral exchange rate is affected by the difference between the inflation rates between the countries. This is necessary to maintain equilibrium between the countries - otherwise, the competitiveness of the products in bilateral trade will be affected. For example, if inflation in Apple is 10 percent per year and 5 percent per year in Banyan, the bilateral exchange rate between the two countries should show 5 percent depreciation of Apple's currency, or 5 percent appreciation of Banyan's. This degree of depreciation will keep the price of traded goods between the countries unchanged despite the difference in national inflation rates.

4.24 If the countries create an union, the exchange rate is fixed. Thus, if the inflation rates differ between the countries, the *real* exchange rate changes, which affects the competitiveness of products in bilateral trade. In this example, Apple's exports to Banyan become 5 percent more expensive each year, and Banyan's exports become 5 percent less expensive for Apple to import. Apple could develop a current account

[78] For some EMU countries, very large adjustments to wages, prices, government expenditures, migration, etc. were needed to deal with imbalances caused by the financial crisis rather than make use of the traditional tool of devaluations – it will be a very interesting economic experiment to see how rapidly these adjustments will occur.

deficit with Banyan, because of this. If the inflation difference continues, Apple's real exchange rate will continue to deteriorate, and Apple will incur a current account deficit.[79] Over time, serious strains could develop that could create instability of the union. The difficulties of the European Monetary System in the early 1990's largely brought on by divergent inflation rates provides an example of such instability. Relatively large real exchange rate divergence between EMU countries also complicated the adjustment of the union to the GFC.

Openness of the economy

4.25 An extension of the OCA theory is that the more open an economy is to trade and capital the more it is affected by international factors, such as changes in international prices. This means that there is less scope for national monetary policy and exchange rate adjustments to affect domestic conditions. McKinnon (1963) argued that nominal exchange rate changes are ineffective for small open economies. A devaluation will raise the domestic price level which will increase pressures to increase nominal wages which limits the devaluation from affecting the real exchange rate. Also, if domestic prices are strongly linked to the exchange rate, the domestic currency is less useful as an unit of account and store of value. Given these two conditions, McKinnon argued that an OCA must have a large untraded sector (only possible in a large union) to be able to set prices in the domestic currency and stabilize purchasing power. By extension, it could be argued that a highly open economy will experience high costs from having a floating exchange rate, and thus it is advantageous to join a currency union.

Economic diversification

4.26 Another element that can affect the prospects for success of an union is the degree of diversification. The more diversified an economy, the more likely that it will be affected by shocks affecting other union member economies – that is, diversification makes common shocks more likely and idiosyncratic shocks less likely. Offering a wide range of exports will buffer shifts in demand and exchange rates, and thus makes joining a currency union feasible. With diversification, it is likely that a smaller exchange rate change will be needed to bring about the needed adjustment.

4.27 It is an empirical question whether EMU membership has contributed to increased diversification. Two opposite effects could be hypothesized following entry into an union – first, greater *inter*industry specialization could result because firms exploit their comparative advantages within larger markets, which reduces trade diversification. Conversely, increased *intra*industry specialization could occur as suppliers link up with industrial customers throughout the union, which will tend to increase trade diversification. In the latter case, increases in overall trade within an union will correlate with increased diversification and result in more symmetric shocks to union countries, which is conducive to union development. This effect of course supports the concept of endogenous convergence within unions.

Exchange rates as a source of volatility

4.28 Views of the nature of exchange rate volatility have changed. In 1961, when Mundell published the OCA theory, the Bretton Woods system still existed with exchange rates fixed in terms of gold but adjustable if needed. It was then held by many economists that allowing a currency to adjust would allow it to gradually and smoothly move toward equilibrium values. The Bretton Woods system broke down in 1971, which hypothetically allowed that sort of adjustment, but exchange markets proved to be quite volatile. It was observed that exchange rates often significantly overshot or undershot equilibrium levels and rates sometimes were out of line with equilibrium situations for long periods. As Böwer comments, "the notion of smooth adjustment under flexible exchange

[79] The IMF has noted that deterioration of real exchange rates between EMU member countries shifts export competitiveness. This is regularly monitored by the IMF in its Article IV surveillance of counties' economic conditions. See Chapter 8 – International for a discussion of IMF bilateral surveillance of exchange rates.

rates, one of Mundell I's key assumption, turns out to be an illusion", and the "ambiguous role" of exchange rates makes it less clear that giving up exchange rate flexibility will create high costs for countries in unions. (p. 4) Thus, this line of analysis undermines the view that countries in fact give up an important policy option by joining a currency union.

Endogeneity

4.29 Endogeneity is the concept that countries within an union converge economically and become more like an OCA and thus are better served by a single monetary and exchange policy. This convergence might be expressed in multiple ways – trade expansion between union countries, production processes spread through the union, shared economic risks due to cross investment between countries, integration of financial markets and opening of capital markets to promote efficient and productive investment. Kenen (2002) also mentions the effects "of a full-fledged monetary union on capital markets and capital movements and … the impact on the ability of households and others to self-insure against various shocks by holding internationally diversified portfolios."

4.30 Probably the best-known study of the endogeneity effect is by Rose (2000) who showed that trade growth between country pairs within unions was twice as strong as between non-union pairs of countries. Others have found similar effects. Kenen (2002; p. 154) concludes that "one must attach great weight to this trade-promoting effect when weighing the overall benefits and costs of a monetary union. It says that a currency union permits its member countries to realize more fully the welfare-raising gains from trade, and it should also promote growth. Furthermore, it has strong implications for the functioning of a monetary union."

4.31 However, the endogeneity view might heavily reflect evidence from Europe where the EU held and strongly promoted the goal of promoting integration of the European economies; that is, convergence was a policy goal in Europe supported by a wide range of actions. It is possible that convergence is not an inevitable consequence of an union, nor would it necessarily be the case that additional convergence follows once some threshold of convergence is crossed. This argument is unresolved, but for future unions, the lesson might be that in order to gain advantages of an union continuing work towards convergence will be needed even after the union is formed.

Loose convergence

4.32 Much of the discussion about the OCA leads to the important issue of what degree of convergence is needed to support union development? Several potential unions are concerned whether an union can be formed first without achieving strict convergence between the potential members as was done in Europe. Can an union be formed if countries are progressing toward convergence, and then complete the convergence process once the union if formed? Similarly, when are conditions suitable to establish an ECU-type system in which countries fix their bilateral exchange rates? Is convergence sufficient, or must convergence be toward strict criteria?[80]

4.33 These questions are critical for regions considering creating currency unions. Long delays might result if strict convergence criteria such as used in Europe were required. There is no formal analysis of this situation, but the general sense of the OCA would be that a high degree of convergence is clearly preferable. For example, national inflation differentials imply that member countries' real exchange rates will change against each other affecting their relative competitiveness – conditions that could destabilize the union. However, if union countries converge toward strict criteria such as a low rate of inflation, such destabilizing forces would be absent.

[80] For example, can an union be effectively formed if all countries have the same inflation rates, but it is too high; for example, around 10 percent in each country? Does the union need to wait until inflation is subdued (such as under 5 percent) in all countries?

Disadvantages of loose convergence

4.34 Reprising some of the points made above, reasons why loose convergence could be disadvantageous are enumerated below.

Inflation differentials. Real equilibrium exchange rates might diverge, changing relative competitiveness in the union and creating balance of payments problems. National interest rates will carry different inflation premia, which might distort investment flows between member countries.

Growth differentials. Economies growing rapidly might need to be cooled down, but other economies might need monetary policy stimulation. It could be impossible to find a monetary policy that benefits diverging economies, or does not damage one of the economies. Also, if union countries have the same marginal propensity to import, rapidly growing economies will incur current-account deficits with other union countries, which could be potentially destabilizing.

Fiscal differences. Different net fiscal situations will channel funds into government liabilities in countries with the largest deficits. This damages investment elsewhere in the union and potentially pulls funds into weaker members of the union. This might undermine international confidence in the strength of the union currency.[81]

Insufficient structural and infrastructure harmonization. Early formation of an union might bring together countries that have major differences in their economic and financial infrastructure, standards, and supervisory systems. Cross-border transactions might face costly frictions. These could impair the advantages of joining an union.

Tax and seigniorage income differences. Each member could follow different tax regimes and rely on seigniorage income to different extents to finance government activities. Joining an union will create common rates of seigniorage income for each member which could be insufficient for countries that previously had the highest rates of monetary growth.[82]

Different structural shocks. If the loose convergence stems from different responses to common structural shocks, this indicates that the economies might be fundamentally different and are thus not good candidates to form an union.

Different adjustment mechanisms and speeds. If countries have different structural conditions and speeds of adjustments, they might respond differently, even to common shocks or policy actions. If loose convergence reflects this, the countries might not be good candidates to join an union.

The common exchange rate is not well integrated into each economy. The ECU existed for over two decades before it was converted into the euro at a one-to-one rate. This caused little shock to the price structure for each economy. These conditions are unlikely under loose convergence conditions.

Advantages of loose convergence

4.35 In contrast, there can be numerous reasons to create an union, even if convergence is not complete.

Once an union is created, numerous common institutions and practices might be introduced which could foster convergence. New union institutions can be seen as important cooperative steps that provide impetus for overall development in line with a common vision. The process of creating the union institutions is also a process that can contribute to improved economic and financial prospects and convergence between member countries.

[81] In the Greek situation, official flows to alleviate the fiscal difficulties in Greece caused serious resentment in other EU countries.

[82] Seigniorage income can be substantial, sometimes equal to 2 or 3 percent of GDP annually.

Evidence has shown that membership in an union promotes greater intra-union trade.

The union currency might be stronger than the currencies of individual members. This can create more stable economic conditions conducive for economic growth.

The strength of the union currency can expand overall demand for the currency and reduce cocirculation[83] of foreign currencies within the economies. This can increase seigniorage income of the union and its member countries.

Creating a currency union can contribute to building trade, tourism, or other types of economic unions. The common currency can facilitate intra-union trade, capital, labor, and other factor flows that create larger, more competitive, more resilient markets.

A currency union creates a larger market, permitting economies of scale and greater competition.

Price transparency increases across borders, which benefits consumers and allows more efficient use of capital.

Regional infrastructure investment (which might be important for overall economic development) is facilitated by denominating investments, costs, and benefits in a common unit. This applies not only to infrastructure investments across different countries in the region, but also to the discounting of costs and returns over time.[84]

Some economies might lack resources or conditions to be able to stabilize economic and financial conditions on their own, and thus are challenged to converge with other members of the union. The union, or larger members of the union, might be able to step in to provide guidance, oversight, or assistance.

There was great uncertainty whether the monetary union would work, and therefore starting the process under the most favorable conditions (including a high degree of convergence) was prudent. The EMU success allows future unions to learn from its experiences (and reveal gaps in the original model) and give some confidence that success is possible with somewhat less convergence.[85]

Risks can be shared within an union, reducing the threats of destabilization to each of its member countries.[86] Additional resources to address instability might be available.

4.36 To conclude, there are many reasons why loose convergence between union members can create problems. The cautions provided in the OCA are well-founded and unions considering starting up before a high degree of convergence is achieved should do so cautiously and aware of the increased difficulties that could be faced.

4.37 However, there are also numerous reasons why loose convergence might succeed. Indeed, convergence might not be possible without a boost from union institutions and policies. *Convergence is good, and convergence with adherence to strict criteria is*

[83] Cocirculation is use of two or more physical currencies within an economy. It can occur due to many factors, but a foreign currency is often likely to cocirculate when the national currency is perceived to be weak. Successful introduction of an union currency would reduce the incentives for holding and using foreign currencies.

[84] Bhattacharyay (2010) argues that a common unit of value or a common currency is a near pre-condition for investment transparency and providing proper price signals to support needed regional infrastructure investment in Asia.

[85] The less-than-strict adherence in Europe to the fiscal convergence tests under the EMU's Stability and Growth Pact has led some planned unions to wonder if this indicates there is some room for flexibility.

[86] For example, Hassan (2009) provides a formal model in which larger countries (and currency unions) provide insurance against world economy, which lowers real interest rates in non-traded sectors. This can stimulate investment and growth.

better, but building an union based on loose convergence cannot be ruled out – it might be the best choice in some situations. Moreover, the idea is gaining acceptance that countries with little integration can benefit from the risk sharing properties of unions and can successfully create unions.[87]

4.38 If countries seek to create currency unions starting with only loose convergence, three things might be requisite.

Conditions amongst potential union countries are similar enough to potentially be handled by the common union policies,

Countries feel confident they can abandon the advantages of independent monetary and exchange policies, and

Countries have access to resources to defend their positions. This can be either their own resources, access to special facilities, or common union resources.

4.39 There are three important cautions, however.

Revocability. The looser the convergence, the greater the advantage of retaining flexibility in case shocks hit or problems develop. Thus, construction of a regional exchange rate bloc might be a good alternative to creating a loose union. Countries can agree on bilateral rates, cooperate on monetary policy, and provide mutual support, but retain their national currencies in order to be able to make exchange rate adjustments if needed.[88]

Strong union institutions. Even though there might be adequate macroeconomic and financial convergence, effective union institutions must be built and put in place before starting the union. This includes both technical institutions, such as settlement houses, but also policy institutions that can provide unbiased and high quality policy direction based on union conditions. Simultaneous institution-building and convergence make sense.

Enhanced surveillance/assistance. Where there is loose convergence, problems might be more likely. Therefore, enhanced surveillance on the more divergent economies is called for, and it can be useful to provide assistance to countries to become convergent as soon as possible. Milestones to move progressively toward convergence should be considered. *Backsliding certainly must be avoided.*

Optimum currency areas – conclusions

4.40 OCS theory has dominated thinking about currency unions for nearly fifty years and it has provided many useful insights, but it has not provided the explicit guidance useful for currency unions now being set up. Much of the discussion about future unions will be couched in the terminology of the OCA and addressed to questions raised by the theory, but the guidance appears uncertain. Numerous regions appear likely to attempt to construct currency unions regardless of what the OCA might be saying. The reversal of some of the conclusions of OCA over the years has made the whole debate less clear.

4.41 For planned unions, the OCA can present some challenging choices.

First, clearly sacrificing monetary and exchange rate sovereignty can present some serious problems in making policy.

[87] "While the initial OCA framework warns countries with asynchronous business cycles about joining a currency due to the resulting loss of national monetary policy and exchange rate adjustments, Mundell II suggests that it is exactly those countries with asymmetric shocks which may benefit most from adopting a common currency and the resulting risk-sharing and income insurance mechanism. In other words, a country that considers joining a currency union, such as the new EU member states, may not want to wait.." Böwer (2006 p.6)

[88] This also permits countries time to get used to cooperating with each other. Also, the regional bloc format permits time for progressively stronger union institutions to be constructed and gradually put into place.

For many small countries the OCA is irrelevant. Countries with weak monetary policy frameworks, or countries neighboring or integrated with strong large countries, could have no choice but to link to another currency or join an union – the only decision is where to set the rate for conversion of the national currency into the union currency. Such countries have little sovereign policy independence to give up.

However, countries with sufficient size and market strength do have an option to set their own monetary policy and exchange rate.[89] For such countries, the issues raised by the OCA are relevant. The advantages of monetary and exchange rate autonomy might be hard to give up. These countries face the question of whether the advantages of an union are large enough to lose standard economic policy tools.

Second, adjustment dilemmas will not disappear in an union. There will be situations in which countries in unions will need to take strong policy actions, but have a limited range of tools to use.[90]

Third, the theory emphasizes the role of wage flexibility, factor mobility, and structural adjustments. This can imply introducing policy changes into politically sensitive areas or contradictory to national policies, such as maintaining a social safety net. This could introduce political frictions that could impede the adjustment processes within the union.

4.42 Faced with such situations, if the benefits of the union do not clearly exceed costs, it is perfectly rational for countries to choose to not join a currency union. They might seek to act independently, or groups of countries could create something like a currency union while retaining the option to make adjustments if they are needed – perhaps agreeing with neighboring countries to form a currency bloc in which bilateral rates are set, but allowed to change by mutual agreement.

4.43 But where countries decide to create an union, the theory is increasingly optimistic by suggesting that the union can support the integration of the countries' markets and share risks. Such unions could be thought of as tools that support the development programs of a cluster of countries. By extension, part of the process of creating a currency union should then include programs for economic and financial integration and the building of a strong and flexible economic union corresponding to the currency union.

4.44 Europe provides an example of such an approach. The EMU, in close support of EU economic and social priorities, took extraordinary steps to promote adjustment, spread economic benefits throughout the continent, and promote physical, economic, and financial integration. Among the many steps that have been taken include; macroeconomic oversight over the economic situations and policies in the member countries, requirements for members to adhere to specific "convergence criteria", rules on fiscal stances, many programs to promote integration of financial markets, freedom of employment anywhere in the EU, programs of infrastructure development to physically integrate the entire continent and eliminate disparities of income, freedom of capital movements, harmonization of financial instruments including government debt securities, creating a large-value money market settlement system to ensure transmission of monetary policy impulses, among many more. *In effect, Europe introduced a very comprehensive set*

[89] Some researchers, such as Dutta, have argued that very few countries actually have the economic strength to retain their own currencies. Most inevitably must join larger unions to avoid being pushed aside in global markets.

[90] For example, it has been argued that Spain and Ireland experienced strong real estate price inflation as a result of being members of the EMU, but without an ability to change exchange rates, tighten monetary policy, or restrict capital inflows there were no effective options to contain an unsustainable asset price appreciation. During the GFC, some Euroarea countries faced very large imbalances without having access to the full range of monetary and exchange policy options.

of programs that facilitate structural adjustments to make its economy more efficient and competitive. As Europe becomes more like a single economy, the types of imbalances and adjustment requirements covered in the OCA become less relevant. Future unions might wish to follow a similar path. [91]

C. Convergence criteria for membership[92]

4.45 A key element in building the EMU was the application of convergence criteria as requirements for membership in the Union. Countries had to meet strict statistical tests designed to show that countries applying for membership had stable macroeconomic and financial conditions that would contribute to the success of the union.[93] Countries that failed to meet the criteria were denied membership. Once in the union, countries are still held to the same standards and continued to be subject to rigorous examination, backed up by the "Excessive Deficit Procedure" that demands remedial action when the countries budgets are out of line, potentially with large cash penalties.[94]

4.46 This system placed convergence criteria at the center of the EMU program by making them high hurdles for prospective members. In effect, the criteria reflect the original concept of an Optimum Currency Area that countries with common economic structures and responses to shocks are the best candidates for a currency union because they can be treated by a single monetary or exchange rate policy.

Purposes for convergence criteria

4.47 Convergence criteria serve many purposes in an union. The cumulative effect of meeting the criteria is that a country will have demonstrated that numerous aspects of its economy are compatible with the goals and policies of the union.

> The overall macroeconomic performance of the economy is balanced and compatible with the union. This is the main reason for their use as a qualifier for membership.

---

[91] However, one possible method of adjustment was not followed in Europe – fiscal transfers between countries. Under the Maastricht Treaty, countries remain responsible for their own fiscal policies and may not take responsibility for debts of other countries. There are several EU programs to support transfers to low-income regions, but for the most part, there is little transfer for adjustment purposes from richer areas, or from where inflationary pressures are highest, to other regions. This differs from the situation within many countries where the central government may substantially move funds from boom areas through taxes to depressed areas in unemployment or welfare payments.

The European limit on fiscal transfers between member states might not be suitable in other regions planning unions. For example, if there is large *intra*-union trade in food or other commodities subject to large price changes, there can be reason to provide compensation to member countries experiencing terms-of-trade shocks against other union member countries. An *intra*-union terms-of-trade shock is asymmetrical in its country-level effects and cannot be readily handled by a single monetary and exchange policy for all countries. Special steps might be needed to cover the divergent results, such as fiscal transfers or negotiating long-term contracts that minimize the price volatility. (The danger here is that needed adjustments may be inhibited because of these transfers, and thus transfer programs may need to be temporary or designed for facilitate adjustments, such as retraining workers.)

Finally, the emergency assistance from EU countries to Greece provides a precedent to provide assistance to countries with fiscal problems, notwithstanding statements that such aid will never again be offered to other countries.

[92] In 2002, the Association of African Central Banks stated "The achievement of macroeconomic stability and convergence in key macroeconomic aggregates is a necessary condition for the evolvement of a monetary union." (Cited in Enoch and Krueger 2002).

[93] The statistical construction of convergence criteria is important in the success of their use. See Chapter 11 – Statistics.

[94] Chapter 7 – Macroeconomics discusses the fiscal convergence aspects of the union, including the Excessive Deficit Procedure and the GSP.

They provide information on the economic response of the union and its members to economic shocks.

They are components of the macroeconomic policy of the union, and provide feedback on the success of policies. For example, a criterion capping inflation rates can provide information on whether fiscal tightening and exchange rate appreciation are reducing inflationary pressures.

4.48 *The use of "convergence criteria" for membership requires early comparisons of data that must be available prior to the start of the union.* Convergence criteria are usually general indicators of overall macroeconomic performance, such as GDP, fiscal position, inflation, and interest rates. Each potential member country must be able to measure how its macroeconomic performance stands relative to the threshold values of the convergence criteria or relative to other member countries. Ideally, indicators should be available on a quarterly basis with good timeliness so that authorities can obtain current feedback on how effectively their policies are bringing the economy in line with the convergence criteria. These statistics must be ready before the start of the union and must be high-quality and harmonized across countries to fairly evaluate each potential union member.[95]

4.49 Convergence criteria will affect the economic behavior of the potential member states prior to the start of the union as countries take actions to bring their economies in line with the criteria. In many cases, the criteria are simply reflections of good financial and economic policy and simply reinforce what the countries should already be doing, but they can significantly constrain policy options in some cases. For example, DeGrauwe (1997) argues that application of the convergence criteria in Europe contributed to slow economic growth because both monetary and fiscal constraints were needed in order to bring economies in line with the criteria. It has also been suggested that during the GFC several Eastern European candidates to adopt the euro were constrained by the criterion that they remain within the currency bands set by the ERM II. Thus, the convergence criteria can have real economic effects and also can subject lagging countries to peer criticism, and thus it is important that they be appropriate and well measured.

4.50 The use of convergence criteria as tests for membership requires early comparisons of GDP, fiscal, inflation, and interest rate data. The requisite nonfinancial and financial statistics need to be high-quality and comparable prior to the start of the union so that valid comparisons can be made that do not prejudice the entry prospects of any country.[96] Such criteria must be well-defined in terms of statistical indicators and in terms of the methodology used to calculate them.[97]

4.51 Where the criteria will be decisive in granting approval to join an Union, the criteria should have legal status and an independent authority recognized by all candidate countries (typically the Union Statistical Office or the Union Central Bank) should be charged with the task of assessing the consistency of the methodology used and the resulting figures. Even if a prior assessment is not called for, the countries will need a set of main macroeconomic indicators based on a common methodology for monitoring the evolution of the Union as a whole and for providing an effective communication tool.

[95] Convergence criteria can also act to induce countries to change their economies in ways that will facilitate the smooth operation of the union once it is established. They also demonstrate that a country is serious about the union process by taking the necessary steps to meet the criteria.

[96] In 1998, the author attended a meeting of the EMI Working Group on Statistics at which one of the representatives from Germany turned during plenary session to his Greek colleague and quite undiplomatically said that he thought that Greek convergence data were bad and that he did not believe them.

[97] Moreover, the quality and comparability of the statistics of the member states will be significantly strengthened if the underlying financial accounting standards for banks and the nonfinancial sectors are improved, made more detailed, and made more transparent.

4.52 The convergence criteria will be among the main macroeconomic statistics for the new Union and will be used for continuing monitoring the individual economies as well as the Union as a whole. They should satisfy the statistical reporting requirements prescribed by international bodies like the IMF, in terms of methodology, coverage, and timeliness.

Euroarea convergence criteria

4.53 The convergence criteria used as tests for member in the Euroarea are listed below. They reflect policy orientations in favor of low inflation, long-term price stability, and fiscal prudence and set rather strict standards for compliance. The European standards generally are the starting model for unions seeking to develop their own criteria.

Euroarea Convergence Criteria

Rate of Inflation: No more than 1.5 percentage points higher than average of the 3 best-performing *EU*[98] member states.

Government deficit: The ratio of the annual government deficit to GDP must not exceed 3% at the end of the preceding fiscal year.

Government debt: The ratio of gross government debt to GDP must not exceed 60% at the end of the preceding fiscal year.

Long-term interest rates: The nominal long-term interest rate must not be more than 2% higher than the average rate in the three best-performing member states (based on inflation).

Exchange rate: Applicant countries should have joined the ERM for 2 consecutive years without devaluation during the period.

Convergence criteria for other unions

4.54 The GCC convergence criteria are listed below, which were modeled after the EMU criteria:

GCC Convergence Criteria

Interest Rates: Average short-term interest rates should not exceed the average of lowest three rates plus two percent.

Inflation: Inflation rates should not exceed the GCC weighted average inflation rates plus two percent.

Fiscal deficit to GDP: The budget deficit to GDP is capped between 3 and 6 percent, based on a formula using international oil prices. The deficit can be higher when oil prices are lower, but at current prices the deficits are effectively capped at 3 percent.

Public debt to GDP: Public debt ratios should not exceed 60 percent for the public government and 70 percent for the central government.

Foreign Exchange Reserves: Foreign exchange reserves should cover goods imports for at least four months.

Exchange rates: Formally pegged to U.S. dollar.

4.55 It can be questioned whether all of the criteria are fully appropriate to the GCC situation and other regions.

> *Interest rates* – The EMU criterion is based on long-term interest rates, which can incorporate a premium based on expectations of long-term interest rates. Markets are presumed to be able to make reasonably valid judgments whether the country has the inflationary situation under control. In contrast, the GCC criterion switched to short-term interest rates, in part because long-term bond markets were underdeveloped in the region

[98] That is, the inflation differential is measured against countries within the large European Group, not against EMU members or close candidates. This makes this quite a strict standard.

(for example, GCC governments – prior to the GFC – did not have substantial borrowing requirements). However, short-term rates are not greatly affected by inflation expectations and because rates in the region are all closely linked to U.S. dollar rates, they all effectively converge to a tight band. If a country's rate differs by more than 2 percent, it is more likely to reflect financial market weaknesses rather than inflation concerns.

In African unions, longer term government bonds might include inflation and default premiums and therefore meaningful comparisons might be made, but other factors might also affect difference between rates, such as relative political stability.

Fiscal deficit to GDP – The GCC formula seems reasonable and recognizes that when petroleum prices are down government deficits might need to increase. Currently high petroleum prices suggest that the GCC will be operating at the 3 percent ceiling, identical to the EMU. An issue will be whether the deficit statistics are estimated correctly, which proved to be a problem in Europe and might also be an issue given the limited statistical resources in the GCC.

In the African unions, fiscal deficits and borrowing needs will generally be higher than in the GCC. Convergence might need to be being defined more loosely. An additional issue is that some African countries receive significant amounts of foreign grants that need to be factored into the formula.

Government and public sector debt to GDP – The level chosen by the GCC is essentially the same as the EMU.

> The GCC distinguishes between the regular government debt to GDP ratio (70%) and the broader public sector (60%), which includes government-owned corporations. The public sector ratio is lower than the government ratio which implies that the public sector's earnings (fees, royalties, sales of goods and services, etc.) make a positive contribution to overall government finances.
>
> The definition of government and the public sector need to be standardized between countries in order to provide valid measures. The IMF statistical standards can provide general guidance, but in order to make valid comparisons future unions will probably need to specifically enumerate and publish a listing of the sectoral classification of institutions as general government, public corporations, or nongovernment corporations.
>
> The status of sovereign wealth funds (SWF) is a specific concern. These should be classified as governmental, reflecting their "sovereign status", but depending on their local legal status and structure might be part of general government, the central banking sector, or perhaps as Nonprofit Institutions Serving Households (NPISH). Often their accounts are often not readily available nor consolidated with regular government accounts. Since their assets, income, and expenditures are often segregated from the general government, and often cannot be used for general government purposes, the treatment might differ for each SWF.

Foreign Exchange Reserves: This requirement is volatile in the GCC countries depending on petroleum prices and spikes in fiscal expenditures; this criterion is clearly applicable in Africa but could prove challenging.

Inflation: This factor is quite relevant for the GCC, especially because Qatar and the Emirates experienced overheating during the late 2000's. This criterion is also valid for African unions.

Exchange rates: The GCC requires that the national currencies be pegged to the U.S. dollar, which effectively links them to each other.[99] The EMU also had a requirement that the countries' currencies be in the ERM, which limited their fluctuations against each other.[100] This criterion helped ensure the intra-union price structure reflects the exchange rate configuration exists long enough that entry into the union will not shock the economic system of the country nor the union.

4.56 Convergence criteria will play an important role in evaluating countries readiness to join an union, and might be decisive in selecting members. They are often also used to evaluate the performance of countries once the unions have started. For these reasons, it is important that the criteria are relevant to the situation and goals of each union. It is also important that the statistics used to estimate the criteria be accurate and compiled according to common standards so that the criteria fairly evaluate each country without bias and allow valid comparisons.

D. Pre-union status

4.57 There will typically also be a defined process or decision-making procedure to elect pre-union countries as full members of the union. It can be expected that in many unions some countries will want to join but are unable to join immediately for various reasons[101];

Some countries do not meet the convergence criteria tests for membership.[102]

Applicant states need time to make legal or structural changes before entering an union.

A successful union gradually expands to include neighboring states that will need time to prepare to join.

Countries building a union adopt a two-track system in which some countries move into the union, but other are permitted to come in later.

There is political opposition to join an union, or a final decision to join an union failed, but substantial technical cooperation and convergence take place.

4.58 In such situations, the pre-union states might go through a period in which they have legal status to join an union, which prescribes rights and obligations for these states, might make them eligible for assistance to prepare to join, and might allow participation in some aspects of the union.

Pre-union states in Europe

4.59 In Europe, pre-union states have a clearly defined legal status within a comprehensive system. *Per* Maastricht, all EU countries would eventually become members of the currency union. Thus, all EU central banks were joined into a single system, called the European System of Central Banks (ESCB). The Maastricht Treaty refers to the ESCB as the collective entity of all EU central banks and establishes in Article 2 the mandate for the ESCB to maintain price stability in Europe and to support the other objectives of

[99] Kuwait has a limited float against the dollar which has had only small fluctuations and has been tolerated by the other GCC countries.

[100] Countries seeking to join the EMU must be members of the ERM II in which currencies are relatively fixed against the euro and the real equilibrium exchange rates of countries are subject to official review. (KKC, 2009) This concern is relevant for other unions.

[101] For example, the author attended a meeting at the Saudi Arabia Monetary Authority when a delegation from Yemen was in the same building negotiating (unsuccessfully) to join the GCC.

[102] A classic case was the failure of Lithuania in 2007 to gain approval for membership to the Euroarea because it failed the convergence criterion for inflation by 1/10th of one percent. Although at the time it was argued that there was some evidence that there could be continuing inflationary problems in Lithuania, when the test was made Lithuania's inflation was lower than numerous countries already in the Euroarea. *The author views this case as misuse of the convergence criteria.*

the union, such as supporting a high level of employment, creating sustainable growth, enhancing competitiveness, and converging in economic performance. Thus, *all EU central banks, whether or not they have adopted the euro, are obligated to support specific EU economic goals*.

4.60 However, not all ESCB members entered into the currency union and adopted the euro. Different sets of rules were needed for countries in the currency union or out of it. For example, countries adopting the euro cede their monetary policy sovereignty to the union; in contrast, the non-union states continue to exercise their own monetary policy and do not participate in the union monetary policy decision-making or operations, but still act to support the EU priorities and converge economically with the other EU countries. Therefore, within the ESCB, a separate subsystem called the "Eurosystem" was created that includes the ECB and the central banks of countries that have adopted the euro. The countries that have adopted the euro are collectively termed the "Euroarea" or "Eurozone". The EU countries that have not adopted the euro are the "Pre-in countries".

4.61 Countries must qualify for Euroarea membership by meeting "convergence criteria". One key criterion is that a country must join the EMS for at least two years, during which time no extraordinary intervention was needed to maintain exchange rate stability. *De facto*, this divides the pre-in countries into two groups – those that have entered the two-year period within the EMS and are actively moving toward union membership, and the rest of the countries. It has been reported that some pre-in countries (like the Czech Republic) are hesitant about actually joining into the Euroarea and thus have delayed entering the EMS.

4.62 Future unions are likely to have countries not fully ready to join the union when it starts, or have countries that seek to join the union once it has started. These unions will also have to define a separate set of rules to cover the rights and obligation of the would-be members, and then define the procedures by which countries can apply for membership and the procedures to approve or reject the application. It is possible that there could be several different classes specified for Pre-in countries, depending on their state of readiness.

Applicants for the Euroarea are evaluated in a convergence report that evaluates the country based on the Euroarea convergence criteria and considers whether the situation is sustainable. If a country meets the criteria, the EU formally votes on membership. Typically, a country is accepted around May so that it has time to prepare to join the Euroarea at yearend. At that time, the conversion rate for the national currency into the euro is also announced. This rate will have to be used by all businesses, government units, and households in order to redenominate values from the national currency into the new union currency.

E. Changing membership

Absorbing new states

4.63 Over time, currency unions might expand to include new countries. This is likely if an union is well constructed and has credible policies because its growth and strength are likely to be attractive to surrounding states. Also, a country might have limited monetary links with the individual countries seeking to form an union, but once an union is formed the aggregate links with the union as a whole might be strong enough to make joining the union worthwhile. Integration into a strong neighboring union can open many avenues for growth and development. This is certainly a strong motivation on the periphery of the EMU, where numerous countries far from the heart of Europe have expressed interest in membership.

4.64 The urge to join also extends to countries wishing to join possible future unions. For example, in 2016 South Sudan joined the pre-union East African Community, and applications have been received from Somalia in 2012 (rejected) and the Democratic Republic of the Congo (DRC) in 2019 (Saddam 2019). The urge of Yemen to join the GCC has already been noted.

4.65 Bringing in new states should be orderly and well thought out to avoid disruptions to the union or to its new members. Legal and economic changes will result, and there will be changes in the governance and power structure in the union. The EMU recognized around 1996 that a number of countries will join after the union was started and therefore the Maastricht plan was modified to set up a formal structure for the late joiners and procedures for how they should join.

4.66 The EU recognized that future members might unilaterally move toward adoption of the euro and took steps to avoid it on the principle that members should engage in all the functions, rights, and responsibilities of adopting the euro and being part of the Eurosystem.

> "Any unilateral adoption of the single currency by means of 'euroisation' would run counter to the underlying economic reasoning of EMU in the Treaty, which foresees eventual adoption of the euro as the endpoint of a structured convergence process within a multilateral framework. Therefore, unilateral 'euroisation' would not be a way to circumvent the stages foreseen by the Treaty for the adoption of the euro." (EC; 2001 p. 21)

4.67 Additionally, treaties, laws, and agreements enacted prior to the accession of new states into the union might need to be modified to reflect the expanded membership of the union. In Europe, a number of special protocols were enacted to do this. In planned unions, if it can be done legally given the local legal framework, it would be useful to insert a provision in the master document for the union that its provisions automatically apply to all new members in all respects, including in agreements made between the union and countries outside the union.

4.68 Future unions should expect that they could expand over time. Learning from the experience in Europe, plans for expansion should be built into the design. Surrounding countries that express interest in joining the union need a clear agenda of steps that they must follow. Their rights or obligations vis-à-vis the union need to be set out. For example, with a few restrictions Pre-in EU countries have the right to participate in the TARGET[103] euro settlement system. They also must make a small capital contribution to the ECB to cover miscellaneous services they receive from the ECB. The General Council, that includes all EU countries, makes decisions that affect the Pre-in Countries. Also, the potential entrants might absorb large amounts of the union currency that will need to be monitored.

4.69 Planned unions therefore must have methods to deal with expansion and to handle the affairs of the union with countries in the process of joining. This can be more *ad hoc* if the number of expected new members is small, using bilateral negotiations. In regions, such as Europe, where multiple new members are likely, more standardized, preset arrangements will be needed.

Associated and peripheral states

4.70 A monetary union is be defined by its core membership, but its reach and use of its currency in other jurisdictions can occur under special circumstances. Some of these cases might be formally recognized in the union treaty or in the regulations of the union. Several such cases are listed below.

4.71 The first category consists of colonies, possessions, associated states, or other special jurisdictions controlled by the member states, but which are not actually union members. Examples include French Guiana which is a part of the EU located on the north coast of South America, and Ceuta and Melilla, which are Spanish enclaves in Africa.

4.72 Several small states or jurisdictions exist within the geographic boundaries of the Euroarea – Monaco, San Marino, and Vatican City. Although they are not EU members, special EU regulations allow these areas to use the euro and have other privileges such as access to TARGET. They are allowed

[103] **T**rans-European **A**utomated **R**eal-time **G**ross settlement **E**xpress **T**ransfer System.

to mint euro coins, although France has not been cooperative in allowing Monaco to do so. These surrounded states must negotiate with the surrounding EU member (France and Italy) on how to operate within the system.

Andorra is another European mini-state that is not an EU member. The euro is used and in 2013 Andorra was allowed to issue its own euro coins.

4.73 However, three large areas surrounded by the Euroarea retain their autonomy and do not use the euro as a legal currency.

The United Kingdom.

Switzerland and Liechtenstein. Switzerland applied for EU membership in 1992 after the plan set out in Maastricht was known. However, membership in the European Economic Area (EEA) as a precursor to EU membership was rejected in a referendum. Since then many cooperative agreements have been made between Switzerland and the EU on a wide range of topics, but Switzerland maintains a separate currency and monetary policy. Liechtenstein is a tiny country on the Eastern tip of Switzerland that uses the Swiss franc and follows the monetary and exchange policy of Switzerland, creating a two-country currency union.

Kaliningrad District of Russia. This territory which uses the ruble is separated from the rest of Russia by the EU countries of Lithuania and Poland. A number of agreements have been made between the EU and Russia to facilitate visa issuance and travel to allow legitimate ties without compromising security issues. The EU has stated that cooperation benefits the development of both Kaliningrad and the Baltic EU countries and has provided technical assistance to support regional development.

4.74 Some states outside a currency area adopt another country's currency. This is sometimes done following a war or major political change when it is convenient to quickly adopt another currency to stabilize the economy. For example, Montenegro adopted the euro when it split from Serbia. Timor Leste (a former Portuguese colony) might have opted for the euro, but settled on the dollar making it part of the U.S. dollar area. There are several areas in Africa where political settlements could result in countries quickly adopting a neighboring union currency rather than setting up their own new currency – this might be done quickly for humanitarian reasons without qualifying according to the regular union procedures.

4.75 Greenland and Faroe Islands are autonomous provinces of Denmark with monetary systems linked to the Danish krone. They use the Danish krone and local versions with distinguishing local markings. Denmark rejected membership in the Euroarea and continues to use the Danish krone, but its value is linked to the euro through Denmark's membership in the ERM II. Thus, the three versions of the krone will move with the rate of the euro, and the areas reflect the monetary policy stance of the Euroarea. There are many other linkages to the financial systems and operations of the EU and ECB.

4.76 Finally, military and diplomatic enclaves comprise territories (such as military bases) recognized by treaty physically located in a different country. They are legally separate and might use the home country currency. This can become relevant if leakage of the currency from the enclave is large and cocirculates in the host economy.

4.77 Elsewhere, although the situations might occur less frequently than in Europe, the above cases demonstrate that the spread of union currencies and its monetary policy stance can extend beyond the formal boundaries of the union. Some cases will involve formal use of an union currency, in which case formal legal recognition is needed. In other cases, the arrangements will be informal but practical arrangements might be made for mutual convenience and to support stable flows. If the total flows outside the union appear substantial, estimates should be made of the balance of payments flows and impact on the money stock. However, there are no general principles that can be derived for such cases because each case could be unique.

Derogation

4.78 "Derogation" is an EU term that indicates that a country has not met the conditions for entry into the Eurosystem. Thus, it cannot adopt the euro and will continue using its national currency and executing its own monetary and exchange rate policy. Countries with derogations retain legal provisions needed to continue their own monetary and exchange rate policy. Conversely, their legal codes do not need to include language in their national legislation needed to adopt the euro and operate within the Eurosystem.

4.79 However, countries with derogations are committed under the Maastricht Treaty to ultimately adopt the euro[104], work towards economic convergence and legal convergence, and introduce central bank independence. That is, countries with derogations commit to moving economically and legally toward adopting the euro, but have not yet reached that stage.

4.80 The status of countries with derogations is reviewed every two years. The ECB and the European Commission prepare reports that are reviewed by the EU Council. If a country meets the entry criteria, the derogation is abrogated and the country must adopt the euro.

4.81 Typically, countries are aware of the state of their preparations to adopt the euro and have expectations a year or more before a review by the EU Council whether they are likely candidates to adopt the euro. During this time period, countries will take steps to comply with any final criteria and begin preparations for the changeover to the euro. The decision by the EU Council takes place at least six months prior to adopting the euro, which has always been at the beginning of following year. If a country's application is successful, the derogation is removed, and the country must rapidly begin preparations to adopt the euro. All necessary legal provisions must be in place before the start date.

4.82 Denmark and the United Kingdom were given derogation status under the Maastricht Treaty. Under protocols attached to the treaty, they are permanently exempted from joining the Euroarea. Each was entitled to choose whether they would adopt the euro, but both announced prior to the start-up that they would not.

> Denmark has the same status of other countries with derogations.
>
> The United Kingdom is exempted from the Maastricht provisions mandating central bank independence and being committed to ultimately adopt the euro. In light of this exclusion, special adjustments were made to the weights used for qualified majority voting in the ESCB to exclude the U.K. share. The decision of the U.K. to formally leave the European Union precludes its adoption of the euro.

4.83 Thus, to conclude, future unions might need to create some a form of partial or transitory membership, similar to the derogation provisions in Europe.

Leaving unions

4.84 The idea of a currency union is that it is irrevocable and that countries will never leave. However, the possibility exists, either because the union mechanism fails (the union as a whole functions poorly, or a country diverges too much from the rest of the union). Many commentators suggested in 2010 that Greece might be forced to leave the Euroarea or

[104] The Protocol on the transition to the third stage of Economic and Monetary Union states, "all member states shall, whether or not they fulfill the necessary conditions for the adoption of a single currency, respect the will of the Community to enter swiftly into the third stage, and therefore no Member shall prevent the entering into the third stage." Press reports have indicated that some of the ten EU members who entered in 2004 are not interested in adopting the euro. It is hypothetically possible to remain outside the Euroarea by failing to take action to meet the economic and legal convergence criteria for membership. Sweden is in this position due to failure to fulfill legal convergence requirements.

might be expelled. Also, the GFC created situations where some countries might opt to have a wider range of policy options than available as an union member – for example, would a country facing double-digit ratios of government deficit-to-GDP decide that it was better off having its own currency so that it could devalue to promote exports and introduce stabilizing monetary policy to attract capital inflows?

4.85 For purposes of this study, the presumption is that joining an union is irrevocable and that if a break-up occurs or a country leaves, it will be only due to very serious, and perhaps unforeseeable and unique reasons.

4.86 Leaving an union would be a highly complex and difficult process given the broad range of rights and responsibilities that exist among union members.[105] An exhaustive financial accounting would be needed in order to redistribute assets and income. Legal arrangements will be undone. If disputes arise, overarching decision-making or judicial authority will be needed.[106]

4.87 The ECB prepared a study in 2009 of the legal situation of countries that might choose to leave the Euroarea or EU. (Athanassiou; 2009) The study concluded that *negotiated departure* from the EU is difficult but not legally impossible (witness Brexit) and if this occurs the country would also have to withdraw from the Euroarea; a country could not *exit* the EMU without also leaving the EU; and *expulsion* of a country from the EU or EMU would be legally next to impossible. However, "even if institutional membership in the Euroarea would not survive a Member State leaving the EU, this would not necessarily prevent it from using the euro." (p. 7)

> The paper argues that practical arguments to remain in the EU and EMU are strong, because the EU has contributed to lasting peace and stability and the EMU as helped avert serious currency crises, contributed to integration and market development, contributed to general prosperity, and improved resilience to external shocks.
>
> Creating a new currency upon exiting from the EMU would "involve considerable risk and complications and entail substantial legal complications, including with regard to the validity and enforceability of outstanding re-denominated contracts". (p. 39)
>
> The paper argues that it would be an "intolerable challenge to EU integrity and sustainability" for a departing country to have "a la carte' arrangements in which some features of the Maastricht Treaty are rejected, but others retained. Thus, departure from the EU and not the EMU is inconceivable. (pp. 39-40)
>
> Consensual euroisation of countries that were former members of the Euroarea is not impossible, following the model for negotiated arrangements for Monaco, San Marino, and the Vatican.

4.88 The conclusion is that withdrawing from a currency union is highly complex, both legally and practically. The EMU discussion shows some of the potential pitfalls, but does point to the need to retain at least some flexibility to deal with what will be a very thorny situation if it ever arises. Future unions might wish to create a streamlined decision-making process for such situations, but must be mindful of the danger to creating too much flexibility to allow

[105] Having observed the complex process of joining the EMU, introducing many structural and legal changes, and facing many uncertainties after leaving the union framework, it has long been the author's view that leaving the EMU is virtually impossible.

[106] A fascinating variation on the issues of leaving an union could result post-Brexit by the possibility that Scotland, Wales, or Ulster might leave the U.K. in order to remain in the EU and thus adopt the euro. Many issues would arise in the course of such a breakup.

countries to pick and choose their situation to the detriment of the union as a whole.[107]

F. Centralized vs decentralized models

4.89 A key variable in joining an union is the extent of national sovereignty ceded to the union, which is a function of the degree of centralization of policy and operations.

The EMU followed a strategy described as centralized policy and decentralized implementation. Maastricht established the "European System of Central Banks" in which the ECB and the preexisting national central banks coexist and cooperate. The countries ceded monetary and exchange rate sovereignty to the union. The ECB is at the center of the system as an independent institution with its own income and capital and endowed with the responsibility to make the single monetary and exchange policies for the union independent of national policy direction. The NCBs of each member country retain their own identities with many differences in their structure and governance. They carry out many union functions in their respective countries in accordance with union policy. The heads of the NCBs have seats on the ECB General Council which sets the policy stance of the union. This arrangement is semi-centralized and requires many complex rules to determine the rights and obligations of each of the parties involved. The NCBs retain their own financial independence and can carry out functions not ceded to the union.

In contrast, the ECCB and the two francophone unions in Africa are fully centralized. The union central bank is a single entity with a central policy and operations office and branch offices in each member country. This is a much simpler structure in which policy is set at the union level.

The Common Monetary Area in Southern Africa is a much looser arrangement in which the member countries retain their own currencies at a fixed rate against the South African rand. The rand can circulate freely throughout the region. Policy is effectively set by South Africa. This is a loose arrangement, with powers distributed very unevenly.

Currently, there are no models in which national central banks, their governors, or other national authorities are directly involved in decision making for the union. For example, a decision to change policy rates could require ratification by three-quarters of member central banks (which could be weighted or unweighted by the size of the economies), to be executed by national central banks, but with some coordination by a relatively weak the central office. This might be similar to the situation during the early years of the U.S. Federal Reserve System in which the Board in Washington, D.C. was relatively weak and regional reserve banks could have different lending rates. Although this model does not currently exist, future unions might find it politically or economically worth trying.

4.90 The degree of centralization in every planned union will need to be set in place when the union treaty is ratified. The history and political preferences in each region will be important in deciding on the arrangement; the nature of policy-making and operations will be affected by the degree of centralization of the structure and it will be important that the technical operations of the union be compatible with the agreed structure. Financial operations will also be affected; Does the center directly own large pools of assets? Does the center exercise effective control over reserve assets owned by member countries? Do countries own their own assets and control their size and composition? How much central monetary control

[107] In 2009 while reeling from severe consequences from the financial crisis, Iceland applied for EU membership (but withdrew it in 2015). This action to come under the umbrella of a stable union suggests that attractiveness and cohesion of an union might actually strengthen during periods of general financial distress.

extends over general government finances or assets of sovereign wealth funds?

4.91 As introduced in Chapter 1, the degree of centralization is one of the key decisions that unions must make early in their constitutional and planning processes because many operations, institutional features, finances, and governance rules will follow from whatever decision is made. The decision will reflect the history, goals, and political climates in each union. The decision will also be made with reference to the experience of the EMU where a hybrid system was put in place initially, but where greater centralization has tended to follow.

Timeline

This schedule is for a small or regional union. Large unions should begin all steps at least one year earlier.

Preparatory period	Preliminary discussions and research amongst potential members
Early actions (four years prior)	Draft and ratify monetary union treaty. Provisional list of union members.
Three years prior	Agreement on Convergence Criteria Convergence reports begin
Two years prior	Country macroeconomic policies support convergence to union criteria
Final 12 months	Preparation of final convergence criteria reports
Final 8 - 9 months	Final decision on membership in union. Conversion rates into union currency set Countries not entering union acquire special status Union central bank created in which countries participate in governance Changeover program begins
Run-up to union	All legal preparations are in place
Union day	New members officially join union

Chapter 5 – Monetary Policy

What is the monetary policy of the Euroarea? How does monetary policy in an union differ from policy in countries not in unions?

A. EMU monetary policy framework

5.1 An important task for building a currency union is selecting and implementing its monetary policy and exchange rate policy. This chapter covers monetary policy issues; exchange rate issues are covered in the next chapter. However, monetary policy and exchange rate policies have many interconnections and the separation of the discussions is somewhat artificial.

5.2 A monetary union creates a single currency that replaces the national currencies of its members. This means that a single monetary policy, single interest rate policy, and single exchange rate policy prevail throughout the union. The member countries must cede sovereign policy-making powers in these areas to the central authority, although they may participate in making policy. This can be a difficult step because the ability to use these tools to regulate the national economy is lost and entrusted to a joint decision-making process.

5.3 This chapter reviews monetary policies in an union and how they differ from national policy settings, some of the policy choices faced by unions, and policy tools available to unions. The choice of the policy framework can have important implications on the institutional setup and operations of the union.[108] [109]

5.4 The EMU monetary policy framework was based on extensive research, discussions, and preparations by the EMI and the monetary policy and operations staffs of the member countries. EU countries had large, well-established professional programs to set and implement monetary policy. They also had an established framework for setting overall macroeconomic and financial goals and forums in the Committee of Governors and the EMI to communicate with each other and understand policies. Moreover, the Bundesbank provided leadership.

5.5 Currency unions can have a variety of goals and need frameworks to achieve them. Common monetary policy goals of unions include;

Stable domestic prices

Economic growth

Employment

Financial inclusion of underserved populations

Limit economic volatility

Financial sector stability

5.6 The EMU monetary policy framework has two pillars – monetary analysis and broad analysis of economic conditions.

Pillar 1 – Monetary analysis

5.7 Monetary analysis seeks to identify the influence of monetary and credit developments to price stability over the medium term. It reflects the view that over the longer-term inflation is a monetary phenomenon, and that monetary movements often anticipate inflation developments. However, in the short term, movements between monetary aggregates and inflation might not be highly correlated, which when combined with uncertainties about the strength and speed of effectiveness of monetary policy actions make it imprudent to attempt to fine tune inflation through monetary policy. Thus, the ECB believes that monetary policy actions should focus on medium-term results and inflation risks. This implies a forward-looking perspective to monetary policy analysis, and suggests caution in monetary policy actions

[108] Much of the description is drawn from European Central Bank. The Monetary Policy of the ECB. 2001.

[109] The Annex to this chapter describes a 2021 ECB statement on its review of its monetary policy framework. The material in this section remains relevant, but is conditioned by policy responses to the Global Financial Crisis and Covid crisis, introduction of new financial technologies, and new EU environmental policy priorities.

and application of judgment in lieu of reacting mechanically to deviations from target values.

5.8 The monetary policy analysis of the Eurosystem is considerably more sophisticated than simply responding to changes in monetary aggregates. A broad set of monetary and financial variables are examined using a range of analytical techniques. The goal is to identify underlying trends in monetary developments and assess their implications for price stability.

Pillar 2 – Broad analysis of economic conditions

5.9 In the monetary policy process, the ECB undertakes a very broad analysis of economic and financial conditions for the union as a whole and for the member countries. "It analyzes all factors which are helpful in assessing the dynamics of real activity and the likely development of prices in terms of the interplay between supply and demand in the goods, services, and labor markets. The economic analysis also pays due attention to the need to identify the nature of shocks hitting the economy, their effects on cost and pricing behavior, and the short- to medium-term prospects for their propagation." (ECB 2001, p. 84)

5.10 This analysis includes fiscal conditions and asset price developments as well as other standard macroeconomic variables and exchange rate analysis. In line with its medium-term monetary policy focus, the ECB also analyzes expectations about interest rates and prices, through surveys and use of sophisticated techniques to extract information about expectations from market information.

5.11 The ECB also uses macroeconomic projections and scenarios, prepared with the cooperation of the national central banks. The exercises are based on a set of assumptions about current conditions to provide guidance to the Governing Council in setting policy.

B. Monetary policy in an union

5.12 The creation of a single currency in an union results in the redenomination of financial and real transactions and assets and liabilities of the member countries, which then are affected by the common monetary and exchange rate policies. In contrast to national monetary policy actions, in an union monetary policy impulses can be quickly transmitted throughout the union and countries cannot effectively isolate themselves from the common currency and the influences of the common policies. Nor can countries exercise their own monetary policy. A new monetary and exchange rate policy framework for the union as a whole must be put in place.

5.13 Different monetary policy frameworks exist (monetary aggregates, credit targets, interest rate targeting, exchange rate stability, inflation targets, hybrid macroprudential-monetary frameworks[110], etc.) that use different targets, instruments, institutions, decision-making schemes, and outcomes. Countries entering an union might have different policy perspectives and monetary policy operations before they enter the union, but these must be reconciled into a single union-wide framework.

5.14 An overarching concept related to the policy choices of currency unions is the policy "Trilemma", or the "Impossible trinity". The Trilemma states that open economies must trade-off between the policy options of free capital flows, a currency peg, and an independent monetary policy. The economy can only achieve only two of the three goals at the same time. For countries in a currency union, the exchange rate

[110] The GFC led to fundamental reassessments of monetary policy frameworks, in which use of macroprudential tools would become nearly coequal with monetary policy. The crisis marked the transition from widespread use of inflation targeting to a new regime in which interest rate policy actions are supplemented by a potentially wide range of macroprudential tools designed to tackle specific financial sector conditions. This is a multi-policy environment in which macroprudential policy comes to the fore. Monetary policy can no longer be premised on existence of a smoothly operating financial system; rather, monitoring of the financial system and intervention in a variety of ways might be needed to bolster the effectiveness of monetary policy; conversely, monetary policy actions can affect financial stability.

will be fixed, and must choose between having an independent monetary policy or free capital movements. In a currency union, capital movements will be free between countries and individual countries give up their monetary policy control to the union.

Central bank independence

5.15 The Maastricht Treaty established the principle of central bank independence, and the ECB has doggedly defended its independence as an important contribution to the policy of maintaining price stability. The Treaty was conceived during a period in which the European countries were struggling to get inflation under control, and economic theory and empirical research at the time were pointing to maintenance of central bank independence as a factor in achieving lower inflation. The rationale was that insulating central banks from political influences allowed central banks to focus on policies to control inflation and lower inflation expectations. This stance stands in contrast to the then accepted view that the high inflation experience of the 1970's stemmed from political pressure to boost economic activity at the expense of higher inflation. The theory argued that the public would come to expect elevated rates of inflation and demand higher nominal wages and other inflation adjustments, and over the longer term inflation expectations would increase and inflation would become ingrained in the economies. "The only way out of this dilemma is to delegate monetary policy to an independent central bank with a clear mandate to safeguard price stability." (ECB 2008d, p. 22)

5.16 Moreover, the ECB has stated that the worldwide reduction in inflation in recent years coinciding with greater central bank independence "represents strong evidence that central bank independence is a precondition for achieving and maintaining price stability. A large number of studies have shown that across countries greater central bank independence is associated with lower average inflation." (ibid, p.24).

5.17 In terms of political influences, the Bundesbank, which followed policies of strong central bank independence linked with a low inflation policy, dominated central bank policy within the European Union during the period when the monetary union was forming and insisted on both elements as part of the policy framework for the union.

5.18 The concept of central bank independence is embodied into the legal and institutional framework of the union in several ways;

> Institutional independence of the ECB is guaranteed in the Treaty (Article 108). It states that the ECB and other organs of the union will not seek or take monetary policy instructions from EC institutions, national governments, nor any other body. The Community institutions and national governments are required to respect this limitation.[111]
>
> The ECB was granted sole competence in monetary policy in the Euroarea making it functionally independent. For example, it was granted a monopoly on issuance of banknotes and could limit all elements of the monetary base.[112] Another aspect of this independence was forbidding monetary financing by the Eurosystem of public sector debt.
>
> The members of the ECB Governing Council were granted personal independence in order to make decisions free of national or other influences. They cannot be sanctioned for their official decisions. The members were also given long-term appointments so that they could consider the long-term benefit of the union free from short-term political considerations. Granting Council members

[111] In the EMI's review of the legal statutes of EU member countries, it advised striking provisions from the statutes of several countries that could compromise the independence of the ECB.

[112] In principle this might preclude privately-issued instruments that could be considered part of the monetary base – an example might be cryptocurrency 'stablecoins' that might substitute for officially-issued cash.

independence was designed to allow them to be freed of obligations to reflect home country views and situations and also permits them the power to criticize ECB policy as a necessary part of the surveillance process.

The Eurosystem was also provided financial resources (capital and ability to retain income) that granted it financial independence and resources sufficient to carry out its tasks.

5.19 In return for granting substantial powers and independence to the Eurosystem, it was expected to live up to democratic principles by providing a high degree of transparency and accountability. The legitimacy of the Eurosystem is considered to be established in several ways;

The Maastricht Treaty and its amendments were voluntarily ratified by the member countries that committed them to participate in the arrangement.

The Governing Council reflects the membership of the union and is subject to extensive steps to establish agreement among the members.

The ECB reports on its policies and transactions to many Community bodies and to the public.

Financial accounting, auditing, and statistical reporting are required.

The system falls under the authority of the European Court of Justice in Strasbourg which has final word on Eurosystem adherence to EU policy and rules.

C. Monetary aggregates and targets

Role of monetary aggregates and targets

5.20 Monetary aggregates are measures of the certain liabilities of the central bank and the banking system (and sometimes other institutions) that are closely associated with economic activity and price levels in a country. The public considers their holding of these financial instruments to be money and usable for transactions, exchanging value, and savings. The aggregates convey information about financial activity in an economy and how it can affect the real economy and prices.

5.21 Monetary aggregates are sometimes used as policy targets. This assumes that a stable relationship exists between money and prices, and that it is possible to control the stock of money so that prices can be controlled over the medium term. Typically, authorities announce that they seek to keep the growth rate of a monetary target within a certain range and will take actions to attempt to keep within the announced range. For example;

An upper limit on growth of an aggregate is announced, such as 8 percent growth in M2 on an annual basis. The financial instruments in M2 will be specifically enumerated and carefully measured.

The recorded growth rate of the aggregate is calculated. For example, it could be estimated that the current rate of growth is 10 percent, which might be interpreted as too rapid and possibly indicating that inflationary pressures are increasing.

The central bank responds by engaging in open market operations that pull liquid monetary assets out of the market, raise interest rates, and slow economic activity.

If all goes as planned, the growth in the M2 aggregate falls below the 8 percent limit, placing the economy in a situation of moderate noninflationary growth.

However, if the target rate is still exceeded, further tightening by the central bank is needed. Additional steps might also be considered, such as slowing the rate of government expenditures. On the other hand, if growth of the monetary aggregates falls too far, say to 1 percent, this could indicate that the central bank has tightened conditions too much and should ease its policy.

5.22 Nearly all countries monitor monetary aggregates because they are believed to convey valuable information about financial and economic conditions. Even countries that do not heavily rely on monetary aggregates in setting policy will often monitor them as potentially useful indicators. Some countries also use credit aggregates as policy targets but prior to the GFC this practice had become less common. (However, following the onset of the GFC credit targets have been increasingly monitored to ascertain whether monetary policy is supporting adequate flow of monetary resources into the economy to stimulate growth.

5.23 One task of union planners will be to assess the nature of the relationships between monetary aggregates and real and financial activity and inflation. This might be solely to learn about the relationships so that the aggregates can provide information for policy setting, but it could also assess whether the relationships are strong and stable and provide a basis for using the aggregates as a monetary target. The following paragraphs describe how those aspects can be assessed.[113] Special conditions affect this process in unions which create greater uncertainty than in a single country case.

Defining monetary aggregates

5.24 Monetary aggregates are empirical relationships. There are no universal or fixed definitions because financial instruments differ between countries, institutional arrangements and market practices differ, policy transmission mechanisms differ, and the responses of markets and inflation to policy changes differ. The openness of the economy and possible use of a cocirculating foreign currency can also be important variables.

5.25 Moreover, monetary conditions and thus monetary aggregates change over time. New instruments are created, markets change, and public behavior in holding and using money change. New instruments and market practices increasingly permit financial assets to be substituted and become fungible, which changes the motivation to hold different types of assets. Thus, a specific aggregate might be useful in one period, but not in later periods.

5.26 Economic research is needed to decide which financial instruments to include in aggregates and how the constructed aggregate relates to economic activity and prices.

Hierarchy of monetary aggregates

5.27 Countries usually compile more than one monetary aggregate because different aggregates can convey different information about the economy. It is common to rank definitions for monetary aggregates from the narrowest to the broadest. For example;

M1 – Narrow money, consisting of currency, current deposits in banks, and other monetary instruments closely associated with transactions.

M2 – Which is usually defined as M1 plus additional instruments with short- or medium-term maturities (such as three-month deposits at banks) that are not immediately available for transactions but which are effectively available quickly when needed by the public.

M3 – Broad money. This could be defined as M2 plus longer term savings instruments, such as deposits up to a two-year maturity.

Special subaggregates might also be calculated. Variations sometimes seen include aggregates such as M2 + certificates of deposits, which adds an additional instrument to the standard M2 definition.

5.28 An important variation in aggregates is whether they include only domestic currency instruments, or also include foreign-currency denominated instruments.

[113] See the IMF's *Monetary and Financial Statistics Manual and Compilation Guide* for a more detailed description. (IMF 2016).

5.29 In the EMU, a range of aggregates is calculated, as described below. M3 is the aggregate that the ECB focuses on for most policy analysis, but the other aggregates are monitored because they convey additional information about monetary behavior and structural changes in the demand for money in the union.[114]

Instruments in EMU monetary aggregates	
M1	Currency in circulation Overnight deposits
M2	*M1 plus* Deposits with maturity up to two years Deposits redeemable with period of notice up to three months
M3	*M2 plus* Repurchase agreements Money market fund shares Debt securities with maturity up to two years

Source: ECB Economic Bulletin.

Currency denomination of monetary instruments

5.30 Research on the monetary aggregates and targets for unions must consider whether foreign currency instruments should be included. In many economies, monetary aggregates include only national-currency denominated instruments. Holdings of foreign currency and foreign-currency denominated instruments are considered to be devoted for use in external transactions with little impact on domestic activity and prices. However, in the Euroarea and some other economies foreign currency instruments are also included because they are used domestically or can be easily substituted for domestic currency monetary instruments. "Holdings by Euroarea residents of liquid assets denominated in foreign currencies can be close substitutes for euro-denominated assets. Therefore, the monetary aggregates include such assets if they are held with MFIs (monetary financial institutions) in the Euroarea." (ECB 2001, p. 33)

5.31 One special issue for unions is the possibility that foreign currency instruments are more important in some member countries than in others. For example, countries serving as entrepots or on the perimeter of the union might have greater than average penetration of foreign currencies. The foreign currencies might be empirically relevant is such countries, but not in the others. This can make the construction of monetary aggregates for the union difficult because it raises the possibility of including foreign currency assets of banks in some countries and not others. This is not acceptable within unions because financial markets should become well integrated and assets should flow freely between countries (as in Europe).

5.32 Cocirculating physical currencies present special problems for construction of aggregates. In up to a quarter of the countries in the world, the public holds and uses significant amounts of foreign currencies. Often, inflows of foreign currencies are neither captured in balance of payments nor monetary statistics, which creates problems in estimating total currency holdings within the country and constructing aggregates. The use of foreign currencies in transactions can affect activity and prices and create problems in monetary policy regulation of the economy.[115]

5.33 Whether foreign currency-denominated assets are included in the national definition of money is a key issue that needs to be resolved. Practices differ and seem to be about evenly split. The EMU definition includes foreign-currency denominated assets. However, as shown below even in a small grouping of closely related countries, such as in the GCC,

[114] Prior to the start of the union, each candidate country compiled harmonized M3 aggregates that – when aggregated – could provide some information about the potential future monetary aggregates for the union.

[115] A discussion of how to measure and deal with cocirculation in an union context is in Chapter 12 – Statistics, Appendix: Cocirculation.

practices differ on use of foreign currency instruments within the national definition of money. In a currency union, agreement is needed on whether foreign currency-denominated assets are part of the common union definition of money.

Components of Broad Money in GCC Countries (2010)		
Country	**Foreign currency deposits**	**Government deposits**
Bahrain	No	Yes
Kuwait	No	No
Oman	Yes	No
Qatar	Yes	Yes
Saudi Arabia	Yes	No
United Arab Emirates	Yes	Yes

5.34 The definition of money is an empirical issue. (IMF 2000) Conditions of monetary circulation and use vary by country and no single standard can apply *a priori*. Moreover, numerous innovations such as new instruments, ATMs, electronic and mobile phone money, new types of institutions issuing money-like instruments, or cryptoassets continually affect usage patterns and mean that definitions evolve, sometimes fairly rapidly.[116]

5.35 Also, the creation of an union itself will cause structural changes that will change monetary behavior. In each country or union an investigation is needed to determine which instruments to include in aggregates to provide the best measures of money as an explanatory variable in prices and economic activity.

Money Issuing and Holding Sectors

5.36 Below, descriptions of the money issuing and money holding sectors are provided. The descriptions are more than statistical artifacts needed to compile data. They convey information about the structure of the monetary system in an union and its member countries. The information is needed to understand who is affected by monetary policy actions and how monetary policy impulses are transmitted in the union. Moreover, the behaviors of these sectors could differ greatly between unions and the information will be needed in order to understand how to execute union monetary policies. For example, monetary holdings of large isolated agricultural sectors with strong seasonal patterns and limited access to formal financial institutions are very different from those in urban settings.

Money issuing sector

5.37 In monetary aggregates, the money issuing sector comprises the central bank, the banking system, and sometimes other financial institutions and government bodies that issue liabilities of a monetary or near-monetary nature. These institutions are critical for the transmission of monetary policy impulses through the economy because the central bank will undertake monetary policy by acting with these institutions. In unions, a common definition must be used and each member country must apply the standards comparably in order to understand the monetary transmission mechanism in the union and thus be able to implement monetary policy.

5.38 *Central bank.* The central bank issues currency, CBDCs, and might take deposits from business and the public that are considered monetary liabilities. Central bank deposits from banks and other institutions in the money issuing sector are not considered part of money because they are not held by business and the public for use in transactions.

5.39 *Banks and similar institutions.* The banking system of a country takes deposits from the public, extends credit, and is central in the transmission of monetary policy impulses through the economy. It's

[116] In many countries in recent years, large changes in the behavior of monetary aggregates have caused the predictive power of money aggregates to decrease. Money aggregates are never ignored, but often less attention is paid to them than in the past. Other monetary policy frameworks, such as inflation targeting, have often taken their place.

liabilities in the form of current accounts, transferable deposits, sight deposits, short-term savings accounts, short-term certificates of deposits, repurchase agreements with the public, etc. are typically considered monetary instruments.

A wide range of institutions can be considered like banks – commercial banks, savings banks, credit unions, microfinance institutions, Islamic financial institutions, etc. depending on whether they issue money type liabilities. Many might not use the word bank in their title. For this reason, the IMF and the ECB use broad definitions for this subsector. The IMF term is "Other Depository Corporations". The Euroarea term is "Credit Institutions".

5.40 Other financial institutions. Practice varies by country, but institutions that issue liabilities readily usable as money or which can easily be exchanged for monetary assets might be considered part of the money issuing sector, as verified through empirical analysis. The institutions and monetary-like practices in this subsector have evolved rapidly in recent years and the list of institutions considered as part of the money-issuing sector should be continually reviewed.

The most common case is money market mutual funds that issue shares to the public that entitle the holder to the income and gains and losses on the portfolio of assets held in the fund. If those shares can be readily redeemed and have "capital certainty", that is fixed or nearly fixed values, they can be considered as equivalent to monetary deposits and can be included in money. (In contrast, shares of mutual funds subject to variable market-based returns, such as a fund that invests in equities, are considered investment companies and not monetary institutions.)

5.41 The Euroarea uses statistical tests to identify monetary institutions. Banks that accept deposit from the public can be readily identified, but it must be empirically determined what other instruments have near monetary characteristics and which institutions issue them. The two text boxes below discuss the process.

Text box: Euroarea definition of Monetary Financial Institutions (MFIs)

In the Euroarea, MFIs are the money issuing sector. It comprises the European Central Bank and NCBs, credit institutions, and "other MFIs", which consist of money market funds. All MFIs must provide harmonized statistical information to prepare the aggregated and consolidated balance sheets for the MFI sector. The balance sheets provide data for the Euroarea monetary aggregates and their counterparts.

The ECB relied on the "credit institutions" legal definition in EC Banking Directives. Credit institutions are defined as "any undertaking whose business is to receive deposits or other repayable funds from the public and to grant credit on its own account." Credit institutions receive funds by incurring monetary liabilities, grant credit to businesses and households, and can receive credit from the central bank, and thus are central to the transmission of monetary policy impulses to the public. Credit institutions are the counterparties to the ECB and NCBs banks in monetary policy operations.

The definition of credit institutions is comprehensive, going beyond the traditional definition of banks and corresponds to a universal banking concept. Consequently, in the Euroarea, the residual grouping of "other financial institutions" is small in comparison to other countries where a large number of nonbank lending institutions might be unregulated and outside the monetary policy framework. Credit institutions are subject to EU-wide banking supervisory standards, as administered by national financial sector supervisors.

The grouping "Other MFIs" (OMFIs) is intended to cover any nonCredit institutions that offer products and services that were traditionally handled by banks. OMFIs include money market funds, which are investment funds that offer liquidity and returns very close to those of banks. In contrast to credit institutions, OMFIs are not monetary policy counterparties.

For planned unions, an issue is whether a comprehensive definition of the money issuing sector should be used, such as the credit union definition used in Europe, or use a narrow traditional bank-based definition. The broad definition brings nearly all institutions providing credit to the public into the monetary policy framework, and it brings a broad range of institutions into the supervisory system which can help support financial sector stability. Conversely, a broad definition might go beyond what is needed for monetary policy implementation, might go beyond traditional practices in a country or region, and could be expensive.

Text box: Identification of Money Market Funds in the Euroarea

The classification of OMFIs covers any nonCredit institutions that offer products and services similar to monetary instruments traditionally handled by banks. OMFIs include a range of funds constructed to serve a variety of investment purposes and are articulated for statistical purposes into money market funds; bond funds; equity funds; mixed bond and equity funds; real estate funds; hedge funds; and other funds such as cryptoasset funds. Money market funds are specifically interesting because they are considered to be monetary in nature, whereas the others are considered to be investment vehicles.

Money market funds are defined as "collective investment undertakings of which the units are in terms of liquidity close substitutes for deposits and which primarily invest in money market instruments and/or other transferable debt instruments with a residual maturity up to and including one year, and/or in bank deposits which offer a rate of return approaching the interest rates on money market instruments." (ECB 2005b, p.11)

Units that meet these requirements are considered part of the money issuing sector and are required to submit statistical reports for construction of the Euroarea monetary balance sheets. Other "collective investment undertakings", better known as mutual funds, that do not meet the strict liquidity and return requirements are classified outside the money issuing sector and do not have to meet the reporting requirements of MFIs.

The definition of OMFI rests on statistical tests to measure the liquidity and return of each mutual fund in the Euroarea. The test measures the degree of capital certainty of investments in mutual funds, and if the fund varies little in value and funds are readily available the fund must be classified as a money market fund. A firm that offers a wide range of mutual funds with different features to appeal to different types of investors must run the statistical tests on each fund separately.

5.42 *Central government liabilities.* Government entities that accept deposits or issue securities that are used like money can be considered part of the money issuing sector. The most common case is government post offices that make use of their widely dispersed office network to collect deposits from isolated populations. Only the specific part of the government that issues such liabilities is considered part of the money issuing sector.

5.43 *Swipe cards and preloaded instruments.* Cards exist with magnetic stripes that can hold value. A payment is made to the issuer of the card, which then can be swiped through machines to transfer the value and purchase goods or services. Usually these are not considered as money, but as prepayments for goods and services that are classified as commercial liabilities of the firm. Deposits in the banking system made by the firm after receiving deposits are included in monetary aggregates.

5.44 *Mobile phones and electronic devices.* A wide variety of electronic instruments are capable of having value stored on them for use in transactions. In some developing countries, mobile phones are very commonly used to hold value and carry out transactions. In these cases, the electronic instruments can be considered as substitutes for deposits or cash that should be included in monetary aggregates. However, if any deposits received by cell phone companies and other electronic holders of value must be deposited in banks (including possibly a 100% deposit), an adjustment is needed to avoid double counting within the aggregate. *Mobile phone-based money has become so widespread in Africa, Asia, and the Middle East, that it probably should be considered part of monetary aggregates.*[117]

5.45 *Electronic money issuers.* It is also possible to create encoded measures of value for use on computers or other devices. These can be transferred for making purchases or other payments. A very long encoded identifier that is virtually undecipherable is used for each measure of value held by the public. These measures of value are held in "wallets" or "electronic purses". A transaction can take place by notifying the issuer to transfer the value to another party, in which case the amount held as electronic money has characteristics of deposits in the banking system. However, if value can be transferred without notifying the issuer, the instrument is more like currency.

5.46 *Central Bank Digital Currencies (CBDC)* CBDCs are digital versions of cash or other central bank liabilities treated as money. A few countries began issuing CBDCs in 2021 and many can be expected to follow; future unions should investigate whether they should officially issue CBDCs. *This is a very rapidly evolving field that all future unions should monitor. See Chapter 9D – The Digital Euro.*

5.47 The identification of the money issuing sector is important because these will be institutions through which the union central bank will exercise monetary policy. Entities in the money issuing sector could be subject to special regulations or requirements, or might need to handle special instruments used to implement monetary policy. They are a key part of the payments and settlements systems of countries. Also, because of the critical importance of these institutions in the operation of the monetary and credit systems of countries, they have a special role to play in assuring overall financial sector stability. They can be subject to supervisory or financial stability rules and might receive special aid or rescues in crisis situations.

5.48 For such reasons, institutions in the money issuing sector should be identified early in the planning process so that officials can explain features of the monetary policy system and to work with them in setting up the arrangements. Once identified, accounting and statistical systems are needed well prior to the start of the union to develop harmonized information on monetary conditions for the new union.

<u>Money holding sector</u>

5.49 The money holding sector includes <u>domestic</u> businesses, households, and nonprofit institutions serving households. These sectors are considered as holding money in order to make purchases of goods and services, and in which the ability to transact might be constrained by the lack of cash. Financial institutions not part of the money issuing sector and government are excluded. Government is excluded because its purchases are not considered constrained by the amount of its money holdings, and because it often engages in many special transactions, adjustments, and offsets that have no counterparts in the private sector. The IMF's *Monetary and Financial Statistics Manual* provides more information on identification of the money holding sector.

5.50 *Nonresidents* are not part of the money holding sector, and their holdings of monetary assets are excluded from monetary aggregates because their stock of money is not deemed to affect domestic economic activity. For this reason, it is important that the statistical reporting system accurately identify holdings by residents separately from nonresidents.

5.51 *Deposits of emigrant workers.* Remittances from nationals working abroad deposited in domestic banks are quite large in some cases. Deposits registered in the name of the foreign worker, but intended for use by the family back home could appear to be accounts of nonresidents, but because of the close links with the domestic economy it is useful to separately compile information on these accounts and to construct supplementary monetary aggregates that

[117] The union itself might even choose to sponsor development of mobile phone money or CBDCs as means to foster development of financial markets and to maintain control over its monetary consequences.

include such deposits. If the accounts of emigrant workers are large, information on them is important in itself for analyzing the national economic situation and should collected for policy analysis.

5.52 *Cocirculation*. Both domestic use of foreign currencies and foreign use of the domestic currency affect the monetary situation of the country. Use of a foreign currency means that the effective size of domestic monetary balances are underestimated, and the national net international investment position is overstated. Conversely, if the domestic currency is used abroad, domestic monetary aggregates are overestimated, and the national net international investment position is understated. Both situations can affect policy. Ideally, adjustments should be made for each, and some countries do so. However, adjustments are often not possible because of lack of reliable information to make the adjustments.[118]

5.53 *Intra-union residents.* As discussed more in Chapter 12, holders of money in unions are dual residents in their own country and in the union. Thus, businesses, households, and nonprofit institutions located anywhere within the union are part of the money holding sector. Two definitions of residency are needed (resident of own country; resident of the union) that must be applied consistently throughout the union.

Empirical changes in monetary aggregates

5.54 Over recent decades, the empirical relationships between money, activity, and prices have shifted in many countries. In earlier periods, the correlation between narrow aggregates and activity and prices was relatively strong, but has weakened in numerous countries. Conversely, correlations with Broad Money have increased. This reflects numerous fundamental and long-term changes in markets, as greater flexibility in moving financial assets has permitted the public to hold more of their assets in longer-maturity interest bearing assets rather than in narrow cash-like non-interest-bearing instruments. For example, availability of automatic teller machines (ATMs), credit cards, and repurchase agreements has reduced the amount of cash the public needs to hold. As a result, in some economies total narrow money has declined despite growth of the economy, while broad money aggregates have grown. In the future, increased use of electronic monetary instruments – and especially CBDCs – promises to introduce further changes in monetary behavior.

5.55 The creation of an union itself changes monetary behavior because money holders can more easily carry out transactions across border and can transfer money and invest in other countries at lower cost and more securely. Greater competition in financial markets and new monetary institutions and practices with the development and deepening of union markets will also change behaviors.

EMU policy on monetary aggregates

5.56 Among the three monetary aggregates (M1, M2, and M3), the focus is on M3 – Broad money. A strong empirical relationship is noted between broad money and the price level. "Money constitutes a natural, firm, and realistic 'nominal anchor' for monetary policy aiming at the preservation of price stability." (ECB 1999, p. 49) Monetary aggregates are considered to convey information about future price developments and therefore contribute to the assessment of prospects for price stability. M3 was chosen as the primary focus because it had the best leading indicator properties for future inflation.

5.57 *M3 is not used as a target, but as a reference value*. That is, Euroarea monetary policy does not respond automatically to movements of M3 outside of a target band. Instead information about M3 is closely analyzed along with other information to gain comprehensive information on prospects for price stability in the union. The components of M3 are also analyzed, individually and as part of narrower aggregates such as M1 encompassed within M3. This permits the ECB to set monetary policy based on the best

[118] Chapter 12 – Statistics, Appendix: Cocirculation discusses how to measure and deal with cocirculation.

information on how to create price stability in the union, which is the ECB's primary goal.

5.58 The EMU concept of monetary aggregates as a reference value is based on the view that growth in monetary aggregates ΔMi is based on relationships between real economic growth (ΔY_r), price changes (ΔP), and the velocity of circulation of money (ΔV), where velocity is the speed with which money moves between holders to support the level of transactions.

$$\Delta Mi = \Delta Y_r + \Delta P - \Delta V$$

5.59 The reference value for M3 was derived from estimates that medium-term annual real growth in the Euroarea was 2 to 2½ percent, velocity declines by ½ to 1 percent, and a policy goal of price inflation of no more than 2 percent per annum. Substituting these values in the formula, the initial Euroarea reference value for M3 was 4½ percent per annum (approximately, ΔMi = 2.5 + 2 – .5). This was set by the ECB Governing Council as the reference rate in December 1998, immediately before the creation of the monetary union. The reference value is published, in part to give the public a benchmark to evaluate the ECB's performance. Although the ECB says it is not obligated to achieve the reference value, it does have an obligation to explain differences to the public in light of its comprehensive analysis of the Euroarea economy.[119]

5.60 The ECB is cautious regarding the use of the reference value because the underlying factors can change or be subject to measurement errors. (ECB 2001, pp. 47-49).

Short-run velocity changes, which measure the relationship between the variables, are possible.

Changes in the banking and financial system structure can create permanent velocity changes.

The creation of the union itself creates a larger market that potentially acts differently than a simple sum of the national economies.[120]

Institutional changes and special factors such as tax law changes can create erratic shifts in data.

EMU policy in practice

5.61 Gerlach (2007) empirically reviewed which indicators the ECB had used in practice to set monetary policy during the first seven years of the union. He tested the importance of inflation, M3 growth, changes in exchange rates, and the general state of the economy in policy reactions. He found that the ECB did not respond to inflationary shocks because they were considered temporary in nature, but that it did adjust policy to changes in the other variables. In

[119] When the union began, M3 was close to the reference value. The early ECB *Monthly Bulletin* published constructed M3 aggregates for 1998, the year before the Euroarea was officially created. The annual percentage changes during 1998 varied between 4.5% and 5.0%, which corresponded closely with the announced reference rate of 4.5%.

However, M3 growth accelerated in 1999, the first year of the union. All months of 1999 recorded rates at 5% or above, and by yearend a rate of 6.1% was recorded. By 2003, M3 growth rates were regularly above 8%. Very rapid growth of money market shares was the prime driver of M3 growth during the first years of the union. By 2008, M3 growth was in the 10 to 11 % range.

By mid-2003, an analyst at the ECB wondered if M3 would ever again fall within the reference rate and complained of the challenges trying to explain M3 growth to the ECB's chief economist.

(During the covid crisis, M3 growth was over 10 % per annum by late 2020.)

[120] Prior to start-up of the EMU, estimates of real growth and velocity were prepared based on compilation of information on a "virtual" monetary union, based on collection of statistics from all potential member countries. Such data reflect a mix of market conditions, policy regimes, and statistical practices and might not perfectly reflect conditions in the actual union. Moreover, union conditions are an average of divergent national conditions.

contrast, policy responses to changes in overall economic activity were strong because they were seen as influencing future inflation. That is, inflation was treated as a medium-term target influenced by both money and real variables; policy actions are initiated using whatever instruments that are likely to affect inflation when they seem to move out of line. Gerlach's empirical results broadly support the description of the policy framework as being based on the two major pillars, but with additional emphasis on exchange rate changes.

Monetary aggregates and targets for planned unions

5.62 From the above analysis, it is clear that the compilation and analysis of monetary aggregates for planned unions, and determination of their future role in a union, is challenging. The process requires construction of data for a virtual union based on its likely makeup and examination of those aggregates. Statistical problems might be serious because of different standards in countries and possibly different quality data. Institutions and policies will differ by country. The economic variables in each country could act differently. And the institutions, policy framework, and market practices in the union itself might differ from those assumed for the virtual union. Within each future member state, holdings of currency of other future states will be converted from foreign currency balances (excluded from monetary aggregates) into holdings of the union currency. Also, financial market integration during the first years of a union will cause economic relationships to evolve and could make estimates of monetary aggregates unstable.

5.63 In future unions the market and institutional conditions between countries might differ more than in the European case. Different types of monetary instruments could exist in different countries, especially for foreign-currency instruments. Behavior will be affected by factors such as the level of income, literacy, rural or isolated populations, access to formal financial institutions, etc.. It is possible that narrow aggregates perform better in some countries, but broad aggregates do better in others.[121] Combining these into an aggregate as a reference or target for policy could be challenging.

5.64 In contrast to Europe, where pre-union experience demonstrated that broad money aggregates were often superior than narrowly defined aggregates, in future unions it might be uncertain which instruments should be included in aggregates and whether narrow, intermediate, or broad aggregates are likely to work best. An added complication not faced in Europe is that in many future unions, transactions in mobile phone money and other digital assets are likely to be significant.

5.65 The degree of economic convergence or non-convergence between potential union member countries could also complicate constructing union monetary aggregates. If growth rates or inflation differ greatly between countries prior to union there might *de facto* be no 'virtual' union-wide underlying monetary behavior. That is in such situations information on the total stock of monetary assets in an aggregate for the future union might have little meaning. Promoting convergence was a high priority for potential Euroarea countries to avoid such problems – whether future unions will achieve a high degree of convergence before entering into the union is unknown.

5.66 Finally, contemporary rapid changes in markets can create complications. Many markets might now be on the cusp of introduction of new monetary technologies, using electronic currency, cell phones, other devices, and perhaps 'cryptocurrencies'[122].

[121] Some future unions have considered whether it will be possible to form unions with less strict convergence between economies than was done for the EMU. Where this might be tried, the variations in monetary practices may be broader than what Europe experienced and therefore greater difficulty could be involved in compiling sensible monetary and credit aggregates for the union.

[122] As covered in Chapter 9D, as of 2021, 'cryptocurrencies', such as bitcoin and many others, are treated as (continued)

Also, globalization and increased openness of markets affect markets. These factors might introduce fundamental changes in the nature of money holding and use that cannot be predicted now.

5.67 Thus, caution is urged in analyzing union monetary aggregates and using them for policy. Uncertainties should be explained to the public. It might take several years for monetary aggregates in new unions to settle down and demonstrate stable conditions, especially if the initial convergence is not strong. It could be a serious mistake to set policy exclusively on monetary aggregates that might not well reflect union conditions and which are subject to errors or uncertainties.

Counterparts of Euroarea M3

5.68 To better analyze influences on growth of broad money, the ECB reorganized data on financial institutions that issue broad money liabilities into "Counterparts of Euroarea M3" that looks at changes in banks' (including central bank) finances that affect broad money. The framework isolates M3 on the liability side; the asset side includes all assets *and* all liabilities other than those in M3. In this format, the asset side of the framework provides an analytical picture of factors that affect growth or shrinkage of the M3 money stock. For examples, increased credit to businesses is an use of the resources banks have received from their M3 liabilities, or increased bond issuance by banks indicates the banks are funding themselves more in nonmonetary financial markets rather than relying on M3 funding.

5.69 The IMF has an equivalent framework called the Depository Corporations Survey (DCS) that reassembles the depository corporations'[123] balance sheet to put all broad money liabilities on one side of the account, and all other assets and liabilities on the other side. (IMF 2016) This framework is widely used to explain factors contributing to changes in broad money and it is recommended that future unions compile similar frameworks.

Flow of funds frameworks

5.70 The ECB realized that simple standard monetary aggregates cover only a small part of financial market behavior, might not be stable during the fluid early period of the monetary union, lacked full coverage of financial conditions needed for monetary policy, lacked key information on credit availability and debt burdens, and could not effectively describe the evolution and development of the single unified financial market.

5.71 To address these concerns, "flow-of-funds accounts", were added to be "a key framework for the analysis of monetary, financial and economic developments and the interrelations between them".[124] (ECB 2009) The accounts are a broad statistical framework that show flows of financial resources into and out of the financial sector; or "from who to whom with what instrument". The 'from who' and 'to whom' data always specify counterpart macroeconomic sectors (corporations, households, government, etc.) supplying or receiving the financial resources, and sometimes the counterparty data can be quite detailed. Early in the new union period,

---

nonmonetary financial assets and are often highly volatile and speculative. However, (1) monetary behavior of the public might be altered by access to cryptocurrencies in ways that could complicate use of monetary policy tools, (2) the underlying digital technology used by financial institutions to transfer money balances could affect the behavior of monetary aggregates, (3) experiments are underway to link some cryptocurrencies to official currencies (stablecoins) which could result in the public deeming them more like 'money', and (4) numerous monetary authorities are investigating possible issuance of digital (crypto) versions of their own currency. At the time of writing, the implications of these trends is unknown, but it is clear that future unions must consider how cryptocurrencies fit into their individual situations.

[123] The IMF term for the banking sector, including the central bank.

[124] Other names are also used, such as 'financial accounts', 'resources and uses table', 'intersectoral accounts', or 'sectoral balance sheets'.

compiling the accounts (under the name Monetary Union Financial Accounts – MUFA) became the ECB's top statistical priority.

5.72 Flow of funds accounts can be compiled at widely different levels of detail, ranging from extremely detailed tables with thousands of cells to highly focused presentations that highlight specific perspectives. (IMF 2016) Information on the banking sector will always be separately displayed within the framework, but if the country also compiles data on other financial subsectors those data can be separately displayed, and also consolidated with the banking data to track the total financial resources and uses of the entire financial sector.

EMU monetary policy instruments

5.73 This section looks at the monetary policy instruments used in the Euroarea and considers their relevance to other regions. The framework for policy instruments was based on research by the EMI on open market operations in all EU countries. (Aspetsberger 1996) This sought to find the most feasible and least disruptive methods of carrying out new forms of policy operations for the union, with recognition that the national central banks would be in charge of most of the operations but that the monetary policy impulses had to spread evenly throughout the union.

Minimum required reserves

5.74 The Eurosystem had a lengthy debate before deciding that there should be a system of minimum required reserves and that they should be remunerated. A system was enacted in November 1998 just before the start of the union.[125] The system requires that each credit institution place reserve deposits at their NCB, but that the deposits are compensated in order to not burden the banking system and to have minimal effects on resource allocations. The requirement is equal in all countries so that it would not cause banks to relocate between countries within the union. The required minimum reserves are based on each bank's reserve base (its liabilities to the general public and government) multiplied by a reserve ratio.

5.75 An important intended function of the requirement was to create a *structural liquidity shortage* for the banking system so that banks need to come to the system for central bank credit. This provides policy leverage for the ECB that allows it to better manage money market conditions.

5.76 The reserve requirements were also intended to help stabilize money market interest rates.[126] Also, changes in the requirement could help dampen medium-term fluctuations in money market liquidity.

5.77 The reserve system operates on a monthly basis, and compliance is based on the average of a bank's daily balances over the month. Each bank must hold reserves over the month so that the average level of reserves meets the required level. Thus, banks can hold daily balances above or below the average level, which provides flexibility and helps reduce volatility in the demand for overnight money market funds.

5.78 Remuneration is paid on the reserve balances (including those above the required minimum). The rate equals the marginal rate of the main refinancing operations during the reserve maintenance period (see next section) weighted by number of calendar days. This rate will be very close to short-term money market rates, and thus banks will be largely indifferent

[125] On one hand, this late decision reflected the need to preserve the policy-making prerogative of the ECB Governing Council, which was only set up in mid-1998. Unfortunately, banks had little time to prepare for the imposition of the requirement.

[126] For example, the reserve requirement limits the full multiplier effect of a sudden infusion of deposits into a bank. Conversely, banks can partially compensate for a withdrawal of deposits by reducing their required reserves. Both effects temper the market impacts of shifts in the banks' reserve base.

between holding reserves or extending credit in money markets.[127]

5.79 Sanctions can be (and have been) imposed for violations. Three methods are permitted; applying a penalty rate of an additional 5 percent to the balances improperly excluded, a payment equal to twice the system's marginal lending rate, or requiring non-interest-bearing deposits at the ECB or NCB up to three times the amount improperly excluded. The ECB has a right (which can be delegated to NCBs) to verify the information used to estimate reserves. It can require submission of documents and explanations and can examine records.

Calculating required reserves

5.80 The reserve base of each credit institution is calculated as the sum of deposit and other liabilities to the general public (households and corporations) and government bodies. Liabilities to other credit institutions and to NCBs and the ECB are excluded – a list of credit institutions within the Euroarea is maintained and available on-line so that credit institutions know which liabilities can be excluded.[128] Articulation by type of instrument is provided because reserve ratios differ by type of instrument. The base is calculated from the monthly monetary balance sheet prepared for statistical purposes.[129]

5.81 The reserve ratio was defined by the regulation to be between 0 percent and 10 percent, with flexibility provided to the ECB to set the level for policy reasons. The ECB sets different ratios for each category of liabilities. Most short-term liabilities have a 2-percent ratio.[130] Longer-term instruments[131] and repurchase agreements have a 0-percent ratio. A 30 percent deduction was made for Debt securities with maturity up to 2 years and Money market paper. Finally, a blanket €100,000 lump sum allowance is made for each bank. This effectively excludes smaller institutions with less than €5 million in liabilities from paying required reserves; larger institutions might also be exempted depending on the structure of their balance sheets.

[127] Remuneration of reserves means that they are not a source of income for the Eurosystem. Other central banks, however, rely heavily on income from reserves and thus may provide little or no remuneration of balances. This of course places a burden on the banks and potentially affects market decisions – the potential risk for an economy is that credit markets move offshore and the implicit cost of reserves represses domestic banking activity. Whether to remunerate will be an important decision for future unions.

[128] Thus, maintenance of a current list of credit institutions within the union is necessary for monetary policy purposes. It matters which institutions qualify for or are exempted from the list of credit institutions. The treatment of branches is especially important – branches of non-Euroarea banks within the Euroarea are included, but branches of Euroarea banks outside the Euroarea are excluded. Electronic money institutions are considered credit institutions subject to reserve requirements. The ECB may exempt an institution upon request if it serves special functions that make reserve requirement counter to the purpose of the system. Also, exemptions may be granted if an institution is being reorganized, is losing or surrendering its banking license, or is being wound up.

[129] See the balance sheet framework in Chapter 12 – Statistics. The use of the statistical system to provide data to calculate the reserve base has several advantages. All member countries apply common statistical standards, use the same articulation of financial instruments, and use the highly efficient system set up to rapidly transmit the information to the NCBs and ECB. The information can be rapidly aggregated to national and union totals for comparison of the base of individual banks to the aggregate base used for monetary policy. The use of statistical standards is also efficient and cost saving.

[130] The enumerated short-term instruments are overnight deposits, deposits with agreed maturity up to 2 years, debt securities with maturity up to 2 years, and money market paper. Repurchase agreements, which can be short term, are exempt from the 2-percent ratio.

[131] Deposits with agreed maturity over 2 years, and debt securities with maturity over 2 years.

ESCB Monetary policy principles

5.82 Principles for the operation of the monetary policy of the Euroarea are provided in the Statute of the ESCB. It states that the system will act in accord with the principle of an open market economy relying on free competition to promote an efficient allocation of resources. (Article 105) It will act based on the following principles;

Operational efficiency, to promote quick absorption of monetary policy actions into money market interest rates,

Equal treatment of financial institutions throughout the Euroarea and regardless of size,

Decentralized operations in accordance with the principle of subsidiarity,

Simplicity and transparency, so that policy actions and the intentions behind them are readily understood,

Continuity, by avoiding frequent or sharp changes of policies, instruments, and procedures so that markets can understand what is being done and the consequences,

Safety, by minimizing financial and operational risks to the system, and ...

Cost efficiency, to keep costs to the Eurosystem and the banking system to a minimum. (Scheller 2006).

5.83 To achieve these goals, the Eurosystem employs a full range of monetary policy operations to both extend and absorb liquidity over a range of maturities.

Structural Operations

5.84 As mentioned above as a function of the minimum reserve system, the Eurosystem seeks to create a structural liquidity shortage for the banking system to provide it leverage to manage money market conditions. The ECB can adjust the structural liquidity position of the banking sector through repurchase agreements, outright operations, or issuing debt securities. This adjusts the medium- or long-term position of banks vis-à-vis the Eurosystem, and could be used as a more flexible option than changing the minimum reserve requirements. As of 2010 this option had not been used.[132]

Main refinancing operations

5.85 This is the most important monetary policy instrument of the Eurosystem, and is used in open market operations to steer interest rates, provide monetary policy signals, and manage overall liquidity. It provides most of the credit from the Eurosystem to the banking system.

5.86 Operations were originally run on a two-week basis, but are now conducted each week and have a one-week maturity. The shorter schedule allows banks to adjust their borrowing more precisely. A standard tender with a pre-announced schedule is used. They are executed within 24 hours from announcement of the auction to communication of the results. Banks anywhere in the union may participate and act through their local NCB.

Longer-term refinancing operations

5.87 Operations with a three-month maturity are also held. These are to provide for longer-term changes in liquidity, and prevent possible volatility by having all the liquidity provided by the Eurosystem turning over every week.

[132] When a new country enters the Eurosystem, it affects the total balance sheet of the Eurosystem and the structural liquidity situation. Entry of a small country will not affect the overall situation, but it could be affected by entry of a large country, such as Poland. Future unions should be aware of the possibility that admission of new members could significantly alter the overall financial situation of the union and require policy adjustments.

Fine-tuning operations

5.88 The Eurosystem needs flexibility to adjust money market rates very quickly in response to unexpected market shifts and to smooth excessive volatility. Fine-tuning operations can be initiated by the system whenever the situation demands, can either provide or absorb liquidity, and might be intended to affect money market interest rates.

5.89 Fine-tuning operations are conducted through "quick tenders" in which an announcement is made to a limited select group of counterparties for conclusion within one hour. Operations can also be made through bilateral arrangements in which the Eurosystem transacts with individual counterparties without announced tenders. This might be done in response to sudden shocks that demand immediate action. Usually, fine-tuning operations will be executed by NCBs, but the ECB also has the authority to execute operations on its own if it chooses.

Standing facilities

5.90 The Eurosystem has two standing facilities that permit individual banks to adjust their positions by their own choice. A lending facility allows banks to borrow overnight funds from the Eurosystem; a deposit facility allows banks to deposit excess funds overnight with the Eurosystem.

> The *marginal lending facility* provides overnight loans to banks against collateral at a predetermined interest rate. The rate is usually set above the money market rate so that banks will borrow only when market funding is unavailable. Banks may borrow as much as they wish from the facility, limited by the amount of collateral they can offer. This unlimited borrowing feature provides a ceiling on the money market overnight rate.
>
> The *deposit facility* allows banks to deposit excess funds in the Eurosystem at a predetermined rate. The rate is below the money market rate and therefore banks make deposits only if other uses are unavailable, which establishes a floor rate for the money market, even though the facility is not heavily used.
>
> The marginal lending facility in conjunction with the deposit facility allows the Eurosystem to set the upper and lower bounds for the money market rate, referred to as the "corridor".

Credit aggregates

5.91 Monetary and credit flows are closely related. Funds flow into monetary institutions as they incur liabilities to the public, which then fund credits to the public which spurs economic activity, which subsequently generates new flows into monetary institutions as businesses and the public demand currency for transactions or to make new deposits. The traditional fractional reserves model of monetary growth describes the effects of this circular flow on the total volume of money in the economy.

5.92 These money and credit flows also can be described in terms of credits of the banking system to businesses and the public, which are the money holding sectors of the economy, to other domestic sectors, and to nonresidents. These are described as the "counterparts to monetary aggregates" that specify the broad flows of credit in the economy, such as lending to corporations and households, but also to government, nonmonetary financial institutions, and the rest of the world. The counterparts' data are part of the regular ECB monetary statistics releases. The ECB states that the analysis of monetary and credit flows has a role in the transmission of monetary policy to price levels, and therefore it monitors both monetary and credit developments closely. (ECB 2001, p. 47)

5.93 The main Euroarea monetary and credit aggregates are presented below. For each of the items, outstanding amounts, transactions, and growth rates are shown.

Euroarea Monetary Aggregates and Counterparts (year end 2008)

Billions of euros

3,982	**M1**	
	4,046	M2 less M1
8,028	**M2**	
	1,379	M3 less M2
9,407	**M3**	
	6,294	Longer-term financial liabilities
	2,562	Credit to general government
	12,986	Credit to other Euroarea residents
	10,785	Loans
	--	*Memo: Loans adjusted for sales and securitization*[133]
	430	Net external assets

5.94 The nature of credit flows is important in understanding the monetary transmission process, since the cost of credit (interest and fees) and its availability affect business and households' decisions and thus affect economic activity.

5.95 The central bank needs to understand the channels by which its policy actions affect the costs, availability, and distribution of credit, and thus the implications of its policy actions.[134]

5.96 Expressing the cycle in terms of credit emphasizes the distribution of credit to different sectors. This is interesting both in terms of broad macroeconomic flows and also flows to specific types of borrowers.

> In a macroeconomic sense, the distribution of credits between major sectors provides important information on the total absorption of funding in the economy, the nature of funding of government, competition for funds between government and private sectors, the funding of investment, or external flows. This information is central to the regular oversight of national economic conditions and policy.
>
> Limitations on credit flows to government are important in establishing noninflationary growth and nonmonetization of government deficits – the original Maastricht rules prohibited the ECB from monetary financing of government deficits[135] and

[133] This is an adjustment to the MFI balance sheet to derecognize loans that have been sold or securitized. This adjustment recognizes that changes in a MFI balance sheet loan position can misstate the actual extension of loan credit because significant amounts of loans might be sold off or securitized each accounting period. Sale or securitization of bank loans is large in some countries and this adjustment is probably needed in some future unions.

[134] Some central banks have responsibility to oversee borrowing conditions, such as accurate posting of borrowing rates, prevention of fraud, prevention of usury, etc..

[135] The Treaty Article 101 states, "Overdraft facilities or any other type of credit facility with the ECB or with the central banks of the member states (national central banks) in favor of Community institutions or bodies, central governments, regional, local or other public authorities, other bodies governed by public law, or public undertakings of Member States shall be prohibited, as shall the purchase from them by the ECB or national central banks of debt instruments."

Under crisis conditions, ECB emergency actions set aside Article 101 restrictions. For example, during the covid crisis, the ECB stated, "The ECB's pandemic emergency purchase programme (PEPP) is a non-standard monetary policy measure initiated in March 2020 to counter the serious risks to the monetary policy transmission mechanism and the outlook for the Euroarea posed by the coronavirus (COVID-19) outbreak. The PEPP is a temporary asset purchase programme of private and public sector securities…. For the purchases of public sector securities under the PEPP, the benchmark allocation across jurisdictions will be the Eurosystem capital key of the national central banks." https://www.ecb.europa.eu/mopo/implement/pepp/html/index.en.html.

public enterprises cannot be granted privileged access to financing by financial institutions.[136]

Some macroeconomic goals might be priorities or prescribed activities in an union, such as promoting funding of the private sector, or providing credit to rural sectors. In recent years, there has been much interest in provision of microcredits to small businesses as a means to break the hold of poverty.[137]

In a microeconomic sense, national policy might promote funding of particular subsectors, industries, or activities. These could include credit for infrastructure development, to low income regions, for high-technology or environmental industries, for microfinance, etc.. For example, in Europe an important goal was lending for infrastructure development to reduce regional disparities; while in the GCC, a goal is diversification of the economies. These are unlikely to be primary goals of a monetary union, but might be part of a broader supplemental range of economic, social, or development goals that the union is expected to support without prejudice to its primary mission.

5.97 From the above, it can be seen that union policy related to credit aggregates and to the promotion or limiting of credit flows is an important supplemental part of the union monetary policy framework. Although of a lesser rank, union officials should compile information on the counterpart credit flows to monetary aggregates and include them as part of the information relevant for understanding the economic picture of the union.

5.98 Also, NCBs might be restricted in lending to governments or public institutions. A statistical framework to monitor restrictions will need to be set up to cover such restricted lending, if any, in all member countries.

D. Inflation targeting

5.99 This framework uses a comprehensive set of information to look at the rate of inflation relative to a published or forecasted inflation target or zone. Recognizing that inflationary conditions often have a certain momentum and are based on market perceptions of future conditions that can be slow to change, inflation targeting advertises a forecast or a goal to achieve a rate that is already low and stable, or which is an improvement over the current rate of inflation. Actual inflation performance is measured against the announced rate.

5.100 Measures of expected inflation and the related premia can be derived from bond markets by subtracting the yield on an inflation-linked bond from the yield on a nominal bond with comparable maturity, assuming both bonds have equal liquidity premia. (ECB 2008a, p.25) This difference can be considered as compensation to investors for their exposures to future inflation. The difference is referred to as the "break-even" rate at which investors are indifferent in holding either nominal or inflation-adjusted bonds. In the context of the Euroarea definition of price stability of inflation not higher than 2 percentage points, the break-even rate for expected inflation also should not exceed 2 percentage points.[138]

---

[136] The Treaty Article 102 states, "Any measure, not based on prudential considerations, establishing privileged access by Community institutions and bodies, central governments, regional, local or other public authorities, other bodies governed by public law, or public undertakings of Member States to financial institutions, shall be prohibited."

[137] The author has had opportunities to speak to statistics compilers from numerous countries that plan on joining the new currency unions in Africa. There is great interest among them in compiling separate information on microfinance.

[138] The ECB closely follows time series for forward break-even inflation rates. Break-even rates ran slightly above the 2 percent goal in 2006 and early 2007, but began to move upward beginning around the time of the market turmoil in the summer of 2007 just prior to the GFC. This was interpreted by the ECB as a genuine increase in inflation expectations. However, part of the

(continued)

5.101 Comparable measures can be derived from inflation-linked swaps, in which payment streams for inflation-adjusted instruments are swapped for payments streams from nominal instruments. In Europe, this measure has corresponded closely with the measure above derived from bond rates.

5.102 Once a inflation forecast or goal has been published, information is gathered on the current state and whether it is compatible with the forecast. The ECB rejected use of simple or automatic responses to deviations from forecasts for several reasons. (ECB 2001, p. 48)

> The inflation forecast does not provide a comprehensive picture of the risks to price stability
>
> Fixed horizons used in forecasting models of inflation and monetary policy are arbitrary and might not reflect feedback from policy actions.
>
> The material from forecast models is hard to integrate with conventional macroeconomic models of inflationary pressures
>
> Uncertainty about the structure of the evolving Euroarea economy made it unwise to rely on a single type of model. Instead, a diversified approach relying on a range of analytical approaches is used.

5.103 Thus, the ECB favors a full information, diversified methodology, in which any information relevant for the interpretation of the current inflation situation is used. Some information is clearly relevant to medium- or long-term inflation, such as information on rapid increases in wage rates, but other information might relate to temporary or reversible effects, such as the impact of an adjustment to tax rates. Under this approach, responses to an inflationary situation could differ depending on the causes of inflationary pressure. As examples, a generalized interest rate response might be ineffective if supply constraints are contributing to the inflationary environment, or cutting fiscal expenditures could provide a better answer in some situations.

5.104 Prior to the GFC, inflation targeting was given high marks for constraining inflation while supporting growth. The credible commitment of central banks to take whatever actions needed to restrain inflation allowed central banks to use their policy interest rate to affect activity and signal intentions. Markets seemingly responded to signals by adjusting their behavior to the interest rate environment. This environment was called the "Great Moderation."

Hybrid macroprudential and inflation targeting regimes

5.105 However, the financial crisis prompted a fundamental rethinking by key central banks and international financial institutions. The view grew that macroprudential tools are needed alongside traditional monetary policy tools to address a range of financial sector stability issues. By early 2010, a change occurred in central banking as macroprudential policy became nearly coequal with monetary policy. A transition evolved from emphasizing inflation targeting as the dominant framework into a new regime in which interest rate policy actions are supplemented by a potentially wide range of macroprudential tools designed to tackle specific financial sector conditions. This describes a multi-policy environment in which macroprudential policy comes to the fore. Monetary policy can no longer be premised on existence of a smoothly operating financial system; rather, monitoring of the financial system and intervention in a variety of ways might be needed to bolster the effectiveness of monetary policy; conversely, monetary policy actions can affect financial stability.

5.106 This shift in the overall framework was simultaneous with many changes in supervisory standards and macroprudential practice, included

---

increase also appeared to have been caused by the financial market turmoil rather than changes in inflation expectations, based on evidence that government bond yields fell faster than nominal yield as investors fled to the more secure and liquid government issues. Such movements and their unwinding will make more difficult the interpretation of these indices as guides to inflation expectations. (ECB 2008a)

applying stress tests on systemically important institutions within the financial sector and analyzing linkages between the condition of the financial system and overall economic and financial activity. The standards and practices are still evolving and much remains to be learned about macroprudential interactions with monetary and credit conditions.

5.107 These are large challenges for future unions. Under any circumstance, much work needs to be done to incorporate macroprudential tools into the union framework, and to develop the linkages with the monetary and credit activity.

E. Monetary policy under pegged exchange rates

5.108 The GCC formally pegged the currencies of its members to the U.S. dollar as a step in its preparations for its future currency union. A common peg supports creation of an union in several ways;

Countries adjust monetary policy in order to maintain the exchange rate peg. Countries can use diverse policies but must achieve the common goal.

By pegging to a common external currency, the configuration of the national currencies is also fixed.

Fixed exchange rates among member countries allows exchange costs between the currencies to fall, resulting in substantial savings for businesses and the public.

Integration of the member countries is supported and time is provided to allow the economies to adjust their cost structures to a common basis.

Interest rates will tend to converge toward the rates of the currency peg country which will often reflect lower sovereign risk than in the union region. Businesses in the union region can borrow at lower costs, which could increase their overall competitiveness.

5.109 Pegging also creates costs – The economies must follow the monetary policy lead of the pegged currency, which will certainly be inappropriate at times for the region as a whole and for individual member countries.

Policy development infrastructure and expertise within the region will be weaker than otherwise.

Ancillary services to support policy development (statistics, economic research skills, dearth of monetary policy instruments, policy communications skills) will also tend be underdeveloped. This infrastructure will need to be built up prior to the start of the union and certainly before the union can introduce any new monetary policy regime.

The nominal peg can disguise changes in the underlying real effective exchange rate (REER) of individual countries because of differences in relative inflation or production costs. Real divergence of the economies can result, but is not captured in the information provided by the nominal peg and thus resolution steps might be delayed.

Cocirculation of the pegged currency is promoted, resulting in shrinkage of the region's central banks and loss of seigniorage. Cocirculation could discourage acceptance of the new union currency and thus could be a serious problem.

5.110 Under a pegged exchange rate regime, monetary policy options are severely constrained. The Central Bank of the UAE (2010) has nicely summarized the situation and described the monetary policy instruments it can follow.

> "The fixed peg of the Dirham to the US dollar … means that local interest rates have to be aligned to those of the dollar across the maturity curve. As a result, the effectiveness of monetary policy instruments at the Central Bank's disposal has been reduced."

5.111 Under these circumstances, the UAE offers a limited range of instruments to adjust liquidity in the banking system and general open market operations are unavailable.

Minimum reserve requirements. (Requirements differ between short and time deposits which can help in adjusting the slope of the yield curve)

Dollar/Dirham swaps for dirham liquidity. (A swap facility was set up at the request of local banks to overcome temporary shortages of dirham liquidity. This could be an indication of an underdeveloped interbank market in dirhams, which of course can impair the effectiveness of monetary policy signals.)

Advances and overdraft facilities for banks. (Advances under seven days are uncollateralized; Advances up to 6 months require collateral.)

Prudential regulation. One option is to change the capital adequacy ratio. Two increases in the ratio in 2009 and 2010 tended to restrict bank lending. Several other ratios or limits on loans are also used – ratio of loans to stable financial resources, limits on personal loans (but credit card loans are exempted), and large exposure limits to individual borrowers and in aggregate.

Central bank issuance of Certificates of Deposit and Repo facilities for CDs. (This has been largely demand driven to provide banks with facilities to invest excess liquidity.) Under a new system begun in 2007, issuance is based on auctions for CDs in Dirhams, U.S. dollars, and euros. Banks can adjust their liquidity situations by repoing their CDs with the central bank, including obtaining dollar term funding. Maturities can extend up to 5 years, which can help adjust the entire yield curve. These facilities also suggest that the interbank market in dirhams is underdeveloped.

Liquidity Support Facility (This is a special facility set up in 2008 in response to the financial crisis.) Banks can submit their securities portfolio to the central bank, which issues guidelines on the types of securities acceptable and sets the value (including haircut) on the eligible securities. Once accepted, the securities can be used on a weekly rollover basis to obtain central bank funds.

5.112 The list above of monetary policy instruments for the UAE shows some of the range of instruments that can be used under the constrained monetary policy environment under a pegged exchange rate. But equally interesting is that *the UAE central bank often appears to be focusing on individual bank adjustments rather than on general market operations*, possibly due to limited interbank operations that allow the market to reflect changes in the overall monetary policy stance. This could be partly due to the focus on the external peg rather than the domestic currency. For future unions, part of the task will be to shift focus to the new union currency to promote its acceptance.

F. Seasonality in money demand

5.113 Total demand for money can change in a regular manner during the course of a year. For example, during tourist season, total money stock might be higher than average because tourists use cash to make purchases, and businesses increase their demand deposits because of increased sales. Conversely, money demand might be lower than average in winter months when business activity is slow. The central bank must actively manage the stock of money to accommodate such changes. Money stock management in unions is usually more complex than in single countries.

5.114 Seasonal money demand implies that there are regular seasonal patterns that can be identified and measured. Knowledge of these patterns supports policy making by allowing authorities to distinguish between short-term seasonal movements and the underlying pattern growth in the money stock. Seasonal information is also needed to handle cash demand because authorities can adjust the supply of currency in advance to meet expected demand. Similarly, currency can be shifted between regions each season to absorb cash from some regions with less business activity and provide it to regions with more activity. Such cash management can be down to the detailed level of demand for each denomination of currency, by region (or by country in unions). For such reasons, estimating seasonality is a major activity of central banks.[139]

G. Islamic monetary policy instruments

5.115 Finally, in some regions Islamic banks exist that make use of a range of 'Shariah-compliant' financial instruments. Islamic financial instruments have some special characteristics – of which the most famous is avoiding use of interest rates – that raise a number of issues in measurement, monetary policy, and financial supervision. Substantial work on the implications of Islamic finance is underway at the time of this writing, but the topic is left aside at this point because it was not a part of EMU history.[140]

5.116 Regardless, future unions in which there is significant penetration of Islamic finance need to consider its implications.[141] In the near term, use of Islamic instruments in monetary policy is difficult because of lack of development of Islamic money market instruments and near absence of standardized Islamic government or central bank-issued bonds for use in open market operations or as collateral. Work in these fields is on-going,[142] but more work and institutional development is needed to provide a basis for use of Islamic instruments as a primary tool for monetary policy. Unless there is a national commitment to heavily or exclusively use Islamic financial instruments, given the present state of development of Islamic financial instruments future unions (other than the GCC) probably should first concentrate of setting up a monetary policy framework based on conventional financial instruments.

---

[139] A discussion of seasonal adjustment methods for the EMU and new unions is in *Chapter 12 – Statistics.*

[140] Also, the topic is complex and involves a steep learning curve. The author recommends that those interested in learning more about the macroeconomics of Islamic finance consult first with the Islamic Financial Standards Board's *Compilation Guide on Prudential and Structural Indicators for Islamic Financial Institutions (PSIFIs)* (IFSB 2019). Also, the joint UN/IMF project on treatment of Islamic finance in the SNA (see last footnote of this chapter) will produce a compilation guide that will have abundant material on Islamic finance and its role within financial systems.

[141] The future GCC monetary union is the one future union in which explicit consideration must be given to the role of Islamic finance in monetary policy. Krueger (2019) describes how Islamic financial institutions in the GCC might be incompletely integrated into the regional financial system which possibly can give rise to financial instability. Also, incomplete integration will have monetary policy implications.

[142] The United Nations and the IMF have a joint task force examining how to treat Islamic finance in the SNA and balance of payments. Because Islamic financial instruments do not provide interest returns, it is challenging to fit them into the SNA framework in which interest is a key financial concept. This work will result in greater standardization of definitions and treatments of Islamic finance.

At the time of writing, it seems as if the basic approach will be to define Islamic financial instruments into their closest conventional equivalents. In addition, given a number of unique features in Islamic finance a separate satellite account for Islamic finance will probably be recommended. Final recommendations, probably including at template for an Islamic finance satellite account, should be ready around 2025.

Islamic finance is found in many countries, and countries using conventional finance also can be affected such as by firms raising funds using sukuk (Islamic bonds). Close monitoring of the Islamic finance subsector is needed in Africa, the Middle East, Central Asia, and Southeast Asia, and at least modest awareness of Islamic financial markets practices is needed in many countries.

Timeline

This schedule is for a small union. Large unions should move all steps at least one year earlier.

Preparatory period	Precursor group sets union policy goals.
Early actions (four years prior)	Survey of monetary and interest rate policies and policy instruments of future members. Establish policy oversight body over members.
Three years prior	Begin research on monetary policy options
24 months prior	Continuing research on policy options Begin discussions with international monetary institutions
18 Months Prior	Documentation and testing of policy instruments Agreement on monetary policy frameworks
Final 12 months	Newly formed union central bank takes direction of monetary policy development
Final 6 months	Union central bank policy operations begin. Monetary and interest rate targets decided Tests of policy instruments Full analysis of macroeconomic and external conditions
Run-up to union	Live tests of monetary and interest rate policy instruments Union central bank decides on initial stance at start of union
Union day	Single monetary policy initiated
Early union period	All union policies are operational. Analysis of lapses or problems Analysis of policies within the union context.
Union steady state	All policies are actively managed

Annex: ECB 2021 Monetary Policy Strategy Statement

In July 2021, the ECB released a statement describing its first monetary strategy review since 2003. (ECB 2021a) It argued that changed economic circumstances have reduced the effectiveness of the interest rate policy tool and ECB policy concerns have become more complex in line with recent priorities in EU policy.

> "Declining trend growth, which can be linked to slower productivity growth and demographic factors, and the legacy of the global financial crisis have driven down equilibrium real interest rates. This has reduced the scope for the ECB and other central banks to achieve their objectives by exclusively relying on changes in policy interest rates. In addition, globalisation, digitalisation, the threat to environmental sustainability and changes in the financial system pose challenges for the conduct of monetary policy."

The statement notes that the Eurosystem will continue to act to maintain price stability and also support EU general economic policies. It reiterated adherence to the HICP as the principal measure of price support but supported gradual inclusion of price measures for owner-occupied housing in the HICP. An annual price increase trend of 2 percent was endorsed to allow flexibility to use lower interest rates as a policy tool and provide a margin against general deflation. Deviations either above or below the 2 percent target were viewed as equally undesirable. It noted that declining equilibrium real interest rates tend to create a lower bound on use of nominal interest rates and thus constrain policy options. When the economy is near the lower bound aggressive steps are needed to move toward the 2 percent target and avoid entrenching deflation.

Use of innovative monetary policy measures is endorsed.

> "In recognition of the effective lower bound on policy rates, the Governing Council will also employ in particular forward guidance, asset purchases and longer-term refinancing operations, as appropriate. The Governing Council will continue to respond flexibly to new challenges as they arise and consider, as needed, new policy instruments in the pursuit of its price stability objective."

The statement continues use of the two analytic perspectives to evaluate policy decisions – economic analysis and monetary and financial analysis.

> "The pervasive role of macro-financial linkages in economic, monetary and financial developments requires that the interdependencies across the two analyses are fully incorporated. This framework reflects the changes that the ECB's economic analysis and monetary analysis have undergone since 2003, the importance of monitoring the transmission mechanism in calibrating monetary policy instruments, and the recognition that financial stability is a precondition for price stability."

It might *de facto* be relevant that the economic analysis leg is mentioned first and the reference to sustaining financial stability is clear.

Climate change is described as having profound implications on price stability. The Eurosystem will employ "an ambitious climate-related action plan" that takes full account of EU climate policy and the strategy of carbon transition, and the monetary policy framework will be adapted to reflect supportive climate disclosures, risk assessments, asset purchases, and collateral rules. Thus, the framework seems to highlight specific interactions with the financial sector that can promote better climate options.

Public communications will be revised to reflect the new policies with outreach to ensure wide public understanding of policy actions and goals. Finally, a five-year schedule for policy reviews was established.

1111111

Chapter 6 – Exchange Rate and International Reserves Policy

What are the exchange rate and international reserves policies of the Euroarea? How are these policies changed in countries joining an union.

6.1. A monetary union creates a single currency that replaces the national currencies of its members. A single monetary policy, single interest rate policy, and single exchange rate policy prevails throughout the union. Chapter 5 covered the monetary policy framework. This chapter provides a history of the EMU exchange rate regime and frameworks for the exchange rate regime and international reserves.

A. Exchange regimes before the euro

6.2. European exchange rates in the years prior to the launch of the EMU were rocky and characterized by frequent failures. The turbulence in exchange rates provided a continuing incentive for European countries to develop a stable and reliable exchange rate system.

Bretton Woods

6.3. The Bretton Woods system was created after World War II to fix the exchange rates between currencies. Each of the European currencies was pegged to the value of gold, and countries were obligated to intervene to purchase or sell gold in order to maintain the value of their currency. Through many of the early post-war years, currency convertibility and cross-border capital movements were restricted and much of the period can be characterized as one in which controls were gradually lifted.

6.4. The system collapsed in August 1971 when the U.S. dollar came under pressure in exchange markets, and the United States suspended convertibility of the dollar into gold and depreciated the dollar. With the breakdown of the system, currencies lost a specific nominal value against other currencies and could "float", or fluctuate in value against other currencies. Following the end of Bretton Woods, countries lacked fixed exchange rates to denominate transactions between countries or for community-wide purposes. A common measure was needed to set the EEC budget, make settlements between countries, administer the Common Agricultural Policy, and measure of future values for investments and their costs and returns over time. (European Communities 1984).[143]

The "Snake" and European Unit of Account (EUA)

6.5. Based on the Werner Plan of 1970, in 1973 the nine member countries of the European Economic Community created the "Snake", which was an exchange rate system in which the nine currencies could fluctuate against each other only within a ± 2.25% band. Each currency could move within the band in response to market conditions, but the total movement was limited. This promised a high degree of stability between the EU currencies that would be conducive to trade development, travel within the region, and long-term cross-border investment within the union. However, as a group, the currencies could move against external currencies, such as the U.S. dollar. A time series chart of the values of the currencies against an outside currency could show large fluctuations for the group, but movements of the individual currencies were in a tight band around the group trend. Visually, this was said to look like a snake.

6.6. In order to bring about greater harmonization of the currency values in the system, in 1975 the EUA was created to serve as a standardized accounting value for multicountry EU projects. The central rate of the Snake was chosen as the EUA to provide the common measure of value. Official transactions could be denominated in the value of the Snake, but since there was no actual currency settlements were made in domestic currencies.

[143] A common unit of value (such as the virtual EUA unit of value) is a natural need for pre-union regional groupings, or for cooperative regional arrangements. In Europe, an internal basket of the participating currencies was used that could float against external currencies; in other regions considering constructing a common measure of value, an external value such as the dollar, euro, or SDR could be used.

European Monetary System (EMS) and Exchange Rate Mechanism (ERM and ERM II)

ERM

6.7. In 1979, the European Monetary System was created to replace the Snake to promote monetary and exchange rate stability and enhance economic cooperation. The EMS was built around the ERM, which was based on the ECU that had evolved from the EUA. For each EU currency, the central parity against the ECU was fixed, which established a "parity grid" between all currencies in the system. The fluctuation bands remained unchanged from the Snake at ± 2.25%, except for Italy's 6 percent band.[144]

6.8. The ERM's early history was erratic, but by the mid-1980's greater success was achieved by policy convergence of a number of the members to promote economic stability and *de facto* alignment of currencies against the German mark as the anchor currency. A period of no realignments lasted from 1987 through 1992, but continuing inflation differentials between countries and the opening of capital mobility with the agreement of Stage 1 of monetary union created strong exchange rate pressures and led to speculative attacks. In short order in 1992 and 1993, Italy and the United Kingdom left the ERM, and the Spanish peseta, Portuguese escudo, and Irish pound were devalued. Under these pressures, the ERM widened its fluctuation bands to ± 15%. The much wider band was designed to deny speculators "one-way bets", because such a large margin could allow currencies to readily move in both directions. In practice, the wide bands hardly defined stable relationships between the currencies. The ERM was effectively a very weak instrument at the time that work began to create the Euroarea in which fluctuations between member currencies would disappear forever.

[144] In 1990, Italy's band was narrowed to ± 2.25 percent to match the other countries.

ERM II

6.9. The ignominious end game of the ERM was superseded by the process of developing the EMU. The ECU continued to serve to set the central rate, and Maastricht was built around evolution of ERM into the EMU and the ECU into the euro.

6.10. A transitional regime to enter the Euroarea was needed for countries that did not initially join or that joined the EU after the start of the monetary union. A new system called Exchange Rate Mechanism II (ERM II) was created based on the ERM and placed the euro at its center.[145] The system was designed to;

Prevent exchange rate fluctuations between the euro and other EU currencies from disrupting economic conditions in the Euroarea.

Help non-Euroarea countries prepare to join the union. The ERM II is similar to the EMU system in that by committing to the euro as the central rate (even with a wide fluctuation band) the countries must use macroeconomic, fiscal, and structural policies to stay within the band. Operating within ERM II successfully for two full years was considered confirmation the country could handle EMU policy successfully after it joins the Euroarea.

Help reduce exchange rate pressures on the currencies because the markets would recognize the firm commitment of the country to respect and maintain the central rate, and because of the possibility of coordinated intervention involving the Eurosystem.

Test whether the central rate is appropriate to fix the irrevocable rate of the currency to the euro.

6.11. Discussions began in 1995 in recognition that not all EU countries would join the union

[145] Multiple countries passed through ERM II, but by 2021 only Denmark remained in. However, the framework might be reactivated in the future if more countries seek to enter the Euroarea.

immediately. In addition to addressing future exchange rate issues, a number of other adjustments to the union plans were made about this time to deal with the forthcoming reality of a two-stage system.

6.12. Maastricht did not provide for a second exchange rate regime. There was a debate at the time whether the new regime should be under control of the Economic Community, reflecting decisions under Maastricht that the ESCB had competence to deal with monetary and exchange rate matters. However, most countries preferred continuing the arrangements under the original ERM in which national governments and central banks retained their competences. There was also preference that decisions to join ERM II would be voluntary. (Jensen 2005)

6.13. ERM II established fixed central rates of each such currency against the euro with a fluctuation band of ± 15%. The band can be narrowed in practice if countries begin to converge with conditions in the Euroarea in order to create a more stable exchange rate relationship[146], although this does not affect the official ± 15% band. Moreover, EU countries are required to treat their exchange rate policies as a matter of common interest, and thus the ECB General Council monitors the operation of the system and promotes the coordination of monetary and exchange-rate policies.[147] In principle, decisions on the central rates and bands can be made through mutual agreement by the ECB, Euroarea finance ministers, and finance ministers of the nonEuroarea countries. There are even procedures for confidential consultations amongst the EU states on changes to the ERM II central rates.[148]

6.14. If the exchange rate of an ERM II country approaches the boundary of the band, the country should intervene automatically and to whatever extent necessary. Intervention before reaching the outer bounds is also permitted. Interventions are coordinated between the ECB and the central bank of the ERM II country. A "Very Short-term Financing Mechanism" (VSFM) was put in place to help provide financing to countries to acquire euros from the Eurosystem if intervention is necessary. However, any financing obligations incurred by the ECB should not affect the primary goal of maintaining price stability – the ECB and the affected country should suspend automatic intervention if there is a conflict with price stability. (Scheller 2006, p. 93) Thus far, interventions under ERM II have not been common.

The euro basket

6.15. Choosing the currencies in a basket and their weights is not simple. The Euroarea largely avoided this task by basing the euro on the preexisting ECU which already had established its independent value against external currencies. The euro itself was allowed to float in markets, with an option to intervene but only under exceptional circumstances. Because the euro would be one of the most heavily used currencies in the world it began its life with substantial economic strength and was in a position to establish its own value in exchange markets. As such, it reflected the view that Europe as a whole was the relevant area for a currency, rather than weighting of values against external currencies.

6.16. The situation will differ for other unions. Will their new currencies be strong enough and liquid enough to be able to sustain an independent float? Or should the value of the new currencies be at least initially defined in terms of external currencies, based

[146] For example, before they adopted the euro, Malta eliminated any fluctuation band and Latvia permitted only ± 1% fluctuation. Denmark (the last remaining ERM II member) has decided to not join the Euroarea, agreed with the ECB to maintain a ± 2.25% band and in practice has remained close to the central rate in order to benefit from the Euroarea policy to restrain inflation under 2 percent which it considered advantageous to the Danish economy.

[147] The agreement creating ERM II states, "each Member State has an obligation to treat its exchange-rate policy as a matter of common interest. The surveillance of Member States' macroeconomic policies in the Council under Article 103 of the EC Treaty will be organized, inter alia, with a view to avoiding such misalignments or fluctuations. (European Council 1997)

[148] Only a few changes of rates within ERM II occurred. Greece revalued its currency once, and Slovakia revalued two separate times.

on current trade patterns or other factors? If an external weighting is chosen, what weights should be used, given that each member country will have different patterns and preferences? If membership in the union changes, should the selection of currencies and weights change?

B. Euro exchange rate policy

6.17. Under the Maastricht Treaty, the ESCB holds and manages the official reserves of the Member States and conducts foreign exchange operations. However, this power is jointly shared with the EU's Economic and Financial Committee (ECOFIN). The ECOFIN Council may "conclude formal agreements on an exchange rate system for the ECU vis-à-vis non-Community currencies" … or may "formulate general orientations for exchange rate policy."

6.18. Maastricht Article 111 provides a framework for setting exchange rate policy, although it has not been used. It states that the EU Council through unanimous action can conclude formal agreements on the exchange rate system defining the relationship of the euro against non-euro currencies.[149] It may also define the general orientation of the euro exchange rate policy, acting through a qualified majority.[150] However, in both cases, the objective of price stability must be supported and frameworks enacted only after consultation with the ECB. The EU Council is mandated to consider the ECB's opinions and to seek a consensus on exchange rate policy consistent with price stability.[151]

6.19. The EU Council decided just before the start of the union that under normal circumstances the exchange rate itself would not be a policy objective, but should be the outcome of economic conditions and policies. In effect, the euro exchange rate would reflect the outcome of market forces and fluctuate accordingly. The Council further decided that setting the general orientation of the exchange rate would be done only in exceptional cases, but still needed to respect ECB independence and the objective of price stability.

6.20. Because the euro's exchange value would ordinarily be market-based, intervention was expected to be rare, but possible. If intervention occurs, the foreign currency reserves of the ECB and the NCBs could be used, which required setting up a mechanism for controlling operations.

Text Box: Intervention to support the euro in 2000

Shortly after the start-up of the EMU, a sharp decline in the euro exchange rate led to intervention in late 2000 to support the euro. Following creation of the euro at the beginning of 1999 at a price of $1.17 per €, the euro fell by up to 30 percent in 2000. Among possible causes of the decline were recorded strong capital outflows, which was the opposite of what many had expected during the euro's initial years.

This decline threatened public confidence in the new currency and acted to raise import prices and push inflation rates in the union above the 2 percent target. Political pressures built to take action to raise the exchange value of the euro.

On September 22, 2000, the G-7 central banks jointly intervened to successfully boost the euro to about 90

[149] Hypothetically, this provision might come into play if a successor international currency arrangement to the current system was set up – for example, a "Bretton Woods III" Agreement. The EU Council would negotiate in that case to determine the role of the euro in the new system.

[150] The qualified majority procedure requires significantly stronger than majority support when deciding major issues.

[151] There is potential for conflict between ECOFIN goals and ESCB monetary or exchange rate goals. As a safeguard, in establishing formal agreements or setting the orientation of euro policy, the ECOFIN Council must consult with the ECB to seek "a consensus consistent with the objectives of price stability; and the general orientation for exchange rate policy "shall be without prejudice to the primary objective of the ESCB to maintain price stability." (Committee of Governors 1992, p. 53) Note that this constraint was set long before the exchange rate arrangements for the euro were established.

U.S. cents per euro. However, the effect was temporary and the euro fell steadily to its all-time low of 82.3 cents on October 26. That prompted a surprise intervention by the ECB totaling around $1 billion. In contrast to the first intervention, the United States, Japan, Britain, and Japan did not participate. Press commentary at the time argued that the United States in particular was hesitant to take actions that would reduce the exchange value of the dollar because the strong dollar attracted capital flows that helped finance the U.S. current account deficit and support domestic economic expansion. However, against this view were concerns that a weak euro might be unsettling for the world economy.

Oversight of the regime

6.21. This section briefly describes the framework for oversight of EMU exchange rates. It was recognized from the beginning that the euro would be a major currency and that the euro to U.S. dollar rate would be the most important relationship in international markets. The primacy of the U.S. dollar in trade, financial markets, and as the main international reserve currency was recognized, but it was recognized that the euro would be important in all these areas, initially and increasingly over time. Therefore, it was important to consider the euro's role within the governance structure of the international financial system, and its roles as an economic policy tool to avoid misalignment, support domestic growth and price stability, and help sustain the stability of the international system. (European Parliament 1999)

6.22. It was further recognized that misalignment of the euro, either too high or low, could damage price stability or economic growth and that volatility could be costly. Moreover, the policy framework embraced the view that targeting a specific exchange rate would require monetary policy adjustments that could compromise the main target of price stability. Thus, the choice of a flexible regime was seen as consistent with the ECB's mandate in terms of the domestic objective of price stability. Therefore, EMU authorities announced that market forces would be allowed to move the rate, and that actions to intervene to affect the rate would be rarely made. (Bini Smaghi 2007)

6.23. Bini Smaghi lists several key aspects in the oversight of the euro exchange rate regime.

Step 1: Monitoring and assessing exchange rate markets and developments, in particular with respect to the underlying fundamentals;

Step 2: Discussing market developments with the other major partners and assessing the configuration of different exchange rate developments and policies;

Step 3: Making public statements on the situation of the foreign exchange markets and on exchange rate policies;

Step 4: Intervening in the foreign exchange markets, either verbally or through market actions.

Step 1- Monitoring and assessing exchange rate markets and developments

The first step of constructing an accurate picture of the situation of the union currency is critical but not straight-forward. It can be difficult to determine if an exchange rate is in line with fundamental equilibrium for the economy or that other exchange rates would be better than the current situation. This should be a matter for continuing research by union and member-country authorities. It is also part of the regular IMF surveillance that looks at changes the real exchange rate of countries, including undertaking econometric investigations or sustainability analyses.

In the EMU, exchange rate developments are continually monitored and discussed at the technical level at the ECB and with the country membership. The ECB holds regular consultations with the Eurogroup, comprised of senior representatives from the finance ministries, on developments and to provide inputs into policy discussions. Amazingly, Bini Smaghi reported that as of 2007 the ECB and Eurogroup had never had technical-level disagreements on developments or the policy situation, and that they often agreed on statements that could be used in discussion with international organizations or the public.

The technical analysis takes a broad view of conditions rather than focus on a single relationship, such as with the U.S. dollar. and includes other major currencies such as the pound, yen, yuan, and Swiss franc. Asian currencies have about as much weight as the U.S. dollar. (Future unions that peg their currencies to a single currency will similarly have to analyze both conditions affecting the nominal peg and conditions affecting the broader effective rate index – equilibrium conditions vis-à-vis one measure might not carry over to the other measures).

Step 2 – Discussions on developments and policy with external counterparts.

Regular consultations are held with the G7 to convey views about exchange markets and policies. The heads of the ECB and the Eurogroup participate, and at the deputy level discussions are held with the U.S. and Japan. Discussions are also held with the IMF through official Article IV surveillance, in which consultations on the exchange rate are held only with the ECB and for which members of the IMF Executive Board from Euroarea countries are bound to the common position.[152] The IMF Mission reports its conclusions directly to the Eurogroup.

Step 3 – Public statements on foreign exchange market developments and policies.

Officials regularly comment on exchange rates in G7 discussion. Both the Eurogroup and the ECB contribute to preparation of the communiqué and views are usually consistent. It is widely recognized the ECB and Eurogroup speak authoritatively for the Euroarea, but sometimes confidentiality about discussions on market conditions and policy options has been broken in public statements by country ministers or heads of state, which can lead to adverse market reactions or reduced policy effectiveness.

Step 4 – Intervention in foreign exchange markets, either verbally or through market actions.

6.24. The power to intervene in exchange markets rests with the ECB, which can assess if and how to intervene given market conditions and the monetary policy stance. The task of moving an exchange rate in a specific direction was seen as technically difficult because strong market forces might be moving in the opposite direction, and it could be hard to move markets and change perceptions to support the desired rate. The authorities must have access to appropriate instruments to intervene and enough resources to effectively intervene. The Eurosystem was set up with what was felt to be enough resources for foreign exchange interventions, backed up with the power to call up additional resources from national central banks.

6.25. Effectiveness of action is increased if coordinated actions are taken, both within the union so that policies of all member countries convey the same message, and internationally so that actions on both sides of the exchange rate support each other. One factor that can strongly increase the odds of successful intervention is that domestic authorities and other countries coordinate their messages and convey a common message that their combined resources will be available to counter adverse movements.

6.26. Also, steps must be taken to establish and retain credibility in exchange actions. If an action is begun, (market interventions, monetary policy actions, fiscal adjustments, jaw-boning, other actions) failure can cause a loss of credibility, which can impair the success of the operation and effectiveness of future intervention. Thus, actions should not be undertaken unless authorities conclude that actions are likely to be successful. The internal consultations and decision making will thus need to be secret until decisions to act are made. Prior to intervening on foreign exchange markets, either verbally or directly, authorities must thus be convinced that they have a high

[152] However, the Euroarea Executive Directors at the IMF are not bound to a common position in their comments on other countries' exchange rate conditions and policies. Also, the Euroarea countries can have bilateral conversations with other countries independently of the ECB views.

probability of success. This will require that adequate resources are in place to take the actions, through use of own resources, through resources gained through loans, swaps or lending from the IMF, or through co-operative intervention with other countries.

6.27. Other than the intervention in 2000 described above, the EMU has not intervened in markets. However, despite the formal ECB commitment to permit market forces to operate, political pressures were sometimes strong to encourage the ECB to move rates, especially during the period of the very high euro exchange rate in 2008. The ECB was certainly aware of such pressures and of course analyzed the full range of views regarding the exchange rate, but the ECB was always careful to assert its policy independence and avoid leaving any impression that its policy actions were taken in response to political pressures.

C. Management of Euroarea reserves

6.28. International reserve assets are monetary gold, SDRs, and foreign currency-denominated assets that are readily available for use in intervention or other balance of payments purposes. Assets that are not readily available, such as direct equity investments, are excluded. Assets denominated in non-convertible currencies are also excluded.

6.29. When the Euroarea was created, holdings of assets issued by other Euroarea countries could no longer be used for international reserve assets. For example, Italian holdings of mark-denominated German government bonds were reserves until the end of 1998, but with the conversion of these assets into euros ceased to be reserve assets because they could no longer be used for intervention or balance of payments purposes between Italy and Germany. That is, the total international reserves of the countries joining the Euroarea suddenly became smaller when the union was started.[153]

ECB reserve assets

6.30. The ECB received an initial transfer of international reserve assets from the member countries. The transfer was 15 percent in gold with the balance in U.S. dollar- and yen-denominated assets, of which 90 percent was in dollars. The Statute of the ESCB called for the EU countries to transfer €50 billion, but because several EU countries did not adopt the euro at the start, only €39.5 billion was transferred. Each country contributed an amount based on its share in the capital of the ECB. When new countries join the Euroarea, they pay up their foreign currency shares to the ECB.[154] The payments create a remunerated euro-denominated claim of the NCBs on the ECB.

6.31. Once transferred to the ECB, they are part of the ECB balance sheet. Changes in reserve holdings will reflect transactions in reserves and valuation changes. For example, despite the intention to allow that value of the euro to fluctuate in markets without intervention, a sharp drop in the value of the euro led to market intervention in late 2000 in which some of the ECB's foreign reserve assets were sold in order to purchase euros.

6.32. In 2005 and 2006, the ECB sold some gold, per a "Central Bank Gold Agreement" between the EU countries that arranged for limited orderly sale of gold. Otherwise, the ECB passively manages its gold holdings. Higher market prices for gold have resulted in a net increase in the value of gold holdings in the ECB balance sheet.

---

[153] See *Chapter 12 – Statistics* for information on the reporting of international reserves under the IMF's *Foreign Reserves and International Liquidity Template*.

[154] When new countries join the EU, such as when ten new members were accepted in 2004, the prescribed transfer of reserves is proportionally increased from the initial €50 billion. The 2004 membership increase resulted in an increase in reserves transferrable to the ECB to €55.6 billion. In this mechanism, the percentage share of existing members in the total transferred reserves decreases because of the new members, but the euro amount of the transfers is unchanged and there is no need to transfer reserve assets back to the NCBs.

6.33. The ECB also has transactions in SDRs, for example when developing countries wish to purchase euros with SDRs.

6.34. The ECB is allowed to make further calls for reserve assets, but must seek legislation by the EU to do so. For example, the EU Council agreed in 2000 that the ECB could replenish depleted reserve assets by an additional call of up to €50 billion, but could not increase its total reserve holdings.

6.35. The management of the ECB's reserve assets must ensure that the funds are secure and liquid to allow their rapid use in time of need. Investment returns on the assets should be maximized but without prejudice to the security and liquidity requirements. The ECB sets specific guidelines regarding currency composition, interest rate return, market and credit risks, and liquidity. Management of reserves must continually rebalance accounts to reflect changes in valuations, transactions, projected transactions needs, and shifts in risks and returns. Strategic benchmarks are set in each relevant area, such as percentage of assets with overnight maturity, with preset fluctuation bands to reflect the need for day-to-day flexibility.

6.36. The risk management and accounting functions for reserve assets are carried out by the ECB.

6.37. Other portfolio operations, including transactions, are done on a decentralized basis by the NCBs under the direction of the ECB. Initially, all NCBs performed these functions, but beginning in 2006 countries could opt out of these duties. This reflected the possibility of increased efficiency and cost savings by having some NCBs carry out reserves operations for other countries. For example, some new EMU member countries have ceded their reserves operations to larger countries on a fee basis.

6.38. NCBs' portfolio management transactions using the ECB's assets are disclosed to prevent routine transactions from being confused with shifts in monetary policy. A portfolio management system uses a secure ESCB communications network to monitor portfolio operations.

6.39. Counterparties for the foreign currency transactions of the ECB are chosen carefully, based on recommendations by NCBs. Creditworthiness must be high, and the counterparties must be able to handle large transactions quickly under diverse conditions at low cost.

6.40. Standard market documentation is used for transactions except for a proprietary master netting agreement that the ECB developed that is used with all counterparties.

NCB reserves and foreign currency assets

6.41. Foreign currency reserves not transferred to the ECB are held by and managed by the NCBs. Intervention is normally undertaken using the ECB's funds, and thus there is less need for individual countries to undertake transactions in reserve assets and given the low returns on such assets the amount of foreign reserves held by NCBs has declined steadily.

6.42. Although NCBs control their own funds, they potentially could act in contradiction with EMU monetary or external policies. Therefore, they must seek prior approval of the ECB to carry out their own operations that could affect exchange rates, domestic monetary conditions, or which exceed limits provided by the ECB.[155] However, NCBs' investments in foreign financial markets do not need prior approval because they are not considered to affect the EMU monetary or exchange rate policy. Also, transactions of countries with international organizations such as the

[155] The EU has also adopted a guideline that the *foreign currency working balances of EU countries, including those outside the Euroarea, are subject to ECB control.* This results in a legally unusual situation in which because of the overarching legal power of the EU countries not part of a currency union are held to the same rules as the member countries. Several NCBs filed suit to increase their control of foreign currency assets they own, but the suit was rejected. The question of who exercises effective control over foreign currency assets could be an area of contention in future unions.

BIS or IMF are exempt from the requirement for ECB approval prior to the transactions.

6.43. Given the more limited role of monetary gold[156] within the Euroarea and lack of interest income on holdings, in 2004 the EMU countries, the ECB, and several other countries (Sweden and Switzerland) agreed on a policy for gold holdings. It stated that gold would remain part of monetary reserves, gold sales should be made through a concerted program over a five-year period, up to 2,500 tons could be sold, and at the end of the period the countries will not have more gold than at the time of the agreement – that is, holdings could be reduced and not increased. Reductions in holdings should be gradual and made in ways that do not disrupt markets.

6.44. This agreement reflects the view that gold has a limited, although not negligible, role in the international reserves and payments system. The situation in other regions could be quite different. Production of gold can be an important part of the income of some countries, and holdings of gold have an important role as collateral to obtain foreign currency usable for balance of payments purposes. Also, strong price increases in gold prices after 2004 (the year of the Euroarea gold agreement) might enhance the importance of gold in the reserves policies of some regions.

6.45. An important exchange policy issue is the level of reserves for the entire union. In the EMU the view was expressed that as a result of creation of the single currency countries could sell off portions of their foreign assets because they were less needed for national intervention or settlement purposes. Badinger and Dutzler (2004) estimated that up to half of total Euroarea reserves could be sold off.[157]

6.46. Future unions will need to set policies on the proper level of reserves, trading off the need for an adequate level of reserves to support the exchange rate, deal with contingencies, and provide a sense to the public of the strength of the union, against the costs of tying up assets in liquid but low-earning portfolios. Some unions might be able to sell off some of their reserves, but others (especially in poorer regions) might want to accumulate reserves during the early period of the union to help build confidence in the union.

6.47. Unions in which SWFs exist present special issues regarding setting the proper level of reserves. Usually, only some countries in an union will have enough foreign-currency reserves assets to be able to divert assets into SWF's, which can provide opportunities to undertake higher return investments instead of high liquidity, low return assets that typically comprise reserves. The countries with SWFs are likely to want to retain control of the assets and their investment strategies, which could conflict with union policies. There are no SWFs among the EMU countries and the EMU rules on management of foreign currency assets effectively prevent countries from forming them, so there is no guidance to be gained from Europe. New unions will need rules for SWFs, what are rights of countries to the assets and income generated, and circumstances under which the union may exercise control.

D. Exchange rate regimes

6.48. In the same way that currency unions can have only a single monetary policy, a single exchange rate policy will prevail for the full union and its member countries. Different exchange rate regimes exist, which will be linked to the monetary policy regime. In broad terms, exchange rates can be pegged to some

[156] *Monetary gold* consists of gold and gold deposits controlled by the central bank and other monetary authorities. *Nonmonetary gold* is all other gold and is treated as a commodity, and hence not subject to the same rules. Gold purchased by a central bank is reclassified from being a nonmonetary commodity into "monetary gold", that is it is "monetized". The reverse process, called "demonetization" occurs when official gold is sold to nonofficial buyers.

[157] Badinger and Dutzler also argued that freeing up official reserves could allow assets held by countries to earn higher returns and permit countries to capture holding gains, which is permitted under Maastricht.

external currency or basket, or float based on market forces or policy actions and interventions. In practice there are many intermediate options. Outside the EMU, the three other existing currency unions have chosen to peg to individual external currencies.

Flexible exchange rate regimes

6.49. In a floating regime, the exchange rate of the union currency against external currencies moves based on market forces, or varies as a result of policy actions. The Euroarea adopted a flexible exchange rate regime in which the euro is allowed to move based on market forces and thus is not an instrument of monetary policy. Pegging the exchange rate to a particular target was seen as incompatible with meeting the internal requirement to maintain price stability. "Price stability is an objective for both monetary and exchange rate policies, by implication there is no exchange rate target. When conducting its monetary policy, the ECB takes into account the exchange rate to the extent that it affects the economic situation and outlook for price stability." (ECB 2008d, p. 25)

6.50. Thus, the ECB allows the euro rate to move based on market forces, which of course reflects the influence of its monetary policy actions. This float was not absolute – the ECB intervened in 2000 when the euro fell to exceptionally low levels. But the general policy was established and has been maintained, in some cases despite considerable political pressure. However, flexible exchange rate regimes can be used as policy tools. Actions to raise or lower exchange rates (intervention, interest rate shifts, capital flows restrictions, shifts in national absorption, etc.) are possible to try to move the exchange rate to desired levels. There are many reasons why countries might wish to move the exchange rate, such as to dampen inflationary pressures, support export growth, etc.. Exchange rate changes could be made in order to try to meet domestic monetary policy targets, such as raising rates under an inflation targeting regime in order to lower inflationary pressures. If this type of regime is followed, there will be ramifications for monetary policies, such as changing interest rates, sterilizing foreign currency inflows, etc. The Euroarea has chosen not to go in this direction, in part because of concerns about the ability to move exchange rates against market forces, but more interventionist exchange rate regimes are possible and future unions might choose to adopt them.

Exchange rate targeting

6.51. Exchange rate targeting involves linking the exchange rate of a national or union currency to another currency or to a basket of currencies.

Single-currency link

6.52. Linking a currency to a single external currency is often appropriate for smaller, open economies that are closely linked by trade, tourism, or remittances with another country. Trade and financial flows between the countries can be normalized, and premia for converting between the currencies can fall to very low levels. Prices comparisons between the economies are easy, and a linked economy can often reflect stable inflation performance of the other economy.

6.53. However, policy independence in many areas might be sacrificed in order to maintain the peg. In order to maintain the peg, the linking economy will have to make adjustments to growth, interest rates, or fiscal policy to maintain the supply and demand relationship between the national and the foreign currency so that the equilibrium value remains at the value of the peg. Excess demand for the foreign currency or supply of the foreign currency can be met by respectively using international reserves to purchase the domestic currency, or by selling the domestic currency to purchase foreign currency.

6.54. For an union, a single-currency link can be used the same as if the union were a single country. The ECCU and the two African currency unions have single-currency links, to the U.S. dollar and the euro, respectively.

6.55. For a regional arrangement, fixing each of the currencies to a common external currency sets the external rate and also the rates between each of the currencies in the arrangement. To the extent that national interest rates and national rates of inflation converge toward those in the country of the external currency, the economies of the countries in the arrangement will converge with each other. For countries planning to join an union, an early link to the union currency prior to joining (such as in the requirement that candidates for the EMU belong to the ERM II for at least two years) will promote convergence – to the union currency and between each other. The GCC countries all formally linked to the U.S. dollar as a step toward monetary union (although Kuwait later switched to a basket peg – albeit one with a heavy dollar weight).

6.56. Following a single currency peg is the easiest exchange rate policy to implement, which has advantages and disadvantages. Advantages include the lowering of costs of conversion, and it could be appropriate where policy analysis and decision-making infrastructure is weak. Disadvantages include placing all the adjustment burden on other mechanisms such as monetary, price, and employment adjustments. Another major disadvantage is that local analysis and policy development infrastructure will not be built up and will be weak, which is not an acceptable situation for future currency unions.

Basket pegs

6.57. It is also possible to peg a currency to a currency basket. A basket peg might reflect the globalization of markets in that countries' export and import markets are becoming more diverse, thus making it less advantageous to link to a single currency.

> In an union, the single exchange rate policy will be set centrally and all countries will necessarily follow the common rate. The basket can only include currencies of countries outside the union.
> In a regional arrangement, each individual country can use the same basket, which sets both the external rates for all currencies involved, but also sets the relationship between the currencies in the arrangement.
>
> The weights used in the basket will be set regionally, such as based on the total external trade of the region, and weights will differ from what each individual country would use if it had its own basket– in this case, each country could have different trade weights from the basket.

In nonunion situations in which there is a regional arrangement of individual currencies (as in the ASEAN), weights for a basket can include external currencies and also currencies of countries within the region (intra-regional currencies). Including intra-regional currencies might more effectively capture the influence of external exchange rate changes on the economies in the arrangement, and in effect dilutes the impact of the countries' exchange rate changes to external currencies.

> The currency basket appropriate for a regional surveillance arrangement is not be appropriate for a currency union. A regional arrangement could have a basket which includes currencies of the countries in the region and thus *intra-regional* rates are used; in contrast an union will only have a basket with external weights. These define two different exchange rate regimes and thus, regions intending to become unions probably should use baskets based on external weights only; whereas long-term nonunion arrangements might choose to include intra-regional weights.[158]

6.58. Both single-currency and basket pegs set the nominal exchange rate only. The real exchange rates for individual countries within either type of peg can differ if inflation rates differ between countries.

The rate for the peg

6.59. New unions will face difficult problems of where to set the initial rate of the union currency vis-à-vis external currencies, and setting the rates for conversion of national currencies into the new union currency. In principle, the rates should be set based on

[158] The monetary policies associated with these two different weighting schemes can of course differ.

the equilibrium real effective exchange rate (EREER) for the union, at which both internal and external equilibrium conditions prevail. However, finding such an equilibrium point can be very difficult given diverse conditions within new unions and because of the structural changes caused by the creation of the union. Indeed, if the member economies are divergent there might not be an underlying effective rate for the entire union. Moreover, authorities may choose as a matter of policy to set the rate a bit higher or lower than an equilibrium level – a higher rate might be set as a demonstration of the strength of the new currency and to show determination to tamp down inflation; a lower level might be adopted to stimulate exports and build foreign currency reserves to provide assets to support the new currency.

6.60. However, problems occur if the peg is set too high or too low so that long-term current account deficits or surpluses result.

> If the peg is set too high (the domestic currency has too high an exchange value), the export price of goods and services is too high for foreign markets and the volume will fall, resulting in drops in export receipts. Conversely, import prices will be low and the volume of imports will rise. This can be favorable to large segments of the population who are able to cheaply buy foreign goods and services. However, it can cause a current account deficit to pay for high net imports. Capital inflows are needed to finance the deficit, or international reserves are used to make payment. Difficulties arise if a country's stock of reserves falls to low levels, or if foreign investors become concerned about the accumulation of international debt and refuse to provide more capital.

> If the peg is set too low, export prices are low for foreign importers and export volume will increase. Conversely, import prices are high, which reduces import volume. Domestic consumption is low and at a relatively high price because there is a net currency account surplus of goods and services moving abroad. Accumulations of foreign currency liquidity can induce domestic inflation, unless sterilized by the central bank. However, the interest cost of sterilization can be high, and might not be sustainable.[159]

6.61. Thus, it matters for a union whether the currency peg is at the right level. There is probably usually a band in which the currency can be pegged without creating difficulties, but a peg outside the band can create macroeconomic problems, and will tend to redistribute benefits and costs between different segments of the economy – exporters, importers, and consumers are affected in different ways. One of the major challenges of setting up a union is set the initial currency peg at the right level to generate long-term noninflationary growth. This is especially important if the peg is intended to be permanent.[160]

Policy under an exchange rate peg

6.62. The economy linking its currency to another currency will also import the monetary policy of the other currency. For example, interest rates will tend to equalize to rates in the country with the pegged currency. If the rates in the linked economy move too high or low capital will flow in or out resulting in equalization of rates. A change in monetary policy in the larger economy will be reflected as changes in interest rates in the linked economy.

> The two francophone unions in Africa are pegged to the value of euro, and previously to the french

---

[159] Sterilization involves central bank absorption of domestic liquidity created by the export surplus by selling securities or taking deposits. If sterilization becomes a long-term condition, the central bank will often have to offer high interest rates to attract the excess liquidity. In some cases, the cost of sterilization has run up to several percent of GDP annually and seriously eroded the balance sheet of the central bank. In such cases, the low currency peg is not indefinitely sustainable.

[160] The Appendix to this chapter summarizes a paper that discusses using the real effective exchange rate as guidance to where to set the union exchange rate peg.

franc. In 1994, the union currencies devalued by a very large 50 percent, accompanied by a series of structural reforms that tamped down a burst of imported inflation following the devaluation and contributed to subsequent stronger growth.

The Eastern Caribbean Currency Union is pegged to the U.S. dollar.

The GCC countries in preparation for their planned union formally pegged their currencies to the U.S. dollar in 2002. The dollar peg was seen as providing a convenient and stable measure of value that has promoted capital imports and development, but beginning around 2006, the peg was seen as introducing problems – the weakening of the dollar contributed to imported inflation and the low interest rate regime in the United States was out of line with the need to tighten conditions in the Gulf regions to tamp down inflation. A vigorous debate ensued in the region whether to maintain the dollar peg at its traditional level to maintain the substantial institutional links to the dollar and to preserve the value of very large dollar-denominated assets, or to revalue the peg or switch to a basket. However, the onset of the financial crisis, increased dollar strength, and lessening of global inflationary pressures caused the debate to subside, but the issue remains valid.

In Asia, following the Asian crisis in the late 1990's, it is said that there is a strong desire to avoid instability in exchange markets and that countries seek to maintain relatively stable intra-regional exchange rates reflecting the close trade and investment ties in the region. There is feeling that if revaluations will occur, it is better that regional currencies move together as a group. (ECB 2005) Steps were taken to bolster intra-regional exchange rate stability such as the Chiang Mai Initiative and the Economic Policy and Research Dialog (EPRD).

Equilibrium real effective exchange rates (EREER)

6.63. The EREER for a currency is a long-run stable value of a country's real effective exchange rate, which is typically calculated by dividing the nominal effective exchange rate index by an index of changes in prices, typically the CPI.[161] An increase in the REER reflects an appreciation for the country's currency, and if the real appreciation is too high the country's external competitiveness is impaired. The equilibrium rate is an underlying long-term REER, which can be measured econometrically or through purchasing power calculations, which is compatible with both domestic and external equilibrium.[162]

6.64. The EREER is highly relevant for the analysis of convergence between the economies of potential members of an union. Despite a period with no currency realignments from 1987 through 1992, beginning in 1993 the EMS experienced severe stress including several currencies leaving the system due to shifts in real exchange rates that affected the relative competitiveness of the European economies. Stable nominal exchange rates were not sufficient and maintaining fixed parity led to competitiveness differentials due to inflation differentials and increased unemployment of the less competitive members. When macroeconomic divergence among the EMS participants rose too high, the absence of devaluation lowered the credibility of a fixed nominal peg rather than raise it. Monetary authorities unable to resist real exchange rate movements might not be able to prevent nominal exchange rates from departing from the central parities. Thus, the adjustment towards the anchor

[161] Data on a country's REER is the multilateral CPI-based real effective exchange rate calculated by the IMF World Economic Outlook (WEO) database. These data are available in the data base for virtually all countries and thus are available to union authorities, but some countries have not granted permission for their dissemination to the general public. Data for REERs are in a table – Real Effective Exchange Rate Indices – in the front of *International Financial Statistics.* The table provides data for about two dozen countries based on use of unit labor cost indices, and for many more countries based on use of consumer price indices.

[162] See KKC (2009) for a demonstration on calculating the EREER.

disappears and exchange rates can become unstable. Bessec (2003) argued that realignments to pull exchange rates based on their purchasing power parity (which can be estimated based on the EREER) can reestablish competitiveness and restore the credibility of the system.

6.65. An implication is that policy credibility of countries seeking to join an union depends both on the ability to maintain nominal exchange rate stability but also on the ability to manage its EREER so that competitiveness is maintained, growth proceeds, and unemployment of resources is low.[163] (Drazen and Masson 1994) Extending this perspective to individual member countries of unions, nominal exchange rates cannot be altered because of the common currency, but real competitiveness can change which affects the ability of member countries to compete with each other. Some EMU countries such as Greece and Portugal experienced real exchange rate appreciations that impaired their ability to recover from recessionary shocks experienced during the financial crisis.

Changing exchange rates

6.66. In addition to deciding on exchange rate policy, the process of moving to the new exchange rate must be considered. Some new unions will likely face the challenge of moving from a fixed exchange rate regime to a flexible regime. For example, the GCC has announced that it's union will begin with a currency linked to the U.S. dollar and then consider moving to a flexible regime. Other future unions might follow a similar path.

6.67. Duttagupta, Fernandez, and Karacadag (2004) analyze experiences of countries moving from fixed exchange rates into floating regimes and the types of market, institutional, and policy steps that facilitate the process. They discuss management of a transition into a float and identify key areas that contribute to a successful transition to a floating regime. They describe a number of steps to follow;

Develop deep, liquid foreign exchange markets

Design intervention policies consistent with a new exchange rate regime

Select an alternative nominal anchor compatible with the regime selected

Support capacity of banks and financial markets to manage exchange rate risks

Build supervisory capacity to regulate and monitor exchange rate risks to banks and other institutions

6.68. In other words, they argue that movement from a fixed nominal rate requires building a flexible institutionally strong foreign exchange market that prices foreign exchange and can handle transactions and risks in a currency that can fluctuate in value.

Implementing exchange rate regimes

6.69. New unions face three major tasks in setting the exchange rate for the new currency. First, the conversion of national currencies into the new union

[163] A real-world example of application of REER analysis is the ERM II, in which countries seeking to join the EMU must participate for at least two years. EMR II currency must remain within bands around a central parity vis-à-vis the euro, without extraordinary intervention. The central rate chosen must reflect the best possible assessment of the EREER at the time of entry into the mechanism (ECB, 2003). The system provided for procedures to formally review the exchange rates, if needed. That is, convergence is based not only on nominal factors, but also was based on the underlying equilibrium real rate. Horváth and Komárek's (2006) estimates of the real exchange rate equilibrium for the new EU members concluded that the misalignment of the currencies' central parities vis-à-vis the euro was low and did not require any adjustment at the time of their research. That is, the nominal exchange rate in fact correlated closely with the EREER. They recommended *not* adjusting the central parity if the real exchange rate misalignment was less than 10%.

The ECB regularly compiles REERs for each member country, as described further in Appendix 3.

currency. Second, deciding on the exchange rate policy for the union. Third, dealing with the practicalities of implementing the new policies, which might include changing between types of regimes.

6.70. Exchange rate regimes range across a scale with at one extreme pure market floats to hard, unchangeable pegs to other currencies at the other extreme. The EMU policy is closer to a pure float, allowing demand and supply conditions in currency markets to move the rate. In contrast, the two African currency unions and the ECCU link their currencies, specifically to the euro and U.S. dollar, respectively. In intermediate situations, numerous other countries allow their currency to float, but seek to to limit currency volatility or to move the currency higher or lower for various reasons.

6.71. In unions pursuing a more constrained exchange rate regime than the EMU, emphasis must be given to resources and instruments that can affect the exchange rate; the adequacy of reserves, availability of suitable exchange rate instruments, active consultations and agreement with major exchange rate counterparties, access to liquid reserves assets and lines of credit, etc..

6.72. Countries often seek greater control over their exchange rate than a floating regime can provide for a variety of reasons. Reasons for a "managed float" to control the exchange rate include;

Limit the economic effects of currency volatility. Individual transactions in goods and services, and long-term investment decisions depend on the prevailing exchange rate and its changes over the life of the transaction - rapid exchange rate changes create uncertainties and make conducting international business more difficult.

Limit the speed of exchange rate changes. Countries might be willing to let the exchange rate change as underlying economic conditions change, but seek to limit the speed of the changes to avoid possible destabilizing large changes and to allow time to adjust.

Suppress destabilizing conditions. Central banks might intervene to stabilize a currency following emergencies or to counter speculative attacks. Currencies with small or shallow markets might be more easily destabilized, creating a motivation to more strongly link to other currencies.

Reduce a trade deficit or trade surplus.

Sustain business relationships with neighboring economies and avoid changes in the price structure in cross-border trade and investments.

Respond to pressure from businesses or the public in favor of certain rates. A wide range of motivations could be involved, from lowering nominal import costs, to export promotion, among many others. Political pressures can prove decisive in promoting particular exchange rate stances. (One advantage of currency unions is that political pressures leading to distortionary exchange rate stances might be less effective.)

Create a currency-account surplus and build international reserves, such as in East Asia following the Asia Crisis.

Avoid exchange rate competition with other economies.

Meet domestic policy goals, such as switching domestic absorption, building a diverse export sector, stimulating employment, or dealing with inflationary pressures, etc..

6.73. Within an union, mechanisms are needed for continuing research on the implications of the exchange rate stance and to set up an inclusive decision-making operation. This will be a major aspect of the policy operations of future unions. If future unions choose a more constrained exchange rate regime than the EMU, they must necessarily give emphasis to policy stances that affect the exchange rate, adequacy of reserves, availability of suitable exchange rate instruments, and on active consultations and agreement with major exchange rate counterparties.

Managed float or dirty float

6.74. In a managed float, the currency is allowed in general to respond to market forces but authorities intervene as needed to influence the direction or speed of adjustment. This is a common policy, and many countries that say that they have a floating currency in fact intervene occasionally or take other policy actions to affect the rate.

Currency board

6.75. A currency board is a very restrictive exchange rate and monetary policy regime, in which countries guarantee that all currency issued is fully backed by foreign exchange reserves. This is intended to provide assurance that the currency is solid and fully redeemable with internationally acceptable assets. A currency board is very restrictive in that money and domestic prices (hence domestic macroeconomic conditions) are held hostage to the stock of reserves. Also, the country cannot act as a lender of last resort in the event of financial system crises.

6.76. Because of their restrictiveness but market credibility, currency boards are sometimes used for stabilization after crises, but countries tend to move away from them once more stable conditions return. An union might begin with something close to a currency board, but certainly would want to move away from it as the union currency gains acceptance and to increase the range of monetary policy instruments available. The box below describes the currency board arrangement used in the Eastern Caribbean as a precursor for its union.

Text Box: Eastern Caribbean Currency Union (ECCU) currency board

In the ECCU, foreign reserve assets continue to serve as backing for the domestic currency in an arrangement much like a currency board. This grew out of a long-term currency board arrangement that eased gradually over time.

The British Caribbean Currency Board started after the Second World War. Each island deposited its foreign currency in exchange for the West Indian dollar at a fixed rate of 4.8 dollars per U.K. pound. 100 percent backing was required with full convertibility. In 1965, the arrangement was modified with the creation of the Eastern Caribbean Currency Authority that issued the East Caribbean dollar, which only required 70 percent backing.

A decade later, the link was shifted to the U.S. dollar and required backing fell to 60 percent, although the actual backing remained much higher. In 1983, the Eastern Caribbean Central Bank was created in which a currency board like arrangement continued but additional services were provided. The ECCB holds a pool of the foreign reserve assets for the member countries, but each country has the right of unrestricted access to the reserves as needed to cover the currency in the domestic economy. Seigniorage is distributed in proportion to the country's share of currency issued.

Official rates

6.77. Countries might set an official rate or rates that must be used by the general public to buy and sell a foreign currency or by segments of the economy for specific transactions. Sometimes, the margins that banks and currency dealers charge might also be regulated. Official rates are used to regulate trading and fees in foreign exchange, to create a unified national market to provide equal access, to raise revenues, and to encourage or discourage trading. In some countries, the official rate is used in conjunction with mandatory requirements that foreign currency earnings be deposited with the central bank in order to build the country's international reserve assets.

6.78. Official rates often differ from available market rates, which implies a subsidy or tax in the purchase price. Official rates are much less common than in the past because they can be distortionary, inhibit adjustment, or become out of date because they might not be changed frequently. Where such distortions build, different segments of the economy could be favored or damaged, and unregulated or black market trading might result, creating new problems.

Multiple exchange rates

6.79. A country might set different rates for different types of transactions or economic sectors. The different rates either subsidize or tax the types of transaction involved. They have been used to capture exporters' earnings, subsidize or penalize imports (for example, encouraging capital goods imports and discouraging consumer goods imports), promote exports, encourage tourism, etc. Because specific types of transactions are affected by the multiple rates, they are often distortionary and encourage unregulated arbitrage trading and thus are generally not recommended. They are much less used than in the past.

Exchange rate band

6.80. Countries might choose to let their currencies float within a specified range, but intervene or take other actions if the exchange rate moves outside the band in order to pull the rate back into the band. Setting a band can recognize that it is can be very difficult to identify a precise exchange rate level and thus market forces are left to set the rate. The central bank is not obliged to intervene continually, but may do so to avoid more extreme changes in the rate. If the commitment to maintain the band is credible, markets will assume that more extreme exchange rates will be pulled back toward the center of the band and will purchase or sell the currency as needed to profit from the movement back to the center – the central bank thus can avoid intervention completely if this occurs.

E. International reserves management

6.81. This section discusses the management of the union's international reserves, which is a key central banking function. Central banks hold and transact in foreign currency assets to support transactions of their economy, to back their currency, to hold precautionary balances for intervention, and to manage the portfolio in ways that bolster security, diversify risk, ensure liquidity, and hold wealth and earn income. The total amount of reserves and their composition is affected by the main purposes of the reserves and the economic situation of the country or union. A complex analysis of liquidity, risk and reward, and national, regional, and global conditions is needed to set the reserves policy of new unions. This will include making judgments of the risk and reward prospects for currencies included in the reserves portfolio.

6.82. All of the functions are affected by specific membership in each union. Member countries should be able to cut back on their holdings of highly liquid, low return assets because of the increased stability of being within the union. Some of the funds released can be used for higher return investments or diverted for other purposes. Conversely, the union itself must build its stock of reserves to cover union-wide uses of reserves.[164] During the early days of an union, it is probably prudent to carry extra reserves in assure markets about the prospects for the union.

6.83. Reserves management should also consider the wider context of its costs and how it interacts with monetary and other economic policies. On the positive side, adequate reserves can assure markets, tamp down volatility, and lower borrowing costs. Conversely, holding large pools of reserves can have high opportunity costs of – both in terms of earnings lost and also in terms denying the funds for alternative uses (which thus might need to be financed by taxes).

6.84. An important demonstration occurred following the Asia crisis where several countries kept their exchange rates low in order to generate current-account surpluses to build large reserve balances. However, central bank purchases of foreign currency export receipts increased the money stock, which was countered by sterilization to sop up the excess liquidity by issuing bonds. The interest payments on the bonds in countries such as Viet Nam became excessively high and greatly exceeded the earnings on the reserve assets acquired, creating large negative carrying costs. In such cases, achieving the reserves target interacted with the exchange rate, monetary policy,

[164] Or, as in the EMU, the union central bank has access to reserves held by NCBs if needed.

domestic interest rates, central bank accounts, and fiscal policy.

Factors affecting reserves management

Transactions demand

6.85. It is common for countries and unions to measure adequacy of reserves by the number of months of imports covered by the reserves. For example, reserves must be equal to or more than the value of three months imports. This measure is sometimes used as a formal convergence criterion. This is a widely followed measure of reserve adequacy and new union probably should adopt it (to an agreed number of months supply) simply because many people expect to see it and will use it as a measure of the soundness of the union and its currency.

6.86. Alternatively, Roger (1993) suggested that the ratio of reserves to current account or capital variability provides a better measure. Roger suggests that developing countries should concentrate on current account variability, but countries more linked to global financial markets should give more weight to potential short-term capital flows. Since his analysis, many more countries have increasingly integrated into global financial markets, which suggests that much more widespread use of capital account flows as an indicator. The GFC demonstrated that international liquidity disruptions can be much more dangerous than previously believed and that the problems were most severe for countries that heavily intermediated international financial capital, and thus this factor must receive greater weight in reserves management analysis.

6.87. The development of digital instruments (including CBDCs) raises the risk of rapid sudden shifts in reserves assets. Additional precautions, higher reserves levels, and rapid information on market conditions might be needed to address increased risks in holdings of digital reserves assets.

Precautionary balances for intervention

6.88. One of the most important purposes to hold reserves is to support intervention in exchange markets in order to affect the exchange rate. Intervention can be two-sided and a country might need to intervene to affect exchange rates not because of its own situation but to assist other countries in their adjustment efforts. Funds for intervention need to be sufficient to support possible attacks on the currency, but policies should recognize that other resources can be called in to assist the effort, as discussed in the next section.

6.89. Funds for intervention must be readily available and situated where they can be used immediately. In the EMU, member countries initially maintained physical positions of assets and stood ready to intervene in support of union policies as directed. Most intervention will be in main money center financial markets and thus a smaller country, such as Portugal, would place reserves in London or New York or wherever convenient if needed for intervention. The EMU later permitted member countries to farm out their reserves management activity to other countries' NCBs with better market access in exchange for fees. New unions will need to manage the physical location of reserve assets so that they can be used effectively. In some unions, market options might be very limited and thus the funds might be placed outside the union and under fairly tight control by the union. (In some existing unions, member countries must deposit all their hard currency export receipts in the union central bank, but these requirements generally have become less strict over time.)

Backing the currency

6.90. Adequate, high-quality international reserves are considered backing for a country's currency. Ample reserves can lead markets to bid the exchange rate of a currency higher, but limited and declining reserves often lead to sell-offs of the currency in markets and subsequent depreciation of the currency. In post-crisis situations, stabilization of a currency might involve creating a currency board in which the entire value of domestic currency issued is backed by foreign currency.

6.91. The amount of reserve assets needed for this purpose will vary based on the general economic situation and credibility of the currency. A currency that has undergone a rough period with political instability or poor fiscal governance might need large balances to recreate confidence. Amounts needed should decline over time with good management and economic results for the economy and currency.

Supply the financial system

6.92. Many central banks are a major or sole source of foreign currency liquidity used by the financial system. Where exporters and banks are required to deposit foreign currency in the central bank, the central bank in return is obligated to manage its stock and composition of foreign currency to supply the legitimate foreign currency requirements of the economy. Receipts and payments can be erratic or subject to seasonal shifts and the composition of receipts might not closely match payments. Some transactions with the government might not be channeled through the private banking system for various reasons. The overall level of reserve assets will fluctuate due to these transactions.

6.93. The central bank will need to take steps to ensure the economy has the amounts and types of foreign currency denominated assets needed. The private banking system might have primary responsibility for this, in which case the central bank might be involved only when special needs or emergencies arise. In other countries, the central bank could be the main source of these funds. Whatever the type of demand, the central bank will need to monitor flows and be able to predict types of demand.[165] Assets must be obtained and supplied where and when needed, without interfering with other functions of reserves. In crisis conditions, the central bank might be forced to allocate or ration foreign currency, with direct effects on economic activity. Arrangements to collect and allocate foreign currency assets must be set up quickly. Low priority activities could be denied funds, but means must be found to supply assets to all segments and regions of the economy. The union central bank might not have a full picture of demand by sector and region and could rely on national or local offices. This knowledge of local conditions was implicit in the EMU decision to maintain the separate identities of the preexisting national central banks.

Diversification of holdings

6.94. Reserve assets should be managed to avoid excessive concentrations of risk and volatility in returns.

> Large holdings of the target currency in a pegged system should be expected. The domestic currency will move with the target currency with little direct effect on domestic monetary conditions.[166] Similarly, maintaining reserves holdings similar to the basket peg for the currency can help avoid costs for the central bank. Also, instruments will be needed to ensure that businesses have access to the currencies in the basket needed for their transactions.
>
> In floating currency situations, or for currencies outside the pegging arrangement, foreign-currency denominated assets are subject to holding gains or losses from exchange rate changes. Large

[165] The private sector often will not cooperate in providing its foreign currency receipts to the central bank and attempt to get more assets out of the system than needed. Oversight and sometimes legal coercion may be needed, which could be a reason for letting the private banking system handle this business if possible.

Foreign currency receipts and demand can be good short-term indicators of economic activity and can provide much data needed for macroeconomic accounts, especially the balance of payments. However, distortions (under reporting export receipts or over reporting payments requirements for imports) have been known to systematically bias this information.

[166] However, the target currency might move against general global exchange markets, which will cause identical movements for the domestic currency. For example, the Gulf countries found that their currency fell sharply against the euro around 2006-8 along with the fall in the value of the U.S. dollar. This had many effects on the Gulf economies, including raising import costs, inducing capital inflows into real estate, and overheating the economies.

losses can severely damage the earnings and balance sheet of the central bank. These cannot be avoided but limiting very large holdings reduces the possibility of large losses. Diversifying holdings can often reduce total volatility in returns by balancing holding gains and losses between currencies.

Commodity risk

6.95. Monetary gold is an official international reserves asset subject to market price movements. International statistical standards require valuing gold at market prices, which affects total reserves. Gold is not actively managed by most economies, but is an important asset for several gold-producing countries.

6.96. However, gold is widely used as collateral under swap arrangements to obtain other foreign currency assets. In this regard, it does provide useful flexibility for management of total reserves.

6.97. Because of its special status, new unions will probably need policies on the use of gold in the union's reserves and its status within member states.

6.98. Other precious metals are also subject to market price risks, but are not classified as commodities and not part of official reserves assets. However, they can affect the overall financial picture of the central bank and thus might need to be monitored. From the perspective of the union central bank the focus is probably how precious metals affect the overall financial picture of the member countries and not how to actively manage them as part of union policy.

Hold wealth and earn income

6.99. The central bank will also be in charge of preserving the assets held as reserves, earning income on them, and hopefully increasing them over time. Income on the assets is part of the net income of the central bank. Part of central bank net income is usually transferred annually as dividends to the government as the shareholder – this income can be an important part of government revenue.

6.100. Central banks often face a tradeoff between maintaining the assets in highly liquid secure assets suitable for exchange market intervention or investing the assets to return higher returns. A key decision will be whether such management will be done within the system or delegated to professional portfolio managers. The experience of many sovereign wealth funds is to rely heavily on outside advice unless they have sufficient experienced resources to do it themselves.

6.101. In some countries, the central bank acts as manager of a national sovereign wealth fund designed to preserve and profitably invest assets. The SWF is usually organized as a legally separate entity from the central bank, but its holdings potentially can contribute to the country's total stock of reserves holdings and might be legally available for use in emergencies to support the exchange rate. (Section E below has more discussion of SWFs.)

6.102. Auditing of returns on international reserves should be expected, especially in unions where income is in lieu of earnings on a national basis and where earnings will be shared with member countries. It can be expected that earnings on reserves assets will be closely watched by member countries, union parliamentary or judicial bodies, and the public.

Valuation of contributions to union reserves holdings

6.103. The initial contribution of reserves assets to the union must be valued at true market value as of the transfer date. All value created prior to the transfer date is retained as property of the member. The value on the first day of the union is recorded on the balance sheet of the union on that date. Changes in value after that date are owned by the union. These changes in value are used to calculate the net profit of the union, which might be later distributed as dividends to member countries.

6.104. In the EMU, most reserves assets are held by the NCBs. Separate books must be kept of the value of those assets when they entered under union ownership and all income earned since. Earnings are property of the ESCB even though the earnings are physically held by the NCB's. The total income of all the central banks will be divvied up between the member countries according to the agreed formula. Because common wealth and income are in the possession of individual country authorities there must be close accounting and auditing of the assets.

6.105. There also can be supplemental contributions to the union after it is set up. These must be under the same rules as initial contributions. One form of supplemental contribution could be contributions by national authorities to cover losses by the union central bank. This will obviously be politically sensitive and the union central bank will need to have accurate documentation of its financial status and need for additional support. This documentation will need to cover policy and investment decisions as well as results of forensic audits into possible criminal activity.

Exchange rate guarantees

6.106. Central banks sometimes provide exchange rate guarantees to banks, other businesses, or the government so that they can carry out business without concern about adverse exchange rate changes. The central bank takes on contingent exchange rate risk as a result. Losses could become severe if large devaluations occur. New unions will need to decide whether this practice is permissible, especially given the possibility that individual countries might provide guarantees that have implications for the entire union.

IMF credit and swap lines

6.107. Countries and unions will have access to supplemental resources for use in cases of balance of payments need. These should be considered when evaluating the adequacy and composition of reserves.

6.108. The IMF has a variety of facilities with large pool of assets that can be used by countries to help finance temporary imbalances.

> Funds are provided in tranches, with the first tranche readily available, but access to additional tranches will usually require a special IMF review of the situation and approval to extend the funds, which will often be contingent on preparation of a formal program in which the country must meet specified conditions "conditionality". Countries are often hesitant to use IMF credit because of a stigma of failure and possible onerous conditions, but the funds are available.[167]
>
> In response to the financial crisis, IMF members sharply increased its resources in order to provide greater amounts of credit to deal with the large liquidity problems caused by the crisis. Lending policies also changed to provide relatively larger amounts of credit and earlier within programs so that more resources are available when problems are more severe.
>
> In late 2009, the IMF allocated 283 billion new SDRs to all member countries. The allocation went to countries that had not previously received SDRs and to all countries to provide a general increase in liquidity available to respond to the financial crises. The increased SDRs became a significant portion of total reserve assets of many countries. This generally eased reserves constraints and because SDRs can be readily exchanged for other reserve assets gave countries added flexibility in adjusting the composition of their reserves.
>
> Existing currency unions are designated as official holders of SDRs and can transact with the IMF and can hold and transact SDRs. New unions will need to negotiate such arrangements.

[167] Following the 2010 IMF Spring Meetings, IMF Managing Director Dominique Strauss-Kahn addressed IMF staff and said that hesitance of European officials to approach the IMF for assistance caused problems to fester and worsen. He said it was important for countries to request assistance on a timely basis. He said such assistance can be low key, such as simply providing advice.

6.109. Swap lines are reciprocal arrangements in which a country needing an international reserve currency exchanges its own currency for a reserve currency. They permit actual borrowing and lending of currencies on a collateralized basis. They are usually negotiated before crises arise and can be quickly accessed as needed, but if crisis conditions arise it is common for lines to be expanded or new lines created. Public announcement of new swap lines often provides support for currencies under attack.

> During the financial crisis, the United States opened massive U.S. dollar swap lines with the ECB and other central banks to allow unlimited borrowing of dollars in order to counter freezes in dollar funding. Central banks exchanged their currencies for the dollar then lent the dollars to their banks to meet the demand.

> New unions should negotiate swap lines with the ECB, IMF, BIS, Federal Reserve Board, and other major central banks prior to the launch of the union.

Intervention

6.110. Central banks can influence exchange rates through direct intervention involving buying and selling the domestic currency with foreign exchange. International reserve assets are used for this purpose. For example, intervention purchases of the domestic currency by using foreign exchange increases demand for the domestic currency and raises the exchange rate. Sale of the domestic currency to purchase foreign currency increases its supply and lowers the exchange rate.

Intervention involves market purchase and sale of the foreign currency on spot or forward markets. This trading will usually be done in major international markets (New York, London, Tokyo, Singapore, etc.) often through a correspondent bank or central bank. Unions need to set up these trading arrangements, similar to what is done by national authorities. Member countries in an union will need to continue trading to handle routine or specifically national transactions, and decisions need to be made whether this will be done parallel to union operations or whether the union will act as an agent for the national transactions. Conversely, union transactions might be handled by the national central banks as agents for the union, which is overwhelmingly the mode used in the EMU although the ECB has the right to intervene on its own.

6.111. Union and national transactions must be fully separate, in decision-making, execution, accounting, and allocation of income, costs, and risk. Moreover, steps need to be in place to prevent markets from construing routine transactions as being due to monetary policy actions or intervention. This can be a problem because the same agents could be used for routine transactions or policy actions. Regular buying and selling of foreign exchange will help convey a sense that transactions are routine and thus policy related actions will not stand out starkly.

F. Sovereign Wealth Funds (SWFs)

6.112. A SWF is a separate pool of assets controlled by central banks or governments that is invested to earn market returns or to finance some future important economic or social project. Typically, high income from commodities or a balance of payment surplus creates accumulations of foreign currency in excess of what is needed for official reserves purposes. Because official reserves typically consist of very safe and highly liquid assets that earn low returns, countries created separate funds that could invest more aggressively in a wider range of investments and earn market returns.

6.113. SWFs present a number of special problems for monetary, exchange rate, and reserves management policies. SWFs did not exist in EU countries when the EMU was set up and thus are not covered in Maastricht. At that time, where they existed elsewhere they were mostly secretive and unnoticed (Norway, which had a highly transparent SWF, was the sole exception). Now, however, SWFs are important in several possible unions. Their size and influences on monetary and balance of payments conditions require that future unions have policies to deal with them.

6.114. SWFs are often explicit consequences of monetary or exchange policy choices that set the exchange rate, accumulate assets, and conduct sterilization operations, etc. As such they must be considered within the monetary, balance of payments, and exchange rate policy mix of the union.

6.115. There are four broad categories of SWFs:

Pure Wealth Funds are endowment funds meant to hold and wisely invest assets in order to transfer assets to future generations. They are often used when a country exploits an exhaustible resource and seeks to gain long-term benefits from the exploitation.

Stabilization Funds are designed to stabilize fiscal revenues to deal with commodity price cycles. A portion of earnings are set aside when prices are high to cover future drops in prices and the resultant downturn and drop in government revenues.

Reserves Investment Corporations are designed to earn higher return on excess reserves, including at times reducing the negative carry of holding reserves. In some countries during the boom times in 2006 and 2007, the assets in these funds grew very rapidly as a result of sterilization of high export earnings, which made the SWFs a key element of national monetary and exchange rate policies.

Pension Wealth Funds hold funds of national pension funds and invest them in order to cover future pension liabilities.

6.116. Most SWFs handle foreign-currency assets, sometimes exclusively. In general, the funds are invested outside the country in a range of assets, government bonds, corporate bonds, equities, and direct investments. Usually, broad SWF investment policy guidelines are provided by the government and the SWF is permitted to make specific investments within the guidelines. As the word "sovereign" implies, the guidelines usually reflect important public goals and are intended to provide broad social benefits. The specific goals, the beneficiaries, and the rules for withdrawing funds can vary widely based on the type of SWF as described above and individual country preferences. SWFs will be held responsible for following the guidelines, ensuring the security of the investment, and earning solid returns.

6.117. Although traditionally many SWFs have invested mostly or exclusively outside their home countries, there have been exceptions where funds are invested in-country for long-term development purposes, and the financial crisis has forced numerous countries to refocus their SWFs to cover domestic investment needs. Thus, currently, SWF activities are more closely intermixed with domestic macroeconomic conditions than in the past, and thus the monetary and financial consequences might be greater.

6.118. If SWFs did not exist, it is clear that the assets held under official control should be subject to macroeconomic surveillance because they can affect monetary and balance of payments conditions, affect the government budget, affect reserves management, influence external sustainability, and affect the exchange rate. These assets potentially could be substitutes for official reserve assets. Thus, for multiple reasons they should regularly be reviewed by national policy officials and fall under IMF surveillance. If the countries are in currency unions, then union-level policy oversight is appropriate.

6.119. The need for oversight is unchanged if the assets are held in SWFs, but the situation becomes much more complex. SWFs are often operated as independent entities operating under guidance by the central bank or ministry of finance, but the assets might be segregated and not subject to regular reporting. Investment policies, risks, nature of flows, and rules for use of the funds are potentially unique to each SWF. Also, some authorities are quite sensitive about disclosure of information about their SWF, even to their own public. Thus, the nature of the oversight or regulation can differ for each SWF. In an union, there could be several types SWFs in different member countries, which means that oversight and regulation will be complex. One potentially sensitive area is where a member country invests some of its SWF assets in other member countries.

6.120. In the same way as the ECB exercises control over NCB's use of foreign assets because they could act in contradiction with EMU monetary or external policies, new unions will need to exercise some control over SWFs. For example, in the Euroarea, NCBs must seek prior approval of the ECB for own operations that might affect exchange rates, domestic monetary conditions, or which exceed limits provided by the ECB. SWFs should also be covered by a similar rule, which must specify the conditions that justify oversight. A tricky situation is whether to follow the European rule that exempts NCBs' investments in foreign financial markets from prior approval because they were deemed to not affect EMU monetary or exchange rate policy.

6.121. Important advances have been made in the oversight and reporting of information on SWFs, including the development of a series of voluntary best practices called the "Santiago Principles" prepared by the International Working Group on Sovereign Wealth Funds (IWG).[168] The *Principles* now comprise the standards for work in the field and thus statistics need to be aligned with them. The information provides the most complete information about SWFs, but its data are tilted toward resource producers. A working group has been set up to continue this work. Unions with SWFs should at minimum insist that SWFs within the union comply fully with the Santiago Principles.

6.122. The IMF inquires about SWFs as part of its regular Article IV surveillance, because of their monetary and balance of payments impacts. In addition, the IMF decided in 2007 on a new policy (IMF 2007b) for oversight of exchange rates which can be construed to cover SWFs. One of the policies suggests initiating discussions with a country about exchange rates if official borrowing (or quasi-official borrowing) is unsustainable or has high liquidity risk, or which involves extensive sterilization or prolonged official or quasi-official accumulation of excessive amounts of foreign assets for balance of payment purposes. The inclusion of the phrase "quasi-official accumulations" covers sovereign wealth funds.

6.123. In conclusion, there are numerous reasons for oversight of SWFs by unions. The Santiago Principles should be applied as part of this oversight. Additional guidance might need to be spelled out, but their nature will depend on the types of SWFs involved. The degree of union oversight or control will depend on the type of SWF and could vary from tight to pretty loose as each case requires.

[168] See Sovereign Wealth Funds Generally Accepted Principles and Practices "Santiago Principles" October 2008, and its companion document Sovereign Wealth Funds: Current Institutional and Operational Practices September 2008. The latter document surveyed a sample of 20 SWFs on legal frameworks, objectives, institutions and governance, investment strategies, and risk management.

Timeline

Large unions should move all steps at least one year earlier.

Preparatory period	
Early actions (four years prior)	Survey of exchange rate policies and intervention instruments of future members.
Three years prior	Begin reviews of exchange rate regime options. Begin design of foreign exchange operations system Initial contacts with IMF, BIS, ECB, and major international financial centers
24 months prior	Continuing research on policy options Negotiate access to IMF and BIS facilities Negotiate swap lines Draft rules for transfer of international reserve assets Draft accounting rules for international reserves Analysis of conversion rates for national currencies
18 Months Prior	Documentation and testing of policy instruments Agreement on exchange rate policy framework
Final 12 months	Members of union selected; Policy adjustment to reflect actual membership Ratification of international reserves accounting rules
Final 6 months	Union central bank policy operations begin Monetary and interest rate targets decided Exchange rate conversion mechanism in place Transfer of assets and reserves to central bank control Foreign currency intervention system operable Foreign currency swap lines put in place Live test of foreign currency intervention mechanism

Run-up to union	Live test of monetary and exchange rate policy instruments Final accounting of national reserve assets for transfer to union
Union day	Single exchange rate policy initiated International reserves redefined on union basis International credit and swap lines in force
Early union period	All policies are actively managed

Chapter 7 – Macroeconomics and the Growth and Stability Pact

How do union macroeconomic and monetary policies interact? What rules were put in place to control economic policies of member countries to support union goals?

A. The EMU policy system

7.1. This chapter reviews the policy apparatus for the Eurosystem and its mechanism to develop policy based on comprehensive analysis of the macroeconomic situation of the union. The policy arm must be capable of sophisticated analysis of conditions within the union and in other economies that can affect the union. This chapter will review the policy mechanism for the Eurosystem, and then discuss the role of fiscal policy within the Eurosystem.

7.2. The complex structure of the ESCB affects the policy operations of the Eurosystem. The ESCB is comprised of the ECB and the NCBs of the member countries. Reflecting the doctrine of subsidiarity, functions meaningful handled on a decentralized basis by the NCBs are retained by the NCBs. The system is summarized in a single phrase – *centralized policy, decentralized operations.* This means that decision-making about the single currency and monetary, interest rate, exchange rate, and reserves policies is made by the ECB; Implementation is done by NCBs on a decentralized basis and which sometimes reflects local conditions.

7.3. The ECB acting through its decision-making bodies governs the Eurosystem. The ECB's General Council, Governing Council, and Executive Board make decisions on policy and implementation, and regulating the system. The Statute of the ESCB spells out their structure and rules.

General Council

7.4. The General Council is the broadest policy body of the system. It is comprised of the ECB Executive Board members and governors of the central banks of all EU member countries. It includes the Euroarea countries and also EU countries that have not yet adopted the euro. It deals with issues that affect all EU countries, such as operation of the TARGET settlement system.

7.5. The General Council has a role only so long as some EU states are not full members of the Eurosystem. It will be eliminated when all EU countries adopt the euro.

Governing Council

7.6. Although the General Council has the broadest membership, the Governing Council, which includes only the Executive Board and Eurosystem members is the main decision-making body. The Governing Council formulates policy related to the single currency, monetary policy, and exchange rate and reserves policy. It also is in charge of implementation of policies and administers the ECB and the operations of the Eurosystem.

7.7. It closely monitors economic conditions within the union and usually meets every two weeks. One meeting each month is devoted to assessing economic and financial conditions throughout the union and making monetary policy decisions. The other meeting each month is focused on other policy issues or administrative matters.

7.8. In order to preserve the independence of decision-making, discussions of the Governing Council are held confidential, but following monetary policy decisions the President of the ECB holds a press conference immediately after the session to explain decisions and their rationale. Thus, it is expected that General Council decisions will be put into effect immediately, and the public notice allows the public and markets to respond quickly and without favoritism to any parties.

7.9. To avoid having the Council become unwieldy as new countries join the Eurosystem, a system caps the total number of members, with rotating participation for smaller countries.

7.10. On policy matters, decisions are based on majority votes, with each member of the Governing Council having a single vote. In the event of a tie, the President makes the deciding vote. For matters requiring a qualified majority, votes are weighted by each NCB's share in the subscribed capital in the ECB and the Executive Board members do not participate.

7.11. The by-laws of the Governing Council can be changed only through unanimous agreement of the Heads of States or Government, acting on recommendations from either the ECB or the European Commission. Thus, changes in the governance rules are difficult to make, but do not require reopening of the Maastricht Treaty itself.

Executive Board

7.12. The Executive Board is comprised of the President of the ECB, the Vice President, and 4 additional members. They are elected for eight years and cannot be renewed. All members have votes in the Governing and General Councils. The Executive Board members are expected to represent the union as a whole and thus they are appointed by accord of the Heads of State or Government of the Euroarea countries. Because they will help formulate policy and administer the Eurosystem, only countries that have adopted the euro participate in their selection.

7.13. The Executive Board administers the ECB and sets priorities and duties for the ECB staff. Thus, it oversees the collection of information on conditions throughout the union and analysis of this information for use by the Governing Council. It makes preparations for Governing Council meetings and participates in decision-making, after which it implements the decisions.

7.14. In addition to policy, the Executive Broad has oversight of ECB exercise of various regulatory powers, such as operating the bank required reserves system and sanctioning those violating the system.

ECB Staff

7.15. The ECB staff supports the decision-making work of the Eurosystem. It operates under the direction of the Executive Board. The President and Vice President have overall responsibility for operation of the ECB and the four other Board members supervise the departments of the ECB. There is regular flow of information and analysis up from the staff to support decision-making and the staff will implement decisions when made. It is important to recognize that the ECB staff does not work in isolation – the ECB has a very active committee structure that results in extensive two-way flow of information between the ECB and the NCBs. This keeps the ECB aware of conditions throughout the union, informs the NCBs about common policies and priorities, and results in peer review of activities.

National Central Banks

7.16. The ECB itself is authorized to undertake many functions, but much of the operational activity of the ESCB takes place at the NCB level under the doctrine of subsidiarity. Acting under ECB policies or guidelines, NCB's handle many operational activities for the system, including amongst others;

Monetary policy operation, including open market operations and operation of standing deposit and lending facilities

Holding and investing international reserves

Intervention in exchange markets

Issuing and retiring currency

Investigating counterfeiting

Bank supervision

Operating the bank required reserves system

Operations of the TARGET system

Collection of statistics and compilation of national aggregates

Collaborating with other central banks, international organizations, and others on areas where the NCB has expertise or vested interests.

7.17. The NCBs also undertake analysis of local and general conditions, including undertaking research

.

7.18. The comprehensive range of activities undertaken by the NCBs contributes to the development and implementation of many Euroarea policies and thus effectively increases the staff, financial, and information resources available to the system. This work for the union done by NCBs is financed by distributing the financial profits of the ESCB as a whole to the NCBs (less a small share for the ECB) based on their capital contribution share at the ECB.

7.19. NCBs can also continue a range of activities outside the monetary union and must have an analysis operation to support these activities.

Overview

7.20. This system described above puts the decision-making core of the system at the ECB, but allows the ECB access to a much wider range of information and analytic and implementation resources than it could maintain by itself – decentralization for the benefit of the system as a whole. That is, the ECB has "recourse to the NCBs to the extent deemed possible and appropriate to carry out operations which form part of the tasks of the Eurosystem." (Statute, Article 12.1)

7.21. The distribution of policy support functions between the union central bank and national central banks will be one of the key decisions for new currency unions. In Europe, financial resources and professional skills were widely spread prior to the start of the union and it made sense to incorporate operating macroeconomic policy systems into the new union. The situation in future unions could be very different and different solutions might result. Some future unions will have minimal resources available at the national level, and thus support of large policy staffs and analytical and policy skills might need to be centralized more than has occurred in Europe.

7.22. Also, in new unions much of the policy staff will be newly recruited and skills, procedures, and decision-making techniques must be built up to full effectiveness. This means that the building of the policy infrastructure should begin early in the process to build its effectiveness and to be able to participate in creating the policy framework for the union.

7.23. As described above, multiple steps are involved in the policy analysis and development process. The union will have to set up systems to cover all steps and properly staff them. This is both a technical and human resource process that should begin early in the union planning process.

7.24. New unions need to build their experience and expertise in policy-making for the union. Among tasks that can be done prior to the start of the union to help jump start the process – analyzing convergence amongst potential union members, estimating conversion rates for national currencies into a new union currency, exploring behavior of different currency buckets, estimating money and credit demand, analyzing real effective exchange rates for member countries, observing then participating in the IMF Article IV consultations with future member countries, and moving accounting, statistical, and financial supervisory systems of potential members toward international standards and best practices and supporting them with up-to-date IT systems. Each of these functions should be done before the start of the union in order to launch the union with suitable analytical and institutional foundations to support the new policy regime.

B. Macroeconomic analytical and policy apparatus of unions

Broad economic analysis

7.25. A currency union must deal with the full range of macroeconomic policy situations facing a national central bank, with the significant complication of covering multiple countries with different macroeconomic, fiscal situations, institutions, and laws. Normally, many aspects of macroeconomic policy are outside the direct control of the central bank, such as the overall fiscal stance (taxes and expenditures), employment, structural changes, infrastructure expenditures, or wage and price policies. Also, government international policies might affect reserves or exchange rates. The central bank will need to develop policy with many of these factors as given, and must also predict their future paths in order to assess future monetary or exchange rate options. In a union, each country might be following different macroeconomic policies, which complicates the task, and with different economic infrastructures it is possible that common monetary or exchange policies could have different effects in different countries.

7.26. A second complicating factor is that the union itself might exhibit new economic behaviors. An union is a larger institution, with new institutions, different public and international perceptions, and new common policies. How the union will react in different situations can be genuinely unknown. The union policy authorities will have to feel their way cautiously to understand the new situation and how policy acts within it.

7.27. Third, international reactions to a new union could be challenging, especially if markets do not have full confidence in union leadership, policies, or economic prospects. As an example, despite intentions at the start to let the euro fluctuate according to market forces, the value of the euro unexpectedly came under pressure and fell sharply during its first two years, forcing the EMU to intervene to stabilize markets.

7.28. A new union will need to deal with such situations, but it begins with a limited policy research and development team. The EMU had an advantage because the EU Committee of Governors already existed that analyzed convergence and exercised policy over the ECU. That group had analytical depth and exercised genuine powers over EU countries. Most future unions already have regional oversight bodies that analyze convergence, but they need significant strengthening to handle the volume and complexity of union operations. Moreover, for regions where exchange rate regimes are fixed, such as in the GCC, there has been little need at the country or union level to develop capacity to deal with complex exchange rate forecasting or policy issues, but this must change once the union is formed. Policy systems will need to be built in a short time.

7.29. A logical framework to build policy expertise for an union is the periodic review of convergence in the potential member countries. These exercises provide opportunities to review conditions in all member countries, including making comparisons of responses to common situations. The analysis should be expanded beyond review of the convergence criteria to a full scale review of macroeconomic conditions in each county and policy alternatives.

7.30. Analysis of convergence must be supplemented by capacity to undertake quantitative analysis. Quantitative or econometric analysis is needed for at least five major purposes – setting the conversion values for national currencies into the new union currency, modeling economic growth and inflation, analyzing monetary and exchange rate behavior, estimating fiscal and external sustainability, and supporting macroprudential analysis.

7.31. A policy decision-making body must also be set up, with rules to assure that high-quality, unbiased decisions are made based on good evidence. Evidence will be drawn from analysis of current conditions such as undertaken in convergence reviews and reviews of international conditions, and also from quantitative analysis. Analysis and decisions must be decisive in policy within the union, but also must participate with equal standing in international policy debates.

7.32. A second avenue to build expertise is to participate in regular IMF Article IV consultations with the member countries. The consultations provide rigorous reviews of current conditions, policy alternatives, prospects for growth and structural development of the country, and financing options. Economic conditions are analyzed in the context of legal and institutional settings. This work analyzes the finances of programs, the interactions with fiscal conditions, and can link to available development finance offered by the World Bank, regional development banks, and others. These are exactly the types of issues in which future unions will need to gain expertise and operationalize responses. Over time, the regional observers will gain in-depth understandings of national conditions, become aware of the differences and linkages between the economies, and hone skills. There might be legal barriers and confidentiality and sensitivity concerns, but to advance union prospects legal or de facto ways to overcome them will be needed.

7.33. A third avenue is for future union officials to actively participate in and gain expertise in international standards and regulatory programs. Relevant areas include financial payments and settlements, financial market infrastructure, financial supervision, financial stability, accounting, statistics, financial and digital technology and associated security and consumer protection issues, central bank digital currencies, insurance, anti-money laundering, etc.. These programs affect all countries and future union authorities should be aware of progress and challenges in individual countries, how cooperative programs can facilitate work, and whether the regional body can gain a seat at the table in deliberations over standards. Each region might organize the work different – perhaps through a consortium of national experts within the region, by industry specialists, or through a centralized system; the authority to introduce standards might follow parallel arrangements.

The work on international standards and regulatory programs is critically important and should proceed regardless of progress on the currency union. All countries will benefit and will help create the financial sector infrastructure to support the process of creating an union when such a decision is made.

Components of the policy situation

7.34. Several distinct steps can be identified in the policy process for unions.

Country situations

7.35. The first step is to understand as fully as possible the macroeconomic policy environment and institutions in each member country. The union must be able to interpret economic conditions in each country in the country's own context. This requires gathering information on national institutions, regulations, and policies. This information will include both qualitative descriptions and statistical information. The information gathering should begin early in the union building process because union procedures should be built to reflect common practices or to deal with divergent situations. In the Euroarea, many diverse national practices could not be fully reconciled prior to the start of the union, but each country was expected to make short-term practical accommodations to meet common needs, with later adoption of "steady state" practices fully in accord with union needs.

Current economic situations

7.36. The first step in actual policy making is understanding current economic and financial situations and problems and the policies currently in place. This requires quick and accurate reporting of a wide range of economic conditions. NCBs, national statistical offices, finance ministries, market regulators, and financial market reporters will all contribute to providing information on national economic situations. The union will need to set up reporting arrangements, sometimes acting through national officials and sometimes collecting information directly. This should be work of the policy committee of the future union, which will prepare an inventory of data needed and its availability from all countries. Standardization of reporting forms and methods can help this process, but this might not be possible because of the short set up period for the union and authority to do so might be lacking.

7.37. Of course, the accuracy and representativeness of the information is important. The union cannot make proper decisions if underlying data are distorted. This requires that members' resources to collect the data are adequate and that steps are taken to ensure accuracy. Also, data compilation procedures are likely to vary considerably between countries, especially early in the union process, and therefore good descriptions (metadata) of the information and how it is prepared should be available in order to permit proper interpretation.

7.38. A wide range of information will also be needed on international conditions and policies.

Collecting, organizing, and transferring data

7.39. The data (descriptive and quantitative) must be collected at the national level, transmitted to the union authorities, and quickly brought together in a usable and flexible form. The information communications process is a separate process that should be planned early in the process. A database needs to be created at the union level to handle the inflow of data and store it in a convenient form that can readily be used for research or for policy analysis. Both processes probably should be handled by a separate working group that includes technicians and key data users.

7.40. Steps in this process include data validation, aggregation or consolidation of the data, and generation of indicators or series used for policy purposes. At times, reported data might need to be supplemented by estimates, projections, or model-generated estimates in order to provide a more complete picture for policy analysis.

7.41. For presentation to policy officials, a specific analytic framework might be introduced – for example, in the United States, a flow of funds and balance sheet framework is used that incorporates projections out five years of financial markets data for use in discussing monetary policy options. Part of the work of setting up the union will be to consider whether to use such frameworks compatible with the policy goals and union institutions.

Policy analysis

7.42. Once information is pulled together, it is analyzed. This will include a detailed review of current conditions, preparation of projections based on continuation of current policy, and evaluations of the various policy options. Often, several options will be evaluated simultaneously in order to distinguish between different results and to report implications to policy officials. This can be high intensity work, with rapid reiterations of work as more is learned about situations or different policy options are suggested. Detailed written and statistical analysis will be prepared for presentation to policy makers.

Decision making

7.43. A wide-range of information is pulled together for presentation of policy officials and for decision-making. Actual decisions are made according to each union's governance and voting arrangements.

7.44. There will be a regular decision-making cycle so that conditions are reviewed and policy courses are altered multiple times during the year. Policy reviews six to ten times per year are common. The schedule for the policy reviews will affect the rhythm of the work flow throughout the year.
Arrangements must be in place for emergency decisions outside the regular cycle.

Implementation

7.45. Once a decision is made, it is implemented. Some decisions might involve public statements and dissemination of the decision in a range of venues, such as is done by the ECB immediately after its policy meetings. Other decisions, such as adjusting market liquidity situations, might be internal and are conveyed without public notice to the operational arms of the union. The behavior of the monetary policy or exchange rate instruments will be watched.

Analysis of results

7.46. After implementation, the effects of the policy should be assessed. This could be directly observed, such as observing changes in market interest rates or exchange rates, but sometimes involves changes in standard statistical macroeconomic indicators (GDP, employment, prices, etc.) and specific indicators (bank capital adequacy ratios, etc.). These assessments determine if policies are achieving desired results or should be adjusted, and thus feed into the next policy development cycle.

C. Fiscal Policy

7.47. Fiscal policy is an important consideration for currency unions. Unlike monetary or exchange rate policy, fiscal policy is exercised by the national government and is outside the direct influence and mandate of the central bank. However, the fiscal policy stance interacts with monetary, interest rate, and exchange rate policy and thus must be aligned with the requirements of the currency union.

Reasons for fiscal convergence

7.48. The Eurosystem takes the view that balanced and sustainable fiscal stances are important for the operation of the monetary union. Therefore, the Maastricht Treaty included provisions to promote sound fiscal conditions.

7.49. Reasons cited for fiscal soundness were to avoid squeezing out private investment, avoid upward price pressure, and limit upward interest rate pressure. Moreover, high returns on government debt stemming from over expenditure in some countries will induce capital movements into the overstimulated economy and out of other union economies. Also, because of the single monetary and exchange rate policies, governments will lack traditional constraints on their borrowing caused by the threat of capital outflows, exchange rate premia, interest rate penalties, and exchange rate pressures or depreciation. Without efforts to promote fiscal soundness throughout the union, EMU planners feared that lax fiscal conditions in some countries could harm the union as a whole and jeopardize its prospects for success.[169]

7.50. As a result of these concerns, two specific convergence indicators were put in place to (theoretically) limit government deficits and debt. Through most of the early years of the EMU countries generally usually remained within the limits or were close, with the exception of a serious breach by Germany due to the costs of incorporating the former German Democratic Republic. This resulted in greater flexibility in the system. However, the GFC in 2008 caused all countries to breech the limits and some had very large and unsustainable deficits. This created severe stresses within the system.

Automatic stabilizers in unions

7.51. Fiscal policy stabilizers continue to play an important role in the EMU, but at the national level. As economic activity recedes in an economy, tax payments fall and expenditures for the social safety net pick up, which both support economic activity in the affected country. This increases government deficits and debt and can cause totals to exceed levels permitted under convergence criteria. Subsequent efforts to constrain the budget to meet the convergence criteria can force tax increases or expenditures cuts, which can worsen the downturn unless the rules have provisions for deeper deficits or debts during recessions. (The experience in the Euroarea *prior* to the 2008 crisis was that the fiscal rules did not effectively constrain the ability of countries to undertake countercyclical fiscal policies, although during the crisis some Euroarea countries suffered large fiscal shocks and became constrained in providing additional stimulus.)

7.52. During the recovery phase there is danger that the deficit and debt levels might have permanently ratcheted up because of tax cuts during the downturn or cuts during the boom when revenues are strong. Unless structural steps are taken to get deficits down during the boom period, the deficit and debt situations could be worse in the next downturn. Thus, there was the view that oversight of the fiscal situation should continue throughout the business cycle.

7.53. In an union situation, the situation can be more complex because overall monetary policy might be out of line with the needs of individual member countries. For example, if the union policy stance is to slow overall growth by raising interest rates, this can harm individual economies that have slack growth. The slack economy could face slower general economic activity and higher fiscal costs because of the higher interest rates needed for the union. Moreover, the affected economy might have less room to counter the slowdown than otherwise because of the weakened fiscal situation.

[169] These concerns were especially strong during the period in which the EMU was negotiated because Europe had experienced a multi-decade struggle to contain inflationary pressures.

7.54. A second problem is a lack of cross-country fiscal stabilizers in an union situation. Even if union countries have identical tax and expenditure policies, stabilizers will operate only in separate economies and countercyclical adjustments might not flow across national borders, unless they are specifically designed to do so. Thus, there can be situations in which high revenues in one part of an union are not passed along to other countries in the union where economic conditions and tax revenues are weak. This contrasts to situations in a single country where fiscal transfers between regions can be large. The fiscal transfer effect has been shown to be strong in the United States, for example, where higher tax revenues from some regions offset increased payments in other regions, which tends to limit the impact on the overall U.S. budget – individual countries in a union do not receive this benefit.

7.55. Thus, membership in an union can put a country in an awkward situation where union monetary policies can potentially worsen fiscal conditions[170] but the country has no access to fiscal redistributions because each country operates a separate fiscal regime. Future unions can consider whether any form of fiscal redistribution and automatic stabilization method can be developed union-wide, but this might not be possible or possible only to a limited extent.[171] [172]

Government bond rate differentials

7.56. The fiscal situations of union member countries can affect the rates governments pay to borrow funds. A country within an union with a large fiscal deficit might pay premium rates to attract funds, which can increase overall interest rates in the union and punish union member countries with sound fiscal situations. Overall economic demand can be affected by the situation of a single union country with a large deficit. This type of situation was examined while designing the EMU and was considered unacceptable and thus was a reason for strict fiscal rules.

7.57. In fact, shortly after the creation of the EMU, government bond rates quickly converged, with investors convinced that oversight of countries' fiscal situations provided assurance that government debt would be repaid. With this assurance, differences in government bond rates were quickly arbitraged away. Divergent government borrowing rates only developed later.[173]

D. Excessive Deficit Procedure and Stability and Growth Pact (SGP)

Overview

7.58. The Maastricht Treaty incorporated language to enforce fiscal discipline in the member countries. The "Excessive Deficit Procedure" (EDP) has specific steps that the EU could take to warn countries that their fiscal situations needed correction and to punish the countries if they failed to correct the problem.

7.59. The SGP is the cornerstone of the budgetary discipline regime. Its aim is to clarify and speed up the excessive deficit procedure so it acts as a genuine deterrent. It supplements the 1993 Regulation laying down the procedures to be followed in connection with excessive deficits.

[170] An union member country with an overheated economy can also be adversely affected by the single union monetary policy if it is too stimulative for the affected country. However, this is likely to result in stronger fiscal conditions and does not create the same types of fiscal problems discussed in the text above.

[171] Two planned unions have considered having fiscal transfers between member countries.

[172] In the absence of a fiscal redistribution mechanism, other more macroeconomic mechanisms might be needed to promote convergence across the union, such as price adjustments that affect trade, labor migration, etc.

[173] The ECB website regularly publishes series on government borrowing rates: "Harmonized long-term interest rates for convergence assessment purposes".

7.60. The SGP was adopted in 1997 to clarify the rules related to application of the excessive deficit procedure of the Maastricht Treaty. The treaty only set the quantitative limits but did not describe the budgetary policy. Also, at the time there had been some concerns that restrictions imposed by the convergence criteria limit national flexibility to promote growth through fiscal policy.

Test box: Stress-induced changes to the SGP

Beginning in 2002 France and Germany began running deficits, which led to a special EU meeting as some countries pushed for more explicit mechanisms to ensure fiscal soundness. The SGP was subsequently modified in 2005 largely to clarify treatment of divergences from the criteria and national responsibilities to return to adherence to the deficit criteria.

The GFC beginning in 2008 caused all Euroarea countries to miss their budget targets. The ECB said, "Given the downside risks to economic activity, the revised pact is likely to be put to the test." (ECB 2008f) Subsequently, a number of specific fiscal rules were introduced.

The 2020 pandemic crisis caused Euroarea real GDP to fall around 8%, raise fiscal deficits to 60% of GDP, and raise the debt ratio to 100% of GDP. Emergency responses included a range of fiscal and liquidity supporting actions – actions to return to more stable fiscal conditions were recommended but with realization that recovery would be drawn out and uneven depending on individual country situations. (European Commission 2020) Changes to the SGP and its surrounding fiscal rulebook can be expected.

7.61. The SGP argued that sound fiscal positions were needed throughout the union so that problems in individual states do not penalize other members by affecting interest rates and undermining overall confidence in the common currency.[174] In 1997, the EU member states signed the SGP followed by two enacting regulations.

7.62. One Regulation, referred to as the "Preventative Arm" of the SGP, dealt with the surveillance of budgetary positions and surveillance and coordination of policies. It required members to strive to follow balanced medium-term budgetary stances that are sustainable and which have a safety margin to avoid short-term government deficits.[175] Countries must also submit "stability and convergence programs".

7.63. Another regulation, referred to as the "Corrective Arm", seeks to speed up and clarify implementation of the Excessive Deficit Procedure (EDP). It imposes strict and timely implementation of the EDP and provides sanctions for lapses.

7.64. The stability and convergence programs began in the fall of 1998, just before the start of the union. Implementation of the SGP ran into problems after several years because Germany and France, the two largest economies in the union, breeched the SGP limits, which resulted in a major reform in 2005, as described in the section *Reform of the SGP*, below.

7.65. The global financial crisis caused all Eurosystem economies to violate the deficit convergence criterion and caused serious deficits in several countries, especially Greece. The EU rescue operations for Greece were accompanied by steps to tighten surveillance and penalties.

Features of the SGP

7.66. The GSP requires members to meet two fiscal requirements – a cyclically adjusted safety margin provides a view of budget sustainability over the cycle, and an actual fiscal balance for use in the applying the EDP. An ECB (2008f) analysis of compliance

[174] In which it anticipated that fiscal convergence at low levels was needed to avoid the type of situation created by the Greek crisis.

[175] This is interpreted to mean that although automatic stabilizers are permitted to operate freely during slowdowns (which increases deficits), countries should have enough reserves to prevent the deficit from rising above 3 percent of GDP.

of countries to both measures concluded that although the requirements contribute to restraining fiscal balances there was considerable lack of compliance.

Preventative Arm of the SGP

7.67. For the preventative requirement, the fiscal safety margin uses a cyclically adjusted fiscal balance (which after 2003 is calculated net of temporary or one-time revenue or expenditure adjustments). This basis is designed to convey information about the budget in which automatic stabilizers are permitted to operate freely during slowdowns, but allow countries to have a large enough reserves to prevent the deficit from rising above 3 percent of GDP. Initially, a calculation of the sufficiency of reserves was made by calculating "minimum benchmarks" based on estimated budget elasticities and output responses to deficits. Later, a stricter interpretation was applied under which cyclically adjusted budgets should be nearly balanced with deficits of one-half percent or less. The stricter standard was intended to enforce long-term budget sustainability in light of the future burdens from an aging population.

7.68. Reform of the SGP in 2005 permitted countries to set their own medium-term objectives. A medium-term budget in near balance or in surplus was sought. The reforms also called for a safety margin to defend the 3 percent deficit ceiling, encouraged rapid progress toward a sustainable position, and allowed room to undertake public investment. The reforms also dealt with the ERM II countries, who were to aim for cyclically adjusted budget deficits of 1 percent or be in surplus.[176] Countries not achieving the target are expected to achieve it during the next cycle. The annual pace of adjustment was suggested at one-half percent of GDP.

7.69. An ECB analysis of the compliance of countries to the requirements of the reformed Preventative Regulation concluded that breeches have been "repeated and persistent" and that implementation has "lacked sufficient rigor and political will". (ECB 2008f, p. 56) Greece, France, Italy, and Portugal never met the requirements. Also, the United Kingdom had not met the requirement during the six previous years. These data did not imply that the SGP's preventative features were ineffective in reducing the overall levels of government deficits, because governments do strive to move toward the targets, and major breeches have led to corrective actions in the following budget or two, but it does indicate that numerous countries have not felt tightly bound by the requirements.

Corrective Arm of the SGP and the EDP

7.70. The balances used for the "corrective" part of the SGP are the actual budget results or the planned actual deficit. The requirement is that the budget deficit not exceed 3 percent of GDP, and breeches are subject to initiation of additional oversight and sanctions. The ECB analysis shows that breeches are not common, but also not rare. The incidence is clearly related to overall economic health within the business cycle, with higher deficits in periods of slow growth.

7.71. The EDP is started if the deficit exceeds 3 percent. The European Commission prepares a report on the country's budget situation. The report notes the size and structure of the deficit and whether the amount of the breech is small, temporary, due to one-time situations, or exceptional in some way. An

[176] "Each Member State shall have a differentiated medium-term objective for its budgetary position. These country-specific medium-term budgetary objectives might diverge from the requirement of a close to balance or in surplus position. They shall provide a safety margin with respect to the 3 % of GDP government deficit ratio; they shall ensure rapid progress towards sustainability and, taking this into account, they shall allow room for budgetary maneuver, considering in particular the needs for public investment.

Taking these factors into account, for Member States that have adopted the euro and for ERM2 Member States the country-specific medium-term budgetary objectives shall be specified within a defined range between – 1 % of GDP and balance or surplus, in cyclically adjusted terms, net of one-off and temporary measures."

exceptional breech might be due to an unexpected economic downturn. If the deficit is not temporary nor explained by exceptional circumstances, the Council will conclude that an excessive deficit situation exists.

7.72. If an excessive deficit situation exists, a recommendation is made to the country to correct it. Correction should occur within the following year. This means that exceptions should not last more than two years. If timely correction does not occur the Council issues a formal notice to the country that opens the way for sanctions. With the easing of the sanctions regime following the reforms in 2005, the Council may repeat issuing notices and can extend deadlines if conditions warrant. Thus, although it should occur rarely, excessive deficit situations could be permitted for several years.

7.73. The ECB review of application of the corrective arm showed that a majority of Euroarea countries had breached their deficit limits one or more times. In several cases, the breech was quickly corrected in line with the intention of the excessive deficit procedure, but during 2003 through 2005 when economic growth was sluggish about half of the countries had breeches. The most notable problems occurred with France and Germany beginning in 2002. Deadlines to correct the problems were set by the Council, but it became clear that neither country would make corrections by the deadline. The Council proposed that a formal notice be issued, but no action was taken, basically suspending action in light of the unwillingness of the two largest Euroarea countries to undertake corrective actions. A deadlock ensued that ultimately led to a review of the SGP and its reform with more flexible features.

7.74. An additional convergence criterion in the Euroarea is that the government debt should be under 60 percent of GDP or should be declining. The failure of numerous countries to reduce the size of their deficits has prevented a number of countries from reducing their total government debt and in some cases caused the debt burden to move in the wrong direction. In 2007, seven of the fifteen Euroarea countries had debt ratios over 60 percent.

7.75. Finally, the ECB review showed that numerous countries often had budget outcomes that differed from the projections, either from expenditure increases during the year or from revenue shortages. These problems have been widespread.

Reform of the SGP

7.76. The GSP was revised in 2005, following the breeches by France and Germany that led to suspension of the EDP and discussions for more flexible application of the rules.[177] A meeting of the European Council of Ministers agreed to a more flexible interpretation of the GSP in which debt sustainability would be considered – countries with low debt levels and hence more sustainable positions would have longer to move toward balance, and periods of abnormally slow growth were added to deep recessions as reasons for forbearance. Also, the deficit procedure was permitted to take into account public investment, investment in research and development, and costs of structural reforms because these were seen as providing long-term productive benefits. Also, the procedure would take into account expenditures linked to the unification of Europe, which reflected the need to address the large costs associated with German unification. The reform also changed the emphasis to state that the purpose of the GSP is "to assist rather than punish" through surveillance and peer pressure.

7.77. A macroeconomic aspect of the reform is that by easing away from rapid implementation of actions to reduce the fiscal deficit, countries have greater flexibility to apply counter-cyclical policies, and thus the SGP would be less likely to further repress economic activity in slack periods.[178]

[177] Some have said that the situation would have been handled differently if the problem countries had not been the two largest in the union.

[178] One major policy action not foreseen in designing the SGP was a call for simultaneous stimulus during crises to pump prime the EU economies as a whole.

Text box: Audits and revisions of fiscal data

A fiscal audit is a thorough independent review of statistical measures of the size and composition of the fiscal situation, identification of vulnerabilities, and recommendations for improvements.

Government accounts are highly complex and often decentralized and poorly organized. The measurement of the overall government deficit and debt is challenging under any circumstance. However, where governments are being rated based on their accounts, such as under the SGP, there can be disincentives to be highly accurate and sometimes information can be hidden. Also, statistical rules for measuring the accounts might not be understood or fully applied.

Both the numerator and denominator in the Euroarea criterion are statistical estimates and subject to error or bias. Both need to be accurate, but errors in the numerator – the deficit – have a greater weight.

In implementing the SGP, several cases occurred where fiscal audits were ordered or statistical revisions made that resulted in new information that countries had breached their limits. This has occurred with Portugal, Italy, and Greece. For Portugal, the structural deficit for preventative purposes was revised upward by 2 percent of GDP. For Greece, an audit found that Greece had breached the convergence criteria limits from 1997 until it entered the Euroarea in 2002. That is, Greece was able to adopt the euro only because poor quality data hid its fiscal deficit. Continuing problems with the Greek data have resulted in Eurostat reviews of the Greek deficit data. In other cases, Spain and Austria had actual deficits above the limit, but were not subject to the deficit procedures at the time because the deficits estimates were revised upward after the fact.

During the GFC, preliminary evidence suggested that Greece's fiscal statistics were very misleading and that actions had been taken that seemingly disguised the size of the deficit. In response, the EU demanded greater transparence and surveillance to ensure better quality data.

These examples indicate that fiscal data quality issues are highly important. Good quality fiscal data are needed for policy planning and to assess the impacts of policy actions. For convergence criteria or where there is some regulatory purpose, data quality can be especially important. Continuing effort is needed to ensure the quality of the data, in terms of accuracy, full coverage, lack of biases, and timeliness. Comparability of data between countries is also important. Special audits or reviews of data quality could be called for.

For such reasons, the union itself might need to take efforts to promote compilation of good quality fiscal statistics in the member countries, through steps such as setting standards, providing technical assistance, providing effective oversight, or undertaking audits. Technical contributions from international standards setters can also help in this effort.

Text box: Sovereign Debt Restructuring

The Greek fiscal crisis that began in 2009 and ran for most of the following decade caused widespread disruption to the Greek economy and led to many emergency economic actions, including loans from the IMF, ECB, and Eurogroup[179], tax increases, and a negotiated 50% reduction in debt to banks, among other actions. The crisis was a dramatic breakdown on the Maastricht discipline under crisis conditions and forced participation of European fiscal and monetary in a rescue of an individual member country. Some commentators saw the crisis as potentially leading to a breakup of the Euroarea. Kawai (cited in Rowley 2010) argued that future unions will have to consider having mechanisms in place to deal with such possibilities.

[179] The Eurogroup is consultative group of European finance ministers that began informally just before the launch of the euro. It was formally recognized in the 2009 Treaty of Lisbon.

Evaluation of the SGP for planned unions

7.78. In summary, the SGP certainly contributed to reductions in the size of government deficits, but in its first real test failed to enforce sanctions on France and Germany, and ultimately faced serious effects from the Greek crisis. Moreover, incidences of breaches have not been rare, and continuing problems are experienced in setting budget targets in line with the SGP criteria and observing projected budgets.

7.79. The ECB drew a number of conclusions about the SGP in a 2008 analysis. (ECB 2008f, p. 64);

> Slippages in controlling government expenditures *per* targets have been "persistent and widespread."
>
> Institutions are needed to promote adherence to fiscal limits, including designing medium-term fiscal frameworks. Effective fiscal management procedures are also needed.
>
> Large revisions and uncertainty over data quality are serious concerns and a sound statistical basis for fiscal information is needed.
>
> EU level institutions should exercise pressure and strictly apply the rules.
>
> Attention needs to be paid to the linkages between fiscal positions and broad macroeconomic conditions, sustainability, and economic imbalances.
>
> Similarly, attention needs to be paid to the relationships between fiscal conditions and long-term growth and employment.
>
> Attention needs to be paid to future fiscal liabilities stemming from aging European populations.

7.80. Lessons for future unions are that the applying rules on fiscal situations as part of the monetary union program will not be easy. There are technical and political challenges to be faced.

7.81. Fiscal planning and management mechanisms need to be strengthened in all member countries and for union institutions. This also contributes to more effective fiscal policy development and implementation, which are important in themselves. This is more important in unions because countries are *a priori* denied access to central bank monetization of deficits.

7.82. Statistical coverage of government and its institutions must be improved. Accurate knowledge of budgetary conditions is necessary for solid policy making and analysis of policy actions. Poor quality information and large statistical revisions will be reviewed by other member countries and union offices and will prove embarrassing.

7.83. Macroeconomic policy research and coordination can be strengthened to highlight the interactions between fiscal actions and macroeconomic conditions and exchange rate and monetary policy choices made by the member countries and the union.

7.84. Sensible targets for deficits and debt reduction need to be developed. Low targets that minimize distortions for policy purposes, such as in the Euroarea, are only suitable where initial imbalances are not large or as long-term goals. They however lose credibility where breeches are common or when routine cyclical economic slowdowns result in breeches. Thus, targets should be set to encourage continuing improvements in fiscal balances.[180]

7.85. The tendency of national authorities to be insufficiently rigorous in enforcing fiscal balances must be recognized and means found to deal with it.

7.86. Finally, future unions need to decide if external grant assistance is included in fiscal balance measures.

[180] This strategy is intended to bring about gradual convergence of fiscal balances for all member countries. Some countries might have low or no deficits. In contrast, in the EMU the chosen strategy is that all member countries needed to reach the targets prior to joining the union.

E. Appendix – Application of SGP Sanctions

This section describes steps taken under the SGP to determine whether an excessive deficit exists and to apply sanctions if needed.

The SGP says that the "reference value" for the government deficit is 3 percent of GDP. Government is defined as "general government", which includes the central government and state/provincial and local governments.[181] A deficit over 3 percent is deemed "exceptional" if it is due to a major unusual event outside control of the government, or results from a severe downturn with negative GDP growth or a prolonged period of low growth. These are deemed temporary if the European Commission forecasts that the deficit will fall below 3 percent when the unusual event is over. (The widespread deficits above 3 percent stemming from the GFC thus were all deemed "exceptional", but most were far from temporary.)

An economic assessment is made of each country's situation, which is summarized in a report passed for a political decision whether an excessive deficit exists. The analysis must consider all relevant information, such as medium-term economic prospects as a measure of potential growth, cyclical conditions, long-term development policies in the Lisbon Agenda and its successor Europe 2020[182], investments promoting research and innovation, and improvements made to improve finances.

After reviewing the situation, the Economic Commission prepares a report for the Economic and Financial Committee which decides based on a qualified majority within four months whether further action is justified. The country is allowed to argue its case before the decision.

If an excessive deficit is found to exist, the Council privately recommends actions to take place within six months to correct the deficit in the following year. It is expected that the minimum annual improvement in the deficit will be .5% of GDP. Revised recommendations are permitted if negative events occur after the initial judgment. However, the excessive deficit procedure is suspended if the country acts in compliance with the recommendations.

The country can be required to report on its compliance with the recommendations. If the country fails to take effective action within six months, the Council can choose to make its recommendations public. Then within two months the Council can give notice that adverse actions can be imposed. A decision to penalize will be made within four months.

The normal schedule should result in action within 16 months. However, if the deficit breech is found to have been deliberate, expedited action can be taken.

Sanctions can be applied if a member fails to take effective action. The first sanction is a non-interest-bearing deposit with the EU. It consists of a fixed component of .2% of GDP and a variable component of .1% of GDP for each percentage that the deficit exceeds 3%, up to a maximum deposit of .5% of GDP. An additional deposit can be applied during the following year if the excessive deficit continues. The deposits are converted into a nonrefundable fine if the excessive deposit is not corrected after two years.

Interest on deposits and fines will be distributed to other union member countries not having excessive deficits in proportion to their capital share in the ECB.

---

[181] General government was chosen for the reference value for two reasons. First, governments are organized in different ways in different European countries and only total general government was comparable between countries. Second, the total fiscal position is often most relevant for macroeconomic analysis.

[182] The Lisbon Agenda created in 2000 was a 10-year agenda to promote greater productivity and dynamic economic growth in all EU countries. A wide range of programs were included. It is largely considered to have had poor success. It was followed by a second 10-year program, Europe 2020.

As is clear from the above description, the SGP sanctions process is long and complex with clauses that can delay or defer sanctions. It is helpful in encouraging countries to comply with the fiscal convergence criterion. Conversely, countries have been hesitant to apply sanctions. Future unions will need to create a system that can encourage fiscal convergence. The SGP can provide some guidance, but it has experienced many problems and thus probably needs to be modified before applying to future unions.

Timeline

Preparatory period	Compile fiscal accounts per IMF *Government Financial Statistics Manual*
Early actions (four years prior)	Agree on convergence criteria for deficits and debt Define compilation standards for fiscal criteria
Three years prior	Implement government accounting standards
24 months prior	Convergence Reports Design union policy quantitative database Set data requirements for NCBs Report on fiscal convergence
18 months Prior	Set up of union policy quantitative database
Final 12 months	Complete set up of union policy quantitative database Full report on adherence to fiscal indicators
Final 6 months	Initiate sanctions regime if applicable
Run-up to union	All elements of fiscal review and sanctions process in place
Union day	Prepare and publish report on fiscal status of union member countries at start of union All elements of fiscal review and sanctions process operational
Union steady state	All procedures operational

Chapter 8 – International Economic Relations of an Union

What will be the international economic role of the union and its membership in international bodies? How does it relate to the policies of member countries?

A. Introduction

8.1. The movement to build currency unions introduces a new type of institution into the center of the global financial system. A currency union involves ceding of sovereignty related to the national financial system from nations (which form the inter*national* system) to a *supra*national (above the nation) entity. The creation of supranational bodies within the global system is nothing new, but within the financial sphere the transfer of control of financial matters at the heart of national sovereignty – currency, reserve assets, and the exchange rate – is unprecedented. Moreover, if all the planned unions come to fruition, the very nature of global financial relationships will change, with a small number of currency unions becoming as important as countries in international financial matters. This chapter looks at how currency unions fit into the global financial system, their relationships with nations and with other international financial institutions, and how they might operate within a changed global financial system.

B. Relations with the IMF

8.2. Countries within unions are also members of the IMF. The IMF is the broadest international financial organization with about 190 members. Membership involves a wide range of obligations and privileges vis-à-vis the IMF, and each member country shares in the governance of the institution. A country's interaction with the IMF is largely a function of its size and level of income – although all members contribute resources to the IMF and are eligible to receive assistance in the event of need, large high-income countries provide more resources and in exchange gain greater voice in policy; in contrast, low-income and emerging economies have a lesser voice in policy and are more likely to be recipients of IMF monetary assistance under policy supervision. This broad split is reflected in the make-up of the EMU versus other current and planned unions – the EMU is comprised mostly of high and middle income countries that provide resources and have a large voice in IMF governance; a GCC union would occupy a sort of middle ground in that it will also be comprised of donor countries but still faces a large development agenda; other current unions and future unions will be heavily weighted toward low or middle income countries likely to need both financial and technical assistance and faee long-term developmental challenges. This split implies that the EMU's relations with the IMF are very different from what most future unions will face.

8.3. Membership of a country in an union does not abrogate its rights with and obligations to the IMF (although they might be modified to reflect practical circumstances). For example, union countries still retain their voting rights in the IMF and all countries remain eligible to receive emergency assistance from the IMF. Countries' obligations to the IMF also continue, such as the obligation to undergo regular surveillance. All members are expected to provide information to the IMF, be subject to surveillance, and abide by the codes of behavior to the international community. (However, practical adaptations can be made to make exercise of these rights and obligations more effective or a better fit for the union situation.)

8.4. Membership of a country in a monetary union changes the nature of the oversight by the IMF. Surveillance of individual member countries continues but with modifications. For example, surveillance of monetary and exchange rate policy must be done at the union level, which is the level at which these union-wide policies are formulated and conducted. Otherwise, the rights and obligations of the member countries vis-à-vis the IMF are legally little changed and IMF oversight over other aspects of a country's situation continues to be conducted at the country level. There is an additional concern that individual countries need to maintain their own economic and financial stability in order to not destabilize the union or other member countries.

8.5. In 2007, the IMF (2007b) reviewed its policies over surveillance of members' exchange rate policies, which included some conclusions about how surveillance should be conducted over member countries of currency unions. Key aspects of that review and the subsequent guidance to IMF staff are listed below.

At the union level:

8.6. The 2007 decision states that it also applies to members of currency unions[183] and that they remain subject to all obligations under IMF Article IV surveillance. This means that each member is accountable for union policies conducted on its behalf. Parallel to the national situation, the IMF assesses whether union exchange rate policies promote external stability, and also if union domestic policies promote domestic macroeconomic stability and thus contribute to the external stability of the union.[184]

8.7. Because of the interplay between domestic and external policies of currency unions and their member countries, surveillance of unions must accompany the surveillance of the member economies. For example, the concept of external stability is defined only in relation to the balance of payments and exchange rate behavior at the union level. Thus, surveillance of exchange rate stability is done only at the level of the union. Similarly, domestic policies implemented at the union level (such as monetary and interest rate policy) are under union-level surveillance.

8.8. Elements of IMF surveillance of unions include;

External stability, fundamental alignment or misalignment of currencies, and observance of principles related to exchange rate policies are reviewed only at the union level.

IMF staff consultations with union officials related to the union level issues.

Reviews of unions consider relevant developments in the union and provide assessments on exchange rate policies. This includes observance of principles and review of union-level indicators. (This obliges unions to compile union-level balance of payments and exchange rate statistics.)

Assessments of the exchange rate level, including whether there is fundamental misalignment. The concept "fundamental misalignment" applies only to the union level. (However, in mid-2009 references to fundamental misalignment were dropped because they created difficulties in eliciting country cooperation for reviews.)

Assessments of the union's external stability[185]

Assessments of monetary policy.
Assessments of other domestic policies implemented at the union level to gauge their impact on external stability of the union and members' domestic situations.

[183] In looser regional organizations, such as CAMC or the CMIM, the primary level of IMF surveillance is at the national level and separate surveillance will not be made at the regional level. However, the IMF might selectively be involved in aspects of the work of regional organizations, to exchange information or to advise. For example, the IMF observes at CMIM Economic Research and Policy Discussions.

[184] By extension, structural vulnerabilities of currency unions that threaten external stability (such as bank supervisory gaps, weak institutional arrangements, vulnerable payments systems, or structural weaknesses in financial markets) could also fall under the IMF surveillance umbrella. However, such items might be more likely to be medium- or long-term issues that could be reviewed under different programs, such as Financial Stability Assessments (FSA). As examples, the ECCU and Central African Economic and Monetary Community countries have undergone FSAs.

[185] External instability at the union level can give rise to disruptive exchange rate movements. It is viewed only at the union level because only union external conditions can cause the disruption. Events in individual countries can affect the external stability of the union, but they are considered to be disruptive only in that they affect the union's external stability. Indeed, union actions might buffer or offset national level disruptions resulting net in no union level external instability.

At the member country level:

8.9. Surveillance of union member countries focuses on matters that influence the current or future external stability of the country. The IMF analyzes the situations and provides advice on matters that affect external stability, which includes exchange rate policies as well as monetary, fiscal, and financial sector conditions that affect the macroeconomic situation. The IMF considers union countries as promoting external stability when their policies support domestic stability, foster domestic growth with price stability, and avoid monetary disruptions.

Surveillance covers individual country domestic policies. Domestic instability[186] that affects overall union conditions is a concern.

8.10. Surveillance also covers individual member country balance of payments. Imbalances at the country level are a channel through which stresses can be transmitted through the union. (This obliges countries to continue compilation of their balance of payments.)

The *real* exchange rate of member countries will be assessed.

This reflects a need to understand each member's overall macroeconomic conditions. This includes the effect of external competitiveness (both vis-à-vis other union members and countries outside the union) on growth prospects. This information is needed to provide advice to individual member countries.

If the real exchange rate of a member country is assessed to be under- or over-valued, the surveillance report will discuss whether the union exchange rate is under- or over-valued. This is needed to determine if policy adjustments are needed at the country or union levels.

No assessment will be made of individual countries' nominal exchange rates.

The IMF states that certain developments indicate thorough surveillance should be undertaken;

Protracted one-way exchange market intervention

Official borrowing that is unsustainable or creates excessive liquidity risks. or which involves extensive sterilization or prolonged official or quasi-official accumulation[187] of excessive amounts of foreign assets *for balance of payment purposes*.

Introduction of restrictions or incentives to affect the balance of payments

Introduction of restrictions or incentives to affect the inflows or outflows of capital to affect the balance of payments

Pursuing, for balance of payments purposes, monetary or financial policies that abnormally encourage or discourage capital flows

Fundamental exchange rate misalignment (as noted above, references to fundamental misalignment have been dropped)

Prolonged current account surpluses or deficits

Large external vulnerabilities, including liquidity risks resulting from private capital flows.

8.11. Some of the above conditions can affect unions as a whole. Unions that have the above developments in their balance of payments can be considered to have a fundamental problem in their balance of payments, which provides a basis for

[186] Domestic stability is defined as "orderly growth with reasonable price stability" and "orderly underlying economic and financial conditions."

[187] Inclusion of quasi-official accumulations means that SWFs are included.

additional surveillance by the IMF of the union balance of payments situation. In effect, the union itself has come under the surveillance umbrella of the IMF, which could provide advice related to the significant problem affecting the union as a whole. This in effect transfers individual country legal obligations to the IMF to the union, even though the treaty signed by the countries with the IMF makes no mention of such a transfer.

8.12. An interesting corollary to this is that if problems arise for a union in those policy areas related to the union as a whole, would the IMF put the union itself under a program, permit it to receive IMF assistance, and monitor its compliance? It would be a major innovation in the governance of the international system if this were to occur.

8.13. Regarding the potential legal implications, Sean Hagan (2009), the IMF General Counsel, in a speech at the ECB said (perhaps anticipating situations that could arise from the then-prevailing financial market turmoil) that it is the Fund view that – regardless of use of a common currency – each union country maintains its own balance of payments and that imbalances can occur that might call for Fund assistance.[188] He said that the IMF has provided assistance to members of other unions.[189]

8.14. In summary, the analysis of balance of payments problems in countries within unions envisions that the causes could stem either from country or union policies, or a mixture. The IMF will engage in policy discussions with countries and unions on appropriate issues and recommend policies. However, currently, the IMF can only provide aid at the national level and not to the union. At some future time, this asymmetry might be addressed, but it would involve a substantial change in the nature of IMF oversight and whether will ever occur is uncertain.

C. Relations with other international organizations

8.15. This section looks at potential relations of future unions with international financial organizations other than the IMF. The types of participation by the ECB provide a model.

Relations with international organizations

8.16. The ECB is actively involved in the activities of numerous international organizations. Often, Euroarea countries are also involved as individual country members of the IO (sometimes as a founding member of the organization). When both the ECB and countries are involved, "pragmatic" arrangements or adjustments are made, which reflect the institutions, the issues at hand, and the relative expertise and resources of the countries and ECB.

8.17. Future unions are likely to become involved in many of the same institutions, either as full members or observers. In some future unions, because the union might have more resources, expertise, or more significant size than many of the individual member countries, the union might have a greater role than individual countries. In many cases, the union might participate where no member country had participated before, which will increase the involvement of developing or emerging economies in the global financial system. This increase could be an important change in the governance and operation of the system and the international financial organizations.

8.18. The *Organization for Economic Cooperation and Development (OECD)* provides a forum for international discussion of a full range of economic

[188] This reinforces the need for union member countries to continue compiling balance of payments statistics and to continue IMF Article IV consultations to assess member countries' balance of payments situations.

[189] At the same meeting, law professor René Smits said that if numerous new unions develop there could be governance changes at the IMF, and that major changes in international governance could occur if the IMF chooses to give appropriate recognition to the new unions. He added that this could significantly increase representation for lower income countries.

and social issues. The membership is limited to major countries, but there are substantial links with other countries. The EC is a standing member, and the ECB participates in matters related to the Eurosystem. The OECD carries out and publishes reviews of the economic situation in the member countries for intergovernmental discussions and recommendations for voluntary national action. The OECD also operates numerous specialized committees, in which the ECB participates along with Euroarea members.

8.19. The *Bank for International Settlements (BIS)* is an international banking organization in Basel, Switzerland owned by central banks that serves as a bank for central banks and fosters cooperation between central banks. It is a counterparty for central bank financial transactions and can act as an agent or trustee in connection with international financial operations – for example, carrying out intervention at the request of a member country. Importantly, it acts as an umbrella for numerous specialized bodies responsible for developing international standards and best practices to operate the international financial infrastructure.[190]

8.20. In 1999, at the invitation of the BIS, the ECB became a shareholder in the BIS with voting rights. Membership was necessary in order for the ECB to be able to carry out international transactions in the same way as other central banks. The ECB participates in a wide range of BIS activities. At that time, the Statutes of the BIS were amended to make eligible for membership "a monetary zone extending over more than one sovereign state"[191], which means that future unions will also be eligible for BIS membership.

8.21. The *G7* is a group of major country finance ministers and central bank governors that meet regularly for informal discussions on economic and financial topics[192] that might lead to policy changes by international organizations. After the creation of the Euroarea, the President of the ECB and the President of the Eurogroup participate in sessions related to macroeconomic and exchange rate policies. The three national representatives from Euroarea countries are absent from these sessions.

8.22. The *G10* is a group of major country finance ministers and central bank governors that focuses on IMF activities and international financial stability. The President of the ECB participates as an observer. The G10 meets every two months at the BIS to discuss international financial conditions. The G10 governors have set up several extremely important committees, in which the ECB participates, and in which future unions will participate, that provide oversight and standards for operation of the international financial system. Some of the groups deal with highly specific technical topics, but which are part of the infrastructure of the international financial system and critical for its smooth operation. Future unions are likely to have to deal with these organizations. They include;

Basel Committee on Banking Supervision (BCBS) is the key international standard setter for banking supervision. Virtually all countries comply with the Basel standards which provide comprehensive goals and best practices for banks and bank supervisors

.

Financial Stability Board (FSB) conducts research and consultations promoting greater

[190] The EMI initially resided at the BIS. Among other important entities resident at the BIS are the BCBS, CPSS, IOSCO, and the BIS Innovation Hub that looks at impacts of technology innovation on the international financial system. Future unions will work with all these and other BIS-sponsored entities.

[191] Statutes of the Bank for International Settlements of 20 January 1930, as amended on November 1999. At http://www.bis.org/about/index.htm.

[192] The G8 was a similar structure that included Russia, but in 2014 Russia was ejected from the group after the invasion of the Crimea.

financial stability and reduction in risk in the international financial system.[193]

Committee on Payment and Settlement Systems (CPSS), which promotes development of strong payments and settlement systems.

Committee on the Global Financial System (CGFS), which examines potential stresses to the financial system and seeks to promote greater efficiency and stability in the system.

Markets Committee, which regularly reviews developments and conditions in financial markets.

International Association of Deposit Insurers. (IADI)

International Association of Insurance Supervisors. (IAIS)

8.23. The *G20* is a new international consultative group that includes major developed countries and key emerging market countries. It was formed to give greater voice in international fora to emerging and developing economies. It gained considerable importance during the GFC because of more aggressive involvement in governance issues and inclusion of China, Russia, India, and other large emerging economies. Both the ECB and the EU Presidency are regular members and participate in preparatory sessions and meetings. The heads of the IMF and World Bank are also members. The G20 is a far more inclusive group than the G7 and includes more than three quarters of world GDP and trade and thus has greater legitimacy in global governance. However, Africa and Central Asia are underrepresented – membership of future unions in an expanded G20 would make the group even more representative and powerful.

8.24. The *Continuous Linked Settlement (CLS) System* and *CLS Bank* is a new system designed to provide efficient settlement services in foreign exchange and a wide range of foreign exchange instruments and derivatives and remove the risk of default on one leg of an international payments transaction. Created only in 2002, the CLS system has become the international standard for effective and secure settlements, while providing large cost savings because of multilateral netting of transactions. Future unions should establish links with the system to provide secure and cost-effective settlements services for their own transactions and for banking systems in the union.

8.25. International payments and settlement arrangements are undergoing rapid change from introduction of new technologies, of which the forthcoming development CBDCs is likely to be the most important. Efficient cross-border payments systems and subsequent increased integration of financial systems are at the heart of the rationale for currency unions – this is an area to be watched very closely.

Regional adherence to global standards

8.26. In recent decades, there has been a major emphasis on defining international standards and best practices and encouraging their adoption. This can improve the operation of the global financial system while reducing or eliminating harmful or unfair practices. For unions, adoption of global practices and standards throughout an union creates a level playing field among union members that can be important for the cohesion of the union and can bring economic benefits for the union. Thus, work on defining and adopting global standards should become a core union function.

FSB Compendium of global standards

8.27. Much recent work with global standards has focused on the stability of the financial sector. When the FSF was founded in 1999, its first major

[193] The FSB was set up in 1999 by the G7 as the Financial Stability Forum in the wake of crises in Asia, Russia, and Brazil as a venue that could help identify threats and coordinate responses. It was reorganized in 2009 as the FSB, with expansion to cover the G20 and shifting functions from consultation to taking a greater role in coordination of responses.

task was to undertake a comprehensive review of international codes and practices related to international financial stability and support of a well- functioning international financial system.

8.28. The FSF produced a Compendium[194] of international standards and actively promoted the adoption and effective implementation of the standards as means to improve soundness and performance of individual economies and the global system. A search was made of possibly relevant standards and dozens of standards and codes promulgated by a wide range of organizations were found. Initially, 12 standards were selected as high priorities for adoption, and programs to support their adoption were set up by the IMF, BIS, and other agencies. The list was later expanded to cover regulation of Islamic banks. The key standards and the responsible agencies are listed below.

8.29. Future unions will need to build expertise in these areas at the union level and by using expertise at NCBs, payments systems, supervisors, accountancy and audit bodies, and the like. The unions

8.30. will need to translate the global standards into local equivalents compatible with local institutions, undertake training, assist in implementation in all union countries, monitor operations and results, and deal with problems. These are expensive tasks that need sustained programs to meet the challenges.

8.31. When the EMU was created, there were few organized global programs to promote adoption of financial sector standards and best practices, adoption was a national prerogative, and thus they were not featured in Maastricht. Also, the EU had power to adopt global standards and thus the monetary union did not need to have explicit provisions. However, the ECB itself has actively promoted the adoption of global financial sector standards. It can be expected that new currency unions will be expected to actively promote adherence to international codes and practices and will be judged based on their programs. Unlike Maastricht, from their inception new unions must explicitly incorporate programs supporting the adoption of global financial sector standards.

Table – Financial Stability Board's Key Financial Sector Standards

Focus	Standard	Issuing Body
Monetary and financial policy transparency	Code of Good Practices on Transparency in Monetary and Financial Policies	IMF
Fiscal transparency	Code of Good Practices on Fiscal Transparency	IMF
Data dissemination	Special Data Dissemination Standard / General Data Dissemination System	IMF
Insolvency	Insolvency and Creditor Rights	World Bank
Corporate governance	Principles of Governance	OECD
Accounting	International Accounting Standards (IAS) (International Financial Reporting Standards)	IASB – International Accounting Standards Board

[194] www.financialstabilityboard.org/cos/index.htm.

Auditing	International Standards on Auditing (ISA)	IFAC – International Financial Auditing Council
Payment and settlement	Core Principles for Systemically Important Payment Systems	CPSS – Committee on Payments and Settlement Systems
	Recommendations for Securities Settlement Systems	IOSCO – Int'l Organization of Securities Commissions
Market integrity	Forty Recommendations of the Financial Action Task Force	FATF – Financial Action Task Force
	Special Recommendations Against Terrorist Financing	FATF
Banking supervision	Core Principles for Effective Banking Supervision	BCBS – Basel Committee on Banking Supervision
	Core Principles of Islamic Financial Regulation	IFSB – Islamic Financial Services Board
Securities regulation	Objectives and Principles of Securities Regulation	IOSCO
Insurance supervision	Insurance Core Principles	IAIS – Int'l Organization of Insurance Supervisors

Text Box: International resistance and acceptance of global standards

Initially, the FSF Compendium of Standards was not enthusiastically accepted by many developing and emerging economies. (Dreszner 2007, pp. 119-148) There was some resentment that the FSF process was tightly controlled by the developed countries and that the developing countries were largely excluded from the process.

In a contentious atmosphere, questions were raised about how implementation should be promoted. One approach recommended by the G7 Finance Ministers was that adherence to codes become a component of IMF surveillance and that access to IMF and other resources should be linked to a country's adherence to the standards. A second approach called for increased transparency of practices in order to promote public oversight of countries' practices. In some fields, such as the recommendations of the FATF covering money laundering and anti-terrorism financing, pressure by governments was applied to bring other countries in line.

Resistance was strong to the first approach (especially by emerging economies) and it was abandoned, but greater transparency and regular reporting of observance of standards became a regular part of the system. One tool introduced was ROSCs, or "Reports of Observance of Standards and Codes" in which reports were prepared (by the IMF and others) and published on countries' adherence to standards. Although the ROSCs are nominally voluntary, as a practical matter, countries came under pressure to undertake ROSC reviews, and the failure of a country to publish the results of ROSCs sent a negative picture about the financial conditions in the country.

However, once the effort began attitudes changed quickly. Countries found the reviews helpful in identifying important problems to address, and public pressure and the influence of the oversight of the international community made it possible for countries to break internal constraints and address long-standing issues. Most countries readily agreed to ROSCs and the publication of results. The process of adherence to standards and public scrutiny of adherence became regular, expected behavior. In the

IMF, reviews of adherence to codes became a regular part of surveillance.

In summary, the early struggle over the appropriate aggressiveness for application of global financial sector standards and best practices has largely been resolved, influenced strongly by onset of the GFC. It has become widely accepted that economies must move toward adoption of many of the standards and that they will be at a competitive disadvantage if they do not. This changeover, which is as profound as the global movement toward creating currency unions, occurred within a short space of a decade. Both trends can significantly change the global financial system.

The Eurosystem strongly supported the adoption of standards (partly reflecting the wishes of its larger members) and they became a regular part of the union program. In future unions a similar path is likely and the union will be a major proponent of adoption of global financial sector standards and best practices, partly because the union itself will be more closely integrated into the evolving global financial system than will many of the member countries, especially in developing or emerging regions.

D. Currency unions as supranational organizations

8.32. Currency unions are increasingly important players in the international financial system. They have received significant powers from their member countries, and the nature and size of their operations give them significant international influence. Two important but related questions are how they fit into the inter*national* system – that is, a system comprised of and operated primarily by individual nations – and how will they relate to other inter*national* organizations – other organizations created by agreement of nations. This section discusses some of the issues that arise in this environment. In some cases, there are no current answers because the continuing evolution of the global financial system and appearance of new unions will change the discussion. The GFC has accelerated the changes and perhaps forced greater cohesion in the face of globalized threats. Future Currency Unions will need to address how they will fit into this rapidly evolving environment.

Concept of primacy of monetary union powers

8.33. As *supra*national organizations, currency unions internally affect their member states and externally assume the lead role for the member countries in monetary and exchange rate policy and often in other important areas. The extent of the union central bank's powers is especially important for unions under construction because potential member countries will want to know types of powers they will cede to the union central bank. The experience of the ECB can provide some indications of the types of issues that might arise.

8.34. In various contexts, questions have been raised about the degree and extent of the powers of the ECB over the international activities of its members. An important instance is the degree of ECB control over management of foreign currency reserves held by NCBs. It has been argued that the ECB exercises substantial independent control over that and many other issues.

8.35. As described in *Chapter 17 - Legal*, a major debate occurred whether EU powers are paramount, or whether the legal principle of independence of the ECB as a supranational central bank enshrined in Maastricht makes it the key regulator in the monetary field and related fields. The legal issues that have arisen are also likely to be faced by future unions and will need to be resolved within the context of each region's goals, legal and institutional framework, and political process. This might be a key factor in whether the union is ultimately successful, but it is largely an internal issue and practices elsewhere might provide little guidance.

The GFC and the Greek crisis demonstrated the primacy of the European Union relative to the constricting features of the Maastricht Treaty. This type of power shift will be an important theme for new unions to address as they weigh the extent of powers of the union and its member countries and what arrangements can best deal with globalization of world financial markets.

Rights and privileges vis-à-vis the union countries

8.36. The bodies of the union have supranational status that provides them with rights and privileges vis-à-vis the member countries, including a broad range of conditions with respect to the host country for the union central bank. In order to carry out union functions in all union member countries, in many areas the union cannot be regulated or constrained by national rules, it must have immunity from seizure of its assets and income, and its staff must be protected from national law in execution of official duties. The interpretation or implementation of the rules might be challenged, and therefore it will be necessary to have judicial arrangements to rule on member country disputes with the union.

8.37. In the Euroarea, there were different levels of rights and privileges. At the top level, the ECB enjoys the rights and privileges of European Union bodies vis-à-vis the member countries, but additional rights and conditions are defined in a formal agreement between the ECB and the Government of Germany as the host country. In contrast, at the national level, the member country central banks retained their own identity and national law prevailed over the NCBs in many respects, but because the NCBs implement many union policies some activities such as the control of income resulting from union monetary policy actions must be exempt from national control. Examples of the types of policies and rights that might be involved are listed below, as drawn from the Agreement between the Government of Germany and the ECB. (Germany 1998).[195] Although not expressly mentioned in the agreement, the Agreement provisions will also apply to local or provincial governments.

Inviolability of Premises – No member of the German government, judiciary, military or police may enter ECB premises except with approval of the ECB President and subject to his conditions. However, entry for emergency protective reasons is granted.

Inviolability of Archives – Similar exemptions are granted to all the records, documents, films, computer files, etc. of the ECB and the information they contain, regardless of their location. The final point means that the information cannot be seized if it is physically outside the ECB itself.

Inviolability of Communications – Similar protections apply to official communications and correspondence.

Protection of premises – The government has an obligation to protect the ECB against intrusion, damage, or impairment of its activities. The ECB can employ armed personnel at its residence, and for protection of ECB personnel outside the building. The weapons will only be used for self-defense or other necessity.

Protection of payments systems – Funds and records of transactions held by the ECB related to settlement within payments systems are also protected from official constraints.

Exemption for direct taxes – The assets, income, and property (including vehicles) of the ECB are exempt from direct taxation.[196] The ECB is exempt from obligations to pay taxes to third parties or to collect taxes from third parties[197], as

[195] A similar arrangement covering the relationship of the EMI and the German government preceded this Agreement.

[196] In effect, this helps create a neutral tax situation between member countries. Otherwise, the host country would receive taxes from the union central bank, which drives up its costs and lowers its net income, which will reduce the distribution of union income to the member countries.

[197] This provision might be deleted elsewhere. In other unions, it might be policy or a matter of efficiency for the union central bank to collect taxes on some types of financial institutions or instruments or transactions.

well as exempt from any reporting obligations. However, there is no exemption for taxes which are in their nature charges for public utility services.

Reimbursement for certain indirect taxes – The government will reimburse the ECB for turnover taxes on goods and services used officially that businesses have charged the ECB and for taxes included in the price of gas, motor fuel, and heating oil.

Reimbursement for turnover and import taxes – The government will reimburse the ECB for any turnover and import taxes it incurs. In return the ECB cannot sell, lease, or rent the goods involved unless it notifies the authorities and pays the taxes involved.

The ECB is not subject to financial supervision by the authorities.[198]

The German Data Protection Act does not apply to the ECB.

Tax exemptions for ECB staff - ECB staff and their families moving to Germany for employment at the ECB are exempt from customs and excise taxes on their furniture, cars, and other possessions. However, taxes can be imposed if the items are resold in Germany.

Identity of employees and registration cards – Each year, the ECB will inform authorities of the names and addresses of its employees. The government will issue staff and their families appropriate identification cards.

Work permits - ECB staff, spouses, and minor children are exempted from holding work and residency permits, even if they are not EU nationals. NonGerman members of the ECB Executive Board and their family members are exempted from German registration laws.

Exemption from Labor and Social Welfare laws.

Eligibility for health insurance after leaving ECB – Staff leaving the ECB are eligible to join the national health insurance scheme upon taking up a new position.

Cooperation – The ECB and government will cooperate to prevent any abuse of the rights and privileges.

The ECB can display its own flag and emblem. Executive Board members and families enjoy all the rights and immunities granted to diplomats and their families.

Either side can request consultations over the interpretation or application of the Agreement.

The European Court of Justice will rule over legal disputes over the Agreement.

8.38. Similar arrangements are needed with other union member countries, with appropriate modifications. Common provisions should be imposed as a condition of membership in the union. However, because the activities of the union can differ in the headquarters country and in other union countries, it might be necessary to enumerate specific institutions and activities involved.

8.39. In effect, the privileges and exemptions of the union and its employees reflect its status as a supranational institution that must operate

[198] An interesting question is whether union supervisory or accounting and audit bodies have authority over the union central bank. In line with the policy of ESCB independence, the ECB is largely responsible for setting the rules for these functions, but in other unions it could be possible for other bodies to carry out oversight of the union central bank. It might even be possible for national bodies to be granted authority to be agents. The global financial crisis radically changed the EU supervisory system by creating new union-wide institutions and powers, in which the ECB plays a key role. The changes make the issue of national supervision of ECB institutions less relevant because the ECB itself has been an integral part of the supervisory system.

throughout the union without interference from local authorities. This parallels the situation for existing international organizations. However, in exchange for exemptions effective controls must be in place to prevent abuses. For example, if a union official travels with his office computer, the computer is exempt from seizure by national authorities because it might contain sensitive official information. However, the computer could be used to support financial crimes and therefore some means are needed to allow investigation and prosecution under circumstances and rules approved by the union.

8.40. Similarly, the rights of employees need to be spelled out. Some ESCB staff might come under the legal framework of the monetary union while others are employed by NCBs. The employment conditions and the rights and protections will differ for each. Within the EMU, for example, governors of the Eurosystem are expected to act on behalf of the union and not their national institutions and thus are exempted from national sanctions – this can include charges of criminal conduct because authorities (including after a change of regimes) might seek to retaliate against their governor's support for an EMU policy decision by having their governor removed under a pretense of bringing criminal changes. Thus, employees of the ECB are granted rights under EU law, which transcends national rules and the ECB rules, and which are adjudicated by the European Court of Justice. In future unions, if such an overarching framework does not exist, the rights might need to be enumerated in the union treaty and involve some form of judicial oversight.

E. Union countries' relations with international organizations

8.41. When a country joins an union, it cedes sovereignty over its external relations in monetary and foreign reserves affairs to the union. Activities in which the member countries have always engaged will be done by the union. Also, the method of participation in international organizations might change. Although the individual countries formally remain members of international organizations, the methods by which they deal with the organizations are affected by the intervening union and in some cases the union might completely take over the activities. This section discusses some of the implications of this situation.

Financial support of international organizations (IOs)

8.42. Usually, individual countries are responsible for the financial relations with international organizations. IOs receive their capital from countries, and might also receive funds from countries for operations. The IOs might pay dividends out of their net annual income back to countries. And if an IO is closed or merged, its capital and net income might be returned to countries.

8.43. The financial power of individual countries vis-à-vis IOs is reflected in voting power and ability to direct policy. Currency unions present a mixed situation in which they receive financing from countries, return income to countries, and are responsible to them in justifying their policies, but have independent powers over setting monetary, exchange rate, and other policies. The ECB retains a share of income to build its own capital and reserves, which is seen to help support policy independence. In future unions, arrangements for power sharing and financing will need to be made in multiple areas. Moreover, because all member countries must receive equal treatment in these regards, the rules must be clearly spelled out. This could involve prolonged political negotiations that protect countries' rights while permitting effective technical operation of the union and protecting its policy independence.

Statistical reporting to IMF

8.44. Member countries of the IMF are required as a condition of membership to give the IMF statistical data needed for the IMF to carry out its surveillance of national economic conditions. The IMF has made clear that the obligation continues if a country joins a currency union – even in a union, it is important to have a comprehensive statistical picture of economic conditions of the individual countries. But as a practical matter, different types of information might be needed, and the mode of delivery to the IMF is likely to change. For example, under a "gateway" arrangement, countries fulfill their monetary statistics reporting requirements to the IMF by sending reports to the ECB which compiles the data and transmits the data to the IMF.[199]

International surveillance of unions and convergence criteria

8.45. Monetary unions undertake regular surveillance of member countries, which will often parallel the types of oversight and consultations undertaken by the IMF, OECD, or BIS. The nature of the surveillance should reflect union-wide conditions and policies, and adjusted to reflect the union policy priorities, including as expressed in the union convergence indicators. For example, an union might require minimum levels of reserve assets as a percentage of imports or the current-account. It is appropriate for international consultations to also cover such criteria as adopted by each union because they represent economic priorities identified as important for the union. Rather than applying one sort of oversight to all union conditions, customization of international surveillance can be better attuned to local conditions and better serve the union.

International deliberations and consultations

8.46. Pragmatically, IOs will deal with unions or their member countries issue-by-issue. The issue or problem could be specific to individual countries or could involve financial matters or expertise of individual countries. Conversely, the issue might involve a competency of the union or could benefit from regional coordination of the union countries that the union can help organize. Whether work is with the union or member countries will be legally affected by the type of problem, the legal relations of the member countries with the IO, and the legal relation of the union with the IO. These all differ case-by-case.

8.47. Increasingly, unions will be represented in deliberations of international bodies and have a "seat at the table". This might be as an observer to provide information or clarify positions, but unions might have voting rights on specific issues. Currently, unions usually are not the sole representative from their region, but this reflects partly the history of most IOs as groupings of countries. However, there are situations where an union or other regional body (in areas such as financial supervision, law enforcement, civil aviation, etc.) is the only entity in a region large enough to have the needed expertise to be seated at the table. This is increasingly true of interactions with international standards setters. The decision to work through an union or member countries will often be done pragmatically issue by issue, such as has been done between the IMF and EMU. Over time, the decisions will become more formalized and many will be codified.

Text Box: Can Euroarea countries borrow from the IMF?

Does union membership abrogate the automatic right of IMF members to draw on a share of their IMF quota and receive IMF assistance? It has been a suggested that Euroarea member countries could be prevented from applying for IMF assistance.

"States that might soon be in need of IMF credit are not allowed to accept them: Spain, Italy, and Greece. Indeed, being part of the Euroarea prevents them from applying for IMF credits." In "Crisis helpers in a crisis" Letter by Detlef Gürtler in Die Welt on August 2, 2008.

The reality turned out very differently. Although the EU, ECB, and Greek officials were very hesitant to involve the IMF to help bail out Greece, ultimately the severity of the problems and the inability of authorities to devise an effective solution, the IMF was called in to help coordinate a solution and provide assistance to Greece.

The legal basis for preventing Euroarea countries from accessing IMF resources could be that it contradicts the ECB common monetary policy and could violate ECB regulations for management of

[199] Chapter 12 – Statistics has an extended discussion of arrangements under which union members can meet their obligations to the IMF to provide statistics needed for IMF oversight.

international reserves. Technically, IMF aid to a country involves a purchase of an international reserve currency such as the U.S. dollar with the national currency – the euro for an Euroarea country. This obviously is related to monetary policy and reserve management of the EMU, with possible effects on overall euro strength. In future unions, IMF assistance might exchange the union currency for other reserve currencies, such as the euro or dollar, which might conflict less with other union policies.

Economically, IMF assistance to an individual member could also affect Euroarea monetary policy because the high degree of financial integration of the Euroarea means that a monetary infusion in one country will quickly be transmitted through the union.

The ECB potentially has authority to forbid members from drawing credit from the IMF if it runs counter to Euroarea monetary or reserves management policies. Hypothetically, this might reflect the conditions at the time of the request, but the ECB might a priori establish a policy that drawing from the IMF is counter to Euroarea policies. For example, the 1998 EMI Convergence Report for Germany stated that it requested that Germany insert language that "makes it clear that the Bundesbank's power to participate in international monetary institutions will be subject to the ECB's approval." Moreover, it said that German legislation has been altered to state explicitly that the Bundesbank may support national economic policy only if it is compatible with the objectives and tasks of the ESCB. (EMI 1998b, pp.310-311) Both these statements were strong indications of the primacy of the ECB and constraints on NCBs. The second statement reflects constraints on the NCBs by limiting Bundesbank actions to those that support ESCB goals and tasks, and in this did not grant more flexible permission for national actions that are not incompatible or prejudicial with the goals and tasks of the ESCB.

For future unions, the relationship with the IMF and access to IMF resources could be important. Countries in future unions might wish to take steps to ensure that they continue to have access to IMF credit, and anticipate how the union will react in such situations. Much might depend on whether the conditions are analyzed to be results of national or union-level problems and policies (e.g., a poor crop year in a country, or fundamental misalignment of the union currency). If the problem stems from individual country problems, a case can be made for IMF support for the country. In contrast, problems stemming from union policies might not be suitable for IMF assistance (even if only some of the countries in the union are affected). How the IMF would react if specific countries are harmed by general union policies could be a thorny issue.

The EMU within the international system

8.48. The creation of the Euroarea affected the relations of the IMF with its member countries in various ways. In effect, it constituted a one-sided revamping of the treaty relations between countries and the IMF. Articles 6.1 and 12.5 of the ESCB Statute state that the Eurosystem Governing Council should be represented at the international level. "The ECB is entitled to participate in international monetary institutions, as are NCBs, subject to Governing Council approval." The Governing Council, comprised of the governors of the NCBs, decided that NCBs should continue to participate in international organizations, but that the ECB should ensure that the ECB is consistently represented where necessary and appropriate. (Scheller 2006, p. 144) Regarding exchange rate policy, the ECB shares responsibility with the EU Council and the Eurogroup.

The Pragmatic Approach

8.49. During the first ten years of the Euroarea, little conflict in dealing with international organizations was generated as a result of the split of rights and responsibilities between NCBs and the ECB. As described by Scheller (2006), in recognition that international institutions were set up to deal with fully sovereign nations as signatories, and without formal provisions for supranational organizations to fully or partly represent them, a sense of practicality has prevailed on both sides in working out procedures and best practices under the new arrangements. The doctrine of subsidiarity also applied because the

NCBs are integral parts of the Eurosystem and their resources should be used. "A pragmatic approach might be the most successful which could minimize the adaptation of current rules and practices provided, of course, that such an approach resulted in an outcome which recognized properly the role of the euro."[200]

8.50. Aspects of the pragmatic approach are;

The ECB is the sole institution entitled to present positions related to the single monetary policy.

Responsibility on exchange rate matters is a shared responsibility between the ECB, the EU Council through ECOFIN, and the Eurogroup. The Presidents of the ECB and the Eurogroup are involved with dealings with third parties on exchange rates and on communications related to exchange rates.

Responsibility for payments and settlement systems is split. The ECB formulates positions related to the responsibility of the Eurosystem to promote smooth and efficient operation of systems. NCBs also participate and can express views reflecting their own responsibility and experience in managing domestic payments systems.

In statistics, the ECB has a formal obligation to cooperate with international standards setters. The ECB formulates positions along with Eurostat.

Also in statistics, the formal country obligation of countries to provide data to the IMF coexists with use of efficient means of data collection via the ECB.

In IMF surveillance, teams continue to visit countries, but hold discussions at the ECB related to monetary policy in the countries. NCBs continue to participate in conferences as appropriate, and NCBs experts are often involved.

In supervision and financial stability, under Maastricht national authorities have competence, but the ECB may participate in meetings and state its positions. However, new EU supervisory arrangements were introduced during the GFC that strengthened EU control over national supervisors. The EU is the main authority, but the ECB and ESCB are mandated to provide a much greater range of support and coordinating services than under Maastricht.

The ECB's consultations with international organizations includes both exchange of information and views with international organizations and carrying out reviews of conditions in other regions in order to understand how the Euroarea might be affected.

The ECB also collaborates with the international community to promote setting of standards and best practices. This work is designed to promote good governance and cooperation within the international financial system as a whole, with each organization contributing within its specific area of responsibility. The application of the standards is often at the national level and sometimes voluntary, but the international community often encourages application and might coordinate efforts.

However, the ECB does not engage in *prior* coordination in monetary or exchange rate policy with policies carried out by nonEuroarea countries. This is viewed as incompatible with the ECB's mandate and its independent status. Policy makers constrained by prior agreements would face a mixture of responsibilities, and could make the ECB less accountable for achieving its goals, such as price stability.[201]

[200] Presidency Conclusions of the Vienna European Council of December 1998, quoted in Scheller (2006) p. 144.

[201] However, in 2007 the ECB along with the United States, Japan, China, and Saudi Arabia participated in the IMF Director's consultation group on exchange (continued)

8.51. The IMF has responded to the founding of the Euroarea in several ways;

The IMF instituted Article IV consultations on Euroarea policies. An IMF team visits the ECB and other EC institutions twice a year.

The IMF modified its Article IV consultations with Euroarea countries by discontinuing national-level discussions on monetary policy and carrying out discussions with the ECB instead.

The ECB is included in relevant discussions as an observer. In December 1998, the IMF granted observer status to the ECB. No changes were made to the IMF Articles of Agreement, which remain based on individual country membership.

The ECB maintains an office at the IMF, with a Director and several staff. It has a standing invitation to attend IMF Executive Board meetings related to Article IV consultations on Euroarea policies and on Euroarea countries, the role of the euro in the international monetary system, and in multilateral surveillance including reviews of the World Economic Outlook (WEO) and Global Financial Stability Report (GFSR).

In IMF Board discussions, the ECB represents the views of the EC on monetary policy. For discussions on exchange rates, where the ECB shares responsibility with other EU institutions, views are presented by the ECB and by the IMF Executive Director representing the current Eurogroup Presidency.

The ECB often attends Article IV discussions for candidate countries for Euroarea membership.

The ECB attends Article IV consultations on the United States and Japan.

The ECB is also invited on an *ad hoc* basis for discussions believed of mutual interest to the ECB and IMF.

The ECB is recognized by the IMF to be a prescribed holder of SDRs.[202]

8.52. Beyond the above steps, creation of the Euroarea is scarcely recognized in a formal sense. Only in 2006, *the IMF's "Medium-Term Strategy" stated that the IMF would deal as necessary with regional organizations in whatever form they happened to take.* Thus, the IMF could interact both with formal unions and with less structured arrangements, such as the Chiang Mai Initiative Multilateralized (which includes the IMF as an observer in its meetings). This could also include the regional institutes of various sorts setting up new currency unions.

IMF Governance and the EMU

8.53. Many proposals have been made to create a single seat on the IMF Executive Board for the EMU or the EU. These proposals are often tied to demands that IMF governance be made more relevant to the changes in the structure of the global financial system and in particular growing economic strength of emerging market economies (such as

rate configurations that was largely intended to address the rate of the Chinese yuan. This type of high-level consultation could result in the types of prior agreement that the ECB formally seeks to avoid. Given the key role of the euro in the global economy, there are good possibilities of the ECB being involved in future consultations of a similar nature, and thus the prohibition on prior agreements seems rather unrealistic.

[202] Beginning in 2001, the IMF and ECB created a buying and selling agreement for SDRs that allows the IMF to initiate transactions in SDRs between the ECB and other countries – this agreement brought the ECB in line with arrangements followed with other countries.

SDRs are an international reserve asset created by the IMF and held by central banks and other prescribed holders that are used for official international settlements. They are originally called 'Special Drawing Rights but that name has been discontinued and 'SDR' is now the legal name.

China, Russia, Brazil, India, South Africa, etc.). A key source of criticism is overrepresentation of European countries on the IMF Executive Board, a legacy of the IMF's make-up when founded after World War II.

8.54. Part of the motivation is to reflect that the ECB speaks for the member countries in key areas of interest of the IMF. The IMF Executive Directors for Euroarea countries are constrained to follow the policy directives of ECB in such areas. Questions arose whether the EMU should have a single seat on the IMF Executive Board representing all the member countries, or should the EU as the overarching legal entity have a single seat on the Board?[203]

8.55. Creating a single EMU seat at the IMF Board would create a complex situation.

> Most obviously, the EMU does not have competence over all financial relationships between the IMF and its member countries – for example, it does not hold the equity capital in the IMF, and although it transacts in SDRs it does not receive direct allocations.
>
> Similarly, in a legal sense, a country is a member of the IMF and it decides on the institutional arrangements for its financial dealings with the IMF. For example, each country decides if its transactions with the IMF run through the central bank or the ministry of finance. Thus, some accounts are handled by Ministries of Finance and are out of direct control by the ESCB, but in other countries the same types of accounts are run through the central bank and are thus potentially more readily fall under control of the ESCB.
>
> The Euroarea rules currently permit countries to undertake transactions with international financial organizations, such as the BIS and IMF independent of ECB control.
>
> The IMF regularly carries out oversight of economic conditions in EMU member countries that are in areas outside of ECB competence.

8.56. In such a complex situation, major institutional and financial changes would be needed to directly seat the ECB on the IMF Board. A more likely scenario is that the ECB becomes authoritative on specific types of issues, but that the Euroarea member countries continue to be represented as countries on the Board.

8.57. Thus, for the foreseeable future national authorities have powers over IMF governance, but with pragmatic accommodations to the EMU when sensible. At some distant point, if currency unions become commonplace throughout the world, the governance structure might change to grant unions greater powers but if and when this might happen is completely uncertain.

8.58. The governance arrangements for the Euroarea will also affect other monetary unions who will seek the same rights. Over time, the pragmatic adjustments might become general international practice and be codified. If the global financial system becomes filled with currency unions, more formal arrangements will be needed covering their roles, rights, and obligations.

F. Special situations

8.59. There are a number of special cases of countries, territories, or possessions related in some way to the Euroarea, but which are not part of the EU or which are outside the national territory of the parent country. Special procedures are needed in these cases, including some likely to be relevant to future unions.

8.60. Unlike Europe, with its specific geography and political and colonial history, most future unions will not face many situations with jurisdictions that require special treatments. However, this

[203] If the EMU or EU held a single seat on the IMF Board, it would have the largest quota share and thus – per the IMF Articles of Agreement – the IMF headquarters would need to move from the United States to Europe.

section might be relevant for future unions because it shows the wide variety of situations that can occur that could need special treatment. New unions will need a flexible decision-making process that can adjust to the special situations and create sensible and legally binding solutions for each case.

Surrounded States

8.61. The EU and the EMU surround several small or micro states that cannot maintain their own currency and therefore use the euro. Prior to the EMU, these states used the currency of the surrounding states. To handle this situation, the EU with the approval of the ECB prepared a declaration on monetary relations with the Republic of San Marino, the Vatican City, and the Principality of Monaco.*204* (ECB 1999b)

> "The Conference agrees that the existing monetary relations between Italy and San Marino and the Vatican City, and between France and Monaco remain unaffected by the Treaty establishing the EC until the introduction of the ECU as the single currency of the Community.
>
> The Community undertakes to facilitate such renegotiations of existing arrangements as might become necessary as a result of the introduction of the ECU as a single currency."

8.62. Andorra later negotiated a similar arrangement to issue its own euros.

8.63. The arrangements allowed the small states to use the euro, subject to the oversight of the surrounding state. They apply the EMU rules on currency quality, counterfeiting, redemption, etc. The countries are allowed to mint their own euro coins using the mints of the surrounding counties, with the allotment taken from the surrounding counties' quotas. (Despite this right, in recent years France has not agreed to mint coins of Monaco.) The arrangement does not permit the countries to participate in ECB deliberations.

8.64. Bosnia, Kosovo, and Montenegro adopted the euro as their legal currency to stabilize their financial systems and permit free movement of capital and payments in euro. All future unions are in regions where their currencies might be used in post-conflict situations, for which special provisions will be needed.

Northern Ireland

8.65. Northern Ireland is part of the United Kingdom and officially uses either the British pound or a local pound with an equal value. However, businesses and consumers are free to use euros, the currency of the Republic of Ireland, which occupies most of the island. Pricing is generally in pounds, but the euro is widely used because of the heavy trade in goods and people with the Republic and the need to denominate goods in euros for trade with the Euroarea. Northern Ireland firms reportedly denominate much of their trade in euros, both for purchases of supplies and sales of their products, which provides a natural hedge for their euro exposures. Because so much of the trade is denominated in euros, a number of firms reportedly can use the euro for purchases of supplies in the U.K.. Some have suggested that the penetration of the euro into Northern Ireland is a step toward use of the euro throughout the U.K. as a cocirculating currency and for denominating many business transactions.

8.66. Thus, Northern Ireland is an interesting example of use of a currency union currency by a bordering country. Use is driven by convenience or commercial necessity, but segments of the economy use the euro to denominate specific types of transactions, creating a true cocirculation situation. Another aspect is that the effect is highly localized within a region and does not affect the entire UK economy, which might be common along the borders of future unions. Cooperation with neighboring economies might be needed to make these situations work – the solutions could differ for each country based on its legal and political situation and how the union currency is used in each neighboring economy.

Territories and Possessions

8.67. A series of protocols were attached to the Treaty to deal with issuing currency or handling monetary affairs in overseas possessions. Each was handled in a separate protocol because each situation was unique.

> "France will keep the privilege of monetary emission in its overseas territories under the terms established in national law, and will be solely entitled to determine the parity of the CFP franc." This provision includes jurisdictions such as French Guiana, Guadeloupe, Martinique, and Reunion.
>
> "Portugal is hereby authorized to maintain the facility afforded to the Autonomous Regions of Azores and Madeira to benefit from an interest-free credit facility with the Banco de Portugal under the terms established by existing Portuguese law." However, "Portugal commits itself to pursue its best endevours in order to put an end to the abovementioned facility as soon as possible."
>
> "The provisions of Article 14 of the Protocol...shall not affect the right of the National Bank of Denmark to carry out its existing tasks concerning those parts of the Kingdom of Denmark that are not part of the Community."

8.68. Such declarations were followed by detailed arrangements to fit the specifics of the actual union, which of course were unknowns when the Maastricht Treaty was ratified.

The CFA area

8.69. A total of fourteen African countries, which are organized into two separate currency unions (Economic and Monetary Community of Central Africa - CEMAC) and West African Economic and Monetary Union - WAEMU), use the CFA (Communauté Financière Africaine, or African Financial Community) franc. Most of the countries are former French colonies, but a former Portuguese and former Spanish colony are included. The CFA franc is linked to the euro.

8.70. Until late 2020, the French Treasury (not the central bank) provided substantial technical support to the unions and guaranteed CFS franc convertibility. In late 2020 this arrangement began to unravel as WAEMU – in anticipation of its eventual merger with the WAMZ – negotiated a separation from the arrangements with France. Reportedly, CEMAC was also interested in ending the arrangement with France.

8.71. The CFA is divided into the separate CEMAC and WAEMU unions in Central and West Africa. Each has its own currency linked to the euro at the same rate. Because of the common rate and guaranteed convertibility, either currency can be used freely throughout the entire CFA area, and thus both unions are considered to be a single currency area. (However, this integration is not perfect and sometimes the CFA francs of each area do not trade at pure par.)

8.72. It was a matter of contention whether the relationship between France and the CFS unions was a bilateral budgetary matter or an exchange rate arrangement that affects the EMU and hence falls under the competence of the EMU. (Hadjimichael and Galy 1997) Institutionally, the French Treasury guaranteed convertibility of the CFA currencies, rather than the Banque de France, which is part of the Eurosystem. In anticipation of the EMU, the European Council reviewed the arrangements and concluded that the technical arrangements of the relationship between the CFA zone and the French franc were not fundamentally changed by the switch from the franc to the euro, the arrangements would not materially affect EMU monetary or exchange rate policies, the operations of the EMU would be unaffected, and thus no obligations were created for the ECB.

8.73. Given these conditions, it was concluded that the preexisting relationship could continue, but the French authorities were required to notify the European Commission and the ECB prior to exchange rate changes, and any changes in the relationship would require Council approval. The requirement of Council approval indicated that the relationship is defined at the EU level and is not primarily a matter for ECB decision-making.

8.74. Key elements of the France-CFA arrangement are/were;

The CFA franc is freely convertible with the euro at a fixed rate with no fluctuation margin.

The rate can be adjusted through consultations and unanimous approval of the member states.

Convertibility is guaranteed because each union central bank sets up an operational account with the French Treasury with market rates of return. The operational accounts can have positive or negative balances. Negative balances are equivalent to an overdraft facility.

Currency and capital mobility exist between the two unions and France.

The foreign currency reserves of each union are pooled with the French Treasury. However, with accumulations of reserves in some oil exporting member countries, it was accepted that countries can retain some of these holdings, which can be considered a type of sovereign wealth fund.

The NCBs are required to deposit at least 65 percent of their foreign currency assets in the operational account, and a reserve must be maintained equal to at least 20 percent of the banks' liquid liabilities.

The central banks many not lend their governments more than 20 percent of the government's previous year's revenue.[205]

8.75. This arrangement with the French government provided several types of support to the African unions – technical operational assistance to operate the system, financial support that permits the convertibility of the CFA franc, and the financing of overdrafts. These efforts tended to extend the euro's zone of influence into Africa.[206]

Timor Leste

8.76. Timor Leste uses the U.S. dollar as its sole currency. Following its independence, both Portugal and the United States sought to introduce their currencies, but more rapid delivery of dollars was decisive in making the dollar the official currency rather than the euro. If the euro had been adopted, it would have been the official currency in a fully sovereign state far distant from Europe.

G. Unilateral adoption of the euro

8.77. Countries on the borders of a currency union might find that the union currency deeply penetrates their economy, resulting in a cocirculation situation. In these situations, neighboring countries might take steps to legalize the use of the union currency. Or, if a neighboring country ultimately intends to adopt the union currency, it could consider unilaterally adopting the currency prior to the formal acceptance into the union. Press stories have indicated that during the GFC the IMF encouraged (without success) the ECB to permit several Eastern European countries to *de facto* adopt the euro as their currency prior to meeting the formal Euroarea admission requirements. (Financial Times 2009) Ecuador and El Salvador have formally adopted the U.S. dollar as their currency, reflecting its widespread use in their economies and economic advantages of operating in the dollar including avoiding translation costs and gaining access to low dollar interest rates.

8.78. Unilateral adoption would require some legal actions, such as legislation declaring the currency to be legal tender, redenomination of

---

[205] This limitation has not always been observed.

[206] Hypothetically, the long-term peg of the CFA franc to the euro could have led to use of the euro as a cocirculating currency. However, this might have been destabilizing for the CFA and use of the euro in the CFA area could have been large enough to affect overall usage and behavior of the euro and Euroarea monetary policy.

securities and contracts, and introduction of currency management techniques. Economically, the country must hold substantial reserves in the union currency, operate monetary policy in the union currency, and supply intraday credit to clearing markets, etc. The country would benefit from the interest rate structure of the union currency, and the stability of the union exchange rate. These could be important advantages in terms of stability and long-term expectations, but could be disadvantageous if the interest and exchange rates were inappropriate for the national economic conditions.[207] The country and its financial system would not have access to the standing monetary facilities of the Euroarea. Countries adopting the euro unilaterally could not participate in the ECB governance framework.

8.79. Another disadvantage of unilateral adoption is that the country adopting the union currency does not issue the currency, and thus cannot control the size of the money stock, easily manage the money stock, and also might not earn monetary income (seigniorage) on the monetary stock. Its central bank could deal with the first problem by agreeing to purchase the union currency and make it available to national markets – this could be important if the currency experiences large seasonal fluctuations in volume. The second problem could be addressed for example by requiring that banks hold unremunerated required reserves in the union currency, which allows the central bank to reinvest those funds to earn seigniorage. The stock of union currency or other currencies within international reserves would also earn monetary income. Thus, there are ways of working around issues of not being the currency issuer, but they might not be straightforward.

8.80. There will also be issues of currency management. New currency must be supplied to ATMs, the costs of inspecting and retiring damaged currencies will be born locally, policy for replacement of damaged currency is uncertain, and counterfeiting problems might be greater outside the union currency's home area. Arrangements should be made with banks or other money handlers in the union area, or with the union itself to devise methods to deal with such issues.

8.81. In these situations, the attitude of the union towards use of its currency elsewhere will be critical. The Eurosystem has requested that it be informed of all cases of established use of the euro outside the Euroarea. It has also set up a correspondent bank relationship with Hong Kong that facilitates use of the euro in the Far East. There are advantages to the Eurosystem to be cooperative – earn seigniorage on currency shipped to other countries[208], tighten controls of counterfeiting, and gain information that helps understand the full economic situation facing the euro. On the other hand, it might have concluded that organized use outside the Euroarea could threaten monetary or exchange rate management and should not be supported.

8.82. Overall, it seems likely that it is advantageous for an union to provide technical support for the use of its currency in other countries because it builds seigniorage income, regularizes currency management, aids anticounterfeiting efforts, and probably helps build the currency's reputation and avoids damage to the reputation of the currency if problems arise. The larger challenge might be policy – will the overall monetary or exchange rate policy of the union be affected? Or will ancillary policies such as maintaining fiscal discipline or price stability be threatened? These might be situations where pragmatic adjustments could be in order to support the smooth use of the union currency in other states so long as its use remains informal and

[207] Around 2005 – 2007, there were many complaints that the U.S. monetary policy was imported into the GCC region because of the peg to the U.S. dollar and caused overheating in the region. The exchange rate for the GCC currencies was deemed too low and the interest rates were too low given the need to cool inflationary pressures. Countries unilaterally adopting another currency can face similar situations.

[208] Logically, the union (or other countries) receiving seigniorage from use of its currency abroad could reimburse the country adopting the union currency for providing what is essentially a free, indefinite maturity loan.

market oriented and legally independent of the union monetary and exchange rate policies.[209]

H. Coordination during the GFC

8.83. The GFC raised new issues about the relationships between governments, currency unions, and international organizations, of which the IMF has been the most important player. Three aspects are important – early warning, coordinating responses to deal with crisis situations, and conditionality in providing aid.

8.84. In crisis conditions, countries experiencing severe difficulties have sought IMF assistance packages. In several cases, efforts were made to collaborate with the IMF to provide assistance to countries in distress but were hesitant to join in rescue efforts until agreement was reached with the IMF. For example, three Scandinavian countries refused to extend emergency loans to Iceland unless an IMF package and economic stabilisation program had been negotiated and approved by the IMF board. (Financial Times 2008c). The crisis appears to have heightened needs for agreements with the IMF, its assistance in stabilizing and reviving economies, and bringing other countries aboard rescue plans. In this atmosphere, plans for rescue packages, swap lines, or other emergency measures developed by future currency unions or other regional arrangements should seriously consider how the IMF should play its role, including possibly making aid conditional on agreement on an IMF package.

8.85. The crisis highlighted the unique role the IMF can play in coordinating international responses to crisis situations. It has moved aggressively to adopt this role, and in Europe the EU and the ECB participated. The ECB for example adopted a proactive stance toward providing liquidity to the Euroarea banking system as the crisis developed.

8.86. This type of situation has been formalized under the CMIM. The IMF participates in the CMIM Economic Research and Policy Discussion process and in the event of a crisis access to swap lines is limited unless there is IMF agreement. Some members of the CMIM reportedly hope to minimize IMF involvement over time and place greater reliance on their own policy analysis and crisis resolution capabilities.

8.87. In such situations, advantages of collaborating with the IMF in regional oversight operations include;

Depth of expertise to analyze problems and experience in preparing packages in response to problems.

Ability to drawn in participation by a broad range of countries or institutions.

Larger resources than might be available to some regions.

Delays could result if local means were tried first.

The IMF can act as a neutral broker. Governments within a region might be unwilling to criticize fellow members or have political reasons for not taking direct actions.

The IMF can take blame for unpopular decisions.

8.88. However, there can be disadvantages on relying on the IMF;

[209] Issues surrounding use of physical euros outside the Euroarea will be replayed once a digital euro as a CBDC is issued, but with addition of new types of risks. Future unions could face monetary policy challenges and risks from any of several possible competitor digital currencies (euro, dollar, yuan, others including possibly privately issued cybercurrencies).

It limits the ability to take anticipatory actions or remedial action early against a problem before it is severe enough to need IMF involvement.[210]

Regional standards for intervening might differ from those of the IMF. Methods to promote changes in policy could differ region by region. IMF involvement can involve delays, or at least a minimum period to make arrangements.

The IMF has limited operational resources to cover 190 countries. There might be a lack of expertise in specific problems faced, or staff might have little time to deal with the issues.

The IMF process can involve political dimensions absent from regional arrangements.

8.89. Future unions will need to build up their infrastructure for analysis of regional conditions and in member countries that might spill over to the union. The need for these capabilities has increased due to the severe threats from the crisis. New unions must build up their information systems and analytical capabilities and techniques to promote adherence to sound macroeconomic policies. This is especially important if local surveillance is intended to substitute for IMF oversight, or if there are important regional issues in addition to purely national issues that will be the primary focus of IMF oversight. However, it is also necessary to provide more frequent and locally nuanced oversight of conditions than the IMF can provide. Credibility of the regional oversight process will be hard to establish and will take time.

I. A world filled with currency unions

8.90. The creation of the euro dramatically changed the functioning of the international financial system. The euro has grown to be the largest currency in the world, the GDP of the Euroarea exceeds that of the U.S., and the euro has become a major alternative to the dollar as an international reserve currency. This section looks at some of the changes resulting from creation of the euro and the future creation of many currency unions that could ultimately cover half or more of the countries in the world.

8.91. Kenen and Meade (2008) discuss how the creation of multiple unions can affect the role of the IMF in the global system.

> "The creation of regional monetary funds...would pose a threat to the primacy of the IMF and would thereby diminish the global influence of the United States." And "The Fund itself has barely begun to respond to the challenge posed by the likely creation of regional rivals – agencies to which governments might turn for larger amounts of financial assistance than those available to the IMF or, more importantly, with fewer or less rigorous policy commitments." They further state that the IMF "has not explicitly confronted the risk that regional arrangements might undermine the rigor of Fund conditionality or the risk that countries with large reserves might lend directly to their neighbors on terms set unilaterally." (pp.194-195)[211]

8.92. Thus, they suggest that the global system will switch from one of separate national states that selectively create "*inter*national organizations" that carry out specialized functions spelled out in their charters into a conglomeration of *supra*national organizations and remaining national states that interact with each other. The *"International"* Monetary Fund was created by national states as an organization to exercise oversight of the global monetary system and provide assistance to countries from a

[210] In May 2010, following the approval of the Greek rescue package that included IMF involvement, IMF Managing Director Dominique Strauss-Kahn addressed IMF staff and expressed regret that countries are hesitant to bring problem situations to the IMF when they were still less than full crises and still could be handled relatively easily. He said that the IMF could be discrete in order to not convey an impression that problems were severe.

[211] However, the IMF role in the Greek crisis and GFC-related large expansion in IMF resources suggests different paths could result from what Kenen and Meade suggested.

pool of funds provided by the member states, and in which the major developed countries have a key role in governance. But in a world filled with currency unions, in many areas supranational organizations will have powers equal to or exceeding those of the nation states (such as the exclusive right of the ECB to deal with the IMF on monetary policy) and the new supranational entities might absorb functions from the IMF and other international organizations (such as surveillance, emergency lending, monitoring of conditionality, etc.).

8.93. Kenen and Meade suggest that in coming decades the IMF and regional "supranational" organizations will share the international financial policy stage. Some roles will be cooperative, but it is certain the modalities of identifying problems, developing policy, and implementing solutions will be different, and in some cases might prove in conflict. The resources and expertise of the supranational organizations might grow to the point where they might have equal weight to the IMF or the BIS. The unions could have advantages in timeliness in identifying problems and quickly and flexibly designing solutions. Moreover, they could have greater regional influence than the IMF, because of better political connections, suasion, or legal powers, and thus they might be in a better position to forge cooperative regional solutions that address the specific problems at hand.[212] [213]

8.94. A noted legal scholar of the EMU, Rene Smits (1997) argued that the growth of monetary unions has fundamentally changed the sovereign nature of countries and because of the transfer of competences to currency unions the unions should have representation in the IMF because they have essentially acquired the powers and functions of states.

"The attribution of powers and the monetary and exchange rate fields to the Community takes away the substance for membership in the IMF. Responsibility in monetary matters, an essential characteristic for Statehood and a condition for the compliance with the obligations resulting from membership in the IMF, no longer lies with the member states. Put differently, the essential conditions for the Member States to remain individual members of the IMF has ceased..."

8.95. Ultimately, these are not issues of who has superior roles in the system, but recognition that in many spheres of economic activity the unions will have a legitimate voice alongside the IMF, they will offer different policy perspectives, will have different methods of providing assistance, and might have different conditionality policies. Examples exist of regional institutions taking views in support of countries' policies opposed by the IMF, and there have been suggestions to transform the CMIM into an Asian Monetary Fund as an explicit counterweight to the IMF. (Truman 2006, p. 57) Competition between unions and the IMF and other international organizations is sure to exist. It can be hoped that this leads to good mutual communication, productive sharing of responsibilities, and joint collaborations when appropriate, but there will always be dangers such as poor communications or conflicts of policies – it will be part of the agenda of the global financial community during the next few decades to create positive interactions and avoid conflicts between existing international institutions and future unions and other strengthening regional entities.

8.96. In a world with many currency unions, a new system will need to be forged, but the topic has received limited thinking. An exception are suggestions by C. Randall Henning (cited in Truman 2006)

[212] Moreover, the IMF faces its own challenges in playing a continuing role within unions, because the IMF itself faces limitations because of a tight operational budget, its remoteness from regions and their member countries, and at least until recently concerns about its dominance by developed country donors.

[213] These of course are the positive attributes of working with neighboring countries on economic problems. Unfortunately, there are ample examples of jealousies and antagonisms between neighbors that might hinder effective operation of a currency union. This of course is an important reason for the currency union to have policy independence and union-wide perspectives that can transcend the national differences.

that the IMF permit membership by currency unions, adopt principles for acceptable regional arrangements, and formulate principles to govern its relations with future currency unions and other regional schemes. Henning argues that new unions would need to comply with the principles, in areas such as strict surveillance and conditionality, in order to be considered legitimate. For example, he argues that the CMIM should adopt principles establishing policies and setting legal rules as to what is or is not acceptable, which can prevent disputes within the regions over the evolution of CMIM policy options. Adherence to the principles could forestall *ad hoc* experimentation on arrangements that could lead to damaging mistakes.

8.97. Recommendations such as Henning's indicate it is likely that regional conditionality arrangements will be closely scrutinized and might be harshly assessed by the international community, financial markets, and academics. New unions can expect they will be under considerable pressure if they adopt policies or surveillance and conditionality models judged not as strict as those of the IMF or the EMU (because it is the global model). Such criticisms can affect acceptance of the new currency. If new unions choose unorthodox or not completely strict policies, they will need excellent analytic support and communications policies to defend their decisions against such headwinds. It will be part of the territory.

J. Conclusions and recommendations

8.98. New currency unions will become important players in the global financial system. Because they will be larger than their individual members they will likely move into roles within the global financial system in which few or none of the member states were involved. These will be new activities for the regions and the global system that must be learned and suitable policy and institutional arrangements made. New G20 roles are developing as emerging economies play larger roles in global financial governance, which bear watching as indications of future directions. Work on this can begin early in the union-building process. It can be facilitated by collaborations with the IMF, the BIS, other international financial institutions, the EMU, other existing currency unions, and other unions being built. However, it must be recognized that the new unions themselves will be introducing changes into the global financial system and its institutions and innovative thinking will be needed on both sides.

8.99. Some specific conclusions from this chapter follow;

Low-income member countries in new unions might need to take steps to assure that they continue to have access to IMF credits or other international assistance. This might create operational problems for the union in its attempts to create a single monetary and exchange rate policy, but is necessary.

New unions should arrange with the IMF to become prescribed holders of SDRs.

New unions should join the BIS and be permitted observer status at the IMF, OECD, and other relevant international organizations and standards setters for matters related to the union, its members, multilateral standards, surveillance of the international financial system, and international financial stability. Even prior to the start of their unions, monetary institutes or other precursors to unions should seek observer status in international fora and involvement in surveillance within their regions – such involvement in the process will help build the infrastructure and capabilities needed to successfully operate the union.

Technical assistance to countries in unions also should be extended to union-level institutions, and also to pre-union monetary institutes and agencies. Assistance to monetary institutes or other precursors during the formative period will contribute to more effective operations later.

Special provisions might need to be made for post-conflict situations on the perimeter of future unions and for territories and possessions outside the formal union, and to deal with use of the union currency in neighboring regions.

Countries outside an union seeking to legalize use of the legal currency or adopt it as the sole national currency, should consult with the union to arrange for liquidity management and other services support, and sharing of seigniorage.[214]

[214] If future growth of unions is strong, smaller states using union currencies on the periphery of unions could become common. The standing of the perimeter currencies and the financial conditions of their central banks could be threatened unless arrangements are made for some form of sharing of seigniorage with the small states.

Timeline

Preparatory period	
Early actions (four years prior)	Set up an External Relations working group within the Policy Committee Begin design of international financial cooperation arrangements
Three years prior	Gather information on use of national currencies and national currency denominated assets outside union area
24 months prior	Begin status negotiations with IMF, BIS, OECD, World Bank, etc.
18 Months Prior	
Final 12 months	
Final 6 months	New union central bank set up and begins official international duties with international organizations and standards setters Central bank gains observer status with FSB and G20.
Run-up to union	
Union day	Become SDR holder Obtain official status at IMF Become member of BIS
Early union period	
Union steady state	

Chapter 9 – Currency

What will be the design and usability features of the currency? How to deal with counterfeiting? What are issues related to cross-border currency flows? How should the conversion from national currencies to the union currency be handled?

Chapter 9D – The Digital Euro should be read in conjunction with this chapter.

A. Introduction

9.1. Since the mid-Nineteenth Century, a country's currency has been a symbol of the country's sovereignty. It also is used to carry out commerce, to denominate values, and serve as a store of value. However, a currency can be threatened by inflation, exchange rate depreciation, and counterfeiting. In establishing a union, a single new currency will replace the currencies of each of the member countries. Successfully launching the currency depends on creating conditions that prompt the population to accept the new currency as its own. This can be done by creating a useful currency for business, creating demand for the currency through policies that support growth and a strong exchange rate, and building trust that the currency is genuine. This chapter covers creating the physical new currency and defending it against counterfeiting.

9.2. The chapter covers the creation of the euro as a physical currency, technical aspects of the design and printing of the euro, and the process circulating a new union currency.

9.3. Two series of euro banknotes have been issued. The original series was issued in 2003 – three years after the formation of the monetary union and introduction of the "virtual" euro which was an accounting measure. The second series, called the 'Europa' series, gradually replaced the original series beginning in 2013.

9.4. Creation of a digital euro as a Central Bank Digital Currency (CBDC) is under consideration. A digital euro would have major impacts on monetary conditions, including affecting use of physical currency. See *Chapter 9D – The Digital Euro.*

B. Creating the euro

9.5. The EMI recognized that creating a new currency would be a long process and work began early in the process of setting up the union. The process from the beginning to circulation of the new currency took about nine years.

Designing euro banknotes and coins

9.6. The physical design and production of the new euro banknotes and coins was recognized as a long-term development project. Work began in 1994 with the set-up of the "Working Group on Printing and Issuing a European Banknote" (later called the Banknote Working Group – BNWG).

Quality

9.7. A decision was made that the euro banknote should be extremely high quality and that banknote production should be continually monitored and improved. This had many advantages – it encouraged acceptance, counterfeiting was discouraged, and use in vending machines and money handling machines was improved.

9.8. Development of high-quality notes also facilitated the production of banknotes within an union in which most countries produced their own banknotes. Prior to launch of the euro, each country applied their own quality standards and security features. The purchasing power of each unit of national currency differed, denominations varied, size, color, and design were different. In contrast, the euro would be a common currency produced in multiple sites and the features and quality standards had to be specified in detail and tightly monitored. Thus, strict production standards were needed and the output of each of the printing facilities in different countries was monitored to ensure quality. This quality assurance process was challenging given the tight production schedule of production of euros and massive number of banknotes to be produced – there was little time to recover in the event of errors.

Naming the euro

9.9. A decision was made that the new currency should be free of national symbols or references and instead capture the spirit of a new continent-wide entity.[215] The decision reflected an urge to convey the unity of the continent under the new currency and also avoid potential problems using banknotes in an economy other than where they were issued. The name euro was selected because of its applicability in all member countries and because it was not named after any current or historical European currencies.

Visual design

9.10. A deliberative, inclusive process was followed to design the new currency.[216] The BNWG held a competition for design themes for the new currency. It collaborated with a group of central bank experts and external experts and set up a Theme Advisory Group. The Group's terms of reference included evaluating themes that cover the family of seven planned banknotes and ensuring that each theme can provide maximum protection against counterfeiting. The BNWG retained the right to modify or reject any recommendation. The Advisory Group was given six months to make recommendations so that the BNWG would have time to reach agreement within a one-year time frame.

9.11. The Advisory Group was mandated to create themes that symbolize Europe and its unity in a visual presentation, be aware of sensitivities of EU countries that remain outside the euro system, meet legal requirements, and serve as a means of payment acceptable to the public. Moreover, themes had to be broadly acceptable throughout the EU, be legible and widely understood, avoid national or gender bias, and have an aesthetic appearance. Finally, because there would be a period in which the new currency would cocirculate with the national currencies, it would need to be immediately recognized and acceptable to the broad public. The European Union flag and stars were accepted as a widely recognized symbol that should be included on the banknote.

9.12. The Advisory Group reviewed 18 different themes of which the most favored was "Ages and Styles of Europe", which featured portraits of ordinary Europeans on the obverse and architectural styles on the reverse. The "paired comparison" method, which each of the Group members ranked each pair of themes on various criteria, was used to rank the top ten choice of theme. In 1996, a design competition was held. Entries were solicited for a common design theme that would run through all denominations of bills. Forty-four entries were submitted, and presented anonymously to a jury of marketing, design, and art history experts, followed by a public consultation. The final design decision was made in 1998, after which the technical production of the banknotes began.

Security features

9.13. Parallel to the work on visual design of the banknotes, a great deal of work was needed on the security or anti-counterfeiting features of the banknotes. The sophistication of counterfeiters and the availability of technology capable of producing very high quality reproductions required that multiple security features be built into banknotes. Some security features must be available for use by the public to make routine inspections that the banknote is genuine. Other features are needed by vendors and cash handlers to verify currency for automatic processing. Some features based on sophisticated technologies might be known only to authorities and can be used to as ultimate tests of the authenticity of the currency.

9.14. A general rule has been that regardless of the precautions taken ultimately counterfeiters can develop passable fake banknotes. However, this

[215] Design of the new euro banknotes began prior to the decision that they should not carry national identification or references. The draft euro banknotes design included a space to the lower left of the map of Europe where national identification could have been made. However, the first position on each note's serial number is an alphabetic character that indicates the country that issued the banknote, but the public is generally unaware of this.

[216] See EMI Theme Selection Advisory Group. "Interim Report on the Selection of a Theme for the European Banknote Series" 1994.

takes time, money, and involve risks. Banknote designers must take extra steps to make the counterfeiting process as difficult and costly as possible so that the cost of producing passable counterfeit banknotes is high enough to be discouraging.[217] Over time, the number of bad notes might gradually increase and it make it necessary to introduce a new version of the currency.[218] New versions provide an opportunity to introduce new security features, which are continually advancing.

Usability features

9.15. The ECB investigated the usability features of the currency in great detail. Color, size, feel, durability, machine acceptability (mechanical or electronic sensing) etc. were examined.

Coin-banknote boundary and gap

9.16. An important decision affecting currency use is the coin-banknote boundary, which is the where the break is made between the largest value coin and the smallest value banknote. The size of the gap between the largest coin and the smallest bill is also an important variable.

9.17. Globally, the boundary varies considerably. In the United States, for example, the largest coin normally used is the quarter, or twenty-five cent coin, which has low purchasing power. (Fifty cent and one-dollar coins exist, but have very limited circulation.) In contrast, the two-euro coin is widely used and has purchasing power about ten times that of the quarter. The Japanese 500 yen coin has about twenty times the purchasing power of the quarter.

9.18. The size of the gap between coins and banknotes also matters. One U.S. dollar banknote is four times the value of the quarter; the 5 euro banknote is 2 and one-half times the value of the 2 euro coin; and the Japanese 1000 yen banknote is twice the value of the 500 yen coin. The banknotes are small multiples of the coins, but have a large range depending on usage patterns and public preferences. If the gap becomes too large, such as setting the smallest banknote to be ten times the size of the largest coin, large amounts of coins need to be carried about for transactions and it is difficult to make change for banknotes. A gap that large could actually inhibit making transactions.

9.19. The choice of the boundary depends on the intrinsic character of coins versus banknotes, patterns of use, and public preferences.

9.20. Coins have many advantages for small purchases, including ease in use in vending machines and durability that allows them to be used indefinitely which saves on production costs. On the other hand, they can be heavy and bulky that can make handling difficult. Also, the intrinsic value of the metal in the coin varies based on market prices, and if the intrinsic value exceeds the face value of the coin, they might be hoarded or melted down for the ore value. Also, they might be relatively easy to counterfeit. If inflation is rapid, the coins can lose their useful value and will be abandoned. Given this mix of characteristics, authorities might want highest value coin have a relatively large value, but subject to constraints of public complaints about having too many coins, expense to money handlers, or increased danger of counterfeiting.

9.21. Banknotes are clearly favored for high value instruments. They are easily used for large purchases or for storing value, but wear out and high denominations are targets for counterfeiting. Also, there is a regular cost of replacing worn out banknotes, and a major cost every decade or so to

[217] Counterfeiting is sometimes used as a type of economic warfare to undermine the acceptability of a currency. This practice might continue regardless of steps taken to attempt to make counterfeiting difficult, but it still remains worthwhile to force the counterfeiters to incur high costs.

[218] A second version of euro banknotes (Europa Series 2 – ES2) was planned from the beginning, but its release was pushed back, in part due to the success of the first series euro being difficult to counterfeit. The series was introduced beginning with the €5 note in 2013 and was completed with the €200 note in 2019.

introduce a new version of the currency. Small denomination banknotes will have a high turnover that make them subject to wear, damage, and dirtiness, and will often need to be replaced at a high cost compared to the face value. Thus, there will be an incentive to make the value of the lowest denomination bank note fairly high.

9.22. The boundary will also be affected by the usage patterns in specific economies. For example, in economies with large low-income populations there might be many mostly small cash transactions daily. Given the constant handling of the currency, coins have an advantage in terms of durability, but market traders often prefer small value banknotes that are lighter and easier to handle; conversely, if only large value banknotes are available, traders are forced to use coins. In contrast, in Europe and Japan, use of high value coins makes it relatively easy to use coins for fairly large retail transactions. In other economies where currency is often dispensed in ATMs, banknotes might be used very commonly while coins are mostly used for making change.[219]

9.23. The coin-banknote gap in the Euroarea has been strongly criticized. At least four countries have requested a one euro banknote, and a majority of the European Parliament has also made this request. These criticisms might grow as more lower income countries in East Europe join the Euroarea. The ECB is seemingly resisting the idea because of the costs involved.

9.24. In the Euroarea, the coin-banknote gap affects the legal issuance of the euro and has fiscal repercussions, because the ESCB is the legal issuer of euro banknote, but national governments issue euro coins. This affects the balance sheets of the institutions, but more importantly affects the amounts and distribution of seigniorage.

9.25. Thus, a variety of trade-offs affect the boundary. For unions, the choice of the boundary is especially difficult because the member countries will have differences in income, average purchase size, usage patterns, and preferences. A choice suitable for a large urban population or tourist zone might be inappropriate in another union member country with large, lower income rural populations. In the extreme, the need to set the boundary at a level suitable for all union countries could mean that the boundary and gap are set very low or even eliminated by overlapping the coin and banknote sizes. Thus, a critical task of the banknote design group will be to gather information on the range of uses and preferences within the potential union to enlighten the decision about where to set the coin-banknote boundary.

Unit size

9.26. The purchasing power of one unit of the union currency needs to be decided. This provides the nominal base from which all other banknotes and coins will be set. The level needs to be set at a point that avoids heavy use of coins for everyday purchases and also avoids having to use high denomination banknotes for small purchases. There is also some prestige value in having a unit currency that has a comparatively high purchasing value compared to other currencies.

9.27. Setting the level is particularly difficult if there are wide income differences between union member countries – a comfortable level in one country could be a nuisance in others. Several methods could be used; calculate the unit value for each pre-union currency in terms of a major external currency then look where values cluster, set the unit to be approximately equal to common consumer purchases such as bread or trolley fare, or adopt the unit

---

[219] Press stories indicate that residents of Slovakia were concerned about the need to use very large amounts of euro coins for transactions, reflecting their low income situation and (in their view) high value of the lower value euro banknote. The lowest value Slovak koruna banknote (20 koruna) prior to the changeover was equal to only 2/3rds of one euro, and thus the lowest value euro banknote (€5) is equivalent to about 150 of the old korunas. That is, the banknote threshold is over seven times higher than previously. (Kubusova, 2009) This type of issue will face new unions with countries with highly varied incomes.

value of a major currency that will join the union and which is used regionally.[220]

Legal specification of the banknotes

9.28. The ECB copyrighted the euro banknotes to prevent a possible range of misuses. It legally defined the banknotes in 2003, which described characteristic features, including the denominations with size, color, and type of design, the symbol of the European Union, the name euro in the Roman and Greek alphabets, the initials "ECB" in all relevant variants, and applied the copyright symbol © and signature of the ECB President.

9.29. The copyrighting and legal specification tightened ECB control over the banknotes and allowed it to better regulate its use, intervene against bad practices, and pursue civil complaints against counterfeiters if criminal evidence is lacking.

C. Currency production

Printing facilities

9.30. A key decision regarding printing was to use existing printing facilities to produce the euro. Eleven sites were used, with each site specializing in production of a limited number of denominations. Concentrating production in a limited number of centers made controls easier, helped coordinate production, helped ensure quality, was more secure, and helped keep costs down because of efficiencies of scale. These advantages were needed to produce the needed number of banknotes under a tight production schedule.

9.31. Printing was complicated because tolerance standards were set higher than usual. For example, in mid-2000, the ECB found that €100 banknotes printed in one of the national printing centers had a slight discrepancy in one of the security features, a slight difference in color of one feature that affected millions of banknotes. The ECB issued a press release stating that no deviation from quality standards would be tolerated and therefore the banknotes would not be put into circulation. However, the problem was corrected and the banknotes were later reprinted to bring them up to quality and were allowed to be put into circulation.[221]

9.32. In contrast to the EMU case where many countries had their own high-quality printing presses and mints and it was a political necessity to involve the national printing operations and mints, future unions will have few or no facilities of their own. Instead, most countries in future unions contract with international printing companies or other national printers and mints to produce their currencies. A key decision for future unions will be whether they will continue to rely on facilities outside the union or attempt to develop their own capacity. In either case, redundancy needs to be built into the system to avoid problems if a production facility goes down. Given the technical sophistication of modern currency printing and minting, a long-term developmental effort will be involved.

Production of the currency

9.33. Following the design process, described above, final designs and technical specifications for the euro were set in February 1988, almost four years prior to circulation of the currency. Production of the printing materials began, including creating dies, films, holograms, and software files, based on manufacturing of printing plates from a single source. Arrangements were made in parallel to obtain raw materials and security devices. Materials were needed to be continuously available and multiple sources were sought to avoid potential bottlenecks. Forty different suppliers of raw materials were involved.

9.34. By September 1998, materials were gathered for test printing of several million banknotes under standard operating conditions. This test established the flow and quality of raw materials, tested

[220] Since 2015, the ECB has authorized NCBs to print €0 (€zero) banknotes to be sold as souvenirs. The notes must meet the same quality standards as real euros.

[221] ECB. "Production of the Euro 100 banknotes". Press Release. July 11, 2000.

the quality management system, and allowed examination of the output.

9.35. The initial production phase rested on efforts of the national central banks, applying the principle of subsidiarity. It also recognized that many of the countries had their own national printing operations that they wished to continue. Each country was responsible for producing or obtaining in own stock for the launch of the union. Banknotes could be obtained from other countries, or countries could pool efforts. The ECB indicated initial production should be 13 billion banknotes, representing about €600 billion in value.

9.36. In 2001, this production model was altered to permit decentralized production, but with pooling of operations. Each national printing office would handle no more than two denominations. This change permitted savings due to economies of scale, and also improved quality controls by reducing the number of production sites. The allocation of production was made by the ECB.

9.37. After the initial launch, the total volume to be printed is decided by the ECB, based on outstanding stock, the estimated amounts for replacement, estimated growth in circulation (which needs to include flows outside the Euroarea), and the need for stocks to accommodate seasonal movements and all other demands. An Eurosystem Strategic Stock (ESS) was also set up to cover exceptional demand or interruptions in supply. The ESS covers 30 percent of the total value of euros in circulation, and 20 percent of the low-value denominations.

9.38. Once printed, the banknotes are sold to other NCBs, as needed, with the financing arranged directly between the banks involved.

9.39. As an example of the production schedule and allocation of by printers, Appendix III shows the approved allocation of the production of euro banknotes for 2009. The schedule was announced in May 2008, and thus presses had 8 months to gather materials and adjust production to the levels for the upcoming year.

9.40. The current system is based on an allocation to existing presses run by national authorities. At least two presses are used for each denomination for back-up.

9.41. Future unions will need to make decisions on who will serve as printer and the production schedules. Existing presses and mints should be used if available, with due consideration for guaranteeing the output quality of each facility. If the region has limited or no facilities, an option is to recognize that banknote and coin production will be ongoing functions of the union, and that production runs will be much larger than under preunion conditions, and thus build production capacity within the region. Initial work could be with small value banknotes or with a few coins. This could save money and help build local expertise and capacity.

9.42. Each euro banknote carries a variety of codes, including identifying the printer, the printing plate, and the individual locations on each production plate. If one of the printing plate is discovered to be defective, it is possible to delete those banknotes from production runs. It is recommended that new unions follow this practice.

9.43. The initial production schedule was lengthy. The schedule was worked up backwards to guarantee availability prior to circulation;

Set the amount of each denomination needed at start-up, including at least a 15 percent reserve. The stock of currency must be in place at least one month prior to the union day.

Added to this was the time needed for distribution to primary handlers (banks, vending machine companies, currency traders, etc.) and for preliminary stocks by the public and businesses. This could be two to six months in length.

The full stock and reserves must be ready by this time before the union date.

Add the time needed to produce the needed stock *of all denominations*. In the Euroarea, the €50 banknote was twice as heavily used as any other denomination, and thus required more printing operations and time produce. Production of the initial stock in Europe took several years. Thus, it can be expected that the initiation of production must begin at least 2½ to three years before the union date.

Once the stock is produced, steady production of bills is needed. The pace will differ from that used for production of the initial stock because smaller denomination banknotes wear out more rapidly and need earlier replacement.

Add four to eight months for the pilot run and evaluation of results and making adjustments.

Add another four to six months to gather materials and set up the production operation. This stage must begin at least 3½ to four years prior to the start of the union. If there are constraints on printing capacity, more delays could occur.

9.44. The schedule will be similar for unions, including those that plan on using a parallel currency approach to introduce the new currency. All times allocated for each step above will be the same except for parallel currencies because the main production run will be shorter because only part of the currency stock will be introduced at the start of the union. However, given the possibility of more rapid take-up of a parallel currency than expected, a larger reserve stock (such as 30 percent) should be included.

9.45. Most future currency unions will not have extensive production facilities. While there might be some regional capacity, much or all of future production will need to be handled on a contract basis with suppliers in other countries. Suppliers could be private firms or public printing offices and mints.

9.46. One problem will be that the demand for banknotes for an union will be large and could exceed the capacity of many individual printers and mints – private or public. One planned union contacted a major private banknote printer and was told that the demand for union banknotes would require the entire production capacity of the firm for several years. In such a case, the choices are to gradually introduce the currency (i.e., abandon the "Big Bang" approach), or involve more than one supplier, which is prudent.[222] On the other hand, using multiple suppliers can create quality control problems, and potentially problems with patents or trade secrets in what is a competitive and secretive industry.

9.47. Similar capacity problems might also exist at the level of the suppliers of specialized paper, ink, printing presses, and security devices. An issue for future unions is whether these matters will be part of the union decision-making process, or whether the union will leave decisions on currency technical aspects to contracted printers.

D. Converting national currencies to euros

9.48. An important issue in creating a new union currency is setting the rates to use to convert national currencies into the new union currency. This rate will be used for converting currency and currency values in all forms into the new union currency. For example, physical Belgian francs were converted into euro, but also every contract denominated in the franc was converted into euros, easily involving redenominization of tens of millions of financial contracts. Setting the rate at the wrong level can have serious consequences for the country and the union. This section covers the method used for setting the conversion rates for the euro.

9.49. The experience described below presents one model but *a priori* it is unclear how much guidance it can provide to other regions. In essence, the European system was based on decades' long experimentation with the ECU that allowed market forces (operating within certain bounds and with occasional resettings of individual rates) to affect the evolution of exchange rates, leading up to the euro. Future unions might not have the inclination or luxury to emulate the method used in Europe.

[222] The EMU has a rule that each denomination euro must be produced by at least two facilities.

Appendix I discusses an econometric method to set the conversion rates that might have advantages for new unions, and in fact it has been applied to the proposed GCC union.

The conversion problem

9.50. The creation of a currency union involves the critical step of converting the individual national currencies into the new union currency.

Redemption of national currencies for the union currency involves turning in the national currency at banks or other exchange stations in exchange for the new union currency. A rate of exchange must be agreed that applies to all residents. For example, (in an union of countries renowned for their trees) citizens of Alder turn in 2 of their Alder dollars to receive one unit on the union currency; whereas citizens of Banyan pay 3 Banyan dinars to receive one unit. The conversion rates are thus; Alder: 2 to 1, and Banyan: 3 to 1.

Redenomination of currency values is also at the same rate. Alder must redenominate all Alder dollar values on boxes of cereal, contracts, deeds, wage agreements, tax schedules, securities, etc. into the new union currency, using the 2 to 1 rate. Banyan must do the same using a rate of 3 to 1.

The rate for each currency must be set and apply to all relevant transactions. It should be set by law using a legally precise number of significant digits so that all parties involved know the value they are receiving in exchange for the value given up.

9.51. The conversion rates used matter.

The rate should be set so that the conversion itself does not create gains or losses in value for any party involved. For example, the relative value of domestic versus cross-border investments prior to the conversion should not change post conversion.

The conversion establishes relative prices of goods and services between member countries of the union, which affects competitiveness. For example, a shirt valued originally at 20 Alder dollars would be valued at 10 units of the union currency, the price at which a consumer in Banyan could buy it. However, if the conversion value for Alder was set at a lower value of 2.5 to 1, the same shirt would then be valued at 8 units, making it cheaper for Banyan to purchase. This directly affects the competitiveness of goods and services between the two economies.[223]

The conversion rate affects the relative wealth of the economies and estimates of the size of the economies. Suppose, for example, that at conversion rates of 2 to 1 and 3 to 1 two citizens of Alder and Banyan, respectively, find that they have equal net value in the union. But if the rate for Alder is erroneously set 2.5 to 1, the citizen of Alder discovers he is 20 percent less wealthy than the fellow in Banyan. Applied to macroeconomic statistics, the conversion rate will determine whether Alder and Banyan are estimated to have the same size GDP or GDPs that are 20 percent different. Applied to financial accounting, the conversion rates similarly affect the value of consolidated cross border investments. Another important area affected is the value of government debt converted into the new union currency. The list can be extended to numerous other important issues, such as the sustainability of external debt positions.

Finally, the conversion rates should not create shocks between the member economies of the union. Countries within unions will have longstanding cross-border trade and investment relationships. They are adjusted to a certain configuration of exchange rates – if a conversion rate is set out of line with the configuration it could unfairly advantage or disadvantage countries, and trade and investment relations for the entire union could be affected.

9.52. Thus, it can be seen that it can matter a great deal what conversion rates are used. A method needs to be found that is methodologically robust

[223] Prior to the start-up of the union, there was widespread concern that a country might suddenly devalue its currency just prior to the launch of the union in order to gain competitive advantages. (De Grauwe; 1997 pp.156-7.) Thus, one of the first acts of the ECB when set up in May 1998 was to set the members' bilateral rates at that point to prevent such competitive changes prior to the Union's formal launch on January 1, 1999.

and delivers estimates of conversion values that all parties involved find equitable. Serious imbalances can result if the rate is not set in line with economic fundamentals.

9.53. The method used in creating the euro is described below. It is a solid option based on the operation of market forces to build the configuration of the exchange rates between the pre-union countries into the macroeconomic environment of all the potential union members, and thus the conversion of that configuration into the union is straight-forward and not disruptive. However, new unions will not face the same market conditions as in Europe and could choose other methods. Appendix I has an alternative econometric method applicable to other unions.

Setting the irrevocable conversion rates for the euro

9.54. A rate used to convert each of the national currencies into the euro needed well-established and clear procedures so that the process could proceed smoothly, procedures were harmonized for both creditors and debtors, artificial gains and losses were not created, disputes over values would not arise, and values were legally enforceable.

9.55. Multiple channels for conversion existed that had to be covered by the rules. To cite only a few examples; physical euro banknotes could be purchased with the national currency; banks could redenominate deposit accounts into euros and pay physical euros when withdrawals were made; securities and contracts written in terms of the national currency had to be converted into euros without replacing the millions of contracts involved; and banks, corporations, and governments needed to convert their full set of accounts into euros. Moreover, the conversions had to apply to instruments held outside the union, or which involved contracts with nonresidents of the union. All these steps required legal rules that established the timing, the mandatory nature of the conversions, the legal status of the euro as the successor for the national currencies in all contexts, and described the procedures for the conversion.

9.56. Procedures for the conversion, as set by the EU finance members and the governors of the central banks follow.[224]

> The EU Council (hence applicable to all EU countries) passed a Regulation in 1997) on aspects of the introduction of the euro.
>
> > Conversion rates were officially expressed as 6 significant digits for all purposes. This meant that the euro value of all converted currencies would be the same for all parties (creditor and debtor) and there would be no gains or losses because of rounding, truncation, or additional precision.
> >
> > Inverse rates should not be used because there is implied rounding that creates inaccuracies.
> >
> > When converting between two national currencies (for example, in a contract between France and Spain), the amounts in one currency should be converted into the euro equivalent and not rounded to less than three decimals, and then converted from euros into the other currency.
> >
> > Rules for rounding conversions into euro were to round up to the nearest cent when the result is exactly half way or above, and round down otherwise. Rounding for conversions from the euro to national currency applies this

[224] The steps described above were set out in Council Regulation 1103/97 on June 17, 1997; a September 1997 meeting of EU finance ministers and central bank governors that agreed on how to implement the Regulation; and the Joint Communiqué of Finance Ministers and Central Bank Governors of the Member States adopting the euro on May 2, 1998. At the time of the 1997 agreement on procedures in September 1997, the list of member countries and the conversion rates were unknown; In contrast, the 1998 Communiqué involved only the countries that would adopt the euro on January 1, 1999.

same rule for the lowest sub-unit of each currency, such as the pfennig for the Deutsche mark.

In May 1998, the list of initial members of the monetary union was announced, which established which currencies would be converted. Until this announcement, work on conversion could not really proceed and banks, corporations, and the public would not commit substantial resources to the conversion process. After this announcement, the conversion became mandatory for the countries adopting the euro and major steps were introduced to make the changeover. This permitted only a short time to undertake all the steps needed to introduce the new currency, which resulted in the public and businesses incurring large costs in the short time before the union was created.

The procedures to set the bilateral conversion rates were announced at the same time. The conversion rate was based on the bilateral central value of each participating currency in the ECU basket. All countries joining the Eurosystem agreed to this procedure.[225]

A Joint Communiqué was published that included a parity grid providing the irrevocable conversion rate for each pair of currencies within the union – for example, the rate between the Spanish peseta and Finish markka was irrevocably set at 3.57345 pesetas per markka. The most widely used market rates were used for each currency pair. This step established the interrelationships between all the currencies that would be converted into the euro, but did not establish the external rates for the euro. (The grid is shown in Appendix II.)

However, between May 1998 and January 1, 1999, national currencies continued in use as legal tender and their value against external currencies fluctuated as a result of movements of the ECU against external currencies.[226]

9.57. The bilateral central rates against the ECU had a long history, which had two important effects.

Over time, they had moved to be compatible with the underlying economy. Thus, their adoption would not influence the macroeconomic conditions in each economy.

They were essentially market rates. They reflected the consequences of market dynamics and the possibility had been removed of overt manipulation of the rates prior to entering the euro.

9.58. The central bank governors announced that they intended to ensure, through intervention if necessary, the convergence between the announced conversion rates and the market rates on December 31, 1998. That is, the bilateral cross rates calculated from each currency's U.S. dollar bilateral rates will be equal to the pre-announced bilateral central rates, on a six-digit basis.

On January 1, 1999 the ECU was replaced by the euro on a one-to-one basis. Legal language stipulated that every reference to the ECU should be replaced by a reference to the euro on a one-to-one basis. Although the external exchange value of the ECU was unknown, the exchange rates

[225] By agreeing on this procedure, the countries could not suddenly change their exchange rates prior to the start of the union in order to gain economic advantages. This pre-agreed stability is a good precedent for future unions.

[226] The ECU basket included currencies of countries that were not in the initial group of countries adopting the euro (Denmark, Greece, Sweden, and the United Kingdom). Thus, the external value of the ECU against nonEU currencies continued to fluctuate somewhat independently of the values of the currencies of the entering countries. Thus, the actual conversion values against external currencies could not be set until the end of 1998, on the close of the day before the introduction of the euro. However, the currencies of the future Euroarea currencies comprised an 84 percent share of the ECU basket, which limited the size of such fluctuations.

were highly stable prior to the announcement and thus approximate conversions factors could be informally calculated, which helped the public in its preparations.[227]

The euro conversion rates were activated and mandatory on January 1, 1999. All transactions and accounts had to be denominated into euros from that point on. On January 1, 1999, the irrevocable conversion factors established;

> The conversion rate was used to substitute the euro for the national currencies
>
> The conversion rate between the currencies of the euro member countries, which were the bilateral central rates published in the parity grid in May 1998.

Text box: The strange case of the Italian lira

The lira left the ERM in September 1992, when a wave of speculation led to a 7% devaluation. Although the political commitment to the exchange rate target was strong, markets viewed the central rate of 760 lira/DM as unsustainable given the Italian unemployment situation and inflation rate. The lira/DM rate fell as far as 1239 per DM, before recovering to around 1000 per DM by late 1996.[228]

Membership in the ERM for at least two years was a requirement for entry into the Euroarea, which was scheduled to begin on January 1, 1999. The Maastricht Treaty requires "the observance of the normal fluctuation margins provided for by the exchange-rate mechanism of the European Monetary System, for at least two years, without devaluing against the currency of any other Member State." Therefore, the lira had to reenter the ERM before the end of 1996 to be eligible to adopt the euro.

Negotiations opened on the rate at which the lira should rejoin the ERM. The lira traded at about 996 per DM at the time. The Italian government and manufacturers sought a rate above 1000 per DM, but the Bundesbank sought a rate as low as 970 per DM. Germany and France reportedly fought for a rate to reverse the Italian export advantage gained when the lira depreciated. A rate of 990 per DM was agreed and the Italian lira was readmitted in November 1996.

Political considerations were strong in setting the conversion rate for the lira. The Italian case stands as a sharp exception to the reliance of countries to the ERM central rates as a reliable, market-based, and time-tested basis for setting the conversion rate.

Text box: Setting the irrevocable conversion rates for the euro

The irrevocable conversion rates were set based on market rates on December 31, 1998. The method followed the existing method to calculate the value of the ECU, called the "concertation procedure".

At 11:30 a.m., December 31, 1998, each NCB recorded its currency's exchange value against the U.S. dollar and communicated the value to the other NCBs. Cross rates were calculated – for example, the peseta markka cross rate was set at (peseta/dollar) / (markaa/dollar). Rates were based on the most liquid markets available and were within the

[227] Several factors contributed to stability in the rates between the exchange rates for currencies entering the Euroarea. Countries accepted into the union had to adhere to the formal convergence criteria, and they remained part of the European Monetary System, which was intended to support such stability. Also, the ECB was created in May 1998 and took over the functions of coordination of monetary and exchange rate policies, which provided a mechanism for supporting exchange stability. Finally, interest rates were converging during the run-up to the union, which tended to remove the influence of interest rate differentials in driving exchange rate changes. These factors resulted in little change in the exchange value of ECU during the interim period between the May 1998 announcement and the introduction of the euro in January 1999.

[228] New York Times. "Italian lira re-admitted into European Union". November 25-26, 1996.

market bid-ask spread, but not necessarily centered within the spread.

The bilateral rates obtained by crossing the U.S. rates were set equal through market intervention to the bilateral central rates announced in May 1998, to six significant digits.

The rates were used to calculate the exchange rate of the official ECU. The overall dollar/ECU exchange rate is calculated as the sum of the U.S. dollar equivalents of the national currency shares within the ECU. The final step is to multiply each of the bilateral U.S. dollar exchange rates by the overall dollar/ECU exchange rate to obtain the irrevocable conversion rate for each currency into euros.

A special meeting of the European Council on December 31 formally adopted the rates. Appendix ii, Table 3 at the end of this chapter shows the irrevocable conversion rates used for the eleven countries adopting the euro in 1999.

Countries adopting the euro later used the same procedures, based on the information needed to set the central rate for their currencies. Thus, for example, the rate for Greece was set based on market rates on December 31, 2000 at 340.750 drachma per euro.

E. Currency demand and usage

Currency usage patterns

9.59. The patterns of usage of banknotes and coins will influence the features of the union currency and its look and feel. The currency must effectively serve many different uses as a means of transactions and store of value. The designers of a new currency need a good sense of currency usage patterns so that the new currency can meet those purposes. For example, in the Euroarea 70 percent of the banknotes are put into circulation through ATMs. (Solans 2000) This meant that euro banknotes needed denominations and features suitable for machine processing. It also highlighted the need to maintain high standards for the quality of banknotes in circulation so that cash handling machines can process them. In contrast, in low-income regions with a limited commercial banking network, banknotes will mostly be processed by hand and the stock of banknotes might consist largely of lower value denominations that must be especially durable in order to circulate for long periods outside of the banking system. For another example, in some countries very high denomination banknotes are used as a store of wealth or to make high value transactions.

9.60. The pattern of usage in the Euroarea reflected the high incomes in the region, its compactness, and the dense commercial banking system. Different conditions will prevail in most other regions which could lead to different conclusions about currency design.

9.61. The currency usage patterns of union countries will differ. Information must be collected on usage patterns and currency needs so that the currency serves the diverse economies of the member countries. For example, the currency might need to provide information in multiple languages. Early in the process, the union's currency committee will need to collect such information from members, such as;

Total stocks in each country

Denominations, and volume of each

Life of bills

Coin usage patterns

Banknote usage patterns, including border and international uses.

9.62. Based on such information, the currency committee will make specific decisions about how usage patterns affect the physical currency and how the currency will be managed. The usage pattern of the union currency will differ from the patterns in any member country before the union – an obvious example is that holdings of currency stocks for cross-border transactions will no longer be needed. Also, new seasonal patterns will emerge requiring transfer of currency stocks across borders to meet seasonal demand changes.

Stock of union currency

9.63. Central banks must supply currency where and when demanded. This section covers several aspects of this process; assessing the total demand for the currency and its distribution between countries; seasonal changes in the demand for currency; the movement of currency across national borders within an union; and demand for the currency outside the union.

Stock of union currency by denomination

9.64. Production of the union currency must be sufficient to meet demand for the full union, with additional reserve stocks. The total stock of union currency needed can be readily estimated by taking the total currency stock in each member country and converting it into the union currency equivalent by using approximate conversion factors from each national currency into the union currency. Unfortunately, in cases where the preunion currencies are not pegged to an external anchor currency the conversion factor is not known and must be estimated. Also, membership of the union might not be set. If the weighting of the conversion factors is based on the actual membership in the union, this could potentially cause large errors if membership is decided close to the actual start of the union. Thus, the total stock of currency that must be produced must be estimated, and a substantial extra reserve should be produced because of the uncertainty.[229]

9.65. Estimation of the number of banknotes and coins by denomination is more complex.

> The first step is to set the steps for denominations. For example, in the EMU the sequence is 1 – 2 – 5. One cent, two cents, five cents; Ten cents, twenty cents, fifty cents; One euro, two euros, 5 euros; Ten euros, twenty euros, fifty euros; 100 euros, 200 euros, 500 euros.[230] The table below shows for each denomination the number produced and total value in 1998.[231] In contrast, in the United States coins effectively jump from the 10-cent dime to the 25-cent quarter to the one dollar banknote[232] – in effect, the quarter takes the place of both the euro 20-cent coin and 50-cent coin.
>
> The second stage is to estimate the demand for each denomination coin or banknote. This involves redenominating into a common base the value of each coin and banknote in circulation in all potential union countries then slotting the resultant values into the closest denomination. Values will be approximate because the final conversions rates are unknown and values might not obviously fall into the common

[229] For example, a year before the start of the EMU it was unknown whether the large countries of Spain and Italy would qualify for membership. However, currency had to be produced for them because it was not possible to print enough banknotes and mint coins for their needs in the short time after they were qualified for membership. Had they not qualified, there would have been a very large and expensive hoard of unneeded banknotes and coins, which would have also created storage and security problems.

[230] An important policy issue is whether the top end of the denomination ladder should be truncated because of concerns that high denomination notes could be used in the underground economy, for tax evasion, or criminal activity. For example, the United States caps its denominations at $100 because of such concerns. (Depending on exchange rates, the €500 banknotes have been valued as high as eight times larger.) As shown in the table above, for whatever reasons the demand for €200 and €500 banknotes has been very large and foreign demand for these banknotes has pulled in €300 billion in assets into the Eurosystem, which is an important fiscal plus for the member countries.

[231] At the time, the €200 banknote was relatively little used relative to the €100 and €500 banknotes. It might have been economical to eliminate the €200 banknote, but instead issuance of the €500 banknote was ended in 2016 due to its heavy use in criminal activity.

[232] A fifty-cent coin exists in the United States, but is little used.

denominations. For example, a coin from a member country might be converted into a value of 34 cents, which does not easily slot into a 20-cent coin or a 50-cent coin. (If this process results in a clustering of values that do not easily correspond to the common denomination ladder, an adjustment to the ladder might be needed.)

Table: Number and value of euros in 2008, by denomination

Euro quantities (millions), outstanding amounts, end of period								
	Total	**€500**	**€200**	**€100**	**€50**	**€20**	**€10**	**€5**
	13,116	530	170	1,381	4,912	2,618	2,030	1,476
Euro value (EUR billions), outstanding amounts, end of period								
	Total	**€500**	**€200**	**€100**	**€50**	**€20**	**€10**	**€5**
	763	265	34	138	246	52	20	7

The third step is to estimate the total amount needed for each denomination by translating the total amount for each banknote or coin for all countries into the common ladder. The total for all countries for each denomination coin or bill will give a first estimate of the total amount of the union currency by each denomination.

The estimate produced as the sum of currencies of each country translated to a common value might not reflect the actual conditions that will develop in the union. Initial union demand could fluctuate as the public and businesses adjust to the new market situation. For example, prior to the union, some Euroarea countries did not circulate large value banknotes, and hence their potential demand for €200 and €500 banknotes was not considered in the calculation of demand by denomination. The demand for large value banknotes has grown strongly every year since 2002. The demand for €500 banknotes, for example, has grown about five times its initial circulation in 2002, while €100 banknotes have more than tripled from its initial level of circulation. This large increase in demand might represent new behavior of households to hold previously unavailable large value banknotes, or holdings outside the Euroarea as foreigners purchase euro banknotes as a form of secure savings, or its convenient use in criminal activity and tax avoidance.

Foreign demand might be difficult to estimate. Before the union started, the amount of each country's currency held out of the country might be limited by small markets for each individual country's currency and greater risk in holding individual country currency. In contrast, the demand for the union currency could be greater than the sum of demand for individual country currencies because of wider usefulness and confidence in the strength of the union currency.

Currency demand

Monitoring currency demand

9.66. Central banks within an union are obligated to provide businesses and the public with sufficient currency and the right denomination to meet demands for transactions and holdings. This is a greater burden in an union than in single countries because distances to obtain currency might be greater, different institutions might be involved in different countries, accounting standards can differ between countries, and there might be extra formalities in crossing borders. Thus, whereas in an individual country it might be possible to assume that cash supply will easily adjust to changes in demand, this assumption might not hold in unions and therefore the union could need to take greater responsibility to monitor demand and anticipate large currency movements.

9.67. A statistical system is needed to track changes in currency supply and demand, in total and by denomination, into national offices of the union system. Potentially, tracking might need to be done on a sub-national level. This tracking allows the system to anticipate demand and move currency where it is most needed. In the initial years of an union there will be little experience regarding cross-border currency movements to draw on. Thus, there is need for large reserve stocks distributed throughout the region and to have reporting systems that can rapidly identify sudden shifts in demand or build-ups of excess supply.

Cross-border cash operations

9.68. Shifts in demand can take the form of large-scale currency movements between union countries. For example, in tourist areas prior to peak periods large quantities of coins might be needed to make change for customers, which creates a massive oversupply of coins following the vacation period. NCBs need to facilitate such large movements of coins and banknotes.

9.69. The ECB found difficulties in large-scale cross-border currency movements that in 2007 led it to take a number of steps to improve cash management. It published a "roadmap" to gradually foster more convergence in cash operations of NCBs and the services they offer to the public and businesses. The roadmap recognized that different economic and geographic conditions required that operations be adjustable to reflect local conditions.

9.70. Key elements of the roadmap were that banks can get access to services of NCBs in other countries, common packaging standards are used (which implies investment in new machinery), common data communications are used, and there was greater convergence on opening hours. The ECB found that a key problem was different rules related to cash transport, especially related to the use of guns, but this dealt with matters outside the Eurosystem's area of competence and could not be covered in ECB rules.

Demand outside the union

9.71. The union currency might also be used outside the union countries. Part might reflect the need for working balances at businesses or small amounts carried out by travelers. Part might also reflect transactions or savings use of the currency in other countries.

9.72. Transactions use means that the union currency is used for business in countries outside the union. This could occur in countries bordering on the union where economic links with union countries are strong and it becomes convenient to use the union currency for a range of purposes. In other cases, for a variety of reasons (including failure to establish a credible monetary regime) countries sometimes use a foreign currency as a circulating currency alongside the national currency, or in some cases as a replacement for a national currency. Both these cases are called "cocirculation", the use of two or more physical currencies in a country.[233] [234] Both cross-border use and cocirculation use can result in significant increases in demand for the union banknotes and coins. This demand can have regular seasonal patterns, as has been shown for euros, which raises issues of the management of regular currency outflows and inflows.

[233] Cocirculation is a special case of the phenomena called "dollarization". However, the term dollarization is also used to describe cases where bank deposit accounts and loans are denominated in a foreign currency, but where the physical foreign currency is not used in transactions. The term is also used anomalously to describe situations where the dollar is not involved, or even more bizarrely to cases such as in Eastern Europe where the cocirculating dollar is being replaced by the euro, where "euroization" is also used.

[234] A number of policy situations can arise in cocirculation situations, possibly including sharing of seigniorage, logistics of currency supply and retirement, and counterfeiting. The ECB monitors use of the euro outside the Euroarea and EU, and has also set up arrangements called the Extended Custodial Inventory (ECI) scheme with banks in several international centers such as Hong Kong for handling of euro banknotes in the region.

9.73. The union currency might also be used as a store of value in countries with unstable monetary conditions, where there is distrust of the formal banking system, as speculation that the exchange value of the union currency will rise, or as a means to hide wealth. The steady increase in demand for €100 and €500 might partly reflect these types of demand. Moreover, the sharp step-up in demand for these banknotes in late 2008 during the financial markets crisis suggests that there probably is hoarding demand.

> Because currency can easily cross borders anonymously, it can be unclear how to separate the demand from outside the union from the demand within the union. However, a variety of accounting, statistical, and econometric methods have been developed to do so. See Krueger and Ha (1995) and the subsequent literature.

Pre-ins

9.74. A special case of the demand for currency outside an union occurs for countries that hope to join the union in the future. The government and public might actively seek to acquire the union banknotes and use them in transactions and savings in anticipation of adoption of the currency as the sole legal tender. The accumulation of these currency balances will also make the ultimate transition to the new currency easier because of familiarity with the features of the union currency, preexisting partial infrastructure to handle the new currency, and a preexisting stock of currency that minimizes the logistics of the changeover. This could be an important additional demand for the union currency. Often the union and the pre-in countries will have a number of arrangements that help in estimating the amount of union currency in cocirculation.

Unilateral adoption of an union currency

9.75. A special case that arises from the global financial turmoil is that countries outside an union unilaterally adopt the union currency. During the financial crisis, this strategy has been suggested for small Euroarea candidate countries to benefit from the exchange rate stability of the euro. (Financial Times 2009) This obviously could affect currency demand for the euro. The union could face multiple issues of whether or how it should support such unilateral adoption of its currency, which might well violate membership rules.

9.76. This issue came to the fore during the GFC when it was suggested that several EMU candidate countries would benefit from early adoption of the euro without waiting for formal approval. The economy adopting the euro would experience greater financial stability because of the stability and depth of euro markets and access to euro interest rates. Moreover, monetary disruption due to the possibility of the population shifting to unorganized use of the euro would be ended. (See Krueger and Enoch 2009)

Conclusions for new unions

9.77. New unions need to estimate demand for their banknotes and coins, in total and by denomination. The process will not be exact and much will depend on which countries initially enter the union. Also, reserves of currency should be distributed throughout the union for contingencies, which creates the possibility that the initial printing and minting of the currency will be too large, which is expensive.

9.78. This situation could exist regardless of whether the currency is introduced in a "big bang" or as a parallel currency that initially cocirculates with national currencies. The initial production needed in the parallel currency case will be smaller and thus expensive over-printings can be avoided, but it will still be important to have enough currency on hand to meet demand – long-run prospects for the union might be damaged if there was demand for the currency, but insufficient amounts to meet the demand.

9.79. Demand for the currency from outside of the union will also need to be considered. The range of uncertainty of course will be larger.

Currency retirement

9.80. Individual banknotes and coins are damaged while in circulation and must eventually be pulled out of circulation and replaced. Banknotes wear out much faster than coins, some of which might survive indefinitely. Arrangements must be made to replace worn out or damaged banknotes and coins, but banknotes are by far the bigger issue.

9.81. Good statistics on the average lifespan of each denomination banknote are needed to plan production schedules and deliver the currency where needed. The information should be broken down by country or region because usage and damage patterns can differ. For example, damage to banknotes can be greater in humid or rainy regions.

9.82. The retirement of each denomination banknote often depends on the size of its monetary value. Low value instruments often are frequently traded hand-to-hand and suffer wear as a result, but they might not be machine processed and there is little danger of counterfeiting. In these circumstances, worn and dirty money might not be a major issue. However, for denominations that are machine processed or are used as stores of value the quality of the notes might be more important – machine processing requires high quality banknotes and the danger of counterfeiting makes it important that high value banknotes be in good condition to allow inspection of security features. For example, in the early 1990's in Russia cocirculating U.S. $100 bills were rejected or deeply discounted by the public if there was very minor damage to the bills because of fear that the damage was hiding evidence of counterfeiting.

9.83. The ECB made a decision that the circulating euro banknotes should be of very high quality and that damaged currency should be removed from circulation. Specific standards were needed to assess the degree of damage requiring removal in order to maintain the quality of the bills in circulation and to avoid situations where member countries used different standards to withdraw currency. A regulation[235] enacted in 2001 required all banks and professional cash handlers to inspect currency received and withdraw it from circulation if there was evidence it was counterfeit or was too damaged. Banknotes reissued in ATMs must be checked using machines tested and certified by the Eurosystem.

9.84. The Framework had the following key features:

It recognized that national practices differed about which bills could be put into circulation using ATM machines. Some countries required that all notes be sent back to the NCB for inspection and reissuance, while other countries allowed the banks to recycle the currency on their own with various degrees of strictness of oversight.

The goal is to create a common cash area in which cash is treated equally throughout the union. A common policy for recycling or withdrawal of banknotes can prevent creating competitive distortions.

Ensure that cash handlers remain diligent to search for counterfeits and help maintain the quality of the banknotes in circulation.

Despite serving the public purpose of maintaining the quality of the money stock, cash handlers are not paid for any costs for implementing the framework.

Inspection of banknotes must be done by machines certified by the Eurosystem or by trained personnel. Staff making inspections were provided information on genuine banknotes during 2000 and 2001 as part of the test runs for the euro.

Banknotes inspected by hand cannot be issued using ATMs, but only by hand over the counter.

---

[235] *Recycling of Euro Banknotes: Framework for the detection of counterfeits and fitness sorting by credit institutions and other professional cash handlers.* Council Regulation No. 1338/2001. June 28, 2001.

The low denomination €5 and €10 notes are subject to high wear and therefore NCBs should regularly supply them to banks and cash handlers in order to maintain the quality of the money stock. Suspected counterfeits must be immediately handed to authorities. The account of the presenter of the banknote should not be credited.

Banknotes that appear genuine but which cannot be fully authenticated because of quality or damage must be presented to the NCB for inspection, but the customer's account can be credited.

Genuine banknotes unfit for recirculation must presented to the NCB for replacement; the customer's account is credited.

9.85. The standards for rejecting soiled or damaged banknotes are strict. Bills with any of the features listed below must be turned over to a NCB for inspection. It is a criminal offence for the cash handler to put a banknote believed to be counterfeit back in circulation.

Dirt across the entire banknote.

Stain covering at least three square millimeters. This is a very small area, but this requirement is in place to prevent counterfeiters from using stains to cover flaws that could identify the banknotes as being counterfeits.

Graffiti or other markings on the bills.

De-inking on part or all of the banknote. This might have the appearance of being bleached or washed.

Mutilation or physical defeat, such as tears, holes, missing parts, or damaged security feature.

Repaired, taped, or glued notes.

Currency lifespan

9.86. Each currency has a limited lifespan. A currency released into the economy typically circulates for only a limited number of years before there is reason to call it in and issue a replacement currency. The new currency becomes the legal tender for the country, and the old currency is retired – sometimes very quickly, sometimes slowly. There are many possible reasons for retirement and replacement of a currency;

A monetary union is created and old national currencies are retired.

Counterfeiting of the old currency had become a major problem. New security features are needed.

The central bank has been reorganized or recapitalized, and the new currency is issued in the name of the new institution.

Inflation or a financial crisis has destroyed the usefulness and public trust in the old currency, and a replacement is demanded.

Inflation has increased the need for higher nominal denomination notes.

Countries merge or break up, or other significant political changes had occurred.

Requirements change for ATMs, cash-handling machines, and vending machines

9.87. Eventually, all banknotes must be redesigned and replaced, to incorporate new features that enhance security or useability, and to remove counterfeits from the system. The schedule for the new Europa-2 series provides an useful summary of the steps and schedule that future unions could follow in changeovers of their currency;

Approval for the new euro series was made in April 2005, and original plans called for issuance in 2012 at the earliest, a lag of over six years. However, issuance was delayed until 2014 because of little evidence of counterfeiting.

The new euro series was issued sequentially, one denomination at a time. The schedule will be affected by the process of incorporating new security features into the design and by the degree of the pressure from counterfeits.

The design work involved extensive consultations with "stakeholders" in the use of euros. Among communities consulted were the European Payments Council, European Security Transport Association, Eurocommerce, consumer associations, and the European Blind Union, the vending machine industry, commercial cash operations centers, and manufacturers of cash operating machinery and sensors. Consultations focused on the usability, functional and technical requirements of stakeholders, and security features of the new banknotes.[236]

Design work, development of technical specifications, and the implementation of the production process began after that.

Pilot production tested and analyzed all processes involved in production. Adjustments were be made as needed.

Large-scale test printing using multiple presses began. At least fifteen printers were accredited to prepare the new euro banknotes, which made it important to verify the quality and comparability of the results from the different operations.

The new issues were issued sequentially and circulated alongside the old issues. An extensive public education campaign was undertaken.[237] Old series notes will gradually be withdrawn from circulation and will fall to low levels of usage. At some point, the ECB will inform the public with ample warning that there will be a date when the old series will lose legal tender status. However, the old banknotes would continue to be redeemed by NCBs for an unlimited period of time.

9.88. The introduction of a new version of a currency involved the same types of issues about how to retire the old banknotes and introduce new notes as the initial issuance. Parallel issuance of both versions of the euro avoids massive production of the new issue needed for the big bang approach. The introduction of a new version of a currency that has distinctly different design, denomination, or security features can create many problems in distribution, handling, and counting banknotes. For example, changes will need to be made to ATMs, vending machines, money counting machines, etc. Introducing these changes can take a long time to establish and publish specifications for machines; design, build, and test machines; and install the equipment. A shorter transition time by introducing a new version currency under the "big bang" approach can make sense and save expenses. In contrast, where most banknotes are small denomination and machine processing is limited, it might be possible to gradually introduce a new currency by a parallel currency strategy.

Seasonality

9.89. Every currency has changes in demand by season as economic activity and incomes change during the year and as special events occur during the year. Seasonality in a currency refers to regular intra-year changes in the demand for a currency above or below the trend in the growth of the currency. For example, currency demand might reach a peak during the harvest season as farmers sell their crops for cash, but average demand falls during winter months when economic activity slows.[238]

[236] Extensive consultations for ES2 contrasted to the situation for the initial euro. In that case, consultations were held with representatives of the blind, but otherwise the EMI basically simply informed banks and cash handlers about the features of the new currency.

[237] The ECB has conducted research that concluded that most users of euro banknotes relied on only a few security devices to conclude whether banknotes are genuine. Features most commonly used were feel, watermark, and security thread. Most users were found to hardly check security features. Therefore, the ECB felt that there was a continuing need to educate the public about security features, especially for new banknote series.

[238] The offset to changes in currency demand is often in bank deposit accounts.

Demand changes can be regular, such as peaks in demand during New Year's celebrations, but can also be affected by holidays or events that move throughout the year, such as an increase during Ramadan. Adjusting the stock of currency to meet these changes in demand is part of the currency management function of central banks. All future unions will need to develop programs to measure seasonal demand for money and build a currency management system.

Demand outside the Euroarea

9.90. In the same way in which the German mark was extensively used outside Germany, the euro is widely used outside the Euroarea. This increases the total demand for the currency. Estimates of the demand for marks indicated that up to 30 percent of the marks might have circulated outside of Germany. This provided a floor estimate of the demand for euros outside the Euroarea, but the amount could be much more because of the much wider use of the euro compared to the mark, and also the potential to hold the euro as a investment instrument reflecting the global importance of the euro. This means that more euros must be printed than needed for local demand. Over time the ECB will gain a better idea of the overall external demand of the euro, the denominations involved, seasonality of currency movements out of and into the EMU, and channels for movements. This will allow the ECB to more precisely adjust their response to external demand. Future unions will need to monitor external flows of currency, for example to monitor cash flows of migrant workers which are known to be large in some cases.

Extended Custodial Inventory scheme (ECI)

9.91. In order to effectively supply the demand for physical euro banknotes, the ESCB created the ECI scheme, under which wholesale banks outside Europe can issue and process euro banknotes on behalf of the Eurosystem. A one-year pilot program was undertaken using two large banks in Hong Kong and Singapore selected through open tenders. Based on the success of the pilot program, a program was launched in Asia in 2008.

9.92. In the ECI, the Eurosystem provides banknotes to an ECI bank under favorable conditions in order to supply the local market. ECI banks are allowed to hold banknotes in custody prior to sale to customers. When sold, the bank is debited and the euros can be considered entered into circulation. Conversely, the ECI bank is credited when it purchases euros from customers. This technique of debiting only upon issuance to the public reduces the cost of the ECI bank of holding banknotes, and thus they can hold large unissued stocks to meet potential customer demand. In return, the bank must provide statistics about patterns of purchases and sales. The information helps the ECB trace and quantify developments in euro cash holdings outside the Euroarea, which is useful in understanding the international role of the euro. The Bundesbank handles the arrangements for the ESCB in providing and receiving euros and holding accounts.

Currency demand in gateways

9.93. Travelers to new currency unions will often seek to hold working balances in the new currency prior to travel. It is convenient if supplies of currency are available in key gateway cities to the union – Paris for francophone African unions, London for SADC or EAC, or Mumbai for the GCC, etc. Officially-promoted exchange points might be more important in smaller gateways or gateways from lower income countries where the formal banking systems might be less well developed and less likely to be well served by banks and money traders.

9.94. Unions might take steps to encourage money traders in a selection of gateway cities to carry the union currency, and ideally should exercise some influence to ensure that fees charged for the new currency are not excessive. Also, an official arrangement can help respond to fluctuations in demand and prevent spikes in demand that could create exchange volatility. An official arrangement might also help in reducing the costs of holding the union currency. As an alternative to setting up exchange points in external gateway cities, the union could guarantee ready availability of the new currency at major entry points, perhaps at official exchange sites. If these arrangements are set up, it would be useful to advertise the availability of the new currency on the central bank web site and locations.

9.95. Money traders will deal in a currency only when there is sufficient volume to generate enough income to make it worthwhile. The pre-union historic patterns for the currencies of union members might *not* provide good guidance on the activity in the union currency because demand for the union currency could be a multiple of the demand for the individual pre-union currencies. That is, trade in the union currency could be profitable for traders, whereas trade might not have been justified in any of the individual pre-union currencies.

Currency flows within the union

9.96. The common currency will move across all member economies, due to tourism, business travel, remittances, repatriation of earnings by cross-border workers, and cross-border depositing in the banking system, among other reasons. The currency is intended to be used by residents for such purposes without incurring the costs of converting national currencies. Also, the central bank or the banking system will move currency across borders to deal with local surpluses and deficiencies of the currency. Cross-border currency flows create issues related to the patterns of flows, accounting, and payment for the flows.

9.97. Strong currency movements are likely within an union. These movements will not be random. For example, EMU residents of the colder countries in Europe withdraw cash in their countries and spend it on vacations in southern countries. The issuance of currency in a country such as Finland increases the assets and income of the Finnish central bank, but conversely increases processing costs and depletes assets of the central bank in countries such as Italy when the currency earned from tourism is retired. In the EMU, these flows are large enough to significantly affect the finances of the central banks involved.

9.98. If future unions treat currency issued as a liability of by the central bank of the country where it was physically issued, then the central bank of a country that redeems the currency has an intra-union cross-border claim on the central bank of the issuing country. The receiving central bank will need to count how much currency is received from each other member's central bank, which requires that the currency can be physically identified by issuing country.[239] The accounting, creating of claims, and settling of payments must be timely to avoid favoring or disadvantaging individual member countries.

9.99. Because of cross-border movements and the implications on finances within the ESCB, a decision was made that the ESCB as a whole would be the issuer of the currency rather than the country where the currency was actually demanded. This has many implications for accounting and financing of central banks that are discussed in Chapter 14 – Accounting and Chapter 15 – Finances. This decision also affects currency management procedures, for example requiring similar standards in all members for handling counterfeit currency or withdrawing damaged currency. Future unions that choose to have currency issued by the union as a whole will need to create appropriate accounting, financial, and currency management rules.

F. Currency design

9.100. This section looks at elements of the design of union banknotes. Many technical features of the currency must be decided. The design process can be long and arduous and require several years of work.

Name of the currency and its symbols

9.101. As simple as it might seem, the selection of the name of the new currency is a sensitive issue. Each country has emotional ties to the imagery and names of its currency and coins, and conversely is resistant to adopting a currency with a name used in another country. If a planned union shares a

[239] The identification can be overt and clearly seen by the public, or could consist of coded messages that are not readily identified by the general public. Machine-readable identifiers are recommended.

currency name derived from common political or social histories (dinar, franc, peso, pound, ruble, schilling, etc.), that name is a logical choice. If not, as in Europe, the choice is more difficult.

9.102. In Europe, a decision was made that the new currency should not have national symbols or references and instead should capture the spirit of a new continent-wide entity. The decision reflected an urge to convey the unity of the continent under the new currency, and to also avoid potential problems using banknotes in an economy other than where they were issued. The name euro was selected because of its applicability in all member countries and because it was not named after any current or historical European currencies. The name of the predecessor monetary unit to the euro, "European Currency Unit" or "ecu", was rejected because it was the same of an ancient French coin.

9.103. In planned unions, the name of the currency should follow this pattern – the name should reflect a positive tone related to the new union, and should avoid national symbols references. Names must be selected for the basic currency unit and its subdivisions or coins; dollar – cent, etc.

9.104. Where the base name is used in countries outside an union, a modifier should be added to distinguish the union currency from similarly named currencies of other countries – East Caribbean Dollar, or East African Schilling, etc.

9.105. The symbols[240] and grammatical rules for the currency need to be decided. If a common historical symbol is not used, selection of the symbol could be a difficult task. The symbol will need to be simple and unambiguous, yet capture some sense of the currency name or origin. It must be easily produced in text, computer transmissions, writing, and graphics. Rules are needed on writing out currency values such as whether decimal points or commas should be used, and the number of decimal places, ($6.26; 3,13; 3/04, etc.), but these might be established quickly through market practice.

9.106. The grammatical usage of the new word "euro" had to be set in each official language, as a noun, adjective, verb, etc.. For example, in some languages nouns have a cases or gender described as masculine, feminine, or neuter. It was decided that the noun for euro would be masculine – "der Euro", and not "die Euro" or "das Euro".

9.107. The selected name should be tested in each potential union member country, to be sure that it is easily pronounced, has no awkward meanings, is not accidently associated with a person, political party, church, etc. The symbols for the currency and its coins (€, sh, $, etc.) also need to be tested. A survey of major currency handlers (banks, vendors, currency dealers) or a more general public sampling should be made, in preference to simply requesting approval by the national central banks or governments.

9.108. The selection of a name needs to be early and announced in advance as advertisement for the coming union.

Security features

9.109. Currency design has become a highly sophisticated exercise that incorporates hard to duplicate elements into the bill. For example, highly detailed and hard to copy elements are built into each bill, and paper supplies and security threads might be available only from a limited number of suppliers worldwide, where they are closely guarded. Counterfeiters might seek to copy the features, but this can be expensive and the results are often detectable as counterfeits. Some features are typically kept confidential (such as the chemical composition of inks) so that even counterfeit bills that are visually identical to real bills can be identified by counterfeit detection laboratories.[241]

[240] The symbol "€", which refers to the first letter in Europe, was inspired by the Greek letter epsilon. Parallel lines were added to represent stability.

[241] The ECB announced that the euro would have more security features than any other currency. It said that up to 90 security features are built into the euro (continued)

9.110. The ability to use the security features to detect counterfeits requires that printing be high quality and that only good quality bills be allowed to remain in circulation. The EMU was therefore very strict in ensuring that banknotes produced in each of the printing centers were identical and also that strict requirements were in place to withdraw notes that were damaged, worn, or dirty.

9.111. Modern technology allows producers of high-quality counterfeits an ability to ultimately duplicate almost any feature of genuine bills, and thus the process of producing currency is to keep ahead of the counterfeiters by incorporating new features, and making it difficult and expensive to duplicate a feature or make adequate copies of all the security features of a currency. Higher denomination bills can have many more security features than low value notes. Also, obtaining materials or expertise to produce a complex counterfeit exposes the counterfeiter of greater risk of arrest. Thus, for example, if it costs a counterfeiter €60 to produce a passable counterfeit €100 bill, with heavy sunk fixed costs in gathering the machinery, paper, designs, and expertise, the counterfeiting can be considered a very high-risk business venture that might not produce enough profit to be worth the effort.

9.112. Conversely, technology has also increased the ability to produce low quality but passable counterfeits. Color photocopy machines are widely available, and can produce counterfeits that might be passable in limited quantities to unsuspecting recipients. Many of the features of modern currency notes are explicitly introduced to prevent this type of counterfeiting. Counterfeits from photocopy machines often are easily detected because the paper has the wrong look and feel, some colors do not reproduce easily, watermarks cannot be photocopied, metallic strips or holograms cannot be copied, and microtext cannot be picked up given the resolution of the copying machine. Also, certain patterns can be printed onto the face of banknotes that can be detected by many color copiers and provide a signal that no copies should be made. Thus, although it might be easy to produce copies of genuine bills, these amateurish attempts at counterfeiting are often easy to detect and shut down.

9.113. Aging of bills makes it harder to detect errors in counterfeit bills, and therefore in countries with problems with counterfeiting the public might be hesitant to accept bills that are aged or dirty. In some cases dirty bills have traded at a discount from their face value. Unwillingness to accept aged or dirty bills can create problems in managing the money stock because usable but somewhat smudged or torn bills might need to be retired early, thereby increasing the costs of maintaining the money stock.

9.114. Some common security features of currencies are listed below. The long, but rather fascinating list of features below highlights the wide range of currency features that might be considered by future unions.[242]

Paper. The use of high-quality banknote paper is often the main feature used by the public to distinguish genuine bills from counterfeits. The Slovakian bills used a natural color paper with visible threads of three colors. The paper had a watermark and fibers that were florescent under ultraviolet light.

Watermarks. Watermarks, which have been used since the 13th Century, are designs pressed into paper when it is made. Different thicknesses of paper show up as lighter or darker fields when light is shown through the paper. Watermark designs printed into the paper often duplicate some of the key visual features of the bill.

banknotes, many of which are not observable by the public, but were incorporated into devices used by vending machines, by money processing centers, or by central banks or anti-counterfeiting labs.

[242] Most of the descriptions are provided by the Slovak Republic Central Bank, which has a nice summary of security features of pre-euro koruna. http://www.nbs.sk/mena/bankovky/oza.htm.

Printing techniques. Different printing techniques can impart a different look and feel to the bill. Genuine bills sometimes use several different techniques to complicate the job of counterfeiters. The Slovak currency used up to four different methods – intaglio, lithography, letter press, and silk screen.[243] The most important for security purposes is intaglio printing which presses ink under high pressure onto the bill, resulting in a raised surface for the ink that can be felt by touch.[244.]

Security threads. These are narrow polyester threads embedded into the paper that are visible when the bill is held up to light. Text, either legible or microtext (such as the denomination of the bill) is often embedded into the thread.

Windowed thread is a more complex version of security thread. These are short visible metallic threads interspersed across the bill that are embedded into the paper. Separating the bits of thread is more difficult to counterfeit than straight security threads, and the metallic surface is hard to photocopy. Microtext visible under certain lights can be embedded into the thread.

Bar codes. Metallic bars are embedded into the paper, serving as a binary code of the value of the note that can be scanned and turned into an electronic signal called Manchester code, which can be used for processing the note.

Check sum. The euro uses a check sum within the unique serial number on each banknote. The formula adds each number in the serial number to see if it adds to the check sum. Many counterfeit banknotes are likely to fail this test.

Latent images. This is an optical effect produced by special arrangements of lines printed by the intaglio technique that is visible only when the note is held horizontally at eye level.

Microtext. This is very small text integrated into the design of the currency that are too small for photocopiers to read and reproduce. The text also might be too small to read with the naked eye. If the microtext is generated by digital means, it is possible to embed serial numbers or information about where or when the banknotes were produced.

Reflective and iridescent surfaces. These are hard to produce and cannot be copied by photocopy machines. The Slovakian high-value denominations used highly reflective gold foil hot-stamped into the paper and a gold-colored strip with an iridescent coating on the back.

Metallic luster ink. Special inks can be used that have a metallic luster. This is hard to photocopy.

Color shifting ink. Intaglio printing using special pigments can produce fields that change color when viewed from different angles. €50 notes and above, change colors when the note is tilted.

See-through images. Portions of an image are printed on opposite sides of the bill so that the total image can only be seen by holding the bill up to light.

---

[243] *Intanglio* printing cuts designs into a metal plate, which are filled with ink that adheres under high pressure to paper placed on the plate. This results in the ink having a raised surface detectable by touch. *Lithography* uses a completely smooth surface in which oil is used to divide the surface of the plate into areas that accept the ink and areas that reject the ink. *Silk Screen* printing uses a fine weave screen through which ink is forced to make an image on paper. A stencil is created by using an impermeable material to cover areas that should not receive the ink. *Letter press* printing uses movable type with raised letters or other types of raised images that are inked and then pressed against a paper to get an image in reverse. *Ink jet* printers propel droplets of liquid ink onto the surface of the bill. This is a low cost, digital method that can produce the fine detail and microtext needed for production of bills. *Laser printing* applies negative charges across a page, then uses a laser to scan across the page to neutralize the negative changes as needed to create a pattern, then uses toner attracted to the negative changes to create the image on the page.

[244] Raised surfaces can help the blind identify bills.

Metallic foil. Pieces of foil with text or images can be hot-stamped onto the bill. In Slovakia, the foil was subsequently partially printed over. If photocopied, the result will be a black surface.

Holograms. A metallic image attached to the banknote that changes design or color as the note is tilted.

Kinegram. This is a proprietary product like a hologram that uses metal foil with images formed by microscopic lines of different thickness and shape. Changing the angle of light changes the image with an effect of a moving picture. In Slovakia, it was used on the highest value bill, where elements of the design moved and transformed.

Security line structure. Fields of lines used as background can be broken up in interspersing lines of different size or character that form a recognizable image.

***Eur**ion constellation.* A configuration of five small yellow or orange circles similar to the constellation Orion that tells color printers to not make copies.

Plastic printing base. As described in the next section, counterfeiting of banknotes printed on plastic base is difficult.

Special currency design issues

9.115. This section deals with several special issues or problems in designing a currency that meets general and special usability needs, such as durability, waterproofing, weight and size, fading, durability, or toxicity, etc..

Plastic money

9.116. In 1988, Australia introduced banknotes printed on transparent polymer plastic. It is hard to counterfeit or copy, the technology is complex and tightly controlled, and it is much more durable than paper banknotes.

9.117. These bills use a nonporous plastic base with a polymer substrate that behaves like paper for printing purposes. It is covered with a protective coating that does not absorb moisture and stays clean longer than paper bills. The special plastic used for the bills is produced by the Reserve Bank of Australia in joint venture with a private firm. The official printer Note Printing Australia also prints plastic banknotes for other countries.

9.118. Polymer banknotes have become increasingly popular because of their durability and ability to include security features not possible on paper banknotes. Many countries have switched to them, including the United Kingdom and the ECCU.

Currency for the visually impaired or blind.

9.119. In Europe, consultations were held with the European Blind Union. Euro banknotes are in different sizes - from smaller to larger as the denomination increases, use large numbers, and are in different colors (with high contrast between consecutive denominations) to assist the visually impaired or blind. Also, raised surfaces created by intaglio printing provide information including "tactile marks" on the two largest denomination bills (although they would be more useful on lower value bills that are much more commonly handled). For coins, each differs in size, weight, thickness, and milling around the edge, permitting identification by the blind.

Toxicity

9.120. The ECB investigated whether the banknotes met the most stringent European health and safety regulations. Tests were made on all denomination banknotes, all printers were investigated, and production materials were tested. This included some special investigations of the use of Tributyltin (TBT) as a possible danger to health of users. The investigation found that TBT was present in euro banknotes but at far too low levels to pose any threats. The ECB has continued investigating health and environmental issues related to euro banknotes.

9.121. Several studies suggested that the one and two euro coins release amounts of nickel that exceed EU standards and can cause skin reactions. It is posited that the use of two metals in the coins can create corrosive reactions. Another study found that excessive amounts of nickel can be found on the surface of both the center and ring parts of the coins.

9.122. Both examples above suggest that future unions should consider possible toxicity problems with their banknotes and coins. Fortunately, the properties of many different features of banknotes and coins are known scientifically, and problems can usually be avoided.[245]

Center holes and stringing

9.123. Coins with holes in their center are used by Denmark, Japan, and others. Coins are lighter, use less metal, and can be strung together or stacked on posts which could be important for transportation of coins in some settings, such as by nomadic tribes. The holes also can be uniquely designed for identification by the blind. Adjusting weights through use of holes can also facilitate identification of coins for vending and coin handling machines. Drilling holes and making them difficult to reproduce can also serve as a security device. The potential advantages of coins with center holes should be seriously considered by future unions.[246]

Composite metals

9.124. A feature that can help easily distinguish coins is to use two or more different metals. This can be done by using a center (called the pill) surrounded by a different metal (called the ring), or by using layers of different metals that can be seen by looking at the edge of the coin. This makes coins harder to counterfeit. The magnetic properties of the coins can also be changed, which can help in vending machines. Disadvantages include higher costs of production and possible corrosive reactions between the two metals. The €1 and €2 coins have pill and ring arrangements. Euro coins also have internal layers that affect their magnetic properties.

Routine changes to banknotes and coins

9.125. As time passes, minor changes will need to be made to banknotes and coins to reflect current information. Typical cases that could affect unions could include;

> Changes in signature of union central bank or other officials with signatures on banknotes. Expansion of the union in maps. Changes to banknotes and coins have reflected the expansion of the Euroarea.
>
> Use of new official languages.[247] Different alphabetic and numeric characters might be needed because of introduction of new countries using different systems. At minimum, these could reflect the name of the central bank, the name of the currency, and the numbers used. For example, the original euro used the Latin and Greek alphabets for the abbreviation of the ECB, but Cyrillic characters became necessary when Bulgaria joined the EU in 2007. In other areas, Hindu-Arabic numerals might need to be added. Any other text on the bills or coins might also need to be changed.

Commemorative coins

9.126. The Eurosystem allows member countries to mint commemorative coins bearing the name "euro". Most of these are intended to commemorate a special event or national feature and also to sell at

---

[245] On April 28, 2020 the ECB released a statement on its finding that euro notes printed on porous cotton are not effective transmitters of coronavirus. In contrast, China has reported it uses ultraviolet light to disinfect banknotes.

[246] Currently, all coins with holes use center cuts, but other possibilities exist – hard to produce irregular holes, or holes integrated into the design on both sides of the coin. This latter feature, for example, would prevent a problem with numerous counterfeit U.K. pound coins, in which the two sides of the coin are askew from each other.

[247] In addition to official languages, use of languages for important minority communities might also be useful to increase usefulness of the currency and enhance its acceptance.

a profit. They have an euro value minted into the design of the coin, which often is a high value such as €50, but they are not intended for general circulation and must be designed so that they will not be confused with regular € coins in circulation. If their design is such that they could reasonably be construed to be an euro coin and might be accepted by the public[248], the design would violate the copyright for the euro and could be acted against.

9.127. For the tenth anniversary of the union in 2009, a special €2 coin was minted. A competition was held in which the public was allowed to vote for the design. The winning design expressed the idea of evolution of trade from prehistoric barter to the euro. All member states were permitted to issue the coin during 2009.

9.128. Beginning in 2015, the ECB permitted printers to produce €0 bills as souvenirs. The bills must have many of the high-quality features of the regular banknotes.

Gold and other precious metal coins

9.129. New unions could decide to issue coins in gold or other precious metals. This is not done by the Eurosystem. Precious metal coins could be used as savings, gifts, or speculation. An advantage of gold coins is that they can earn substantial income for the issuing country or union.

9.130. The first question is who is the legal issuer of the currency and thus pockets the income. The country producing the metal might be the legal issuer of the coin, in which cases the union does not benefit, or the union could be the issuer which allows it to control the issuing conditions and denomination and creates income for distribution throughout the union. Given the amounts involved, this could be a contentious issue.

9.131. Two pricing strategies could be followed.

The coins could be minted on the basis of weight (such as one troy ounce of fine gold) and sold for the market value of the gold (and sometimes a small premium for the artistic merit of the coin). This makes them suitable for savings or for speculation based on the price of the gold content. Coins sold this way are often made through an arms-length sale by the government that frees it from any future obligation, although it might take steps to prevent counterfeiting that could ruin the sales potential of the coin.

The coins could be sold at a fixed price in the union currency that exceeds the intrinsic value of the metal content, but with a guarantee that the coin can be resold for the national currency at its face value. For example, the coin could sell at 100, but only have an ore content worth 60. It could be resold to the central bank at any time for 100. This strategy increases the profit for the government, but increases the danger of counterfeiting of the coin, and creates an obligation of the central bank to accept the coins in exchange for national currency and will also create an accounting liability for the premium on the coins. The central bank might also guarantee that it will redeem the coin for national currency at market price if it rises above the face value.

G. Counterfeiting and copyrights

9.132. This section deals with steps to deal with counterfeiting of the union currency and protection of the image of the currency which is considered important to promote acceptance of the currency and avoid damage to its reputation.

Anti-counterfeiting procedures

9.133. Prior to the start of the union, the ECB issued a report (1999b) that warned that counterfeiting could increase in an union. Among reasons cited were widespread circulation outside the Euroarea, new widely available reproduction equipment, differences in countries' detection and policing

[248] This could be a situation if, for example, someone attempts to market a €10 coin. It is not a counterfeit of a real coin, but it could be acted against as a violation of the copyrights or other statutes.

capabilities, different legal structures controlling counterfeiting, and lack of familiarity of the new currency and its security features. Future unions will need to follow similar practices, especially because some countries in new unions might have limited capabilities to investigate, police, and prosecute counterfeiting.

9.134. The ECB set up the Counterfeit Analysis Center (CAC) as a common investigation center and database and laboratory on counterfeit banknotes and coins. Initial investigation done at the national level would determine if a counterfeit was a known variety. The CAC handles possible counterfeits from outside the EU. If a new version counterfeit banknote is found it is forwarded to the CAC which will investigate then provide the information to all NCBs, mints, and the police. A separate center was established for possible counterfeit coins. In addition to the need to create a centralized entity for the technical work on counterfeiting and to support national efforts, there was also a need for coordination of police work at the EU level. Much of this activity goes through Europol, which has been given authority to deal with counterfeiting and forgery of other means of payment, that can support anti-counterfeiting activity of national authorities.

9.135. Europol requires that each country set up a single liaison office to deal with it. Moreover, the Geneva anti-counterfeiting convention requires that a central office coordinate investigation in each country. Thus, both requirements contribute to centralization of information on counterfeiting, which contributes to centralization of information within a currency union. This was backed up in the EU by rules that the police or the NCB must forward counterfeits and a complete set of information to national analysis centers and the ECB analysis center. These arrangements are supplemented by a system that provides information on whether arrests or convictions have been made and thus whether a specific episode of counterfeiting has been closed.

9.136. The report also reviewed national rules covering obligations of banks and other money handlers to hold counterfeits and surrender them to authorities. It found that ten countries did not have any requirement to hold counterfeits and surrender them to authorities. The ESCB felt that there should be a legal obligation to surrender counterfeits to prevent them from continuing in circulation. This ultimately led to introduction of rules describing obligations of banks and money handlers to scan for counterfeits as part of its regular money handling operations and to prevent them from going back into circulation.

Copyright protection and legitimate reproduction

9.137. Copyright protection for euro banknotes was also sought. The ECB sought a copyright to prevent possible misuse of the currency and its designs and other steps that might "adversely affect the standing of euro banknotes." The copyrighting of the euro banknotes allows civil proceedings to be initiated, including the possibility of taking action against counterfeiters when criminal evidence is weak. The ECB established a rule covering the copyright of the euro, but it was felt that comparable legislation was also needed at the national level to ensure application throughout the union. A legal opinion was provided that the copyright was valid even though the © copyright symbol was not used on the euro banknote, but it was agreed that it was useful to use the symbol to warn the public about reproduction. It was agreed that NCBs could exercise enforcement actions against parties violating the copyright on euro banknotes. This could include legal sanctions and seizure of unauthorized reproductions.

9.138. There are cases where reproduction of the image of the euro banknote or parts of the euro could be made for innocent purposes, such as informing the public about the bills prior to circulation or providing information on security or usability features. In principle, this might violate the copyright or perhaps could be construed to be counterfeiting. Thus, rules were needed to distinguish between innocent use of the image and cases where the purpose was illegitimate or criminal. Common rules were sought for all countries. This led to a set of rules (ECB 2003) covering permissible reproduction of the euro image. Reproduction was permitted if the result cannot reasonably be mistaken by the general public for a real banknote. This could be through actions such as changing the size of the image, printing it on material with a color or material not representative of real banknotes, printing a specific feature but with a background not resembling a banknote, and electronic images can be used provided the word specimen is prominently printed and the resolution is not greater than 72 dots per inch.

9.139. New unions should copyright their currency. The ECB rules establish a reasonable basis of protection of the image of a union currency and they are recommended for new unions. Actions to defend the copyright and use of the image of the currency will be needed, both within the union and outside the union.

Anti-copying devices

9.140. The report stated that it would be useful if photocopying devices are not permitted in the EU if they lack devices to prevent the copying of banknotes. Singapore forbids such devices. At the time of the report, no EU countries had such prohibitions.

9.141. An international Central Bank Counterfeit Deterrence Group (CBCDG), which includes the ECB and many other central banks, promotes voluntary adoption by hardware and software producers of use of counterfeit deterrence systems that prevent their devices from being usable to make counterfeits. This effort has resulted in a significant drop globally in the volume of counterfeits produced by computer and copy-machine methods.

Anti-theft devices/Replacement of damaged banknotes

9.142. Banks and other professional money handlers can use anti-theft devices that can discolor or mutilate banknotes if a robbery is attempted.[249] This either prevents the robbers from obtaining the cash or prevents putting the cash back in circulation. The ECB (2003) devised rules covering damaged cash retrieved from a robbery or attempt.

9.143. If a bank has or receives damaged or mutilated banknotes it will present them to its NCB for replacement. The NCB receiving the banknotes will inspect and analyze the causes of the damage and judge whether the legitimate owner is requesting replacement. More than 50 percent of the original banknote must be presented for replacement, or proof provided that missing parts were destroyed. Replacement is made without charge if damage stems from robbery or attempted robbery. However, to minimize the possibility of the money handlers damaging the banknotes through misuse of the anti-theft devices, NCBs may charge a fee for such damaged banknotes when they are presented for replacement.

Withdrawal of banknotes

9.144. An extension of the sole authority of the Eurosystem to issue banknotes, it can also establish rules for withdrawing currency. This covers rules for withdrawing damaged or worn currency, and for replacing the union currency with new versions.

Counterfeiting of coins

9.145. Anti-counterfeiting work was also undertaken for coins. The European Technical and Scientific Facility has a Counterfeit Coin Experts Group (CCEG) that reviews suspected counterfeit coins. Procedures similar to those for banknotes are used to collect suspect coins, test and catalog them, and report information to cash handlers and police. An annual report is made to the public (European Anti-Fraud Office; 2008)

9.146. The Group has found that there have been numerous efforts to counterfeit the 50 cent, €1, and €2 coins, with €2 coins by far the more common. The total amount of counterfeit coins has not been large in the total volume of coins in circulation. A recorded increase in detected counterfeits might

[249] For example, an anti-theft system might be designed as a currency pack with embedded electronics and a chemical pack. If the pack is given to a robber it can transmit information on location or to initiate emergency calls or take other actions. It could also set off the chemical pack that could release dyes, colored smoke, or tear gas. This can help identify the criminal, make the currency unusable, and often cause the cash to be abandoned.

partly reflect increased detection efforts so the trend is uncertain. However, the number of detected counterfeits is significantly lower than the counterfeits circulating in the Euroarea countries prior to the union.

9.147. When a counterfeit coin is identified, it is put into a specific "class", where each class represents an identifiable individual illegal mint. Each class has variants, representing different national sides, denomination, or year. This research reveals that there at least 75 independent illegal operations in business. Six operations that account for about 80 percent of all counterfeits have been long-term problems. Thus, although illegal minting operations are closed each year there is a continuing problem that reflects "intense and continuing activity of counterfeiters" (ibid, p. 7)

9.148. The CCEG works with mint directors and international technical and legal groups and cash users to try to prevent counterfeiting of coins. A special effort is being made with operators of coin operating machines. These include running tests with manufacturers to improve methods to detect and reject counterfeit coins. As a result of such work, technical means have been found for machinery to reject all known types of counterfeit euro coins. Moreover, a proposal has been made for mandatory inspection for counterfeit coins be made by cash handlers.

9.149. The experience in Europe shows that counterfeiting of coins is a real problem, especially for high value coins. Thus, planned unions will also need to develop facilities to deal with counterfeit coins, create machines to detect and reject them, and initiate law enforcement. The problem will be exacerbated if some regions of the union have limited access to detection equipment or if illegal minting is done outside the region. Like the EU experience, there is a need to establish common rules for detecting counterfeits and handling them, which might require changes to national laws.

Substitution of foreign coins

9.150. The use of foreign coins in vending machines raises an additional problem. With so many different types of coins in the world, it is possible that coins can be found that can substitute for genuine euro coins in vending machines. This could lead to situations where inexpensive foreign coins could be imported in large quantities for use in machines, causing large losses for businesses.[250]

Legal protection of banknotes and coins

9.151. Prior to the issuance of the euro, the ECB undertook surveys and prepared reports on the legal status and protection of banknotes in the EU. (ECB 1999b) This was a joint project of the Working Group on Banknotes and the Working Group of Legal Experts. Among issues addressed were counterfeiting, copyright protection and production of images of banknotes and coins, introduction of anti-copying devices, redemption of damaged or worn banknotes, rules for withdrawals of banknotes, and the status of banknotes not issued by the ECB or NCBs including issuance of non-legal tokens or banknotes denominated in euros (called "fancy banknotes"). The review was made on an EU-wide basis, recognizing that the euro would be expected to be widely used throughout the union and all countries are required to protect the banknotes of other member countries.[251]

[250] For example, the Eurosystem found that a planned series of Turkish coins could pass for €1 and €2 coins. Negotiations and tests resulted in slight changes in the Turkish coins and adjustments to coin processing and coin validation machines so that they could identify the Turkish coins and reject their use.

[251] The International Convention for the Suppression of Counterfeiting Currency of 1929 states "No distinction should be made in the scale of punishments for offenses...between acts relating to domestic currency on the one hand and foreign currency on the other."

9.152. The first step was surveying national standards against criminal counterfeiting. The intent was to obtain a complete picture of the anti-counterfeiting framework within the EU. Specific matters surveyed included the types of activities deemed punishable, legal descriptions of crimes, burdens of proof, methods of prosecution, interpretation of legislation by courts, and strictness of penalties. Both criminal and administrative offenses were covered.

9.153. The reports found that counterfeiting and falsification (creating a high value banknote out of a low-value note), procuring, possessing, transporting, and transacting were all punishable offenses. A number of countries had laws against importing counterfeits. Most countries had laws prohibiting production and the holding or sale of machines used for making counterfeits. In some countries, adapting machines so that they could be used for counterfeiting constituted attempted counterfeiting.

9.154. Counterfeiting was subject to long-term imprisonment, and some countries also impose fines. The range of penalties varied, but in some countries counterfeiting was among the most severely punishable crimes. In some countries, the laws state that punishment will be less severe for less serious cases.

9.155. The review concluded that the differences in national practice (including the application by the courts) were not fundamental and thus the matter was being handled by national practice. However, the report concluded that there was scope for a common convention for EU countries to set the minimum elements of anti-counterfeiting practice and to develop common criminal law to deal with technological innovations in counterfeiting.

9.156. In future unions, a similar survey of practices should be made, and a reasonable degree of uniformity in restrictions and their application needs to be assured. This might be through *de facto* convergence of practice between countries, designing minimum standards as proposed in Europe, or by fashioning a common legal code.[252]

9.157. Some countries had laws forbidding mutilation of banknotes or stamping or writing on them, which is a practice that new unions should adopt. Cutting coins to serve as a lower denomination currency should also be outlawed.

Protection of quality of banknotes

9.158. The mandate to protect the integrity of the euro banknote as a means of payment implies that it is in a condition that permits its use, such as for purchasing train tickets from a machine. Thus there should be "competence to adopt a common regime under with the NCBs are prepared to exchange mutilated or damaged euro banknotes."[253]

H. Legal issuance of banknotes and coins

9.159. An union must decide who is the legal issuer of the banknotes and coins used in the union. The issuer incurs a legal liability for currency issued and is responsible for redemption of currency. The legal issuer will record currency issuance on its balance sheet as a liability, and each holder has a legal claim on the issuer.

9.160. In the Euroarea, the ESCB is the legal issuer of banknotes but the national governments are legal issuers of coins. This has important financial implications, including the amount and distribution of seigniorage, and production and retirement expenses.

[252] Because counterfeiting in any union member country is a crime against the union as a whole, there is a case for centralized prosecution of counterfeiting related crimes. Also, some countries with limited infrastructure might need investigative and prosecutorial assistance from the union.

[253] Creating a uniform standard also prevents situations where different NCBs face unfair burdens and expense in terms of retiring damaged banknotes.

9.161. Because the euro is the currency of the union as a whole and circulates freely in the union, special procedures are needed to adjust the legal liability for euro issuance and the distribution of seigniorage.

For banknotes, issuance is allocated based on each country's capital share in the ECB, with an adjustment that 8 percent of total issuance is allotted to the ECB. The amount calculated by the formula is entered as a liability of each NCB, regardless of the actual amount of currency put into circulation by the NCB.[254]

For coins, the amount each NCB is allowed to mint each year is decided by the ECB, based on its analysis of needs. This limits the amount each country can issue.

I. Electronic money (e-money)[255]

9.162. In the mid-1990's, central banks began taking interest in the development of electronic money, which could be defined as encoded measures of value that could be used by computers or other electronic devices to store value and make transactions. There was concern about how various proposals for electronic currency worked, the regulation of electronic money and electronic money companies, the impacts on monetary policy, and implications for law enforcement. In 1997, the EMI reviewed the state of work on electronic money and provided an opinion to the European Commission in March 1998 that concluded that electronic money could significantly affect monetary policy in the future and that rules governing its issuance are needed.[256]

9.163. Electronic money was defined by the EMI as an electronic store of monetary value on a technical device used as a prepaid bearer instrument for making payments for undertakings other than with the issuer without necessarily involving bank accounts in the transactions. In order to be considered e-money, such devices must operate as general-purpose payment instruments. The definition excludes instruments that involve one-time prepayment for specific goods and services, such as a card that stores value only for use on a transportation system. Another important difference is whether the value on the card debits the value from the system and must be recharged, or whether the value can be transferred between electronic money systems without involving banks to debit and recharge value to the device. There are many prepayment systems in existence and some of them can be used by a wide range of vendors, so the differences between them and e-money systems is not always clear cut. Both types of systems can have monetary policy impacts – either could substitute for use of physical currency and thus raise monetary policy issues.

9.164. A wide variety of e-money devices have been developed or proposed.[257] One strong prospect for widespread future use in less developed areas are cell phone devices, in which a means of storing value is linked with a communications device.

This technology is linked to current communications practices and much physical infrastructure

[254] However, the IMF felt that information on the actual amount of currency issued in each country is useful for analysis of overall conditions and therefore it requested that this information be provided to the IMF. The data are regularly published in the IMF's *International Financial Statistics*. Future unions can also expect to be required to provide these data to the IMF.

[255] Also see *Chapter 9D – The Digital Euro*. A digital euro could have profound impacts on monetary behavior and policy. It might, for example, cut heavily into demand for physical banknotes.

[256] EMI. "Opinion of the EMI Council on the issuance of electronic money" transmitted to the European Commission. March 2, 1998. EMI Annual Report 1997. pp. 74-75.

[257] The ECB is investigating creating a digital euro as a "central bank digital currency (CBDC) as an official currency liability of the ECB. Chapter 9D, which immediately follows, describes a possible future digital euro and other CBDCs.

is already in place. Adoption could occur quickly.

Electronic money systems can be operated by computer software companies or telecommunications companies as extensions of their existing businesses, which could dramatically change monetary conditions and bring in new types of monetary institutions.

This technology appears to be well suited to facilitate financial transactions in rural and developing areas where transportation is limited and few formal banking institutions exist.[258] Thus, electronic currency can be one component of development of banking systems that can reach many millions of people without access to formal bank facilities.

A group of mobile phone operators with networks in about 100 countries and with about 600 million customers have plans to set up systems for international transmission of remittances between cellphones. These arrangements will require linkages between international payments companies, such as Mastercharge, and between local banks and cell phone operators. It is expected that the high costs of international remittances can be dramatically cut and service will be quicker and more convenient.

9.165. Other types of e-money systems exist, such as for transfers over the internet or other special e-money devices. Moreover, simple prepaid cards often can be accepted by a wide range of vendors giving them a quasi-monetary role, and they can often be easily reloaded with value, making it hard to draw a sharp line between genuine e-money devices and close competitors. Some definitions of e-money include prepaid cards. Thus, efforts to develop or regulate e-money systems should be viewed as covering a range of different channels and devices that will evolve quickly. This means that rules should be general to cover a range of systems and flexible enough to deal with innovations and new markets.

9.166. The wide availability of these devices could bring about major changes in money and financial markets. First, they can make access to financial markets available for much wider segments of populations. Second, they compete with banknotes and coins for use in transactions, which can cause structural changes in the demand for money and in seigniorage. Third, new types of financial institutions might evolve which can increase market competition, lower costs, support product innovation, and force changes in regulation and oversight. New instruments and changes in the channels of transmission might change monetary relationships in the economy and loosen the control of authorities over monetary conditions.

9.167. New forms of risk might develop. There will be new forms of operational risk because of the use of sophisticated electronic systems to handle the e-money. Interoperability of systems will be needed to prevent the possibility of failures of transactions between operators of systems. Electronic theft or fraud must be treated as possibilities and security systems developed to deal with them. There could also be a wide range of new issuers or agents for e-money, which will require new rules to register them, supervise them, and guarantee their proper operation.

9.168. The ECB also felt that the introduction of the euro could make cross-border transactions easier and less costly and facilitate a shift towards use of electronic money.

9.169. E-money systems raise the possibility of privately operated systems, including telecommunications companies, becoming competitors in issuing money to the official monetary system based on use of central bank money and official oversight.

[258] For example, in lieu of fixed line phone communications in Africa, there are estimated 100s of millions of mobile phone users who could be provided payments services through e-money facilities. The Governor of the Central Bank of Kenya has said that 85% of all bank transactions in Kenya are done using mobile phones. (bitcoin.io 2021)

The central bank and government could lose their ability to control the monetary base and the monetary stock, with potentially major effects on monetary and economic policy.

9.170. Finally, electronic money potentially seriously threatens the seigniorage income of government if it results in reduced demand for banknotes and coins. In light of the concerns above, in 1998 the ECB published "Report on electronic money" (1998), that built on the EMI's analysis. It covered reasons for regulation of issuance of electronic money and issuers of electronic money. It also addressed the role of electronic money in payment and settlement systems and prudential supervision. The ECB set out minimum requirements for electronic money systems;

Issuers of electronic money must be subject to prudential supervision

Issuance must be subject to sound and transparent legal arrangements

Technical security must be assured, including the ability to detect counterfeits

Protection against criminal abuse is needed

Monetary statistics reporting is required and companies must supply information needed for monetary policy purposes

Issuers of electronic money must be legally obliged upon request to redeem electronic money against central bank money at par

Central banks can impose reserve requirements on all issuers of electronic money

Electronic money systems should be interoperable, and

Insurance, loss-sharing schemes, or guarantees are needed to protect the holders of electronic money.

9.171. The ECB concluded that the easiest solution was to absorb electronic money schemes into the existing union monetary and institutional framework by limiting issuance of electronic money to credit institutions. The existing mechanisms for control of credit institutions were extended to cover electronic money companies. Also, the ECB is authorized to place reserve requirements on credit institutions. Therefore, electronic money companies were classified as "credit institutions" subject to the same regulatory regime as banks.[259]

9.172. The ECB argued that all issuers of electronic money should be legally obliged to redeem electronic money at par value. Redeemability is needed from the monetary policy point of view to preserve the unit-of-account function of money, to maintain price stability by constraining issuance of electronic money, and to control the liquidity conditions and short-term interest rates set by the ESCB. This feature, combined with a requirement for interoperability and common insurance arrangements, meant that electronic money could operate as a single market linked with the official monetary market. This avoids the possibility of the market operating with different liquidity or risk conditions from the overall market or between systems. Interoperability widens consumer options, reduces costs to consumers, increases competition to lower costs for customers and encourage innovation, allows switching between services, and improves efficiency.

9.173. Such conclusions led to development in 2000 of a EU regulatory framework for electronic money companies (called electronic money institutions – ELMIs) (EC 2000) that ….

Limited ELMIs to issuing electronic money, providing related financial and non-financial

[259] Communications companies are actively involved in setting up e-money systems. Following the EMU example, regulation will be needed for the e-money activities of these companies. Organizing the e-money activities as a separate subsidiary is useful in avoiding mixing regulated e-money activities with communications activities.

services, issuing and administering other means of payment, and storing data on electronic devices on behalf of other undertakings or public institutions.

Prohibited ELMIs from granting credit.

Put ELMIs under the scope of the EU money laundering directive.

Required redeemability with banknotes and coins with charges limited to the cost of the operation.

Required initial and minimum ongoing capital, set at a low €1 million level.

Required investments related to electronic money liabilities to be in highly liquid assets with 0% or 20% Basel risk weights. Activity in financial derivatives was limited to hedging of market risks. Individual countries can put limitations on extent of exposure to market risks.

The capital, liquidity, and market risk limitation requirements are subject to review by authorities at least twice a year.

The company must be operated in a sound and prudent manner, with internal accounting and controls.

However, some waivers were permitted for systems that handle only small amounts.

Implications for future monetary unions

9.174. Future currency unions should consider supporting the introduction of electronic money schemes, especially in unions where large populations have limited or no access to formal financial markets. It could be done either through operation of private schemes under close regulation such as in the Europe framework or as an official function of the union. There are strong reasons for introducing electronic money;

It is an important innovation in markets that will be widely adopted worldwide. New unions are capable of being competitive with other economies or even establishing leadership in the field.

Creating an electronic currency could be quicker, less costly, and easier to introduce to the public than a physical currency. For example, if a virtual currency is used prior to issuing physical currency, as was done with the ECU and for three years with the euro, initially issuing the currency as electronic money might facilitate adoption of the physical currency by the public.

Electronic money can facilitate cross-border remittances, which are often costly, difficult, and unsecure for large populations of migrant workers. Large segments of populations in unions could directly receive large financial benefits from cross-border electronic money remittances. This could be a major service of the union that would support its acceptance.

Payments can be made more rapidly, less expensively, and more securely than cash or mail payments.

Electronic money can effectively expand the market by allowing payments to be made over larger areas.

Electronic money can be a gateway for provision of basic financial services to large populations who do not have access to them. The system could be linked to current and savings accounts in formal banks that could provide secure and convenient savings methods for the public, and also establish channels for extending credit to e-money customers

.

Electronic money can, if desired, be used to document financial transactions to support business requirements for populations lacking access to the formal financial system.
Electronic money can facilitate settlements which can significantly reduce risks.

Electronic money can be more secure and less prone to theft or loss.

Systems can be fashioned to handle small transactions and accounts that are often uneconomical for formal banking institutions.

Cautions

9.175. However, there are many potential problems with electronic money schemes that need to be carefully considered before initiating electronic money schemes in an union. Existing systems need to be studied to draw lessons.

Growth of electronic money schemes in the EMU was much less rapid than many expected.[260] The reasons need to be understood and caution is in order. To allow for experimentation in setting up systems that work best, pilot projects might be appropriate or several systems might be allowed to compete for a period of time. (However, very rapid growth of e-money systems in Africa, such as M-Pesa[261], seems to indicate that systems that meet consumer's needs can grow rapidly.)

Operational risk is very high. Failure of electronic money systems can cause large losses, freeze transactions, and be economically, socially, and politically disruptive. Backups and redundancy must be built in. Electricity or communications failures are major threats.

Initial investment might be large to set up hardware, software, communications infrastructure, and introduce the systems to businesses and the public. There is a danger of investing in very expensive systems that have problems or which become obsolete.

Electronic systems might be suitable for areas with large populations, a high volume of transactions, and good infrastructure, but might not be feasible in many regions including most rural areas. Different degrees or speed of introduction in different regions of an union could be both an economic and political problem.

Public education will be important. Systems cannot be too complex to be adopted by large segments of the population.

The technology will evolve. The system must be able to deal with innovations and introduction of new methods.

Smaller or poorer countries might be less capable to independently operate electronic money systems, and therefore systems might need to be operated by corporations acting across borders, by the union itself, or perhaps public-private partnerships.

Criminal use of electronic money is potentially a major problem.

Security of users' systems is a major concern. Systems must be made as immune as possible to theft or fraud.

Public resistance might be high. Although systems might be very useful in particular niches, the general public could resist use of electronic money for a variety of reasons.

Electronic money will need to be usable on multiple platforms. For example, the same measure of value potentially could be used in mobile phones, computers and across the internet, or on prepaid cards (either single purpose of multipurpose).

Conversion to physical currency needs to be assured.

[260] Growth of electronic money in the Euroarea has been slow, presumably because other instruments serve public needs well. It comprises only a small part of total money. Using the ECB's limited definition of e-money, only €800 million in euro-denominated e-money was circulating in the Euroarea at the end of 2008 and less than €20 billion in 2020. A heavy majority of this was hardware-based. https://sdw.ecb.europa.eu/reports.do?node=1000003509

[261] M-Pesa was launched in Kenya, but as of 2021 has extended to a number of other countries, although it failed to catch on in several countries. Various studies on its impacts on inclusion, economic growth, and consumer protection have split between positive and negative conclusions.

Rules and laws need to be established covering usage, right of refusal, recovery of value if systems fail, etc.

Compatibility with international systems needs to be considered.

Money demand and behavior will be affected. There could be a large loss of seigniorage income unless arrangements are made to capture it in the new system.

9.176. To conclude, electronic money systems offer some important advantages for new unions, but could also have major problems and expenses. They are an important area of monetary innovation and unions might need to adopt them for their economies and financial systems to remain competitive. Electronic currency has the potential of becoming a central component of the union's monetary system. Planned unions should undertake a study early in their process of how electronic money might be used. The study will also need to consider how diverse preexisting systems and different national systems fit into the union arrangement. In light of the dangers and expenses a cautious approach might be best, perhaps focusing on a few niches (cellphone transfers, remittances, etc.) where the need is high, results can be monitored, and experience can be gained.

J. Introduction of the new currency[262]

9.177. Banks and professional money handlers must have early access to information about the new currency so that they can modify their systems to deal with the new currency. Therefore, the ECB and national central banks provided information to such entities on the new currency and its security features beginning in 2000 in preparation for the actual introduction of the currency in 2002.

9.178. Education and training of cash handlers will be important in new unions. Cashiers, clerks, bank tellers, payroll officers, toll collectors, and the like are the interface between the new currency and the public. They must be fully prepared to handle distribution, collection, and payment on the first day of circulation of the new currency. Programs to train cash handlers must be set up by the central bank, working with banks, retailers, government offices, and numerous other entities.

9.179. Training materials for cash handlers must be available in all relevant languages. Thus, in Europe, comparable materials were prepared for the official languages of all EU countries, and also in the languages of several countries that might join the union later or were considered likely to use the euro as a cocirculating currency, or would be likely to receive euros from visitors or for other reasons. (Cyprus, Czech Republic, Estonia, Hungary, Poland, etc.).

9.180. Cash handlers were provided with high quality color materials that showed the currency, its key identification features, and the main security items. For banknotes, a Trainers Guide provided information on many of the features. [263] For coins, similar descriptions of security features were provided, including size, weight, color, composition, and milling around the edge.

Notification of the public

9.181. The public reception of a new currency depends greatly on their confidence about whether the currency is genuine. It is necessary to have a public campaign to describe the currency and its security features before its release. This must be done early enough to permit knowledge of the new currency to spread widely. However, very early release of the new design and release of highly detailed

[262] Also see *Chapter 18 – Transition to the new currency* for more information.

[263] In 1998, prior to the start-up of the union, the printing plate for holograms for the euro was stolen. It was replaced with a new version. Because of the very large volume of banknotes to be printed, loss of the hologram to counterfeiters later in the production process could have created major problems in releasing the new euro currency.

images should be avoided to gain a jump on counterfeiters who could float forgeries before the public is familiar with the new currency.

Recycling of Currency – the Banknote Recycling Framework

9.182. The Eurosystem created a "Banknote Recycling Framework" (BRF) that requires companies handling cash to check that it is in good condition and is not suspect before putting it back in circulation. This section covers the process of collecting, testing, and recycling the currency; the next section covers how to deal with damaged currency and possible forgeries uncovered in this process. In 2002, guidance was given on procedures to detect counterfeits and on minimum sorting standards for currency which regularized the recycling by banks of currency back into circulation.

9.183. Practices for recycling currency in Europe vary because of national traditions, but one common practice is for banks to only supply currency received from the central bank, unless cash is recycled after authentication and fitness-checking by machines tested by the Eurosystem. The BRF is designed to create harmonized standards and clear requirements to detect counterfeits and pull damaged currency out of circulation, and to avoid competitive distortions in the process.

9.184. Elements of the BRF included;

The framework defined various types of automated cash handling machines. All machines are required to automatically identify and separate suspect banknotes, and create packages of banknotes.

Rules for recirculation of banknotes were established

Criteria for fitness sorting were established.
Separation into batches (authentic, unauthenticated, suspect, fit, unfit, etc.) was required. Batches with mixed attributes must go to the national central bank for further processing.

It is recommended that national central banks regularly supply €5 and €10 notes because these are subject to most wear.

National central banks should continually monitor the condition of currency and provide advice to the ECB on changes to fitness standards to maintain the good condition of the currency.

Standards are set for crediting accounts when banknotes are suspect or not authenticated. For suspect notes, accounts cannot be credited and the notes must be sent to the national central bank within 20 days along with information on the customer. For unauthenticated notes, information must be kept for 8 weeks.

Video surveillance of transactions was encouraged.

Common testing standards were established for money processing and authentication machines. Once a machine passes the test, it can be used anywhere in the Euroarea.

Cash handlers are responsible to install the latest hardware or software needed to meet current standards or threats.

Manufacturers are requested to inform NCBs of new procedures that help identify new types of counterfeits. This information will be covered by non-disclosure agreements.

9.185. The NCBs must monitor implementation of the BRF by collecting general information on recycling practices, statistics, information on the machinery, and information on remote processing sites where manual authentication is used. The NCBs can carry out tests of the machinery in use.

9.186. Banks and other cash handlers were granted up to two years to implement the changes, and a transitional timetable was set for countries expected to join the Euroarea. However, numerous countries requested one-year extensions, and some countries requested up to three years. Thus, an average implementation period of about four years might be expected to make these ambitious changes.[264]

9.187. *Summary of the BRF* – The Euroarea has established a comprehensive system and very high standards in order to maintain the high quality of euro currency and to suppress counterfeiting. The detection of counterfeits is facilitated by maintaining a high-quality stock of currency. Maintaining the common currency requires the application of common standards, especially for operation of money handling machines which have a prominent role.

9.188. For future unions, the highly automated currency processing environment that exists in Europe does not exist, or the financial system is bifurcated with a modern automated sector and a nonautomated sector where institutions are smaller and heavily dependent on hand processing. The programs in future unions will thus probably need to be more oriented toward visual inspection and hand processing, but more sophisticated facilities must be in place throughout the union with reasonable availability to carry out more technical examination of the currency.

Collection of damaged or suspect banknotes and coins

9.189. Cash handlers are required to take steps to identify possible counterfeits. Prior to the euro's release, EC Council Regulation No. 1338/2001 (June 28, 2001) required all professional money handlers to withdraw currency from circulation if they suspect it is not genuine and immediately hand it to national authorities. Entities that fail to do so are subject to sanctions. In 2002, guidance was given on procedures to detect counterfeits and on minimum sorting standards for currency to regularize the recycling currency back into circulation.

9.190. Most currency is examined by currency processing machines; manual inspection is required if machines are not available. The currency may be reentered into circulation only if it passes these tests. Similarly, all currency handled by the national central banks is examined by automated processing machines before being returned into circulation. Reasons to withdraw banknotes include dirt and stains, markings or notations, de-inking due to washing or chemical contact, mutilation, taping or gluing, or suspected counterfeiting.

9.191. When banknotes are identified as damaged and unsuitable to recirculate, cash handlers must send them to their NCB for replacement. Redemption is free of charge, except when the bills are damaged by anti-theft devices.

9.192. Suspect banknotes are to be sent to NCBs within 20 days of receipt, along with as much information as known on who provided it.

9.193. The ECB publishes information about counterfeits on its website semi-annually, and in annual published reviews, on the number of counterfeit banknotes taken from circulation. As this number is small relative to total circulation, the release of this information instills confidence in the public regarding the soundness of the currency. In 2006, 565,000 counterfeit bills were detected out of a total of 11.3 billion banknotes.

Currency outside of the union

9.194. The announcement of a new union currency will tend to pull back currency that has gone abroad, is hoarded, or is used for black market purposes. Reportedly, very large amounts of deutschmarks were returned to Germany prior to issuance of the euro. The mark was held globally, but was considered to be concentrated in East Europe, Turkey, and the Balkans. As much as 100 billion DM was estimated to be outside the country, of which the Bundesbank estimated that up to 30 billion DM was related to criminal activity. (New York Times 2001) Deutschmarks that could not be openly

[264] If banks choose not to introduce changes that will permit them to recycle currency, they were expected to make use of the cash handling procedures of their NCB.

deposited and exchanged for euros had to be smuggled back to Germany where they could be used for a legitimate purpose such as buying real estate, jewelry, or vehicles. The German police made random searches of cars for returning cash and reportedly discovered a sharp increase in inflows. But much might have reentered successfully because of a large number of 500-mark and 1000-mark bills returned to the Bundesbank in the year before the changeover to the euro. Conversely, there was reportedly an outflow of cash from Germany by domestic tax evaders to place the funds in foreign bank accounts where they would be automatically converted into euros when the changeover occurred.

K. Retiring currency

9.195. This section covers procedures to retire old and worn banknotes. This is a pure cost to central banks that cannot be recovered. Also, printing and introducing new banknotes removed is also expensive.

Retiring the union currency

9.196. Retirement of currency is a regular function of central banks. What is different about union situations is that cross-border movements of banknotes can seriously skew the costs that must be borne by each national central bank. Moreover, there is a special issue of who bears the responsibility and cost of redemption of the union currency circulating outside the issuing country.

9.197. Cross-border movement of the union currency will result in NCBs retiring currencies issued in other parts of the union. This incurs costs for the NCB retiring the currency. An equitable method of distributing the costs is needed.[265] This needs to be part of the intra-system accounts that deal with the costs of issuing currency, the accounting of income generated from assets acquired to issue the currency, the distribution of seigniorage, and the costs of retiring the currency.

Retiring legacy currencies

9.198. *Under the Big Bang approach* for changeover to the new currency, there will be an initial short period of dual currency use after which the legacy currency is no longer usable for transactions. It can be expected that the public will exchange the vast majority of their holdings for the union currency quickly in order to meet regular cash transactions needs. The transition program of the union will have to have specific arrangements to collect and retire almost all of the national currencies within a short period.

9.199. *Under gradual approaches*, allowing either parallel use of the old and new currencies, or replacement whenever the legacy currencies are deposited in formal institutions or are retired because of condition, there can be a surge of replacements at first followed by a long period during which old currencies are gradually taken out of circulation. The portion of the legacy currency retired might differ between countries.[266]

9.200. *In either case*, the public might hold small amounts of the pre-union national currencies for extended periods. Arrangements must be made to retire the national currencies for years. During the first year, it is recommended that all banks be required to accept the national currency in exchange for the union currency. Thereafter, only a small number of redemption points are needed, perhaps at NCBs' offices. It is important that the arrangements for redemption of legacy currencies be announced before the changeover, including the length of time

[265] This is a major problem. In Europe, euros issued in Northern Europe regularly migrate to Southern Europe for vacations, resulting in countries such as Spain or Malta incurring high expenses to retire damaged euros. Serious problems can also occur where laborers work in one country, but regularly migrate (perhaps at the end of a crop year) with cash back to their home countries.

[266] This complicates accounting because countries with a larger issued stock of national currencies continue to earn seigniorage on the currency. Without a mechanism to induce changeover to the union currency, individual countries have an incentive to delay retiring the national currency.

in which currency can be exchanged and with clear descriptions of how it will be handled in each country.

9.201. It is also recommended that arrangements be made for banks to accept other member countries currencies. Because of the common legal and accounting elements of the union countries, arrangements can be made for member central banks or the union central bank to collect notes for other member countries, and potentially carry out the destruction of the currency. There could be several options;

> Each NCB agrees to collect the currency of other member countries. Each could either then ship the currency back to the home country for reimbursement, or certify that the withdrawn currency is destroyed and receive payment based on verified certification.
>
> Each NCB could collect the currency of other member countries and transfer it to the union central bank, which would make settlements between the recipient and issuing central banks, which could be on either a gross basis or on a multilateral net basis.

Because there will be less familiarity with a currency outside the home country, arrangements for retirement in other union countries might be made upon verification by the home country that the currency received is genuine.

Timeline

This schedule is for a small or regional union. Large, or continent-wide unions should move all steps at least one year earlier.

Preparatory period	Compile data by country on currency demand, denomination, seasonality, purpose Report on national currency management practices
Early actions (four to five years prior)	Set up Currency and Printing Committee Initial contact with printers and mints Information gathering visits to unions, major countries, and vendors Investigate use of plastic banknotes Investigate use of electronic currency Decision on common, own, or vendor production Draft legal framework for common currency
Three years prior	Consultations on user needs Establish currency themes and denominations Set coin-banknote boundary and denomination ladder Select security features Decisions on currency design and features Public review or survey on currency and designs Consultations with industry on ATMs, money handling, and vending machines Draft standards for machinery Final decisions on design Decisions on electronic currency Begin work on anti-counterfeiting regime and detection centers Discuss anticounterfeit enforcement with Interpol Union and all member countries subscribe to Geneva anti-counterfeiting convention. Survey country anti-counterfeiting practices
24 months prior	National legal implementation Printing masters prepared (6 months) Arrange for purchase of materials Report on usage outside of planned union Preparation of materials for cash handlers Begin developing training materials
18 months prior	Begin training of cash handlers Test runs under operational conditions Evaluation of test and corrections Decision on initial volume Begin production of banknotes and coins, with stock for testing purposes Set up anti-counterfeit network, testing labs, and legal framework for national adoption Live run testing of machines

Final 12 months	Full production of banknotes and coins underway Shipments begin to central banks and distribution points
Final 6 months	Final decision on membership Final decision on intra-union conversion rates for national currencies into union currency By 6-month point, central banks must have working stock on hand
Run-up to union	Distribution to banks,cash handlers, and government offices Distribution to external users Distribution to central banks or distribution centers outside of union Loading of ATMs 20% reserve in the field by startup date
Day before Union day (U – 1)	Calculate final external conversion rates for new currency
Union day (U)	New currency becomes legal currency of union Monitor experiences
Early union period	Evaluate performance of machines Priority oversight of possible counterfeits Measure uptake of currency, by country Measure retirement of national currencies Initiate currency handling procedures Pull old currency out of circulation Prepare report on changeover experience
Union steady state	Complete collection of remaining legacy currency Report on collection of legacy currencies Financial accounting report on legacy currencies

Appendix I – Conversion rates from national currency to the union currency

This appendix describes various methods to calculate the conversion rates from national currencies into the new union currency, which conversely describes methods to undertake on-going analysis of the alignment of new union currencies with underlying economic conditions. This should be a major research and analysis effort for each union, and a clear decision-making process should be employed so that union members and international markets have confidence that the rates were well-chosen and based on sound economic evidence. Given the importance of this issue, new unions might test multiple methods and compare results.

Euroarea method

The Eurosystem was based on decades' long experimentation with the ECU that allowed market forces (operating with certain bounds and with occasional resettings of individual rates) to drive the evolution of exchange rates. The long development of the system allowed time for the relative price configuration of the European exchange rates to be integrated into the domestic price structures of the economies so that intraregional trade could evolve based on relative national prices. Ultimately, the configuration of exchange rates built into the ECU established the conversion rates for the euro because the ECU was converted into the euro one-to-one. The EMU method is sound in concept, but *a priori* it is unclear how much guidance it can provide to regions that will not have a long gestation period for their unions nor the same degree of real economic integration that existed in Europe. Thus, future unions might be forced to adopt alternative methods.

Gulf Cooperation Council dollar peg

As preparation for their currency union, the countries of the GCC pegged their currencies to the U.S. dollar, but at different rates for each country. This established the *nominal* relationship of each currency vis-à-vis the dollar and with each other GCC currency. This arrangement has been very effective in reducing conversion costs between the Gulf currencies and provided a method to set the conversion values for the new union currency. A tentative decision to continue the current dollar peg until the start of the GCC currency union means that the nominal conversion rates have already been set.

However, using the rates for the *nominal* peg might not be optimal for the *real* exchange rate. For example, if during the time since the peg was set a Gulf country experienced rapid domestic price inflation relative to the other GCC countries, it experienced real exchange rate appreciation against the others that makes the economy less competitive. Such a change in relative prices occurred in Qatar and the UAE during about 2006 – 2008 that markedly changed the real exchange rate between the Gulf currencies. Moreover, such imbalances could be intrinsic to the peg because the peg effectively imports U.S. monetary policy potentially leading to macroeconomic imbalances.

KKC Method [267]

A method developed by Krueger, Kamar, and Carlotti (2009) can be used to estimate conversion rates in new unions that do not have a market-based arrangements as used in Europe, (ERM and ERM II). The method sets the conversion rates based on estimates of each country's real equilibrium exchange rate (REER) and its degree of misalignment from a common reference value. KKC provide a detailed presentation of the method suitable for rigorous testing. [268]

The notion of a country's equilibrium exchange rate as guidance for setting the conversion rate into the euro was introduced in ERM II for new entrants to the Euroarea. ERM II requires countries seeking to

[267] The attributions on the working paper fail to capture the lead role of Bassem Kamar in developing the method.

[268] The method can also address changes in real exchange rate between the GCC currencies because of different rates of inflation in the countries.

join the EMU to hold their currencies within specified bands around a central parity vis-à-vis the euro for at least two years. It also requires that the central rate chosen should reflect the best possible assessment of the equilibrium exchange rate at the time of entry into the mechanism. The ECB says that the assessment should be based on a broad range of economic indicators and developments. (ECB 2003)

Identifying the equilibrium exchange rate at the conversion date is therefore essential. If an exchange rate is misaligned (overvalued or undervalued) at the time of the conversion into the union currency, it will be frozen at that misalignment leading to economic distortions across union members. An undervalued conversion rate provides higher competitiveness for the country in comparison with its partners in the currency union, and will require a higher than average inflation rate throughout the union to reduce the misalignment. An overvalued entry could involve significant costs in terms of unemployment and bankruptcies (Wren-Lewis 2003). Therefore, accurate assessment of the misalignment for all potential members of the union is crucial.

The KKC method provides a comprehensive approach to determine the conversion rate, taking into account the notion of exchange rate equilibrium. It focuses on *forecasts* of macroeconomic conditions and equilibrium exchange rates and thus has an advantage of providing policy makers seeking currency union with a framework to help identify the required exchange rate adjustments in the future when the union is expected to be formed.

The methodology has three steps:

> The first step identifies the year in which the economy was closest to its internal and external equilibrium. Several methods can be used;
>
> Use economic judgment to select a period in which there is apparent domestic and external equilibrium, based on indicators such as near-full employment, constrained price pressures, exchange rate stability, and a sustainable current-account balance.
>
> Use the IMF standard methodology to estimate the equilibrium exchange rate conditions. Three methods are used by the IMF, as described in *IMF CGER Exchange Rate Assessment Methodologies*, below.
>
> Use the real exchange rate equilibrium approach that links the exchange rate to its long-term fundamentals. The lowest deviation from equilibrium (the lowest misalignment) in the recent years is an indication of the equilibrium year.[269]
>
> The second step estimates the real exchange rate equilibrium and misalignment of *each* currency vis-à-vis the prospective anchor currency for the union, or vis-à-vis the REER if the anchor is a basket of currencies or if the objective is for the new currency to float freely.[270] Forecasted values of the real exchange rate and its fundamentals are used to allow for forward-looking perspectives.
>
> The final step consists of normalizing the equilibrium exchange rate from Step two above to have a value of zero in the year of equilibrium identified in Step one. The forecasted real exchange rate misalignment calculated in step two will serve as a measure of the necessary nominal exchange rate (NER) adjustment for the conversion rate.

These methods can be used to determine if the existing exchange rate configuration of the pre-union currencies is robust or should be changed. Small measured misalignments (such as less than 5 percent or 10 percent might be considered "close

[269] The KKC study uses this method in order to obtain nonsubjective, country-specific measures of exchange rate alignments.

[270] The countries seeking to create a GCC union have linked their currencies to the U.S. dollar – misalignment in the real exchange rates can be measured vis-à-vis that common measure. Other unions also have fixed pegs to the dollar or euro. However, other unions that wish to peg their currencies to a fluctuating currency basket or allow the union currency to float will not have a fixed nominal peg and instead can adjust to the REER using the method described here.

enough" and left unchanged. Larger misalignments should be corrected.

Text box: Euroarea harmonized competitiveness indicators (HCIs)

HCIs are REERs of each Euroarea country against major trading partners to measure their relative competitiveness in export and import trade. Applying common methods for each country allows the relative competitiveness of each member country versus other members. A common methodology is used with narrow and broad groupings of trade partners and multiple deflators (consumer prices, manufacturing unit labor costs, GDP deflators, and total economy unit labor costs). HCIs can be used to either compare competitiveness of a member country vis-à-vis other members or against countries outside the Euroarea.

The ECB methodology is well-documented (ECB website or Buldorini (2002)) and can provide guidance to statistical programs in emerging regions.

Because the conversion to the new union currency is a prospective event that will occur in the future, the methodology uses forecasted data for all the variables and proxies in the models. Data for each GCC country from the IMF's World Economic Outlook forecasts were used because they are available for many countries for five future years in a harmonized fashion. However, other forecasts can be used for comparison of results.

For example, a forecast misalignment of each exchange rate is based on the information identified in points one and two. For each prospective union country, the equilibrium bilateral real exchange rate is set to equal zero at the equilibrium year identified in step 1. Then the misalignment estimated in step 2 is used to get the required percentage of adjustment for each year following the initial established rate – which because of the use of forecast data is forward looking. For example, if the REER was at equilibrium in year 2006, and the misalignment in year 2010 is estimated to be +27% (i.e., overvalued by 27%), 23% in 2011, and 17% in 2012, the exchange rate needs to be devalued by 27% if conversion into the currency union takes place in 2010, by 23% if the currency union takes place in 2011, and by 17% if the common currency in established in 2012.

One reason for using this approach is that each prospective union will face challenges to its credibility and the new union currency might be subject to speculative attacks. Information from this method can impart a view to the public that exchange rates are based on fundamentals, which can contribute to greater stability for the currencies. The rigor needed to apply the method requires that authorities carefully organize their research and analytic program to compile the range of relevant data from all the prospective union members and carefully analyze the data and produce defensible results. By doing so, the researchers and union authorities will be very familiar with conditions in each country and the conditions that favor or hinder the use of any specific conversion rate. This expertise can contribute to public confidence that the proper exchange rate has been used. Each prospective union should undertake such investigations, ideally starting well before the official beginning date of the currency union.[271]

Moreover, the information generated will provide key insights on the convergence process, especially real convergence, that can help evaluate the process of union building. One possibility is to apply different scenarios to the underlying parameters to reflect possible policy or exchange rate regime options.

IMF CGER exchange rate assessment

The IMF has a standard method for assessing exchange rate conditions called the Consultative Group on Exchange Rate (CGER) approach. The

[271] In all regions, data issues will present challenges to all methods to calculate conversion rates. Historical time series going back well before the planned start-up date for the union will be needed. For this reason, programs to compile the relevant statistics under common standards should begin in all potential member countries early in the process of developing the union. A centralized database is required to make use of the data to estimate the conversion factors.

CGER uses a multi-country panel to estimate equilibrium trade conditions. The use of a panel permits application of the results to a wide range of countries and therefore the method is easy to apply, but it lacks precision that can result from focusing on variables affecting individual countries. Assessments of exchange rate misalignments based on CGER will always need to be informed by country specific factors that are difficult to incorporate into studies based on large cross-country datasets.

Surveillance over the exchange rate policies of its member countries is a central responsibility of the IMF. In late 1994, the IMF took a step toward making its surveillance more effective by initiating more extensive and systematic assessments of current account positions and exchange rates of the major industrial countries, incorporating both the perspectives of the IMF's area departments and calculations derived from a multilateral framework implemented by the IMF Research Department. In 1995, the interdepartmental CGER was established to strengthen and extend this work, and provide greater discipline and consistency in the staff's judgments about exchange rates. CGER's general approach for assessing the current accounts and exchange rates of the major industrial countries was reviewed by the IMF's Executive Board in October 1997, and a description of the methodology was subsequently made public.

Abiad, Kannan, and Lee (2009) describe three complementary approaches used in the CGER: macroeconomic balance approach, reduced form equilibrium real exchange rate approach, and external sustainability approach.

> The **macroeconomic balance (MB) approach** calculates the difference between the current-account balance projected over the medium term at prevailing exchange rates, and an estimated equilibrium current-account balance or "CA norm." The latter is a function of medium-term determinants of the savings-investment balance, such as demographic factors (population growth and old-age dependency), the fiscal balance, and level and growth rate of output per capita. The exchange rate adjustment that would eliminate this difference over the medium term—a horizon over which domestic and partner-country output gaps are closed and the lagged effects of past exchange rate changes are fully realized—obtained using country-specific elasticities of the current account with respect to the real exchange rate.
>
> The reduced-form **equilibrium real exchange rate (ERER) approach** estimates an equilibrium statistical relationship between the real exchange rate for each country and macroeconomic fundamentals, such as net foreign asset (NFA) position, relative productivity differentials between the tradable and nontradable sectors, and the terms of trade. The exchange rate misalignment is then calculated as the difference between the estimated equilibrium real exchange rate, based on medium-term projections of the fundamentals, and its current value.
>
> The **external sustainability (ES) approach** calculates the difference between the current account balance projected over the medium term at prevailing exchange rates, and the balance that would stabilize the NFA position of the country at some benchmark level. Using the same elasticities as in the MB approach, this difference is translated into the real exchange rate adjustment that – over the medium term – will bring the current-account balance in line with its NFA-stabilizing level.

The three misalignment estimates are then combined to give an **overall assessment**, using simple criteria. If the average of the three misalignments is within five percent of zero, or if each of the three misalignments are less than 10 percent in absolute value, then the currency is assessed to be broadly in line with fundamentals. Otherwise, the approximate midpoint of the three estimates (when all three estimates are within 10 percentage points of each other) or a range encompassing all three estimates (when the estimates are at least 10 percentage points apart) is used as the assessment.

Cross-country price comparisons

Although unlikely to be the primary method of setting conversion rates, information on relative prices of traded goods can provide important supplemental information on the price structure in the new union conversion rates. The use of price information in based on the concept of purchasing power parity which says that, with allowance for differences in shipping costs, the price of identical goods traded between countries converted by a exchange rate should be equal. A corollary is that if they are not equal, arbitrage will take place to shift purchases to where the goods are less expensive. This shift in demand for goods between countries can lead to changes the exchange rates until the point is reached where parity is restored. In a classical economic environment, movements in exchange rates that cause deviations in PPP will be short-lived.

This basic concept has been thoroughly empirically reviewed, but most important for this purpose is the International Comparison Project (ICP; 1975) and the numerous follow-up studies). The ICP is a major international statistical initiative needed to produce price measures for national income measurement and to measure poverty and wealth. It uses the concept of PPPs to convert national expenditure data into a common currency. *The body of research for the ICP has shown that movements of exchange rates can cause significant and persistent deviations in exchange rates from those that result from PPP.*

Another aspect of the ICP is that converting purchasing power in different countries by *exchange rates systematically understates the purchasing power of the currencies of low-income countries.*

> *This makes per capita incomes of low-income countries look lower than the reality.*[272] *For new unions, a wide dispersion of incomes among prospective members could indicate misalignments away from PPP, which is ultimately one of the goals of creating an integrated economic area within the union. The challenges of finding the best conversion rates will be greater under these circumstances.*

These conclusions are very important for new currency unions. *It cannot be assumed that PPP conditions will exist between countries joining an union.* Whether PPP exists can be empirically determined using the ICP methodology, and mechanisms can be sought to encourage greater integration of the price structure in the planned union, through market mechanisms such as use of the ECU in Europe or other methods such as the KKC method above.

Fortunately, the ICP program is being widely applied and good information on prices of comparable goods is available for many countries, including in Africa. As these data will continue to be needed for future unions, continuing support for the ICP is needed.

Planned unions might consider applying the ICP methodology across future member countries to better obtain information specific to their future union.[273]

[272] The real rate – although better than the estimated income level – might still not be good and the poverty being described is still very real, but at least it is being better measured. For example, a higher more accurate estimate of the starting point will tend to show that improvements in poverty are less rapid than shown with the less accurate data.

[273] *Chapter 12 – Statistics* has further discussion on the ICP.

Appendix II – ERM bilateral central rates

This appendix presents three tables used in estimating the conversion values of national currencies into the euro. The uses of these tables are described in section D, above.

Table 1 presents the matrix of bilateral central exchange rates used to set the central rates for the ECU that was used to set the final irrevocable conversion rates for the euro.

Table 1 - ERM bilateral central rates used to set the irrevocable conversion rates for the euro

	DEM100 =	BEF100 =	ESP100 =	FRF100 =	IEP1 =	ITL1000 =	NLG100 =	ATS100 =	PTE100 =	FIM100=
Germany:	1.00000									
Bene/Lux[274]	2062.55									
Spain:	8507.22	412.462								
France:	335.386	16.2608	3.94237							
Ireland:	40.2676	1.95232	. 473335	12.0063						
Italy:	99000.2	4799.90	1163.72	29518.3	2458.56					
Netherlands:	112.674	5.46285	1.32445	33.5953	2.79812	1.13812				
Austria:	703.552	34.1108	8.27006	209.774	17.4719	7.10657	624.415			
Portugal:	10250.5	496.984	120.492	3056.34	254.560	103.541	9097.53	1456.97		
Finland:	304.001	14.7391	3.57345	90.6420	7.54951	3.07071	269.806	43.2094	2.96571	

Table 2 presents the calculations used to set the irrevocable conversion rates for national currencies into the euro. The data in Table 2 are sample data for yearend 1997 (the year before the actual conversion) as published May 2, 1998 in the *Joint Communiqué of Finance Ministers and Central Bank Governors of the Member States adopting the euro* to show the calculation that would be used to set the actual rate for the euro. The actual irrevocable conversion rates based on exchange rates at the end of 1998 are shown in Table 3, immediately below Table 2.

[274] Belgium and Luxembourg used a single currency.

Table 2 – Calculation of exchange rates of official ECU against the EU currencies in the Euroarea
Sample data for December 31, 1997

	National currency units in ECU basket ($weight_{NC}$)	US$ exchange rate on Dec. 31, 1997 (NC/$)	Dollar equiv. of national currency amount ($weight_{\$}$)	ECU exchange rates
	(a)	(b)	(c) = (a) / (b)	(d) = (*USD/ECU*) × (b)
DEM	.6242	1.7998	0.3487541	1.97632
BEF	3.301	36.92	0.0894095	40.7675
LUF	.130	36.92	0.0035211	40.7675
NLG	.2198	2.0172	0.1089629	2.22742
DKK	.1976	6.8175	0.0289842	7.52797
GRD	1.440	282.59	0.0050957	312.039
ITL	151.8	1758.75	0.0863113	1942.03
ESP	6.885	151.59	0.0454186	167.388
PTE	1.393	183.06	0.0076095	202.137
FRF	1.332	5.9881	0.2224412	6.61214
GBP	.08784	1.6561	0.1454718 *	.666755
IEP	.008552	1.4304	0.0122328 *	.771961
ECU basket = Sum of dollar weights above			*ECU = 1.1042128**	
FIM		*5.4222*	1.1042128	*5.98726*
ATS		*12.59*	1.1042128	*13.9020*

Table 3 – Irrevocable conversion rates
Actual rates derived from December 31, 1998 exchange rates,
Using the methodology in Table 2

Currency	Six-digit conversion rate
Austrian schilling	13.7603
Belgian franc	40.3399
Dutch guilder	2.20371
Finnish markka	5.94573
French franc	6.55957
German mark	1.95583
Irish pound	.787564
Italian lira	1936.27
Luxembourg franc	40.3399
Portuguese escudo	200.482
Spanish peseta	166.386

Appendix III – Euro banknote production in 2009

Denomination	Quantity (millions of banknotes)	Value (€ million)	Producing Countries
€5	930.00	€4,650	France; Netherlands
€10	1,170.00	€11,700	Germany, Greece, France, Austria
€20	4,228.28	€84,565	Cyprus, Estonia, France, Germany, Ireland, Greece, Luxembourg, Malta, Netherlands, Portugal, Slovenia, Finland
€50	2,700.00	€135,000	Belgium, Germany, Spain, Italy
€100	700.00	€70,000	Italy, Austria
€200[275]	none	n.a.	n.a.
€500[276]	none	n.a.	n.a.
Total	**9,728.28**	**€305,000**	

[275] At various times, €200 notes have been printed by Belgium, France, Germany and Italy. Due to limited demand, no production was needed in 2009.

[276] Austria and Germany printed €500 notes. No €500 notes have been printed since 2014, and in 2016 a decision was made to end its production.

CHAPTER 9D – THE DIGITAL EURO

Central Bank Digital Currency (CBDC) – In 2021, the ECB announced it is investigating issuing an official digital version of the euro. Issues creating a digital euro are perhaps as complex as creating the physical euro. A CBDC mu st be fully compatible with an union's physical currency as described in Chapter 9. A digital euro and its possible spread outside the Euroarea might (along with the rise of other CBDCs) induce other unions or future unions to create their own CBDCs.

This chapter draws on current investigations into a digital euro as well as EU work on legal and supervisory frameworks for digital assets. The chapter discusses some aspects of bitcoin and other cryptoassets that gave impetus to create CBDCs, but cannot provide a comprehensive picture of that complex and rapidly evolving environment and its technologies.

The many diverse digital projects underway, in combination with the severe disruptions and price collapses in private cryptoassets in mid-2022 ("crypto winter"), create relevant news almost every week. This chapter provides a picture in time (early to mid-2022) and readers are advised to keep up-to-date with changes since the chapter was written.

"Given the potentially far-reaching consequences of CBDCs, policy makers must apply the utmost prudence."[277]

A. Introduction to CBDCs

9D.1. A CBDC is a digital equivalent of cash issued and backed by the central bank.

9D.2. CBDCs can be constructed either as general-purpose (retail) legal tender used like cash or deposit account money at commercial banks, or as (wholesale) intrafinancial-system instruments for use in the regulated monetary system (the central bank, commercial banks, and other authorized users).

9D.3. In July 2021, the ECB formally announced a project to create a "digital euro", an electronic version of the cash euro. The digital euro is an example of a Central Bank Digital Currency (CBDC). This chapter gives some history on reasons to create it, describes advantages or risks, and summarizes some possible lessons for future monetary unions.

The digital euro will revolutionize the European monetary picture, with global consequences.[278]

The digital euro can meet demands for efficient, inclusive instruments to support the European economy and facilitate cross-border transactions. It will change market dynamics, require new institutional and legal arrangements, and raise new types of risks.

Internationally, the digital euro and other CBDCs could drive regional monetary and payment arrangements to take advantage of its efficiency and cross-border flexibility, but could also penetrate and threaten smaller national currency markets. A plausible response might be for other countries and regions to accelerate work on monetary unions to create their own digital currencies.[279]

B. Background

9D.4. Many countries and the international financial community are investigating and testing creation of CBDCs – of which a digital euro would be a global leader.

9D.5. A digital euro would be a complex instrument that merges elements of cash and payments instruments. It can introduce efficient services and lower costs, but might induce financial disintermediation, soundness risks, and monetary policy dislocations. It affects many aspects of the financial system and paths ahead are still uncertain. Authorities analyzing CBDCs will need a multifaceted and balanced approach that promotes the benefits, but guards against negative results and disruptions.

9D.6. As of yearend 2021, work on a digital euro and other CBDCs is moving rapidly and the ultimate results are unknown. National and regional officials will need to monitor the ongoing work closely and be prepared to adjust frequently.

9D.7. This volume has suggested at various points that a new currency union could promote adoption of its new currency by first issuing a digital version. For example, in the Euroarea, the euro existed electronically in bank and government accounts for three years before physical euros were issued. During that period, the public, businesses, and financial institutions had time to become familiar with the new currency, reprice goods and financial contracts, and otherwise prepare to transition to the physical

[277] World Economic Forum. (2020)

[278] In January 2022, the U.S. Federal Reserve Board issued a paper requesting public comments on whether a digital version of the dollar should be created and how it might operate and be regulated. (FRB 2022) In March 2022, U.S. President Biden issued an executive order mandating that government agencies investigate numerous aspects of crypto markets, including possible development of a U.S. dollar CBDC and policies promoting investor protection, financial stability, and prevention of illegal use of cryptoassets.

[279] For example, the ECCU has already created its own digital currency called "DCash". Among larger countries, China already has a CBDC in limited circulation. Cambodia has a system called Bakong, and several other early CBDCs have been floated.

currency. Future unions might do something similar by for example beginning with a virtual version of the union currency for mobile phone transactions.

9D.8. Today, electronic transactions are intermediated by supervised financial institutions that maintain reserves and other accounts with the central bank. In contrast, CBDCs are direct liabilities of the central bank that are issued either as;

a general-purpose *retail* equivalent of cash that the public can use for transactions, or as

a *wholesale* instrument used between the central bank and financial intermediaries.

9D.9. As simple as the concept of an electronic version of cash might seem, many issues – technical, legal, institutional, policy, and consumer protection – need to be resolved. *Creating a digital currency might be as complex as creating a physical currency.*

9D.10. The complexity arises because cryptoassets can have features of cash, payments systems, securities, investment funds, or even commodities. They often fall outside of existing regulatory and tax rules and legal jurisdiction over them (by country or by topic) often is unsettled. These uncertainties are heightened for cross-border transactions.

9D.11. The ECB and many other central banks are now researching how to create CBDCs, investigating their possible impacts on the economy and public, and reviewing how to manage policy. China is a leader in developing a CBDC, but the ECCU and a handful of other countries already have CBDCs, and many others will surely follow. Many options are still in play and eventual directions are unknown.

9D.12. International flows of CBDCs (for tourism, cross-border income flows, remittances, general capital flows, etc.) could be large. Countries will need to adjust monetary and payments systems to receive such flows and monetary policy changes might follow. Ease of transacting in CBDCs might overwhelm smaller national currencies or result in other countries' CBDCs cocirculating along with national cash systems or national CBDCs. All countries (including future unions) will need to consider how CBDCs could affect their systems and whether they should launch their own CBDC.[280]

9D.13. As will be discussed below, issues surrounding CBDCs are quite complex and deserve a high priority in work of future monetary unions. Handling the complexity might be beyond the resources of many small or medium-sized countries, which argues for adoption of coordinated regional approaches or international interoperational systems. Thus far the implications of CBDCs for recipient countries appear to have been little considered, but this will become important for many countries.

C. Why create CBDCs? Some History and Terminology

9D.14. A digital version of the euro was always a possibility, but new technologies have transformed and accelerated the likelihood. This section briefly scans several developments since creation of the euro that help explain why CBDCs became interesting.

9D.15. A history (in rough chronological order) leading to CBDCs includes;

- Bitcoin and its imitators – bitcoin was a breakthrough technical innovation that spurred many new instruments and market developments,
- "Altcoins" that enhance the bitcoin framework,
- "Stablecoins" which are altcoins that have value linked to a currency or basket of underlying items,
- "DeFi" (Decentralized Finance), which builds on a bitcoin type network to handle many banking and securities functions,
- Recognition of bitcoin's energy demands,
- Libracoin, which was a stablecoin intended to directly challenge national currencies,

[280] The cross-border aspects of CBDCs are significant and have led countries to adopt various strategies, including taking steps to prevent foreign CBDCs from entering as well as preventing nonresidents from holding the domestic CBDC.

- EU actions to encompass digital instruments within its regulatory framework, *and finally….*
- CBDCs.

Bitcoin

9D.16. Bitcoin (market symbol BTC) began in 2008 following publication of a paper authored under the pseudonym Satoshi Nakamoto, "Bitcoin: A Peer-to-Peer Electronic Cash System." Bitcoin was designed as a fully anonymous not-state-controlled instrument transferable by digital devices (computer, mobile phone, etc.).[281]

9D.17. Bitcoin mixes cash-like features (anonymous holding of value usable for transactions) and payment and settlement features (quick, low cost, verified transfers including international transfers) allowing it to be used for many legitimate reasons but also for tax avoidance and criminal reasons.

9D.18. Bitcoins can be used to transfer value quickly, inexpensively, and anonymously. They have no intrinsic value; their value is based on their acceptance by a community of holders that holds and trades them for their unique properties. Bitcoin's price is based on supply and demand conditions – because the supply of bitcoins is strictly controlled (by the algorithm that generates them), changes in demand create volatile prices.[282]

9D.19. Bitcoin operates through a global network of "miners" (also called "nodes") which are independent data processing centers that verify transactions and create new bitcoins. Miners are compensated under a 'proof of work' basis that rewards miners with fees[283] and with new bitcoins for verifying transactions and embedding an encoded record of transactions into a permanent 'blockchain'.[284]

9D.20. Bitcoin miners employ a 'distributed ledger technology' (DLT)[285] in which encoded records of transactions are sent electronically to miners throughout the world to verify. The system is described as "*permissionless*" meaning that any entity willing to invest in and operate the required computer

---

[281] This section goes into some detail regarding the bitcoin system because it is the dominant instrument and established many practices related to cryptoassets. However, digital instruments have gone in many different directions from bitcoin, only some of which are discussed in this study.

[282] The supply of bitcoin used for trading is significantly less than total issuance because many are hoarded as stores of value and a good number have been lost.

[283] Fees to miners are based on the size of transactions handled. For example, a rate of 0.00000048 bitcoin per byte, could generate a total fee for a transaction of average length that might range between €5 and €20 depending on the bitcoin market price. Also, a paper by the U.S. Federal Reserve Board (2022) cited original bitcoin processing speed as only about 5 transactions per second and costs up to $60. Such speed and prices are prohibitive for small-value transactions, but less expensive than correspondent banking fees used for larger international transactions and remittances.

[284] The bitcoin verification system relies on majority votes by the global community of miners to avoid cases of spending a bitcoin (which is only a string of computer code) multiple times. Miners are compensated on a so-called '*proof of work*' basis by processing a large number of transactions and solving a very difficult mathematical problem. The process to communicate and verify globally is slow and takes 10 minutes or more to complete. (New competitors to bitcoin claim faster processing times.)

Alternatively, verification can be done on a '*proof of stake*' basis that weights miner's votes based on the size of their investments (as measured by their capacity to process transactions, which is largely a function of the size of their investment in specialized computer chips) – this system often involves fewer miners and thus uses less energy.

A third alternative is *'proof of authority'*, in which a few authorized and trusted verifiers (such as central banks) are used. These systems are fast and use much less energy than the original bitcoin model. A CBDC can operate on a proof of authority basis and thus be much more efficient than private systems.

[285] Gonzalez (2021) has a brief introduction to DLT.

facilities can mine bitcoins for profit or set up exchanges that allow the public to buy, sell, or store bitcoins. A permissionless system requires a mechanism to review and approve by majority vote all transactions handled by individual miners – which increases the resources employed to verify transactions and slows processing.

9D.21. The alternative is a "*permissioned*" system operated by smaller groups of miners based on their size of investment stake in the system or their authority (such as central banks).

9D.22. The record of verified transactions is embedded in a 'blockchain'. The blockchain provides proof, verified by the bitcoin mining community, of who owns a coin – it is designed so that the coin cannot be copied, spent more than once, nor owned by more than one party.[286]

9D.23. Miners comprise a truly global network in which they operate over the internet anywhere in the world. The actual processing process uses large banks of specialized computer chips[287] that generate large amounts of heat and which must be cooled by air conditioning or by placing facilities in cold climates. The main cost of mining is the cost of electricity to run and cool the system and thus processing is concentrated in areas of cheap electricity or cold temperatures. The industry is mobile and if costs or regulatory/political situations change, miners can move.

9D.24. The general public does not transact directly within the bitcoin system. The public pays for bitcoins using national currency at 'exchanges' that charge fees to purchase the coins or make transactions. Customers' holdings are held in 'wallets' that record the owner and an amount of coins held. (The wallet contains the amount of coins - not the equivalent national currency value of the coins).[288] The value of the coins in the wallet or used for transactions reflects the current market value of the coins on an exchange.[289]

9D.25. Finally, bitcoin is not 'currency'. Unlike cash, it lacks official backing, is too volatile to be a stable store of value, does not have general use for transactions, has limited public acceptance, and with rare exceptions is not legal tender for use in official transactions (such as for taxes).

'Cryptocurrency'

9D.26. The term *cryptocurrency* was originally applied to bitcoin because advocates argued it could substitute for or even replace official national currency. The term however has come to be applied loosely to many different types of digital instruments that are not currency. Thus, *the term 'cryptocurrency' is generally considered misleading and it is*

[286] A key innovation of the blockchain is that it acts as a ledger that verifies that each bitcoin is held by a unique owner and that a transaction irrevocably transfers ownership, thus preventing a holder from copying it and using it more than once.

[287] Mining involves a very large number of calculations in order to monitor and verify transactions. In one example, one Chinese mining pool said it was expanding its capacity to handle an *additional* 18 quintillion calculations (18,000,000,000,000,000,000) *per second.*

So many calculations use a lot of electric power – global bitcoin mining uses more power than entire countries. This demand for power has been widely criticized as environmentally damaging – excessive power demands were cited in 2021 among the reasons for shutting down blockchain mining in China (which prompted major shifts in mining into Kazakhstan, the United States, and elsewhere.). Energy consumption was also cited in a Russian central bank proposal to ban bitcoin mining. (Reuters.com. 2022)

[288] The holder (or the exchange) must retain a record of the coins held – if that record is lost (including by the exchange or theft from the exchange) any value from the coin is permanently lost – the same as if cash were destroyed. A significant number of bitcoins are believed to be permanently lost.

[289] The public purchase and sell coins at exchanges based on the coins' national currency market values. National currency prices of a bitcoin can differ between exchanges.

recommended that it not be used – either as a general description of widely diverse instruments nor especially in comparisons to CBDCs which will be true currencies.

Altcoins

9D.27. The pathbreaking bitcoin framework quickly fostered many different crypto instruments, often referred to as "altcoins" (alternative coins). Most of these changed various features of the bitcoin model to enhance speed and usefulness or serve additional functions. Also, "native coins" were designed for exclusive use in specific or proprietary payments systems or to serve specific clients.

9D.28. By mid-2021, the global total value of altcoins began to rise above the total market value of bitcoin. Because altcoins are embedded in many specific financial niches, they will continue to exist in some form regardless of what might happen to bitcoin. The diversity of altcoin experiments complicates their treatment as economic instruments, which can affect accounting, tax treatment, supervisory oversight, policy action, and analysis. Many altcoins have failed, but thousands still exist.[290]

9D.29. Future unions will need to follow developing definitions of instruments and international guidance on their treatment, and in union settings countries must agree on common treatments.

Text box: Mining income

Bitcoin and many subsequent DLT systems are based on a global network of independent miners that operate processing facilities that record transactions in the blockchain. Miners earn income in two ways – creating new coins that are credited to their accounts and earning fees for processing transactions.

Creating new coins. In the bitcoin system, miners compete to solve a very difficult mathematical computation in which the winner is rewarded with a number of newly created bitcoins. In 2021, 6.25 bitcoins were awarded for each iteration of the process, which occurs about every 10 minutes. Because a reward is made only to the first miner with the solution, miners often form pools to increase chances of gaining a reward which is then shared between pool members. Large groups have formed to the point that mining is dominated by only a handful of groups.

Processing fees. The second source of miner income is fees for processing transactions. In a typical situation, a customer approaches an exchange to handle the transaction. The exchange announces to miners that it has a transaction to process along with information about the fee the customer is willing to pay.

Based on the length of the transaction (measured in terms of bytes of data) and the fee offered, miners decide whether they will accept it. Fees reflect the number of coins offered per byte processed, which must be sufficient to cover miners' variable costs, which is usually mostly electricity.

Fees also vary because of the limited processing capacity of the system. In 2021, an average ten-minute session handled just over one million bytes of data. If capacity is reached, miners accept transactions offering the highest incentive fees; customers offering low fees can see their transaction delayed or ignored. Transactions with highest fees are handled in the next ten-minute session, but those with lower fees are processed later. Fees rise at periods of high demand or when system capacity is stretched – for example, very sharp spikes in fees occurred around yearend 2018 and in mid-2021. The possibility that during financial stress the system cannot handle panic demand and thus generates fee spikes is a clear threat to the soundness of the system.

[290] Bitcoin dominated the crypto market during the first dozen years. Altcoins began slowly but many new altcoins appeared beginning around 2017 and during the bitcoin price spike in 2021. Over time, altcoins with more advanced features, less energy consumption, better consumer protection, or better governance features might overtake bitcoin in general usage or become lead instruments within some market segments or for certain functions. Two largely parallel markets have developed – one for the original bitcoin and entities directly derived from it, and the second focused on altcoins and their use for general business purposes. Although daily price movements between bitcoin and the leading altcoins are often closely correlated, bitcoins and altcoins probably should be analyzed separately.

In summary, bitcoin processing fees are high relative to other retail payment systems and take 10 minutes or more to settle, both of which are unacceptable for many commercial applications.

Stablecoins

9D.30. Stablecoins are an important type of altcoin linked to the value of a currency, currency basket, or basket of noncurrency assets (commodities, securities, derivatives, etc.). The first stablecoin, which was U.S. dollar linked, was issued in 2014; it remained fairly inactive until bitcoin began to rise in value in 2017, at which time many new stablecoins were created.

9D.31. Stablecoins linked to a single currency can be exchanged for that currency and must have ready backing in that currency. Stablecoins linked to a currency basket will vary in value with changes in the value or composition of the currencies in the basket.

9D.32. Single currency stablecoins reflect the value and returns of the underlying currency, but break direct links with central bank money or formal banking institutions. An example might be a mobile phone company creating its own digital coin to facilitate transactions between its customers.[291] On a wholesale basis, a stablecoin could facilitate international transactions, settle interbank balances, temporarily park assets outside of the formal banking system or outside regular operating hours, or handle transactions within closed proprietary systems.

9D.33. A multicurrency stablecoin could be relevant in multiple situations.[292] Many questions arise in constructing a basket (currency weights, changes in exchange rates, trading bands, portfolio "hardening", interest returns and remuneration of holders of the basket, among others).

9D.34. The type, extent, and liquidity of reserves backing stablecoins is critically important – a stablecoin can be judged by its reserves backing and can be subject to the same risks as its reserves.[293] Reserves of some stablecoins include other stablecoins or crypto-derived instruments, which can be correlated with bitcoin or other altcoin prices; thus, under crisis conditions[294] demands for stablecoins' reserves could correspond to drops in the value of reserves, thus transmitting financial stresses between coins or creating market instability.[295] [296]

[291] This example might be relevant as a means to enhance financial inclusion - mobile phone systems in developing countries have increasingly provided basic banking services to many without easy access to banks and other formal banking institutions. A proprietary stablecoin might be used in lieu of using banking facilities – but it would have many economic and policy implications.

[292] For example, had the technology existed prior to the founding of the EMU, a multicurrency stablecoin could have been used to emulate the ECU as a weighted measure of the participating currencies prior to release of the physical euro; or future unions could explore creating one as a step to create their new union currency. Also, a digital SDR-equivalent stablecoin is possible. (Chapter 3 covers the ECU, which had properties analogous to currency basket stablecoins.)

[293] Similar issues rise for central bank reserves and commercial bank capital, which are subject to stringent capital adequacy standards. Stablecoins in contrast are largely unregulated, lack transparency, and lack backup liquidity and swap facilities available to the formal institutions.

[294] Given the speed of digital transactions, demands to convert stablecoins into an underlying currency potentially could arise very quickly, making the liquidity of a coin's reserves quite important.

[295] Reflecting potentially high volatility in the value cryptoassets held by banks as reserves, the BCBS has proposed very high capital requirements for bank holdings of such assets.

[296] CBDCs avoid this issue because they are fixed price central bank liabilities, and banks holding the CBDCs can be supported by central bank emergency lines of credit.

9D.35. Also, some stablecoins back their coins using algorithms that weight multiple reserve assets to statistically provide full backing for the coin. The reserves might include digital assets, which individually can be volatile, and thus supervisors and the public can be unclear about the quality of reserves. (A 2022 crisis arbitrage-based algorithmic stablecoins highlighted this issue.) (CNBC.com 2022a)

Smart contracts and Decentralized finance (DeFi)

9D.36. Many altcoins build upon the flexibility of the blockchain to create new applications or append programs to the chain. Thousands of variations have been created.[297]

9D.37. An important feature is the ability to program "smart contracts" or applications ("apps") into the system that automatically document and execute transactions as conditions are met, or take alternative actions if conditions are not met. Smart contracts can initiate transactions with full finality when conditions are met and record the transaction in the blockchain.[298] Other conditions are possible, such as transferring ownership rights, releasing collateral on completion of transaction, or charging a sales tax on applicable store purchases. This flexibility can be used to create complex financial instruments, create derivative-like instruments, customize altcoins, create proprietary systems for individual firms or industries, or handle special market conditions.[299] [300]

9D.38. In effect, it has become feasible for users to use apps or smart coins to create their own altcoin for use in transactions processed on a blockchain. Securities, commodities, or real assets could be represented in an easily transferable form similar to standard financial assets. This can reduce costs and can be done independent of banks and official financial infrastructure.

DeFi

9D.39. The term 'decentralized finance' or 'DeFi' is used to describe techniques that effectively emulate bank lending or other formal financial activities. The full complement of cryptomethods (coins, stablecoins, DLT, smart contracts, etc.) can be used

---

[297] A sematic distinction sometimes made is that a digital "coin" is a unit used within the system that created it, while a "token" is a digital package that can be used in multiple systems.

[298] The smart contracts are embedded in the blockchain, establish a permanent record, and cannot be changed. Likewise, records of market events that initiate transactions are also embedded into the blockchain. For example, a contract could pay the difference between a market price for oil – on a specified market and time – and a strike price, which is equivalent to a financial future.

[299] Consumer protection aspects of smart contracts are very important because transactions can be initiated automatically with full finality. A phrase sometimes applied to such contracts is "Code is Law" which implies that programmed smart contracts can provide firm guarantees in a positive sense or harmful actions without recourse in the case of poorly constructed or fraudulent contracts. A specific danger is that contracts can be agreed and enforced without involving lawyers and legal oversight. More generally, they have been described as 'unregulated investment funds', which of course should attract supervisory scrutiny. Building oversight and remediation systems over smart contracts will be a thorny problem for future regulators. (Section C below describes the EU's proposed "Digital Operational Resilience Act; Markets in Crypto-Assets (MiCA)" that begins to address these concerns.)

Rigidities in such systems were shown in fall 2021 when a programming error mistakenly sent $162 million in tokens to depositors' accounts. The protocol could not retrieve the funds and recipients were asked to voluntarily return funds less a 10% reward for their honesty. (CNBC.com 2021)

[300] Hypothetically, major commercial digital platforms could use smart contracts to create national digital currencies customized to individual country needs. This option could allow countries to contract for their CBDCs to take advantage of the expertise and infrastructure provided by global firms. (There does seem to be some competition by digital service firms to sign such contracts.) This option might prove quick and efficient, but creates operational risk of dependence on a single supplier.

to carry out conventional financial activities (lending, securities, derivatives, financial transactions, settlement, etc.) without working through banks or other regulated financial institutions.[301] Numerous DeFi schemes with many different features have been created – creating regulatory, legal, and policy challenges.

9D.40. Because DeFi can operate outside the regulated financial system, the rights, obligations, and legal certainty associated with DeFi operations are uncertain and might not be covered in existing regulatory and legal frameworks. Accounting and statistical reporting of DeFi positions and risks might be incomplete or nonexistent. Also, monetary policy control could be affected and banks and existing financial institutions might be destabilized if financial activity shifts to unregulated channels.[302]

Libra

9D.41. Libra was proposed in 2019 as a stablecoin backed by a multicurrency basket to be a direct competitor to the central bank monetary system. Libra was intended to be rapid, inexpensive, inclusive, and capable of handling the very large volume of transactions that occur globally each second.

9D.42. Libra was designed as a digital coin for use by a consortium of banks, payment systems, credit card companies, computer and mobile phone operations, and other financial businesses that interact with the public and then conduct settlements between themselves using Libra within a permissioned distributed ledger system. Libra was to be backed by multicurrency reserves contributed by consortium members. The responsibilities of meeting financial regulatory rules would remain with the individual members of the consortium.

9D.43. Libra was quickly and strongly criticized by numerous central banks and finance ministries.[303] The Finance Minister of France said that Libra would not be allowed to become a sovereign currency that could threaten countries' monetary sovereignty and raises serious risks in the areas of consumer protection, privacy of customer's finances, money laundering, and financing of terrorism. (Munster 2019) The U.S. Federal Reserve Board said it had serious concerns about Libra's impacts on money laundering, consumer protection, and financial stability. (Barber 2019) The U.S. President's Working Group on Financial Markets (2021) has also cited potential concentration of power due to stablecoins, such as Libra.

9D.44. The sharp criticisms quickly forced changes in the proposal. The concept of a multicurrency stablecoin was dropped in favor of single-currency backed coins, the name was changed to Diem, and issuance deferred until regulators' concerns are resolved.

9D.45. The Libra announcement had two immediate effects – central banks accelerated work on CBDCs and to strengthen the regulatory regime over cryptoassets. For example, the BIS put out a consultation proposal in June 2021 that classified different types of cryptoassets and their risk treatment in bank capital – in light of the inherent price risk of bitcoin it proposed a punitive risk weight of 1,250% on bank holdings of bitcoin (which when multiplied by the 8% required capital ratio means that a bank must hold capital equal to 100% of its bitcoin holdings).

9D.46. The ultimate shape of Libra/Diem and its regulatory regime is unknown at present. But dealing with stablecoins will be an important project that future unions will need to monitor. International regulatory bodies are quite active in this area, which is

[301] For example, a DeFi system might use a proprietary stablecoins for all internal transactions, but use a currency-denominated stablecoin to interface with the general public to handle cross-border payments transactions.

[302] During "crypto winter" in mid-2022, many DeFi systems collapsed with major losses to investors. Some systems introduced voting systems for depositors to allow changes to the arrangements in order to survive the crisis.

[303] The international financial community (IMF, BIS, G20, etc.) had begun investigating cryptoassets prior to the first bitcoin price spike in 2017, but the announcement of Libra raised the imminent possibility of a private digital currency – which spurred quick and widespread action.

likely to develop guidelines on how individual countries and regional bodies should handle cryptoassets. Moreover, given the global reach of cryptoassets, coordinated international standards and actions are likely to be needed.

Three EU initiatives on digital assets

9D.47. In late 2020, the EU put out three proposals that seek to create a comprehensive financial sector framework that includes cryptoassets not previously covered in the EU regulatory system.[304] The proposals seek to lever the innovative features of the new financial technology, but also address the broad range of risks and protections associated with cryptoassets – consumer protection, investor protection, legal finality of transactions, money laundering, criminal activity, financial stability, and monetary policy implications.

9D.48. The proposals established a new foundation for the European financial sector by recognizing the multifaceted aspects of the new digital technologies – communications, storing value, transacting, making payments, and settling positions. Each aspect of the system must operate efficiently and securely to support the European economy and its growth, provide customer protection, facilitate monetary policy action, and maintain financial soundness.[305] Digitalization and its diverse and interrelated impacts are global phenomena – other countries often will need to take steps to reform their financial systems similar to the actions being introduces in Europe.

Digital Operational Resilience Act (DORA)

9D.49. This Act bolsters the robustness of information and telecommunications infrastructure used by the European financial sector and prevent serious disruptions in operations. It explicitly brings digital service providers under regulatory control of financial sector supervisors. EU-wide standards are proposed to prevent divergences between national efforts. Authorities gain power to request information, conduct inspections, issue risk management rules, and issue recommendations subject to fines for failure to comply. Importantly, it forbids European financial firms from using infrastructure not located in the EU but which is critical for operations within the EU. A common reporting arrangement is set for reporting of infrastructure failures or attacks.

Markets in Crypto-Assets Act (MiCA)

9D.50. A mid-2022 EU agreement (CNBC.com 2022b) to enact MICA in 2024 is intended to bolster innovation and competitiveness in the EU financial system by supporting initiatives in digital finance while providing protections against the new risks involved. Investigations found that existing EU financial services rules did not cover most cryptoassets and could inhibit instruments based on DLT. Also, regulation was fragmented by legislation enacted by individual countries. A common EU framework was felt needed to address such concerns, provide consumer protections, strengthen market resilience, and build larger and more competitive crypto markets.

9D.51. Priorities cited in MiCA are;

> Provide legal certainty for all forms of crypto-assets within a common EU framework,[306]

---

[304] Elsewhere, the 2019 ASEAN Digital Integration Framework covers many of the same issues as the EU regulations. Although it does not address cryptoassets directly, it provides a long list of institutional actions related to digital assets that can help provide a sound foundation for future CBDC transactions.

[305] The European Systemic Risk Board has described how high level of "interconnectedness across financial entities, financial markets and financial market infrastructures, and particularly the interdependencies of their ICT systems, might constitute a systemic vulnerability since localized cyber incidents could quickly spread." ESRB (2020).

[306] The agreement focuses on crypto-asset firms and exchanges. Bitcoin is not covered (because it is not issued by a firm) and crypto-asset mining is not prohibited. NFTs are not covered, but the EU Commission was mandated to investigate whether regulations are needed.

Support financial innovation,

Provide consumer and investor protections,

Maintain financial stability,

Address environmental concerns, and

Provide "Safeguards to address potential risks to financial stability and orderly monetary policy that could arise from stablecoins".

9D.52. MiCA notes that the "structure of stablecoins is complex and comprises many interdependent functions and legal entities." Thus, it seeks to "create a comprehensive and holistic EU framework on stablecoins, capable of mitigating the risks identified ... in particular financial stability risks.

9D.53. MiCA states regulations should be proportionate to their need and risks addressed. It says the "proposal imposes more stringent requirements on 'stablecoins', which are more likely to grow quickly in scale and possibly result in higher levels of risk to investors, counterparties, and the financial system."[307]

9D.54. The strategy for stablecoins calls for legislation (largely based on FSB recommendations) that addresses stablecoins' risks[308] and extending the Electric Money Directive to cover stablecoins because they have many characteristics of e-money, are stores of value, and can be used for payments. Placing stablecoins under the E-money umbrella also helps prevent arbitrage between the conventional and digital regulatory regimes. Reserves were required to cover mass withdrawals and daily (€200 million) limits on transactions were agreed.

9D.55. MiCA has over 120 articles that can serve as a possible model to other countries and regions seeking standards for crypto-assets markets and how they should be regulated.[309]

Pilot Regime for Market Infrastructures based on Distributed Ledger Technology (DLT)

9D.56. Given the complexities and rapid changes in cryptomarkets, this EU proposal lays out an evolutionary process in which actions to support innovations in the market (while adhering to the MiCA priorities and protections) will be adjusted as new financial practices develop and experience is gained in the oversight of the markets.

9D.57. The project focuses on three market innovations; cryptoassets, the "tokenization of traditional financial assets, and use of DLT in financial services. Financial assets are broadly redefined to include financial instruments based on DLT, crypto-assets not covered by existing EU financial regulations, and e-money tokens.

9D.58. The project mandates that the various European Supervisory Authorities review how their regulations apply to cryptoassets, identify areas for improvement, and consider strategies to make the framework friendly for innovation.

9D.59. It is recognized that some existing rules would inhibit development of DLT instruments[310] – especially those requiring centralized registry of financial instruments and activities which clashes with the decentralized transacting and recording under DLT. The pilot regime would seek to overcome such obstacles,

[307] MiCA. Section 2. Legal Basis, Subsidiarity, and Proportionality.

[308] Parallel to the FSB concept of globally systemically important financial institutions, the term "global stablecoin" foreshadows the possibility that stablecoins might become systemically important within the global financial system and become risks to global financial stability, and thus require special oversight.

[309] An important feature to limit misuse of crypto-assets is to require reporting of transfers over €1000 between crypto exchanges and individual wallets.

[310] "Existing financial services legislation was not designed with DLT and crypto-assets in mind. This means that there are provisions in it which sometimes restricts and even prevents the use of DLT."

"With a common EU pilot regime for the experimentation of DLT market infrastructures, firms within the EU would be able to exploit the full potential of the existing framework, allowing supervisors and legislators to identify obstacles in the regulation, while regulators and firms themselves gain valuable knowledge about the application of DLT".

Also, the regime allows "adequate flexibility for supervisors to determine which provisions to disregard for a market participant's test, to allow different test cases. The pilot regime will enable regulators to remove regulatory constraints that can inhibit the development of DLT market infrastructures, which could enable the transition to tokenised[311] financial instruments and DLT market infrastructures, enabling innovation and ensuring EU's global competitiveness." [312]

9D.60. The regime would require harmonized requirements to issue cryptoassets or obtain authorization to provide services for cryptoassets. It would also would harmonize operational and disclosure requirements for service providers. These steps would allow firms to operate across the single market which should increase their efficiency, reduce complexity of instruments and operations, simplify burdens for consumers, and provide better and simpler consumer and investor protections.

[311] "Token" has multiple meanings in crypto-lingo but in general it might be defined as an encoded messages that stands for something else. In this case, it might refer to a blockchain-tradable version of an underlying financial instrument.

[312] Prudential Regime. Section 2. Legal Basis, Subsidiarity, and Proportionality.

[313] In the Euroarea and most other countries, commercial bank money is mostly in the form of electronic entries in customers' bank accounts.

D. Central Bank Digital Currencies (CBDC)

What is a CBDC?

9D.61. A CBDC is a direct liability of the central bank issued as a digital equivalent of cash. Before the concept of CBDCs arose, 'central bank money' comprised physical cash and reserve balances of banks at the central bank. 'Commercial bank money' is comprised of the public's accounts at banks backed by the banks' reserves at the central bank.[313]

9D.62. CBDCs can be constructed either as general-purpose (retail) legal tender used like cash or deposit account money at commercial banks, or as an instrument used within the regulated monetary system (wholesale), that is, the central bank, commercial banks, and other authorized financial institutions.

9D.63. A retail CBDC, as a direct public claim on the central bank, could substitute for physical cash or deposit accounts at commercial banks. If a CBDC can provide similar or better services than cash or banks,[314] cash use could decrease or disintermediation of banks might result and affect monetary and credit conditions or financial stability. Similarly, if CBDCs can provide quick and inexpensive cross-border transactions, balance of payments flows can be affected, potentially unsettling financial conditions in both the CBDC selling and purchasing countries.[315]

9D.64. A wholesale CBDC would be a riskless asset used between financial institutions that could

[314] Store of value, use in transactions, high liquidity, simple person-to-person transfers, low processing costs, etc.. (Conversely, anecdotal reports from China have suggested that the public is largely satisfied with existing payments arrangements and might be in no rush to adopt the e-CNY.)

[315] For example, asset shifts of the CBDC of Country A into neighboring Country B which does not have a CBDC could create monetary and international payments policy problems in both countries. The management of cross-border CBDC flows is an important policy challenge. (A solution within a region is to create a monetary union with a region-wide CBDC.)

be cheaper and faster that existing transactions, that provides settlement finality, that might be well-suited for cross-border transactions, and that provides access to innovative digital financial instruments and services.

9D.65. Experiments are underway with CBDCs and many more can be expected. Different models are being tested and it is too early to know which approaches will prove technically most successful or be most widely adopted.

First CBDC Experiments

Eastern Caribbean Currency Union: DCash

9D.66. The ECCU has a CBDC pilot project called "DCash" which trades at par with the ECCU dollar (EC$).[316]

9D.67. The program is part of an overall strategy to increase use of electronic payments throughout the union with increased use of debit and credit cards and DCash substituting for cash and checks. DCash is intended to permit transfer of funds throughout the ECCU faster and at lower costs than present methods. Specific issues being addressed are high costs of payments and banking services, inadequate banking services for some customers, and slow settlement of checking transactions – especially inter-island transactions. DCash was adopted gradually beginning in March 2021 by half of the ECCU states, then by all but one by the end of the year.

Text box: Botswana warnings on Crypto assets

In November 2021 the Bank of Botswana put out a warning to the public that summarizes some of the potential consumer protection problems that can arise from cryptoassets. (Bank of Botswana 2021) It acknowledged receiving public questions about their use in Botswana, the regulatory framework, and consumer protections. Among key points;

> *There is no prevailing legal or regulatory framework and thus funds are at complete risk similar to other investment assets.*
>
> *It is prudent to investigate the registration and legality of entities offering cryptoassets, as well as their sources of income.*
>
> *There is general concern that some activities are similar to pyramid schemes and other scams which could cause participants to unwittingly participate in criminal activity and expose themselves to legal risk and loss.*
>
> *"Cryptocurrency" is a misnomer since it lacks fundamental characteristics of currency.*
>
> *Other than the existing general bank legal framework, "The public would have no recourse to the Bank of Botswana for redress pertaining to fraud, misconduct, or financial losses emanating from or associated with participation in the crypto assets business".*
>
> *It is recognized that effects of financial markets and mandates could be pervasive and significant and thus continuing monitoring is needed.*

The Bank of Botswana has crafted a simple and direct statement that might be widely applied.

9D.68. DCash is being distributed through financial institutions and authorized agents. Financial institutions handle usual documentation requirements for customers to receive regulated financial services.[317] These customers are given 'registered-based wallets' (RBWs) that have flexible ceilings based on customers' individual profiles.

[316] As a cash equivalent, DCash has a fixed value to the EC$ and cannot pay interest. However, instantaneous rollover into banking accounts might be feasible; thus, excess funds in wallets might be 'swept' daily into interest-bearing bank accounts.

[317] Know your Customer (KYC), Anti-Money Laundering (AML), and Countering Financing of Terrorism (CFT) rules, among other national rules such as tax reporting.

9D.69. In addition, an effort to include users without accounts at financial institutions allows them to obtain 'value-based wallets' (VBW) from authorized agents (such as mobile phone operators). VBW accounts are limited to EC$2,700 (US$1,000) per month.

9D.70. Customers load their wallets by trading in physical cash or transferring funds from existing bank accounts. Balances in wallets can be converted back to cash or credited to accounts at financial institutions.

9D.71. The central bank will transfer DCash upon request to financial institutions and service providers, but total issuance is subject to a limit.

9D.72. Mobile phone service providers will provide digital wallets to store DCash and handle customer transactions. Records maintained by the providers permit restitution of funds if wallets are lost.

9D.73. In a typical transaction, a user accesses a vendor's 'Quick Response' (QR) code[318], types the amount into the wallet, authenticates, then completes the transaction. The transaction is instantaneous with the user's wallet immediately debited and the vendor's wallet immediately credited. A record is created that allows users to track their inflows and expenditures.

9D.74. Transactions between customers and bank and service providers, while not fully anonymous, are likely to be confidential at about the same level as bank transactions, but they might be strengthened by additional regulations. While person-to-person transactions might have more confidentiality than those involving institutions, they are unlikely to be as completely anonymous as cash.

9D.75. The pilot program operates using business-oriented blockchain platform based on a DLT platform. Unlike the original bitcoin-type platform that involves global access to an encoded blockchain, the ECCU system limits access only to processors granted permission. The system also has flexibility to program in applications, such as limiting the size or types of transactions, holding funds in escrow, accommodating 'smart contracts', etc.). Also, the platform can track and reverse transactions.

9D.76. The 2020 IMF Article IV consultations with the ECCB commented on the DCash plan, pointing out advantages and risks;

> "The digital currency pilot project should proceed cautiously as planned. The authorities view the digital currency as an option to reduce excessive reliance on cash and cheques; improve the efficiency of the retail payment system; and support economic development by reducing financial frictions. To contain vulnerabilities, important safeguard measures are embedded in the design of the digital currency, such as the limited size of its holding and transaction values, no interest accrued; and does not include foreign currency transactions. That said, the digital currency could expose the ECCB and the financial system to various risks, including those related to financial intermediation, financial integrity, and cybersecurity. The pilot will provide the opportunity to examine these risks, test the design of the digital currency, and assess any policy gaps. After the pilot, the ECCB is planning to thoroughly review its results, and more work may be warranted, especially to further test the digital currency system, strengthen cybersecurity and AML/CFT operations, and update legal and regulatory frameworks."

9D.77. In summary, the ECCU DCash pilot project provides a working example to how future systems might be developed.[319] The process is clearly complex, and could challenge the resources of

[318] A QR code is a visually readable (such as by a mobile phone) square containing a barcode of information folded into a square shape. The encoded information can quickly convey information about a party in a transaction.

[319] The developer of DCash was also chosen for Nigeria's CBDC, called eNaira, issued in late October 2021.

smaller countries or those with weaker legal/regulatory systems.

The Bahamas: Sand Dollar

9D.78. The Bahamas launched the sand dollar in October 2020. The official website (sanddollar.bs) cites advantages as; (1) providing faster, more efficient, and secure payments services, (2) enhancing financial inclusion in the small islands comprising the country, (3) providing nondiscriminatory access to payments systems, and (4) defending against money laundering, counterfeiting, and other illicit activity.

9D.79. Holding is limited to residents, who can integrate it with existing bank accounts, and visiting nonresidents, who are subject to limits on holdings and monthly transactions. External transactions will continue to be handled through commercial banks, thus maintaining central bank controls.

Cambodia: Project Bakong

9D.80. The National Bank of Cambodia launched a quasi-CBDC system in 2020 that links a DLT system with existing bank accounts and mobile phone wallets to provide inclusive retail payments. The public loads wallets with riel or U.S. dollars then makes payments using QR codes that are cleared within the system and verified using a permissioned DLT platform designed by a Japanese company. Transactions are quick, interbank fees are low, and transactions by users are free. Due diligence and other supervisory tasks continue to rest with the member financial institutions.

9D.81. Project Bakong is explicitly intended to reduce the use of U.S. dollars; with the project launch the National Bank of Cambodia ceased distribution of U.S. $1, $2, and $5 banknotes.

9D.82. Thus far, the project appears only moderately successful, with 1.4 million Bakong transactions and about 6 million uses of on-line apps linked to the system during the first half of 2021. (Takemiya 2021) If it continues to operate successfully and becomes more popular it could become an important model for other countries to follow.[320]

China e-yuan (e-CNY)

9D.83. In 2021, China gradually introduced a retail digital currency through a pilot project, which began in several cities and reached about 10 million users in mid-2021. At this time, it is intended for domestic retail use with access for visitors; existing payments systems continue in use for international transactions.

9D.84. Given the size of the Chinese economy and its strong economic ties to Southeast and Central Asia, the e-CNY has potential to become a major international reserves and transactions instrument.

9D.85. In sharp contrast to the official promotion of the e-CNY, the central bank has sharply restricted private crypto operations. In 2021, private cryptocoin mining operations were forbidden[321] as well as many crypto exchange services. A Deputy Governor of the central bank said that the private coins had fostered destabilizing speculation and facilitated illegal activity and money laundering, and that stablecoins could affect international payment and settlement systems. (Bloomberg News 2021)

El Salvador Bitcoin Experiment

9D.86. CBDCs, bitcoin, and stablecoins are potential competitors as monetary instruments. An interesting experiment is El Salvador's decision in mid-2021 to declare bitcoin as legal tender. Because El Salvador is fully dollarized and does not issue its own currency, El Salvador would have two legal currencies. Among motivations were to increase

[320] Laos is investigating a similar scheme using the same Japanese platform, with assistance from the Japan International Co-operation Agency. (Ma 2021).

[321] This immediately closed around half global bitcoin mining. Mining operations then began migrating to other countries.

financial inclusion and reduce the cost of remittances into the country, which could directly benefit many Salvadoran households.

9D.87. A law introducing bitcoin as legal tender required all businesses to accept it unless they lacked the technology. To encourage use, a wallet called Chivo was created that instantly converts the bitcoins into U.S. dollars. Transactions using Chivo are intended to be commission free. Each Chivo is preloaded with $30 worth of bitcoins as an incentive to join. 200 ATMs are being installed and arrangements made with 50 bank branches to load or use Chivo.

9D.88. The regional development bank, Central American Bank for Economic Integration (CABEI), is providing technical assistance to help draft a legal framework for bitcoin as a currency. CABEI reportedly is interested in whether bitcoin can cut the cost of sending remittances.

9D.89. However, hesitancy about the scheme exists. Prior to the launch, El Salvador officials made statements that acceptance of bitcoin was not mandatory. An international ratings firm said that holding bitcoin would probably be a negative factor in insurers' ratings because of its volatility, accounting and legal uncertainties[322], and additional costs involved – overall the decision was described as "unnecessarily rushed". (decentralized.trading 2021) In January 2022, the IMF Board advised El Salvador to remove bitcoin as legal currency, and a survey in March 2022 found that it was little used in transactions. (Bloomberg 2022a, 2022b)

9D.90. The initial experience thus has been somewhat rocky – the project continues, but at a rather subdued rate and many adjustments have been made to deal with problems. (Pymnts.com 2021) What happens in El Salvador will be closely watched. If remittances costs are significantly reduced and problems recede, other countries might also adopt bitcoin (in lieu of creating a CBDC). However, it remains to be seen if the public fully adopts the project or if rushed incomplete preparations threaten the project.

m-CBDC Bridge

9D.91. In early 2021, China, Hong Kong, Thailand, and the UAE[323] announced a joint project ("m-CBDC Bridge") to test a concept of a multi-CBDC system for continuous multicountry cross-border foreign exchange payments-vs-payments (PvP). The project is intended for "move central banks in Asia as well as other regions to jointly study the potential of DLT in enhancing the financial infrastructure for cross-border payments." (Hong Kong 2021) Also, the project is "strongly supported by the BIS Innovation Hub Centre in Hong Kong." Thus, the project is being given serious consideration as a prototype international CBDC transactions system specifically to address frictions, high costs, and legal and regulatory complexities of cross-border transfers, trade settlements, and capital market transactions.

9D.92. If the project proves successful, a *de facto* international standard and infrastructure might be established in relatively short order. *All countries considering CBDCs should monitor this highly promising work which that might establish an international model for cross-border payments.*

Marshall Islands' SOV

9D.93. The Marshall Islands, a Pacific Island microstate with links to the United States, has announced a bitcoin-like scheme for a digital currency (the SOV) to cocirculate alongside the U.S. dollar.

9D.94. The IMF strongly criticized the move as risky and beyond the legal and administrative resources of the country. An IMF spokesperson said issuing the SOV as legal tender would "raise risks to macroeconomic and financial stability as well as

[322] *Chapter 3 – The ECU* discusses legal issues associated with parallel currencies, such as bitcoin in El Salvador which was adopted without consideration of the issues.

[323] This form of monetary cooperation was investigated in the Saudi/UAE "Project Aber", which produced favorable results. Its fully documented results provide an excellent summary of how the m-CBDC Bridge could operate.

financial integrity." Specific risks cited included jeopardizing the country's last U.S. dollar correspondent banking relationship, potential anti-money laundering and combatting the financing of terrorism risks, "potential cost of SOV issuance will likely outweigh the expected benefits", and "the legal, regulatory, and institutional framework is not yet ready to accommodate the SOV issuance and manage associated risks." The problems identified by the IMF could be relevant to many small economies.

E. The Digital Euro

9D.95. In October 2020 an ECB paper (ECB 2020) covered rationales for a digital euro and possible implementation strategies.

9D.96. The paper cited multiple reasons to introduce a digital euro.

Support digitalization of the European economy to promote productive innovation and efficient payment systems. A digital euro can help support interoperational payment systems[324] throughout the union thus advancing integration within the union.

Deal with the significant drop in use of physical cash that could undermine the sustainability of cash services in the union. A digital euro would help guarantee public access to riskless public money.

Counter possible deep penetration of the European economy by other countries' CBDCs or private digital instruments (such as stablecoins). These competitors could affect monetary transmission, create risks and foreign exchange exposures, and affect retail channels.

Support monetary policy options, which included mention of the possibility to remunerating the digital euro in line with more general interest rate policies.[325]

Build resilience and back-up capabilities into the digital euro to mitigate dangers of cyberattacks, natural disasters, power cuts, or shocks that could affect other systems.

Support the international role of the euro. The report suggests this could involve cooperation with other central banks to create interoperable systems between CBDCs, which addresses international payments frictions without giving nonresidents direct access to the digital euro.

Improve the cost structure and ecological footprint of monetary and payment systems.

Market impacts of a digital euro

9D.97. The report looked at the market impacts of a digital euro and how it could affect Eurosystem functions. Impacts were expected to vary depending on whether the public directly holds digital euros, or whether they are intermediated by banks and other financial institutions.

9D.98. The report reviewed the possibility of financial instability because of disintermediation if the public shifts deposits away from banks into safe digital euros.[326] In particular, the public could shift into the digital euro very quickly, which might increase both the likelihood and severity of bank runs.[327]

---

[324] Digital payments systems within the union are supported by a 2014 EU Regulation that established standards for electronic IDs and signatures. This ancillary legislation will be needed in other regional arrangements.

[325] Monetary policy was not a major focus of the report.

[326] Such shifts might be accelerated during periods of negative interest rates on deposit accounts if the digital euro is like cash with a fixed 0% interest return. A number of analyses have been made of possible deposit to CBDC shifts – all have shown some effect, but size estimates vary.

[327] In the face of deposit withdrawals, banks could compensate by raising their offered rates, borrowing from capital markets, or borrowing liquidity from the central bank (continued)

9D.99. Second, the digital euro could affect the balance sheet, income, and condition of the central bank. Among possible impacts cited were substitution of the digital euro for cash, the net change in central bank liabilities, whether it would be remunerated, the impact on seigniorage, the types of access (if any) by nonresidents, the type, extent, and liquidity of assets (including official reserve assets) held against the digital euro liabilities, and possibility of lending to banks losing deposits because of the digital euro.

9D.100. Costs of issuing a digital euro need to be considered – how will new infrastructure and operating expenses be covered? Will fees be charged? Can seigniorage cover the costs? Will the entire system or specific parts of the system be subsidized?

9D.101. Also, the central bank might gain responsibilities, costs, and risks of operating a retail payment system, including constructing failsafe systems to handle emergencies. In future unions, promoting financial inclusion could be a key motivation for a retail CBDC, but this might involve creating new systems for small-scale transactions or systems that would be uneconomic for existing banks to operate. Building in standardization of procedures and interoperability of systems will be critical.

9D.102. In a retail payments system, existing institutions could be affected or new institutions and payment patterns might be needed.

9D.103. A variety of new legal arrangements might be needed to facilitate new payments arrangements and settle the rights and obligations of the parties involved.

9D.104. International exposures of the digital euro can vary depending on whether retail or wholesale systems are set up and if any restrictions placed on international transactions and exposures. The report says possible digital euro cocirculation in nonEuroarea countries that could unsettle their exchange rates, markets, and 'monetary sovereignty'.[328] [329]

9D.105. The report says that conditions on use outside the Euroarea are useful to avoid volatile flows and exchange rate instability. Decisions will also be needed on any remuneration of nonresident holdings and any sharing of seigniorage. Holdings outside the Euroarea might also facilitate criminal activity.

9D.106. A final concern is to build in the highest levels of resilience and redundancy to withstand shocks, protect data, and recover values if needed.

Legal Considerations

9D.107. The report describes some of the legal implications of creating a digital euro and guaranteeing its use as legal tender. Four different use patterns for the digital euro are covered; it concludes that each will have a different legal backing;

> The digital euro is only used as a monetary policy instrument with central bank counterparties,
>
> It is a settlement instrument between eligible counterparties,
>
> It is available to Euroarea residents through accounts held with the Eurosystem, and
>
> It is equivalent to a banknote available without restriction.

9D.108. The report states, "Retail access of the digital euro entails considerable legal novelty."

(which would require banks to hold collateral against their liability to the central bank).

[328] Currency substitution effects within potential regional unions might inhibit union development if a regionally dominant country's CBDC spreads throughout the region and suppresses options for the union to create its own CBDC. For example, the eNaira as the CBDC of Nigeria, Africa's largest economy, could become competitive throughout much of Africa.

[329] Staunching such international digital currency substitution suggests creating m-CBDC Bridge systems (described in section D) that use defined channels between separate countries' CBDC systems.

Moreover, some options would involve private distributors which would require legal arrangements for private entities integrated with official rules and regulatory procedures.

9D.109. Designing the legal system for the digital euro will be complex given existing rules, multiple system options, diverse public and private actors, different country legal arrangements, multiple European market supervisory institutions, and levels of legislative action. It is apt to be even more complex in future unions whose legal frameworks are less unified than in Europe.

Design Considerations

9D.110. Design choices for the offline and online versions of the digital euro must be compatible and probably should be issued simultaneously.

9D.111. An important aspect is user privacy. Unlike cash, the report states that existing rules do not permit anonymous digital transactions and full anonymity might not be possible.[330] Also, systems that involve private entities need strict rules on access to private information.

Limiting investment holdings of the digital euro

9D.112. In addition to limiting holdings to slow disintermediation from existing financial institutions, the ECB specifically raises the issue of how the digital euro interacts with negative interest rate monetary policy. If the digital euro is unremunerated like cash, "It does not seem feasible under current circumstances to offer unlimited holdings of digital euro to corporate entities at zero interest rates" because unrestricted access would disrupt monetary policy.[331]

Channels for cross-border flows

9D.113. Noting the serious risks from unrestricted international use of the digital euro, the paper (p. 24) calls for investigation of an approach in which countries establish supervised channels between separately operated CBDCs. This allows any two countries to maintain their monetary and exchange rate policies, while permitting international flows that can be monitored in order to take compensatory actions if necessary.

Accounting and Verification

9D.114. The digital euro system needs a mechanism to ensure that only legitimate instruments are transferred and transactions are credited to the right parties. As was described in Chapter 9, the cash euro imbeds many features to prevent counterfeiting and permit private cash processors to verify authenticity. In contrast, "a similar level of security in the digital environment with multiple sources of cyber risk *is much more complex, and this risk is not yet fully understood*." (p. 25)

9D.115. The paper discusses account-based systems in which transactions are verified by the central bank, by private supervised entities, or bearer systems. In bearer systems, responsibility to verify transactions rests with the two parties involved, or it is suggested that payment devices in the Euroarea might include built-in restrictions on certain transactions – moreover, it suggested that central bank rules limit issuance of payment devices to entitled users which would require then to confirm their identities.

Some conclusions of the paper

9D.116. The paper provided a highly ambitious program to design a system, educate the public, set up supporting infrastructure, design policy instruments, introduce the legal framework, set up

[330] Among official reasons for limited anonymity are possible restrictions on holdings by nonresidents, limits on large transactions, tracing for criminal investigations, as well as KYC, AML, and CFT rules.

[331] The idea of limiting holdings of euros is not new. To deter money laundering, corruption, financing of terrorism, etc., several Euroarea countries already have limits on euro *cash* transactions and consideration is being given to creating an EMU-wide €10,000 limit on cash transactions.

accounting and statistical systems, coordinate with private entities, negotiate international arrangements, and implement the full system. The program outlined has scale and complexity similar to the original launch of the union and the euro two decades ago.

Two-year digital euro project

9D.117. The proposed system was complex and needed testing. In late 2020, the Eurosystem began a series of experiments to test the key aspects of possible systems and conducted a large-scale survey of public views. The investigation covered four main areas; creating a digital euro ledger, privacy and anti-money laundering defenses, limiting euros in circulation, and facilitating inclusiveness and users' offline access.

9D.118. In July 2021, the ECB announced that test results had been favorable and no technical problems were found.[332] The 'throughput' (processing speeds and volumes) of TARGET and blockchain technology were tested and both found to be able to process 40,000 transactions per second.[333]

9D.119. In response to the positive results, the ECB Governing Council launched a two-year "digital euro project" to design a prototype technical system, consider how to distribute the digital euro, consult with user communities and industry groups, interact with legislators, consider how to adapt the EU legal framework, examine market impacts, and more.

9D.120. Following these investigations, a decision can be made whether to proceed to launch the digital euro.

Text box: Testing TARGET against a DLT blockchain

In 2018, the TARGET system introduced a system for rapid processing and settlement of transactions called TARGET Instant Payment Settlement (TIPS). It is designed to permit instant payments between bank accounts anywhere within the Euroarea.

In TIPS, banks place reserves into an account at their NCB that can be used for settling transactions instantly using central bank money. A bank sends a payment order to the TIPS system which validates the order then transfers funds to the receiving bank.

Transactions usually are sent and settled within 10 seconds. TIPS transactions are very cheap, fast, and available 24 hours a day.

TIPS was designed to be scalable to meet demand and thus it was tested and successfully handled a large volume of digital euro type transactions.

Tests were also made using a blockchain system with similar positive results.

Experiments were then made (with successful results) on how the centralized TIPS system could interact with a decentralized blockchain system to efficiently process very large numbers of CBDC transactions.

BIS Annual Survey of CBDCs

9D.121. Outside the Euroarea, many other countries are actively investigating CBDCs. The BIS annually surveys central banks about their research and intentions for CBDCs, with over 60 central banks covered in the 2020 tally. (Boar and Wehrli 2021)

---

332 The system was also found to consume negligible amounts of energy compared to DLT bitcoin processing.

333 The throughput of TIPS resulted from a two-decade long evolution to create a unified, rapid, and efficient payments system for the Euroarea. The original TARGET system for monetary policy operations and interbank euro transactions was built upon national payments systems because of lack of time to build a new system before launch of the union. In 2007-8, a centralized TARGET2 (T2) system was created to provide real time gross settlement (RTGS) payments between banks using central bank money. In 2017-8, TARGET2-Securities (T2S) was created to harmonize securities transactions across the Euroarea. T2S supports rapid delivery of securities upon payment (DvP) of central bank money with full settlement finality. The digital euro test showed that the TIPS system built upon this hard work is highly efficient and competitive with any new digital system.

9D.122. In 2020, 86 % of polled central banks were investigating CBDCs.[334] Responses were grouped for "advanced economies" versus "Emerging market and developing economies" (EMDE). However, few responses were from Africa and Central Asia and thus the information is incomplete for some regions actively working on monetary unions.

9D.123. The report indicated that most work is on *general-purpose retail systems* to produce digital equivalents to cash for use by households and business. The most important motivation cited by EMDEs was for general-purpose CBDC systems[335] to promote financial inclusion; in contrast, advanced countries listed financial inclusion is the least sought motivation (presumably because existing financial institutions already effectively serve most needs of the population).

9D.124. Relative to advanced economies, EMDEs are also more interested in CBDCs to improve domestic payments systems, implement monetary policy, and support financial stability. In contrast, both advanced economies and EMDEs gave only modestly high scores for use of CBDCs to improve efficiency of cross-border payments, which might be taken as an indication that to date most of the focus has been on how domestic monetary situations will be affected.

9D.125. The report says that some comments by EMDEs stressed (1) that CBDCs can support 'monetary sovereignty' in contrast to 'digital dollarization' or adoption of private digital currencies, and (2) they can maintain public access to central bank money despite declining cash use.

9D.126. Overall, the survey suggested that overall EMDEs feel greater urgency to introduce CBDCs to improve inclusion and domestic payments infrastructure…

> "seven out of eight central banks in advanced stages of CBDC work are in EMDEs. In these jurisdictions, the focus is generally on CBDC for domestic payments. However, larger EMDEs with ongoing pilot programs do also consider cross-border payments efficiency as important." (p. 9)

9D.127. Finally, the survey queried central banks about their attitudes regarding cryptocurrencies and stable coins….

> "Cryptocurrencies…central banks continue to see these as niche products with no widespread use as a means of payment. Conversely, developments in stablecoins are closely watched given their potential for rapid adoption by consumers." (p. 14)

9D.128. The survey highlighted different focusses of Advanced Economies versus EMDCs. The Advanced economies (which includes the financially already well-served Euroarea) give greater weight to CBDCs to ease frictions in cross-border transactions and serve as a defensive mechanism to counter declines in cash use and penetration by other CBDCs or private cryptoassets and stablecoins. The EMDCs have these same needs, but more urgently need to boost financial inclusion and improve their domestic financial infrastructure.

9D.129. The BIS survey reveals that all potential monetary unions, especially those in Africa, must improve financial inclusion by creating retail CBDC systems.

[334] Footnote 3 to the report notes that alternative quasi-CBDC models are under consideration. These might be privately organized or involve prepayment into the system using regular cash or bank accounts (similar to existing prepaid cards). It can be speculated that although such systems might not fully qualify as CBDCs, some might serve as alternatives or competitors to CBDCs – that is, at this early stage it is premature to narrow the boundaries of possible digital monetary and payments systems.

[335] Results are similar for wholesale systems, with the notable exception of financial inclusion for advanced countries which scored quite low for advanced countries.

9D.130. Inclusion means providing payment mechanisms for large portions of the population, often geographically dispersed, frequently not linked to existing payments infrastructure, and perhaps literally not speaking the same language. A retail CBDC plan must decide on payments devices and media, creating digital IDs, creating personal wallets or other stores of value, educating target populations, and actual implementation - tasks comparable to launching a cash currency. Prioritizing the retail CBDC option also involves more complex requirements than for the wholesale option.

9D.131. In areas such as Africa existing mobile phone and point-of-sale systems might *de facto* be primary media for introducing CBDCs rather than introducing new channels and devices. In monetary union situations, systems will also have to prioritize *intra*union cross-border transactions to help unify financial markets through the union.[336]

9D.132. In these tasks, regions creating a currency union should watch the euro experiment closely. Options could be foreclosed, new modes created, standards for supervision of digital instruments developed, and best options for cross-border digital transactions solidified. Future unions can learn much from Europe - including borrowing from EU legislation on market and supervisory infrastructure,[337] but will have different priorities and challenges.

F. CBDC scenarios for future unions

9D.133. This section outlines priorities that could be followed by future unions in designing their CBDC systems and three scenarios that they might choose given their economic and political priorities and technical resources. Among priorities are;

Enhance financial inclusion

Facilitate remittances and lower their cost

Integrate financial markets

Adopt financial technology; increase market efficiency

Facilitate cross-border transactions and settlement

Use as a monetary policy tool

Maintain seigniorage income

Bolster financial stability

Counter decreased use of cash, and

Defend against penetration by other CBDCs and cryptocurrencies

9D.134. Given such multiple priorities, which scenarios are most likely and how are monetary union prospects affected?

Scenario 1 – No coordination

9D.135. In broad terms, EMDEs prioritize financial inclusion and cutting remittances costs, while politically capturing some of the enthusiasm surrounding cryptoassets. These priorities could induce some countries to independently go forward with domestic *retail* CBDC schemes.

9D.136. Within any particular region multiple countries could independently develop retail CBDCs. These efforts might divert focus away from deepening regional financial integration or unions.

9D.137. Union prospects could be impeded as multiple nonharmonized CBDCs could have diverse impacts on their home countries and complicate cross-border transactions within the region.

9D.138. Although domestic benefits can arise from this scenario, independent experiments undertaken so far suggest that countries must take significant actions to impede threats from various risks.

---

[336] Outside Africa, potential regional arrangements in more prosperous areas (GCC or Southeast Asia, for example) also need to improve inclusion, but might be able to give earlier emphasis to the cross-border aspects. These areas might end up more closely following the future digital euro model.

[337] See Section C "Three EU Initiatives on Digital Assets".

Monetary and exchange rate policies and financial soundness can be affected due to the potential speed and ease of shifts in CBDC holdings.

An effective outreach campaign is needed to build public and business acceptance and to avoid fraud or other misuse of the system.

The technical ease of creating a CBDC might outrun building suitable market infrastructure, building supervisory and legal frameworks, and designing monetary and balance of payments policies.

Even relatively small-scale independent CBDCs must take cyber and operational risks very seriously – which means creating redundancy and backup arrangements and restitution of public and business losses from operational failures.

9D.139. Countries must carefully weigh benefits, costs, and risks from retail CBDCs, and whether the country infrastructure can support the many aspects of CBDCs. *Introducing a CBDC that is not publicly accepted, that creates financial risks and instabilities, impairs monetary control, or that fails operationally could prove economically and politically intolerable. Creating an independent CBDC might not be feasible for some countries. It might also complicate existing or future regional monetary arrangements.*

9D.140. Fortunately, a lot of information is available from early experiments and ongoing research in Europe and elsewhere. Active review by international organizations might begin setting standards and outlining feasible approaches.

9D.141. Moreover, it is unknown whether individual small country CBDCs can successfully compete against major outside CBDCs or stablecoins. If digital euros, dollars, yuans, or stablecoins become deeply embedded, monetary control of countries *and* the region could be impaired – making creation of an union more challenging.

Scenario 2 – m-CBDC Bridge

9D.142. If m-CBDC Bridge arrangements become feasible, many cross-border complications might fade away and could allow countries to establish their own retail CBDC systems that maintain domestic controls and capture seigniorage yet gain more efficient cross-border transactions.

9D.143. Scenario 2 might be widely appealing; domestic markets benefit from the national CBDC, but country cross-border frictions can be eased, fewer intermediaries are involved, settlement can be faster with better certainty, and cross-border transactions' costs reduced. If international minimum requirements are developed (perhaps by the BIS Committee on Payment and Market Infrastructure, or by SWIFT), individual countries' CBDCs might be easily tradable with multiple other countries.

9D.144. Scenario 2 is close to a union-like situation with endpoints in different countries encompassed in the system. It is complex because it requires some harmonization of domestic and cross-border payments and settlements between financial institutions. The Saudi/UAE Project Aber successfully tested a wholesale payments scheme along these lines. (SAMA 2020) [338]

9D.145. More ambitiously, the m-CBDC Bridge project now underway with four unlinked currencies (China, Hong Kong, Thailand, and the UAE) might have more global applicability.

9D.146. Scenario 2 might accomplish many of the goals of a monetary union and thus might reduce the rationale for completing a full-scale monetary union.

Scenario 3 – Single union-wide CBDC System

[338] Project Aber was between two countries whose currencies were already linked in the GCC quasi-monetary union. It used a joint CBDC created by the Saudi and UAE central banks. Aber tested payments between financial institutions within a country and in different countries with ensured settlement on each end of the transaction.

9D.147. In this scenario, movement toward monetary union accelerates in order to (1) capture efficiencies of an union-wide digital monetary instrument, (2) avoid diverse impacts of monetary policy, interest rate, and legal systems that remain within a m-CBDC Bridge arrangement, and (3) counter pressures from outside CBDCs or private cryptoassets.

9D.148. Explorations underway in the EAC to improve the operations of its regional cross-border payments system highlight how CBDCs might promote currency union prospects. (bitcoinke 2021a) A common CBDC could integrate RTGS systems in all the six member countries. It would help overcome limited stocks of partner member states' currencies needed for settlement, challenges from diverse national payments systems, and lack of centralized liquidity and collateral management.[339]

9D.149. Scenario 3 is the most complex option because it encompasses the full range of currency, monetary policy, interest rate, exchange rate, payments, supervisory, and other tasks addressed by monetary unions. All member country currencies would be merged into a single union currency, in both cash and digital forms.

G. The path ahead

9D.150. Many central banks, including some considering creating a monetary union, have begun CBDC projects. A frequent element in the CBDC reviews is their role in improving payments systems. Indeed, CBDCs might be thought of as integrating the monetary and payments aspects of regional arrangements – *a "digital payments union" becomes equal partner with the "currency union".*

9D.151. Countries investigating creating their own currency/payments union need to watch the euro experiment and other countries' experiences closely. They can learn much from Europe, but must recognize their different priorities and challenges and innovate appropriately.

9D.152. Smaller and developing/emerging economies also face a distinct threat that other countries' CBDCs will disruptively penetrate their economies. Countries could be forced to introduce digital currencies, but this might be feasible only on a regional level given the complexities and resource commitments involved which can exceed smaller countries' resources. And many countries will also want to upgrade their financial infrastructures and rules to meet international standards and best practices, much as Europe has done.

9D.153. Importantly, it appears no country can ignore competing CBDCs (especially major-currency CBDCs), other cryptoassets, or stablecoins. These instruments have potential to penetrate and disrupt domestic financial systems and international financial relationships. Countries will need to choose a path to follow, each offering various benefits, costs, risks and challenges.

9D.154. The research underway on the digital euro, other investigations, and results of early CBDC experiments need to be reviewed to illuminate possible paths ahead. The Annex to this chapter gives two lists of features desirable for retail CBDCs that countries and future unions should carefully consider before launching their own CBDCs. Countries taking a dispassionate looks at CBDCs might conclude that they should not launch a CBDC alone and need to work with others.

9D.155. The digital financial revolution underway might result in near universal adoption of CBDCs – it remains to be seen whether this results in many individual country CBDCs, or in a smaller number of regional arrangements. Will technology and market forces lean toward – or even accelerate – movement toward monetary unions?

9D.156. It will be interesting if potential unions, such as in East and West Africa choose Scenario 2 as an intermediate or even a final regional integration step. It addresses financial inclusion relatively

[339] These are issues already addressed in the Euroarea, but are continuing challenges already recognized in developing the EAC monetary union.

quickly and could be a more feasible option than tackling the many additional tasks involved in moving to a full union. The key factor might be whether all potential union members have the resources and sufficient policy, supervisory, and legal frameworks to float their own CBDCs or will have to rely on centralized resources offered in a monetary union.

H. The virtual euro redux?

9D.157. During its first three years the euro was virtual. Chapter 2 describes the 1999 launch of Stage 3 of the union in which the euro was created as an accounting identity with the exchange rate of each national currency irrevocably linked to the euro. The virtual euro was used for official purposes and by the banking system. Only in 2002 were national currencies withdrawn and physical euro banknotes and coins circulated.

9D.158. Perhaps a similar path will be followed by future currency unions using CBDCs. The ambitious current experiments suggest that – as a first phase – national *wholesale* CBDCs can be created fairly quickly for use within closed systems involving the central bank, the government, banks, and payment and settlement systems. The efficiency, rapid settlement, and cost advantages of digital instruments can be put into practice, including for cross-border settlements. This might be done more rapidly than addressing the same issues using the existing nondigital financial technologies under existing monetary union plans.

9D.159. In contrast, creating retail systems (even as a second less-rushed phase) is more challenging – designing systems capable of handling diverse tasks, educating the public, creating physical devices, and handling the large-scale transition phase. Very high degrees of consumer protection and system robustness are needed to ensure acceptance of the CBDC and avoid disastrous system failures.

9D.160. Over time, CBDCs and physical currency systems will fully interact. CBDCs will partially replace physical currency, with diverse impacts on monetary conditions and policy, soundness of financial institutions, and public behavior. Impacts might be simultaneous with launch of the retail system or might be revealed over time.

9D.161. A scenario based on an initial wholesale CBDC seems plausible and could reflect the technical and practical challenges and risks ahead. But *it scarcely reflects the high priority placed by many countries on introducing retail systems to enhance financial inclusion.* CBDC advantages and risks might prove difficult to balance against real economic and social needs. It seems best to conclude with the opening statement:

"Given the potentially far-reaching consequences of CBDCs, policy makers must apply the utmost prudence."

Annex: Features needed for retail CBDCs

This annex shows two lists of requirements for retail CBDCs. Retail CBDCs are a high priority for Developing and Emerging Economies, but they are more complex than wholesale CBDCs, more challenging to put into place, and potentially create risks for the public and businesses. Future unions are strongly advised to implement retail CBDC programs only after the points listed below have been satisfactorily answered.

This list summarizes core attributes of retail CBDCs as recommended by the Group of Central Banks, which comprises the ECB, the central banks of Canada, England, Japan, Sweden, Switzerland, the United States, and the United Kingdom, plus the BIS.[340]

Core Attributes of Retail CBDCs ***Recommended by the Group of Central Banks***	
Instrument features	
Convertible	The CBDC exchanges at par with cash and bank accounts
Convenient	The CBDC should be as convenient as using cash
Accepted and Available	The CBDC should be usable in same types of transactions like cash. There must be ability to make offline transactions.
Low cost	Low cost or no cost is needed for users. Technical investments are low cost.
System features	
Secure	Users and infrastructure must be *extremely* resistant to cyber attacks. Instrument must be protected from counterfeiting.
Instant	Final settlement must be instant or near instant
Resilient	The system must be *extremely* resilient to operational failure, natural disasters, and electrical outages. The system must permit off-line payments.
Available	The system should never be closed.
Throughput	The system must speedily process a very large volume of transactions.
Scalable	The system is able to expand to meet demand.
Interoperable	The system interacts with private payment systems with easy flow of funds between systems. It potentially interacts with systems in other countries.
Flexible and adaptable	The system can adapt to new instruments, new conditions, and policy changes.
Institutional features	
Robust legal framework	A central bank should have clear authority to issue a CBDC.
Standards	The system, its institutions, and participants will conform to prudential and regulatory standards equivalent to those covering firms offering cash or digital money services.

[340] Group of Central Banks. "Central bank digital currencies: foundational principles and core features", Joint Report, no 1, October 2020.

The Monetary Authority of Singapore released the following list of issues to resolve before issuing CBDCs. It comprised a list of questions for a competition among developers on how a retail CBDC system address various problems, introduce CBDCs distribution to the public, and create related infrastructure.[341]

1. New Functionalities vs Inclusivity

Can a retail CBDC system be embedded with additional functionalities beyond a basic transfer of value without requiring users to use smartphones (or other expensive/complex hardware)

2. Security vs Accessibility

Can the design of a retail CBDC system be highly secure for users (e.g. one that prevents unauthorised uses and illicit transactions) without compromising the ease of use? Would such a system be able to cater to the varied needs of the elderly, minors, and those with disabilities?

3. Availability vs Risk of Disputes

Can offline transactions be enabled in areas with no or limited internet connectivity? What safeguards against double-spending and counterfeiting can be embedded to minimize disputes related to offline payments?

4. Recoverability vs Anonymity

In the event of theft, damage or loss of a wallet, card or instrument, can a retail CBDC system adequately trace transactions, limit the loss or support the recovery of lost funds without compromising user identity?

5. Widespread Frictionless Use vs Control

Are there technological features that can be incorporated into a retail CBDC solution to minimise the risk of significant and abrupt outflows from bank deposits to the CBDC, while ensuring that the use of the CBDC is as seamless as possible?

6. Personal Data Protection vs System Integrity

Can the retail CBDC solution protect personal and consumer transactions data, while allowing for monitoring, detection and prevention of illicit activities on the network (e.g. money laundering /terrorism financing, fraud, scams and corruption)?

7. Expanding Access to Financial Services vs Guarding against Data Monopolies

How can the design of a retail CBDC solution allow participating firms to harness payment data to enable the offering, customizing, or improving the pricing of financial services (e.g. credit, insurance) to users, while avoiding the undesirable effects of data monopolies on consumer welfare over time? How might users retain control over use of their data?

[341] Monetary Authority of Singapore (2021). Key international financial organizations also backed the competition.

8. Coexistence vs Integration Complexity

How can a retail CBDC infrastructure be made more resilient to single points of failure? Can concentration risks be minimized through decentralization? How can we develop a safe, stable and sustainable governance model for such decentralised infrastructure with clear lines of responsibility and accountability?

9. Decentralisation vs Accountability

How can a retail CBDC solution allow financial institutions to distribute CBDCs to the end user in a manner that leverages existing national payment rails such as a country's payment systems, while keeping participation cost competitive at minimal disruption? How can it process payments between users on different payment systems without introducing the need to involve additional intermediaries, or needing custom integration for onboarding?

10. Extensibility vs Operational Resilience

Can a retail CBDC infrastructure be flexible yet robust, allowing for computationally intensive use of programmable functions and addition of new capabilities without incurring additional overheads in terms of cost, operational performance or introducing system vulnerabilities?

11. Privacy vs Performance

Can a retail CBDC infrastructure incorporate privacy preserving capabilities while remaining high performing, with fast response time, low latency and scalability to support large deployment?

12. Interoperability vs Standardization

How can interoperability be achieved across different instruments of digital money and across different technologies without a commonly accepted standard?

Chapter 10 – Integration of Financial Markets

"Most financial systems are small" [342]

What programs promote integration of financial markets to create competitive markets and support effective union-wide monetary policy action?

[342] World Bank (2009) Global Monitoring Report, p. 21.

A. Introduction

Currency unions change financial markets

10.1. The statement "Most financial systems are small" describes all but a few financial systems in the world. Almost all financial systems in countries planning on creating currency unions are small. Small systems have some inherent drawbacks including limited liquidity, volatility, high fees, and limited competition. Almost all small systems are now undergoing rapid changes as they become exposed to larger, globalized markets. Small financial firms often cannot compete with larger international firms, offer limited services, and might protect their markets at the expense of domestic businesses and consumers. Creating a currency union transforms a cluster of smaller national financial systems into a single larger integrated financial system encompassing all the member countries. Markets will become more competitive, firms can grow larger and provide more services, banks can better compete against external firms, price signals are better, and costs of financial services fall for business and consumers. Thus, among important purposes of a currency union are creating larger, more competitive, and stable financial markets.

10.2. At the same time, new risks can emerge, with the particular risk of contagion of financial stresses across union countries. Issues arise of who is responsible for dealing with firms operating across borders and who pays the costs dealing with financial distress.

10.3. Planners for the EMU were aware of both the opportunities and risks. They felt that integration of financial markets was a key advantage of the union that would potentially provide large benefits to businesses and consumers in terms of access to new services, lower costs, and more stable markets. A wide variety of programs were initiated to promote financial market integration. This integration was also seen as promoting the sense of Europe as a single, unified entity that encompasses political, social, and cultural elements in addition to the economic elements. All these elements will come into play in future unions, who will need to plan programs for financial market development that seize the opportunities and deal with the risks.

10.4. This chapter focuses on EMU programs to integrate markets and create new opportunities. *Chapter 11* on payments and settlements systems describes technical systems that contribute to overall financial integration. Chapter 13 on supervision of financial institutions and markets deals with the elements of risk in union financial systems.

The role of financial integration

10.5. The central role of integration of financial markets into a single market is not well known to the public. However, it is critical in understanding how the EMU operates. Building a single integrated financial market with deep penetration into all union economies helps…..

Transmit monetary policy impulses throughout the union.

Provide proper signals to investors to help channel investment and credit into the most productive investments and projects to support the overall development of the union and to make it more competitive globally.

Reduce or eliminate financial barriers so that efficient and inexpensive markets can develop

.

Support development of long-term bond markets and equity markets to support building of the productive base of the union.

Reduce business' costs for financial transactions to support their operations anywhere within the monetary union.

To extend the advantages of competitive and inexpensive financial markets to the public and businesses so that the costs and range of available services are equal within domestic markets and in cross-border transactions.

Facilitate cross-border investments in infrastructure and private direct investments.

Reduce risks and simplify finances for travelers and cross-border workers.

10.6. The integration of financial markets is a key part of the European Union program. It is the culmination of the process of integration of markets underway since the 1950's. The integration of markets has proved highly successful in creating bigger and more competitive markets that advanced the overall development of the European economy, raised incomes, reduced inequalities between the regions of Europe, and made Europe more competitive in world markets. An EU-wide framework for financial market integration and development called the Single European Act was enacted in 1986. Thus, the framework for regional financial integration was established before work began on the monetary union, which then was subsequently promoted by the ECB.

The Euroarea and financial sector integration

10.7. The ECB (2001a) examined the impacts of the creation of the euro and found numerous areas where it had or was expected to have very quick impacts. "The Eurosystem encourages and promotes market initiatives fostering the development of the single Euroarea market." (p.10)

10.8. For example, securities markets rapidly developed "The euro-denominated bond market is much more homogeneous than in 1999."

A single market was developing for European equities. Large issuers could appeal to a larger pool of investors and small investors had new opportunities to list.

The TARGET clearing system played a key role in this development, including facilitating arbitrage that led to equalization of pricing throughout the Euroarea.

Money markets rapidly integrated and standardized. The nonsecuritized deposit market and derivatives markets were fully integrated by 2001.

Market integration proceeded more rapidly in banking markets than in retail markets.

Credit risk rose in relative importance in pricing of financial market instruments.

Virtual cross-border markets in debt instruments and repos through electronic trading developed, which often replaced over-the-counter domestic trading. Many mergers and alliances between securities markets developed.

Rationalization of securities settlements occurred though linkage arrangements or mergers and alliances. Ease of cross-border transfers increased.

From the start of union, the correspondent central banking model (CCBM)[343] assured availability of collateral for monetary policy operations and for TARGET. However, the CCBM could only collateralize central bank debt and therefore arrangements for other cross-border transactions needed to be developed.

Success was rapid in creating a system to distribute liquidity throughout the union, including providing liquidity from ESCB refinancing operations. This fostered development of area-wide transactions in unsecured money market instruments, which by 2001 comprised half of the entire money market.

10.9. To conclude, the creation of the Euroarea (even before creation of a physical currency) had very rapid impacts on a range of financial activities and quickly promoted integration of the individual country financial systems. This quickly provided new opportunities for Euroarea banks and businesses, increased competition and reduced costs, and made markets more efficient. This was exactly the type of response sought. Although these changes are rarely

[343] The CCBM is described in Section F on collateral.

noticed as functions of the currency union, they were clearly successes for the union.

B. EU comprehensive program for financial sector integration

EMU and EU programs

10.10. The EU and the EMU have a very comprehensive program to promote creation of a single financial sector for the union. It is intended that over time distinctions between domestic and cross-border transactions disappear and that businesses and the public throughout the union have equal access to financial services anywhere in the union. The enhanced competition in a single market will lead to introduction of new services, reduce costs for consumers, and open new investment opportunities. It will also enhance effectiveness of monetary policy.

10.11. Many of the initiatives for financial integration are set by EU policy, but the ECB and the NCBs contribute to policy making, development of rules and regulations, implementation, and oversight. Thus, although the programs can extend beyond the Euroarea (for example, to include the EEA economies preBrexit United Kingdom, or Sweden), the ECB and other Euroarea institutions play a big role. The ECB adopted the role of implementer and supervisor of many financial integration initiatives.

10.12. The Single European Payment Area (SEPA) extended to retail markets a 2001 EU regulation to harmonize financial institution's fees for euro transactions. SEPA was designed to carry the financial integration process to retail markets to generate benefits for businesses and households. The ECB was a prime mover of the initiative, but SEPA is an EU-level initiative that applies to all EU countries and countries in the European Economic Area.[344] It also covers the broad financial sector, not just the banking sector.

10.13. A key objective is to remove frictions affecting cross-border financial transactions. Several years into the monetary union, separate payments systems continued in the member countries, resulting in non-harmonized procedures, inefficient or delayed transactions, and higher costs for customers. Customers wishing to carry out cross-border transactions needed to approach a bank or local institution and pay a relatively high fee in order to complete the transaction. Diverse standards made it hard for firms operating in multiple countries to centralize and streamline operations. As a result, cross-border transactions within the EMU remained only a few percent of total financial transactions.

10.14. The failure to integrate retail markets was considered inadequate for a currency union under the rationale that a financial transaction should be treated equally anywhere within the union – a resident should face similar conditions and costs for domestic and cross-border transactions. SEPA was set up to aggressively foster such integration, to simplify the interface with customers and create more efficient cross-border transactions – including the possibility of using a single cross-border payments platform instead to dealing with two national payments systems.

10.15. Among the objectives are to standardize payments in euros, set time limits for transactions, establish "straight-through processing" in which transactions are processed electronically from start to finish, create efficient and cost-effective processing systems, enhance competition between service suppliers, create equal levels of fraud control, and erase cost differences between national and cross-border payments using credit cards, debit cards, direct debit, or electronic bank transfers. Pan-European Clearing Houses (PEACH) are an important component of the system. SEPA was also designed as a platform for "e-Government", the use of electronic procedures for more efficient delivery of public services. Large gains in

[344] The EEA extends the EU single market to several closely linked states (Iceland, Liechtenstein, and Norway). Switzerland considered joining, but choose not to; however, it has since signed many bilateral agreements with the EU similar to various EEA provisions.

efficiency were anticipated, as high as 2 percent of GDP.[345] [346]

10.16. Implementation of the single euro payments concept was initially slow. National implementation lagged and banks and other brokers were hesitant to introduce changes that would cut into their margins. Expectations that market participants and national payments systems, responding to public pressures for greater efficiency, would quickly make the system operational were not met. Subsequently, the banking industry in 2002 created the European Payments Council to create a roadmap and time table – three years were allocated to agree on standards and design the technical system. In 2007, the EU passed the Payments Services Directive, which required each member country to introduce legal changes and set maximum execution times for introduction of Pan-European instruments, such as credit cards, credit transfers, etc. The system became operational in 2008 with full migration to the new system in 2010. A second Directive in 2015 extended coverage of internet and digital payments, enhanced consumer protections, and increased oversight over retail fees.

C. The Many Faceted Financial Integration Programs

10.17. Two tables below list the many financial sector goals and functions carried out by the ESCB and also some of the large number of programs underway. The tables list many of the ESCB programs that contribute to overall financial integration, with an emphasis on payments systems. The systems should contribute to smooth and secure payments that serve business needs, contribute directly to monetary policy implementation, support financial stability, and permit seamless cross-border transactions within a single integrated European market.[347]

10.18. The initiatives and programs listed below extend well beyond the scope of this volume, but can provide designers of future unions a sense of the scope of financial market integration aspects that can contribute to the effective operation of monetary union. Fortunately, many of the programs are technical in nature and move countries toward adoption of international standards and best practices regardless of whether or not an union is created. Achieving the goals will develop regional teamwork and facilitate the eventual operation of a future union.

[345] RTE 2007. Also, ECB 2007a

[346] One interesting aspect of SEPA is that by reducing the cost of financial transactions and making them more accessible, a structural reduction in use of cash was expected. One aspect of this is that criminal uses of cash and tax evasion were expected to become more difficult.

[347] The information comes from a presentation at the 7th ECB Seminar on Payment and Settlement Issues for Central Banks, September 4-7, 2007 at the ECB.

Table 10.1: Financial Integration Goals and Functions in the EMU

The ESCB contributes in three ways – service provider, market oversight, and market development.

Service provider

Cash settlement and real time gross settlement systems
Settlement for securities' payment (including DvP[348])
Central depository for bonds
Large value payment systems
Retail payment systems
Check clearing
Settlement agent in net payment systems
Operate interbank funds transfer systems (IFTS)
Provide intraday credit to smooth market functioning
Replace functions of correspondent banking systems[349]

Market Oversight

Ensure safety and efficiency of payment and settlement infrastructure
Ensure system soundness and liquidity (including systemically important payments systems – SIPS)
Set standards for design and operation of systems
Regularly assess of operations and soundness
Enforcement, which is often decentralized
Cooperation with international authorities
Deal with financial consolidation and globalization, and potential gaps and leaks
Crisis communications and coordination

Market development

Information exchange and cooperation among market institutions
Promote harmonization through standards for systems and user interfaces
Own use of best practices and leading by example

---

[348] DvP (Delivery versus Payment) is a settlement mechanism that transfers securities only after payment.

[349] In correspondent banking, banks provide payment services to other banks based on bilateral contracts fashioned by market practice. Payments are often through reciprocal accounts (loro/nostro) to which credit lines might be attached. Correspondent banks typically use IFTS to settle between themselves. Correspondent systems are often used for cross-border settlements. Correspondent banking can be expensive and slow, as each leg of a transaction must fully verify transactions.

In 2018, the TARGET system introduced a system for rapid processing and settlement of transactions, called TARGET Instant Payment Settlement (TIPS). It is designed permit instant payments between bank accounts anywhere within the Euroarea.

In addition, the expected development of a digital euro direct liability of the Eurosystem would also provide rapid transactions and settlement.

Table 10.2: EMU Financial Integration Programs

Monetary Policy Implementation – Transmission of monetary policy impulses
- TARGET/ TARGET2 – Large € transactions throughout the area. Transmission through the banking system
- TARGET Instant Payment Settlement System (TIPS)
- EBA's Euro1 System is a bank-sponsored euro settlement system.[350]
- Monetary policy "corridor" – Standing deposit and funding facilities to set interest rate floors and ceilings
- Collateral (Eligibility standards and cross-border acceptability)
- Repo facilities
- Service provision – cash settlement and RTGS systems
- Securities settlement (including DvP)
- Central depositories for government bonds
- Supervisory oversight
- Continuous Linked Settlement (CLS) – foreign exchange settlement system
- Standards for fees (cross-border the same as domestic)
- EBA (European Banking Association)
- CEBS (Committee of European Bank Supervisors)
- SIPS (Systemically Important Payments Systems)
- Enforcement (common standards, but decentralized application)
- Central bank money (including a digital euro in the future)

Long-term capital markets
- Servicing of long-term instruments
  - Large value payments; Bond depositories; Repos; Credit transfer
- TARGET2-Securities (T2S)
- Securities Settlement Systems (SSS)
- Standardization of instruments
- Legal framework and oversight (in cooperation with IOSCO)
- Oversight of stock exchanges
- Securitization
- SPV (Special Purpose Vehicle) Legislation
- Oversight of fiscal situations (national risk premium has sharply narrowed)
- Inflation targeting (inflation premium has narrowed)

Retail (Single Euro Payments Area - SEPA)
- SEPA credit transfer
- SEPA direct debit
- SEPA card framework
- PEACH – Pan-European Automated Clearing House [351]
- On-line payments
- Mobile payments standards
- E-invoicing

---

[350] Euro1 is a multilateral netting system with over seventy clearing banks. End-of-day settlement is through TARGET. The system has a liquidity pool at the ECB and a loss-sharing agreement.

[351] STEP2 is an EBA sponsored PEACH owned by EBA Clearing Corp. for mass payments of euros. Gross settlement originally was made in Euro I, but has migrated to TARGET 2.

Implications for future unions

10.19. The long list of projects above provides a sense of the complexity of designing a program for financial market integration. There are many channels of financial payments within an economy with diverse institutions and instruments and a wide range of transactors and overseers. In an union, the complexity is increased because cross-border transactions involve diverse practices, institutions, and legal arrangements. These factors can severely impair operation of financial systems unless there is a focused program to harmonize practices and rules. Future unions will need a substantial program for financial integration that covers each important financial market instrument, sets up market institutions, harmonizes rules and practices across countries, and manages oversight, etc..

10.20. In future unions, promoting market integration might involve actions or services beyond what is typically handled by private financial institutions, and thus government incentives or direct actions could be involved. The union itself could become a service provider, much as the ECB developed TARGET specifically to promote market acceptance of the euro and to handle official transactions in euros. Similarly, future unions probably should join the CLS foreign exchange transactions system in order to provide the union's markets with access to superior foreign exchange transactions services. Union operation of a mobile money phone-based system for financial transactions is a realistic future prospect. If a future union chooses to operate a major financial market system, major implications for the union building program result;

The gestation periods for projects can be lengthy. Work must begin early to set technical standards, build infrastructure, recruit and train professional staff, pass implementing legislation, integrate programs into private financial markets, test operations, and educate the public and affected businesses. *The start-up of the union might need to be delayed until after technical infrastructure and oversight systems are operational*[352]

Technical complexity – Market systems will be technically complex which requires that the union have substantial technical skills or purchase access to such skills. Future unions are likely to lack the trained staff and preexisting technical infrastructure that existed in Europe and thus must build programs from scratch or purchase services.[353] [354]

The union itself will become a service provider with income and expenses related to the service. Setting the fee structure will be important to cover costs, encourage acceptance of the system, and compete with or subsidize private markets and consumers. These could be politically sensitive issues.

Policy operations need to be supported by the systems, which might affect the features of the systems and the design of policy operations.

10.21. Such considerations mean that a future union must decide early what types of systems it will support. It also should be decided whether the system will be a foundation component of the union (such as TARGET, collateral arrangements, and standing facilities were in Europe) or is a separate initiative that contributes to the union (which permits greater scheduling and institutional leeway).

---

[352] For example, the EMU would have been delayed if technical issues had held up the start-up of TARGET.

[353] Prudence suggests having two or more back-ups or suppliers of critical market infrastructure elements. As mentioned in *Chapter 9D – The Digital Euro* this can be especially important with increased use of digital financial instruments. This redundancy can create coordination issues and be expensive, but failure of a single node in the process could be disastrous.

[354] For example, the African Development Bank is supporting the development of payments systems in the EAC and WAMZ. The projects are technical and quite expensive. Without such assistance, the start-ups of these unions might be indefinitely delayed.

10.22. Future unions will also have different market conditions and needs than in Europe, and thus might go in different directions. For example, systems for workers' remittances and mobile currency systems for rural and low-income populations are two major services critical for future union financial markets and the welfare of the unions' populations that were not issues during the building of the EMU. (Other issues more relevant to future unions could include credit registers, credit insurance facilities, exchange rate insurance for external transactions, and oversight of services offered by external firms, etc.).

10.23. Thus, compared to Europe, new unions face different and more comprehensive financial market development and integration challenges, but begin with fewer financial, infrastructure, and professional resources. Private markets are less likely to be able to offer support. *A comprehensive review of the directions, schedule, and interactions with union policy operations is needed early in the union-building process. The union program might need to be adjusted based on the results of this review.*

Monetary policy and financial integration[355]

10.24. The rules and procedures for union monetary policy can influence prospects for financial integration. There are two main activities in this regard – the construction of a system to spread monetary policy impulses throughout the union, and the selection of counterparties for monetary policy actions.

10.25. *Spread of monetary policy impulses.* Chapter 5 – Monetary policy discussed the importance of creating union procedures that permit quick and widespread transmission of monetary policy actions throughout the union. A variety of innovations were introduced to support monetary policy that also promoted integration of the financial systems of the member economies into a single financial system.

10.26. *Monetary policy counterparties:* A currency union must identify the financial institutions eligible to participate in monetary policy operations. The selection should be made to ensure that the monetary policy stance is quickly transmitted through the banking system to all member countries. Effective regulation of the counterparties is critical. The selection can affect overall financial integration.

10.27. The Euroarea has an inclusive definition of institutions eligible to participate in monetary policy operations. Firms designated per EU law as "credit institutions" that take deposits or close substitutes and supply credit to households and firms[356] are eligible as counterparties for ECB monetary policy operations. All institutions covered have various rights and obligations – participation in monetary policy operations, reserve deposit requirements, accounting and statistical obligations, etc. Rights under the system include access to standing facilities to make overnight deposits at the central bank and borrow overnight funds against collateral, and to participate in fine-tuning monetary policy operations. By making a very broad range of institutions eligible to participate, national short-term money markets quickly effectively merged, facilitating the movement of capital between countries. [357]

10.28. The use of a broad common definition of counterparty facilitated the implementation of monetary policy. Comparable institutions in all member

[355] See ECB. The Monetary Policy of the ECB. 2001.

[356] Credit institutions are defined as "an undertaking whose business is to receive deposits or other repayable funds from the public and to grant credit for its own account."

[357] "The money market plays a crucial part in the transmission of monetary policy decisions, since changes in monetary policy instruments affect the money market first. A deep and integrated money market is a precondition for an efficient monetary policy, since it ensures an even distribution of central bank liquidity and a homogeneous level of short-term interest rates across the single currency area. In the Euroarea, this precondition was met almost immediately…when the national money markets were successfully integrated into an efficient Euroarea money market.". (ECB 2001, p. 23)

countries were captured as part of the "money issuing sector". Also, because a broad definition was used, problems were avoided of missing specific subsectors that might be important in some countries but not others. Without this broad approach, the definition of the monetary sector of a union is difficult, which makes monetary policy difficult and potentially impedes financial integration.[358]

10.29. Future unions should consider how the selection of monetary policy counterparties could affect the integration process. Counterparties need to be spread throughout the union territory and provide services to major market segments. Moreover, the monetary policy instruments and procedures must be set so that all potential counterparties can participate in actions. For example, collateral should not be restrictively defined so that for example only larger urban banks hold the types of securities usable for collateral. Constructing a suitably inclusive definition of counterparties and monetary policy instruments might not prove easy.

D. Successive financial markets directives[359]

10.30. The EU has implemented a series of plans covering financial markets beginning just before the launch of the monetary union. As EU plans, they applied to the monetary union, noneuro EU countries, and in this case also to EEA countries. The plans provide specific guidance to EMU officials on market infrastructure and practices, but also guarantee coherence of the same standards in a number of nearby markets, thus expanding the size and competitive strength of the market.

10.31. The Financial Services Action Plan (FSAP) launched just before the start of the monetary union was designed to create fully integrated financial services markets in the EU that are efficient and stable. The European Commission began work in 1998 to identify apparent deficiencies in integration in European wholesale and retail financial markets.[360] Overcoming the obstacles and creating a more integrated market would help secure the benefits of euro markets and contribute to efficient operation of markets. Key elements of the plan were creating a single wholesale financial market, create open and secure retail markets, and implement sound prudential rules. (Löber 2006, p. 10).

10.32. Priorities in the wholesale market included improving issuance and trading of securities, creating common rules for exchanges, and providing for raising capital across the entire union. These goals were supported by a series of specific Directives[361] and regulations that included;

> *Markets in Financial Instruments Directive (MiFID)* that created a "European passport" that allows financial services firms to offer services

[358] In particular, in IMF monetary statistics the appropriate definition of money and the money-issuing sector is an empirical concept – measures that empirically best correspond to economic activity and prices within each economy. They can differ between economies. *In an union such variation in the effective definition of money between economies is an absurdity.* The creation of a union with a single monetary policy implies that the nature of money must be effectively identical in all member countries – if not so at the outset, efforts are needed to bring about such unity. (This implies that integration of the financial sector is endogenous to the creation of the union.)

[359] Aspects of the plans are closely integrated with plans for payments and settlements systems discussed in the next chapter.

[360] European Commission (1999).

[361] The directives constituted a paradigm shift in the EU to promote explicit harmonization of practice across the union by enacting specific rules that promote an integrated single market. This replaced an earlier focus on minimum harmonization across countries or mutual recognition that allowed a wide range of practices to coexist with the union.

The directives are described in Chapter 16 on legal issues because of the important legal changes they embody. The directives offer financial market rationales that could also apply to future unions.

throughout the union based on home country approval, while enhancing mechanisms for cooperation between supervisors to protect investors.

Directive on Prospectuses, which allowed prospectuses approved by one member state to be used in all countries.

Transparency Directive, which covered disclosure requirements for listed securities.

Regulation on the application of International Accounting Standards (now International Financial Reporting Standards) required application of the standards.

Settlement Finality Directive set out rules to ensure that payments, including netted payments, have legal finality.

Directive on Collateral, to ensure that market participants have access to cross-border collateral to cover transactions.

10.33. Over 40 specific measures were included in the FSAP. Future unions could review the elements of the FSAP to see if they can be adopted in their unions. Intensive effort will be involved to understand the elements of the FSAP, interpret their relevance to the local situation, decide on priorities, and implement. This probably should be a joint project of future unions' payments and settlements committee and monetary policy committee.

10.34. In 2011, partly in response to the GFC, the European System of Financial Supervision was created. It includes the European Systemic Risk Board (ESRB) that oversees overall financial soundness of the system, European Banking Authority (EBA), European Securities and Markets Authority (ESMA), and European Insurance and Occupational Pensions Authority (EIOPA), and national supervisors in each of these fields. Overall, the degree of EU-level authority increased. This change established that the *full financial sector should be treated as a integrated whole subject to coordinated supervision.*

Lamfalussy Approach

10.35. An approach for securities regulation and supervision to support the market integration process was called the "Lamfalussy Approach" (after its chairperson, Alexandre Lamfalussy) developed by a Committee of "Wise Men". The approach is sometimes called the "Comitology Approach", based on the operation of committees to carry out the implementation of the framework principles. It is a complex system built on several layers of rules and operating entities. It is relevant for future unions because it deals with the challenges of creating harmonized systems starting from diverse national rules and decision-making processes. The Approach includes;

Applying framework principles from EU legislation. This is referred to as "Lamfalussy level 1". Setting out the technical details of implementing the EU legislation, involving consultation with committees of representatives of ministries of finance and national supervisors. [362] (Level 2)

Countries adopt legislation incorporating the details and processes developed by the EU. (Level 3) Countries implement the approved standards and regulations. (Level 4).

Supervisors increase their cooperation to promote more uniform application of the EU rules.

Enforcement implementation is strengthened, especially through EU actions.

10.36. Rene Smits (2005, pp. 207-209) points out the complexity of this process, which involves five layers for setting, interpreting, and implementing standards. Five steps are involved before a change in

---

[362] In the draft European Constitution, the EC stated its intention to consult with national experts in preparing European regulations for financial services.

international standards works down to where market practices are affected. Even at the end of this process, full convergence in practice is not guaranteed because there is room for diverse national interpretations or application of country-specific rules.

10.37. Smits cites several initiatives that were under consideration to enhance convergence. These include a database on regulatory decisions, creation of mechanisms to establish one decision-maker in selected fields, creating joint teams of supervisors, etc. In one example, the ECB has called for standardized implementation of Basel supervisory standards at the national level per Lamfalussy level 2.[363]

10.38. Smits states that the ECB called for Lamfalussy level 2 rules to be recognized "as the main body of rules applicable to EU financial institutions. At the same time, those aspects that could be more appropriately dealt with in EU legislation could be transferred from national legislation to Level 2 acts. The ECB is convinced that such a harmonized, simplified set of European rules would contribute significantly to further integrating financial markets, would considerably reduce regulatory costs for financial institutions, and would enhance consumers' rights in relation to financial services."[364] (Smits 2005, p. 110)

10.39. Smits called for union wide supervision of banks for multiple reasons; (p 211)

Synergy in information exchange between central banks and supervisors

Central bank focus on systemic risk and system soundness

Central bank independence

Central bank expertise

Historic involvement in supervision at multiple central banks[365]

Central banks' effective communications network across the continent

Efficiency in reporting to a single agency

Clarity for home country supervisors and firms

10.40. Conversely to Smits' views, it can be argued that overconcentration of power at the center should be avoided, that national regulators are better attuned to national market conditions, and the political difficulty of coaxing countries to cede their powers.

10.41. Ultimately, the GFC and its severe threat to the financial system ended up creating a more centralized system of financial market supervision in Europe, including bringing many supervisory functions under the ECB.

10.42. The argument in Europe over the Lamfalussy rules will seem hopelessly euro-centric to other unions and could be dismissed as just another confusing example of the European penchant to over-organize and create committees on top of committees and rules

[363] The EU has mandated adoption of Basel III standards and will continue to introduce the most recent versions of the standards. In future unions, moving all member countries up to the most recent Basel standards could be challenging and central authorities might need to selectively introduce the most important new standards.

[364] All countries should introduce the Basel standards (and related systems for securities, insurance, etc.) compiled in accordance with the IFRS as the foundation of their supervisory systems. Common programs to implement Basel can benefit regions by promoting efficient and cost-effective implementation, dealing in a harmonized manner with cross-border issues, and helping with integration of the banking sector. Fortunately, adherence to the Basel standards has become nearly universal, although not all countries are applying the most recent standards.

[365] It has been suggested that the strict separation of the central banking and supervisions function under Maastricht reflected the German model and the political strength of Germany to push the point.

on top of rules. All that is true, but new unions will also need to work out their own effective arrangements to agree on when union or national authority applies in setting the rules, implementing them, and adjudicating them. Moreover, the rules are likely to differ depending on how closely a function is a core functions of the currency union – greater centralization will be required for core and near-core functions, but subsequent concentric circles of financial sector regulation farther from the core monetary policy functions can be – and perhaps should be – more flexible and open to national control.

E. Cross-border securities markets

10.43. Corresponding closely with the development of the Euroarea was a trend in securities markets in Europe to move toward interconnected systems, or for mergers between national securities markets. This trend was supported by the ESCB with the ultimate goal of building a single gateway securities market infrastructure that could provide access to all Euroarea securities to all market participants.

10.44. Cross-border trading in the Euroarea is now extensive, with electronic trading for debt instruments and repurchase agreements. Stock exchanges have merged or forged alliances. This increases market access for the public and builds market liquidity.

10.45. An important stimulus to development of the market was the decision prior to the start of the union to convert all government debt into euros and use common technical standards. Finance ministers decided that to promote the development of financial markets all government debt including existing debt should be denominated in euros and that issues would conform to a common technical standard. The decisions made issues in different member countries comparable and more substitutable. It reportedly created a competition by national governments to get benchmark status for their bonds. Spreads on government debt issues quickly converged to very low levels regardless of the issuer.

10.46. These steps in effect created something like a single market for euro-denominated government debt comparable to the U.S. market. This created secondary market liquidity and supported the growth of underwriters, which reportedly had a powerful spillover effect for corporate debt. (Kenen and Meade 2008, pp. 63-64) However, the effective unification of government debt markets collapsed during the Greek crisis when market traders began to discriminate between issuers, with spreads of Greece and several other countries rising much higher than the benchmark German "bund" issues, as investors began a "flight to quality" and sold off issues with an apparently higher risk of default.[366]

F. Collateral

Eligible collateral

10.47. The Eurosystem requires that all monetary policy operations or use of intraday credit in TARGET be fully collateralized by eligible collateral. The collateral eligible for such actions is defined by the ECB. The collateral regime had multiple stages;

> *Start-up* – At start up, two lists of eligible collateral were used. The first list consisted of high-quality (A- rating or above), generally accepted instruments that could be used anywhere in the Euroarea. The second list consisted of instruments accepted by the NCBs as suitable in their own countries. These instruments might be in languages not used elsewhere and could have features unique to each country, both of which made them less suitable for widespread use outside the home country. The use of the second list also avoided creating major shocks to existing collateral arrangements at the start of the union.

[366] The GFC caused fiscal crises in Greece, Ireland, Spain, Portugal and other countries who had difficulty refinancing government debt issues, and ultimately led to rescue operations by the ECB, the IMF, and a newly created European Financial Stability Facility (EFSF) that was a temporary facility that issued bonds in its own name to finance purchases of the distressed countries' debt.

2007 innovations – The second stage occurred in 2007 when the system moved to a single list of eligible assets and eliminated the second tier. Eligible issuers were limited to those domiciled in the EEA and issues by international institutions.

Crisis-related changes – The financial crisis led to a number of changes in collateral rules. In response to the emergency need to provide liquidity during the financial crisis, the acceptable credit rating was dropped from A- to BBB- and the list of eligible collateral was expanded on a temporary basis to include;

Euroarea-issued securities denominated in U.S. dollars, British pound, or Japanese yen

Debt including Certificates of Deposit (CD) issued by credit institutions traded on some non-regulated markets (with a 5-percent haircut)

Subordinated debt protected by guarantees (with a 10-percent haircut plus an additional 5 percent if nonmarket valuations are used), and Fixed-term deposits held with the Eurosystem.

Modification of collateral based on the Greek rescue package – In May 2010, the minimum credit rating requirement for Greek government debt was suspended for marketable securities issued or guaranteed by the Greek government. The change was introduced based on EU approval of the financial rescue plan linked to a monitored program of financial adjustment. The ECB General Council ruled that this was sufficient assurance of repayment and thus other collateral rules could be suspended.

Subsequent changes – Subsequently, as the Euroarea worked through the GFC and its aftermath, many changes in collateral rules occurred. The ECB has put out a good summary of the "Eurosystem collateral framework" (ECB 2017) that provides a good picture of the legal complexities of operating the system. The ECB maintains an on-line data base of all acceptable collateral that is updated daily and can be used by credit institutions to identify eligible collateral.

Correspondent central banking model (CCBM)

10.48. The transmission of monetary policy impulses throughout the union requires that all banks anywhere in the union are able to participate in monetary policy operations. A specific problem is that credit institutions wishing to borrow from their own NCB might have placed their collateral in a securities depository in another economy and thus lack available local collateral to borrow from their own NCB. The Eurosystem created the CCBM to assure availability to all market participants of collateral for monetary policy operations or for TARGET. In the CCBM, NCBs act as custodians for each other, which allows participants to use all eligible assets regardless of their location within the Euroarea.

10.49. Under the CCBM, a credit institution can deposit collateral with any NCB in the Eurosystem. The NCB oversees the securities settlement system used by the credit institution. The NCB will hold the security as collateral, verify its eligibility and value, and notify the credit institution's home central bank that it is okay to extend credit to the credit institution. The system has been considered a major success that has fostered an extensive repurchase agreement market.

10.50. The ECB began work on a CCBM2 as a common centralized platform to manage collateral, but abandoned that project in order to address some technical issues and focus of development of TARGET2 Securities (T2S).

G. Nonbank financial institutions

10.51. Nonbank financial institutions (NBFI) are increasingly important components of a financial system. The Euroarea's comprehensive definition of "credit institutions" as monetary policy counterparties meant that relative few types of financial institutions (such as mutual funds) were not brought under ECB oversight. However, all institutions were subject to a range of oversight by the EU and oversight was significantly strengthened during the GFC when the

European Financial Supervisory System (EFSS) was created. Various features of the SEPA (Single European Payments Area) also helped harmonized NBFI practices and their contributions to an integrated financial market. Future unions will need to consider how NBFIs will be regulated and supervised and how they fit into an union integrated financial system.

H. Insurance

10.52. The insurance industry (including pensions) is a distinct type of NBFI that can be an important component of financial sector activity – with liabilities and credits often seen as remote from monetary policy. Insurance often has separate supervisors and reporting requirements and separate regulators. The special character of its liabilities and reserves meant that analytically it was not easy to aggregate insurance activity with other financial industries.

10.53. Mauro Grande (former head of the ECB's Prudential Supervision Directorate) has stated that the original reason for the exclusion of insurance from ECB oversight – its remoteness from central bank functions – is no longer valid in light of developments in financial markets. (Smits 2005, p. 212) This conclusion was reinforced by the problems of the insurance sector during the GFC, and subsequently insurance supervision was incorporated into the new European Supervisory System. Supervision is now considered as a key component of the overall financial market situation and the sector's activities and its impacts are regularly monitored. The FSB has recognized the soundness importance of insurance and designated several "Globally Systemically Important Insurers" (GSIFIs) that are subject to additional oversight and capital standards.

10.54. Many lower income countries now in unions or potentially in unions have small or limited insurance sectors and thus have given little thought about how it fits into integrated monetary union financial markets. However, insurance has an important development role as a channel for savings, purchaser of long-term government securities, provider of long-term development finance, and source of high-quality liquid securities used for bank supervisory purposes.

10.55. Future unions will need to examine whether insurance companies have a systemic role across the union and, if necessary, introduce common regulatory and supervisory policies.

I. Islamic financial markets

10.56. Islamic banking and finance is significant in several potential unions in Africa, Asia, and the Middle East. Islamic finance has some unique characteristics that distinguish it from conventional finance, of which prohibition on receipt or payment of interest is best known, among other differences. Islamic finance had no role in designing the EMU, but it has to be considered in several potential future unions.

10.57. Islamic finance presents interesting problems in designing a monetary union with well-integrated financial markets because Islamic banks and other Islamic financial institutions are constrained to transact only in "Shariah-compliant' financial instruments. This can *de facto* partially separate the Islamic finance subsector from the conventional finance subsector, which can impair the smooth transmission of financial signals and financial flows through the economy, complicate monetary policy, and potentially create financial stability issues.

10.58. Only in the past decade has much work been done to gather information and analyze the behavior of Islamic finance within an economy. Very little work has been done examining how it affects regional integration programs.[367] However, the focus has changed and work underway at the IMF, IFSB, Accounting and Auditing Organization of Islamic Financial Institutions (AAOIFI), UN, World Bank, and elsewhere can provide some insights into the role of

---

[367] One exception is the author's analysis of challenges integrating Islamic finance into the planned GCC monetary union. (Krueger 2019).

Islamic finance in future monetary unions and regional integration programs.

10.59. The UN and IMF have created a joint task force to investigate treatment of Islamic finance in the SNA and Balance of Payments statistics. This initiative is likely to result in greater standardization of work on Islamic finance and awareness of its potential economic importance that can help future unions better understand how to integrate Islamic finance into their monetary union plans. [368]

J. Conclusion

10.60. Strong and effective integrated financial markets will permit more efficient and productive investment and help make the union competitive in global markets. The EMU considered such benefits as an important benefit of the union and thus aggressively promoted financial market integration rather than leave the process to market forces. Likewise, future unions that face the simultaneous challenges of developing and integrating financial markets should not treat the tasks passively, but should work systematically to promote financial market integration as an important contribution to the eventual success of the union.

[368] Recognizing that Islamic finance has multiple unique features that distinguish it from conventional finance, the UN/IMF group is also considering recommending preparations of an "Islamic finance satellite account" that captures macroeconomic information on the behavior of the Islamic finance subsector. It is recommended that future unions with significant Islamic financial activity consider compiling the satellite account to better understand how the subsector could affect union financial behavior and integration.

Timeline

Schedules to promote financial market integration will often parallel the schedule for clearing and payments systems described in Chapter 11. Also see that schedule, as relevant.

Preparatory period	Comprehensive surveys of financial market conditions, financial transactions costs, and market frictions (payments systems, securities transactions, collateral, etc.) Compile information on legal frameworks
Early actions (four years prior)	Identify monetary policy requirements for union-wide operations. Design payments systems required for monetary policy Identify monetary policy counterparties Decisions on e-money and interoperability. Identify legal barriers to cross-border transactions. Survey market participants on impediments to cross-border transactions Investigation of CLS system; review of barriers to adoption
Three years prior	Draft legal provisions permitting cross-border transactions. Draft legislation needed for CLS
24 months prior	Enactment of legal changes permitting cross-border transactions
18 Months Prior	Enactment of legal changes permitting cross-border transactions
Final 12 months	Harmonized financial legal framework implemented. Implement rules of pricing of cross-border financial services.
Final 6 months	Monetary policy payments system operational Other critical systems operational Finalization of CLS arrangements
Run-up to union	
Union day	Monitor experiences
Early union period	Evaluation of results
Union steady state	Implementation of noncritical systems

CHAPTER 11 – CLEARING AND PAYMENTS

What clearing and payments institutions will be created to further the integration of markets, to support the effective application of monetary policy, and to serve financial markets?

A. Introduction

11.1. The Maastricht Treaty states that "The ECB and NCBs provide facilities, and the ECB may make regulations, to ensure efficient and sound clearing and payments systems within the Community and with other countries."

11.2. This chapter reviews the role of payment and settlement systems in the EMU, and the role of payment systems in planning new currency unions.[369]

> In designing the EMU, the efficient and safe operation of clearing systems for money market instruments was considered critical for monetary policy and effective transmission of monetary policy impulses. This led to creation of a new union-wide system called TARGET – "**T**rans-European **A**utomated **R**eal-time **G**ross settlement **E**xpress **T**ransfer System" – for large value euro payments.
>
> Moreover, development of efficient and sound clearing systems for securities and retail payments was considered important to allow businesses and the public to benefit from the creation of a single integrated financial market for Europe.
>
> Based on such considerations, the Eurosystem is responsible for oversight of all euro payment and settlement systems. (ECB 2001) It operates key aspects of the system, promotes development of integrated systems throughout Europe, and exercises oversight.

11.3. Although payments systems attract little public attention, in the Eurosystem they were considered critical components of the overall framework. TARGET had to be operational for the start-up of the union in order to carry out monetary policy operations. Following the successful launch of TARGET and the integration of European money markets emphasis shifted toward an aggressive program to create an integrated European financial market with payments systems in which distinctions between domestic and cross-border payments ultimately disappear.

11.4. TARGET, and its successor TARGET2, will be reviewed as the primary means for integration of euro-denominated money markets critical for the execution of monetary policy. The chapter also discusses securities settlement systems and retail settlements systems that are part of the Single Euro Payments Area (SEPA) initiative. The Continuous Linked Settlement (CLS) system for foreign exchange transactions, which has become the global standard, is also discussed. Application of international standards and best practices in payments systems is important for economies to successfully integrate into the global financial system, and therefore key standards are also discussed in this chapter.

B. Role of payments systems

11.5. Clemente (1999) provides a concise description of why payments systems are important central banking activities.

> "Payment systems have traditionally stood at the heart of Central Banking concerns. Almost all Central Banks either run their country's key payment systems, or exercise some form of oversight over them. There are a number of strong reasons for that. *First*, Central Banks actually evolved from being bankers to the banking system, and the liabilities of the Central Bank, whether bank notes or transfers across the commercial banks' accounts at the Central Bank, remain the means of final settlement in almost all currencies. *Second*, it is as the marginal provider of liquidity to the banking system that monetary policy operations work. *Finally*, in a market economy almost all economic transactions involve, ultimately, the use of a payments system to transfer value. So, the failure of a major high value payment system….would disrupt

[369] This chapter does not deal with the digital euro and other CBDCs, which are effectively hybrid monetary/payments instruments. They will have many impacts on payments and need to be addressed by future unions. They are discussed in *Chapter 9D – The Digital Euro.*

monetary policy, as well as the financial system, and involve real economic costs."

11.6. The above statement summarizes why operation and oversight of payment and settlement facilities is central to the operation of a currency union. It is through operation of the payment system that the union currency becomes the means for final settlement. The payments system is central to the operation of monetary policy. Efficient operation of the payments system supports business and the productive allocation of capital. A crisis in payments systems threatens the banking system, the economy, and the exchange rate. Additional roles for payments and settlements systems in unions are to transmit monetary policy impulses throughout the union, integrate markets, and remove frictions between national financial systems. Thus, payments and settlements systems of unions are more complex than national systems, requiring new tasks and functions. Planning for these new features and putting the necessary infrastructure in place before the union starts requires that planning on systems begin at least four years before the start of the union.

11.7. These tasks are even more important in an union, where cross-border payments which are traditionally subject to a wider range of risks and uncertainties than in domestic payments. Cross-border transactions for countries outside a currency union face issues of currency risk, settlement risks due to differences in time zones, different systems, different procedures and standards between countries, and when disputes or defaults occur issues of choice of law and conflicts of law. The process of creating an union will involve making diverse and idiosyncratic national payments systems, each of which addresses all these issues, into an integrated operable system. The new system will create structural changes in markets and introduce dangers of contagion of risks across the economies while at the same time making national oversight from a national perspective more difficult – conditions that make regulation and oversight by union-level institutions critical.

11.8. Innovations in payments instruments are occurring rapidly. New forms of electronic instruments are affecting retail customers, businesses, and banks and other financial institutions. Digitalization, as discussed in Chapter 9D, is creating many new opportunities and risk. Moreover, cross-border instruments are becoming more common. These raise important challenges for payments systems and force systems to continually innovate.

11.9. Thus, the tasks of a currency union include developing payments systems to handle the new common currency, foster compatible systems in all member countries, construct efficient systems that support business and public needs, and manage risks in all important payments systems, domestic and cross-border. New instruments must be continually incorporated. These are challenging tasks.

11.10. The mirror side of payments systems is the operation of securities settlement systems (SSS). Many payments are made in conjunction with securities transactions, in three important ways; the purchase or sale of securities, the use of securities for collateral, and the use of securities for monetary policy implementation. The EMU has moved aggressively to promote more effective SSS operations. One important driver for enhancement was a decision by the Eurosystem to require collateral for all credit-providing operations in order to protect itself from losses. This meant that to carry out monetary policy securities markets throughout the union must be efficient with ready access to SSS in order to participate in monetary policy actions. Disturbances to SSS could impair monetary policy and block the operations of the TARGET payments system by denying users of intraday credit from the Eurosystem needed for transactions. Thus, SSS must be seen as another component of the EMU infrastructure.

11.11. An important aspect of development of payments systems is to incorporate as fully as possible recent important advances in international standards and best practices. As far as possible, new payments systems should reflect the BIS's *Core Principles for Systemically Important Payments Systems* (SIPS) that provide guidance on creating efficient systems that promote integration and economic growth, and also deal with risk management and the stability of the financial system. Systems that meet international standards will contribute to the acceptance of the new currency, but systems that lag might impair prospects for the new union and expose the union's markets to new types of risks.

C. EMU payments systems

11.1. This section looks at several major payments systems in the Euroarea.

TARGET and TARGET2

TARGET

11.12. TARGET ("***T**rans-European **A**utomated **R**eal-time **G**ross settlement **E**xpress **T**ransfer System") is the Euroarea's central system for large value euro payments. One purpose is to make sure that banking institutions throughout the Euroarea have equal access to monetary policy operations so that monetary policy impulses can move quickly throughout the entire union so that money market rates converge and are equal in all markets. TARGET was also designed to promote widespread acceptance for the euro by providing a low cost and highly secure interbank settlements system. It was also intended to help build integrated markets and provide market depth and efficiency.

11.13. TARGET is a Real Time Gross Settlement (RTGS) system, in which payment orders are processed individually on a continuous basis. Therefore, it provides immediate and final settlement for all payments, provided that the payer has sufficient funds or access to overdraft facilities with the payer's NCB.

11.14. When set up, TARGET was designed with three guiding principles;

> Market principle – Use of TARGET is required for monetary policy transactions and for government transactions, but the public has the right to use TARGET or other systems – correspondent systems and private clearing arrangements – as they wish.
>
> Decentralization – The system was built by linking national settlement systems, but the linkage required adoption of many common practices in all member countries.
>
> Minimum approach – The most streamlined system possible would be used, compatible with the basic requirements for monetary policy. Time involved and costs were to be minimized by retaining national RTGS systems, which could retain unique features and potentially offer somewhat different services. Harmonization was to be kept to a minimum, but had to include common practices in providing intraday liquidity, operating hours, and pricing. In line with the minimum approach, domestic payments in national RTGS system were permitted to vary, but cross-border transactions used a common central bank correspondent model in which reciprocal accounts were credited or debited based on each payment order.

11.15. TARGET is decentralized. It might have been possible to set up a centralized system run by the ECB, but this would have required making more substantial changes than might have been prudent for a new type of system and given the already large demands on resources to prepare for the union. Also, some national clearing systems had made significant efforts to upgrade or modernize and were not eager to change systems so quickly. (Scheller 2007) The decentralized system consists of a new payments mechanism of the ECB linked with the national RTGS systems run by each central bank. All systems are interlinked to provide a uniform platform and uniform pricing for euro payments.

11.16. All EU countries are members of TARGET, which allows EU countries that have not adopted the euro such as the United Kingdom to participate in the euro market. This helps build market strength and liquidity for the euro and also helps support intraEU trade in goods and services which is a key purpose of the EU.

11.17. TARGET was designed to minimize risks within the system. As a RTGS system, systemic risk is reduced and settlement risk and credit risk are eliminated through settlements using central bank money. Settlements have legal finality, which came about through enactment of the Settlement Finality Directive, which required that all EU countries enact legislation ensuring that settlements are final.[370]

Text Box: U.K. Admission to TARGET[371]

The United Kingdom received a derogation exempting it from adopting the euro. Prior to the Eurosystem launch there was debate whether the U.K. should be admitted into the TARGET euro payments system.

At issue was whether TARGET was a monetary policy entity operated by the Eurosystem and available only to its members, or an EU initiative payments system open to EU members. The U.K. would want to join TARGET for competitive reasons, fear of exclusion from Euroarea business, and possible migration of banks out of London.)

If TARGET were classified as a commercial payments system, as an EU member the U.K. could join based on Single Market rules that forbid discrimination in commercial matters. But if treated as a monetary policy entity used to control the stock of euros, provide intraday credit to smooth markets, adjust minimum reserves (which were not required in the U.K.), and facilitate lender-of-last-resort actions.

Thus, the argument focused on whether parallel systems could effectively operate - one influenced by monetary policy considerations, and the other with a commercial orientation. Given free capital movements, it could be expected that euro-based financial markets would develop in the U.K. – these might take a different form than in the Euroarea, could be supervised differently, react differently to financial stresses, and potentially affect the stock of euros. Information on conditions in the U.K. euro markets and whether they could be adjusted could be important in setting and executing policy in the Euroarea.

In July 1998, just before the launch of the euro, the ECB granted the U.K. access to TARGET and allowed British banks to use sterling assets as backing for borrowing euros. Also, the ECB decided to remunerate required deposits, in part to avoid disadvantaging Euroarea banks competing against British banks that did not make required deposits.

Later, beginning in 2007, TARGET2 was launched by the ECB, but the U.K. choose to not participate.

11.18. TARGET was an immediate success and handled a tremendous volume of domestic and cross-border settlements from its start without problem. It became one of the largest payments systems in the world, handling more than 300,000 payments instructions per day with a daily value over 2 trillion euro. It handled about 90 percent of all large value euro payments in the Euroarea.

11.19. Processing is open to banks and their customers acting through the bank, but during the last hour each day only interbank transactions were made in order to allow banks to complete their net settlements for the day. The transactions during the last hour are much larger than the average through the day.

11.20. TARGET allowed participants access to unlimited collateralized intraday credit from the NCB to cover liquidity demands of gross settlements trading.

11.21. TARGET is run by the Eurosystem. The ECB Governing Council has decision-making responsibility. The Payment and Settlement Systems Committee (PSSC) administers the system through a sub-group, the TARGET Management Working Group. The Working Group monitors the performance of the system and makes recommendations on improvements to it. The operation of the clearing system itself is handled by the NCBs' payments and settlement departments and a coordinator at the ECB. When problems arise in the system, they are first addressed at the local level, but can be referred up the chain to the ECB Governing Council, if necessary.

[370] "Settlement Finality Directive" (98/26/EC) enacted by the European Parliament.

[371] See Kaminska (2016)

TARGET2

11.22. In early 2008, TARGET2 replaced the initial decentralized TARGET infrastructure with a single platform. The new system was intended to provide harmonized services for domestic and cross-border payments using common pricing to further enhance cost efficiency and allow for expansion to include new EU members. Supervised banks anywhere in the EU and European Economic Area can participate by operating through direct members in the system.

11.23. A key feature is introduction of a single technical infrastructure, called the "Single Shared Platform", which is operated cooperatively by Banca d'Italia, Banque de France, and Deutsche Bundesbank on behalf of the full EU. The single platform allows banks anywhere in Europe to have access to the same services at a common price. Multicountry businesses are able to consolidate their financial operations into a single system with important cost savings and thus manage their liquidity more efficiently.

11.24. Under TARGET2, each payments message enters the interlinked shared platform, where all NCBs participate simultaneously. This facilitates the batching of payment instructions by banks to reach counterparties throughout the entire Euroarea – for example, the payment of dividends to holders of securities anywhere in Europe. This is in contrast to the original TARGET system in which transactions between two banks are settled between the systems of the two national central banks involved in the transaction with the linkage provided by the SWIFT messaging system.

11.25. TARGET2 also provides harmonized settlement services for nonbank financial systems based on access to central bank money, referred to as "ancillary systems" such as retail payments systems, clearing houses, and securities settlements systems. This permits systems to access any account on the single platform using a standardized interface. This is efficient in that systems do not have to maintain separate balances to operate in multiple systems.

11.26. Although procedures under TARGET2 are much more harmonized than under TARGET, banking institutions continue to transact with their NCBs.

11.27. Reflecting the multi-country operations of banks within the Euroarea, TARGET2I provides several different types of membership in the system;

Direct participants have full access to the system and maintain a RTGS account in the system. They bear full responsibility for any transaction sent into their account.

Indirect participants include supervised banks in the European Economic Area that can transact with the system through a direct participant.

Addressable BICs (Bank Identifier Codes) are branches and correspondents of direct participants that have a specific identification code in the system and who can transact using the account of the direct participant. This permits individual locations of large banks to send and receive payments instructions by operating through the parent's account in the system.

Multiaddress access permits individual branches and offices within a banking group to transact directly with the parent's account in the system without involvement of the parent. This permits a bank to manage its payments flexibly, including creating specialist centers to handle specific types of business for the entire banking group.

11.28. The introduction of TARGET2 was handled in an interesting manner. Each participating country and the ECB were assigned to a group organized around one of the countries operating the single platform – Germany, France, and Italy. The German group migrated into TARGET2 in late 2007, and the other two groups migrated on separate dates in 2008. A fourth migration date was also set for contingency purposes.

11.29. The development and implementation of TARGET2 was lengthy. Work on specifying its elements and standards began in late 2004 and continued into early 2006. Development of the system, its legal framework, and contractual arrangements began in early 2005 and ran until early 2007. Most of 2007 was spent testing the system, prior to migration which began in November 2007 and ran for six months into 2008, with a built in three-month contingency period appended at the end. Following the migration, NCBs still had up to four years to continue to process transactions in their own systems, but ultimately had to move to TARGET2. (ECB 2007d, p.15)

11.30. Future unions should budget equally long development periods for their systems.

Text box: TARGET and the GFC

The solid construction of TARGET and TARGET2 was demonstrated during the GFC, when despite major shocks to the European financial system, payments operated without difficulty, thus demonstrating their contribution to general financial stability.

Recognizing the critical importance of continued smooth operations of payments systems under stressed conditions, in 2001 the ECB adopted the "Core Principles for Systemically Important Payment Systems" developed by the BIS, and in 2014 enacted a Regulation mandating application of revised BIS standards issued in 2012.

EBA payments systems

11.31. The Euro Banking Association (EBA)[372] is an association of European banks that runs an euro payments system called Euro1. It is owned by a separate company called the EBA Clearing Company, which is owned by the banks. It handles several hundred thousand mostly medium-sized transactions daily, totaling around €200 billion per day.

11.32. Euro1 is a multilateral net settlement system, in which each participant has a single position against all other participants in the system. Settlement is made at the end of each day using TARGET and a settlement account at the ECB.

11.33. Risk in the system in mitigated through bilateral and multilateral limits for each participant. A loss-sharing agreement covers defaults between the clearing banks in the system, which must meet financial requirements. A liquidity pool at the ECB can cover the single largest position in the system.

11.34. The bank-owned EBA also runs an automated clearing house called STEP2, referred to as a PEACH, or "Pan-European Automated Clearing House", which covers transactions across the Euroarea. It handles several hundred thousand transactions per day, most with a size of several thousand euro. It uses batch processing for instructions received on D-1, the day before the transaction. Instructions are sorted by the receiving bank and gross settlement is made the next morning. Initially, payments were made through Euro1, but were later transferred to TARGET2

Offshore euro payment systems

11.35. The importance of the euro in international trade and finance led to development of euro payments systems outside the Euroarea. Reasons include processing in different time zones and to include the euro in specialized foreign exchange market trading. By far the biggest offshore system is the CLS foreign exchange trading system (described below) in which euro turnover is about 20 percent of total transactions. Smaller systems exist in Switzerland, Hong Kong, and Dubai, and several other countries.

11.36. Offshore retail euro payment systems have also been set up in EU countries that are not planning to join the Euroarea or which are not yet included in order to allow customers to settle business accounts in euro. These systems are small.

[372] Just to be confusing, the European Banking Authority (also EBA) is an official regulatory body over banks.

Securities settlement systems (SSS)

11.37. A securities settlement system handles the sale and delivery of securities against payment. Safe, efficient, quick, and low-cost settlement is important for the success of a monetary union. In an union, an additional requirement is that settlements can be handled across borders so that monetary policy impulses can be transmitted throughout the union for implementation of monetary policy and to improve price signals and effectiveness of financial markets. SSS are also links to the global financial system and are subject to international standards for safety and operations, and therefore must be developed in accord with international standards and practices. Finally, the GFC raised important new issues of how systems affect financial stability and the types of oversight needed.

11.38. Many variations of SSS are possible and one important task in planning for a currency union is to make sense of what are likely to be different systems in each country, and possibly multiple systems within each country for different types of clients or financial instruments. Some systems will be systemically important to operate the union and must be changed or improved prior to start-up of the union. Other systems might not be critical, but as part of the union program they must meet modern standards of safety and efficiency (such as meeting the CPSS-IOSCO principles for financial market infrastructures) and do not create threats to general financial stability. Solutions might call for creation of a single system for the union (which is certainly an option for small unions) or linking existing systems.

11.39. Changing SSS is a long and complex process. New systems must be designed, legal arrangements agreed to permit harmonized operation of the new systems, financial infrastructure put in place, operational changes introduced, and changes made to systems in central banks, banks, and businesses. This process will be long and might need to be done in stages, introducing changes critical for the union first, then proceeding over time to address less central systems and to make long term structural changes.

11.40. The process for setting SSS arrangements in the EMU described in the next section is instructive because it faced multiple systems, critical initial needs, and long-term development issues.

Euroarea SSS

11.41. The EMU supported enhancing and linking of the securities settlements systems throughout the union. The EMI recognized that enhanced development of SSS would be needed for the settlement of assets used in monetary policy operations, which placed work on SSS on the agenda for the future union. Strengthened SSS was also seen as contributing to more effective and competitive financial markets as a benefit of the union and create to more stable markets. The EMI's *Working Group on EU Payments Systems* was responsible for this work as part of its general EU function of coordinating central banks' activities in the field of payments systems and preparing for functioning of payments systems for the EMU.

11.42. The Eurosystem supports the integration process in securities markets in several ways;

Contributing to the removal of obstacles to integration through cooperation with both the private and public sectors

Setting standards as a major user of SSSs for Eurosystem credit operations

Promoting the cross-border use of collateral
Enhancing the integration of the regulatory and oversight framework, and

Promoting financial market integration, including providing efficient settlement services using central bank money.

11.43. The first step taken by the EMU planners was assessment of the suitability of the existing systems and their technical operations to handle monetary policy operations. Information on existing SSS systems in all EU countries was collected and published a 1996 volume (EMI 1996c) that ran over 700 pages.

Recommendations for SSS

11.44. Ideally, securities transactions are done on a Delivery versus Payment (DvP) basis, which makes delivery only when payment is guaranteed and removes danger of default from both sides of the transaction. A typical DvP transaction involves a securities depository putting a hold on the securities then sending a payment instruction to the central bank. The central bank transfers funds from the buyer's reserve account to the seller's reserve account and sends confirmation to the depository. Upon receipt of confirmation, the depository records the change in ownership of the security. (Sometimes, the cash side of these transactions is handled by the depository on behalf of the central bank.)

11.45. Ideally, these transactions are done in a dematerialized electronic form that facilitates matching of orders with securities and accelerates processing.

11.46. Securities transactions and payments can be done on a gross or net basis. For example, both the sale of the security and the payment can be on a RTGS basis; or the securities sale could on a gross basis and payments on a net basis; or both could be on a net basis.

11.47. An important variation is whether the securities transfer and the payment are integrated and run by the settlement agent; or whether the securities and payments sides are separate. In an integrated system, the securities depository or settlement agent handles the cash payments on behalf of the central bank. If a separate system, the depository or settlement agent handles the securities side, and the central bank handles the funds transfer – this requires communications between the agent and the central bank indicating that the securities are escrowed for delivery and that the payment has been made.

11.48. The situation becomes more complex for cross-border securities settlements. Many variations are possible, including the possibility that the depository or settlement agent is in a third country. There are potentially five levels involved in national transactions – customer, broker, depository, bank or settlements agent, and central bank; in cross-border transactions, the cross-border linkages could be at any of those levels, which could create problems in establishing authority to participate and agree on legal arrangements. It is possible that legal or institutional arrangements can differ between countries and thus different types of cross-border linkages could exist within the same international securities settlement system. In the event of disputes, it s who has standing, the country in which proceedings take place, and how conflicts of national laws are dealt with. These are complex issues that future unions will need to deal with – obviously, the greater the degree of harmonization that can be introduced among the union member countries, the easier will be this task.

11.49. Oversight of cross-border SSS can be challenging. The rights and responsibilities of home and host country supervisors and central banks need to be settled, and a central supervisor is preferred in order to have oversight of the entire system including operations in different countries. Central oversight is especially important in unions where national supervision is weak or limited because of the small size of the economies or lack of resources to effectively carry out the supervision. Such oversight of the system exists within the Euroarea, but might be difficult to achieve elsewhere.

11.50. A particular problem for international systems is how to manage systemic risks, such as failure of one institution causing other institutions to fail or failure of the system, or if liquidity problems within a single country feed into the system. The authorities in the country in which a problem starts should have primary responsibility to correct it, but might have limited capacity or the problems could become generalized. Also, with cross-border banking, it might be difficult to decide in which country the problem originated. Devising solutions to deal with such situations could be difficult – each situation will differ and solutions could differ. Here union-level solutions have advantages, but mechanisms can be developed for collections of national systems, although this could be more difficult.

11.51. A currency union will have special standing in dealing with cross-border securities settlements to promote greater harmonization of national practices and legal recognition of the cross-border claims. This will contribute to the financial integration of national markets within the union, which supports financial deepening, economic convergence, and general development, and can assist in the implementation of monetary policy by helping create a common interest rate benchmark throughout the union. Such motivations were strong within the EMU.

11.52. In cross-border trading, an additional issue arises about the relationship between the customer and his broker, who takes the instruction to buy or sell a security and then places the order in another country. Home country brokers do not want to lose business by allowing national customers to place orders directly with exchanges or brokers in other countries. This has been an issue in Asia that has held up cross-border trading of securities, and for which proposals have been floated to create "tunnels" that allow home-country brokers to accept business and provide straight-through electronic processing for transactions in exchanges in other countries.

11.53. Subsequently, TARGET2 – Securities (T2S) was launched with work beginning in 2007 and effective in 2014. It is discussed below in the section on SEPA – Single Euro Payments Act.

Foreign exchange payments – Continuous Linked Settlement (CLS)

11.54. The CLS system is an international standard system designed to provide efficient settlement services in foreign exchange and a wide range of foreign exchange instruments and derivatives and remove the risk of default on one of the legs of an international payments transaction.[373] A particular risk addressed by the CLS system, which has grown due to globalization of markets, is settlement between countries in different time zones.

11.55. Since its launch in 2002, the CLS system has become the international standard. It addresses both the need for market participants to have an effective and secure settlement system and concerns of regulators and central banks about risks within the very rapidly growing foreign exchange market. CLS handles an extremely large value of transactions, equaling half or more of global foreign exchange payments.

11.56. The CLS provides major improvements in the efficiency and liquidity of markets through multilateral netting for Settlement Members. The CLS Bank has estimated that multilateral netting reduces funding needs by over 95% each day compared to gross transaction-by-transaction funding. That is, for each trillion of value settled, CLS Settlement members fund less than US $50 billion in cash. Payment risk is also reduced because of a large drop in the number of pay-ins and pay-outs between Settlement Members and CLS each day – on average, only 26 payments are made each day per 10,000 instructions settled, a 99.75% payment volume reduction. (CLS 2008)

11.57. The system is owned by its members, who are shareholders from leading foreign exchange trading banks, which cover over half of foreign exchange transactions worldwide. Central banks are eligible to be members, but do not need to contribute capital. All members have equal votes.

11.58. The system operates through CLS Bank, which is organized in the United States as a limited function bank regulated by the US Federal Reserve System. It provides foreign currency settlement services, for which it maintains an account at the Fed for each of 18 eligible currencies.

11.59. The Federal Reserve is lead supervisor, operating with a cooperative oversight arrangement with the central banks whose currencies are settled by CLS Bank. A separate sub-group of the CPSS has

[373] This particular risk is known as "Herstatt risk," named after Bankhaus Herstatt that experienced such a crisis in 1974.

been set up for oversight of the system. CLS Bank observes the Core Principles for Systemically Important Payment Systems published by the CPSS.

11.60. CLS Settlement Members are the first line participants in the system. They must be shareholders in the system. Settlement members each have a single multi-currency account with CLS Bank. They may submit payment instruction on their own account or for their customers. Each settlement member must prove that it has financial and operational ability to handle its business with CLS Bank.

11.61. Central banks can also be Settlement Members, but are not shareholders. Central banks have somewhat different requirements reflecting their special status, but are still scrutinized by the CLS for eligibility and must provide information on their capital position, profitability, and rules for profit distribution.

11.62. A second group consists of *User Members* that are sponsored by a Settlement member and transact through the Settlement members account. User members can write payment instructions on their own account or for their customers. The Settlement member is responsible for covering all obligations in its customers' accounts, and therefore User members might need to post collateral or margins with the Settlement member.

11.63. The acceptance of a currency into the CLS system means the effective internationalization of a currency. A demanding process is applied for acceptance, which applies a series of criteria that create conditions for settlement finality. One requirement is strong support of central banks.

11.64. A total of eighteen currencies are in the CLS system - Australian Dollar, Canadian Dollar, Danish Krone, Euro, Hong Kong Dollar, Hungarian forint, Israeli Shekel, Japanese Yen, Korean Won, Mexican peso, New Zealand Dollar, Norwegian Krone, Singapore Dollar, South African Rand, Swedish Krona, Swiss Franc, UK Pound, and US Dollar.

11.65. The text box below describes eligibility requirements for a currency to be part of the CLS. All currency unions should strive to meet these criteria so that their currencies can be accepted into the system[374] – membership in CLS facilitates development of integrated money markets, provides a valuable service to residents of the union, and contributes to the international acceptance of the new union currency.

Text box: CLS currency eligibility requirements

CLS Bank has received a written request by two or more CLS Shareholders to designate the currency as an Eligible Currency;

CLS Bank has received indications from at least three institutions of willingness to act as Liquidity Providers for the currency on commercially acceptable terms;

The currency's payment systems meet CLS Bank's requirements as an Approved Payment System, including opening hours that sufficiently overlap with the Settlement Period for all Eligible Currencies;
The cost of inclusion of the currency in the system is reasonable;

Adequate risk reduction would result from the designation of the currency to justify the investments necessary to include the currency;

Any exchange restrictions or similar conditions on the transferability of the currency are acceptable to CLS Bank;

The convertibility, liquidity, and historical volatility of the currency, the stability of the banking system, and rule of law applicable in the jurisdiction of the currency, and other mitigating issues are acceptable to CLS Bank;

[374] The requirements are strict and some large economies are not eligible to join the system, often due to the lack of settlement finality. (Hartsink, 2007)

The relevant Central Bank has agreed to (i) allow CLS Bank to establish a special account with the Central Bank solely for the purpose of facilitating transfer of an Eligible Currency from and to Settlement Members, (ii) permit a means of operational access to the account acceptable to CLS Bank, and (iii) contractual arrangements made that are satisfactory to CLS Bank;

CLS Bank has received a legal opinion in form and substance satisfactory for addressing finality of payments made to and from CLS Bank's account with the relevant Central Bank and such other legal considerations as might be required; and

Legislation or regulation provides for finality of (i) the Settlement of Instructions and (ii) Pay-Ins and other Settlement payments received by CLS Bank through the relevant payment system for the currency.

Operations of CLS

11.66. CLS handles transactions on a payment versus payment (PvP) basis, which means that it settles both sides of transactions simultaneously from available funds from both sides of the transaction, per instructions regarding the value date. This eliminates settlement risk. Settlements are done on a multilateral basis for all obligations for a value date.

11.67. The system uses straight-through processing so that entries are only made once, with no interventions as transactions move between parties handling the transactions, or for authentication, matching, and settlement. Both counterparties must be already enabled to use the system, and transactions can only be in the accepted currencies. The processing is highly efficient and is estimated to cost as little as seven hundred-millionths of the transacted value.

SWIFT

11.68. SWIFT is the Society for Worldwide Interbank Financial Telecommunication, a member-owned cooperative with over 8300 banks, exchanges, and other financial institutions in virtually every country as members. SWIFT is headquartered in Belgium and therefore the Banque Nationale de Belgique is its lead overseer. The Banque is part of the ESCB and therefore the EMU has an important responsibility related to SWIFT. SWIFT provides a platform for transmitting encoded financial messages between members. Several million messages are transmitted each day.

11.69. Swift does not handle financial transactions nor transact on its own account. Also, it does not manage accounts nor store financial information. Its role is to provide a necessary messaging service for the financial sector. SWIFT's standards are accepted world-wide and banks and central banks must belong to the system. SWIFT is also involved in development and marketing of network applications and in research and development, and marketing and sales of terminals and related software.

11.70. SWIFT is owned by shareholding banks. The system was originally limited to banks, but restricted access is now granted to non-owner "participants" which include securities brokers and dealers, related institutions such as Euroclear, and domestic clearing systems.

11.71. SWIFT's core service is handling the exchange of financial messages. This was originally done over a proprietary network (computer facilities, switches, leased lines, related software, and customer-level terminals), but in 2005 under the 'SWIFTNet' it shifted its customers to a secure Internet Protocol. Additional elements of the transition to an internet platform are continuing. In July 2021, SWIFT Go was launched as a low transactions value payments system.

11.72. SWIFT accepts, validates, stores until delivery, and delivers financial messages 24 hours a day, seven days a week. About 3 billion SWIFT messages are sent annually, which typically cover banking activities, payments orders, foreign exchange confirmations, and deliveries of securities. Each message is highly structured and customized to the types of information needed for the transaction, and as a result there are over one hundred different types of messages handled.

11.73. SWIFT is critical to the payments and settlement architecture of Europe. It provides the interlinking message service for the ECB and national central banks participating in TARGET. It also provides messaging services for the Euro1 and STEP2 payments systems run by the private Euro Banking Association. It also provides messaging services for national central securities depositories, including Clearstream, Euroclear, and the London Clearing House.

11.74. SWIFT works on development of new standards for message formats, in which each bank has a Bank Identification Code (BIC) as a universal identifier of each bank. The technical standards are agreed by the banking community shareholders and are often developed cooperatively with international standards setters, and thus provide standards that are used by outside bodies and can be adopted as standards for national financial messaging systems.

11.75. The SWIFT system is designed to ensure confidentiality. Messages are automatically encrypted when they enter the system, and banks have an option to encrypt their messages within the flow from their in-house terminals and the SWIFT access point. Each message is authenticated based on bilateral code keys known only to the sender and receiver to identify the sender and receiver and which can provide a guarantee that the message was not modified during the transmission. The system can provide information back to senders on their overall activity and on the status of individual messages.

11.76. SWIFT has a contractual responsibility and financial liability for carrying and delivering messages. Rules for the use of the system and SWIFT's and users' responsibilities are set out and are binding on users. The rules and the enumeration of responsibilities for timely transmission of messages and delivery are often taken as the basis for standards for correspondent banking relations. *Unions and union institutions will thus become legally involved in the SWIFT operating rules and responsibilities, and thus must design their systems to be compatible with the SWIFT standards.*

11.77. A SWIFT message differs from messages in domestic large-value funds transfer systems because under its rules SWIFT itself does not create an irrevocable obligation for the sending bank. Banks using SWIFT messages must arrange clearing and settlement themselves through bilateral correspondent relationships or by forwarding incoming payments orders to domestic interbank funds transfer systems. This has been addressed by banks through introduction of "straight-through processing", with automatic links between the bank's SWIFT connection and their computer systems linked to domestic payment system. Also, SWIFT messages are sometimes treated by banks as authoritative. Thus, SWIFT messages might become integral parts of interbank funds transfer systems by forwarding them to the clearing house. This is more common for international payments, such as was done under the ECU Clearing and Settlement System where SWIFT had a key role. SWIFT messages are also customized to interface with TARGET.

11.78. SWIFT has recently instituted a feature called Fin Copy and Fin Inform which allow messages to automatically be copied and sent to third parties. Reasons for copying include authorization for the transaction, initiating some type of processing, liaising with corporate treasury operations, custodian's reporting to clients, reporting to regulators, anti-money laundering monitoring, or creating back-ups, etc.. Fin Copy permits central authorization for a single payments message, where Fin Inform is for information purposes only and allows multiple parties to be informed about a message. These services fit naturally with use of straight-through processing, for greater control over transactions, and increased reporting requirements. The systems are largely intended for banks transacting within closed user groups (such as TARGET or CLS) with a central institution. Currently over 50 RTGS systems use Fin Copy in their operations.

11.79. SWIFT is a critical component of the international payments infrastructure. It has an important role in linking together central banking and payment and clearing operations in the member countries of an union. For this reason, it has an international oversight group comprised of the G-10 central banks, the ECB, and the BIS that deals with policy issues, technical standards, and operations.

11.80. Payments infrastructure for future unions will need to be compatible with SWIFT standards, platforms, and legal responsibilities, and should be designed to take advantage of the services available from SWIFT. The process of setting up SWIFT systems for messages between organs of an union central bank and with the banking community can be based on the EMU role model, where there is considerable technical expertise to draw upon.

11.81. Future currency unions and their organs, as appropriate (NCBs, payments systems, depositories, etc.), will need to be shareholding members of SWIFT. Unions should participate in SWIFT deliberations and standards setting as a representative of the central banks within the union, and to reflect the needs of the banking community within the union. The payments and settlements functions of future central banks will probably be based on SWIFT services for linkages between central bank organs and linkages with payments systems, SSS, exchanges, and financial institutions.

Key Euroarea financial integration initiatives

Single Euro Payment Area (SEPA)

11.82. The SEPA initiative, launched in 2007[375], is designed to carry the financial integration process to retail markets to generate benefits for businesses and households. One key objective is to remove frictions affecting cross-border financial transactions. Several years into the monetary union, separate payments systems continued in the member countries, resulting in nonharmonized procedures, inefficient or delayed transactions, and higher cross-border transactions costs because customers had to approach a local bank and pay a relatively high fee in order to complete the transaction. Diverse standards made it hard for firms operating in multiple countries to centralize and streamline operations. As a result, cross-border transactions within the EMU remained only a few percent of total financial transactions.

11.83. Under SEPA, pressure was applied on the private banking industry to develop retail payments systems that provide cross-border clearing houses, credit card systems, debiting systems, etc. with the same efficiency and costs as national systems

11.84. The failure to integrate retail markets was considered inadequate for a currency union under the rationale that a financial transaction should be treated equally anywhere within the union – a resident should face similar conditions and costs for domestic and cross-border transactions. An aggressive program was set up to foster such integration, to simplify the interface with customers and create more efficient cross-border transactions – including the possibility of using a single cross-border payments system instead to dealing with two national payments systems.

11.85. Among the objectives are to standardize payments in euros, set time limits for transactions, establish "straight-through processing" in which transactions are processed electronically from start to finish, create efficient and low-cost processing systems, enhance competition between service suppliers, create equal levels of fraud control, and erase cost differences between national and cross-border payments using credit cards, debit cards, direct debit, or electronic bank transfers. Pan-European Automated Clearing Houses (PEACH) were introduced. SEPA was also designed to be used as a platform for "e-Government", the use of electronic procedures for more efficient delivery of public services. Large gains in efficiency are anticipated, which have been estimated to be as high as 2 percent of GDP.[376] [377]

[375] Payments Services Directive (EU) 2007/64/EC, followed by regulations in 2009 and 2012.

[376] RTE 2007. Also, ECB 2007b.

[377] One interesting aspect of SEPA is that by reducing the cost of financial transactions and making them more accessible, a reduction in use of cash is expected, creating a structural change in the behavior of money. One (continued)

11.86. SEPA covers the full range of retail payments arrangements, including credit transfers, direct debiting, a framework for credit and debit cards, and setting up PEACHs, such as the STEP2 system operated by the Euro Banking Association.[378] It is expected that private initiatives based on these platforms will begin providing value-added services to customers (such as e-invoicing, online payments, payments services) that will provide the service providers with a steady income flow while offering customers efficient and low cost payment services.

11.87. Although the creation of the EMU was the trigger for SEPA and although the ECB is a prime mover of the initiative, SEPA is an EU-level initiative that applies to all EU countries whether inside or outside the Eurozone. The vision for SEPA was developed by the ECB and the European Commission with the expectation that the market participants and national payments systems, responding to public pressures for greater efficiency, would make the system operational by 2008. The system was to be run by the banking industry, which was deemed best placed to design requirements and schedules aligned with the industry's needs.

11.88. However, implementation of SEPA was slow, extending into 2014. National implementation was slow and banks and brokers were hesitant to introduce changes that would cut into their margins. In 2007, the EU passed the Payments Services Directive, which mandated each member country to introduce legal changes and set maximum execution times that will permit operation of Pan-European instruments, including debit cards, credit cards, credit transfers, etc. Although there is strong official support for SEPA, the financial industry did not appear very enthusiastic. As late as November 2008, the ECB issued a statement that the financial sector turmoil should not be used as an excuse to delay adoption of the initiatives. (ECB 2008e; p. 4) The first elements of the system became operational in 2008 when the frameworks for credit and debit cards and for credit transfers were put into place. Delays in introducing national enabling legislation to create direct debit systems also delayed implementation of the full system.

TARGET2 Securities (T2S)

11.89. Corresponding to the SEPA initiative, the Eurosystem created T2S, a centralized single European SSS for central securities depositories (CSDs).[379] The new platform for cross-border and domestic settlement of securities uses central bank money - claims on the central bank – that can be used for settlements in payments systems. Participating CSDs continue their regular relationships with their clients.

11.90. T2S addressed the lack of harmonization in cross-border transactions and much higher costs for cross-border transactions than for domestic transactions. T2S was intended to increase cost transparency and provide equivalent services throughout the union, allowing customers to choose local securities service providers on the basis of costs and services rather on the location of the security.

11.91. T2S is an example of the Eurosystem's direct involvement in promoting financial sector integration by providing central bank services to CSDs and acting as a catalyst for private sector actions. Both the direct involvement of the Eurosystem and the promotion of private sector action (in which the Eurosystem is both a customer and overseer) are

---

aspect of this is that criminal uses of cash and tax evasion are expected to become more difficult.

[378] The Euro Banking Association is owned by a consortium of banks. Its EBA Clearing Corp operates a PEACH that is an essential component of the payments and settlement infrastructure for the euro.

[379] The system is highly complex and had a substantial lead time. Research on T2S began in 2006 to see how to best handle demands for integrated European settlement infrastructure with harmonized practices and to reduce settlement costs for cross-border transactions or where low volumes resulted in higher costs. Detailed specifications for the system (technical features, pricing, governance, and legal requirements) were developed around yearend 2009.

inferred from the Maastricht Treaty provision that the Eurosystem should promote the smooth operation of payments systems.

11.92. T2S handles securities transactions using central bank money. It is also a multicurrency platform open to EU nonEuroarea countries and Switzerland. T2S is built on TARGET2 system by combining payments and securities settlements.

11.93. Following the model for decentralized implementation of TARGET2 by several central banks, four central banks (France, Germany, Italy, and Spain) agreed to implement the system. T2S received final approval in mid-2008 following agreement on technical features and strong support by CSDs, and was fully implemented after a long delay in 2017.

Over-the-counter (OTC) derivatives

11.94. The turmoil in financial markets that began in 2007 highlighted the importance of over-the-counter (OTC) derivatives in generating instability as well as the inadequate infrastructure for their settlement which contributed to a lack of transparency and the instability. OTC trading was viewed as nonstandardized, based on bilateral relationships, and involving a considerable manual processing. In large part this reflected the customized nature of many OTC products designed to fit the specific customer needs and frequent use of proprietary instruments.

11.95. A particular area of OTC risk was in credit default swaps (CDS) that had grown massively prior to the GFC. CDS are a form of insurance against defaults by corporate borrowers. Many financial institutions took positions in CDS based on long-term very low default experience of many borrowers, but when the financial turmoil hit defaults increased and some financial institutions took very large losses.

11.96. CDS introduced new financial sector risks and directly contributed to market instability during the crisis. (ECB 2008e; p, 5) First, they are nontransparent and facilitated undetectable shifts in credit exposures. Second, exposures are highly concentrated and large relative to the capital of financial institutions, which made holders vulnerable to defaults by major counterparties. And third, the lack of official oversight of the market allowed institutions to take imprudent credit exposures.

11.97. Key regulators agreed on the urgent need to create regulatory and settlements infrastructure for CDS. One of the first priorities was to set up central counterparty facilities (CCPs) for CDS. CCPs help in diversifying risk exposures, their strict margining requirements help cushion shocks, 'and positions become more transparent and known to regulators. The European Commission took the lead in establishing a CCP in Europe within only a few months.

11.98. Thus, the GFC fostered rapid development of new payments arrangements and requirements for additional oversight of derivatives and OTC contracts. Future unions will need to consider how this change might affect their payments and settlement infrastructure, whether it be by promoting derivatives exchanges and CCP within the union or by linkage to entities outside the union.

D. Supporting legislation

11.99. The discussions above noted that differing legal standards create difficulties in setting up cross-border payments systems. Currency unions have a vested interest in promoting harmonization of legal standards related to payments systems to promote ease in making cross-border transaction, then prevent and resolve disputes. Absent legal harmonization, businesses and investors are inhibited in making cross-border transactions, which inhibits growth of integrated markets, creates cross-border risk premia, prevents development of an union-wide interest rate benchmark, prevents movement of capital to most productive investments, and in general diminishes the effectiveness of the union in promoting economic growth and development.

11.100. The importance of supporting legislation is shown through the uncertainties that can be created for cross-border payments systems needed for effective monetary policy implementation. For example, the legal and operational environment in each country, including insolvency law, can affect the timing of the finality of transfers. Asymmetries in settlements and their finality between countries can create systemic risks (Herstatt risk) Often, individual institutions cannot alter their payments system infrastructure and procedures without changes to the legal framework in which they operate. Creating symmetry across countries will require adoption of common legal arrangements by the countries involved. (EMI 1996c; p.676)

11.101. The EMU benefitted from substantial legal convergence due to the overarching legal framework of the European Union. However, additional legislation specifically aimed at harmonization of practices in payments systems was also needed – settlement finality, collateral, and netting. These were accomplished through use of EU "Directives" described below that mandate countries introduce legislation to accomplish the goals of the Directive within the context of their own national legal frameworks.[380] The Directives had to be implemented prior to the start of the union. The EMI had authority to review legal convergence in the EU countries to ensure that national legislation was sufficiently convergent to support the union.

Settlement Finality Directive

11.102. In 1998, Directive 98/26/EC on Settlement Finality in Payments and Securities Settlement Systems was enacted. It cited the finding in the 1990 Lamfalussy report that important systemic risks exist in multiple legal settings.[381] A particular problem identified was dealing with netting in insolvency proceedings in determining applicable laws and recourse to collateral. The Directive further stated that harmonization in finality would contribute to efficient and low-cost operation of systems to reinforce the freedom of movement of capital with a single European market.

11.103. Key features of the directive follow;

The payments system must indicate to countries in which it operates whose law is applicable for participants in the system.

Transfer orders and netting are legally enforceable and binding on third parties, even in the event of insolvency proceedings, if transfer orders were entered into a payments system before the moment of insolvency proceedings open.

Transfer orders entered after the moment of opening of insolvency proceedings and carried out are legally enforceable and binding on third parties only if it can be proven that the agent or clearing house, etc. prove that they were not aware, nor should have been aware, of the opening of proceedings.

It is not possible to unwind a netting by applying laws, regulations, or practices for transactions completed before the moment of opening insolvency proceedings.

11.104. The Directive established that the netting and settlements of the payments system are legally enforceable in all EU countries, including in cases where bankruptcy or insolvency proceedings are initiated, and that the settlements cannot be unwound through national actions. The law governing participants in each payments system must be declared. These features establish regular features for settlements that allow participants throughout the EU to understand the conditions in which transactions will take place and establish the legal arrangements covering them. Also, by ensuring that settlements are

[380] For example, the Directive on Settlement Finality states "Member States shall bring into force the laws, regulations and administrative provisions necessary to comply with this Directive before 11 December 1999. They shall forthwith inform the Commission thereof."

[381] A bank's settlement exposure for foreign exchange deals is defined as equal to the full amount of the currency it has purchased, and lasts from the time at which its payment instruction for currency sold can no longer be cancelled unilaterally until the time when the currency purchased is received with finality. (EMI 1996c, p. 676)

final, it allows market participants to use assets immediately after concluding the settlement, which facilitates the liquid free flow of capital within the market.

11.105. For future unions, the issues of settlement finality will be very important. The unions might be in different time zones from the money market centers in which they commonly transact financial business, might have a large geographic spread over multiple time zones with little overlap over opening times, might have different deadlines for cancellation of orders, or have different volumes of transactions which affect batching and processing times. These issues will need to be addressed by each union based on its particular situation.

Collateral Directive

11.106. The Collateral Directive (2002/47/EC) was enacted to create a uniform framework for use of collateral to limit credit risk in financial transactions. The Directive reduced formal collateral requirements to make them more uniform throughout the EU.

11.107. Among the purposes of the Directive were removal of barriers to use of cross-border collateral so that collateral arrangements between two parties could include collateral in any EU country, create clear rules, limit legal and administrative burdens, legally recognize risk mitigation techniques used in markets, allow reuse of pledged capital after a transaction is complete, and create legal certainty.

11.108. Collateral provides assets to guarantee the performance of an obligation and recourse in the event of default on a transaction. The Directive accepts two forms of collateral; 1. Assets provided by transfer of full ownership to the collateral taker, which includes title transfers under repurchase agreements, or 2. transfer of possession to the collateral taker under a "security right" such as a pledge or lien where full ownership of the assets remains with the collateral provider. In the second case, after default the collateral can be taken under the terms of the pledge. The ECB felt that the first definition was clearer and easier to enforce, but the second definition was accepted because of existing national practices.

11.109. The Directive provided the right of countries to exclude from collateral some types of claims on the collateral provider itself, such as shares in the collateral provider or its affiliates, or shares in undertakings related to the collateral provider's business operations. This provision provides assurance that the collateral has value independent of the condition of the collateral provider.

11.110. The Directive requires removal of certain procedures that create burdens in setting up collateral arrangements, including formal acts and excessive procedures to create, value, enforce collateral arrangements such as statements by notaries, registration requirements, public announcements, and formal certification, etc. Not only do such procedures impede use of collateral and create costs in complying with different national procedures, but the legal certainty of arrangements can be impaired if complex procedures are not completed to the letter of national law.

11.111. The Directive requires that enforcement actions to take control of collateral or to use it to set-off obligations can be initiated without various actions that could create delays, such as giving prior notice, getting court authorization, auction of assets, or setting a waiting period.

11.112. The Directive focused on a limited form of netting – bilateral netting, but needs to expand its coverage to deal with multilateral netting used in many European payments systems and netting by a central counterparty. (Löber 2006; p. 63)

11.113. Finally, collateral arrangements are especially important in unions with substantial Islamic financial instruments because some common Islamic instruments involve use of collateral. As a result, the Dubai International Financial Center set up a separate operation to handle collateral associated with Islamic bonds and other Islamic instruments.

Conclusions regarding legal frameworks

11.114. The Settlement Finality and Collateral Directives are examples of secondary legislation that contributes to the operation of the currency union. Both greatly facilitate the operation of the union, but are not core attributes of the union.

11.115. These types of issues affect unions and integration of various nonunion regional schemes. For example, the ASEAN is setting up or is discussing several financial integration programs similar to some in the EMU.

11.116. An union might have legal authority to impose provisions on its membership, but as these matters are secondary such powers might not explicitly exist in the union. In contrast, the power to introduce secondary legislation is unlikely to exist for some regional integration arrangements, although standards can be recommended. Thus, enacting secondary legislation could be a challenge. In this regard, the concept of a "Directive" seems relevant in both union and non-union situations – a legal instrument that sets goals for countries to implement, but which permits countries to implement within their own legal frameworks. As was done in Europe, this flexibility needs to be monitored by a central authority to ensure that the national implementation does not accidently or purposefully fail to provide the harmonized results sought.

E. International standards and best practices

11.117. To facilitate its operations, the Eurosystem set standards for Eurosystem credit operations with all EU securities settlement systems and their links. (ECB 2001a; p. 15) Principles for the standards were;

- Equal treatment for all institutions
- Promote soundness of the systems
- Promote efficiency of systems
- Eurosystem standards for SSS are used in Eurosystem credit operations
- Legal soundness
- Settlement in central bank money
- No undue custody risks
- Regulation or control by competent authorities
- Transparency of risks, and conditions for participation in a system
- Risk management procedures
- Intraday finality of settlement
- Hours and days of operations
- Operational reliability and availability

11.118. Application of standards such as the above reflected a strong commitment by the EU, its member countries, and ultimately the ESCB to support modern payments systems that provide high degrees of protection against risk and reflect the best international practices. Such protection was felt necessary to provide confidence of the success of running cross-border settlement systems for the new currency to support acceptance of the euro; Conversely, difficulties in payment systems would reflect negatively on the euro.

11.119. Two important international standards applied to the Euroarea payments systems are described below.

Lamfalussy Report

11.120. In 1989, the G10 established a high-level committee to analyze issues related to cross-border and multicurrency netting systems. The committee was headed by Alexandre Lamfalussy, and its report issued in late 1990 is known as the "Lamfalussy Report."

11.121. The Report addressed several potential credit and liquidity risks affecting netting arrangements for interbank payments, forwards, and foreign exchange contracts. Netting arrangements permit the pooling of receipts and payments so that only a net payment is made, which can be efficient, inexpensive, and less error prone. The Report also reviewed several policy issues on netting and interbank settlements, settlements and monetary policy, interbank trading, and supervisory responsibilities for cross-border netting.

11.122. The Report concluded that netting can improve the efficiency and stability of interbank settlements, reduce costs, and reduce risks. However, the report noted that achieving these results depends on whether legal arrangements create binding net exposures immune to legal challenges. This is particularly problematic for cross-border settlements, and thus comprehensive legal arrangements were needed to facilitate cross-border netting.

11.123. The report also covered risk management arrangements. It discussed a spectrum of possible arrangements in which risk is covered either by the central provider of the netting services or by the participating banks. (Lamfalussy 1991; p. 2)

> In a centralized system, risks are covered by the provider of the netting services, usually backed up by customers posting collateral against the system's exposure.
>
> In a decentralized system, each customer remains responsible for credit losses within the system through pro-rated allocation of losses among the nondefaulting customers. The risk control mechanism consists of bilateral limits on exposures to other participants.

11.124. The report discusses the policy framework for oversight of payments systems and lays out a set of minimum standards for cross-border and multicurrency payments systems. The report is clear that it provides minimum standards, not necessarily best standards or practices. Countries were permitted to develop more stringent standards and in particular were encouraged to create systems capable of handling multiple defaults.

11.125. Also, national payments systems linked to TARGET were evaluated for their adherence to the Lamfalussy Standards.

Core Principles for Systemically Important Payment Systems

11.126. The TARGET payments systems and several other Euroarea payment systems were assessed for their compliance with the *Core Principles for Systemically Important Payment Systems (CPSS; 2001)*. The CPSS were developed by the G10 countries' Committee on Payment and Settlement Systems.

11.127. Beginning in 1988, work began to develop general principles based on the early Lamfalussy standards that important payment and settlement systems should follow. General principles were developed to not impose a specific type of system on countries, but to allow countries to evaluate their own systems to see if they successfully performed key functions and promoted safety and stability. Following an initial draft of the principles in 1999, the group working on the principles was expanded to bring in a wider range of countries and the ECB. The final statement of principles was published in 2001. Six of the ten standards were restatements or rewordings on the earlier Lamfalussy standards, and the ECB quickly adopted the principles, organized an assessment of all systems within TARGET and some other important systems, and published results. (See ECB 2004b)

Text box: Core Principles for Systematically Important Payment Systems[382]

I. The system should have a well-founded legal basis in all jurisdictions.

II. The system's rule and procedures should enable participants to have clear understanding of the system's impact on each of the financial risks they incur through participation in it.

III. The system should have clearly defined procedures for the management of credit risks and liquidity risks, which specify the respective responsibilities of the system operator and the participants and which

[382] The four new Core Principles not in the Lamfalussy Report are IV, VI, VIII, and X.

provide appropriate incentives to manage and contain those risks.

IV. The system should provide prompt final settlement on the day of value, preferably during the day and at the minimum at the end of the day.

V. A system in which multilateral netting takes place should, at a minimum, be capable on ensuring the timely completion of daily settlements in the inability to settle by the participant with the largest single settlement obligation.

VI. Assets used for settlement should preferably be a claim on the central bank; where other assets are used, they should carry little or no credit risk and little or no liquidity risk.

VII. The system should ensure a high degree of security and operational reliability and should have contingency arrangements for timely completion of daily processing.

VIII. The system should provide a means of making payments which is practical for its users and efficient for the economy.

IX. The system should have objective and publicly disclosed criteria for participation, which permit fair and open access.

X. The system's governance arrangements should be effective, accountable, and transparent.

11.128. In mid-1993, all Euroarea NCBs assessed systems in their country, including all RTGS systems linked to TARGET. The ECB assessed TARGET as a whole. Work was coordinated by the Payment and Settlement Systems Committee to ensure consistency of results. [383]

11.129. The review found that a high degree of compliance with the principles, but only one system within TARGET was fully compliant. Where not fully compliant, most systems were partly compliant. Deficiencies in compliance were to be addressed during the transition to TARGET II.

11.130. Less than full compliance was most often for Principle VIII – practicality for users and efficiency for the economy. This principle examines the objectives of the system, the capacity of the system to handle demand, pricing policy, and cost efficiency. Most of the systems were only broadly compliant because of some issues regarding their cost recovery methodology, and the ECB itself was only partly compliant because of its large overcapacity which could generate higher costs than necessary. However, this degree of less than full compliance regarding cost compliance was somewhat misleading. The IMF review had found that the same systems were compliant, but additional work on cost recovery in preparation for the TARGET2 system had shown some inconsistencies. Thus, the deficiencies noted were more nominal than effective.

11.131. Principle VII – security and operational reliability – was less than fully compliant for half the countries, mostly because backup facilities were physically too close to the main facility.

11.132. It is strongly recommended that future currency unions' clearing systems be brought into compliance with the Core Principles. Also, regular compilation of statistics on payments system for the union and their publication in the BIS *Redbook*384 is also recommended. The successful operation of monetary policy requires that monetary policy impulses be transmitted quickly and evenly throughout the union, which is effected through the payments system. Moreover, confidence in the currency rests upon a

[383] Many of the systems had also been evaluated under the IMF's Financial Sector Assessment Program, which conducts comprehensive reviews and evaluations of the strengths and vulnerabilities of major financial institutions and markets of countries.

[384] The BIS's CPSS publishes an annual compilation *Statistics on payment and settlement systems in selected countries* with data on payments and payments systems, called the Red Book. Future unions should begin compilation of the data series in the Red Book during the earliest stages of planning for the union.

sense that payments in the union currency are transacted efficiently, reliably, and securely. Such important goals of an union can only be achieved if the payments system operates in accord with the highest international standards. Moreover, less than full compliance should be corrected as soon as possible. In Europe, the lapses were not significant and could wait for correction, but this should not be considered the norm.

11.133. For other regional integrations schemes, bringing all systemically important payment systems, especially cross-border systems, up to the Core Principles standards can make an important contribution to making the regional financial system more efficient and building confidence in it. This can be supported by requesting an IMF review of compliance with the core principles early in the union planning process to provide an agenda of tasks to address prior to launching the union.

11.134. This recommendation needs to be applied in two ways. The payments systems itself should be brought up to international standards, and participants in the system should understand that they are expected to operate in accordance with the standards. Second, harmonization of national legal codes and market practices is needed to overcome existing barriers. This harmonization requires creating a set of standards in line with international best practices, promoting national enabling legislation, and carrying out a review of legal convergence to ensure sufficient harmonization of national practice.

Giovannini Committee

11.135. In 2001, an EU committee examined barriers to cross-border clearing and settlement systems. (Giovannini, 2001) The Committee identified fifteen key barriers to cross-border clearing and settlement systems, divided into three categories – technical requirements, tax differences, and legal uncertainty.

Technical Requirements

Operating hours, and settlement deadlines
IT platforms and interfaces
Intraday settlement finality
Settlement periods
Restrictions on locations of payments and settlements
Remote access
Rules on corporate actions (votes, dividends, etc.)
Restrictions on primary dealers and market makers

Tax barriers

Withholding taxes
Efficiency of tax collections

Legal Barriers

Lack of an EU-wide framework
Legal treatment of bilateral netting and need for multilateral netting
Conflicts of laws

11.136. The legal barriers were considered especially intractable because they reflect “basic and intimate parts of the legal systems of Member countries, and to change them has many ramifications.” (p.54)

11.137. One issue left unsettled was locus of rights when intermediaries hold securities for investors in a book entry form – does the depositor of a security retain full rights to the specific security, or is it similar to a bank cash deposit in which depositors have only a general claim along with other creditors. The Group recommended a “Legal Certainty Project” designed to introduce provisions into the national statutes to provide a sound legal infrastructure for clearing and settlement of securities held in a book entry form.

11.138. The Group set responsibility for addressing each barrier and proposed a specific schedule for removing all fifteen barriers as well as the public and private parties responsible for the actions. Scheduling was done in recognition of the differing importance of the barriers and interactions between some of the barriers. The intent was to schedule removal of barriers over two- to three-year periods in ways that minimize market disruptions.

11.139. Coordinators were designated if the actions required cooperation by several parties. In some cases, introducing modern market practices required substantial changes to national laws to reflect the nature of the underlying transactions.

11.140. Future unions will face the same sorts of ambiguities as they try to better integrate national financial markets into a cohesive whole. An approach similar to the Giovannini Group's seems appropriate – first carefully document the barriers to integration, then create mandates for countries to correct them, then verify status of work. Regular oversight of the process will be needed if it is to move forward. This process can proceed independently of any momentum toward monetary union, but it ultimately supports the union effort whenever it proceeds.

Timeline

Preparatory period	
Early actions (four years prior)	Set up Payments and Settlement Committee Compile information on all payments and settlement systems within region, including treatment of e-money Compile information on national laws and regulations on payment systems Compile information on volume of settlements, costs, institutional arrangements, *per* BIS Redbook Initial IMF Review on Observation of Standards and Codes (ROSC); Set priorities for work
Three years prior	Consultations on user needs, including special needs Draft legal framework Draft technical standards for machines, ATMs, and vending
24 months prior	Initiate purchase orders of hardware and software systems Implementation of legal changes Review of system pricing and competitiveness
18 Months Prior	Purchase hardware and software systems. Preliminary tests on individual systems. Decisions on system pricing Reiteration of ROSC; initiate remedial actions
Final 12 months	All legal changes made
Final 6 months	Full-scale test of monetary policy systems Full test of all market systems
Run-up to union	
Union day	Start up Monitor experiences
Early union period	Evaluate performance of systems
Union steady state	

Appendix: The private ECU Clearing and Settlement System[385]

The pre-Euroarea ECU Clearing and Settlement System was a private multilateral net settlement system that cleared and handled payments denominated in private ECUs. Because some unions are considering using parallel virtual currencies similar to the ECU as a step toward setting up their unions, the experience with the ECU settlement system could be instructive.

When the ECU was first created, a small group of commercial banks set up a clearing system for private ECU transactions called MESA (Mutual ECU Settlement Accounts). It was quickly realized that the arrangement was inadequate given an increase in private ECU transactions and number of banks handling transactions. In 1983, banks approached the BIS and The Committee of Governors of the EC Central Banks (COG). (The BIS acted as a clearing center for payments systems, and the COG was responsible for administration of the ECU system.) In March 1983, the COG issued guidelines that stated that the private ECU system must remain exclusively within the BIS framework for commercial banks and that actions of the system must not conflict with national monetary policy objectives.

The system was managed by the ECU Banking Association located in Paris, which was created under French law in 1985. Commercial banks with headquarters or branches in EU countries with significant involvement in ECU transactions and interested in the development of the system could be members. Several banks were selected to become clearing banks for the system. SWIFT handled communications and netting of transactions for calculating net positions.

The BIS as agent for the clearing banks handled settlements for the system. Each clearing bank maintained an ECU sight account and a clearing account with the BIS.

> The ECU sight account was used only for the settlement of operations and did not bear interest nor permit negative balances, and therefore the BIS did not assume any credit risk in the ECU system. The sight accounts could be credited either by sale or purchase of ECUs from other banks, or by transferring all ECU component currencies to special accounts (arranged by the BIS) at central banks whose currencies are components of the ECU – in this arrangement, the BIS itself did not incur a direct liability for ECU positions created.
>
> The clearing account is used for clearing and debited or credited with each day's final netting balances – it thus represents the position of each bank against all other banks in the system.

The netting was handled in several phases each day;

> Until a fixed time each afternoon, the netting process occurred with clearing banks by exchanging ECU payment orders through the netting center operated by SWIFT. All payment messages are intercepted and copied to a netting computer.
>
> Immediately after the daily cutoff time, the netting center calculates preliminary balances, informs clearing banks, and reports the information to the BIS.
>
> During the next phase which lasted about an hour, clearing banks borrow and lend with each other. Per a rule the sum of preliminary debits must equal preliminary credits and creditor banks must lend funds to debtor banks so that debit balances do not exceed 1 million ECU. Alternatively, banks transfer to the BIS all ECU component currencies required to cover the ECU debit. This is a form of presettlement of balances.
>
> Final netting balances are calculated, each bank is notified of its position, and information is reported to the BIS. The BIS verifies that settlements can be made without incurring debit positions in any of the sight accounts. The BIS

[385] See Lichter 1988.

executes the settlement by crediting or debiting each banks clearing account with final netting balances, and as appropriate debiting or crediting each bank's ECU sight account.

Next, if any clearing bank is left with a debtor position of 1 million ECU or more it must request assistance from the BIS to help arrange borrowing to settle the final balance. Any funds transferred at this stage are considered overnight loans bearing interest equal to the next day ECU interest rate calculated by the BIS from information reported by the clearing banks. Based on these loans, the BIS will settle the books. Based on this calculation, each clearing bank undertakes to transfer funds by value date +2 to other clearing banks.

Ultimately, if outstanding debits cannot be covered, an "unwind" procedure occurs. The entire clearing for the day is carried over to the next day and all payments to and from the debtor bank are withdrawn from the day's clearing transactions and new balances calculated for settlement the next day. This next day procedure creates a systemic risk in that beneficiaries of payments will not receive usable funds until the completion of clearing on the next day, but this possible risk never occurred.

If future currency unions seek to create a new currency through a staged, parallel currency approach following the example of the ECU, a payments and settlement arrangement will be needed, which might follow some of the steps used in the ECU Clearing and Settlement System. A key element of the system was the involvement of the BIS as the effective settlement agent, but without creating an official ECU liability for the BIS because the liability was passed back to the central banks of the component currencies of the ECU. This arrangement is not necessary for future unions (that might wish to have an institution with direct liabilities for the new currencies), but might be considered.

A second important aspect of the ECU arrangement was the preagreement that the system would not compromise national monetary policies. Similar concerns would be important in future union situations, but there might be more concern now for regional monetary policy implications than during the ECU period. The information gathered by a regional payments system for a parallel currency would provide valuable information on usage patterns of the new currency and its possible monetary policy implications.

CHAPTER 12 – STATISTICS

Statistics – How will monetary, external, and macroeconomic statistics be collected in a harmonized manner to provide information for policy analysis and to assess policy effectiveness?

A. Development of statistics in the EMU

12.1. Statistics are at the heart of any currency union. A good and timely set of statistics is needed in order to understand the economic and financial conditions in the union, to make policy and monitor its results, and to coordinate a complex range of tasks. Given the diverse conditions in member countries, the task of statistical systems is to create a harmonized overview of conditions in each country in order to provide policy makers a current overview of the union as a whole so that they can make and implement correct policies for the union and monitor policy effectiveness. Above all, statistics must be timely so that decisions and the monitoring effects of policy actions are based on current conditions.[386]

12.2. The Europeans had a comprehensive approach going back to the early 1980s. (Bull 2004) Recognizing that development of statistical systems can be long and complex, work began very early in the planning process. It involved not only a range of committees and numerous consultations with statistics users and national statistical officials, but also interaction between the EMI (the predecessor to the ECB)[387] and Eurostat, the EU agency covering the broad range of macroeconomic statistics. This early committee work resulted in broad agreement on many – but not all – aspects of the union. During the early statistical work, many policy and institutional aspects of the shape of the union were unknown, and thus the early work examined options that might or might not be used and required flexibility to deal with later policy or institutional changes. However, a key aspect affecting the early work was an expectation that statistics needed for policy at the union level would parallel those already used by the national policy officials.

12.3. In 1991, the Committee on Monetary, Financial, and Balance of Payments Statistics (CMFB) was created by the European Council to help set the direction of statistical programs, especially regarding the allocation of responsibilities between central banks and national statistical offices. Its oversight responsibilities continued throughout the period when statistics were under development.

12.4. In 1992, the EEC Committee of Governors established the Working Group on Statistics (WGS), composed of the heads of statistics functions of the central banks. This working group was supported by a small group of statisticians—most seconded from central banks and based at the BIS in Basel, Switzerland. The WGS began putting into effect the statistical programs, based on the options for the strategy of the future single monetary policy of the union. The strategy was defined by the policy arm of the EMI and would ultimately be decided by the ECB when set up.

12.5. Eurostat, the EU-wide official statistics office in Luxembourg, produces a wide range of statistics that support the currency union.[388] Prior to the WGS, Eurostat collected data from national authorities and produced monetary and interest rate statistics, balance of payments statistics, and financial account statistics. Because these tasks were closely related to the future work of the ECB, they were ultimately transferred there. Discussions were held on the boundary of responsibilities between the agencies and

[386] The authoritative study of statistics for the EMU is *The Development of Statistics for Economic and Monetary Union*, 2004, by Peter Bull, former Director of the ECB Statistics Directorate. This chapter draws heavily from that source, but selectively pulls away from the European experience to highlight principles that might have more general applicability. Future monetary unions could have very different structures and policy frameworks than existed in Europe.

[387] The EMI/ECB itself was not permitted to compile statistics until just before the inauguration of the monetary union.

[388] Eurostat handled GDP, price indices, and fiscal statistics needed to compile the "convergence criteria" for each country. The convergence criteria determined which EU countries were eligible to join the currency union. Eurostat also compiled a very broad range of macroeconomic statistics used in support of the EMU. It also has joint responsibility with the ECB for producing balance of payments statistics for the Euroarea.

modalities for ongoing cooperation in producing statistics were discussed.

12.6. The EMI Statistics Division became the ECB Statistics Directorate, and the WGS later became the ECB Statistics Committee (STC) in which senior statistical officials from each country oversaw the direction of overall statistical policy. The STC usually met once a quarter. It continues to operate.

12.7. For each of four topical areas of statistics, the WGS/STC established a working group of technical officials—in monetary, balance of payments, general statistics, and information technology. Each group developed statistical practices and rules that were subject to STC review and approval. Each group had a secretary at the EMI, who frequently communicated with each country. Meetings were held as often as six to eight times a year, the working groups would also call *ad hoc* meetings when needed.

12.8. In addition, *ad hoc* task forces were created as needed to address specific issues. Membership was voluntary and usually included about four to six people with key expertise from statistical departments in the member states. The task forces were asked to investigate issues and arrive at solutions quickly.

12.9. The EMI/ECB and national statistical authorities followed a decentralized approach, applying the core EMU doctrine of *"subsidiarity."* In this doctrine, activities are handled by national authorities operating independently to the extent possible. Reliance on NCBs to collect the basic information was believed to speed data collection, reduce reporting burdens, and make use of existing infrastructures and large corps of trained staff. A corollary was fashioning of a *"layered approach"* to statistics. In this approach, the national central banks collect a common set of statistics in their countries based on the statistical practices appropriate for that economy. They then transmit the data up a layer to the ECB for aggregation and consolidation into union-wide statistics.[389]

12.10. The layered approach to compile statistics required convergence to common statistical standards, producing data that could be transmitted rapidly in a common format to the central statistical office. Much of the EMU systems was explicitly fashioned on the standards of the European System of Accounts, which is based on the statistical System of National Accounts (SNA). The linkage of the EMU standards to the national accounts allowed for construction of many currency union statistics from preexisting systems. It also facilitated the comparison of the union-related data with the set of macroeconomic statistics maintained by each country, which helps evaluate the performance of the monetary policies.[390]

12.11. In recognition of the critical importance of statistical harmonization across the countries in currency unions and the need to link to the SNA, the Statistics Department of the IMF initiated training in statistical harmonization of monetary statistics in preparation for currency unions and regional arrangements in African and Central America. [391]

B. Principles for statistics for a currency union

12.12. This section reviews key principles that authorities can consider in developing statistical programs for a currency union. The principles are not intended to lay out a specific path for union statistical programs. Those paths will be affected by where each country starts and where the union wants to end up.

[389] Centralizing statistics compilation applies both to monetary statistics, which are typically compiled by central banks, and to general macroeconomic statistics, which are used for analyzing general economic conditions of the union. The latter statistics might be collected by institutions outside the central bank, such as Eurostat.

[390] In contrast, the statistical foundations of the African and Caribbean currency unions are based on application of common financial accounting standards for banks operating throughout their unions, which facilitates aggregation of the data.

[391] This harmonization also supported greater harmonization in statistics to facilitate processing by the IMF and better policy analysis by producing statistics with greater cross-country comparability.

Unknowns will be faced, and decisions will be made along the way that will affect the overall result.

12.13. In particular, there is the possibility that some unions might adopt a relatively loose, more consensual approach to creating the union, which would contrast sharply with the EMU model. In creating the union, the principles mentioned below can be considered, but they should be accepted or rejected as appropriate to each union's particular situation and goals. The EMU arrangements differ from the other existing currency unions in Africa and the Caribbean, and new unions will certainly have unique features that will affect their statistical requirements.

Key Principles[392]

12.14. *The key idea – the operation of a currency union requires that a single common monetary policy exists and that the policy officials have reliable, current information about the common policy and the policy instruments used to operate the union.* The choice of policy is largely a political decision, but whatever the chosen policy, it cannot succeed without information about the condition of the union and the policy instruments available. Statistics provide the information needed to permit the successful operation of the union. Statistics are also the public face of the union, providing the information that the union members and the world at large need to judge the success of the union.

12.15. Statistically, once the currency union is in place, a new entity exists: *the union as a whole*. This means that alongside reliable and comparable statistics of the member countries, statistics for the union as a whole are needed.[393] Compilers will produce the union data mostly via aggregation and, when needed, consolidation of the national data. This implies that the national data should be designed or fine-tuned to allow such operations. Statistics should also be available in a timely manner, implying a further effort at coordination between the national compilers. In addition, a need for longer historical series will emerge with respect to the union, back to periods before the union existed – the available national statistics will be the only source to build historical series for the union.

12.16. *The statistics of the member countries must be added (aggregated) and consolidated to provide a unified picture of economic activity and the operations of the common monetary policy.* Although a currency union is comprised of many countries, its policy is carried out union-wide. Thus, it is necessary that statisticians construct some statistics as if the union were a single country. This principle has many implications for the statistics programs of the union and its member countries. An important corollary is to introduce a new statistical requirement to distinguish between positions with other member countries of the union and countries outside the union.[394]

12.17. *A common set of statistical standards is needed* to be able to aggregate and consolidate data, which must be applied by all member countries.

12.18. *It must be decided whether statistical programs will be centralized or decentralized.* The centralized approach is followed by the currency unions in Africa and the Caribbean—the union central banks operate throughout the region, and the national agencies are branch offices of the central bank. In this situation, one organization handles the official

[392] Much of the material in this section is drawn from Krueger and Kovarich (2006).

[393] Parallel construction of good statistical systems for the union and in each of the union members is critical. Good-quality statistical systems need to exist within each member country to meet a continuing demand for national statistics and to contribute to the union statistical program. Union-level oversight of national statistical systems might be needed to ensure that the overall quality is not imperiled by poor-quality data from some union members.

[394] In Europe, this meant that banks needed to compile separate data on their asset and liability positions vis-à-vis residents of other monetary union member states (MUMS) and all other nonresidents (non-MUMS). This was a challenging task.

compilation of statistics. In contrast, Europe had a decentralized approach.

12.19. *Laws or other regulations might need to specify matters central to the production of the core statistics of the union* to ensure that application is fully consistent across the union. Further, some regulatory activities might be directly tied to statistics, which means that statistical standards begin to carry the force of law.[395] Linked to that, an effective system of sanctions (fines) can help dissuade reporting agents from not complying with the reporting requirements. Thus, future unions might follow the European example and decide to introduce compulsory reserve, capital, or liquidity requirements, and could decide to use statistical measures to generate the information to operate the system. This decision could imply significant savings of reporting burden and gains in data quality.

12.20. *National statistical activities are likely to be constrained by the application of the common methodology, institutional structures of the union, or legal requirements.* A need will continue for good-quality national level statistics, but the nature of the statistics might change because of the membership of the country in the union. For example, the meaning of monetary aggregates or reserve assets at the country level will change. In addition, many methodological changes will be introduced to monetary, balance of payments, and other statistics, to be able to produce harmonized union-level statistics.

12.21. *Structures and procedures must be set up to establish rules and coordinate the actions of the union and national statistical compilers.* Regardless of the specific form the arrangements take, it is important that the rights and obligations of each party involved be clearly specified and that the components function smoothly as individual entities and as part of the larger framework.

12.22. *The use of "convergence criteria" for membership requires early comparisons of GDP, fiscal, inflation, and interest rate data.* Convergence criteria are indicators of overall economic performance used to establish whether a country can enter the union (and are also often used to evaluate general economic conditions once the union is formed), which requires that the requisite nonfinancial and financial statistics be high-quality and apply a well-defined common methodology prior to the union's start-up. In this way, countries can make valid comparisons that do not prejudice the entry prospects of any country.

12.23. *The needs of users should be surveyed and the feasibility of meeting those needs must be conveyed back to users.* This helps efficiently develop the needed statistics within given resource constraints and also helps users understand the prioritization that must be undertaken. This was an important part of the process in Europe, and provided some specific guidance to the statisticians as early as 1992 on the directions for the development of statistical programs.

12.24. *Review of the existing situations and practical implementation experiences* helps ensure the consistency of the results. The EMI sent many surveys to the member countries to ask about the existing conditions, feasibility of proposals, and experiences in applying statistical standards. Working groups reviewed the surveys and discussed the results. Based on this process, the authorities frequently revised the rules and procedures. Monitoring of implementation became a continuous activity, and several formal implementation reports were prepared that set out the status of work and the gaps that needed priority attention.

12.25. *Flexibility and a focus on the essentials are needed because some key decisions will not be made until late in the process.* Statistical programs might need to be developed before the final shape of the union is known. For example, when statistical work began in Europe the eventual membership of the union, the policy instruments, and bank reserves policies

[395] In the EMU, this situation occurred because of a decision to (1) apply required reserves to the same institutions that comprise the statistical money-creating sector, and (2) calculate banks' required reserves based on statistical information on resident's deposits.

were unknown. Flexibility was important, and statistical options were prepared that might not be used. Also, some political decisions might come quite late in the process, requiring very quick statistical adjustments.[396]

12.26. *Flexibility is also needed to deal with statistical practicality.* Some information is unavailable on a timely basis or not available at all due to resource constraints. In Europe, one technique to deal with this was to distinguish between statistics compiled under a "short-term approach" versus "steady-state statistics." The short-term approach mostly used existing nonharmonized data to give a rough idea of conditions needed to carry out policy. Over time, a steady-state approach was introduced to produce harmonized statistics based on careful research on what should be done. Under the steady-state approach, countries are required to introduce changes to their statistical systems, if needed.[397] Another aspect regarding flexibility is that as work proceeds statistical issues or problems will be uncovered that need to be addressed.

12.27. *Statistics will require more resources and should have a high priority.* There is a clear danger that the resources allocated to union statistics will not be sufficient to address the demands for more output, better quality, and more timely statistics. Although some reprioritization might take place between the production of statistics for the home economy and for union purposes, authorities cannot assume that the resources needed for national statistics will diminish and become available for production of union statistics.

> Sturm and Siegfried (2005 p.55) suggested that significant staffing is needed at the supranational level to move the process forward and that "simply entrusting staff working for national authorities with the tasks and trying to foster cooperation in committees and working groups might not be sufficient to ensure that the necessary supranational perspective is given due consideration".

12.28. *Data must be collected and transmitted to a central statistical operation and statistics prepared quickly in order to be useful for policy.* Data providers must collect the information quickly and accurately, and statistical compilers must complete their work in a timely fashion. Timeliness plays an important role because a complete statistical picture of the union is unavailable until the last reporting agent has fulfilled its requirements. This fact puts pressure on data providers and statistical offices, who must operate on fixed schedules. Procedures must be in place to deal with gaps created by unavailable or late data.

12.29. *An early view on the money issuing sector is needed by defining the universe of monetary institutions early in the process* so that statisticians can begin to work with them. Statisticians should work early with banks and other money issuers to make them aware of statistical needs when they are adopting accounting systems or creating databases. This undertaking can greatly facilitate the ultimate process of collecting data needed for compiling statistics.

12.30. *Statistics must be communicated between central banks, national statistics offices, and the central statistical operation based on a common messaging format or data exchange protocol.* The EMU addressed this need by creating a new, highly flexible electronic data exchange system, known as GESMES/CB, which NCBs were required to use to communicate with the ECB. For this purpose, technicians also developed a standard data-coding system, used throughout Europe.

12.31. *Analysts and the public will expect historical time series for newly developed series.* This

[396] For example, the decision on allocation of seigniorage in the EMU came after the inauguration of the union, which required changes in the accounting for issuance of currency by the NCBs.

[397] Some observers felt that a general shortage of resources in the national statistical offices led to a higher priority being placed on monetary statistics, to the detriment of work to improve other statistics. Observers felt these statistics lagged the monetary statistics and initially were not up what they should have been.

enhances the usefulness of newly developed data. However, the historical time series can be quite difficult to compile, and innovative methods will often be needed.

12.32. *Dry runs should be undertaken prior to the start of the union* in which all relevant data should be supplied and attempts made to compile the consolidated union statistics. These dry runs will test procedures and provide policy officials with a first look at the union-wide data.

12.33. *The messages coming from the union and national sources must be coordinated.* Unions will need to develop procedures to determine who can release information and when. The statistics coming from national authorities might need to be compiled in special ways to ensure consistency with the information from the union.

12.34. *Provision of data to the IMF for surveillance, publication, and other purposes will change.* For the EMU data, a "gateway" approach was developed under which the ECB voluntarily sends the IMF monetary data for all the EMU countries. This procedure guarantees that the data are timely and that the data used at the IMF are fully consistent with the data used for policy in the EMU. It also reduces reporting burdens for national authorities. Following the creation of the union, an Euroarea page was introduced in the IMF's *International Financial Statistics* covering monetary, reserves, and other statistics for the union as a whole. It was later followed by pages for the Central and West African monetary unions and ECCU.

12.35. *Expansion of the union is a possibility.* Whatever holds the countries together hopefully is a glue that can be used flexibly in the future if other countries seek to join, and not a shell that excludes others. Each expansion of the union creates new challenges for statisticians who must help new members' statistical programs catch up with existing members. The statisticians also should be able to construct historical time series based on the expanded union membership. In Europe, the definition of the Euroarea had to be regularly expanded because of the accession of new members. This expansion occurred for Greece, which joined the EMU two years after the start of the union, and for each of the subsequent entrants.

12.36. Preexisting statistical practices are probably not optimal. Before joining their unions, the statistical systems of countries have developed around specific national standards, practices, institutions, personalities, and historical accidents. They are unlikely to be well set up for extensive international cooperation and adherence to a common program – many changes will be required, which will require time, effort, and expense. New staff will probably need to be recruited. Complacency about this should not be permitted – prior to the start-up of the EMU, the IMF Statistics Department visited the monetary statistics programs of all the new countries and found unexpected problems in many of the countries visited.[398]

12.37. Many of the above points about the role of statistics were summarized in the study by Sturm and Siegfried in their review of the prospective program for the GCC Currency Union (2005; p.53), but the points are relevant to other planned unions:

> "An absolutely crucial issue for GCC convergence criteria is the quality of the statistical data on which the monitoring and assessment of the criteria are based. First, data for all indicators used must be available in a timely manner. Second, data need to be sufficiently reliable. Third, data must be comparable between member states, as otherwise no meaningful conclusions can be drawn...and comparisons might even be misleading. The European experience shows that even in countries with a generally sound data basis, a major effort is needed to meet the statistical

[398] Reviews of the statistical systems of all potential union countries by the IMF or other outside experts could result in important improvements the overall quality and usefulness of the ultimate union statistics. However, this is expensive and might be impractical on that basis – alternatively, extensive reporting by national programs on the extent of the preparations might be used.

requirements for monetary union, in particular regarding data comparability".

12.38. The crucial message of the principles above is that ***statistical preparations for a currency union must start early.*** Statistical preparations for the EMU at Eurostat and the EMI began six to seven years before the start of the union. It took that long to establish standards, set up the central operations, and introduce new standards and program changes at the national level. Even so, just prior to the launch of the EMU, statistical operations were very hectic, and some things could not get done. The unambiguous message is that the statistics work must start early, long before the public notices, and long before some key decisions are made that will affect the ultimate shape of the union. And as reinforced by Sturm and Siegfried, "steps toward the harmonization of concepts and the preparation of appropriate aggregation and consolidation methods have to be taken in good time prior to the start of Monetary Union. Their implementation in all prospective participating countries has to start sufficiently far in advance, as it generally involves a significant lead time" (p. 68).

Statistics needed for a currency union

12.39. Statisticians might distinguish among several types of statistics relevant for unions: convergence criteria that serve as tests before countries can join or to monitor countries' continuing macroeconomic performance; the core set of statistics to operate the union; statistics on external aspects of a currency union; a broad set of macroeconomic and market statistics to evaluate general conditions and monetary policy and assess its effectiveness; the new topic of statistics on financial inclusion, statistics disseminated to inform the public and serve as the public face of the union; operational statistics, and specialized statistics related to the economic and institutional conditions within the union.

<u>Total union macroeconomic statistics</u>

12.40. Macroeconomic statistics for the entire union need cover activity of all member countries *and* union entities. For example, Euroarea monetary statistics are compiled based on the monetary positions of all NCBs in the union, plus the positions of the ECB. Union-level totals are compiled by aggregating all union and country data or consolidating out intragroup positions and transactions from the aggregate data. The concept is straight-forward for monetary statistics, but also applies for other major types of statistics – balance of payments, international investment position, government finance, GDP, international reserves, etc..

12.41. When union-level institutions have significant transactions, they must be included in the total union statistics. This is obvious for the ECB, which itself issues currency, holds substantial assets, lends to banks, etc. and thus statistics must be compiled for the ECB itself harmonized with the member country statistics and suitable for aggregation or consolidation to produce union totals. When significantly large, data must also be compiled for other union-level institutions and integrated into the total union statistics. Because the union itself will be new, it is likely that new reporting arrangements will be needed. This can include;

Fiscal accounts of the union government – Union government institutions (for example, the European Commission, Eurostat, European Court of Justice, etc.) themselves might tax, earn income from services, hold assets, purchase goods and services, make transfers, etc..

Nonbudgetary union accounts – Union institutions might channel international assistance flows, operate utilities or other services, operate employees' pension schemes, etc. These need to be picked up (but with caution that some such flows such as utilities could be, or should be, reflected in local data.)

Union-level development banks and specialized banks – Europe has numerous EU-sponsored financial institutions that can borrow in markets or from governments and lend for infrastructure, development, social cohesion purposes, etc.

Government or central banking SPVs – Governments or the central bank might transfer assets and liabilities off their balance sheet and place them in special purpose vehicles (such as for the European Financial Stability Facility) that might not be captured in regular statistical reporting. Large positions and flows might be involved that need to be captured to construct a full picture of the union's economic and financial situation.[399]

Monetary and financial statistics

12.42. Monetary and Financial Statistics constitutes the core of union statistics. The specific statistics could vary depending on the specific policy framework adopted in each Union. For example, if the preservation of domestic price stability is selected as a prime goal of the union, as in the EMU, then price indices are required. In other unions, this indicator might only be useful supplementary information, not a key element of policy.[400] Also, the widely followed inflation targeting framework takes a comprehensive, full information view of economic conditions that requires collecting a broad range of data to inform the policy discussion in numerous individual areas.[401] And recently, the view that effective application of monetary policy requires complementary actions to bolster the soundness of the financial system implies that a broad range of macroprudential indicators also need to be compiled.

12.43. Monetary statistics are derived from the banking systems, which usually offer timely and accurate data. Challenging tasks include harmonization of the data collected by the national banking systems, defining the coverage of financial institutions, collecting the level of detailed information needed, and implementing uniform timeliness for all reporting agents. Banks' income statements and balance sheets include most of the information needed to assess the evolution of liquid, and less liquid, assets within the union. If national data are comparable and provide the needed breakdowns by instrument and counterparty, compilers can aggregate and consolidate data at the union level to generate measures of money and credit.[402]

---

[399] In some future unions, SWFs might fall into this category. SWFs did not exist in the Euroarea; Norway, which is in the European Economic Area, has a large SWF.

[400] Other information that might be required to operate an union could include fiscal statistics or information on capital adequacy of banks.

[401] Examples of demands for comprehensive data collection and analysis for policy purposes can be found in numerous articles in the *ECB Monthly Bulletin* during the first few years of the Euroarea. For example, "The Two Pillars of the ECB's Monetary Policy Strategy" (November 2000) describes the second pillar as analysis of a wide range of economic and financial indicators to broadly assess risks to price stability and to help provide a medium-term forward-looking perspective to deal with the time-lags in transmission of monetary policy.

Other studies described the ECB policy perspectives—monetary aggregates and price stability, short-term economic indicators for assessment of price developments, the institutional framework of the ESCB, external accounts of the Euroarea, Euroarea international reserves, monetary presentation of the Euroarea balance of payments, international use of the euro, GDP growth and output gap, monetary policy under uncertainty about the state of the economy and structural changes due to creation of the union, and the information content of interest rates for monetary policy, among others. These analyses required extensive data and supporting information to bolster the quality of the research and policy discussion.

Also, the collection and dissemination of a range of data used for policy analysis helped ensure transparency over policy decisions and build public confidence in the soundness of the policy process.

[402] In many countries, this data collection applies only to the banking sector. If nonbank financial institutions provide substantial credit, the picture presented from compilation of data from banks only can be misleading. (However, the Euroarea broad definition of 'credit institution' encompassed entities that might be classified as nonbank institutions in other countries.) Also, even if credit from nonbank institutions is not large in the total picture, the distribution of credit could be important – for example, credit flows to rural areas. A broad flow of

(continued)

12.44. Once established with a homogeneous reporting population, a common methodological framework, harmonized reporting requirements, and agreed reporting timeliness, the union has a sound base of monetary statistics, allowing economic and monetary analysis for the purposes of the single monetary policy. The final step would be to introduce the consolidation procedures to allow the production of union statistics and the calculation of union monetary aggregates.

12.45. In this respect, another challenging methodological aspect is to derive flows from changes in the reported stocks. Reported balance sheet data are end-period stocks. For many purposes of economic analysis, statisticians need to derive flow data by netting out all nontransactions changes in volume (revaluations, devaluations, loan write-offs, catastrophic loss, etc.).

12.46. Among the most relevant outputs of the monetary statistics datasets are:

Balance sheet for the central bank, compiled according to statistical standards. The balance sheet is a component of the monetary and credit aggregates of the union and is needed to track policy actions. (It differs from the financial accounting statement for the central bank.)

Consolidated balance sheet for commercial banks. This is a component of the monetary and credit aggregates of the union, and tracks the interactions of the banking system with the public and the external sector.

Consolidated balance sheet for the central bank and commercial banks. This is used to calculate the monetary and credit aggregates of the union and provide a picture of overall monetary activity.[403]

Clearing system statistics. A currency union will have a unified method to clear interbank transactions and cross-border transactions in policy securities. The ECB, for example, collects statistics on the TARGET clearing system.

Policy interest rates

Transactions in securities and deposits used for policy.

Required bank reserves.

Currency issuance and retirement, and movements between union members of currency and negotiable instruments included in the money stock. In Europe, currency issuance and retirement statistics are also used for the important purposes of allocating seigniorage income and allocating the expenses of retiring used currency.

International exposures of the banking system.

Statistics on the external aspects of a currency union

12.47. A currency union creates a single currency, for which international reserves and exchange rate policies must be developed. Thus, the union needs statistics on the following:

The exchange rate (market rates, nominal and real rates, and effective rates against broad groups of currencies).

The international reserves of the union.[404]

funds framework covers situations where broad sectoral information is needed.

[403] If nonbank financial institutions also issue monetary liabilities, they need to be captured in the money and credit statistical scheme.

[404] The international reserves of members of a currency union differ from reserves of individual countries, because claims formerly in currencies of other union members will no longer be part of union reserve assets and because the union might exercise some control over the assets held in individual countries. The IMF's *Data Template on International Reserves and Foreign* (continued)

Balance of payments

International investment position.[405]

Use of the union currency outside the union.

12.48. As described in Chapter 6, the IMF monitors the balance of payments situations of individual members of currency unions as part of its regular Article IV surveillance. This was confirmed in a 2007 decision by the IMF Executive Board on bilateral surveillance (IMF 2007b). Thus, there is a continuing requirement that individual union countries continue compiling balance of payments statistics. The decision also required that real exchange rates of union members be monitored in order to assess the international competitiveness of the economy and competitiveness of each economy against other union members. Thus, union member countries must also compile price indices in order to estimate the real exchange rates.

Statistics on the macroeconomy and the effectiveness of policy

12.49. Analysts need a wide range of macroeconomic and financial market statistics to carry out policy analysis or to evaluate the effectiveness of monetary policy. Statistics must be compiled quarterly and on a timely basis in order to provide information useful for policy development.

12.50. Once the EMU was established, interest steadily increased for a very wide range of macroeconomic statistics to support the ECB's policy analysis, resulting in many new demands on member country authorities for statistics. These included;

Financial accounts – In Europe, a major program was established to compile the Monetary Union Financial Accounts (often referred to as MUFA, or 'flow of funds accounts'), covering the financial assets and liabilities of the major sectors of the economy.[406] (ECB 2009c)

Asset prices – Real estate[407], equities, and debt securities.

Financial market statistics – The ECB has a comprehensive database of securities markets and interest rates.

GDP and its components.

Fiscal accounts – Government debt and deficit are monitored annually as a condition for membership in the Euroarea.

Statistics for dissemination to the public

12.51. The public and financial market participants will demand a wide range of statistics on the union and its member countries. Rapid and reliable data dissemination via the Internet will be expected. Statisticians need to make special efforts to ensure that statistics released by the union and by its members convey the same message and that the sequencing of release times for statistics does not confuse or mislead statistics users or provide unfair advantages

Currency Liquidity is an internationally accepted framework that probably should be used.

[405] The transactions and positions between union members must be netted out in the consolidation process, which requires that statisticians apply a common classification system to the external statistics of each country and reconcile bilateral discrepancies in the external accounts.

[406] The financial accounts show flows of financial resources into and out of the financial sector and other macroeconomic sectors; in a "from who to whom with what instrument" table. Chapter 5 on monetary policy describes their role in the Eurosystem's analysis of the trends in and development of the financial sector.

[407] Information on real estate prices and the exposures of the financial system to real estate is critically important in understanding trends in the cost of living, asset price movements, and financial system exposures. Often real estate price booms are associated with capital flows from abroad, which can abruptly reverse creating both balance of payments and real estate crises, and broad financial disruption.

to certain segments of the market. Statisticians can expect strong pressure from analysts and the public to produce historical time series.

Macroprudential and financial stability statistics

12.52. At the time of the founding of the EMU, financial supervision was excluded as a function of the union and macroprudential and financial stability statistics were a new field that was not part of the original statistical program of the ESCB. However, work on aggregate statistics on the condition of the financial sector grew rapidly, and with a spur from the financial crisis it is now a major activity of central bank statistical programs worldwide.

12.53. Macroprudential statistics are a major separate branch of statistical activity that new unions must address in order to have information needed to defend the financial stability of the union. The section *Macroprudential indicators and supervisory statistics* below provides more information on the types of indicators to collect.

Operational statistics

12.54. Statistics are also needed on operations of the monetary union. These will include a range of financial accounting aspects, such as the income statement and balance sheet, but constructed based on statistical standards and in a time series form. This allows for easier comparison of how activities of the monetary union affect general economic activity. Statistics can also include data on the number of banknotes[408], by denomination and country of issuance or retirement. Information on staffing and payroll could also be monitored. Also, many operations must be monitored at the time of the changeover from national monetary systems into the union to see how they are affected – presentation of the information in statistical time series contributes to the analysis. Like in the EMU, statisticians might also be tasked to maintain current registers of monetary financial institutions and counterparties.

12.55. In the Euroarea, monetary statistics are also used for calculating official reserve balances of banks.

12.56. Statistics might also be used to calculate market indicators used for monetary policy operations, such as average interest rates used for compensating deposit balances, price changes used for indexing wages or prices, distributions of seigniorage or customs unions revenues, etc..

Financial Inclusion statistics

12.57. A new policy priority for many countries is promoting better access to financial services to populations that have lacked ready access to banking facilities and sources of credit that can support economic development and poverty elimination. This is an important priority for many countries that might join unions, and something that might be included in the union program.

12.58. The international community (IMF, World Bank, etc.) has data collection programs underway, that are described in more detail in *Section H – Statistics on Financial Inclusion.*

Electronic money (e-money) and central bank digital currencies (CBDCs)

12.59. Innovations in electronic money (which comes in many forms) is causing important changes in the structure of financial markets. The new development of "crypto" instruments, and especially introduction of CBDCs, is rapidly changing the field and new statistical definitions and data collections are needed. *Chapter 9 – Currency* covers the Euroarea approach to broadly defined e-money, which began soon after the euro was created. *Chapter 9D – The Digital Euro* covers cryptoinstruments and the recent work on CBDCs, which has become so important that a separate chapter is devoted to it.

12.60. E-money and CBDCs are major issues affecting monetary control and policy. *This area is sufficiently important that all future unions and most central banks need to monitor the field on an on-*

[408] And probable future issuance of digital euros.

going basis. International investigations need to closely followed.

<u>*Specialized statistics*</u>

12.61. Specialized statistics can support the operations of the union and the analysis of its performance. Some of these could take statisticians into areas of statistics where little previous work has been done:

Petroleum statistics. For the GCC union and other potential unions, the extent of petroleum and natural gas exports in total trade and their price volatility make it important to collect and separately analyze information on them. The IMF has investigated statistical work in this area that encouraged additional metadata (information about statistics sources and methodologies) to promote knowledge of practices in oil and gas statistics. The work also encourages transparency initiatives, such as the Joint Oil Data Initiative and the Extractive Industries Transparency Initiative.

There have also been demands for separate estimates of GDP for the petroleum/gas sector and for all other sectors. The rationale is that in some countries major differences exist between the growth, income, fiscal implications, price movements and volatility of the petroleum sector (or other major extractive sectors) versus other sectors. Total GDP might disguise serious problems in the nonpetroleum sector that can only be revealed by separate information on it from information on the more prosperous commodity export sector. Also, fiscal convergence criteria could distinguish between the petroleum sector and the balance of the economy.[409]

Other commodity statistics. For some unions, other commodities (gold, other ores, sugar, coffee, etc.) play important roles in much the same way as petroleum does in other regions. Special measures, such as construction of commodity GDP and non-commodity GDP, might be developed.

Workers' remittances and Hawala transfers. Information on these flows can be important for understanding capital flows as well as domestic investment. In some countries, remittances are large enough to influence overall public consumption and balance of payments flows. The channeling of these flows outside standard banking channels creates major statistical problems.

Workers transfers can be quite large for some economies within likely future unions, both between union member countries and externally. An union might create formal transfer and settlement mechanisms for worker transfers in order to make this activity more secure, lower costs, and provide worker protection. Formal activity is relatively easy to measure, but there continues to be a need to attempt to measure informal transfers. Four international organizations have collaborated to publish a compilation guide on remittances statistics. (OECD 2009)

Islamic Financial Institutions (IFIs). As they grow in importance, the role of IFIs in financial systems need to be followed. Significant methodological issues are involved in attempting to incorporate information on IFIs into a standard statistical framework. The Islamic Financial Services Board (IFSB) has programs to construct prudential indicators similar to FSIs, and sectoral income statements and balance sheets for IFIs. The UN and IMF are investigating the treatment of Islamic finance in the national accounts and balance of payments and might recommend compilation of a separate "satellite account" covering Islamic finance. Several future unions probably should initiate statistical coverage of Islamic finance and how it

[409] Estimation of petroleum GDP can be challenging. A key problem is the extent to which the petroleum industry (or other commodity industries) will be measured. The easiest is primary production, looking at extraction, sales of crude petroleum and gas including exports, and tax revenues. However, this does not measure the full influence of petroleum in the economy, which is harder to measure because it becomes intermixed with other activities, such as secondary activity (processing, storage and distribution) and tertiary activity (the multiplier effect on employment and income, investment in roads and other infrastructure to support production, housing for staff, ancillary services, and the like. Measuring secondary and tertiary activity is likely to involve challenging definitional issues and measurement problems.

might affect monetary and other macroeconomic behavior.

Real estate and asset price information. Real estate conditions play an important role in overall economic activity, price movements, and financial stability. Surprisingly, relatively little information is collected by most countries, or data are compiled using widely differing methods. Although this is not a new area of statistics, for many countries major new investigations will be involved and new forms of data collections will need to be defined and implemented. Over the past two decades multiple international organizations have begun to focus on better compilation of real estate price indices (IMF 2005), (European Union 2013), and (OECD 2020).

C. Convergence criteria

Introduction

12.62. One of the most important functions of union statistical systems in production of high-quality, unbiased "convergence criteria". Convergence criteria are general indicators of overall economic performance based on GDP, fiscal, inflation, exchange rate, interest rate, or similar macroeconomic data that are used to establish whether a country can enter a union. Alternatively, the indicators can be used not has hurdles for entry, but as "convergence benchmarks" that are general guidelines for monitoring countries' performance either prior to membership or once countries are in the union. Criteria can also be constructed to reflect the integration strategy of the union to prompt countries to restructure their economies to meet the goals of the union. Criteria can also be used to promote specific macroeconomic goals, such as in one case promoting more effective tax collection to help assure that the government has sufficient resources to meet its needs.

12.63. Whatever the goals and targets of the convergence criteria, the indicators require high-quality nonfinancial and financial statistics constructed according to a well-defined common methodology. They must be available prior to the start-up of the union. High-quality, unbiased statistics allow countries to make valid comparisons that do not prejudice the entry prospects of any country, or that can be used for regular monitoring whether a country is converging with the common economic targets.

12.64. As discussed in the section on loose convergence in Chapter 4, the criteria can also provide information on the speed of convergence or whether countries are diverging, which is a threat to the union. Indeed, if countries begin unions with less than a high degree of convergence, there is increased danger of imbalances within the union and divergence over time – which could even lead to application of "divergence indicators" (such as the spread between country indicators is growing or shrinking). (Krueger and Enoch; 2009)

12.65. Convergence criteria are used to ensure that the macroeconomic performance of each member is reasonably close to the performance of other countries so that major imbalances are not introduced into the union to the detriment of overall monetary policy, or to prevent asymmetries between countries in reactions to economic shocks or to application of the common monetary policies. Ideally, indicators should be available on a monthly or quarterly basis with good timeliness so that authorities obtain current feedback on how effectively their policies are bringing the economy in line with the convergence criteria.

12.66. Where the criteria are decisive in granting approval to join an union, the criteria have legal status and an independent authority recognized by all candidate countries (typically the union statistical office or the union central bank) should be charged with the task of assessing the consistency of the methodology used and the resulting figures. Eurostat was given this role in Europe.

12.67. Even if convergence criteria are not used to make decisions on joining an union, union-member countries need a set of main macroeconomic indicators to monitor the evolution of the union and provide an effective communication tool. Convergence criteria are among the key macroeconomic statistics for the new union and to monitor the individual member economies. The criteria should satisfy international statistical reporting requirements in terms of methodology, coverage, and timeliness.

Euroarea convergence criteria

12.68. The EMU used convergence criteria as hurdles for countries seeking to join the union. The criteria were ratified in 1991 in the Maastricht Treaty to promote price stability within the Eurozone prior to and after the start of the union. Countries must meet the criteria prior to acceptance into the union, and the goals were intended to remain valid even if new states joined the union. Countries were evaluated in comprehensive reports prepared by Eurostat, the EU Statistical Office that looked at the levels and sustainability of meeting the criteria levels.

Euroarea Convergence Criteria[410]

Rate of Inflation: No more than 1.5 percentage points higher than average of the 3 best-performing European Union member states.

Government deficit: The ratio of the annual government deficit to GDP must not exceed 3% at the end of the preceding fiscal year.

Government debt: The ratio of gross government debt to GDP must not exceed 60% at the end of the preceding fiscal year.

Exchange rate: Applicant countries should be in the ERM for 2 consecutive years without devaluing during the period.

Long-term interest rates: The nominal long-term interest rate must not be more than 2% higher than the average rate in the three best-performing member states (based on inflation).

[410] Chapter 4 has rationales for the criteria. All Euroarea criteria are nominal measures, but experience has shown that real convergence, as represented in each country's real effective exchange rate (REER), is an important indicator. The REER reflects information on the rate of inflation and the exchange rate.

Statistical issues affecting convergence criteria

12.69. An important statistical issue affecting convergence criteria is their degree of harmonization across countries. The criteria will be used to measure the performance of each of the economies against other union members in important ways, such as determining membership or assessing penalties on errant countries. Poor comparability thus can have serious economic and political effects. Also, convergence criteria must be comparable in order to aggregate them to the union level to provide measures of the overall union performance. For such reasons, common standards, applied with oversight, are important for compilation of high-quality convergence criteria. The statistical program of the union must undertake this task simultaneously with setting up its own program, and assist and prod building of effective national statistical programs that can produce such comparable statistics.

12.70. A second issue is whether the criteria are technically measuring what they claim to be measuring. For example, when the Euroarea criteria for fiscal debt enumerated types of debt included in the measure, trade debt was inadvertently omitted. This exclusion significantly affected the fiscal convergence criterion of one applicant country. A second example was the HICP exclusion of the cost of owner-occupied housing in the measurement of real estate services on the grounds it is an investment cost. This is a serious omission because housing costs are a significant part of households' expenditures and prices had moved rapidly in some countries. Moreover, monetary policy can affect house prices and thus affect housing costs. In this case, there can be serious question whether the current Euroarea price measure is the most appropriate measure.[411]

[411] Similarly, in the GCC, the inflation convergence criterion was based on "core" measures of inflation (that exclude some volatile prices such as rents) rather than the overall measure. The core measure might be a more stable measure and thus facilitate comparison between the countries, but it is not the measure of inflation that directly affects the public and volatile prices can (continued)

12.71. For future unions, the convergence criteria need to be relevant to the region and the structure of the union, and the Euroarea criteria should not be simply followed. Several examples follow;

The Euroarea interest rate criterion was based on long-term rates to capture information about long-term inflation expectations for the country. However, in the GCC for example, a similar criterion exists but the market is dominated by short-term rates that reflect the U.S. interest rates because of the exchange link to the dollar and limited short-term borrowing by GCC governments.

The GCC inflation criterion is hard to interpret because of the structure of the economy with three distinctly different consumer populations – citizens who receive many goods and services at subsidized prices, immigrant professionals and business people who pay market prices, and contract workers with low incomes and constrained consumption profiles. See *Text box: The International Comparison Program*, below.

The GCC has decided to use a core measure of inflation that excludes volatile items such as real estate rental prices. It must be determined whether the core index validly provides information relevant for monetary policy purposes. A general index that includes volatile prices directly affects public consumption and might have important influences on economic behavior.

The fiscal criterion in Africa is affected by grants, which can be a significant portion of government expenditures. Simple application of the EMU 60% debt criterion makes little sense in this situation. Should the criterion include or exclude grant income and expenditures? Also, grant income flows are likely to be erratic and possibly not easily controlled.

Commodity exporting economies (such as in the GCC and many African countries) will have fiscal situations heavily affected by shifts in commodity prices. The fiscal balances might be sharply affected by the commodity price movements, and might not be easily controlled. Another question is how sovereign wealth funds (SWFs) created out of the commodity export earnings are treated in the criterion.

Late penalties

12.72. An aspect of convergence criteria is that creation of the union itself can create difficulties for later applicants to meet the same criteria met by the original members. This happened in Europe.

Inflation criterion

12.73. The Euroarea inflation criterion based on comparisons with other member countries effectively changed as the number of members increased. "No more than 1.5 percentage points higher than average of the 3 best-performing *European Union* member states." This criterion was appropriate for selection of the original members of the union, but was seriously flawed for later applicants for at least four reasons.

The distribution of observed inflation changed as more countries entered the EU. The tail distributions became thicker and thus it is more likely that three countries would have very low inflation rates.

"European Union" is not the relevant measure for later applicants. Original members had their inflation performance compared against other EU members. However, for later applicants this comparison creates a problem in that they should be compared against the performance of union members. In 2006, Lithuania was rejected for Euroarea membership although it met all convergence criteria except inflation – even though one EU non-Euroarea country (Sweden) was in the comparison, Lithuania's inflation was lower than in some Euroarea countries and the entry of Lithuania would

subsequently affect the core measure and thus be a reason to change monetary or other policies.

have actually lowered the level of inflation for the Euroarea as a whole.

The ECB goal is that inflation for the union will not exceed 2 percent. Thus, the weighted mean of the distribution will be very low, giving new applicants a difficult target to achieve. Early applicants did not have to meet any specific target.

Prospective members of the Euroarea will experience capital inflows and a shift to use of the euro as a parallel currency, which creates upward pressures on asset prices and inflation. The original applicants did not face these conditions.

Interest rate criterion

12.74. The interest rate criterion (nominal long-term interest rate must not be more than 2% higher than the average rate in the three best-performing Euroarea member states based on inflation) was affected by the creation of the EMU.

12.75. Macroeconomic stability as a result of union membership led to a drop in the country risk premium in the interest rates of the member countries. (Country risk premia in government borrowing rates of the Euroarea countries quickly dropped to trivial levels during the first few years after the union was created – although the risk premia reemerged during the fiscal crisis caused by the GFC.) Late applicants do not benefit from this advantage.

12.76. Financial integration and the absence of exchange rate risk in the Euroarea permits capital to freely flow into countries with higher interest rates, lowering rates for those countries. Late applicants do not benefit from these specific advantages that would tend to pull them toward the interest rate levels of the Euroarea.

12.77. The net consequence of these effects cannot be precisely measured but it is clear that late applicants to the Euroarea face greater challenges than the original candidates. They must try harder and might need to apply stricter monetary and fiscal policies than otherwise.

12.78. The above examples demonstrate that convergence criteria should be reviewed periodically to assure that they reflect the relevant conditions and that the creation of the union has not effectively altered their meaning.

D. Price indices for unions

12.79. The central role of price stability in the Euroarea placed the statistical measurement of prices at the center of policy deliberations.

Harmonized Index of Consumer Prices (HICP)

12.80. The HICP is the inflation measure for the Euroarea. Eurostat does the conceptual work on harmonization of indices in collaboration with national statistics offices. Standardization in all countries is needed so that the data can be aggregated to produce a measure of inflation for the entire union. Many of the standards are reflected in EC regulations and must be followed in all countries.

12.81. The HICP excludes the cost of owner-occupied housing on the grounds it is the cost of an investment item. This is a serious omission in that housing costs can be a significant part of households' expenditures, and also because the costs have recently risen rapidly in some countries. Planned unions are urged to not follow this European practice and instead include owner-occupied housing in their indices.[412]

12.82. The overall HICP is split into goods and services as the major components. Goods are subdivided into four major components – unprocessed food, processed food, energy, and nonenergy industrial goods. Each of the components was chosen to reflect the influence of different economic factors.

[412] Diverse methods have been proposed on how to include owner-occupied housing in price indices. Arriving at a suitable conclusion will involve review of international investigations on the topic and weighing of different needs for national accounts statistics and for monetary policy.

Unprocessed food is affected more by short term factors such as weather, global market changes, and seasonal shifts; in contrast processed food reflects manufacturing costs more and is less influenced by the above factors. Energy prices obviously are highly volatile.

Overall and core inflation indices

12.83. Should inflation indices focus on overall price changes or on a subset of prices that exclude the most volatile items? For example, in discussions of convergence criteria for the proposed GCC union, Qatar proposed using core measures of inflation that exclude volatile components that are likely to be reversed or will subside. For example, real estate rental price increases, which were rapid at the time of the proposal, were viewed as representing acute shortages of housing for Qatar's rapidly growing population, but were believed likely to slow because of a large number of units under construction. The Qatar proposal was accepted and research was undertaken on how to construct such a measure.

12.84. It is likely that unions will need both overall and core measures of inflation, which serve different purposes.

> Indices of overall price changes, such as the HICP, which are often called "headline indices" because of the way they are announced in newspapers, provide information on how price changes directly affect consumers and their cost of living. This is important information about changes in public welfare, and it often has political implications. Also, overall changes could become part of the underlying inflationary structure and become permanent – for example, a spike in grain prices when overall inflation and inflation expectations are low can have a passing effect, but in a more inflationary environment could be seen as more evidence of inflation and might be quickly be incorporated into long-term inflationary expectations.

> Core measures are designed to look at the underlying inflationary process and provide a medium-term perspective. This perspective might be best for assessing medium term prospects when making monetary policy, or might be suitable for convergence criteria. For these uses, there should be some confidence that current price movements in the headline rate are unlikely to become part of the underlying inflation process. This requires that the public has confidence in the reliability of the core index and that it is not simply an after-the-fact device to make a bad situation look better. Authorities should communicate regularly and clearly why the core measure is more appropriate.

Consumer indices versus broader indices

12.85. The HICP focuses on households' consumption of goods and services and thereby provides measures of how price changes affect overall public welfare. However, broader measures are possible. For example, the price of inputs to capital investment affects costs of industrial plants, housing, or infrastructure development, etc. Or rising wage levels affect the cost of providing government services. These parts of the overall inflation picture can be missed by focusing solely on consumer prices. The most available broad measure is probably the GDP implicit price deflator, which is the measure of the price differences between gross domestic product (GDP) at current nominal prices and real GDP using prices from some base period. The implicit GDP deflator provides the broadest possible measure and might correspond to the growth of the total money stock.

> Ideally, the overall implicit GDP deflator should be constructed from detailed measures for sectors or subsectors of the economy, because price information will be better at less aggregated levels. One possible distortion is that price inflation for the export sector will be built into the overall deflator, but it will not directly affect domestic inflation.

> In many developing countries, methods of estimating GDP are rudimentary and the results are of questionable reliability. GDP estimates might be available only annually and only after a long delay. In such situations, measures of consumers' prices are preferred for monetary policy deliberations.

Text Box: The International Comparison Program (ICP) [413]

The ICP is a global program to measure and compare prices of goods and services using a purchasing power parity (PPP) method. It compares prices and consumption for nearly every country by demographics and major product breakdowns.[414] *Regional measures can be constructed by comparing economies using PPP weights rather than the standard exchange rates.*

Different consumption patterns can exist within a population. In the GCC, for example, three main population segments have very different consumption patterns. Citizens receive many subsidized goods and services; businessmen and immigrant professionals pay full market prices; contract construction and service workers receive low incomes and often consume only a very constrained basket of goods and services. The consumption weights and the prices faced by each group are completely different; combining them into a composite inflation measure is challenging. It is unclear whether the aggregate measure correlates with monetary aggregates, or whether subindices[415] *might work better.*

Price collections often focus on urban areas. Rural and low-income populations could be ignored or poorly measured.[416] *Subdivision of aggregate price and consumption measures by region or product (such as in the ICP) can provide valuable information on who is most affected by price changes.*

GulfStat, the statistical office of the GCC, has experimented with PPP weighting of national CPIs[417] *as a first step toward constructing a harmonized measure of GCC consumer inflation in anticipation of a GCC monetary union. Harmonization is "prerequisite for meaningful monitoring of regional monetary policy in the context of already agreed GCC monetary union, as well as for use as a key macroeconomic indicator in its own right for various national and regional decision-makers." (Manninen 2015)*

2021 is the base year for the next ICP round. All future unions should seize the opportunity to review how the new information can help compile regional price indices used for union monetary policy.

12.86. The overall conclusion for future unions is that price indices are important pieces of information to assess current economic conditions, assess the effectiveness of monetary policy actions, and measure key variables such as the real exchange rate and external competitiveness. However, in many planned unions, serious problems exist in production of price indices. They present long-term structural challenges that cannot be quickly resolved. Conceptual work, commitment of resources, and institution building are needed for extended periods to improve data collection and the comprehensiveness and quality of the indices. In this situation, planned unions cannot rely on

---

[413] The section *Cross-country price comparisons* in Chapter 9 also discusses the ICP and PPP.

[414] See *Purchasing Power Parities and the Size of World Economies: Results from the 2017 International Comparison Program*. Washington, DC: World Bank. © World Bank. World Bank. 2020.

[415] Such as, businessmen and immigrant professionals at market prices, plus weights for citizens using unsubsidized prices.

[416] Rural or low-income populations areas often have different consumption patterns (partially monetized, more consumption based on own production or barter, etc.) and information collection can be difficult or expensive, intermittent, or based on small samples.

[417] The six GCC countries will presumably produce more harmonized price indices as they introduce the standards published in the *Consumer Price Index Manual: Concepts and Methods* (2020) by six international statistics organizations, including Eurostat. Applying common coherent methods, in conjunction with new data from the ICP, could provide a firm basis to improve GCC CPI measurement useful for the eventual monetary union. Other future unions can also adopt this strategy.

price indices to provide fully accurate unbiased information. They should be treated as guidelines and indicators rather than precise measures used as targets.

Inflation at the start of monetary unions

12.87. In the Euroarea, there were frequent fears that the changeover to the union currency would be used to hike consumer prices. Although broad indices of consumer prices might show little change due to the changeover (as occurred in Europe), it is often suggested that many of the most consumed items (milk, bread, bus fare, haircuts, neighborhood restaurant meals, etc.) might experience excessive price increases. This could be due to simply rounding up prices that convert unevenly into the union currency, but it could also be due to actual attempts to increase profits.

12.88. These fears occurred frequently enough that special efforts are needed to determine whether price hikes occurred and publicly report results. This special effort might focus on the most commonly consumed products, and might sample prices with greater than normal frequency just before and just after the changeover. Or special regulations could be enacted regarding price changes and statisticians tasked to collect information needed to enforce the regulations.

Asset prices measures

12.89. One issue that has caused concern regarding the start-up of unions, or when countries join an existing union, is that a surge of capital inflows will drive up land and real estate prices, including the possibility that premium and high-prestige domestic properties will be grabbed up. The inflows could reflect opportunities to take advantage of large differences in assets prices between existing union countries and countries joining the union. Equity prices also can be affected.

12.90. In an union, capital inflows to new member countries can be expected as part of the integration process that will gradually bring about greater equalization of prices of goods and services and assets. However, large rapid capital inflows and rapid reversals and outflows can be seriously disruptive.

12.91. Asset price increases and the takeover of domestic properties can be important political issues. National authorities might wish to compile information on asset price changes for this reason and in order to understand more about the general economic implications of joining the union.

12.92. Construction of real estate statistics is notoriously difficult, because of the wide diversity of properties, quality differences, and high costs of compiling the detailed data needed. It is recommended that collection of real estate price indices for residences and commercial real estate be collected as a regular part of national price index programs. Special surveys of the impact on land and real estate prices related to joining the union can be considered. One important step in constructing good real estate indices is creating a baseline picture of the stock and condition of real estate, which requires efforts to take benchmark censuses and sometimes cadastral (airplane) surveys. Unfortunately, other projects often have priority.

E. Seasonal adjustment in money demand

12.93. Estimating seasonality in economic time series is a major activity of central banks that is usually handled by statisticians in conjunction with policy experts. This section describes estimates of seasonal demand for money, but similar seasonal methods are needed for many financial and economic time series.

12.94. Total money demand can change in a regular manner during the course of a year. For example, during tourist season, total money stock can be higher than average because tourists use cash for purchases and businesses increase their demand deposits because of increased sales. Conversely, money demand might fall in winter months when business activity is slow. The union central bank must actively manage the stock of money to accommodate changes to the money stock and demand in individual countries.

12.95. Seasonal money demand implies that there are regular seasonal patterns that can be identified and measured. Knowledge of these patterns supports policy making by allowing authorities to distinguish between short-term seasonal movements and the underlying pattern growth in the money stock. Seasonal information is also needed to handle cash demand because authorities must adjust the supply of currency in advance of expected demand. Similarly, currency can be shifted between regions each season to absorb cash from some regions with less business activity and provide it to regions with more activity. Such cash management can be down to the detailed level of demand for each denomination of currency, by region (or by country in unions).

12.96. Stable seasonal patterns are in theory easy to describe. Assume for example that the underlying stock of money grows at a constant rate each year and has a consistent seasonal pattern every year. In each first quarter, the seasonal influence increases currency demand 10 percent higher than the trend, expressed as + 10%. Every year the seasonal influence in the second quarter is lower than the trend, at – 5 %. The third quarter is + 3 %. The fourth quarter is consistently – 8 %. By definition, the sum of seasonal influences within each year must equal zero (10 - 5 + 3 - 8 = 0). That is, $\Sigma S_i = 0$, where i is the number of the quarters (or months, etc.). In this example, seasonal changes in demand are related solely to the regular patterns that occur each month, quarter, etc..

12.97. Directly observed data from the markets, which includes the influence of the 10 - 5 + 3 – 8 pattern, are called the "*original series*" or the "*seasonally **un**adjusted series*". From such information, the authorities can expect the money stock to grow between the second and third quarters each year by a total of 8, from 5 below the trend to 3 above the trend.

12.98. However, because unadjusted data can be hard to interpret, and affect estimates of the target growth rate for the money stock, "*seasonally adjusted data*" can be estimated to obtain information that subtracts out the seasonal influences. The seasonal adjustment process subtracts the seasonal factors above from the raw data series to obtain an estimate of the underlying trend in the data. For example, the first quarter seasonal factor (S_1) of 10 is subtracted from the original first quarter data (0_1) to estimate the trend value for the first quarter T_1, and the second quarter seasonal factor of 5 (S_2) is added to the original second quarter data, etc.. The resulting seasonally adjusted trend data can be used to estimate the growth rate for the monetary target.

12.99. The simple example above uses *additive seasonal factors*, which are subtracted from the raw data to get the adjusted data. It is more common to use *multiplicative seasonal factors* expressed as percent deviations from the trend. The multiplicative seasonal factors are divided into the raw data to obtain adjusted data. That is, the corresponding multiplicative factors are 1.10, .95, 1.03, and .92. Multiplicative seasonal factors usually work better if the level of the trend changes over time, which is common in many time series. But additive factors must be used if the raw data series includes both positive and negative values.

12.100. Seasonal adjustment can be done at various *periodicities*, such as quarterly, monthly, or weekly periods. Or nonstandard periods can be used, such as three periods per month, or even varying periods such as four periods with varying lengths in months if there is an analytical reason and data are available.

12.101. The paragraphs above give a simplified description of seasonal adjustment used by central banks. However, three other sources of variation are often removed from the raw data to obtain better estimates of the underlying trend.

A "Holiday adjustment" (H) is often made for changes above or below the trend corresponding to a moving holiday or other event. For example, money demand might increase by 20 percent during Ramadan, but the calendar period for Ramadan changes each year. The size of the holiday adjustment can be estimated by creating a dummy variable for the event in whichever period it falls, then estimating the average size of the dummy variable using the seasonally adjusted data.

A "Trading day adjustment" (TD) can estimate the changes in the data associated with the number of business days in a period. For example, sales data for February in a leap year will be on average 3.6 percent higher than February data in other years because of the extra day. The number of regular workweek days or weekend days can also matter.

Finally, there are "Irregular factors" (I_i), which are residual changes in the series after all the other identified factors have been subtracted out. Irregular factors include unscheduled special events (change of government, natural disaster, dock strikes, etc.) that affect the time series.

> Starting with 0_i as the original observed series, the combined Trend and Irregular influences $T_i + I_i = 0_i - S_i - H_i - TD_i$. In some cases, the influence of an irregular factor, such as a storm that affects overall commerce, can be identified and subtracted from the raw data to improve the estimate of the trend.
>
> However, estimation of the size of the irregular factor is often an internal research-based exercise to improve policy analysis, and it is common to publish data including the irregular influence (that is, $T_i + I_i$). Subtracting irregular factors from the published data might open authorities to charges of manipulating the data, and there is always an option to publish descriptions of the influence of the irregular factor to the public but without adjusting the published data.

If we can assume that the irregular factor represents random movements in the data that statistically cancel with a zero mean value over time, (that is, $I_i \rightarrow 0$) then the equation can be redefined to represent an estimate of the trend, $T_i = 0_i - S_i - H_i - TD_i$.[418] However, many countries only estimate the seasonal factors, that is, $T_i = 0_i - S_i$.

12.106. Estimating data for analysis of trends in monetary growth (and other economic variables) is obviously complex. It is a specialized activity undertaken by central banks, and can include a variety of methodologies, statistical tests, and techniques not discussed here. When this adjustment process is considered reliable, seasonally adjusted data are often preferred as being more useful for analysis or for policy purposes. Because the adjustment process changes the values reported for the series, it is important to be transparent about the procedures and the factors used to avoid charges of manipulating the data. It is common to publish projected seasonal factors for a year in advance to avoid such problems. At the end of the year, seasonal factors will be re-estimated using the actual data and revised seasonally adjusted series will be published.

12.107. Several statistical software packages exist that greatly ease the process of estimating the seasonal and other factors and the trend series. These packages also provide a battery of statistical tests of the quality of the seasonal adjustment. Quality tests are crucial because original series always includes the influence of irregular factors. The process of averaging data for seasonal factors thus always includes some irregular influence. If the irregular influences in fact reduce to zero or near zero, then good quality seasonal factor estimates can be obtained.

12.108. However, if irregularities are large relative to seasonal influences, then statistical irregularities will be systematically embedded into the estimated seasonal factors and the seasonally adjusted series. At some point, more bad information is provided by the seasonally adjusted series than good information. Thus, *seasonal factors and seasonally adjusted data should not be published if they do not meet rigorous statistical quality standards. Biased and misleading information could be published if series do not meet such tests. Unadjusted data should be used instead.*

12.109. Also, seasonality might not exist in the data. If tests indicate this, the unadjusted data must be used.

---

[418] However, the irregular series might contain economically important information that should be further analyzed. For example, the irregular series contain structural breaks in series that affect the original data, and also includes the impact of sudden shocks that affect the series such as a port strike. If such events can be identified and quantified, it is preferable that they be defined as a new series I_i' that should be subtracted from the original series to estimate the trend.

ECB Seasonal Adjustment Procedures

12.110. The ECB initiated sophisticated seasonal adjustment procedures during the early years of the EMU. (ECB 2000b) A special committee was set up comprised of experts from NCBs to devise methods to seasonally adjust the new data for the union. Because the membership of the union was unknown until 8 months before it started there was no historical experience with the seasonal behavior of the monetary and economic aggregates of the new union. New series for the union were constructed and the seasonal patterns estimated. (A proxy for union seasonal factors might be estimated by adding seasonally adjusted series of the major countries in the union.)

12.111. A composite series for the Euroarea was needed that was long enough to exhibit statistical properties needed for seasonal adjustments. This required construction of monetary series reflecting the composition of the EMU back into periods in which it did not yet exist. This problem is reiterated as new countries join the EMU because historical series reflecting the expanded composition of the union need to be reconstructed. However, the new countries have been small relative to the size of the members already in the EMU, and thus they had little effective impact on the adjustments.

12.112. Seasonal adjustment is largely a judgmental process, with the researchers selecting different models, interpreting results differently, and trading off between more precise but laborious estimates and more routine procedures that can process many seasonal series less expensively. The process of setting the seasonal adjustment framework for the EMU was not without tensions.

Procedures for new unions

12.113. New unions need to introduce methods to estimate seasonal demand for money and credit and their components to better inform the public about underlying financial conditions, to separate seasonal influences from trend changes to improve policy development, and for currency management.

12.114. All potentially relevant data should be reviewed to see if they are suitable for adjustment. It is recommended that a team be set up in either the statistics department or monetary department to review seasonal adjustment methodologies and to run tests on series to see which are candidates for adjustment.

12.115. It is desirable to construct composite series for the union prior to the start-up of the union. This might involve estimating seasonally adjusted series for larger countries in the union then aggregating them to the union level. A program to test the seasonal adjustment of series should be set up, covering seasonal adjustment in each member country of any size, and also deal with seasonality of the union-level series. The testing process should be documented and formal recommendations on methods, specific series to adjust, and publication procedures should be presented to the policy board of the union. If seasonally adjusted series are published, a summary of the recommendations of the report should be released with the data.

12.116. Seasonality will continue to be needed for each country, but the estimation procedures can vary by country. Financial conditions might vary between countries and different models might work in different countries. What is needed is the original data series and the estimated seasonally adjusted series for each country, which can be added up to union totals. The difference at the union level between the original and seasonally adjusted series will give the implicit seasonal factor for that period for the union. This information can help union authorities set up money and cash management procedures in response to seasonal movements.

12.117. Each year, seasonal factors should be reestimated using the actual data for the year. A revision of the seasonally adjusted series should be made and important variables reestimated and published, if significantly large. At this time, estimated seasonal factors for the upcoming year should also be published and held constant until the next annual review.

12.118. New unions should however remain cautious about making any seasonal adjustments. Statistically reliable adjustments usually require series at least six years long, and if markets are shallow or underlying national data are not good quality it might not be possible to produce good data. Moreover, creation of a union itself can cause structural changes that can affect seasonal patterns, and thus it might not be possible to identify reliable seasonal factors. *Series should not be adjusted if the statistical tests fail to indicate that the adjustments are statistically reliable.*

F. Financial Soundness Indicators (FSIs) and supervisory statistics

FSIs - First wave

12.119. In the decade following creation of the Euroarea awareness grew of the critical importance of soundness of the financial sector in supporting economic growth and effective implementation of monetary policy. Conversely, breakdowns in financial soundness can damage an economy and impair monetary policy. Shortly after the Asian Crisis in the late 1990's, the international community, led by the IMF, began a program to compile indicators of the strengths and vulnerabilities of countries' financial sectors.

12.120. FSIs are aggregate measures of the current financial health and soundness of a country's financial institutions and of their corporate and household counterparties. The ECB strongly agreed on the importance of this work and made important contributions in the development of the methodologies for FSIs and in the compilation of indicators.

12.121. The Asian Crisis in 1997–98 revealed major gaps in statistical coverage of countries' financial sectors that permitted serious vulnerabilities to remain undetected. National authorities in central banks or financial supervisory offices lacked information to take steps to prevent crises from happening or at least ameliorate their effects.

12.122. An important step in development of FSIs was the 2006 IMF *Compilation Guide: Financial Soundness Indicators* that described indicators and the methodologies for their compilation. The *Guide* describes a "core set" of indicators that all countries should compile, and an "encouraged set" of important indicators that countries might choose to compile depending on national circumstances or needs. The Guide was substantially revised in 2014 to reflect experiences from the GFC and new Basel III global bank supervisory standards.

12.123. To support countries in implementing the standards in the *Guide*, and to help with compilation of indicators, promoting cross-country comparability, and to increase transparency and strengthen market discipline, the IMF launched a Coordinated Compilation Exercise (CCE) with voluntary participation of 62 systemically important countries. Participating countries were requested to compile series for the common period 2005 along with extensive metadata (information about the data). The exercise tested the feasibility of the methodology and the use of a common period allowed international comparison of the results.

12.124. All Euroarea countries and other EC countries participated in the CCE, with the ECB playing an active role. This indicated the importance the Eurosystem attached to understanding the condition of the financial sector in order to be able to strengthen it. The ECB began collecting indicators very similar to the FSIs for its own use and use by financial supervisors. The ECCU also actively participated in the developmental work on FSIs support their work to bolster financial sector stability in their union. Future unions should compile FSIs to submit to the IMF and also publish a customized set aligned with their union's priorities and institutions.

FSIs - The next wave

12.125. The GFC that began in mid-2007 raised questions about threats to and the resilience of financial sectors. Many countries, often with international assistance, extended emergency liquidity support to financial institutions to prevent possible severe or total financial market collapse. The crisis reinforced the importance of compilation and analysis of FSIs and prompted development of an expanded set of indicators more focused on issues raised by the crisis. The new indicators tended to focus on new Basel III supervisory measures of bank capital and liquidity, and broader views of financial and real estate markets, and market concentration and systemic importance[419] of individual financial institutions.

12.126. The crisis revealed important gaps in regulatory systems and information about risks. One important gap was absence of information on credit risk transfer (CRT) instruments, such as credit default swaps, that allowed parties to transfer credit risk in markets to others willing to accept the risk in exchange for fees. These instruments had become very popular because they allowed banks to lower their capital requirements. A second important factor contributing to the crisis was securitization of assets by many credits of banks and other financial institutions – huge markets in securitized instruments developed. Both these trends transferred great amounts of credit, market, and exchange risk into securities markets, but left little evidence of who holds the risks and the extent and types of risks.

12.127. In the EU, the creation of the new European Supervisory System fostered a demand for a wide range of data on the financial system as a whole in order to support the analysis of risks and policies supporting soundness.

12.128. In light of international agreement on the need for aggregate indicators of financial sector soundness, the close interactions between financial soundness and monetary policy implementation, and urgent needs to strengthen this type of information, it is strongly recommended that planned unions build a strong regional statistical program to compile FSIs. In regions in which Islamic finance is significant, the union also should compile Prudential and Structural Indicators for Islamic Financial Institutions (PSIFI) promulgated by the IFSB that closely parallel FSIs.

12.129. Building a regional program involving collaboration between central banks, supervisors, and other officials to collect information on financial soundness or vulnerabilities and addressing how to support stability is too important to await the formal start of union programs. Cooperative efforts to support stability can build institutional relationships that might contribute to building unions at some later date. For example, all three of the African regions planning unions are setting up FSI-type programs to support the operation of their supervisory systems.

Prudential microdata within a macroeconomic context

12.130. An important advance in contemporary statistics is the ability to use the internet to cheaply and quickly collect raw data for individual reporters (microdata), then use flexible computing power to aggregate the information into macroeconomic statistics. The ways that new unions can collect statistics are now very different from in the past, especially for collection of data from banks, which will be one of the most important sources of information needed by currency unions.

12.131. Many aggregate macroeconomic statistics are derived from information about individual financial institutions and firms. Although *micro*economic information about individual firms might be structured according to different rules and for different purposes than *macro*economic statistics, it is common for individual micro-information to be collected and aggregated to a macroeconomic level. For

[419] Systemic significance of individual financial firms indicates the influence they can have on the overall financial system. The GFC demonstrated that economic stresses from large banks or insurance companies in trouble could affect entire economies. This prompted international financial regulators to create a statistical system to monitor "global systemically important banks" (G-SIBs) and insurance companies and require additional capital cushions. Systemically importance is particularly important in smaller countries, which comprise most of the membership of monetary unions, because smaller economies tend to have fewer banks and more concentrated banking systems in which impairment of a single bank can have widespread consequences. Thus, countries (and future unions) should consider monitoring and enhancing supervision of their "domestically systemically important banks" (D-SIBs).

example, information on banks compiled on the basis of the International Financial Reporting Standards (IFRS) is often used for statistical purposes, even though valuation and sectorization standards differ. It is the job of statisticians to reconcile the two data sets so that the best possible statistical series can be constructed.[420]

12.132. Importantly, work on FSIs has shown that in many cases simple aggregations of data on individual firms can hide important information. More detailed information on the activities of individual firms is necessary to understand the dynamics of risk concentration and transmission. A key issue is how likely is it that extreme results will occur, which requires information on the distribution of the data (standard deviation, skewness, range, etc.) that cannot be obtained from macroeconomic statistics that provide totals or average amounts. (The revised FSI system requests compilation of such distribution measures.) Some important contemporary frameworks for analyzing systemic risk, such as "contingent claims analysis" are based on analysis of distribution information.

12.133. Data collection can now compile micro information on all firms and use it to generate information on distributions or to compile macroeconomic statistics. Fortunately, computers can now collect information on large samples of firms and flexibly manipulate the information to provide structural information about the firms or information on totals. This is a fundamentally different way of compiling statistics from traditional techniques in which flexibility in manipulating the individual data to address specific research needs was often not available. Several examples demonstrate possible interactions between microdata and macroeconomic statistics.

> In the United States, the individual bank data collected by the Federal Financial Institutions Examination Council (FFIEC) system can be used for supervision of individual banks, research on distributions and the structure of the banking sector, and compilation of macroeconomic statistics. The FFIEC collects computerized data on all banks, including detailed identification series that allow the data to be accessed in many ways. Every piece of thousands of data items can be quickly accessed. Data with complete historical detail are stored in a large database. Individual bank examiners in the field can call up the entire data set for the bank on which they are working; Government researchers and policy analysts can compile the data quickly to answer research questions using the identification fields to extract the institutions and data they need; and macroeconomic series can be compiled for the entire banking sector.
>
> The flexibility of the FFIEC system can be readily duplicated. Similar systems have been created in the WAEMU and ECCB unions using the computing power of desk top computers. These examples show that *all* future unions can create highly flexible and useful microdata-macroeconomic data systems.
>
> In response to the needs for information on the distribution of risk in the banking sector, the deLarosiere Report (2009) proposed creation of an "International Risk Map", which would make use of both microdata and the associated macroeconomic data.

12.134. An ECB Board Member, Lorenzo Bini Smaghi (2009a), has described the importance of interactions between micro and macro data in dealing with the financial crisis. With reference to the International Risk Map, he said

> "The starting condition for implementing a comprehensive macro-prudential function is an adequate information basis. The first part of the information basis is a good system of continuous market intelligence, which gives a hands-on picture of

[420] Incompatibilities will often be found that prevent supervisory series from being compiled in complete concordance with statistical standards. In such situations, "metadata", or written descriptions of statistical series and their methodologies should be used to explain the issues to users.

current market developments and expectations through direct contacts.

The second part consists of the regular collection of macro-prudential data and statistics, such as those relating to the macroeconomic environment, financial markets and related infrastructures, payment and settlement systems, regulated and unregulated intermediaries, non-financial corporations and households, as well as to the relationships between the main economic and financial sectors.

The third part consists of the regular collection of firm-level information and data, in particular for large and complex financial institutions. This relates to specific items of information regarding on- and off-balance-sheet items, with appropriate breakdowns of exposures related to the asset and liability sides (geographical, sectoral, currency, etc.), including the identification of counterparties. For the identification of interlinkages between major intermediaries and the assessment of contagion risks, an international "risk map" – as proposed for example in the de Larosière Report – would be particularly helpful.

Lastly, for the large and complex groups, micro-prudential information about liquidity and risk management models would be required." (Bini-Smaghi 2009)

12.135. The new European Supervisory System (ESA) has an arrangement in which each of the three new European Supervisory Authorities (covering banking and financial institutions, securities markets, and insurance) will collect *micro*prudential information from all institutions they supervise, which then will be compiled into aggregate statistics. The statisticians of the ESCB will provide the expertise and facilities to aggregate. The data will be made available to the European Financial Stability Board for statistical purposes and for providing information to concerned international organizations. Thus, there will be complete set of microdata available for all financial institutions in Europe and comparable aggregate data.

Stress testing of individual banks is being taken up to help ensure that weakness of banks does not become systemic weakness and also to gain confidence that official support provided to banks goes to institutions that have strength to survive. A great deal of individual bank information is gathered in this process that can support general macroprudential analysis.

A key aspect of this process is a decision by international banking supervisors and the IASB to use an industry standard internet language XBRL (Extensible Bank Reporting Language) that allows statisticians or the general public to almost costlessly and instantaneously collect the data posted in XBRL by individual firms.

12.136. New unions should create a fully flexible micro-macro data system, for both macrostatistical and macroprudential purposes, as well as oversight of systemically important institutions. This will involve an alliance between statisticians, supervisors, and information technology specialists to introduce the physical technologies, organize accounting systems to produce the information, and then make use of the data. These are large and complex tasks, but with great rewards.

Data needs during financial crises

12.137. A financial crisis creates extraordinary demands for information on the condition of financial institutions and the causes of the crisis. Intense demands arise for very rapid production of new types of statistics. Once the crisis is over, crisis statistics are likely to become part of the regular data collection.

12.138. As described in *Chapter 13 - Supervision*, European supervisors recognized that they needed a standardized information framework to assess cross-border threats before and during financial crises. They negotiated a MOU that provides a common framework for organizing data needed for understanding the build-up of risks in the system and operating during a crisis. Union statisticians might be tasked to prepare the data or to advise supervisory offices on statistical issues.

G. Statistics on Financial Inclusion

12.139. Over the past two decades, strong international interest has grown on how to provide basic financial services to all populations in an economy – globally, billions of people lacked any or affordable access to financial tools needed to save, invest, and carry out transactions, which can suppress economic activity, growth, and economic development. New demands grew for statistics on financial inclusion, including on availability of microfinance and use of new electronic technology to provide services.

12.140. In response, the IMF designed a Financial Access Survey (FAS). It looks at channels to access financial resources in an economy – banks (and their branches and ATMs), credit unions and cooperatives, microfinance institutions, insurance, credit and debit cards, as well as mobile and internet banking.

12.141. The new data have shown that financial inclusion is improving very rapidly, which is a major structural change in the global economy. The many current projects in developing and emerging economies to develop central bank digital currencies to further advance financial inclusion demonstrates the priority being given in this area – future unions will need to give statistical coverage on this topic.

H. International statistical standards

12.142. Union statistical systems will involve collection of information from multiple countries and compilation of union-level aggregates from such data. The only practical method to achieve this is for the union and its countries to apply internationally recognized statistical standards. By each country following such standards, broadly comparable data will be constructed in all member countries. Achieving such comparability can be a long-term challenging process because each country might need to create new reporting systems in a wide variety of areas, and in each area high-quality reporting is needed. Finding the staff and resources for this work will be difficult.

12.143. Unions and their member countries can take advantage of the common need for comparable statistics in accordance with international standards. They can participate in common training on the standards or compilation methods, draw on resources of international authorities, compare information on cross-border positions, exchange information on methods, or create institutions that operate in multiple countries.

> For example, unions will need comparable price indices across the union, which might be achieved by creating a single agency to sample prices in all union countries. Individual countries might not have the expertise or resources to undertake surveys on their own, and data collected can be efficiently centrally processed.
>
> Also, integration of union banking systems means that reporters need information on classification of the cross-border positions with other banks or government agencies. The union should compile a list of all such institutions in all countries and share it throughout the union. The union statistical office might operate an on-line database that lists banks, government agencies, financial instruments, etc. with their statistical classifications that can be used across the union.

12.144. Thus, there can be strength in numbers of countries addressing the same task simultaneously and modes of cooperation should be sought.

12.145. The specific standards that should be applied are well known. The overarching framework is the System of National Accounts (SNA). Compatible systems in topical areas include monetary and financial statistics, balance of payments statistics, government fiscal accounts, consumer price indices, real estate indices, and their related subsystems. Unions need to become operational in all these areas, and should be be included in international deliberations on the development of such standards. Outside the macroeconomic family of statistics there will be standards on financial accounting, bank supervision, securities markets, payments systems, and insurance, etc.. In the area of data communications, there is convergence on use of XBRL for data communications and dissemination of bank reports and financial accounting reports, along with a compatible system for statistics called SDMX (Statistical Data and Metadata Exchange) promoted by the major international statistical agencies.

I. Revisions policy

12.146. Policies must be in place to cover revisions to data. Union-level statistics merge together national-level statistics that might have different cycles for collection of data, or different types of data might only be available after a delay. Surveys should be made of when each major type of data can be received, data gaps, data subject to delay or revision, and where quality problems exist. It is also important to know when additional source data become available that can replace preliminary information. Each potential union country should be surveyed, first to set the schedules for data collection and statistics compilation, then for understanding the revisions cycle, and as needed to focus assistance and resources to statistical problem areas.

12.147. Once the union starts, data and methodologies can be compared across countries, which can improve methods of collecting data and reconcile differences. For example, differences in intra-union balance of payments flows between countries became apparent – in one major case, it was discovered that export trade with other EMU countries always exceeded the recorded imports of the same countries, which implied that every EMU country had an upward bias in its current-account and GDP estimates. To adjust, the ECB revised downward its balance of payments estimates from 1997 into 2000; and indeed the estimate of the current account for 1999 was changed from a surplus to a deficit. This indicates that each union should conduct reconciliation exercises once the union starts to attempt to resolve discrepancies and improve the overall accuracy of the accounts.

J. Statistical reporting to the IMF

12.148. Member countries of the IMF are required as a condition of membership to give the IMF statistical data needed to carry out its surveillance of national economic conditions. The IMF has made clear that the obligation continues if a country joins a currency union – even in a union, comprehensive statistical picture of economic conditions of the individual countries is needed. This section discusses arrangements under which union members can meet their obligations to the IMF to provide statistics.

12.149. As a practical matter, it was easier and cheaper to collect statistics on the EMU and its member countries from the ECB than from the individual countries. The ECB collects data on its member countries and aggregates and consolidates them as needed to compile the union level statistics. It was efficient for the IMF to collect the data directly from the ECB, under what is called the "Gateway" procedure. Resource costs are less on both sides, the data reflect the ECB validation efforts, data are the same vintage at both the ECB and IMF, and errors are not introduced.

12.150. This is done as a practical step, and the use of the Gateway did not alleviate any country of the obligation to supply required data to the IMF. Luxembourg continued to send its data directly to the IMF in recognition of the direct Luxembourg-IMF relationship of rights and obligations that are part of its membership in the IMF.

12.151. The gateway arrangement has also been applied for collection of statistics from other currency unions in Africa and the Caribbean.

12.152. Over time, countries have increasingly insisted on arrangements for only one-time submission of data for all receiving agencies in order to save costs and improve data quality.

12.153. As described in *Chapter 8 – International*, in 2007 the IMF introduced a new regime for surveillance of members' exchange rate policy that defined the types of information needed from unions and their member countries for surveillance.

> At the union level, statistics for surveillance include measures of external stability, union balance of payments, fundamental alignment or misalignment of exchange rates, and monetary conditions. A full set of macroeconomic statistics is needed, on both current and real bases, and thus there is a need for good quality price statistics.

At the member country level, the IMF will still conduct surveillance over countries' domestic policies and financial stability conditions because they could affect overall union stability. Surveillance will also cover individual member country balance of payments as the channel through which stresses are transmitted through the union. The real exchange rate must also be monitored to understand changes in countries' competitiveness. This means there must be continuing compilation of a broad spectrum of macroeconomic statistics, the balance of payments, and real exchange rate indices.

12.154. Within a monetary union, certain types of monetary and reserve assets information become less important or change at the national level and new types of information on the union as a whole become relevant. For example,

Money stock information at the national level might no longer be relevant because currency and other monetary instruments can readily move across borders within the union. In the case of the Euroarea, only union money stock figures are considered relevant for monetary policy.[421]

National monetary policy instruments are no longer relevant. Union-level policy interest rates are relevant; information on interest rates for policy instruments is no longer needed.

Management of reserves is at the union level, and thus information on union level reserves is needed. However, reporting by countries of nonreserve foreign currency assets and liabilities remains important for numerous reasons and thus continuing reporting, as in the IMF's Reserves Template, should be continued. Special procedures might be needed for sovereign welfare funds, in part because they often have important monetary policy roles.

12.155. The IMF has changed its format for presentation of data from Euroarea countries to reflect the changes above, the framework of the Euroarea monetary balance sheet, and classification of financial instruments. The new IMF format reflects data at both the national level and at the union level. The changes reflect that the analytic and policy framework of the Euroarea has changed and that it is meaningful for the IMF to convey the information in a way relevant to the analytic methods actually used in the Euroarea.

12.156. Several additional data items are requested by the IMF to bridge from the Euroarea to aggregates used at the IMF. A requirement that the Euroarea countries provide the supplemental data has been put into an ECB regulation, guaranteeing that the countries will supply the statistics.

K. Conclusions

12.157. Statistics play a special role in the operation of unions. They provide information on conditions throughout the union on a current harmonized basis and are compiled into union-wide aggregates on money and credit, economic activity, and inflation. Statistics are also used to collect information on instruments for monetary or exchange rate policy and help track the influence of policy changes on the economy. Statistics can have a direct influence on behavior through their use as convergence criteria, which are mandatory indicators that prescribe targets for activity.

12.158. For the above reasons, and many others, unions require high quality statistical systems. Data must be current and accurate to inform policy deliberations, and because they are the public face of the

[421] Regardless, researchers have remained interested in activity in monetary instruments at the country level. Therefore, data on instruments within the Euroarea money stock are available at the national level and are referred to as "national contributions to the Euroarea money stock". Thus, the IMF requested that Euroarea countries still provide information on issuance of banknotes and coins even though the currency itself will move between countries once in circulation. This information on issuance is published for each country as a memorandum item in the IMF's *International Financial Statistics.*

union must be considered trustworthy by markets and the public. Building high quality statistical systems requires a commitment of resources and long and diligent effort, which should start at the earliest stages in the planning for the union.

12.159. There is no single formula of building statistical systems for unions because each union has a unique structure, reflecting different histories, philosophies, institutions, and policies. But whatever the ultimate specific structure and policies of each union, the union and its member countries must create sound statistical programs that can flexibly address the requirements of the union.

12.160. The process will require professionalism and institution-building at both the national and union levels. As described by IMF Managing Director Rodrigo de Rato with reference to the GCC countries, thought might be given to "creating an institution perhaps along the lines of Eurostat in the European Union to provide the GCC countries with high quality statistical information."[422]

> This involves creating a statistical infrastructure specifically suited for compilation of monetary, reserves, and other statistics needed for a currency union. Initially, statistical work might be done in a separate institution or as part of the Eurostat-like structure, but ultimately the authority and responsibility for collecting monetary and financial sector statistics for the union will probably need to reside within the union's central bank.[423]
>
> Subsequently, in 2014 a GCC central statistical office (GCC-Stat) was created in Oman. It parallels Eurostat in that its GCC-wide coverage is broader than the countries currently planning on joining the regional monetary union.

12.161. Serious consideration should be given to creating an union-level statistical institution early in the union planning process. This provides an opportunity to build infrastructure and professional staff, develop modes of cooperation and decision-making for the union, and develop a culture of reliable statistical reporting by banks and other financial institutions. This organization can usefully perform regional functions such as supporting customs unions data collection or providing regional policy information to regional groups such as the CMIM. And the organization could make an important contribution to the success of the union by presenting the public with an institutional face for the union as an operating organization.

12.162. The ultimate statistical demands of the union will be large, and substantial lead time is needed to build the institutional and legal infrastructures for statistics and to begin the methodical collection of information and compilation of statistics. Throughout this process, statisticians should collaborate with international statistical authorities and apply international standards and best practices in their work.

12.163. Finally, as ECB President Jean-Claude Trichet has said,

> "Statistics are like the glasses through which policy-makers and all other economic agents view macroeconomic reality. If the glasses are totally reliable, well-polished, and easy to handle, we may hardly notice that we are wearing them and we do not realize how vital they are for our clear view of reality. Surely, we only start to complain when the glasses are out of focus and we want to have a new pair when glass-making technology proceeds."[424]

---

[422] De Rato (2005). See also Dziobek and Al-Mansouri (2006).

[423] The union system for monetary and financial statistics must also be matched by systems for other macroeconomic systems and demographic and social indicators. These might be done by other agencies, but in small unions perhaps only a single statistical office is feasible.

[424] "Euroarea statistics and their use for ECB policymaking," Speech by Jean-Claude Trichet delivered at (continued)

Statisticians will need to work diligently to construct such eyeglasses, and once they have them and the union is operational, will find that – if the experience in Europe is any guide – that they will be thrust into the center of analytic and policy work of the union and will be asked to construct ever more new sets of specialized glasses.

Text box: Customs union statistics as precursors

In several regions, currency unions are seen as an culminating step in a long-term regional integration process. Customs unions are a common early step in this process. Typically, customs unions remove duties and other formalities on trade between member countries; inspect and impose customs duties at the first port of entry; then share customs revenues between member countries. This system requires a statistical system to track the goods entering the union, duties assessed, destination of the goods, and payments received and disbursed.

Several unions have sought advice on how to set up such systems – the South African Customs Union sought advice from the IMF, and the GCC sought advice from a private consultancy firm. The GCC for example had difficulties in arranging the distributions of revenues, which caused delays in implementing the plan.

New unions should treat setting up the statistical system for their customs unions as an opportunity to build an effective and professional statistical system that can serve as an example of how to build a statistical system suitable for their future currency union however far in the future that might be.

---

the Second ECB Conference on Statistics, Frankfurt-am-Main, April 22-23, 2004. The author can attest that some ECB statisticians were very pleased when the above statement was made.

Timeline

Large or continent-wide unions should move all steps at least one year earlier.

Preparatory period	Build resources and professional expertise of central bank statistical office and national statistics institute. Conduct benchmark survey of consumer expenditures and prices, in urban and rural areas. Survey of NCB and national statistical offices strengths and gaps
Early actions (four years prior)	Set up Statistics Committee
Three years prior	Compile list of banks and financial institutions in the money issuing sector. Begin building IT system to collect monetary and financial statistics from member countries. Inform monetary policy and open-market counterparties and other reporters of statistical obligations. Intense training of staff in international standards and best practices begins
24 months prior	Agree on statistical standards; begin drafting statistical compilation guides. IT systems are purchased and installed
18 Months Prior	Specify the data transmission language Implement legal changes to promote statistical harmonization and mandatory filing Consultations with IMF, BIS, and other agencies on data provision
Final 12 months	Union and country IT systems become operable
Final 6 months	Test live data collection of all union and country systems In-house preparation of union monetary and credit aggregates, balance sheet. Union data flow procedures in place Adjustments to statistics to reflect final decisions on policy framework Presentation of statistical framework to markets and public
Run-up to union	Live production of full set of internal data needed for policy Arrangements for IMF reporting put in place
Union day	Union statistics come into effect. Monitor experiences
Early union period	Publish full set of macroeconomic and financial statistics; Statistical press releases Compile and publish statistics on uptake of union currency, and retirement of national currency, by country Measure retirement of national currencies Reconcile cross-country positions and modify methods, as needed. Begin work on steady state methodologies

Appendix 1: Cocirculation[425]

Cocirculation refers to the use of two or more physical currencies within an economy. It is not uncommon and many economies make extensive use of the U.S. dollar, euro, ruble, and other currencies alongside the national currency.[426] [427]It raises numerous issues of policy and monetary control and also has major statistical implications. Cocirculation is relevant for this study because;

> It describes the parallel currency approach for introducing a new union currency,
>
> Prospective union members and countries on the periphery of unions will often adopt the union currency as a cocirculating currency.
>
> It can create a bifurcated economy in which multiple numeraires of value exist and which affect different sectors in diverse ways.
>
> Similar statistical problems affect economies with cocirculation and countries in a currency union in which currency and other bearer monetary instruments can freely move across borders.

Cocirculation raises many policy questions and monetary control issues, including the important issue of loss of seigniorage income. Some cases are discussed in this volume, but most policy issues are outside the scope of this study.[428] This appendix focuses on statistical issues surrounding cocirculation.

Cocirculation can create severe statistical problems that are hard to resolve. Large scale cocirculation creates multiple statistical biases – mismeasurement of the effective monetary base and money stock in both the currency exporting and importing economies, balance of payments flows and international investment position misestimates, difficulty in compiling sectoral balance sheets, misestimates of the underground economy and thus overall GDP, and difficulties in making price measurements. Moreover, changes in exchange rates cause hard-to-measure diverse effects on sectors depending on which currencies are held.

In an union, the free movement of currency across borders is equivalent to a cocirculation flow. Because such flows are common in the EMU, the ECB held that individual member country money stock data are no longer relevant and thus the money stock should only be analyzed from the view of the union as a whole. Also, in unions, cross-border currency flows affect estimates of the stock of money which in turn affects seigniorage income.

---

425 The term "cocirculation" is often associated with "dollarization" because many countries use dollars as a cocirculating currency or for formal bank depositing and lending. This study uses the narrow term cocirculation because (1) dollarization does not correctly describe the use of other currencies – such as "euroization" in some Eastern European countries – and (2) the focus is on physical currency rather than general redenomination of financial instruments and bank accounts. The IMF's *Compilation Guide on Monetary and Financial Statistics* includes material on statistical treatment of dollarization and cocirculation. See also Krueger and Ha (1995).

426 Kamin and Ericsson (1993) documented that use of the U.S. dollar in Argentina was probably the largest component of the money stock of Argentina. Following the break-up of the Soviet Union, similar situations probably prevailed in Russia, Poland, and several other East European countries.

427 The advent of CBDCs could accelerate cross-border movement of currencies and cocirculation.

428 The extensive academic and empirical literature on dollarization provides many insights on the policy implications of cocirculation. Some examples include Baliño *et al* (2004) – "Monetary Policy in Dollarized Economies"; Berg and Borensztein (2000) – "The Pros and Cons of Full Dollarization"; Gulde *et al* (2004) – "Financial Stability in Dollarized Economies"; and Winkler *et al* (2004) – "Official Dollarisation/Euroisation: Motives, Features, and Policy Implications of Current Cases".

Early work at the U.S. Federal Reserve Board concluded that cocirculation of U.S. dollars abroad had caused massive amounts of U.S. dollars to exit the country without documentation causing a very large balance of payments discrepancies. Krueger and Ha (1995) documented numerous serious statistical discrepancies caused by cocirculation and reviewed methods for statistically estimating cocirculation and corresponding cross-border flows of currency. Subsequent research on cocirculation often focused on Eastern Europe and Latin America, but it is more widespread. Other work has focused on the seigniorage aspects of cocirculation – for example, Ha's unpublished 1993 estimates of the circulation of the South African rand in Swaziland were intended to help allocate seigniorage. Others have made estimates of the amount of seigniorage income gained by the United States because of use of the dollar abroad.

Multiple methods to estimate cocirculation have been suggested. The methods to use depend on a range of issues including the causes of the cocirculation, patterns for currency flows, data availability, and skills of the compilers. No single method is superior in all cases. In practice, multiple methods can be tried and results compared. Among methods suggested have been;

Comparisons of national money stock (per capita or per GDP unit) with closely related countries

Shifts in seasonal demand for money given changes in underlying economic activity of known magnitude

Econometric estimates of demand for money

Tracking time series of currency usage to identify breaks in patterns

Surveys of money holdings by public, business, or banks

Examination of the stock of currency by denomination to identify unusual patterns

Tracking identifiable cross-border flows of currency through banks, money changers, etc.

Tracking repatriation of currency back to the home country after tourist outflows or seasonal migrant labor movements.

And, someday, the computer technology used to record issuance and transactions in central bank digital currencies might permit it to be accurately tracked in cocirculation situations.

Estimates of cocirculation and associated cross-border currency movements are difficult to make and are likely to be subject to a large range of uncertainly. Statisticians face challenges deciding on whether the data are sufficiently accurate to be used in on-going statistical reports, or whether the information should be only used for supplementary analysis or only internally. Both strategies are followed – the U.S. and Russia put some rough estimates of flows into their balance of payments data, but other countries have chosen to publish their analyses without making changes to published statistics. This will be a judgment call – the data will never be very accurate, but it will sometimes be better to incorporate rough information in the statistics (along with warnings to readers) than to say nothing. Pressures could be intense to produce estimates where the allocation of seigniorage is involved.

Appendix 2: Measuring financial sector integration

Financial market integration can be measured in several ways. Three common methods are measuring the extent of cross-border financial flows, applying the law of one price for financial assets and interest rates, and similarity in financial markets. (See Mongelli 2002, p.20)

Cross-border financial flows

Information on integration can be derived from examining the extent to which domestic financial assets are used relative to cross-border assets. A low level of integration is revealed as a "home country bias" in which residents use domestic markets in preference to foreign markets. Home country bias can result from simple familiarity with domestic markets and use of established business ties, but it also can result from exchange rate risk or impediments in cross-border transactions and uncertainties in using foreign markets (taxes, language, different procedures, legal uncertainty, etc.). The costs of such bias can include higher borrowing costs, loss of competition in markets, less efficient investment, etc.

It is useful to have statistical measures of the intensity and trends of cross-border financial flows. Two components of this information are statistical estimates of balance of payments flows of financial assets and the international investment position. Balance of payments estimates of aggregate flows (which are often derived from estimates of the change in positions in financial assets) should normally be available from regular balance of payments reporting. Even in isolation from other information, the balance of payments data can provide general indications of how much an economy is financially linked with other economies, and the strength of growth of cross-border assets. Also, an indirect measure sometimes used is the ratio of per capita current account balances to GDP.

Detailed information on counterpart countries for financial flows, and on the types of financial instruments used is very useful for analyzing trends in integration. However, such information might not be readily available, or if it is used for statistical compilations might not be published on a detailed basis. Special data collections might be useful.

For unions and future unions, it is important to understand the intensity of intra-union financial integration. Therefore, data should be regularly collected on financial account transactions within the union separately from information on transactions with the rest of the world. This information should also include detail on financial instruments, at least at the level needed to compile consolidate monetary aggregates for the union. Thus, the monetary balance sheets used by the EMU, which detail intra-union positions by financial instrument, provides a good model for the type of data needed to estimate financial sector integration.

A number of regions with regional schemes have set up harmonized regional monetary and financial data gathering systems to provide analysts a coherent picture of regional financial sector activity. These data also potentially provide good information for measuring the intensity of cross-border financial activity.

In addition to the cross-border information, it is very useful for comparison purposes to also collect information on domestic holdings of financial assets and liabilities. Such information comes from SNA-based financial accounts and flow of funds statistics that provide balance sheets for the economy and its major macroeconomic sectors. Compiling balance sheets can be challenging, but there is increasing recognition of the importance of analysis of national and sectoral balance sheets for monetary and financial policies and to understand the macrofinancial linkages within economies. Many countries compile such data, and numerous countries are establishing new programs. Also, the IMF has recognized the importance of balance sheet analysis for surveillance and the IMF statistics department encourages countries to compile financial balance sheets.

Law of one price (cross-border price convergence)

This measure looks at differences in yields of comparable instruments across countries. If markets were highly integrated, differences in yields provide opportunities for arbitrage by buying assets with higher yields in other countries. Increased demand for financial assets with higher yields causes their prices to increase and thus lowers the yield. With perfect integration, differences in yields would fall to zero; less prefect integration results in larger differences which might reflect differences in the risk of the assets.

> In principle, integrated markets within currency unions should eliminate yield differences between union member countries.[429]
>
> Yields on money market instruments, such as short-term certificates of deposit traded between banks, converged very rapidly following the start of the EMU. Similar results occurred for Euroarea government bonds (although later diverged when fiscal problems developed in some countries). The rapid convergence reflected near perfect opportunities for arbitrage following the elimination of currency risk, the high degree of security for banks and government debt, and the ability to move capital freely within the Euroarea.

Similarity in markets and institutions

Numerous different measures of similarity or differences of markets have been used. One measure closely related to the analysis of the monetary transmission mechanism is the sensitivity of lending or expenditure to interest rate changes. Other examples include differences between countries in the maturity structure of debt, or the availability of nonbank financial intermediaries. Other measures are more descriptive in examining differences in legal or market structures; size of fees at banks and intermediaries.

A major difference between financial systems is the proportion of the population without access to modern banking services. Outside the developed countries,[430] as recently as two decades ago, areas of Africa and Asia as much as 80 percent of the population lacked access to formal banking services. These populations rely on other sources such as traditional money lenders, suppliers' credit (to finance working capital for agricultural or home production), trade credit, or increasingly on microfinance mobile phone facilities. Quite obviously, countries with large unbanked populations have low overall measures of financial integration, but some market segments (import merchants, urban professionals, etc.) might have good access to financial services. The lack of access is a serious impediment to economic development and tightens the grip of poverty. The monetary policy transmission mechanism is also affected because monetary policy actions undertaken through the banking sector can be transmitted to the nonbanked sectors only with lags. Any economy with such populations faces major structural issues in its financial sector that might significantly affect the speed of adjustment to economic shocks, from rapid reactions in small, shallow formal financial sectors, to slow reactions for the economy as a whole.

The extension of financial services to nonbanked segments of any economy is a valuable contribution to overall economic welfare that is increasingly recognized as a priority of the international community. For example, the IMF and World Bank in 2010 collaborated in creating a financial access survey (described above) asking all countries about access to basic banking services. *Future currency unions should include on their agendas how their programs can help extend financial services to all segments of their populations and help integrate the financial sectors of the economies within the union.*[431]

[429] Assets with underlying risk differences should not have identical yields because higher yields should be required to absorb the higher risks of some instruments. Care should be taken to compare only instruments with the same or nearly the same risk.

[430] Holland, for example, has more than one bank deposit account for every resident, children included.

[431] Because financial access programs will often be new, the union might piggy-back on them to introduce the new currency or financial infrastructure programs supporting the new currency.

ECB indicators of financial market integration

The ECB has developed a series of indicators of financial market integration. In general, they show that markets in deposits and short-term instruments necessary to ensure the effective transmission of monetary policy quickly became highly integrated across the countries of the EMU following the creation of the euro. Markets in longer term markets are much less integrated. Individual indices listed below provide a sense of the types of integration considered important in Europe. The list might also provide guidance to countries building unions on which markets should be given priority to more effectively create integrated markets.

In 2007, the ECB published *Financial Integration in Europe*, (2007e) which included a detailed statistical methodology of markets being assessed and the indices, with graphs for each of the indices.

Money market indicators

Interbank lending rates – Standard deviation of rates for cross-country bank loans.

Average interbank rates for repurchase agreements – Rates for bank to offer euro funds to other banks secured by securities repurchase agreements.

Cross-country holdings of short-term debt securities.

Share of cross-country payments in the TARGET system, by number of transactions and by value.

Bond market indicators

Government bonds – Standard deviation of bond yield spreads for maturities of two, five, and ten years.

Government bonds – Correlation across countries of coefficients for yields on ten-year bonds

Government bonds – Difference from coefficients implied by complete integration for ten-year bond yields.

Government bonds – Variance for ten-year bond yields

Chapter 13 – Supervision

What will be the role of the union in overseeing the soundness of banks and other financial institutions, in suppressing contagion, volatility, and other market risks, and in acting as lender of last resort?

A. Introduction

13.1. This chapter deals with the supervision and regulation of banks and other financial institutions within currency unions. Under the original Maastricht model national supervision was primary and the ECB role was limited, but this changed sharply under financial crisis conditions. Future unions will be more likely to follow the latter approach and be much more involved in supervision in order to assure the stability of the union financial system for several reasons:

Financial integration within a currency union requires creation of common mechanisms to deal with cross-border issues.

Macroprudential factors are increasingly seen as relevant to ensure the stability of the financial system and carry out monetary policy.

Many central banks outside Europe have long traditions of involvement in financial supervision.

The GFC showed weaknesses in the European system and led to major changes. Greater centralized supervision introduced in Europe is likely to be relevant for many future unions.

13.2. The crisis identified weaknesses of the European system to predict and prevent crises and coordinate crisis responses. Failures were recognized and major innovations were introduced. The changes provide some guidance for future unions on the types of supervisory system appropriate for a currency union, and thus they are discussed in some detail.

B. Euroarea financial sector supervision

13.3. This section first describes the supervisory framework set up under the Maastricht Treaty, then describes the new European Supervisory System created to deal with problems identified during the crisis.

The System defined under the Maastricht Treaty

13.4. The Maastricht supervisory system was decentralized with the ESCB playing a supportive role, with no direct responsibility for supervision. National authorities had primary responsibility, which meant that each country had both a central bank and a separate financial supervisory authority. Moreover, there could be more than one supervisory authority if supervision was broken up by line of activity, typically banking, securities, insurance, and guarantors including deposit insurance.

13.5. There was great diversity in supervisory institutions, philosophies, and practice in Europe. For example, in Germany there were two layers of super ision, with each German state ("Land") operating official local "Landesbanks" that had key roles in supervision. The Bundesbank itself had a limited role in supervision. Translated into the Maastricht context, this meant that the primary responsibility for supervision was placed outside the NCB. The split of responsibilities is also in line with the Maastricht concept of subsidiarity.[432]

13.6. The split reflected a view that different approaches are suitable for supervision and monetary policy. The responsibility for monitoring the soundness of *individual* banks and other financial institutions was seen as resting with local authorities, who can apply a highly sophisticated set of financial standards when monitoring the individual banks. In contrast, monetary policy should be concerned with the operation of the *system*, in which monetary policy impulses are smoothly transmitted through individual banks that are each assumed to be sound enough to participate in monetary policy operations.[433] The

[432] Maastricht did not create a supranational supervisory organization parallel to the ECB, despite some proposals to do so. Areas considering creating unions should consider such an option, especially in light of a common movement in many countries to create a single financial sector supervisor for banks, other financial institutions, securities markets, derivatives, and insurance, etc.

[433] However, the reality of the monetary policy/supervisory split can be hazy and affected by general market conditions and by mutual interactions between the (continued)

system was intended to avoid policy conflicts in which possible central bank support for individual banks could conflict with overall monetary policy.

13.7. The above philosophies are reflected in Maastricht Treaty Article 25 that defines a limited role for the ECB in supervision of the banking and financial system. It states in its entirety,

> "The ECB may offer advice to and be consulted by the Council, the [European] Commission, and the competent authorities of the Member States on the scope and implementation of Community legislation relating to prudential supervision of credit unions and to the stability of the financial system. In accordance with any decision of the Council under Article 105 of this Treaty, the ECB may perform specific tasks concerning policies relating to the prudential supervision of credit institutions and other financial institutions with the exception of insurance undertakings."

> Article 105 referred to above prescribes the goals of the ESCB in general terms. The only language relating to supervision is in paragraph 5,

> "The ESCB shall contribute to the smooth conduct of policies pursued by the competent authorities relating to the prudential supervision of credit institutions and the stability of the financial system."

13.8. The provisions above provide no specific guidance and clearly indicate that the ESCB roles will be limited. However, the language could be interpreted narrowly or broadly. Prior to the startup of the EMI, the COG put out a proposal for a more active ESCB role in supervision, but this was rejected and abandoned. The EMI established a Banking Supervision Committee (BSC) that it hoped would be an active forum for discussion of supervisory matters, but practice proved more limited. In this context, and given the many other tasks of preparing for union, little further work was done at the EMI to promote bank supervision. An "enabling clause" in Maastricht gives the ECB some competence in the area, but was never activated. [434]

13.9. Although a strong supervisory center was precluded, the planners recognized the importance of a strong financial system (sound banks, liquid capital markets, reliable payments systems, etc.) to support the monetary policy operations and to contribute to economic growth. An impaired system hinders transmission of monetary policy signals and makes monetary policy less effective, restricts credit flows, causes losses for depositors and other investors, creates distortions in markets, generates volatility, fails to intermediate risks, and potentially results in serious losses. Extreme financial instability can create long and deep economic and balance of payments crises.

13.10. Thus, although the condition of the financial system was recognized to have important influences on monetary policy implementation, responsibility for financial sector stability remained decentralized and primary control was exercised by national authorities. National financial supervisors had direct oversight, with participation by finance ministries, who ultimately had responsibility to cover financial losses and costs of lender of last resort operations. The ECB would only facilitate the national policies, provide advice, exchange information, etc.

---

system and individual banks. The general monetary policy environment can affect the soundness of individual banks; conversely, weakness of larger banks or the risk of contagion between banks can limit monetary policy options. This tension between supervision and central banking has numerous implications in designing the institutions and policies for a currency union.

[434] Maastricht ¶105(6) states that "*The Council may, acting unanimously on a proposal from the Commission and after consulting the ECB and after receiving the assent of the European Parliament, confer upon the ECB specific tasks concerning policies relating to the prudential supervision of credit institutions and other financial institutions with the exception of insurance undertakings.*" This provision provided authority to expand the ECB supervisory role. The process is not easy to implement, but because the language existed, the treaty itself did not need to be revamped to later expand the ECB's supervisory powers.

13.11. However, many supervisory policies were set by EC regulation and were common to all countries. It is the responsibility of national supervisors to implement the common policies and carry out the ongoing supervision. Thus, the Eurosystem, in theory, could focus on how overall financial stability affects monetary conditions and policies, and on where it can provide common services to national authorities.

13.12. The EMI set up a Prudential Supervision Committee. There were hopes that it could play an important role at the union level in promoting financial stability, but some national authorities objected to any significant diminution in their roles in financial supervision. The hope that the Committee would become a key forum for deliberation on financial stability issues did not advance far. (Scheller 2007)

13.13. When the ECB was created in 1999, its Banking Supervision Division had only four employees, reflecting its limited role in the system. However, it grew rapidly during the early years of the Euroarea, as the macroprudential aspects of supervision gained greater recognition.

Implications of different national rules

13.14. Like the post-Maastricht situation, some new unions are likely to begin with supervisory systems that are at least partially and sometimes fully decentralized. This can create problems of coordination and inconsistent rules and implementation. Alternatively, in smaller counties central banks might have to handle both policy and supervision.

13.15. Countries building unions might start with different supervisory institutions and rules and carry them into the union unless specific steps are taken to harmonize the rules. Also, divergence in national supervision might reflect different practices in implementing the Basel Supervisory frameworks and their choices of supervisory options.

> In 2004 the more complex Basel II system was introduced and countries had options to adopt. Some countries might need assistance to move toward more common union-oriented regulatory regimes. Smaller countries especially might choose to continue use of a modified Basel I approach rather than fully adopt the more complex Basel II framework, which might be beyond some supervisor's resources. (This diversity in applying approaches later continued when a Basel III model was introduced in 2009).

13.16. In an union, if national supervisory systems are retained there must be mutual recognition that the decisions of each supervisor are valid elsewhere. The European system was based on mutual recognition in which a license granted to a bank permitted it to operate anywhere in the EEA. Similarly, each supervisor would monitor its own banks' capital adequacy and liquidity ratios, which provided assurance that the bank was suitable for depositors throughout the union, to participate in union monetary policy operations, post collateral for clearing operations, etc.

13.17. Unfortunately, application of national rules can result in significantly different economic situations for banks in different countries. For example, differences in recognition of impairment, provisioning, derecognition of securitized assets, valuation of collateral, application of fair value methods, and others, can create large differences in recorded income statements and balance sheets. Information drawn from such sources might not be comparable between countries, which can impair policy analysis. Moreover, cross-border investment and depositing might be inhibited because of the uncertainties, which sacrifices some of the benefits expected in a currency union. The EMU sought to bring about a relatively high degree of common practices by issuing banking directives, but these permit variations in national practice as long as the common goals are met, and it was agreed that quite a bit of national variation remained.

13.18. However, fortunately, the application of international rules for supervision, accounting, licensing, disclosures etc. pushed national supervisory offices toward convergence of practice. The Basel II process, for example, included some modifications of the Basel I capital adequacy framework that increased convergence, and all Basel I countries were required to take steps to enhance their supervisory oversight (Pillar 2 of Basel II), and introduce greater disclosures

(Pillar 3). The introduction of the IFRS has promoted greater accounting harmonization in valuation, recognition of income, provisioning and impairment, recognition of the sale of assets, etc. These are very important forces to promote convergence, although they do not cover all differences in national practice.

13.19. If national supervisory practice is retained within a union while markets are integrated and funds can move between countries without exchange rate risk, regulatory arbitrage is possible allowing funds to move into jurisdictions where oversight is weakest or at least to avoid some supervisory oversight in the home country. Inflows into weaker jurisdictions, or volatile capital inflows through a weaker system, can result in an union-wide increase in risk and threat to financial stability. Thus, there is a common interest to promote good supervisory practice in all union countries. Although decentralized, it should be expected national supervisors recognize the need to address common issues and promote convergence in practice, and construct some form of consortium to deal with common issues.[435]

Post-Maastricht supervisory changes

13.20. The supervision system set out in the Maastricht Treaty came under steady criticism for the first eight years of the union due to apprehension that national supervisors would be unable to adequately assess risk in a multi-country integrated market and concerns that fiscal costs of rescue actions could not be fairly distributed. Initially there were few major challenges to overall systemic stability and the system remained broadly unchanged, although there were modest efforts to enhance coordination and clarify responsibilities of fiscal authorities.

Evolution prior to the financial crisis

13.21. Louis (1995) reviewed the decentralized supervisory framework and concluded that a framework of national responsibility over home country banks in conjunction with bilateral cooperative arrangements for cross-border supervision could not possibly guarantee systemic stability. Also, risks were certain to increase under the currency union. Some centralization compatible with the general principles of subsidiarity was needed, and Louis saw a case for central supervision of larger banks. A key element could be to create a financial supervisory agency parallel to the union central bank with supervisory power over all types of financial institutions and markets. Full centralization was not implied; national supervisors could still exercise substantial authority but coordinate through an union body.

13.22. Shortly after the launch of the EMU, the Lamfalussy Report (2001) provided guidance on speeding up the financial sector integration process in the EU along with proposals to strengthen the banking, securities, and insurance supervisors, referred to as the "Level 3" Committees".[436] It sought to build supervisors' technical expertise, encourage convergence in practices, increase communications and transparency, and increase political accountability. The Committees, however, lacked legal powers over national supervisory practice and – absent majority decision-making processes – found introducing changes difficult. In this environment, little progress was made because of lack of national cooperation or efforts to protect or promote national interests. A number of supervisory differences remained between countries, including divergence in applying Basel II framework, such as incomplete convergence in risk modeling and oversight over securitizations.

[435] A consortium of country supervisors can help carry out peer reviews, review common issues, be a clearing house for technical assistance, and promote joint practices. It can facilitate cross-border inquiries by national supervisors. It could promote data collection and compilation of financial soundness indicators. Also, the union level consortium may represent the union in matters with international organizations – for example, advising on new international standards, or arranging training by the Financial Stability Institute for union members.

[436] See Chapter 11 regarding the Lamfalussy levels.

EU Memorandums of Understanding (MoU) on Supervisory Cooperation

13.23. Recognizing that mechanisms were needed to deal with cross-border supervision in crisis situations, the EU negotiated two memorandums of understanding (MOUs) between EU supervisors, central banks, and finance ministries. The first in 2005 was prior to the crisis, but it was strengthened in June 2008 when the crisis was underway. The MOU recognized that the development within the union of integrated financial markets and large cross-border financial groups increased the possibility of contagion across borders and financial sectors. In this environment, the responsibilities for crisis resolution and incurring the costs of resolution could be difficult to pinpoint. The EU held that the situation was one of union concern and that all potential parties needed to be involved in the arrangements. EU-level principles were needed to lay out the rules and procedures for crisis resolution.

13.24. The second MOU (European Commission 2008) provided a set of principles for management of cross-border financial crises, set out an analytical framework that all countries should use as a basis to agree on strategies to address the crisis, and also provided specific guidelines for crisis management. *This MOU enumerates numerous specific steps in crisis management that could be relevant for future unions.* (Appendix I presents the principles.)

13.25. The MOU recognized that crises could develop quickly in unexpected ways and therefore it was important to have an ongoing information base to assess situations and views on resolution. Thus, assessments should be made using a common analytic framework that provides information on current conditions and uses a common terminology amongst the parties involved. The assessments would be made by supervisors and centrals banks, with finance ministries being kept fully informed.

13.26. The MOU did not create new institutions, nor change responsibilities for the parties. Supervisors, central banks, and finance ministries were the three relevant parties to the agreement, but it was recognized that other institutions could be involved, such as deposit insurers, competition policy authorities, law enforcement, or other authorities.[437]

13.27. Importantly, the MOU "does not create any legal environment for any of the parties to intervene in favor of anyone affected by the financial crisis." (p.2) Thus, it does not introduce commitments to rescue financial institutions, businesses, or the public harmed by the crisis, although these possibilities always exist.

13.28. Although the MOU was not legally binding, the parties pledged full cooperation in dealing with assessment of risks and management of crises. In non-crisis times this would include;

Setting up a framework for cooperation

Exchanging information and using the common analytic framework

Communicating with the public

Conducting stress testing and simulations

Developing contingency plans.

13.29. The MOU would come into effect whenever a situation involves a banking group with major cross-border activity that threatens severe systemic problems or might go bankrupt. The goal is to protect financial system stability and minimize economic damages at the lowest overall collective cost. *The MOU explicitly states that preventing bank failures is not a goal.*

13.30. The MOU had a market orientation. It states that "primacy will always be given to private sector solutions....management will be held accountable

[437] Also, authorities in the EEA countries were invited to associate with the MOU.

....shareholders will not be bailed out....creditors and uninsured depositors should expect to face losses." Moreover, "the use of public money to resolve a crisis can never be taken for granted and will only be considered to remedy during a serious disturbance in the economy and when overall social benefits exceed the cost of recapitalization at public expense." Also, intervention must preserve a level playing field between countries and must comply with EU rules on competition and state aid.

13.31. The sharing of fiscal burdens in crisis resolution was seen as needed. "If public resources are involved, direct budgetary net costs are shared among affected Member States on the basis of equitable and balanced criteria, which take into account the economic impact of the crisis in the countries affected and the framework for home and host countries' supervisory powers."

13.32. This formulation does not provide obvious answers on sharing of fiscal burdens – each crisis will have unique elements, institutions with different degrees of cross-border activity will be involved, the economic impacts might be difficult to assess or might develop over time, culpable actions might be involved that need to be adjudicated, the ability of states to incur burdens differs (which was shown clearly by the crises in the smaller countries of Iceland and Ireland), there will be political hesitance to come to the aid of nonresidents, and perhaps most important actions might not be taken quickly enough to address urgent domestic problems.

13.33. Crisis resolution steps will need to be flexible, but should operate within the frameworks of existing supervisory arrangements. In particular, home country supervisors retain their role as coordinator of actions over global consolidated enterprises.

13.34. The MOU used "colleges" which are groups of supervisors and other authorities that are responsible for supervising the different parts of cross-border financial groups. Although such arrangements were appropriate for the situation, there had been general agreement before the crisis that the colleges were not sufficiently diligent in identifying potential problems. The MOU also indicated that the European level supervisors of banks, securities, and insurance can be involved, as well as various ESCB committees. Because issues might arise with regard to specific financial groups involving specific countries, "Voluntary Specific Cooperation Agreements" (VSCA) could be negotiated to deal with the specifics of each situation and how it should be supervised. Where a VSCA is in place, a common database should be created with both public and proprietary quantitative and qualitative data relevant to the situation.

13.35. The MOU modified this by requiring designation of a Cross-Border Coordinator, who would generally be the national coordinator for the home country of the affected financial group. Any party in the MOU can request that the Coordinator activate the crisis procedures, which triggers notification of all relevant parties in all involved countries. Thus, the triggering process for crisis related action was quick and easy.

13.36. As an example of how the mechanism might work, if a liquidity problem (which is a central banking problem) affected a financial group, the central bank of the home country of the financial group coordinates actions of all affected central banks. The ECB and Eurosystem might also be involved. The central banks would work with the supervisors and immediately inform finance ministries if emergency liquidity assistance might be needed. If systemic issues arise potentially involving use of public funds, the home country finance ministry will act as coordinator.

13.37. As can be seen, the system is designed to quickly involve the relevant players who would take coordinated actions in line with EU rules and MOU guidelines. However, the system remained largely decentralized, and thus its effectiveness might depend on the foresight, effectiveness, and resources of the home country authorities.

13.38. Finally, the MOU provided a template for assessing systemic risks with public and private information needed to understand the situation. The template included all relevant public statistics and financial accounts, supervisors' assessments, information on contagion channels and linkages, and results of stress tests and simulations. Each template had sections covering the condition of banks and other financial institutions, securities markets conditions, conditions in financial infrastructure (clearing and payments systems, deposit insurance, etc.), macroeconomic conditions, and contagion information. In each of these areas, conditions are ranked from not affected to very severely affected, and a heat map is constructed showing the areas of risk and the intensity of the risk by color.

de Larosière Report

13.39. The ink was barely dry on the MOU when worsening of the crisis in late 2008 forced additional strengthening of the system. At the height of the crisis, the EC set up a high-level committee headed by Jacques de Larosière, which prepared the *Report of the High-Level Group on Financial Supervision in the EU* in early 2009 on reforms to the EU supervisory system. (de Larosière 2009) The proposals were intended to apply throughout the EU. *The ECB in its role as an EU institution gained roles throughout the EU.*

13.40. The Report cited three factors at the heart of the problems with the EU supervisory system;

> Lack of adequate process and guarantees for host country depositors and policy holders[438]
>
> Lack of a clear framework on cross-border burden-sharing at the EU-level
>
> A lack of trust among EU supervisors, which it believed had worsened because of the crisis.

13.41. The Report also stressed the importance of closing supervisory gaps over nonbank financial institutions that comprise the "parallel banking system", standards for derivatives and securitized financial instruments, improved methods of burden-sharing of crisis resolution efforts, among others.

13.42. The Report did not make recommendations for Europe in isolation. It envisioned close interaction between European supervisors and international bodies who would provide global standards and coordinate responses. It also supported giving the IMF a larger role in the global financial system.

Text box: Potential supervisory conflicts with union monetary policy

The de Larosière Report presents a case of potential conflict between crisis resolution needs and the competence of the Eurosystem to have sole competence in monetary policy.

> *"Furthermore, there could be cases where Member States disagree with the monetary policy choices made elsewhere in the EU, seeing them as too lax and jeopardizing the stability of the financial system. Given the impact of excessive credit expansion, especially in some host countries, safeguards for such countries could be justified. If the host supervisor detects such deviations, it should be able to act by tightening credit conditions or increasing reserve requirements."*
>
> *Specifically, for "significant mismatches in terms of borrowing in foreign currencies, the host supervisor should have leeway through appropriate regulations to curb those currency mismatches in both subsidiaries and branches" and "particular attention should be dedicated to the appropriate degree of liquidity of branches and subsidiaries of branches and subsidiaries in host countries."*

These types of powers considered useful for host supervisors appear to potentially place restrictions on liquidity conditions of local affiliates in conflict with ECB "single passport" policies in which home country supervisors establish the prudential standards for intra-EU operations.

[438] One issue specifically cited is host country concern that regulatory capital levels are decided by home country authorities.

Also, crisis responses involving large liquidity infusions financed through government borrowing could contradict EMU monetary policy.

C. New European supervisory system

13.43. As the GFC gripped the European financial systems major changes were introduced into the supervisory system. The urgent needs were highlighted by continuing difficulties in the banking system. In late 2011, the ECB issued €489 billion in emergency loans to banks that helped avoid a "major, major credit crunch" in the words of ECB President Mario Draghi. A year later, similar loans exceeding €500 billion were issued.

13.44. The de Larosière Report recommendations were enacted in 2014. Under the new rules, national authorities retain primary responsibility for supervising individual financial institutions, but important new initiatives covered macrofinancial risks and regulation. It is a two-pillar regulatory system, with a microprudential pillar covering individual institutions (largely administered by national authorities), and a more centralized macroprudential supervisory system that monitors the financial system as a whole.

13.45. The ECB was granted power to supervise banks operating in the union and to directly bail out banks in trouble. Over 100 large banks came under direct ECB supervision; smaller banks remained supervised by national authorities with the ECB as the overarching regulator. The increased ECB role was balanced by a new system of oversight by the European Parliament.

13.46. Elements of the microprudential supervision pillar included;

An European System of Financial Supervision (ESFS) with supranational authority to strengthen oversight of all major cross-border EU financial firms.

Three new independent supranational regulators affiliated with the ESFS covering banking and finance, securities markets, and insurance.

A number of specific regulatory changes including broader coverage of financial institutions, Basel II-related changes to reduce pro-cyclicality, and controls over rating agencies.

Numerous improvements in technical oversight and risk management including improved modeling and risk measurement methodologies to better cover asset quality and credit risk, maturity risk, and liquidity risk; new rules covering mark-to-market valuation and valuation of illiquid assets; better transparency and rules for off-balance-sheet vehicles; proposals for centralized clearing systems for securitizations and derivatives, requiring issuers of securitizations to hold significant exposures; strengthen the definition of "own funds"; and increase minimum required capital including introduction of counter-cyclical "dynamic provisioning".[439]

13.47. Elements of the macroprudential pillar included;

The European Systemic Risk Board to identify risks and provide macrofinancial oversight. The ESRB would be governed broadly, including the European Commission, the ECB, the EU Central Bank Governors, and the heads of European Banking, Securities, and Insurance Regulators. Thus, it was intended to involve the key regulatory and financial policy actors and provide them with a current assessment of systemic threats and provide policy recommendations.

Expand the IMF role to operate early warning systems (EWS), have greater power to implement its recommendations, and conduct compulsory FSAPs. The de Larosière Report recommended that the IMF develop an "international risk map" that will be a very large data base of micro- and

[439] Dynamic provisioning is designed to cover credit risks over the full economic cycle. Reserves are built up during the expansion phase of the cycle when loss experience is low, but risks might be building in the system.

macroprudential risks to the global financial system, but also recommended that the EU create a risk map if the IMF does not.

Expand the Financial Stability Board and continue its roles to identify risks and gaps in the global regulatory system and push for convergence in international financial regulation.

European Systematic Risk Board (ESRB)

13.48. The European Council approved an ESRB that will collect and analyze information needed to identify and assess systemic risks, issue warnings about risks, give recommendations, monitor national follow-ups to its recommendations, and liaise with the IMF, FSB, and authorities in other countries. Findings and recommendations of the Board can be made public.

13.49. The Board has a major role in collecting information to assess risks. It is tasked to "define, have access to and/or collect as appropriate, and analyze all information relevant for identifying, monitoring, and assessing potential threats and risks to financial stability in the EU that arise from macro-economic developments and developments within the financial system as a whole." (Council, 2009 p. 2)

13.50. The Board makes recommendations based on its analysis of risk, and informs the Council if it feels country responses are inadequate. The Council represents the highest level of authority within the EU and thus the intention is to devise a system that guarantees that problems get serious attention and appropriate responses are made.

13.51. The ECB is tasked to provide administrative, logistical, analytical, and statistical support. It can draw advice from NCBs and national supervisors. With this, the *ECB clearly transcends its role as the central bank for a currency union.*

13.52. The Board is expected to report regularly to the Council and the European Parliament.

13.53. An interesting feature of the Board is that it does not have a separate legal personality and should undertake duties without prejudice to duties of other existing bodies.

European System of Financial Supervisors (ESFS) – European Supervisory Authorities (ESA)

13.54. In order to strengthen supervision throughout the financial system, the Council transformed its committees of supervisors into the "European Supervisory Authorities" which have legal personality under EU law.[440] Three separate authorities cover banking and other financial institutions, securities, and insurance. National supervisors retain responsibility for supervision of individual institutions, but the supervisor could deal directly with troubled banks during emergencies with approval of EU finance ministers. (BBC 2010). Duties of the ESFS include;

Ensure that harmonized supervisory rules are applied at the national level

Issue guidelines on supervisory practices

Coordinate analysis of risks to financial institutions and groups

Conduct peer group analyses

Participate in deliberations of supervisory colleges to foster consistency

Develop common training

Interact with international authorities

Collect micro-prudential information in a central European database.

[440] For example, the European Banking Authority adopted binding technical standards and carries out regular bank stress tests.

Ensure application of EU rules, with the power to require national authorities to take specific actions.

Serve as primary supervisor for pan-European institutions, such as credit rating agencies and central counterparty clearing houses.

Coordinate responses to crises.

The above activities, however, should not impinge on the fiscal responsibilities of the EU countries.

13.55. The new system includes a relatively straight-forward model of macroprudential oversight. (Wredenborg 2010) It consists of three steps – identification of key types of risks, monitoring of indicators of potential systemic risk, and identification of channels of contagion.

Potential sources of systemic risk – Analysis of both endogenous sources of risk (weakness in financial institutions, market volatility, structural weakness in financial infrastructure, etc.) and exogenous shocks (macroeconomic imbalances, unexpected shocks, volatility, etc.)

Monitoring of indicators – The ECB identified three types of tools to monitor the condition of the financial sector;

A set of financial stability indicators that will be continuously compiled and reviewed. The ECB has a set of indicators similar to the IMF's FSIs, that can be supplemented by short-term market indicators to monitor day-to-day stability or stress in financial markets.

A comprehensive framework to provide early warning signals, including measuring the likelihood of risks materialising.

Market intelligence drawn from continuous monitoring of financial markets and contact with financial market participants.

Assessment of contagion channels, the potential severity of risks identified, and the system's ability to absorb shocks. Tools include contagion models and macroeconomic stress testing.

13.56. Future unions will need to set up a framework for macroprudential analysis. The EMU began setting up this framework late, but the activities and tools described above now being used by the ECB might provide useful guidance for new unions.

Text box: Hybrid prudential-monetary policy

The financial crisis resulted in fundamental rethinking about central banking policy and financial system soundness and risk. By Spring 2010, once the greatest dangers of the financial crisis had passed, central banks and international regulators began to consider what lessons could be drawn from the crisis and what changes should be made to central bank policy and financial regulatory frameworks.

In effect, central banking experienced a paradigm change in which macroprudential policy became nearly coequal with monetary policy. The period prior to the crisis had been termed the "Great Moderation", in which inflation targeting policies had contributed to fairly widespread growth, low inflation, and sustainable debt. However, financial sector risks had built up with excessive leverage and insufficient concern about liquidity threats to the financial system. The resulting disruptions to the financial system caused massive economic costs, impaired the ability to carry out monetary policy, and ended the belief that a focus on interest rates as a single monetary policy variable is sufficient to engender financial sector stability.

New prudential policies are coming into place. For example, a new Basel bank supervisory regime, under the general rubric of "Basel III", was introduced. The new regime is viewed as more cautious and in effect turns back the clock to require simpler and more ample capital and liquidity buffers. Accurate and relevant dissemination of financial information is part of the new regulatory mix. A number of new or modified prudential buffers and indicators were introduced that include a new leverage indicator, dynamic provisioning, additional capital to the regulatory capital ratio, and liquidity requirements. Systemically important institutions were singled out for special attention because they could be large enough to affect overall financial markets and monetary policy.

Such regulatory changes, and more, are intended to be included in a new type of policy regime in which interest rate policy actions are supplemented by a potentially wide range of macroprudential tools designed to tackle specific financial sector conditions. This is a multi-policy environment in which macroprudential policy comes to the fore. Monetary policy can no longer be premised on existence of a smoothly operating financial system; rather, monitoring of the financial system and intervention in a variety of ways might be needed to bolster the effectiveness of monetary policy. Conversely, monetary policy actions can affect financial stability.

If hybrid macroprudential-monetary policy regimes become widely accepted, future unions will be expected to undertake aggressive steps to monitor and preserve financial sector stability in order to support their monetary policy regime.

D. Lessons from crises for future unions

13.57. The crisis severely tested the European supervisory system and showed that the system devised under the Maastricht Treaty was not adequate to deal with the crisis. The creation of the EMU resulted in a high degree of integration between markets and cross-border banking, but supervision remained a national responsibility. Individual national supervisors had limited access to information about operations and risks of financial institutions throughout the union and had limited powers to affect institutions' activities in other countries. Lack of common policies, such as coverage under deposit insurance, created problems. Moreover, individual countries retained control over fiscal actions related to the crisis such as paying deposit insurance, or recapitalizing the banking system. And policy reactions to the crisis were uncoordinated or incompletely coordinated.

13.58. The forced introduction in Europe of new institutions and policies to handle the crisis indicates that future unions must design their unions to be capable of handling similar problems. New powers will be needed at the union level to deal with common problems, gather information and assess risk, standardize rules throughout the union, and coordinate policy responses. The union also might take on duties interfacing with international organizations and standards setters. And there might be fiscal roles for the union or coordination of burden-sharing.

13.59. Organizationally, the new EU model might appeal to new unions. Other models might also work, but in some manner macroprudential work must be taken on board.

13.60. The changes in the EU can provide some guidance, and the degree of financial stability witnessed thus far during the Covid crisis gives some confidence that the new supervisory regime has functioned well. The lesson appears to be that new unions need a much broader range of microprudential and macroprudential supervisory functions than attempted by the EMU at its start. But with limited resources in many potential union countries, the process will be challenging.

13.61. Planning for the supervisory systems needs to begin early in the process – at least four steps seem needed;

Enhanced information sharing between central banks and supervisors so they understand each other's perspectives and can act appropriately.

Monitoring and adopting evolving international standards and best practices in supervision and financial accounting, which can include union-level and key country participation in deliberations.

Launching a macroprudential program to assess systemic soundness and risk and crisis resolution options.

Recognizing that monetary policy and macroprudential oversight are now fundamentally intertwined and incorporating this into the union policy stance, institutions, and governance arrangements.

13.62. In the new environment, unpleasant tradeoffs might be faced. Issues of emergency liquidity, LOLR, crisis resolution, and potential recapitalization cannot be ignored. Such actions can stabilize markets and avoid large economic disruptions, but might destabilize monetary policy and could be very costly – potentially running up to several percent of GDP. Actions could involve multiple union countries or authorities outside the union. The problems might be external in origin, but demand a local response to avoid damage within the union. The balance sheets of the union central bank and NCBs could be seriously affected and national treasuries might be called on. Assets of sovereign wealth funds, where they exist, might be reprogrammed to support the domestic financial system. Contingent international lines of credit might be needed. These are actions that authorities would like to avoid and undertake only when absolutely necessary.

13.63. Resolution of such crisis situations in a multi-state union can be particularly challenging because responsibility might be hard to assess, allocation of costs is uncertain, and individual states might need to cover common problems. The resistance of the public in Germany to aid Greece during its crisis is a salient example. The union-level authorities will need to coordinate and facilitate working out solutions under challenging circumstances. The union could also take the lead in coordination with the IMF or other providers of external assistance. These are challenging tasks that require that union authorities have high degrees of professionalism, political skill, independence, and trust with member country authorities.

Setting up an union supervisory system

13.64. This section covers the set up of supervisory systems with macroprudential oversight. There is much that new unions can draw on – the BCBS in particular has extensively discussed international best practices. Also, the Financial Stability Institute offers extensive training programs that can benefit unions and their member countries.

Centralized vs. national supervision

13.65. A lesson of the financial crisis is that supervision in future unions will probably be more centralized than under Maastricht, but there can be many decisions on how to implement specific arrangements. For example, there are extensive established rules on home country versus host country supervision that might be adjusted to reflect the role of a regional supervisor, including the possibility of changes in fiscal support to resolve bank crises. How much responsibility should be taken on at the center? Are there dangers of remoteness and overconcentration of supervisory activities?

13.66. Two types of expertise are needed that create a tension between central and national control. National supervisors are commonly in daily contact with banks and understand the local markets and the bank problems and strengths and are able to provide quick corrective advice – tasks probably done effectively through local supervision. On the other hand, supervisory expertise is hard to obtain, especially as more complex rules are introduced. In some regions, relatively few resources might be available and thus should be centrally located at the union to be available for all member countries.

13.67. Responsibility for costs is an issue. Are countries, regions, or financial industries expected to finance the supervisory infrastructure? Will resources come through the central bank, or is there a parallel supervisory system to support. Who pays for emergency assistance?

13.68. In terms of standards to apply, the trend toward application of common global standards can be expected to continue, to be implemented in all union member countries, which results in greater harmonization of practice. The number of areas where local supervisory discretion is permitted is shrinking, and regional authorities might further restrict national discretion and thus promote greater harmonization.

13.69. Language is an issue in some regions. Documents need to be translated and an ability to verbally communicate complex supervisory concepts and rules is also needed. National supervisors are likely to have advantages in this regard, but cross-checking will be needed to ensure that translations are telling the same story.

13.70. Common clearing and payments systems in the union will also promote harmonized national supervisory practice.

13.71. Regions might have common judicial arrangements, at least at the appeals level, which also supports more harmonized national supervisory practice.

Supervisory colleges

13.72. One issue to address is supervision of cross-border financial institutions. The general international standard is that the supervisor of the country where a financial institution is organized ('home country') has primary responsibility to supervise the world operations of the institution. The 'host countries' can supervise activities in their own countries, but they have more limited information and no power to affect the banks operations in other countries. In order to overcome this asymmetry, "colleges of supervisors" are set up among interested supervisors to handle oversight of individual international banks by exchanging information on home and host country policies and conditions. This helps construct a better picture of the full range of vulnerabilities and soundness of the global enterprise. When specific questions arise they can be channeled through the college.

13.73. The theory is good, but in practice the colleges have often proved less effective than hoped. Meetings become routine and staff assigned might not have the necessary rank or influence. One conclusion of reviews of problems associated with the global financial crisis is that the colleges for the major international banks had not been as effective as necessary – it was commonly held that the college system in Europe did not function well – and that they should be strengthened.

Institutional arrangements

13.74. In designing supervisory systems for new unions, different institutional strategies are possible. Each seems to have pros and cons and thus a decision point for each union will be to decide which arrangement fits each union's needs and situation.

13.75. Topical supervisors – This typically means that each of the three major segments of the financial system – banking, securities markets, and insurance – has its own supervisor.[441] This is the system chosen by the EMU in response to the crisis, perhaps because it most closely reflected the model used by many of the EU countries for their systems. It also reflects the setup of the international regulatory agencies (BCBS, IOSCO, IAIS). Some further specialization might be useful, such as supervision of international banking or Islamic institutions. However, the topical approach can face difficulties handling institutions following an universal banking model (as is common in Europe) in which financial institutions are free to engage in all forms of financial activity.

13.76. Supervision by function – Supervisors could specialize in specific activities. For example, one supervisor could have responsibility for prudential

[441] Systems with more than three supervisors are also possible. The US, for example, has separate supervisors for banks, securities, commodity futures, and deposit insurance, and supervision of insurance is handled at the state level. In other countries, different government levels might have their own supervisory functions, such as supervision by German "Landesbanks". This might also reflect that financial accounting constitutes a separate form of regulatory activity with its own international authority; the International Financial Accounting Board is the overarching authority, supervision of Islamic Financial Institutions is a special case where standards follow those of conventional institutions where relevant but can differ to cover some unique Islamic financial practices. Supervision of microfinance institutions might be separate. Supervision of e-money and crypto institutions might have technical reasons for separate supervision.

oversight to ensure that individual financial institutions or markets are sound; another could be responsible for supervising the behavior of institutions and markets, such as an agency monitoring consumer lending by banks. This system avoids potential compromises between policies to ensure soundness and policies to regulate market behavior.

13.77. Financial supervisory authorities (FSA) – In this increasingly common approach, a single supervisor is responsible for oversight of all financial market activities in recognition of the fungibility of financial activity and universal banking. In small or lower income regions, this might be a practical necessity because of limited resources available. This system also potentially avoids gaps in supervision for financial institutions that cover multiple financial subsectors.

13.78. Supervisory wing of the central bank – In some smaller countries, the central bank is the only institution that can feasibly handle banking supervision. Typically, it is done by a separate wing or section because of the complexity of supervisory functions and to avoid conflicts of interest in allowing prudential concerns to affect monetary policy.

13.79. The choices are not clear cut for new unions. Supervision by topic reflects the structure of the international standards setters, allows expertise to be built in each set of complex rules, and might correspond to institutional arrangements in the country. Changing an existing multipart structure could be politically difficult. Certainly, new unions will need to develop expertise and authority in all areas. On the other hand, limited resources in new unions might force a single institution to cover all areas and might be best to deal with cross-sector activities of institutions. The supervision of large complex institutions needs be done on a comprehensive basis.

Text box: Financial supervisory trilemma

In the midst of the financial crisis, ECB Board member Lorenzo Bini Smaghi (2009b) discussed supervisory challenges in a currency union. He noted that the EU system revolves around the responsibility of home country supervisors having primacy in supervision because their national authorities pay for resolving problems at their banks. However, the creation of the union and the crisis challenges undermined the validity of this system.

Financial integration has extended to the point that a bank failure in any country can affect other countries. This occurs by weakening affiliates of the troubled bank in other countries, but also through contagious disruption in cross-border money market financing.

Bini Smaghi felt that EU harmonization efforts under the Lamfalussy framework had not created a level playing field and supervisory rules and practices had not converged enough.

Despite the push to create a single financial market, national competition continued which had encouraged regulatory competition. National banks might get favorable treatment in order to make national markets more attractive to financial institutions. Weak links could exist that might introduce problems that can spread through the system.

He posited a supervisory trilemma: financial integration, national supervisory autonomy, and financial stability cannot coexist. Greater integration implies a common set of rules, a "Single rulebook", that should supersede national discretion. It must be matched with political and juridical systems to resolve conflicts in treatment of cross-border institutions. An important implication is that resolution costs can affect host countries, not just the home country of the troubled institution.

Bini-Smaghi's analysis is important for future unions because it makes clear that national differences persisted despite strong efforts in Europe to integrate markets and their oversight. Also, region-wide problems can result from such national differences operating in a partially integrated environment.

Supervisory life-cycle

13.80. Supervision involves three major stages in the life cycle of financial institutions – licensing to permit institutions to operate in the economy, supervising on-going activities to promote soundness of the institutions and protection of the public and the financial system, and handling the demise or closure of institutions. International standards (Basel Standards, IOSCO Objectives and Principles of Securities

Regulation, and IAIS Insurance Core Principles) deal with each of these of these phases. Unions will be judged internationally by the quality of supervision in building and supporting the integrity of their financial systems, including how effectively they adopt international standards and best practices. These qualities also support effective operation of union monetary policy and provide opportunities for economic growth and financial integration.

13.81. Tackling these tasks should not wait for start-up of the union. Substantial effort is required to build supervisory infrastructure and introduce standards. The work should begin well before the union starts and many elements put in place as soon as feasible. Introduction of international standards builds greater comparability in practice between member countries, but a key is whether regional authorities are in place to contribute, promote training and build capacity in all countries, encourage additional harmonization, and facilitate building ancillary juridical and legal arrangements.

Deposit insurance

13.82. Deposit insurance is part of the process of dealing with insolvent banks. Deposit insurance provides protection to depositors in the event that a bank fails. Insurance prevents depositors from losing their money, but also helps prevent runs on banks when fearful depositors suddenly withdraw their funds thus causing the bank to fail. Since 1994, the EU Deposit Guarantee Directive (DGD)[442] required member states to have minimum coverage of €20,000 deposit insurance. Typically, banks make insurance premium payments to the government (often a specialized agency) equal to a certain percentage of deposits, which creates a pool of funds to pay depositors if the bank fails. Because the insurer has funds at risk, it inspects banks to ensure that they act to avoid failure and losses for depositors.

13.83. In a broad sense, the calculus is that owners/investors in a bank should face losses if the bank fails, but depositors that have innocently put money into the bank believing it is secure and have also implicitly paid an insurance premium in the form of lower interest returns deserve protection. Thus, there is a distinction, which can in theory be sharply drawn, between insured guaranteed deposits, and other funds placed in the bank that are subject to loss if the bank fails.

13.84. In Europe prior to the crisis, only the first €20,000 was guaranteed – any deposits over that amount must be sought by filing a claim during the bankruptcy proceedings, and only partial returns can be expected on those funds. Among reasons for such limits were to;

[442] The 1997 Investor Compensation Directive (ICD) complemented the DGD by establishing a right of compensation for customers to cover losses due to default of licensed investment firms and insurance companies. Customers were entitled to compensation equal to the lesser of €20,000 or 90 percent of the losses due to default. For insurance, compensation covered the greater of paid-in premiums or loss on a claim, up to the limits. Only private investors or small firms were protected.

All types of investment firms (investment firms, stock exchange firms, insurance firms and brokers, etc.) were required to participate in investor compensation schemes. The scheme also covered products of firms run through other intermediaries, who must contribute to an insurance-like fund. A number of EU countries created specialist companies to receive contributions and set up arrangements to quickly compensate clients after a default.

The ICD was designed to protect innocent customers from loss, similar to deposit insurance, but with less emphasis on mitigating systemic risk. The ICD acted to prevent customers from mistakenly purchasing uninsured instruments offered by banks rather than making insured deposits, and also covers bank-like institutions not in the deposit-insurance scheme. This latter provision was important because nonbank institutions were increasingly offering near banking services. The ICD also covered licensed sellers of financial products to the public, recognizing that granting a license is often taken by the public as a guarantee that the firm is trustworthy to hold funds and has capital as a cushion against risks.

Encourage depositors to be prudent about where they place their funds, as a form of market discipline on banks to avoid risky behavior

Limit potential liability to the guarantee fund, and

Lower the cost of insurance premiums.

13.85. The GFC changed the situation in 2008 when withdrawals from Irish banks forced the government to increase deposit insurance to €100,000 per depository per institution. This action put severe pressure on other deposit insurance schemes and increased the danger of runs on banks in other member countries. In March 2009, the Deposit Guarantee Schemes Directive (DGSD) was enacted to bring about more common practices in the EU. Maximum insurance rose to €100,000, depositors were guaranteed more rapid access to funds, national deposit insurance schemes were required to cooperate, and failure to cover deposits was linked to quick action to determine if an institution is in default.

Text box: The Irish deposit insurance crisis[443]

The GFC came to a head in September 2008 as crises hit financial systems in multiple countries (U.S., Germany, Iceland, Ireland, Greece, and more). A crisis in the Irish deposit insurance system was especially dramatic; it partly reflected large prior inflows into Ireland after creation of the EMU with opening of cross-border financial markets and simultaneous reduction in apparent country risk, and in turn demonstrated that the new environment demanded regional solutions in supervision and willingness of fiscal authorities to support financial systems.

Irish banks entered the period relatively exposed, with loans (especially in real estate) well in excess of their deposit base and thus banks were heavily reliant on short-term market funding. Although authorities were already concerned about market stresses and were investigating options, the crisis rapidly developed and overwhelmed the banking system. After Lehmann Brothers failed, withdrawals began from Anglo Irish Bank and other Irish banks.

Rapid withdrawals caused Anglo Bank to breach its liquidity requirements and forced it to request liquidity assistance from its regulator by pledging some of its loans as collateral for a central bank loan. Many options were considered, but finally to calm markets the deposit insurance limit was raised from €20,000 to €100,000 and the government announced it would "protect the whole financial system, secure its stability and ensure that all deposits in Irish financial institutions are safe", thus implicitly guaranteeing deposits beyond the limits of the deposit insurance system.

Later, concerns were raised that the central bank's reserves were insufficient to cover substantial losses, and the central bank was reportedly hesitant to provide assistance to avoid damaging the reputations of individual banks. In this situation, a more general government guarantee appeared appropriate, but concerns were also raised that the guarantee would damage the country's credit rating and shelter weaker banks and thus benefit stock holders who in principle should bear losses.

As conditions worsened, nationalization of one or more banks was considered. Eventually, to avoid immediate collapse, a large government guarantee was extended over deposits. Subordinated deposits – which would not normally be covered – were included to avoid rapid withdrawal of funds that had been attracted into Ireland by unusually high interest rates offered by the troubled banks.

The government extended loans and very large lines of credit to several banks and took equity positions in some, which would convert to majority ownership if the banks defaulted. The guarantee calmed markets and funding eventually returned to the system. Later, Ireland received regional and international assistance from the EU and IMF.

[443] This box benefits from a day-by-day description of the developing crisis by Simion Carswell (2010).

An asset management company was set up to exchange bad bank loans at a 30% discount for government securities that could be resold in markets to help reliquefy the banks' balance sheets. The company was set up as a SPV majority owned by the public – a situation that created many accounting and statistical issues, including how to value the "long-term economic value" of its assets, whether it was a financial institution or part of government, and whether its obligations were part of national government debt. Ultimately, it was ruled to be governmental.

This action made Ireland the first country during the crisis to put a blanket guarantee over the financial system, which imposed a massive burden on the public - banking system bailouts totaled 45 percent of GDP. (IMF 2021)

The Irish deposit insurance crisis contributed importantly to reworking the Maastricht supervisory framework; hybrid monetary-supervisory action became a norm, government support in financial crises became an expectation, the need for forward-looking oversight and crisis preparations became recognized, the EU raised its deposit insurance coverage, and new rules abounded. The Maastricht boundaries separating the monetary, supervisory, and fiscal spheres were decisively overridden.

Text box: Financial failure and moral hazard

The deposit insurance concept contrasts to a model in which authorities focus on keeping the whole bank in business. The European Shadow Financial Regulatory Committee has said that in Europe deposit insurance has been little used because the focus has been on trying to prevent failure of the bank itself. If banks are routinely kept in business, "moral hazard" can become an issue. In the concept of moral hazard, depositors and the bank management and owners come to believe that there is an implicit guarantee from the government that the bank will not be permitted to fail, and thus depositors might imprudently put their money in weak institutions which might ultimately increase the possibility of failure. (CEPS 2007)

This issue also arose in the context of the results of stress tests in 2010 on about 90 major European banks comprising about two-thirds of total European bank assets. The tests were designed to bolster the resilience of the European financial system by demonstrating that banks have sufficient strength to survive in the face of plausible threats. Banks failing the stress tests would need to find additional capital or face closure. Prior to announcing results, statements were made that some banks failing tests could be recapitalized by public funds, including possibly using the new European Financial Stability Facility in addition to national funds and EU funds. Several weeks prior to the announcement of the results, a group of European finance ministers indicated that they would take action to support the banks if needed, and were willing to put pressure on one recalcitrant country. (Agence France Presse 2010.)

The attitude regarding stress tests indicated that the European governments were prepared to actively provide support to stave off possible instability under crisis situations. This contradicted the bias toward nonintervention promoted during the pre-crisis period. Ultimately, these situations involve a weighting of advantages of taking actions (for example to avoid another Lehmann Brothers crisis response) against disadvantages of moral hazard. The choice is not easy, but clearly options could change depending on the degree of stability in the system.

13.86. The above issues take on a somewhat different tone in the currency union context. In an union, increased cross-border competition could foster tighter margins and greater odds of bankruptcies. Different insurance premiums in different union countries, or different coverage, could create distortions and shifts in activity between countries. Also, different standards for closing institutions could affect the extent to which the insurance fund is used. The ease of making cross-border transactions within an union will tend to make such effects more likely or larger; Conversely, the application of minimum standards will tend to reduce such possible distortions. However, it can be difficult to define a standard that provides effectively similar relief in countries with very different income levels or depositing practices – such as the case in the EU after the admission of Eastern European countries. A maximum limit suitable in higher income countries might effectively cover nearly all deposits in a lower income country, thus removing any market discipline aspects of the deposit insurance.

13.87. Deposit insurance typically does not provide coverage above a specified amount, subordinated debts, and often excludes wholesale deposits, deposits by financial institutions, securities, and liabilities to miscellaneous creditors such as trade credits. Such limits can cap the size of losses if a bank becomes insolvent, and also help to inculcate market discipline because larger, more sophisticated investors presumably will place their funds only in institutions they feel to be sound, providing that there is no implicit guarantee that the government would cover all debts.

13.88. In future unions, there will have to be explicit consideration of dealing with weak banks, closing insolvent banks, and operating deposit insurance. As banks become weaker there is a strong case to be made for "prompt corrective action", in which supervisors actively intervene with weak banks before they become insolvent. This can pull weaker banks out of difficulty, thus saving the public from losses if deposit insurance is limited, save the insurance fund from losses, and prevent general economic distress from the failed bank.

E. Crisis management and Lender of Last Resort (LOLR)

13.89. The GFC led to fundamental reconsiderations of the adequacy of the decentralized supervisory framework in Europe. A member of the Governing Council of the ECB (Orphanides, 2009) stated that the model for separating supervision from the central banks was inadequate to deal with the crisis. The British system in which regulation is shared between the Bank of England, the Financial Services Authority, and the Treasury was cited as a case where responses to the crisis could not be coordinated and led to the collapse of Northern Rock. He said that there were serious gaps and that "The financial crisis has shown that countries whose central banks had immediate access, and detailed knowledge of the supervisory framework of the entire banking sector, both on a macro-economic and on a micro-economic level, were better placed to successfully deal with the consequences of the crisis." He also said that supervision must be totally independent and free of political influences, and that supervisors had been affected by political influences and interference which made the crisis worse.

13.90. The complexity of crisis management reflects the reality that each financial crisis is unique, stemming from different causes, affecting different market segments, and requiring diverse solutions. It also reflects concerns about moral hazard, the risk that private financial institutions will engage in riskier behavior if they believe that there will be official rescues. Countries might have different tools available and major differences can exist in the size of fiscal resources available for crisis resolution. Also, political ideologies and pressures differ between countries.

13.91. Such complexity means that there are no simple off-the-rack solutions or strategies in crises. It might be that the best case is for union members to have available attributes that will help find innovative solutions when needed. This includes a good statistical framework, effective communications, a venue for consultation at the union and national levels, and a battery of legal powers so that action can be quickly initiated. To these attributes, access to adequate liquid resources is helpful – either within countries, or through regional agreements, international bank lines, international swap lines, or IMF resources.

F. Financial Soundness Assessment Program (FSAP)

13.92. The FSAP is a joint IMF/World Bank program to undertake detailed assessments of financial market strengths and risks. Teams of specialists visit the country, make comprehensive reviews of areas of potential risk, conduct financial system stress tests, and prepare detailed recommendations. The assessments also evaluate countries' adherence to international financial standards and best practices, such as the Basel Core Principles for Bank Supervision. A FSAP assessment has a "shelf life" of about four to five years until conditions are considered sufficiently changed that a reassessment is needed. At that point, an "update" is undertaken, which tends to be more focused than the original assessment.

13.93. The program is considered a major success in helping countries understand where they stand in creating a strong financial system, identifying areas for action, and evaluating adherence to international standards. Countries obtain detailed recommendations to guide their work in buttressing financial soundness, and the comprehensive information developed is useful for financial markets to assess national financial conditions. Moreover, the pressure from international financial organizations and the public information available for the FSAP can cause countries to undertake reforms they otherwise might have neglected.

13.94. Given the benefits of the FSAP in strengthening markets and providing transparency on national market conditions and infrastructure, it is recommended that all union countries undertake FSAPs at least three years prior to the start of the union. Early assessments will allow countries to make improvements prior to start-up, help harmonize practices between member countries, and ensure more effective operation of the financial system, which in turn supports better implementation of monetary policy. It would also be appropriate to have a FSAP assessment for union level programs and institutions to focus on how regional soundness can be supported. A review early in the process benefits from expert oversight and provides time to make modifications.

G. Financial Soundness Indicators (FSIs)

13.95. Indicators of the soundness of financial systems are now considered critically important to maintain sound financial systems that can support economic growth and help effective implementation of monetary policy. Shortly after the Asian Crisis in 1997–98, the international community, led by the IMF, began a program to compile FSIs of the strengths and vulnerabilities of countries' financial sectors. The crisis revealed major gaps in statistical coverage of countries' financial sectors that permitted serious vulnerabilities to remain undetected. National authorities in central banks or financial supervisory offices lacked information to act to prevent crises from happening or at least ameliorate their effects.

13.96. In response, the IMF launched an initiative that included FSIs to improve coverage of potential financial vulnerabilities.[444] FSIs are aggregate measures of the current financial health and soundness of financial institutions and their corporate and household counterparties. The ECB strongly agreed on the importance of this work and made important contributions to the methodologies for FSIs. The ECB prepared similar indicators for its membership more attuned to the institutions and policy goals in Europe.

13.97. The IFSB has also prepared FSIs for Islamic Financial Institutions, called Prudential and Structural Indicators for Islamic Financial Institutions (PSIFIs). They closely parallel the conventional FSIs, but diverge as needed to reflect unique features of Islamic finance. As of mid-2021, 24 countries (including the United Kingdom) compiled PSIFIs.

13.98. An important step in the development of FSIs was publication in 2006 by the IMF of the *Compilation Guide: Financial Soundness* Indicators and a revision in 2019.[445] that described indicators and methodologies for their compilation. The IFSB simultaneously published a revision of their *Compilation Guide: Prudential and Structural Indicators for Islamic Financial Institutions (PSIFIs).*

13.99. The ECB, all Euroarea countries, and other EU countries have actively supported compilation of FSIs. The ECCU also actively participated in the developmental work on FSIs to help support their work to bolster financial sector stability in their union. In

[444] *Chapter 12 – Statistics* also discusses FSIs.

[445] The *Guide* is available in English, Arabic, Chinese, French, Russian, and Spanish. Thus, descriptions of the rationale for indicators and their methodology are accessible to audiences in most of the possible future unions.

early 2022, only half of the six GCC countries compile FSIs, but all compile PSIFIs.

13.100. Work on FSIs continues to evolve due to the introduction of new regulatory standards and to address problems identified during the financial crisis. New "Basel III" supervisory standards are reflected in a number of new FSIs, as published in the 2019 IMF and IFSB Compilation Guides. New emphasis is placed on liquidity measures, which was an area in which performance in the crisis was judged to have been particularly poor. Greater emphasis is also given to monitoring of systemically important financial institutions. All these matters will need to be on the plate of the new unions.

13.101. Given international agreement on the need for aggregate indicators of financial sector soundness, the intimate interactions between financial soundness and monetary policy implementation, and also urgent needs to strengthen macroprudential information during the current financial market turmoil, it is strongly recommended that planned unions begin building a macroprudential analysis system, including compilation of FSIs (and PSIFIs in at least 5 different potential union regions). Indeed, building a regional program involving collaboration between central banks, supervisors, and other officials to collect information on financial soundness or vulnerabilities and addressing how to support stability is too important to await the formal start of union-building programs. Work to strengthen macroprudential supervision should not wait for the union start-up, and cooperative work between countries to support stability might help build institutional relationships that can later contribute to building unions.

H. Supervision of E-Money

13.102. Unions will face new types of challenges in supervising e-money institutions and operations. E-money firms have extensive telecommunications activities that are outside traditional supervisory scope, can be highly technical, and are not covered by existing regulatory frameworks. The process is compounded because e-money could become a very important source of financial services for large portions of the population, especially low-income populations and segments without ready access to traditional financial intermediaries. E-money systems can have high operational risks and an operational failure could have devastating effects on large populations and result in severe economic disruption.

13.103. Thus, the task for supervisors is to provide extraordinary supervisory oversight in the face of rapid innovation, technical complexity, and absence of general standards and best practices. Experience in these areas is quite limited globally and thus unions will need to collaborate closely with each other and with international initiatives in order to develop and maintain an adequate supervisory framework.

13.104. The advent of CBDCs as an official form of e-money system that raises similar complex issues. The evolution of regulatory and supervisory institutions over CBDCs, as described more in Chapter 9D, bears close scrutiny.

Timeline

Many supervisory activities can begin independently of the start-up of the currency union. Early implementation is encouraged.

Preparatory period	Decision on degree of centralization of supervision of financial institutions, financial markets, and insurance Decisions on status of supervisory bodies in central bank or as independent entities
Early actions (four years prior)	Review gaps in implementation of Basel Pillar II (building the bank supervisory system) Review of plans for supervisory systems related to e-money and CBDCs. Review deposit insurance schemes Review schemes for closing financial institutions Review crisis resolution rules including cross-border
Three years prior	National improvements in Pillar II implementation Begin review of Basel III and elements that might be adopted Initiate preparation of FSIs and PSIFIs as needed
24 months prior	National legal implementation Agreement on rules for deposit insurance Agreement on rules crisis resolution Agreement on rules for closing financial institutions Publish FSIs and PSIFIs Draft standards and procedures for cross-border supervision and crisis resolution.
Final 12 months	National implementation of deposit insurance rules Set up information framework for supervision of cross-border institutions
Final 6 months	Union central bank set up Union supervisory body set up and legal framework in place
Union day	Monitor experiences
Union steady state	Continued strengthening of supervisory systems

Appendix: Common Principles for Cross-Border Financial Crisis Management

In response to the GFC, the EU introduced measures to enhance cooperation between countries in managing cross-border financial crises. In October 2007, the ECOFIN Council adopted "*Common Principles for Cross-Border Financial Crisis Management,* which lay out a clear, strong philosophy for crisis resolution;

> The objective of crisis management is to protect the stability of the financial system in all countries involved and in the EU as a whole and to minimize potential harmful economic impacts at the lowest overall collective cost. The objective is not to prevent bank failures.
>
> In principle, primacy will always be given in crises to private sector solutions which as far as possible build on the financial situation of a banking group as a whole. The management of an ailing institution will be held accountable, shareholders will not be bailed out and creditors and uninsured depositors should expect to face losses.
>
> The use of public money to resolve a crisis should never be taken for granted and only considered in order to remedy a serious disturbance in the economy and when overall social benefits are assessed to exceed the cost of recapitalization at public expense. The circumstances and the timing of a possible public intervention cannot be set in advance. Strict and uniform conditions shall be applied to any use of public money.
>
> Managing a cross-border crisis is a matter of common interest for all Member States affected. Where a bank group has significant cross-border activities in different Member States, authorities in these countries will carefully cooperate and prepare in normal times as much as possible for sharing a potential fiscal burden. If public resources are involved, direct budgetary net costs are shared among affected Member States on the basis of equitable and balanced criteria, which take into account the economic impact of the crisis in the countries affected and the framework of home and host countries' supervisory powers.
>
> Arrangements and tools for cross-border crisis management will be designed flexibly to allow for adapting to the specific features of a crisis, individual institutions, balance sheet items and markets. Cross-border arrangements will build on effective national arrangements and cooperation between authorities of different countries. Competent authorities in the Member States affected by a crisis should be in a position to promptly assess the systemic nature of the crisis and its cross-border implications based on common terminology and a common analytical framework.
>
> Arrangements for crisis management and crisis resolution will be consistent with the arrangements for supervision. This consistency particularly refers to the division of responsibilities between authorities and the coordinating role of home country supervisory authorities.
>
> Full participation in management and resolution of a crisis will be ensured at an early stage for those Member States that might be affected through individual institutions or infrastructures, taking into account that quick actions might be needed to solve the crisis.
>
> Policy actions in the context of crisis management will preserve a level playing field. Especially, any public intervention must comply with EU competition and state-aid rules.
>
> The global dimension will be taken into account in financial stability arrangements whenever necessary. Authorities from third countries will be involved where appropriate.

CHAPTER 14 – ACCOUNTING

Accounting - *What accounting standards and information will be needed to support the official work of the union and its members, and what will be the standards for public and private enterprises within the union?*

A. Introduction

14.1 This chapter looks at accounting requirements for currency unions. A currency union is a complex institution with very large financial assets and myriad internal transactions across the union, with the domestic banking systems, the rest of the domestic economies, and the rest of the world. Complex international financial transactions must be accounted for, large pools of financial assets must be managed, the union has current and contingent financial obligations exist, and diverse types and channels of income and expenditures occur. Accounting standards track the flow of income and holdings and common standards are needed across the union in order to ensure that each participant's obligations are fairly incurred and each receives an equitable share of income or other benefits. Effective accounting will support the governance structure of the union and promote smooth operations.

14.2 Compared to regular national accounting standards, additional accounting standards are needed in unions to cover assets and liabilities under union control and for operations of the union itself.

14.3 Because of diverse accounting standards among potential union member countries, complexity of union operations, and the lengthy process of implementing accounting standards, work to harmonize accounting standards among union members must begin early in the planning process. In the EMU, accounting was identified as one of the areas where long-term developmental work was needed, and therefore creating an accounting working group was one of the first steps in planning for the union.

14.4 This chapter describes the overall legal framework for accounting work in the Euroarea and the evolution of work on the accounts of the ECB and the Eurosystem as a whole. The balance sheets and income statements of the ECB and the Eurosystem are presented, with commentary on the specific items used to convey information about the operation of the union. Certain items that future unions will deal with, such as allocation of seigniorage, are discussed in some detail.

14.5 The chapter also covers the harmonized accounts for the banking system needed for the union, and information requirements for policy oversight, such as accounting needed for required reserves. Auditing issues conclude the chapter.

B. Accounting for the ECB and Eurosystem

14.6 Legal authority for the ECB and ESCB accounting frameworks is straight-forward. The Statute of the ESCB states that the fiscal year will correspond to the calendar year, the ECB will prepare annual accounts according to standards agreed by the Governing Council, a consolidated ESCB balance sheet will be prepared (covering NCB assets and liabilities that are part of the ESCB, but not other assets solely held by NCBs), and the Governing Council will establish the necessary rules including for reporting by NCBs.

14.7 As the work to create the union progressed, several major accounting steps occurred. In general, the major accounting changes were accompanied by publication of revisions of a *Guideline on the legal framework for accounting and financial reporting in the ESCB*.

> The EMI developed accounting rules for the ESCB, based on principles approved by the EMI Council in 1996. The rules established the basis for internal controls, external reporting, liquidity management, and meeting statistical needs. The framework was largely complete a half year prior to the creation of the ECB and a full year prior to the start of the monetary union. The ESCB thus had time to implement the standards and produce harmonized accounts to consolidate to the union level prior to the start of the union. In some cases, late decisions, such as on the distribution of monetary income, meant that some accounting rules continued to evolve.
>
> Creation of the ECB in 1998 resulted in (1) winding up of the EMI accounts and transfer of its assets to the ECB, (2) ending the ECU system, and (3) creating a new ESCB accounting system.
>
> The creation of joint operating arms of the union, specifically TARGET, called for means of

cooperative oversight. At first, the TARGET Audit Group was formed, comprised of the auditors of the ECB and NCBs for oversight of the TARGET payments system. Later, given the need for oversight of management of the ESCB's decentralized foreign reserves assets in 1998, an Internal Auditors Committee (IAC) was created to cover ESCB accounts and activities in general.

Transitional accounting rules, incorporated in a *Guideline* enacted in 1998, were needed to cover restatement of positions and transactions that occurred at the start of the union and during the period prior to the release of the physical euro.

> The *Guideline* separated realized and unrealized gains and losses of NCBs prior to the start of Stage 3 (because they were under national ownership) from gains and losses after the start of Stage 3, which might be part of joint ESCB income. Each NCB had to separate valuation gains and losses for instruments on their books on December 31, 1998 and retain them on its own books according to the rules that prevailed under Stage Two.
>
> Gains and losses from irrevocable fixing of bilateral exchange rates among Euroarea countries were treated as realized under national rules because foreign exchange risk disappeared when the euro was adopted.

14.8 A number of amendments made during the first years of the Euroarea were incorporated into a single *Guideline* issued in 2002. Some changes reflected accounting for the issuance of the new euro physical currency and the need to have harmonized accounts for all NCBs related to the issuance of the currency, intra-system claims and liabilities generated, and the allocation of income related to the currency. Each of these items reflected joint participation of the ECB and all NCBs, which required application of a fully harmonized accounting using common definitions, methods, and valuations.

> In 2006, a new *Guideline* was approved that reflected an important shift to using an economic approach for recording foreign exchange transactions and positions and for related accruals.
>
> In December 2009, the 2006 *Guideline* was amended (ECB; 2009a) to deal with three situations arising from the GFC; provide legal authority to purchase covered bonds issued to provide liquidity to the Euroarea financial systems, clarify that monetary policy liabilities incurred prior to joining the Eurosystem will be recorded under 'Other liabilities to Euroarea credit institutions denominated in euro', and specify treatment arising from defaults by Eurosystem counterparties.
>
> In 2010, an amended *Guideline* further set rules to standardize accounting for NCBs and clarified valuation rules for monetary policy instruments. Several additional *Guidelines* have been issued but seem to have little interest here.

Balance sheet and income accounts of the ECB

14.9 The 2000 ECB balance sheet is below, from the Annual Report. Key items relevant to the union finances are described. An important variable in the presentation is the distinction between "Euroarea residents" (counterparties within the monetary union) and "non-Euroarea residents", which comprises residents of all other countries including EUcountries outside the Euroarea.

14.10 The ECB accounts convey meaningful information, but they represent only a small part of the financial condition of the system.[446] The consolidated accounts of the Eurosystem (next section) provide the full picture of the financial strength of the union.

---

[446] "The balance sheet of the ECB by itself is effectively irrelevant and uninformative as to the financial strength of the Euroarea monetary authority." (Buiter 2010)

ECB Balance Sheet as at 31 December 2000[447]

Assets	**2000**	**1999**
1. Gold and gold receivables	**7,040,906,565**	**6,956,995,273**
2. Claims on non-Euroarea residents denominated in foreign currency		
Balances with banks and security investments, external loans and other external assets	**37,475,047,829**	**41,923,041,208**
3. Claims on Euroarea residents denominated in foreign currency	**3,824,522,571**	**2,595,090,860**
4. Claims on non-Euroarea residents denominated in euro		
Balances with banks, security Investments, and loans	**698,252,463**	**3,002,567,659**
5. Other claims on Euroarea credit institutions denominated in euro	**288,143,000**	**565,724,243**
6. Securities of Euroarea residents denominated in euro	**3,667,731,194**	**3,537,141,285**
7. Intra-Eurosystem claims		
Other claims within the Eurosystem (net)	**13,080,794,017**	**0**
8. Other assets	**1,263,554,616**	**902,479,111**
8.1 Tangible and intangible fixed assets	64,168,178	42,589,467
8.2 Other financial assets	81,758,341	76,083,163
8.3 Off-balance-sheet instrument revaluation differences	51,564,471	0
8.4 Accruals and deferred expenditures	862,316,142	777,032,332
8.5 Sundry items	3,747,484	6,774,149
9. Loss for the year	**0**	**247,281,223**
Total assets	***67,338,952,255***	***59,730,320,862***
Memorandum item		
Forward claims denominated in euro	**2,885,697,468**	

[447] The ECB balance sheet grew dramatically after the financial crisis began in 2008. At yearend 2007, total assets were €126 billion (a bit more than twice as large as in 1999) – by yearend 2008 assets more than tripled over 2007 to €384 billion. Heavy euro-denominated borrowing from creditors outside the Euroarea supported massive lending from the ECB to other members of the Eurosystem (i.e., an increase in "Intra-Eurosystem claims).

Liabilities	**2000**	**1999**
1. Liabilities to Euroarea credit institutions denominated in euro	**288,143,000**	**265,724,244**
2. Liabilities to other Euroarea residents denominated in euro	**1,080,000,000**	**1,080,000,000**
3. Liabilities to non-Euroarea residents denominated in euro	**3,421,112,123**	**301,656,911**
4. Liabilities to non-Euroarea residents denominated in foreign currency		
Deposits, balances and other liabilities	**4,803,381,255**	**4,708,950,946**
5. Intra-Eurosystem liabilities	**39,468,950,000**	**41,189,887,646**
5.1 Liabilities equivalent to the transfer of foreign reserves	39,468,950,000	3 9,468,950,000
5.2 Other liabilities within the Eurosystem (net)	0	1,720,937,646
6. Other liabilities	**1,678,027,878**	**1,274,608,403**
6.1 Accruals and deferred income	1,626,022,228	1,237,727,166
6.2 Sundry items	52,005,650	36,881,237
7. Provisions	**2,637,039,135**	**21,862,239**
8. Revaluation accounts	**7,972,626,864**	**6,860,539,710**
9. Capital and reserves	**3,999,550,250**	**4,027,090,763**
9.1 Capital	3,999,550,250	3,999,550,250
9.2 Reserves	0	27,540,513
10. Profit for the year	**1,990,121,750**	**0**
Total liabilities	***67,338,952,255***	***59,730,320,862***
Memorandum item		
Forward liabilities denominated in foreign currency	**2,885,697,468**	

14.11 Key items in the ECB balance sheet relevant to union finances are described below.

As noted above, the presentation distinguishes between "Euroarea residents" (counterparties within the Euroarea) and "non-Euroarea residents". The definition of "Euroarea residents" corresponds to the membership on each accounting date. The distinction is analytically interesting, but is also needed for compilation of consolidated accounts for the full Eurosystem that consolidate the accounts of the ECB and all NCBs.

Assets, lines 1 and 2, *Gold and gold receivables* and *Claims on non-Euroarea residents denominated in foreign currency* record as assets the holdings of gold and foreign currency-denominated assets transferred from the NCBs to the ECB when it was founded. These provide a fund for intervention by the ECB and for carrying out balance of payments-related transactions in foreign currencies.

Assets, line 5, *Claims on non-Euroarea residents* and line 6 *Other claims on Euroarea credit institutions* cover positions in the ECB's own funds, which are segregated from the other accounts. Segregation of the information means that changes in these accounts will not provide false signals about the monetary policy stance or its results. These accounts consist mostly of deposits at banks and repurchase/resale agreements.

Assets, line 7, *Intra-Eurosystem claims* consists mainly of balances of NCBs in the TARGET system against the ECB.

ECB Balance Sheet: TARGET-related positions

	2000 ***€ million***	**1999** ***€ million***
Due from participating central banks In respect of TARGET	59,011	7,698
Due to participating central banks In respect of TARGET	(45,930)	(9,418)
Net position [448]	***13,081***	***(1,721)***

[448] The large change in the net position between 1999 and 2000 was due to intervention purchases of euro with foreign currencies that were settled in the TARGET system.

Text Box: Shift in TARGET accounting in November 2000

A major change in TARGET accounting occurred in November 2000. In the initial TARGET accounting, positions between participating NCBs were calculated on a gross bilateral basis. Under this basis, each clearing operation estimated bilateral positions with each other NCB by crediting bilateral accounts within TARGET. This resulted in accumulations of very large gross positions because bilateral settlements did not necessarily cancel out over time. Balances could increase indefinitely because of regular one-way chains of transactions within the system. That is, if A owed amount x to B, B owed amount x to C, and C owed amount x to A, the net would equal zero because the amount x in each link of the chain is equal. However, on a gross basis, gross claims are 3x and gross liabilities are 3x. Exactly this type of situation existed in the Euroarea and was revealed once the clearing system was pulled into a single accounting presentation.

The new system netted each day all bilateral TARGET claims and liabilities between NCBs and between NCBs and the ECB and novated a new single net position of the ECB vis-à-vis each NCB. The position shown on the ECB balance sheet therefore represents the single net asset or liability position of the ECB against all NCBs.

Future currency unions are likely to face similar situations, which might make regular novation of bilateral positions into single multilateral positions a practical necessity.

14.12 Assets, line 8.2, *Other assets: other financial assets,* includes among other assets holdings of 3000 shares in the BIS (recorded at an acquisition cost of €38.5 million). Future currency unions will probably have share-holdings in the BIS. This account is comprised mostly of the ECB pension fund, which is segregated from other accounts.

14.13 Assets, line 8.3, *Off-balance-sheet revaluation differences* represents the off-balance-sheet offset to on-balance-sheet foreign exchange swaps. The on-balance-sheet spot transactions are revalued identically with off-balance-sheet forward positions, resulting in no net change to the balance sheet.[449]

14.14 Assets, line 8.5, *Sundry items,* includes claims of the ECB on the German Ministry of Finance for recoverable taxes (value added and other indirect taxes) because of the immunity of the ECB from taxes of the host state as stated in the Statute of the ESCB. Future currency unions will need to include this accounting entry if their central banks and its organs have similar immunity.

14.15 Liabilities, line 1, *Liabilities to Euroarea credit institutions, in euro*, consists of the counterpart to repurchase operations as a result of investment of the ECB's own funds.

14.16 Liabilities, line 2, *Liabilities to other Euroarea residents, in euro*, consists of balances of the Euro Banking Association used as collateral for EBA payments settled through TARGET. The EBA, which is owned by European banks, operates a private euro settlement system for their customers but clears transactions between the banks through TARGET. Future unions might have a similar system.

14.17 Liabilities, line 3, *Liabilities to non-euro residents, in euro*, consists of deposits of EU non-Euroarea NCBs that arise from their participation in the TARGET system. All EU countries can participate in TARGET, but special rules apply to non-Euroarea countries.

14.18 Liabilities, line 5.1, *Intra-Eurosystem liabilities: Liabilities equivalent to the transfer of foreign reserves*, consists of liabilities created by the transfer to the ECB of gold and foreign reserve assets at the start of the union and when new countries join the euro system.

---

[449] Currency swaps involve on-balance sheet delivery of one currency for another, with an off-balance-sheet forward to re-exchange the currencies in the future. The spot and forward positions are revalued identically so that there is no net change.

14.19 Liabilities, line 6.1, *Other liabilities: Accruals and deferred income,* is mostly accrued interest owed on the liabilities shown in line 5.1.

14.20 Liabilities, line 7, *Provisions*, is mostly a special provision set up against possible losses due to exchange rate and interest rate risks. A large €2.6 billion reserve was set up, given the uncertainty whether regular revaluation reserves could cover future losses.

14.21 *Memorandum items, forward claims, and liabilities, in euros*, includes identical values on both sides of the balance sheet for outstanding foreign exchange contracts. This is simply the amount of swap contracts outstanding at yearend, but because the value of claims and liabilities are equal there is no net effect on the balance sheet.

14.22 Finally, there is a short note at the end of the published accounts that "No material contingent liabilities were outstanding as at 31 December 2000." This is important information. Contingent liabilities can have a major impact on the effective condition of the balance sheet. It would be better if there were an enumerated liabilities account item, *Contingent liabilities,* or a titled disclosure paragraph describing if there are contingent liabilities, and if so, what are their nature, likely incidence, and magnitudes.

14.23 *Post-balance sheet events*. ECB accounting rules require disclosure of significant events occurring after the accounting period that can affect the subsequent interpretation of the accounts. For example, in the *ECB Annual Report 2000*, the implications of the entry of Greece into the union on January 1, 2001 were disclosed – the accounts disclosed that Greece provided an additional €97.7 million in capital, and €1,278 million in foreign currency reserves.

14.24 An additional memorandum item that might be added in some future unions is *Arrears,* that is, central bank claims on NCBs or financial institutions that have not been paid when due. This has not been a problem for the EMU, but it might be an issue in some future unions where parts of the financial system are remote, might have poor communications, and might not have good financial messaging systems. This might also occur if there is some sort of systemic breakdown in the system.

ECB Profit and Loss Account for the year ending 31 December 2000

	2000	**1999**
Interest income on foreign reserve assets	2, 507,164,892	1,733,987,854
Other interest income	4,657,469,867	3,122,690,418
1.1 Interest income	*7,164,634,759*	*4,856,678,272*
Remuneration of NCBs' claims in respect of foreign reserves transferred	(1,375,110,826)	(913,067,289)
Other interest expense	(4,375,476,075)	(2,988,344,639)
1.2 Interest expense	*(5,750,586,901)*	*(3,901,411,928)*
1. Net interest income (1.1 – 1.2)	**1,414,047,858**	**955,266,344**
2.1 Realised gains/losses arising from financial operations	3,352,768,266	(466,056,435)
2.2 Write-downs on financial assets and positions	(1,084,563)	(604,920,383)
2.3 Transfer to/from provisions for foreign exchange rate and price risks	(2,600,000,000)	0
2. Net result of financial operations, write-downs and risk provisions (2.1 – 2.2 – 2.3)	**751,683,703**	**(1,070,976,818)**
3. Net income from fees and commissions	**673,498**	**232,200**
4. Other income	**904,158**	**436,898**
Total net income (1 + 2 + 3 + 4)	***2,167,309,217***	***(115,041,376)***
5. Staff costs	**(80,275,827)**	**(61,022,091)**
6. Administrative expenses	**(82,808,524)**	**(60,748,855)**
7. Depreciation of tangible and intangible fixed assets	**(14,103,116)**	**(10,468,901)**
Profit/(Loss) for the year (Total net income – 5 – 6 – 7)	***1,990,121,750***	***(247,281,223)***

Distribution of ECB Net Profits or Losses

	2000 *€ millions*	**1999** *€ millions*
Profit/loss for the year	***1,990***	***(247)***
Withdrawals from/allocated to general reserve fund	(398)	28
Transfer from monetary income pooled	0	35
Direct charge on NCBs	0	185
Distributable profits	1,592	0
Distribution to NCBs	(1,592)	0
Total	***0***	***0***

14.25 Most of the items in the profit and loss statement correspond closely to standard statements and no explanation is needed. However, a few key items in the ECB profit and loss statement relevant to union finances are described below.

14.26 Line 2.1, *Realised gains/losses arising from financial operations*, recorded substantial gains from exchange market intervention by the ECB in the fall of 2000.

14.27 Line 3, *Net income from fees and commissions,* includes receipts from penalties imposed on credit institutions from noncompliance with reserve requirements. In new unions, sanctions of various sorts might be needed to induce banks to follow new procedures. Separate identification of monetary penalties received provides useful information on the effectiveness of union operations. The best case is that such penalties disappear over time; the worst is that they increase and banks fall into arrears in payment.

14.28 The ECB is not required to publish a statement on the distribution of profits, but does so for information purposes. The structure is simple;

The profit or loss is taken from the income statement. Up to 20 percent is transferred to a general reserve fund, subject to a cap that the fund cannot exceed the capital of the ECB.

If a loss is incurred, such as in 1999, the ECB can take a portion (seigniorage) of the general monetary income generated that year, and – if insufficient to support ECB activity – can directly assess the NCBs. For the 1999 fiscal year, the ECB used both techniques, transferring in €35 million from the monetary income of the Eurosystem and assessing the NCBs an additional €185 million.

The balance, if any, is distributable profits. Distributions are made to the NCBs in accordance with their paid-in capital. EU NCBs outside the Eurosystem are not eligible to receive distributions.

14.29 The loss experienced by the ECB during its first year (1999) should provide a warning to future unions that their union central bank could experience similar problems, and thus provisions must be made to deal with the possibility. This is most likely during the first few years of the union when reserves of the union are small and there is uncertainty about the currency and potential volatility, which could result in exchange market intervention.

Consolidated balance sheet of the Eurosystem

14.30 A balance sheet is also prepared for the consolidated Eurosystem, comprising the ECB and the member NCBs. In line with the phrase that Eurosystem decisions are centralized, but operations are decentralized, this balance sheet is in some respect more important than the ECB's because it captures information on the full interface between the Eurosystem as a whole and the Euroarea economy and the rest of the world. It encompasses the combined resources of the ECB and the NCBs of member countries, and thus provides an overview of the financial strength of the Eurosystem as a whole.

14.31 It includes several key macroeconomic variables. such as the total international reserves of the system, currency issued, the monetary base, the capital backing of the system, etc. It is also articulated to show monetary policy relevant activity in lending to the banking system and deposits and other liabilities to credit institutions.

14.32 The consolidated balance sheet is constructed by adding up (aggregating) the balance sheets of the ECB and all member central banks, then eliminating both sides of any positions between any of the reporting units. This is possible because each unit must follow common accounting standards that use the same standards for valuation, recognition, timing, articulation of instruments and institutions[450], and which identify all positions between the reporting units (*which will be a requirement for all future unions*).

14.33 As a result of this process, the consolidated balance sheet presents the position of the Eurosystem against all other counterparties within the regional economy (credit institutions, other financial institutions, government bodies, households, etc.) and against counterparties in all other countries (including those against EU countries outside the Eurosystem).

14.34 Positions with governments of Euroarea countries and with institutions of the union itself (legislatures, courts, inspection offices, etc.) are all classified as resident in the Euroarea. International organizations, such as the BIS, IMF, FAO, are all classified as positions with nonresidents, even if offices are physically within the Euroarea.

14.35 The balance sheet is shown below, drawn from the year 2000 *ECB Annual Report*. Many of the definitions of series are identical with the ECB Balance Sheet. A few key series relevant for currency unions elsewhere are discussed following the balance sheet.

[450] Because NCBs are permitted to engage in banking activities and functions that do not interfere with the functions of Eurosystem, it is possible that any particular NCB will have unique types of positions. These have to be included within the consolidated balance sheet. Thus, the rules for classification and treatment of positions must be flexible enough to cover and incorporate all possible types of situations for all NCBs without being hopelessly detailed.

Consolidated Balance Sheet of the Eurosystem

Assets	31 December 2000	31 December 1999
1 Gold and gold receivables	**117,073**	**116,610**
2 Claims on non-Euroarea residents denominated in foreign currency	**258,825**	**254,882**
2.1 Receivables from the IMF	26,738	29,842
2.2 Balances with banks and security investments, external loans and other external assets	232,087	225,040
3 Claims on Euroarea residents denominated in foreign currency	**15,786**	**14,385**
4 Claims on non-Euroarea residents denominated in euro	**3,750**	**6,050**
4.1 Balances with banks, security investments and loans	3,750	6,050
4.2 Claims arising from the credit facility under ERM II	0	0
5 Lending to Euroarea credit institutions related to monetary policy operations denominated in euro	**268,648**	**248,815**
5.1 Main refinancing operations	222,988	161,987
5.2 Longer-term refinancing operations	45,000	74,996
5.3 Fine-tuning reverse operations	0	0
5.4 Structural reverse operations	0	0
5.5 Marginal lending facility	608	11,429
5.6 Credits related to margin calls	53	404
6 Other claims on Euroarea credit institutions denominated in euro	**578**	**1,842**
7 Securities of Euroarea residents denominated in euro	**26,071**	**23,521**
8 General government debt denominated in euro	**57,671**	**59,180**
9 Other assets	**87,559**	**81,567**
Total assets	**835,961**	**806,853**

Liabilities	31 December 2000	31 December 1999
1 Banknotes in circulation	**371,370**	**374,964**
2 Liabilities to Euroarea credit institutions related to monetary policy operations denominated in euro	**124,642**	**117,301**
2.1 Current accounts (covering the minimum reserve system)	124,402	114,672
2.2 Deposit facility	240	2,618
2.3 Fixed-term deposits	0	0
2.4 Fine-tuning reverse operations	0	0
2.5 Deposits related to margin calls	0	10
3 Other liabilities to Euroarea credit institutions denominated in euro	**305**	**283**
4 Debt certificates issued	**3,784**	**7,876**
5 Liabilities to other Euroarea residents denominated in euro	**57,047**	**61,762**
5.1 General government	53,353	56,470
5.2 Other liabilities	3,694	5,292
6 Liabilities to non-Euroarea residents denominated in euro	**10,824**	**9,048**
7 Liabilities to Euroarea residents denominated in foreign currency	**806**	**927**
8 Liabilities to non-Euroarea residents denominated in foreign currency	**12,414**	**11,904**
8.1 Deposits, balances and other liabilities	12,414	11,904
8.2 Liabilities arising from the credit facility under ERM II	0	0
9 Counterpart of SDRs allocated by the IMF	**6,702**	**6,534**
10 Other liabilities	**72,215**	**54,222**
11 Revaluation accounts	**117,986**	**106,782**
12 Capital and reserves	**57,866**	**55,249**
Total liabilities	**835,961**	**806,853**

14.36 Assets, line 2, *Claims on non-Euroarea residents denominated in foreign currency,* includes official international reserve assets of the Eurosystem and other foreign currency assets. Some of the other foreign assets could be used as reserves for balance of payments purposes if the need arises, but other assets such as holdings of illiquid currencies or holdings as collateral for specific transactions are not part of reserves. The foreign currency assets shown in this line can provide backing for the international strength of the euro. As a matter of policy, a minimum level of foreign currency assets is considered necessary. Claims on the IMF of all countries are shown separately. The ECB can have such claims, but most result from the bilateral relations between member countries and the IMF; bilateral positions of the IMF with member countries will mostly be *un*available for use for union exchange rate policy purposes.

14.37 Assets, line 5, *Lending to Euroarea credit institutions related to monetary policy operations denominated in euro*, provides total Eurosystem credit provided to banking institutions within the union, with a detailed breakdown on the type of facility used. This allows the public to obtain substantial information on how monetary policy is being executed.

14.38 Liabilities, line 1, *Banknotes in circulation,* provides information on total banknotes in circulation issued by the Eurosystem.[451] Because the banknotes can freely circulate within the union, special rules are used to record how much banknotes are considered to be issued by each NCB. These rules deserve a full discussion, which is provided in the section on Intra-Eurosystem accounts, below.

14.39 Liabilities, line 2, *Liabilities to Euroarea credit institutions related to monetary policy operations denominated in euro*, consist of liabilities of the Eurosystem to credit institutions related to monetary policy operations. The account is articulated to identify major types of monetary policy operations.

14.40 Liabilities, line 9, *Counterpart of SDRs by the IMF,* represents the accounting entry recorded by NCBs for receipt of SDRs issued by the IMF. Member countries have received several allocations on SDRs from the IMF, which are a form of reserve asset created to facilitate transactions in reserves. The ECB can hold SDRs and use them as part of its international payments transactions, but does not directly receive allocations of SDRs from the IMF. Per ESCB rules, SDR allocations are classified as unallocated "other assets" outside of capital and not treated as a liability to nonresidents.[452]

C. International Financial Reporting Standards (IFRS)

14.41 Over the past two decades, new standards for financial accounting have become globally accepted. Originally called the International Accounting Standards (IAS), they are now called the International Financial Reporting Standards (IFRS). The International Accounting Standards Board in London establishes the standards in consultation with accounting bodies and international organizations.

14.42 The IFRS introduced revolutionary changes to financial reporting, moving toward much greater use of economic rationales for recognition and valuation of assets (including use of "fair value accounting") and putting out more specific standards for presentation of data. The adoption of the IFRS has resulted in much greater comparability between the accounts of individual banks and between reporting for countries. However, there a number of complexities and permissible options and thus differences remain.

14.43 The IFRS are designed to be general purpose accounting statements that serve many public

[451] In the future, Eurosystem issuance of digital euros as a central bank digital currency would probably be shown in this item. Digital euros might be an important policy instrument and thus separate detail on its issuance would be valuable.

[452] In August 2009, the IMF methodology was changed to redefine allocations of SDRs as transactions creating a liability of each central bank, rather than as a capital contribution included as part of the central bank's shares and other equity. This change was made retroactive.

purposes. However, it recognizes that there might be special requirements that do not fit into the framework, and thus national (or union) authorities could introduce additional requirements. Also, it recognizes that there can be several acceptable options – in such cases a preferred "benchmark" is designated, but the others can be used.

14.44 The financial crisis led to recognition that the IFRS suffered from some problems. A number of major changes were introduced, including;

Valuation standards reduced from four different treatments to two in which all financial assets are classified as valued at fair value with changes in value taken to profit or loss, or at amortized cost.

Impairment standards changed to move from an incurred loss basis to one based on expected losses of financial assets and liabilities.

Rules on consolidation of units clarified.

Rules on derecognition and securitization of assets clarified.

14.45 The IFRS also has worked to promote better communication of the accounts to the public. In this regard, it has promoted use of the XBRL internet communications language. XBRL is a highly flexible language that allows users to access individual data items along with metadata (descriptions about the data). The IFRS and the BCBS are jointly promoting use of XBRL to enhance access to bank reports. Future unions should be able to handle XBRL-provided data, including possibly adopting it as the primary means to collect statistical information on banks.

14.46 The IFRS are now true global standards and new unions should act to ensure their adoption by all member countries. The union-level accounting authority should seek to participate in the deliberations of the IASB, either as the sole representative for the union or alongside other union countries.

Text Box: Islamic finance accounting standards

In some countries planning unions, Islamic Financial Institutions (IFIs) coexist with conventional financial institutions. The Islamic activity might be conducted either by a separate institution or a separate "Islamic window" within a conventional institution. In both cases, there must be regular IFRS-based financial reporting but there could also be reporting under Islamic accounting standards. Because Islamic institutions use unique types of financial instruments with unconventional names, cash flows, and counterparty rights and obligations, special accounting instructions have been developed on how to report them.

One problem will be dual reporting of activity under conventional and Islamic standards. For example, a conventional bank operating a separate "Islamic window" must report activity of the window within its regular consolidated financial accounts, but also separately report the activity of the window under Islamic accounting standards. The depiction of the window under the two standards will differ – whether differences are material is an empirical question. This will be costly, could prove confusing, and raises prudential oversight issues.

Two institutions help set accounting standards for Islamic institutions – the Islamic Financial Standards Board (IFSB) in Kuala Lumpur, Malaysia, and the Accounting and Auditing Organization for Islamic Financial Institutions (AAOIFI) in Bahrain. Future unions that will have Islamic Financial Institutions should set up a special body to investigate the particularities of IFI accounting and reporting.

D. Intra-Union accounts of the Eurosystem

14.47 This section provides more detail on several important intra-union accounts of the Eurosystem. Future currency unions might create similar accounts to handle positions and transactions between participants in the system. Even future unions that operate as a single organization with branches spread throughout the union might need similar ledger entries between branches.

Capital of the ECB

14.48 The ECB's own capital was initially provided by transfers from the member countries of the ESCB. After the initial transfer, the ECB was responsible to maintain and increase its capital through its own operations. The earnings of this capital are intended to support the ECB's operations.

14.49 Each ESCB must provide a share of the capital to the ECB, according to specific rules. The initial capital contribution of the ECB was designed to be €5 billion. Each country contributed capital based on its *"capital subscription key"* based on its GDP and population.[453] Countries in the Eurosystem paid their full share; EU countries not in the Eurosystem paid a small 5 % portion of their capital subscription. Because not all ESCB countries entered the Eurosystem at the start of union, the initial paid in capital was just under €4 billion.

14.50 When a new country joins the EU, it enters the ESCB and makes a contribution of 5 % of its *capital subscription key* to cover some of the operational costs of the ECB. Thus, the capital of the ECB is automatically increased. The prevailing amount of subscribed capital is multiplied by the ratio that includes the weight of the new member's NCB and the weights of the current ESCB-member NCBs. For example, in January 2007, Bulgaria and Romania joined the EU. At this point, the two NCBs paid 5 % of their capital subscription key requirement, which resulted in an increase in the total ECB capital from €5.565 billion to €5.761 billion.

14.51 Subsequently, when a country enters the union and adopts the euro, it pays the remainder of its capital requirement. For example, when Slovenia joined the Eurosystem in January 2007, it paid the remainder of its capital contribution to the ECB.

Harmonized intraunion accounts

14.52 Certain items on the balance sheets of NCB had to be harmonized, specifically banknotes in circulation, net intra-Eurosystem claims and liabilities, and monetary income. These items are truly joint in nature and cannot be calculated except in a harmonized manner.

Banknotes in circulation

14.53 The value reported in the accounts of each NCB is calculated from two parts.

> The unadjusted amount of euro banknotes in circulation is calculated, using either of two methods.
>
> (1) BC = BP – BD – S
>
> (Banknotes in circulation (BC) equals amount printed(BP), less amount destroyed (BD), less amount stored in vaults (S)).
>
> (2) BC = BI – BR
>
> (Banknotes in circulation (BC) equals value of banknotes put into circulation (BI) less the value of banknotes received (BR).

14.54 An adjustment (+ or –) is made to the national estimates of banknotes in circulation based on the "banknote allocation key".

> The *banknote allocation key* is defined in Regulation ECB/2001/15. The decision on the allocation of currency issuance proved politically difficult – in large part because it affected the seigniorage income for each NCB. It was resolved only just before the startup of the union when it was decided that the allocation of euro banknotes in circulation would grant the ECB 8% of the total value of euro banknotes in circulation. The balance of 92% went to NCBs in proportion to their paid-up shares in the capital of the ECB. That is, the banknote

[453] The shares of NCBs in the ECB's capital key are weighted according to each member country's share in the total population and GDP of the EU. The weights are adjusted every five years and whenever new countries join the EU.

allocation key is the same as the "capital subscription key" except for the adjustment for the ECB.[454] The key must be adjusted when new members join the union.

Euroarea banknote allocation key (2009)

European Central Bank	8.0000 %
Austria	2.5595 %
Belgium	3.1975 %
Cyprus	0.1805 %
Finland	1.6530 %
France	18.7495 %
Germany	24.9630 %
Greece	2.3590 %
Ireland	1.4630 %
Italy	16.4730 %
Luxembourg	0.2305 %
Malta	0.0835 %
Netherlands	5.2575 %
Portugal	2.3075 %
Slovakia	0.9140 %
Slovenia	0.4336 %
Spain	10.9465 %

14.55 For example, for Portugal the value in the key is 2.3075%. This means that Portugal's balance sheet will record as currency issued an amount equal to 2.31% of the value of all banknotes issued by the Euro system, and will receive an equivalent amount of monetary income.

14.56 The allocation of euro banknotes among Eurosystem members gives rise to intra-Eurosystem balances, as explained below. The remuneration of intra-Eurosystem balances directly affects the income of each NCB. Income is distributed to each NCB in proportion to its share in the subscribed capital key.

Monetary income

14.57 Monetary income accrues to NCBs as a result of performing monetary policy functions. As defined in the statutes of the ESCB, each NCB's monetary income is equal to income derived from assets held against notes in circulation and deposit liabilities to credit institutions. The assets acquired with the funds from these liabilities and the accrued income are earmarked by NCBs in accordance with guidelines from the Governing Council. Prior to 2002, monetary income included assets based on NCBs' monetary policy liabilities to credit institutions, but income generated from issuance of national banknotes was retained as the sole property of each issuing NCB. With the issuance of banknotes in 2002, income from assets acquired from banknotes in circulation was added.

14.58 Thus, from the 2003 financial year onwards, the formula for estimation and distribution on monetary income was;

> Each NCB earmarked assets acquired as a result of monetary policy actions, specifically from issuing banknotes in circulation and accepting deposits and other policy-related liabilities to banks.
>
> The total income earned by all NCBs and the ECB on these assets is treated as monetary income of the Eurosystem.
>
> Each NCB's monetary income was then reduced by interest paid on the monetary policy liabilities.
>
> The sum of monetary income for all NCB's is added.
>
> The share of each country in the monetary income is applied by using the capital key.

[454] The published balance sheets of the NCBs reflect the allocation of banknotes based on this key. The rationale is that regardless of the country in which the currency is actually issued to the public, the banknotes can freely move throughout the union.

Alternative methods to account for currency liabilities of NCBs

14.59 The Euroarea treats banknotes as a liability of the ESCB as a whole, without linking banknotes to the individual NCB where they were issued. However, future unions might treat union banknotes as liabilities of individual central banks. In this case, each banknote of the common currency issued must be identified by the issuing central bank.[455] The currency can be used throughout the union, but the ability to identify the country of issuance of each banknote allows it to be repatriated back to the issuing central bank when withdrawn from circulation in another union country.

14.60 For example, a union currency banknote issued by the central bank of country A (NCB_A) can be used in country B by a tourist. The banknote might ultimately be deposited in B's NCB (NCB_B). This creates a claim of NCB_B claim on NCB_A, which issued the banknote.

> NCB_B could send the banknote back to NCB_B in exchange for some sort of payment from NCB_A, such as NCB_A crediting NCB_B's correspondent account.
>
> NCB_A and NCB_B could do a net settlement of their mutual currency holdings. For example, NCB_B could count up all the banknotes it holds issued by NCB_A, and NCB_A could do the same with NCB_B's banknotes. The net liability between NCB_A and NCB_B can then be settled by a single payment. The single net payment will be smaller than the two gross payments, which is less expensive and more secure than making two shipments of currency.
>
> However, in a multimember union, claims as a result of currency issuance might follow a circular pattern of large gross flows with little netting of flows between individual country links in the chain. For example, NCB_A might have a claim on NCB_B, who has a claim on NCB_C, who has a claim on NCB_A. The system as a whole will be in balance, but large gross claims exist within the system. The intra-NCB accounts generate large gross claims and liabilities. On settlement, large gross payments must be made, which can be expensive with possible security risks.
>
> If a union handles banknote issuance and retirement in this way, there are regular costs to examine and identify each banknote by issuing NCB. Separate accounts with each other member central bank will be needed.[456]

14.61 The treatment of union banknotes as liabilities of individual central banks has comparatively simple accounting. Each NCB issues currency and records a liability for it. The assets earned by the central bank from the sale of currency can be treated as its own sole property that it manages and invests to earn income. The earmarking of assets acquired from issuing banknotes is unnecessary, nor is it necessary to earmark income earned, and no reconciliation between NCBs of monetary income generated from issuance of banknotes is needed.

14.62 This alternative requires that NCBs receiving and holding banknotes issued by other NCBs actively identify the source of the banknotes it holds and quickly make settlement. Until settlement is made, the issuing NCB increases its balance sheet and gains income from the use of assets gained, while the receiving NCB has a smaller balance sheet and loses income because of the payments made to purchase the banknotes.[457]

---

[455] When the euro was designed, a space was left at the lower left side of the map of Europe side for possible use of a national symbol or identifier of the issuing NCB. However, a decision was made that euro banknotes would not carry any national identifiers and would be liabilities of the ESCB as a whole.

[456] This accounting would be easy in future unions that create a CBDC because balances can be tracked electronically.

[457] An advantage of this processing of banknotes for accounting purposes is that each bill can be inspected and (continued)

E. Accounting for monetary policy counterparties

14.63 It will be important that banks, governments, and other counterparties to union monetary policy actions and positions use common or harmonized accounting standards and practices. This helps ensure that all parties affected by union actions respond in a similar and nondiscriminatory manner.

Required reserves

14.64 The EMU applies a system of required reserve assets, in which the reserves must be deposited by banks with their NCBs based on their liabilities with some standard deductions. Collection of reserves in a nondiscriminatory fashion requires that all member banks classify their liabilities in the same way and use identical standards for valuation, recognition, and timing of liabilities.

14.65 The ECB decided that the best way to do this was to use monetary statistics standards[458] (rather than financial accounting standards). Thus, banks provide authorities with all the information needed to calculate required reserves when they prepare their statistical reports. This is efficient and also allows the analysis of required reserves within the general statistical framework used for monetary policy analysis. Timely reporting is also required in order to adjust reserves quickly based on current conditions.

14.66 One consequence of the calculation of reserves based on statistical reporting is that the statistical reports acquire an important regulatory role and directly affect the income and expenses of the reporting banks. Moreover, reporting must be comparable between banks across the union, which means that union statisticians exercise regulatory power and thus their decisions must be made with awareness of legal consequences. Effective oversight of the statistical reports must be set up, and audits performed periodically. An important by-product of this oversight is that statistical quality will be improved.

14.67 The European decision to use statistical standards has proved to be easy to apply and cost effective, but other unions might not choose to use statistical calculations for reserves calculations, or financial accounting standards derived from principles different from those applied in Europe which might not fit into a statistical framework. In this case, an alternative system is needed to guarantee similar comparability in terms of valuation, recognition, and reporting obligations.

Collateral, settlements, and clearing

14.68 An important component of the EMU system is that financial markets should be fully integrated so that monetary policy impulses move quickly to all parts of the union and economic agents anywhere in the union have access to good, current signals of financial reward and risk. This means that traded financial instruments be valued and recognized based on common economic principles, which should be carried over into financial accounting statements.

14.69 As integrated into the ECB accounting guidelines, an economic approach should be used for recording many transactions and positions and related accruals. Certainly, the economic value should be used for each financial instrument used for collateral, clearing and settlements, and monetary policy operations and those values should be carried over to financial accounting statements. However, in financial reports, in line with the IFRS, there will continue to be exceptions to valuations standards for loans and other financial instruments that do not trade and which

counterfeits and damaged currency can be removed from circulation.

[458] IMF monetary statistics are based on the SNA international statistical standards which applies an overarching set of standards to all countries to compile the macroeconomic accounts of countries. SNA rules require that both sides of each transaction be treated symmetrically in terms of classification, timing, and valuation which acts to avoid discrepancies between both sides of the accounts, which allows counterparty asset and liability positions to be aggregated. This was an important reason why SNA-based statistical data were selected for compiling the monetary balance sheets of the Eurosystem.

reporters intend to continue to hold to maturity – these will continue to be reported at amortized cost.

Government

14.70 Harmonization of the accounts of the central government units is important for calculation of convergence criteria and for union policy analysis. The convergence criteria for government deficits and debt are important for monetary policy analysis to determine the degree of stimulus and restraint implied by the fiscal situation, and prospects for sustainability. Within each country, government accounts should be complete, timely, and in accordance with international standards such as those in the IMF's *Government Finance Statistics Manual.* The country data need to be aggregated across the union and combined with information on union-level institutions (taxes, other income, and expenditures and grants of the union secretariat, parliament, judicial system, etc.).

14.71 Also, as discussed in the section on IMF safeguards assessments below, fiscal reporting to the IMF is an important part of IMF assistance programs to member countries.

14.72 Many countries are far from achieving high-quality fiscal accounting systems. Moreover, tax and expenditure practices often differ considerably between countries so simple adding up of accounts of countries or simple comparisons of country ratios might not prove useful.

14.73 Dealing with government accounts is a long-term, very challenging project often constrained by political considerations. However, the information is useful and needed for convergence analysis; thus, reasonable comparability should be achieved before the start of the union. Rationalizing government accounting should be on future unions' agendas for early action. The damage done to the credibility of the Euroarea because of poor fiscal accounting by Greece should be a lesson to future unions.

Private institutions' preparations

14.74 Training and outreach to private financial institutions to introduce financial accounting changes is needed for the currency union. Important requirements include *harmonization* of standards and procedures followed by banks and other financial institutions, *timely* reporting, and *full coverage* of monetary institutions and policy relevant financial institutions.

14.75 *Harmonization* of standards and procedures is needed to ensure comparability of data and statistics across institutions and between countries. Harmonization might involve introducing specific practices in all member countries through new legislation or regulatory actions, or it could involve complete replacement of national accounting frameworks with a single common framework.

Use of a common framework might often be needed because variations in accounting standards in areas such as valuation, recognition of income, securitization, consolidation of affiliates, and provisioning and impairment can fundamentally change financial results and preclude effective aggregation of the information for monetary policy purposes.

The introduction of IFRS contributes to overall harmonization and greater comparability of accounts between institutions and countries.[459]

Introduction of harmonized accounting can be a lengthy and resource intensive. Designing standards, legally ratifying the changes, sequencing changes into the accounting cycle, and allowing time for institutions to introduce changes can take several years.

The financial crisis led to some major changes to international accounting standards, in areas such as valuation, impairment, consolidation, and derecognition of assets, etc.. Future unions should follow the development of standards and require

[459] The IFRS are designed to be a general-purpose framework. Within a currency union, additional common requirements will be needed to cover specific union policy or information needs, for example, to compile required bank reserves.

introduction of the new standards as soon as possible.

14.76 *Timeliness* of the information is also critical. Banks and other financial institutions must provide information to their NCBs or union offices rapidly for use for policy purposes. Statistics must also be current to meaningfully inform the public. Therefore, a union might introduce requirements such as production of monthly monetary statistics within 25 working days after the end of an accounting period, or production of income statements and balance sheets within 45 days. A common reporting platform might be introduced to facilitate rapid processing of reports from multiple countries. Institutions might need to change operational and information technology in order to meet requirements. Speed in production might require purchase of new computer facilities and data transmission hardware and software. These changes could be expensive and time consuming, and some financial institutions within a currency union could be hard-pressed to meet the requirements.

14.77 *Full coverage* of relevant institutions is also important. Monetary statistics have traditionally covered regulated banking institutions, but increasingly many other types of financial institutions carry out banking-type functions and should be included within the reporting universe. In some economies, virtually all financial institutions might be relevant to monetary union policy. However, regulatory, accounting, and statistical coverage has often been limited, inadequate, or absent for nonbank financial institutions, which sometimes are explicitly exempted from reporting. Introducing the legal power to cover nonbank financial institutions might involve new legislation and establishing new institutions such as a Financial Supervisory Authority. Once authority exists, designing and implementing the reporting requirements and allowing time for their introduction can sometimes take years.

14.78 All the above tasks are important for the success of the accounting and statistical systems of a currency union. They are also important for policy operations, such as calculating required reserves, valuing collateral, or estimating foreign currency positions. Many of the actions are difficult, time-consuming, and potentially expensive. The ability of financial institutions to make the changes is important for union effectiveness, and therefore a key part of the union-building process is to make sure that the private institutions can effectively meet requirements.

14.79 Most of the burden for ensuring these results will fall on the union's accounting working group, (perhaps in collaboration with the statistics working group). Information must be gathered on the current state of national accounting systems and differences between systems, identify elements of accounting systems that must be harmonized, determine the costs and feasibility of proposals for implementation by financial institutions, design standards, regulations, or legislation to introduce the changes, and monitor progress for implementation.

14.80 Systems need to be on line prior to the start-up of the union for testing purposes[460] and might need to be in place in time to compile the accounts for the previous year for comparison purposes and to operate the system for a full year. Where preferred methods are not feasible or cost-effective, scaled-back demands or temporary fixes might be needed.

14.81 Thus, early contact by the union with financial institutions is needed to ascertain conditions, evaluate feasibility, support implementation, and ensure comparable implementation. This work can be done through contacts with individual banks, associations of banks and other financial institutions,

[460] For example, the ECB compiled the union monetary statistics months before the start of the EMU in order to test the effectiveness of operations and get a first view of the monetary situation of the union as a whole. This required that reporting banks have accounting and communications in place, that the NCBs receive, verify, and process information into aggregate national statistics, and that the national data be transmitted to the ECB for verification and compilation of the union-wide statistics.

accounting authorities, and through outreach by regulatory authorities. Because all countries must be at similar states of development at the start of the union, monitoring of implementation by countries and enforcing application of common rules or procedures will be an important duty of the Accounting Working Group. Technical assistance might be needed to bring lagging countries up to speed.

14.82 This will include formal steps such as passing laws, modifying accounting standards, or establishing reporting deadlines. This will also require extensive training of managers and staff of financial institutions to familiarize them with new standards and procedures and to support their introduction of new methods. Operating procedures of financial institutions need to be changed, and staff across a wide swath of banks and other financial institutions need to be trained and organized to produce the needed data on a tight schedule. This could be challenging for new unions who might lack the extensive regulatory infrastructure that existed in Europe.

Aggregate balance sheet of Monetary Financial Institutions (MFIs)

14.83 For statistical and monetary policy purposes, MFIs must prepare monthly accounting statements according to standardized statistical rules. These are compiled for each country by NCBs and forwarded to the ECB. The ECB then compiles aggregate accounts for the Euroarea as a whole. The ECB also supplies these data to the IMF.

F. Audits and assessments

14.84 An audit is a thorough review of the accounts and activities of an organization to assess performance, adherence to policies, correct errors, and detect problems including illegalities. Regardless of the care exercised in operations, controls, and quality of governance, regular outside oversight is needed to minimize loss of funds from waste or theft and to spur efforts to improve the efficiency of operations. This requires regular audits of the union central bank, of union-related activities of national offices or NCBs, and of other union transactions or activities. More intense audits will be required where problems are found, in areas of highest risk, or where governance is weak.

Audits in the Euroarea

14.85 The auditing process of the Euroarea has four separate layers – audit of the ECB as an EU institution, ECB internal audits, coordinated audits between the ECB and NCBs, and national level audits.

14.86 Audits of EU organs such as the ECB are carried out by the Court of Auditors, consisting of 12 members with independent authority. The Court of Auditors carries out audits of selected ESCB functions, which vary each year. The Court reviews the effectiveness of various functions, the control system, and whether they fulfill their mandate, rather than review the balancing of the accounts or seek out fraud or abuse. For example, in 2001 the Court of Auditors looked at the efficiency of ECB management operations, which was considered a priority in the run-up to issuing the physical euro.

14.87 The Statute of the ESCB mandated that the accounts of the ECB and the NCBs shall be audited by external accountants nominated by the Governing Council and approved by the EU Council. Auditors have full power to review all books and accounts and to receive full information about transactions.

14.88 Internally, the ECB carries out audits in accordance with the "ECB Audit Charter" (ECB 2007c) that set up an internal Directorate for Internal Audit (D-IA). The Directorate operates independently to provide additional confidence in the efficiency and appropriateness of operations. It also provides consulting services to improve operations by systematically reviewing and evaluating controls, processes, risk management, and governance. All ECB activities are subject to audit.

> Independence of the Directorate was achieved by placing it directly under the Executive Board with reporting to the President. The auditors have no responsibility for any activities that they audit.
>
> The auditors are guided by a code of ethics and the International Standards for the Professional

Practice of Internal Auditing promulgated by the Institute of Internal Auditors. The auditors are expected to have a high degree of professionalism.

Topics to investigate are based on an audit plan based on a risk-based methodology and approved by the Executive Board.

Audits are undertaken, which can involve coordination with external auditors and the Court of Auditors.

Auditors have full access to all staff, records, and systems.

Information provided must be truthful and timely.

The Executive Board is informed of any attempts to hinder the auditors.

Results of audits are reported to the Executive Board and to the units investigated.

The auditors monitor and evaluate implementation of recommendations and report results.

14.89 Among the tasks undertaken in the audits are;

Auditing annual statements

Evaluating internal controls

Evaluating the identification and analysis of risks and the risk management systems

Auditing controls over information systems and their security and back-ups.

Testing operations and performing stress testing operations

Conducting special investigations of fraud, loss, or other problems

Providing advice on projects during development

14.90 Audits related to interactions between the ECB and NCBs are performed in accordance with the "ESCB Audit Policy". (ECB 1998) Special rules and procedures were needed to deal with joint projects to define responsibilities, lines of responsibility, and objectives. A framework was needed to ensure that all levels of activity are properly covered, work is coordinated, and applies common principles, and effective exchange of information occurs. An Internal Auditors Committee comprised of the ECB auditor and auditors of NCBs with the ECB serving as secretariat was established to handle this coordination.

Auditors for each NCB are responsible for auditing the systems and operations of their NCB, including the local component of ESCB-wide systems.

The ECB auditors are responsible for auditing the ECB's information systems, the ECB component of ESCB-wide systems, the ECB balance sheet and its related operations, and functions located at the ECB or which enter the ECB profit and loss account.

Joint ESCB projects are audited using a common approach, under the coordination of the Internal Auditors Committee. The IAC will establish a plan for audits each year, but only for tasks and risks that cannot be handled at the local level.

Special audits can be ordered at any time, in which case lower priority projects will be set aside.

The IAC coordinates preparation of joint reports and their submission for action.

Due to subsidiarity, the organization, methods, and philosophies of auditors in different NCBs can vary. The Internal Auditors Committee coordinates as needed.

14.91 Audits related to areas of sole responsibility of NCB are done by national-level auditors.

14.92 The four-level structure of audits for the Euroarea highlights the different types of audits that potentially need to be done within future unions. A unitary central bank in which one central bank operates in all member countries will need a much simpler arrangement with internal audits and periodic external audits. However, where distinct NCBs exist, or where other union institutions exist (clearing organizations, separate foreign reserves offices, deposit insurance offices, etc.) different levels of audit will exist and a coordination mechanism is required. Core currency union functions must fall under direct control of the union central bank auditing arm, or be coordinated such as is done with through the ESCB's Internal Auditors Committee.

Forensic audits

14.93 A forensic audit is an investigation that could result in legal action or criminal prosecution, either against individuals who engage in wrongful acts, or against the organization being audited, or against its directors for lack of oversight, poor controls, fraud, etc..

14.94 Obviously, central banks responsible for safekeeping, managing, and transacting very large sums must be prepared to investigate and prosecute as needed. A careful audit of trails of transactions and collection of information suitable to bring legal action is needed. One question is whether regular audit procedures, such as annual audits by outside auditors, can effectively serve this function. Does an union central bank need to initiate special actions to investigate and prosecute illegal actions? And how should this be done in a multi-country situation within an union?

14.95 There is uncertainty to what extent a regular external audit is expected to engage in forensic auditing. Organizations ordering audits typically believe that auditors have an obligation to detect substantial fraud as a normal part of the audit, and thus additional special investigations are not necessary. In contrast, organizations such as the International Organisation of Supreme Audit Institutions (INTOSAI) have made statements to the effect that their role is largely preventative and should focus on matters such as control weaknesses, poor record keeping, mechanical or arithmetic errors, unusual transactions that might indicate fraud, improper expenditures, unauthorized actions, and waste and inefficiency. Thus, a regular audit does not guarantee detection of illegalities. Special investigations, including cooperation with regulators, police, or tax authorities might be needed in addition to standard audits.

14.96 Thus, there is potentially a large gap between what firms expect auditors to do, and what auditors view as their role. For union central banks, it must be clear what degree of oversight of fraud and illegal transactions will be provided by audits, especially in light of poor controls or fraudulent behavior that has been known to exist within some central banks that might ultimately join unions. Thus, the union central bank needs to have regular audits over its monetary and exchange policy actions and over the institutions that execute them, but also should have the power to conduct forensic audits or order them. The effectiveness of forensic audits must be ensured, which can become an issue in cross-border situations. Who is entitled to gather evidence? And if outsiders, how does this relate to central bank independence? Following the review, it must be determined who has the right to review results and make recommendations, and ultimately which legal system will take the lead in acting against problems.

14.97 These are not easy issues to resolve. The legal committee working in conjunction with the financial committee might need to take up these issues and incorporate recommendations into the monetary union treaty or other documents accepted by all parties.

Safeguards Assessments and the PRGF[461]

14.98 The IMF conducts "Safeguards Assessments" for countries receiving certain types of assistance that are intended to provide the IMF reasonable assurance that a central bank's control procedures, reporting standards, and auditing are adequate to safeguard the funds provided, to ensure the integrity of financial operations, and for reporting information to the IMF. (IMF 2002) With permission of the central banks involved, reports can be shared with the ECB,

[461] IMF Poverty Reduction and Growth Facility

World Bank, and donors can be briefed regarding funds they have provided.

14.99 The methodology for the assessments looks at five areas with the acronym "**ELRIC**" (**E**xternal audit mechanism, **L**egal structure and independence, financial **R**eporting, **I**nternal audit mechanism, and internal **C**ontrols).

14.100 A large number of assessments have been completed under the program, covering over 90 central banks, including the three existing currency unions outside Europe and their membership. Moreover, there is on-going monitoring of over 50 central banks, representing over 70 countries.

14.101 Monitoring continues as long as the IMF has credit outstanding to a country. Most monitoring is conducted from IMF headquarters and is intended to identify new vulnerabilities at an early stage

14.102 A heavy majority of the assessments were for countries receiving aid under the IMF's PRGF, which provides low-interest loans to the poorest countries to support poverty reduction programs. The PRGF also requires preparation of comprehensive strategy papers to strengthen institutions and governance to support prudent macroeconomic policy development, public funds management, transparency, accountability, and to consider the social and poverty impacts of macroeconomic and financial policies.

14.103 For unions planned in low-income regions, assessments should be sought to assist the union central bank and the member countries in managing and securing funds received, supporting policy development, and strengthening governance.[462] The assessments will also contribute to strengthening the union's monitoring and control over member countries' external and reserves transactions, which is a component of the external policy of the union. The assessments also contribute to central banks' frameworks for risk mitigation. These goals were largely achieved in Europe through self-development over long periods of strong operational controls and through application of common EU rules, and these goals will necessarily be a focus of new unions in attempting to create operationally effective institutions. New unions should consider recommendations of Safeguards Assessments in designing their operational controls. An assessment specifically focused on union-related institutions and controls should be requested, and it would be helpful to have an assessment prior to the start-up of the union to provide some outside analysis of the union plans.

Fiscal reporting

14.104 Safeguard assessments are only made for central banks, but there is a risk of improper use of funds that might ultimately be received by national governments for execution of a program. When the Safeguards Assessment Program was initiated, many countries had significant problems in reporting of fiscal data. The size, breadth, and diversity of fiscal activities made it very difficult to undertake valid assessments for the fiscal sector. Also, frequent revisions of fiscal accounts complicated statistical reporting (which impairs policy formulation) and auditing.

14.105 To address this situation, the IMF has several initiatives to improve the quality of fiscal data and reporting. This includes the IMF *Code of Good Practices on Fiscal Transparency*. Country adherence to the *Code* is part of another IMF program what examines the degree to which national authorities comply with international codes and best practices and reviews the fiscal institutional framework, the quality of fiscal statistics, and the quality of budget estimates. Results are presented in "Reports on the Observance of Standards and Codes (ROSCs)."

14.106 In addition, the IMF Statistics Department has developed a *Government Finance Statistics*

[462] Currency unions have been subject to Safeguards Assessments. For example, a Safeguards Assessment for the ECCB in 2007 found that it had fully adopted the IFRS and had appropriate control mechanisms in place.

Manual with a comprehensive framework for fiscal statistics for reporting purposes and for use in policy analysis. The IMF provides technical assistance to improve reporting and the annual Article IV teams frequently provide advice on how to improve reporting. Regardless of these efforts, the process of improving the quality of fiscal statistics can be long and challenging with continuing uncertainties over the actual level of expenditures or accounting.

14.107 The IMF initiatives broadly parallel the efforts of the Euroarea to improve fiscal reporting, and improvements in fiscal reporting will contribute to more effective implementation of Fund Assistance programs or Euroarea monetary policy. For new unions, the lesson is that improvements over fiscal reporting contributes to the operations of the union. Moreover, within an union, the additional requirement for harmonization of fiscal accounts across countries is important in order to make comparisons between member countries in convergence reports and to compile consolidated measures of fiscal conditions and GDP for the union.

Corruption

14.108 An additional specific concern is corruption and criminal activity. Within a union, union funds are potentially at risk in all member countries, and there can be losses to the union as a whole if specific member countries have severe problems with corruption, misuse of funds, skimming receipts, misreporting the value of assets, etc. Union central banks should institute strict controls and reporting for monetary policy and reserves transactions, but might have limited means to influence the broader fiscal accounts or behavior. However, an action by the EU could be instructive: in 2008, the EU cancelled two large programs for Bulgaria (totaling €780 million) because of its failures to address corruption and organized crime. There was fear of funds being diverted by crime syndicates. The cancellation was also seen as warning to other Balkan countries that they need to deal with corruption before becoming eligible for EU membership.

Timeline

Early actions (four years prior)	Set up Accounting Committee or Board Initial contacts with national accounting and auditing authorities Initial contact with government accounting bodies Contact IFSB and AAOIFI if Islamic institutions are involved.
Three years prior	Prepare reports on state of convergence to IFRS and auding standards; catalog divergences and flexibility options Determine areas of necessary convergence Preliminary statement of union accounting standards Public comment period
24 months prior	Outreach to accountants and auditors National legal ratification begins Implementation by NCBs begins
18 Months Prior	Bank and other corporate application Adjust fiscal years to common basis
Final 12 months	Report on changes to accounts of NCBs Implementation of Intra-Union Accounts Preparation of historical accounts for union
Final 6 months	Construction of union central bank and system accounts Close books of monetary institute and transfer assets to union central bank
Run-up to union	Last day: closing of accounts of NCBs. Audit of closed accounts
Union day	Opening of new accounting period for union central bank and NCBs
Early union period	Accounting and audit of phase out of national currencies Publish new accounts for union and members Publish historical accounts for union
Union steady state	Continue improvements to fiscal accounts

CHAPTER 15 – EUROSYSTEM FINANCES[463]

What will be the capital of the union institutions and how will their income and expenses be handled? What will be distribution of seigniorage and the costs of maintaining the currency?

463 This chapter summarizes financial arrangements for the Eurosystem. Substantial detail on many of the topics in this chapter can be found in the chapters on organization of the system, accounting, statistics, and monetary and international policies.

A. Introduction

15.1 The finances of a currency union involve all of the internal financial issues of a single central bank plus several major additions – financial relations between the union bank and national institutions, the financial transition through several stages of union evolution, intra-union accounts, and denomination of accounts and valuation. This adds complexity and creates a need to clarify the financial rights and obligations of each of the parties involved and to provide full and transparent accounting to all parties.

15.2 The chapter reviews the major accounts of the ESCB and discusses several key types of transactions in more depth. Several special types of transactions are covered not treated explicitly in the Maastricht Treaty or which occur only outside the Euroarea – such as fiscal transfers. sovereign wealth funds, emergency crisis assistance, reserves transactions with international financial institutions, and borrowing from the IMF.[464]

B. ESCB financial accounts

15.3 In contrast to the EMU's centralized decision-making system, many ESCB financial operations are decentralized. This requires that all parties use a common accounting framework with common valuations and accruals so that both sides of internal transactions are identical and positions can be netted bilaterally. For the union as a whole, transactions and financial positions of all members must be additive to union totals and in the EMU multiple types of transactions are netted into single positions, which makes the need for comparable standards more imperative.

15.4 The ECB is required to prepare annual accounts for review by the Governing Council and subsequent publication. Consolidated accounts of the ESCB are also compiled. The Governing Council is tasked to prepare accounting and reporting standards to standardize reporting for this purpose. The accounts of the ECB and NCBs are audited by independent auditors, who have full power to examine all books and accounts and to request full transactions information.

Capital and income of the EMI

15.5 The EMI was financed by an initial allocation of capital from the ESCB members. The income generated by the assets was used to cover the expenses of the EMI in preparing for the union. The EMI experienced deficits in its final years, and when the EMI was dissolved in May 2008 a special assessment to the NCBs covered the net deficit. Assets of the EMI were returned to the shareholding countries, but usually were rolled over to be part of the countries' contributions to the ECB's capital.

15.6 Future unions are likely to need similar procedures to close the books of their monetary institute planning the union, returning assets and any net income to the institute's shareholders, then putting new funds into the new union central bank. Because the legal frameworks and memberships of the institute and the union central bank are likely to differ, perhaps the best strategy is to decisively close the monetary institute, reimburse the countries, then have a new financing process for the union central bank.

The allocation of capital to the ECB

15.7 The capital of the ECB is set in the Statute at €5 billion. The Governing Council with a qualified majority can increase the capital. NCBs are the sole subscribers to the ECB's capita, and cannot transfer their shares. The Governing Council can decide how much of the capital will be paid up and in what form. The capital shares key is adjusted every five years, which changes the relative size of holdings of NCBs, and could result either in calls for countries to

[464] This chapter should be read in conjunction *with Chapter 14 – Accounting.*

increase contributions or refunds of capital back to the NCBs.

15.8 The formula for the capital contribution to the ECB is called the "key". Each NCB's contribution to the ECB was based 50 percent on the population of the country in the year prior to the start of the union (1998) and 50 percent on average GDP during the five years prior to the year before the start of the union (1993-1997). Rules are provided for the statistical data to be used for the calculations. The key is clearly designed to give greater weight to the larger countries – Germany is easily the largest economy in Europe and has the biggest weight, followed by France. The two provide just over 40 percent of the ECB's capital.

Capital key of the eleven original Euroarea NCBs		
Central Bank	**€ millions**	**Percentage Share**
Deutsche Bundesbank	12,247	24.49
Banque de France	8,417	16.83
Banca d'Italia	7,448	14.90
Banco de España	4,447	8.89
De Nederlandsche Bank	2,139	4.28
Banque Nationale de Belgique	1,433	2.87
Oestereichisches National Bank	1,180	2.36
Banco de Portugal	962	1.92
Suomen Pankki	699	1.40
Central Bank of Ireland	425	0.85
Banque Centrale du Luxembourg	75	0.15
Total	**39,468**	**78.94**

15.9 The original eleven NCBs held a little less than 80 percent of the total subscribed capital of the ECB. Four EU countries not members of the Eurosystem – Denmark Greece, Sweden, and the United Kingdom – held a bit over 21 percent of the capital. These countries only contributed 5 percent of their subscribed capital, on the presumption that they gained some benefit from the services of the union. Between the Eurosystem members and the nonmembers, about 80 percent of the subscribed capital of the ECB, or €4 billion, was paid in at the start of the monetary union.

15.10 New unions need a mechanism to provide capital to the union central bank. If all countries join at once, each country will contribute the full amount of capital at the start of the union. If however countries join gradually, a system similar to the EMU's might be followed.

15.11 The EMU designed the system to provide the ECB with sufficient initial capital to operate based on its earnings. Future unions might follow this model, but might operate by providing partial initial capital which would be supplemented by regular contributions. This choice might be chosen because poorer countries might not have funds to make large capital contributions at the start of the union.

15.12 Future unions must provide enough initial capital to give international markets confidence in the new currency. A new union central bank must have capital to intervene in markets and to provide international confidence that the union has sufficient capital to support the currency – small contributions might compromise this goal.

Management of ECB's own funds

15.13 The ECB seeks to separate the management of its own funds from monetary policy actions. ECB capital funds are invested in euro-denominated assets, creating a situation in which routine portfolio management transactions in the funds might conflict with monetary policy decisions. The ECB has stated that "it is of the utmost importance to prevent any interference with the Governing Council's monetary policy decisions." (ECB 2001, p.71) Two steps were taken to avoid this conflict – own funds are strictly physically and functionally separated from other ECB funds, and the ECB follows a passive investment approach in order to not generate what might be considered as monetary policy signals. The Governing Council sets the overall policy for management of the funds, with a goal of maximizing the return, consistent with effective risk management.

15.14 The NCBs held their own capital prior to the founding of the Euroarea. As separate corporate entities entitled to own assets and engage in transactions on their own, the NCBs retain their capital under the union. From 1999 on the accounts were denominated in euro. All components of NCBs' balance sheets denominated in the national currency were translated into euro using the six-significant digit national currency-euro conversion rate, and thus no relative gains or losses were experienced to NCBs' capital because of the restatement into euros.

15.15 Nationally controlled financial positions are not owned by the ESCB. NCB's own funds must be segregated from union funds held by or managed by the NCBs. This requires that NCB financial positions on the day before the union launch must be fully identified and valued, including all holding gains and losses. Financial assets and liabilities should be assessed at fair value. Audited closing balance sheet of the pre-union positions of the NCBs should be published.

Seigniorage and monetary income

15.16 Seigniorage is the income earned from the investment of assets received from the circulation of currency. Seigniorage income can equal as much as several percent of GDP each year and is an important source of income for the central bank and fiscal balances because of central bank profit remittances to the government.

15.17 In the ESCB, the term "monetary income" is used to describe the net earnings from union operations. It includes seigniorage earnings and all other earnings from union operations, such as net interest on monetary policy operations, fees, penalties, and interest earned on holdings of required reserves. All monetary income related to union activity must be carefully segregated from other financial transactions of the central banks.

15.18 An interesting issue for future unions is whether seigniorage should be shared with candidate countries. (The EMU does not have any system to share seigniorage income with candidates.) Countries seeking to join an union will generally seek to stabilize the value of their currencies against the union currency (which is a requirement under ERM II) and it is likely that the country's firms and population will increasingly use the union currency. The union will earn seigniorage income on the currency used in the candidate countries, and conversely the country using the union currency will have its seigniorage income reduced. In such situations, new unions could share seigniorage income with candidate countries to compensate for the shift in seigniorage income. In an extreme, the seigniorage shift could prove destabilizing for the candidate country and possibly even delay the acceptance of the country into the union.

15.19 The share of seigniorage income might be determined by multiplying the estimated stock of union currency in use by an applicable interest rate. The stock might be measured as the sum of documented holdings of the central bank, financial corporations, government, and public corporations, etc., but this misses general public holdings. Alternatively, statistical or econometric methods might be used to prepare estimates. Such estimates should focus on amounts held throughout the year, not just seasonal peaks. Because of the uncertainties of such estimates, the amounts calculated might be discounted.[465]

In return to receiving the seigniorage income, the receiving countries should be expected to comply with anti-counterfeiting initiatives and currency management programs.

C. ESCB intrasystem accounts

Net income of the ECB

15.20 Each year, the ECB prepares annual financial accounts for itself and for the consolidated Eurosystem.

15.21 Per Statute 33.1, the ECB can retain up to 20 percent of its net profits, to be transferred to its general reserve fund. The amount is decided by the General Council. The general reserve fund is capped to not exceed the amount of the ECB's capital. Remaining amounts are distributed to the NCBs, which are the ECB's shareholders.

15.22 Losses by the ECB can be covered by an allocation from the general reserve fund. If this is insufficient, the General Council can allocate funds from the ESCB monetary income for the affected year. For example, in an extreme case, a large loss incurred by the ECB as a result of holding losses on foreign currency reserve assets could hypothetically exceed the total monetary income of the ESCB and result in transfer of the entire monetary income to the ECB.

Allocation of income of NCBs

15.23 Per Statute Article 32, income of NCBs earned as a result of their implementation of ESCB monetary policies is allocated annually. The amount of each NCBs income will equal its annual income derived from assets held against banknotes in circulation and deposit liabilities to credit institutions. These assets and the income derived must be earmarked by the NCBs in accordance with ECB guidelines, and segregated from other NCB accounts. Each NCB's monetary income is reduced by an amount equal to interest paid by that central bank on deposit liabilities to credit institutions, to generate net income.

15.24 NCBs' total net monetary income will be allocated to each NCB in accordance with its capital key, as described above. That is, the net income of the total Eurosystem as a result of monetary operations is divided amongst the NCBs based on their share in the capital of the ECB. The rationale is that the monetary policy actions affect the entire union and the particular country in which policies are implemented is not relevant – no country should benefit because union-linked operations happened to take place in it. Therefore, income is divided according to a formula.

15.25 Expenses of NCBs for implementing monetary policy actions of the Eurosystem are not reimbursed. The NCBs receive an allocation of income from total net earnings of the Eurosystem, but are expected to cover their own expenses. This is intended to promote efficient operations by putting financial pressure on each NCB to keep its costs under control.

15.26 Problems with this approach are that income allocated according to the key might have little relevance to the extent of monetary actions undertaken by a country and costs it incurs. Thus, the net income received could differ greatly between countries. The ECB Governing Council can choose to reimburse NCBs for costs they incur in connection with issuing banknotes or for specific losses arising from monetary policy operations.

Text box: Seigniorage income under the parallel currency approach

The Eurosystem formula for distribution of seigniorage income does not apply when countries use a parallel currency approach to introduce an union currency. Under the Eurosystem's "Big Bang" changeover scenario, all countries moved quickly to the

[465] *Chapter 12 – Statistics* discusses methods to estimate currency held outside the issuing country, which provides information on the potential size of seigniorage shift.

union currency and large differences in absorbing the union currency did not occur.

In contrast, under a parallel currency approach, acceptance of the union currency, and the concurrent retirement of the national currencies, can differ between countries. For example, in country A, 75% of the national currency might be retired and replaced with the union currency, but in country B only 20% might be changed over. Logically, Country A should receive a larger share of the seigniorage generated by the union currency to replace the large loss of income from retirement of the national currency. In contrast, Country B still has large earning from the national currency and deserves only a smaller share of the union seigniorage income.

Given this reality, unions following a parallel currency approach need to monitor the degree of retirement of national currencies, and national issuance of the union currency, as proxies for the use of the union currency. The allocation of seigniorage from the union currency would then be based on that proxy.

D. Transfer of foreign currencies to the ECB

15.27 The NCBs provided the ECB with a stock of foreign reserves assets. NCBs were liable for up to €50 billion in foreign currency reserves, in proportion to their share in the subscribed capital to the ECB. The Governing Council decided how much should be paid in immediately and how much later. Actual transfers, as shown in the 1999 Consolidated Balance Sheet of the Eurosystem, item 9.1 – "Liabilities equivalent to the transfer of foreign reserves", totaled €39.5 billion.

15.28 During the first week of the union, the ECB received 15 percent of the total in gold and the balance in securities, 90 percent denominated in U.S. dollars, and the rest in Japanese yen. The ECB had full rights to use the amounts transferred to it. The amounts transferred are not capital contributions, but create a claim of the NCBs on the ECB. Amounts received were recorded as assets of the ECB and were deducted from the holdings of the NCBs. The claims of the NCBs for foreign currencies transferred are euro-denominated, and hence NCBs do not incur exchange rate revaluations. The ECB bears the exchange rate risk.[466] The NCB claims are remunerable at the short-term refinancing rate for the Eurosystem, adjusted to reflect a zero rate for gold.

15.29 The NCBs retain many of their rights to use foreign currencies to meet their international obligations. They may continue relations with other central banks and international financial institutions, transact in spot and forward transactions in foreign exchange assets and precious metals, hold and manage such assets, and conduct all forms of banking transactions in other countries and with international organizations. Future unions will need to clarify rights and restrictions on national use of foreign currency assets.

15.30 To ensure that NCB transactions in foreign currency are consistent with union exchange rate and monetary policies, countries' use of foreign currency assets in excess of those transferred to the ECB and amounts for working balances above certain limits are subject to approval of the ECB. The Governing Council issues guidelines on uses.

15.31 The ECB's holdings of foreign currency assets transferred from NCB's holdings are recorded on the balance sheet of the ECB, offset by a liability to the NCBs. The ECB can hold IMF reserve positions and SDRs.

[466] However, a special provision [never used] was made by the Governing Council that during the first three years of the union if the ECB experiences large unrealized exchange losses on holdings of reserve assets and has insufficient net income and reserves to cover the loss, then the ECB's liability to the NCBs can be reduced down to as low as 80 percent of its original value. That is, during the first years of the union, the NCBs had a contingent liability to cover a portion of foreign reserve exchange rate losses, which provided a bit of protection for the ECB during its early period. (Although this provision was not used, it does indicate that for the long-run good of the union there might need for special provisions that insulate the union central bank from major threats to its assets or income.)

15.32 Consolidated reserves data for the Eurosystem are published, using the IMF's international reserves and foreign currency liquidity template. Gold comprises most of the reserves, but the IMF standard presentation excludes gold as a reserve asset because it is effectively relatively illiquid and will not be actively exchanged for balance of payments purposes. In mid-2010, total reserves excluding gold totaled about \$280 billion (U.S. dollar equivalent value), of which about \$194 billion was in foreign exchange. The second largest category was SDR holdings of about \$70 billion, which had grown very sharply from about \$6 billion in 2009 because of the new allocation of SDRs in late 2009. This increase in SDRs increased the availability of liquid funding available for balance of payments purposes, but did not involve a direct contribution of the resources from national sources to the Eurosystem.

E. Costs of new unions

15.33 As described in *Chapter 2*, setting up the EMU was quite costly, both to set up the central union operations and for the central banks and governments of the member countries. Europe is a rich region that could afford the costs and had extensive legal arrangements that facilitated financing the venture. With the exception of the planned GCC union, in future unions some or all of the potential member countries might face serious challenges in paying the costs of setting up a new union. In some regions, the costs of setting up a fully configured union could be too high and only a more limited regional arrangement might be possible.

15.34 Costs facing new unions include;

Capital contributions to the new central bank. NCBs lose interest income on these assets.

Meetings of technical committees. Hundreds of meetings were involved during the six years' preparations for the EMU. The meetings required heavy commitments of EMI staff. The EMI spent over 10 percent of its budget for goods and services needed to hold meetings to set up the EMU.

Official consultations and meetings.

The costs of travel to the EMI and hotels and expenses were borne by the countries. The costs of attending meetings could be much greater for future unions because some regions are much less compact than Europe.

Costs of a secretariat or council setting up the union. This includes the costs of acquiring and outfitting union buildings.

Translation costs. The working language of the EMI was English, but the EMI and countries incurred large costs translating into English or translating legal texts into the countries' languages. Much of the cost was borne by the NCBs.

Computer and communications systems. This includes large-scale systems for the union as a whole, individual staff systems, and software.

Design and preprinting of the currency stock

Payments systems infrastructure.

Security

Public facilities for meeting, training, etc..

Training and information sessions; for staff, member country officials, businesses, and the public. A public relations campaign for the changeover to the new currency must be prepared. Information outreach beyond the region itself is also needed.

15.35 Clear rules are needed on who is responsible for costs – the union, member countries, or banks, businesses, and the general public.

15.36 Costs increased steadily in Europe as the preparations for the union intensified and the ECB exhausted its available funds. The view was taken that costs necessary to set up the union had to be paid. Ultimately, the ECB charged the NCBs for the extra cost. *Costs incurred by the NCBs have never been compiled.*

Cost of meetings to set up an union

15.37 The Eurosystem experienced major costs holding meetings to set up the union. Costs were substantial at the EMI/ECB and for member countries. Future unions will face similar costs, but often might have fewer resources to pay for the consultations.

15.38 To reduce costs, future unions will often rely on virtual on-line meetings (which are now much more accessible than when the EMU was set up) and written communications. On-line meetings will be especially important during the final run-up to the union because of the need to quickly resolve issues among a potentially wide group of stake holders and decision makers.

15.39 On-line communications are encouraged, but it must be recognized that virtual meetings often do not provide good opportunities for in-depth investigations of conditions and discussions leading to the best possible decisions. The author strongly encourages at least quarterly in-person meetings in order to allow participants to focus on the issues at hand, learn from others' experiences, review progress in candidate countries, apply peer pressure to maintain progress, and continue forward progress toward union formation.

15.40 In-person meetings are needed and should be scheduled and structured in ways that minimize costs for all involved. For example, it was standard EMI and ECB practice to end the last day of meetings early enough to allow attendees time to get to the airport and avoid an additional overnight stay. A permanent liaison from each potential member country is obviously costly, but it could eliminate a lot of travel from the field to the central planning office. The situation in each future union will differ, but the need to hold down meeting costs is just another of the many issues to address.

F. Audits

15.41 The finances of the ECB, NCBs, and other arms of the monetary union are subject to audit, as described in *Chapter 14.*

Timeline

Preparatory period	
Early actions (four years prior)	Agreement on areas of central or dispersed funding Funding of monetary institute Funding for headquarters building Agreement on capital budget Agreement on seed money for tasks
Three years prior	Seed money for currency design; payments systems, IT systems Draft rules for financial management of system Draft implementing legislation
24 months prior	Agreement on capital contributions Agreement on budget of union central bank and union clearing body Seed money for central bank and clearing entity Seed money for currency printing
18 Months Prior	Complete implementing legislation
Final 12 months	System financial accounting system in place
Final 6 months	Capital contributions to union central bank Transfer of reserves assets to union
Run-up to union	Day before union, all NCB financial positions are valued.
Union day	Monitor experiences Currency liabilities absorbed by union Bank required reserves transferred
Early union period	Calculation of monetary income of union and member NCBs Initial distribution of income
Union steady state	

CHAPTER 16 – LEGAL

What will be the legal framework for union institutions and member countries within the union? How much legal power is transferred from member states to the union? How are legal changes made to adapt to changing conditions?

A. Introduction

16.1. This chapter describes the legal framework for the creation and operation of the EMU and draws lessons for future unions.[467] [468] [469] The framework was constructed over a long period during which the overarching EU legal framework was created that covers the Euroarea as well as the broader group of EU member countries and institutions. Much of the framework existed before the start of work on the monetary union and provided common standards in numerous areas that could be applied in constructing the EMU. Legal materials are extensive and detailed. Most of the material is available on line, but the volume of material, its complexity, the extended development, and the multiple sources make it very "user unfriendly". It offers "bewildering complexity" (Lastra 2009)

16.2. Although complex, the system is "robust", in that it has worked well, is highly internally consistent, and covers many new situations or is flexible enough to apply broadly. Overall, (until challenged by the global financial crisis and accompanying fiscal distress) it has been successfully applied in all the member countries, where widely differing legal frameworks exist.

16.3. It has also successfully met its major challenge of creating a new form of international public law covering the large-scale transfer of sovereignty to a supranational body and successful operation of the new system. The principles the EMU legal framework established thus could provide much of the legal basis for future monetary unions. This conclusion can be taken only so far because new unions face different situations or new areas where new legal principles need to be developed. For example, new unions are more likely to be involved in supervision of banks and other financial institutions than in the original Maastricht framework, which will create a mix of monetary, supervisory, and fiscal arrangements for the legal system to handle. Or growth of multiple new unions might change formal governance of the international financial system beyond the *ad hoc* pragmatic adjustments sometimes used for the EMU. As new unions develop, strengthening and legal codification of international governance arrangements becomes more likely, including the possibility of creating new international bodies.

16.4. Further problems exist due to some inconsistencies or asymmetries in the framework, the need to define the rights and responsibilities of the multiple actors involved, and handling the resultant complexity. Also, the financial and Greek crises created new challenges that forced changes to the legal arrangements.

16.5. For future unions, building the legal framework will be a major part of the process. It is likely that many principles or elements of the EMU framework will be adopted, but major differences will emerge which could include....

Reducing the complexity of the EMU system.

Bringing the framework into a single text.

Incorporating the goals and principles of regional parent organizations.

---

[467] This chapter benefitted from conversations with Erwin Nierop who was part of the legal team of the EMI and ECB. He continues to advise potential future unions on a variety of topics.

The author cannot match the legal skills of the experts cited in this chapter. Any errors in fact or interpretations are solely the author's.

[468] An excellent overview of issues affecting the complex Eurosystem legal system was compiled by Aicorum and Garavelli (2005).

[469] In this chapter, the terms 'Maastricht Treaty' and 'Treaty' are used to describe the basic requirements of the system. The terms as used here encompass the Statutes for the EMI and for the ESCB and ECB, since they were attached as protocols to the Treaty although later separately enacted. The explanations are clearer without precise attributions by document and paragraph, which nonspecialized readers do not need.

Eliminating references to European laws and practices.

Covering different policy regimes than in Europe.

Integrating new macroprudential perspectives into the policy framework.

Creating rules for membership and governance.

Creating rules for new types of financial arrangements.

Applying different standards for centralization of policy decision-making and implementation.

Dealing with financial supervision

Dealing with new situations in international governance

Dealing with the absence of the EU's overarching legal framework as a means to introduce cross-comparability between union members.

Fostering adherence to the growing body of international standards and best practices in numerous technical areas that could support effective operation of the union.

Covering a transition from loose or partial arrangements early in the process to comprehensive, stricter standards for the completed union.

Creating judicial systems to regulate the union bodies and resolve cross-border business disputes related to union actions.

Potentially including special conditions appropriate for ethnic, language, or religious communities.

16.6. This is obviously a very heavy agenda. A key challenge in building a system in the shadow of the European experience is winnowing from the mass of material the core information relevant for other regions. Moreover, some potential unions begin with diverse fully sovereign legal systems that must be merged together from scratch – new legal foundations are needed, not just creating a new type of central bank.

16.7. One possibility is to use the legal framework as the organizing structure for the union-building process – similar to the SADC model legal code for the union for adoption by all of sixteen possible future member countries. This is a plausible approach, but it faces the challenges listed above and fitting into a wide range of existing legal systems and local institutions and practices.

16.8. *Approached from this angle, the choice is whether to tackle the full legal challenges or to identify the minimum legal requirements to construct a monetary union – if those can be identified, a program can be created for construction of the legal foundations for an union.*

16.9. *Or, if legal complexity precludes developing a full union structure, a decision could be made to aim for some lower level of regional integration.* This could take various forms; create a customs union or trade bloc, create mechanisms for mutual macroeconomic oversight, or promote regional adoption of key international technical standards that could de facto lead to convergent practices within the region. [470]

[470] Such as the Basel bank supervisory standards, Chiang Mai-style reserves swap lines, codes of fiscal transparency, accounting and auditing standards, securities clearance systems, UNCTAD trade documentation simplification, etc. Each such action can be beneficial in isolation, but also can create a regional atmosphere in which prospects for eventual formation of a union are bolstered. An important focus of such efforts should be to address each of the dozen *Key Standards for Financial System Soundness* developed during the GFC by the FSB. The Standards lay out an ambitious agenda for adoption by all countries, and provide a good model for regional efforts to promote financial sector development and soundness. Nearly all the *Standards* deal with cross-

(continued)

Levels of financial integration redux

16.10. In this section, the taxonomy of levels of financial integration presented in the Introduction is reprised because different legal structures apply.

16.11. A critical variable underlying the framework will be the degree of centralization of the union central bank and NCBs.

> If the plan is to create a single central bank for the union and for all member countries, a relatively simple framework is possible. The single central bank can decide on its own procedures in many spheres and implement them in all countries. Rules are not needed on independent behavior of NCBs.
>
> If the system is decentralized, the rule-making process between the union central bank and NCBs must be clarified, rights and obligations of each bank spelled out, income and expenses divided, and operational procedures set. More complex legal arrangements are needed to define the interrelationships between the central banks within the union and to relate the central banks to different national legal standards.

16.12. *Chapter 1 – Introduction* presented a taxonomy of different levels of integration. The Euroarea has a very high level of integration with a single monetary and exchange rate policy and an organization (European System of Central Banks - ESCB) comprised of the ECB and all NCBs of the member countries that enacts policy throughout the union. Substantial national sovereignty over financial policy was ceded to the new union. But agreements with lesser degrees of integration are possible. A group of countries could choose to coordinate or integrate some functions, or might wish to maintain greater national control than permitted in a pure monetary union. Also, new unions might pass through these stages on their roads to create their unions, and thus will have evolving legal arrangements.

16.13. Four levels of financial integration are;

I - Independent national financial market development

16.14. This describes a situation in which each country, acting independently, seeks to create financial sector infrastructure and effective markets. International or regional standards and practices exist and can be followed, but this is done through national initiative.

II - Coordinated policy research and decision-making

16.15. In this stage, countries continue to act independently, but have procedures for regular consultations and agreements over policy and standards. Decisions are made through multi-country consultations in which each country participates.

16.16. Agreements can have degrees of strictness, from agreement to adhere to voluntary codes, memos of understanding, to full treaties. Implementation is the responsibility of the individual countries. Examples include the original CMI, in which Asian countries agreed amongst themselves to behave in certain ways, including carrying out regular consultations and making reserves swap lines available.[471] The CAMC is also at this level of integration.

III - Transnational oversight

16.17. Countries agree by treaty or other mechanism to set up a transnational entity with specified powers over the participating states. Powers could be broad or tightly defined.

16.18. The IMF is an example – it holds resources provided by the members, carries out regular overview of country situations and policies, and can

border activity in some form and thus are something every future union must address.

[471] In May 2008, the Chiang Mai Initiative was strengthened to substantially increase the swap lines between countries for use during exchange rate emergencies, create a single document, and make the arrangement mandatory. This strengthening effectively transformed the initiative into Level III

extend resources with conditions and sanctions.[472] The aborted Asian Monetary Fund would also have been an example. Authority might be broad, or it might be limited to a specific area, such as being a standard setter for clearing systems operations, a regional transportation authority, or monitor implementation of agreements or technical standards. A country can belong to multiple Level III arrangements handling different topics.

IV - Monetary and financial union

16.19. In a full-fledged monetary union, countries cede substantial sovereignty to a transnational entity and integrate activities so that a single standard prevails or national differences are reduced or disappear. The Eurosystem, which is a single system operating in all countries using the euro, controls monetary policies as if national markets no longer exist. At this level of integration, important binding decisions can be made at the transnational level.

Corresponding legal systems

16.20. Different legal frameworks apply to the different levels of financial integration.

16.21. At level I, *Independent national financial market operation,* there is no explicit integration. In fact, independent national sovereignty is recognized by the international community, through steps such as the right of each country to choose its own exchange rate regime, or to issue its own currency.[473] No convergence or harmonization of legal systems is necessary. However, there is increasingly some degree of harmonization in practice as countries follow international standards or best practices. For example, virtually all countries apply the Basel capital adequacy standards for banks. However, the decision to do so and the implementation of standards is national. Moreover, the Basel standards and numerous other international standards permit options or flexibility in national applications. National legal practices can differ widely under these circumstances.

16.22. At Level II, *Coordinated policy research and decision-making,* countries retain decision-making authority, but come together in various fora to set common goals, coordinate actions, or resolve differences. Legal systems can be different between countries and different methods can be used to move toward common goals. However, countries also can agree to change legal provisions – for example, all countries could agree to common rules against counterfeiting. Implementation could be voluntary by each country, or various degrees of strictness can be applied including signing a full treaty, but the impetus to agree and to apply the rules remains national.

16.23. Level III - *Transnational oversight.* Countries agree by treaty or other mechanism to set up a transnational entity with specified powers over the participating states. Powers could be broad or tightly defined. At this level, specific legal commitments are required. Countries must cede authority to a supranational entity that must have a governance system that includes; financial backing, a decision-making process, clear rules on members' obligations, dispute resolution procedures, etc. Each of these actions could involve specific legal provisions, which might be included in a common central document and often are reflected in implementing provisions in each member country.

16.24. A key variable in transnational oversight is how broad or tight are the duties of the transnational entity. Only a strictly limited set of functions might be involved that require few legal changes to national systems, or a broad range of powers with complex legal requirements could exist. As more functions are

[472] The IMF General Counsel has said that membership in the IMF requires accepting obligations and constitutes a limitation on monetary sovereignty in exchange for the benefits of membership. Sovereignty is limited to promote international cooperation and the common good. (Gianviti 2004).

[473] The issuance of the national currency is protected from counterfeiting under the 1929 Geneva Treaty on Suppression of Counterfeiting Currency.

incorporated related to money, foreign exchange, settlements, market infrastructure, etc, the closer the entity becomes like a monetary union.

16.25. A broad form of transnational oversight is provided by the IMF, which obligates countries in ways that limit sovereignty, such as requiring countries to engage in transactions in SDRs as part of its membership in the international system. Similarly, although countries are not permitted to manipulate exchange rates to prevent balance of payments adjustment nor act in ways that harm the international financial system, countries retain substantial rights such as the right to choose which exchange rate regime it wishes to adopt and have rights under international law to change the value of their currencies.[474]

16.26. Level IV – *Monetary union*. At the highest levels of integration, a monetary union can be formed in which countries cede control of monetary and exchange rate policies to a supranational entity. Legal powers must be explicit, detailing the rights and duties at the union level and at the member level.

16.27. Although monetary unions cede substantial sovereignty to the union, the obligations of the member states remain mixed. For example, union member countries remain obligated under their commitments to the IMF simultaneously with obligations to the union or mutual obligations with each other. Countries can still exercise sovereign powers in other spheres such as fiscal policies or bank supervision. Legal systems, of course, need to specify the various rights and obligations involved, as well as deal with conflicts.

16.28. Broadly speaking, new unions might advance along this 4-stage path, beginning at stages where greater latitude in national actions is permitted and moving toward greater central or supranational control. Unions being planned are usually in type II or III situations and moving toward IV. However, flexibility is possible. For example, a group of countries could pledge to peg their currencies to a single external currency, such as the GCC has done, or to a large regional currency, such as to the South African rand in the CMA, then allow each country to implement the adjustments needed to sustain that peg.

16.29. The legal arrangements for each level of integration above could differ widely. The path chosen for union and the endpoint itself could differ. Obviously, such differences need to be reflected in the legal arrangements.

B. EMU legal framework

16.30. This section provides an overview of the EMU legal framework. It is the most comprehensive legal framework used in any of the existing monetary unions.[475] It covers many different tasks and relationships, and thus can be a guide to the types of legal issues that other union might face. However, the system grew organically out of very complex institutional arrangements in Europe and much is not relevant elsewhere.

The European Union

16.31. The EMU exists within the framework of the European Union (EU), and therefore is covered by EU legal provisions. The EU itself was the product of decades of development in which progressively more comprehensive organizations with supra-national powers developed. The creation of the monetary union has been called the crowning achievement of the development of the EU framework.

16.32. The term supranational is important. The prefix *supra* implies something that is legally above or superior. Thus, a supranational entity is superior to

[474] This right, now widely accepted by the IMF membership, did not apply under the original IMF Articles of Agreement, under which countries obligated themselves to set the par value of their currencies in terms of gold and to intervene to maintain the currencies within a tight band around the par values.

[475] Although the Andean Union, which is a free trade area, has adopted many of the institutional arrangements of the EU and might look a bit like it on the surface.

a national entity and its laws have priority over national laws. A supranational entity is created by countries coming together and agreeing to cede part of their sovereignty to the union.

16.33. In a multi-country setting, such as in Europe, it was advantageous to have a superior body whose decisions must be followed by member countries. This supported comparability of practice between countries or sometimes introduction of common practices. It also allowed for common legal arrangements to cover multi-country issues, such as integration of financial markets, dispute resolution, free transit between countries, and many more.

16.34. The EU supranational institutions, laws, and practices are not superior in a dictatorial sense. EU level institutions and rules are derived from consultative or legislative processes in which all member countries or their populations have a voice. Also, many of the EU level rulings allow variation or flexibility at the national level or even establish that national level authorities have primary authority in some spheres, such as in bank supervision under the original Maastricht rules. And finally, there are numerous areas where national legal practice prevails – setting national legal holidays is one small example. Thus, the EMU is a component of a larger framework, but with a complex mix of union-level and national level institutions, laws, and practices.

16.35. The EU *supra*national framework above the EMU with an established body of "Community law" can be contrasted to an *inter*national framework. An international framework is based on agreement by separate national, each acting in a sovereign manner. Decisions are made by sovereign nations and implementation remains a sovereign national responsibility.

16.36. The EMU could have been created by a treaty among sovereign states in which it acts in accordance with treaty provisions without elements of supranational power. However, the EMU was created by a treaty that placed it within the EU framework in which supranational power exists, and the EMU was given authority to exercise that power in the field of monetary policy alongside the general EU powers. In the "Olaf Case" the European Court of Justice ruled that the "ECB is a creature of Community Law, which falls squarely within the Community framework"[476]

16.37. The creation of the EMU within the EU legal framework provided important advantages.

Much of the legal framework for the EMU already existed and was implemented in national law and did not have to be created anew.

Community law could be used to introduce additional legal changes needed for the monetary union that were unclear at the time of the Treaty.[477]

Other EU institutions, such as the EU statistical office or courts, cooperate with the monetary union.

Broader goals of the EU (including social and environmental targets) provided direction to the monetary union.

---

[476] (Lastra 2009). See also *Chapter 8 – International Economic Relations of an Union* for a discussion of monetary unions as supranational entities.

[477] A generic title used for additional legal rules to serve monetary union purposes was called "secondary legislation", which covered laws not central for operation of the union, but which created the environment in which the union could operate successfully. Rules set by various EU bodies can effectively serve the same functions. Examples of laws or rules applied for the EU include the common definition of a bank, accounting standards, deposit insurance standards, or rules for dealing with bankrupt banks, methods of compiling interest and fees, public disclosures, instituting claims across borders, and bank reserves and liquidity requirements, etc..

Financing rules and contributions at the union and national levels can be mandated at the union level.[478]

16.38. Where planned unions have similar arrangements to the EMU, they should be incorporated into the local framework. However, comparable institutions might not exist – they might need to be created from scratch and their functions will perhaps need to be explicitly included with the union legal framework.

The Maastricht Treaty

16.39. The EMU core document is the *Treaty establishing the European Community*, better known as the Maastricht Treaty ratified in 1991. It advanced the program for political, trade, and financial integration in Europe, and included the legal provisions that enabled the creation of the monetary union. The provisions for monetary union were referenced in the main treaty, but in a more detailed form were attached to the Treaty as a protocol with equal force of law called the *Statute of the European System of Central Banks and of the European Central Bank.*

16.40. All EU member countries signed the Treaty, in which they ceded substantial sovereignty over monetary policy to the new European System of Central Banks (ESCB) that included the national central banks (NCBs) of all EU countries with the ECB as its central body. Countries agreed to make changes to their economic situations and legal systems to support the operation of the new union. A new currency was to be created that would circulate in all countries. A single monetary and exchange rate policy was to be introduced throughout the new monetary union. National members agreed to cease operations of their own monetary, exchange rate, and foreign reserves policies. The EMI, was set up to make preparations for the start of the union.

16.41. The EMI was given supranational powers in several respects, but in other ways it continued to share powers with national members.[479] Under the doctrine of *subsidiarity,* functions remained at the national level unless there were specific reasons for them to be done at the union level. The union was permitted to access the resources of the NCBs to carry out operations, which is a substantial supranational power.

16.42. Maastricht placed the EMU within the EU framework. The ECB and other monetary union bodies reported to EU executive and judicial bodies; and the monetary union was required to respect the goals of the EU and work with other union bodies.

16.43. Maastricht laid out two major features for the central banking regime in the new union – price stability and central bank independence[480] as an important tool supporting price stability. The concept of central bank independence fostered an uniquely powerful role for the union;

Union policy makers and union institutions were to be free of national political interference.

The ECB had independence to make decisions for the union as a whole and not as a reflection of

[478] The fiscal aspects of EU supranational powers were very important in finding paths through the GFC, the fiscal crises, and the Covid crisis.

[479] The entity planning the new union will *de facto* have large powers to introduce practices into the union. The union treaty will necessarily be incomplete and must leave many operational details to this entity, which might have already been granted some forms of supranational authority. This can be politically tricky and it will be advantageous to have fairly strong public oversight of this institution, as well as legal constraints on its actions.

[480] "The choice of a specific article demonstrates the desire of the Treaty's authors to underline the independence of the monetary authorities of the Community. Nevertheless, they are part of the Community's overall legal order…The provisions are inserted into the EC Treaty." (Louis 2005, p. 32). Louis also notes that ECB acts can be reviewed by the European Court of Justice.

national conditions. It would set policy that member NCBs must implement.

The ECB could create regulations and make decisions for member countries to follow or implement in their national legislation. The ECB could call on the EU to enact secondary pieces of legislation needed for effective operation of the union.

The ECB has independent finances, which was seen as a necessary condition for policy independence.[481]

16.44. The Maastricht Treaty transferred powers in the monetary field to the EMU, but other economic policies remained under national control. A key issue was how broadly should the monetary field be interpreted. In the strict terms of the Maastricht Treaty, a narrow interpretation includes operation of the single monetary policy, exchange rate policy, holding and managing reserves, oversight of payments systems, and issuing banknotes.[482]

16.45. In September 1995, a Working Group of Legal Experts (WGLE) was set up by the EMI, with a mandate to report on all relevant legal issues with particular reference to preparations for Stage 3 of the union. This group acted independently of the legal team at the EMI. The EMI group translated decisions in various topical areas into legal language for use in various rulings, directives, and the like. In contrast, the WGLE reviewed the EMI language and could comment on any aspect, including identifying problems, clarification of terminology, inconsistencies, clashes with EU level or national legislation, etc., areas in which it is credited with making some important contributions. It also provided a channel for informing national legal bodies about the legal developments at the EMI – it was felt that the EMI on its own could not have properly informed countries about the legal aspects of creating the union.

Derogation

16.46. "Derogation" is a Maastricht Treaty term that indicates that a country has not met the conditions for entry into the Eurosystem, and cannot enter the monetary union as a full member. Countries with derogations have special legal status and retain their legal provisions needed to continue their own monetary and exchange rate policies. Conversely, their legal codes do not need to include language needed to adopt the euro and operate within the Eurosystem.

16.47. However, countries with derogations are committed under Maastricht to ultimately adopt the euro[483], are obliged to work towards economic and legal convergence, and introduce central bank independence. Countries with derogations are in effect part way into the union and must have legal provisions in place for this status. For example, countries with derogations are members of the TARGET system, are members of the ESCB, and must make small contributions to the capital of the ECB. Legal provision must be made for each of these cases.

[481] "Budgetary independence was, and still is, held to be inherent in the nature of an independent central bank." (Louis 2005, p. 37).

[482] *The ECB took the view in 2003 that a narrow and technical interpretation should not be made*: in its comments on the draft Constitution for Europe, it said that its powers included all exclusive competencies related to the euro. "Opinion of the ECB of 19 September 2003 at the request of the Council of the European Union on the draft Treaty establishing the Constitution for Europe", as quoted in Louis (2005, p. 29).

[483] The Protocol on the transition to Stage Three states, "all member states shall, whether or not they fulfill the necessary conditions for the adoption of a single currency, respect the will of the Community to enter swiftly into the third stage, and therefore no Member shall prevent the entering into the third stage."

Press reports have indicated that some of the ten EU members who entered in 2004 are not interested in adopting the euro. It is hypothetically possible to remain outside the Euroarea by failing to take action to meet the economic and legal convergence criteria for membership. Sweden is in this position due to failure to fulfill legal convergence requirements.

16.48. The status of countries with derogations is reviewed every two years. The ECB and the European Commission prepare reports that are reviewed by the EU Council. If a country meets the entry criteria, the derogation is abrogated and the country must adopt the euro. At this point countries must rapidly take steps to be sure all necessary legal provisions are in place before the start date.

16.49. *Future unions that will have some form of partial membership will need to have legal provisions that allow the countries to participate to the extent allowed, with specified rights and obligations.*

Legal tasks preparing for the EMU

16.50. The 1996 EMI Annual Report cites areas of legal work in preparation for the union;

Revaluing and redenominating

Secondary EU legislation to implement the preparatory work for the union

Legal convergence

Project support

Advice on national implementation legislation or rules to ensure compliance with Treaty provisions.

Administration.

Revaluing and redenominating

16.51. The replacement of the national currencies of union countries with a single union currency requires legal instruments that mandate that currencies be converted into the union currency for all uses and that specify the rate of conversion. Thus, for example, the EU enacted rules that the ECU should be converted into euros at a rate of one-to-one. This obligates all EMU countries and all private parties to recognize the conversion.

16.52. One thorny question regarding conversion is whether rules changes within the union are accepted extraterritorially, for example by traders outside the union. Gianviti (2004) states that when the ECU was converted into the euro, New York and other U.S. states enacted laws that recognized the conversion and the rate. This was unprecedented and preemptive, forestalling possible challenges to the power of the EU to enact changes that have extraterritorial effects. (For example, instead of accepting euros, could a party with a contract in ECU demand payment in the form of the currencies comprising the ECU basket?)

Secondary EU legislation

16.53. The EMI provided advice to the European Commission on legislation to introduce the euro. For example, in mid-1996 it submitted material for new regulations covering the replacement of the ECU by the euro and national substitution of the euro for national currencies. Once the regulations were in a draft form, the EMI again commented in late 1996. At that time, it found that there needed to be greater specification of the timing of introduction of banknotes and coins and further work on issues related to redenomination into euro of government debt and bonds and securities traded in financial markets.

16.54. Other examples of advice on Community legislation included preparing draft texts on collection of statistical information, application of required minimum reserves, and the power of the ECB to propose sanctions.

Legal convergence

16.55. The Maastricht Treaty required member countries to eliminate provisions in their laws incompatible with the treaty, a process referred to as "legal convergence". The treaty also required the EMI review the legal convergence process similar to reviewing economic convergence criteria.

16.56. In 1996, the EMI published a report "Progress towards Convergence" (EMI 1996b); and half of the final convergence report used to select EMU members was devoted to legal convergence. (EMI 1998b) Three areas of focus of the convergence reviews were NCB independence, legal integration of the NCBs within the ESCB, and other legislation including banknotes and coins, foreign reserves management, and exchange rate policy, etc.

Project support

16.57. The creation of a currency union involved completion of perhaps two hundred different steps, each of which might have numerous components. Each step must be completed with the appropriate degree of harmonization – be it full agreement between countries, agreement on principles that are applied by national practice, mutual recognition, or some other degree of comparability. Different forms of legal infrastructure are required for each. This means that the union level legal staffs, national central bank legal staff, and key counterparties in countries need to work out legal arrangements – for each project as it affects each country, in a manner compatible with other projects, and with the appropriate degree of enforceability.

Advice on national implementation

16.58. National authorities were required to consult with the EMI on draft legislation related to the EMI's areas of competence to ensure compatibility with the Maastricht treaty. (The arrangement is legally a bit strange in that the EMI's views formally were not considered binding, but if a country failed to consult on legislation in a relevant topic the legislation was considered to be invalid.)

Administration

16.59. The legal staff also contributed to setting up the legal framework to administer the union and set rules for operations.

C. Elements of legal convergence

16.60. This section discusses some details on the elements of legal convergence between countries monitored by the EMI and ECB.

Institutional independence of the NCBs

16.61. The Treaty expressly prohibits the ECB, NCBs, and Governing Council members from seeking or taking instructions on monetary policy from European institutions, national authorities including central banks, and other bodies. The Treaty also prohibits such entities from attempting to influence the members of the Governing Council.

16.62. Independence is required in four central policy areas – monetary policy, exchange rate policy, foreign reserves management, and payments systems. In other fields, independence was not believed necessary. Thus, NCBs can perform tasks outside the range envisioned in the Treaty, and take instructions in these tasks (unless the Governing Council rules by a two-thirds vote that the activity interferes with ESCB goals and tasks). For example, a NCB could be directed by its government to serve as agent for collection of securities transactions taxes.

16.63. The EMI broadly defined central bank independence to include institutional status, personal independence of authorities, functional/operational independence, and financial independence. It also prepared a list of practices it thought incompatible with independence. These lists provided guidance to legislators adapting national laws to reflect Maastricht provisions. Legal independence was required by the time the ECB was created so that its independent judgment could be used in policy making.

16.64. The list of features of independence were based on three assumptions (EMI 1988b, p.291);

Central bank independence is required to carry out the duties prescribed in the Treaty.

The list of attributes is not additional legislation beyond the scope of the Treaty, but a tool to facilitate the assessment of independence.

Independence cannot be judged mechanically, but must be assessed case-by-case.

16.65. Types of violations of central bank independence include;

Giving instruction to NCBs or their governors

Rights to approve, suspend, defer, or veto decisions

Rights to censor decisions on legal grounds

Participating in NCB decision-making bodies with a right to vote

16.66. A right exists for consultation prior to NCB decisions.[484] Dialog, even when based on statutes, promoting exchange of information and views is acceptable as long as it does not interfere with independence, the ECB's competencies and accountability are respected, and confidentiality requirements are respected.

Personal independence

16.67. The NCB Governors were expected to perform key roles in formulation of monetary policy and it was considered important that they be able to act independently with regards to the union as a whole and not solely as a representative of national situations or policies. For example, in reviewing legislation covering the Bundesbank, the EMI recommended adding language that the Bundesbank president as a member of ECB Governing Council is independent of instructions from the Bundesbank Central Bank Council.

16.68. A NCB governor is required to have a minimum five-year term, with protection against arbitrary dismissal.

Legal integration into the ESCB

16.69. The Maastricht Treaty states that member NCBs will become integral parts of the ESCB and are required to comply with the ECB's rules and instructions. In many cases, this conflicted with existing national legal language authorizing the national central bank to engage in certain actions or to be the sole authority for actions. One common example was granting the national central bank sole authority to issue currency. In these cases, legislation often needed to add statements establishing the competence of the ECB or Eurosystem, and often the nature of the relationship between the Eurosystem and NCBs. These legal provisions (which often had operational aspects) needed to be in place by the start of Stage 3, when the euro was created and the single monetary and exchange rate policies were introduced.

Adaption of other national legislation.

16.70. A wide variety of other legislation could be affected – banknotes, coins, finances, accounting, statistics, audits, etc. These steps were taken relatively late during the preparations for the union. In early 1997, the EMI noted that work on adapting statutes for NCBs was proceeding, but there had been little done adjusting other legislation and thus action should not be postponed further. (EMI 1997, p. 81)

16.71. In judging convergence, the EMI permitted national legislation to reflect local conditions and practices so long as it was not incompatible with the Maastricht Treaty. In the language of the Treaty, national legislation needed to be only "compatible". It was not necessary that the legislation be fully "harmonized", which was the term used to indicate that provisions were close to identical or unified across countries.[485] Countries might express the legal concepts in different ways or with reference to local institutions, but the results must achieve Maastricht

[484] The ECB Governing Council is viewed as the relevant authority to undertake dialog at the Community level.

[485] In the EU, different types of legal actions at the union level have different levels of applicability and harmonization. For example, an EC "Directive" tells national authorities to take some type of action, but allows countries leeway in how the legislation is expressed at the national level. In contrast, an EC "Regulation" applies to all member countries and is specific in its language that all countries must use. It is a source of debate which EU-wide initiatives should permit local variation or apply to the union as a whole and are identical in all member countries.

An additional question is whether union-wide regulations need to be reflected in national codes. Incorporating them into national codes allows for the national code

(continued)

Treaty goals and ECB rules and procedures. Also, NCBs can take actions not specified in the Treaty that do not interfere with ESCB goals and tasks, which will result in differences between national legal texts. Also, countries were permitted to introduce compatibility in different ways; by deleting offending provisions, making reference to Treaty obligations, by incorporating the Treaty language into national text, or some combination.[486]

The legal nature of EU Directives[487]

16.72. This section describes several EU Directives enacted to facilitate the operation of the monetary union. Although spurred by creation of the monetary union, they apply throughout the EU. They are important (1) as descriptions of the major types of secondary issues that the EU felt were needed for effective operation of the financial system, and (2) as examples of more direct legal intervention over national standards to require common treatments throughout the union. These directives moved the EU from mutual recognition of national legal practices toward greater use of common standards. This evolution might apply to other regions that might begin by accepting more flexible legal frameworks between countries as a first step in creating an union. This legal flexibility could be politically necessary, could allow time to experiment before committing to final arrangements, or simply reflect an inability to completely harmonize legal systems during the time available before the union is launched. Conversely, future unions might question whether a flexible first step is needed if market pressures, expectations of adherence of widely accepted international standards, and efficiency push for more common legal frameworks, and thus might try to introduce a common legal framework from the beginning.

Banking Directive

16.73. The Banking Directive enacted in 2000 is the main instrument to create a single market for banking institutions. (Löber, p. 29) It created a single license for banks anywhere in the EU, applied home country supervision, and a common capital requirement based on the Basel Standards. Its definition of banking institutions includes credit institutions as already established in EU practice and also includes all institutions that engage in any of a list of activities, including securities safekeeping and administration. EU states are also required to permit the activities in the list to be carried out in their country, which thus for example permits banking institutions to carry out securities safekeeping and administration throughout the union.

Settlement Finality Directive (SFD)

16.74. The SFD guards against risks to the solvency of the union's financial systems. Because many financial transactions are part of chains of transactions that occur quickly one-after-another, the failure of a single transaction puts many transactions at risk. Failures in chains of transactions can create serious systemic

---

to be complete and can work the regulation into the national language and legal framework in a logical manner. Conversely, re-expressing a legal code into many different national setting is resource intensive and could introduce errors or differing interpretations. Also, the results should be reviewed, which can be cumbersome. Practical considerations may come into play – small economies, or economies that have recently recast their legal frameworks, might have limited advantages in embedding union-level regulations into national legislation, and a simple reference to the higher-level regulation might suffice.

[486] One complication is that Maastricht only covered cases of national legislation incompatible with the Treaty provisions themselves, and did not cover subsequent Community or ECB "secondary legislation" that enters into force at the beginning of Stage 3. Importantly, case law of the European Court of Justice established that national legislation must be brought in line with the secondary legislation. (EMI 1998b, p. 289) Future unions should include arrangements to incorporate union-level legal changes into national legislation.

[487] This section covers legal aspects of several directives to facilitate financial integration. Their roles in supporting EMU financial policy goals are discussed in Chapters 10 and 11.

risks. Ensuring finality of settlement and netting ensures that this risk cannot occur.

16.75. The Directive's scope was tightly limited, covering supervised financial institutions, public entities, central counterparties, and clearing houses and settlement agents. Limitations were introduced to not create far-reaching exemptions to general bankruptcy laws. Thus, in effect, insolvency within the financial sector is governed by a special set of rules.

16.76. The Directive applied a single set of rules for an integrated union financial market.

> "With the SFD, the Community stepped away from its traditional legislative approach of mutual recognition and introduced the harmonization of certain rules of substantive insolvency law, international insolvency law, and private international law" (Löber 2006, p.16)

16.77. Under the Directive, payment orders and netting are final and irrevocable, even under insolvency proceedings. This contradicts generally applied insolvency rules, which permit transactions be completed before initiating insolvency proceedings that can reverse or cancel transactions.

16.78. A second exception to standard practice stems from a provision that a foreign participant in an EU settlement system falls under the law governing the system, which supersedes a principle in private international law that the insolvency rules of the country of the participant apply. Thus, the settlements system is protected from application of foreign insolvency law.

16.79. A provision covers collateral in conflict-of-laws situations. For example, collateral used by an exchange in country A might come from the country B, where the collateral giver resides or where his accounts are kept. Indeed, the EMU's "correspondent central banking model" (CCBM) permits this so that transactors anywhere in the union can post collateral at any exchange. The Directive established that the relevant law is where the relevant account records the right of the collateral taker.

16.80. The Directive explicitly covers transfer orders and netting and protects them from legal challenges.

> *"The success of this mechanism is conditional upon the proper designation of one law for the whole system, insulation against any foreign law, and the irrevocability and finality of transfer orders and netting." (Löber, p. 18)*

16.81. The directive is tightly defined and does not cover the underlying transaction or instrument. Thus, the underlying instrument might be subject to judicial review, for example because it is fraudulent, and could be declared invalid. This obviously would be a legally messy situation if it arises.

16.82. SFD implementation was required prior to start-up of the union. It was considered critical to reduce systemic risk in payments and settlements systems and had to be in place to permit proper operation of union money market arrangements.[488] [489]

---

[488] In 2006, the SFD was reviewed to ensure that it had kept pace with market changes and deal with technical clarifications. Among policy questions were how to deal with an increase in multijurisdictional situations because of cross-border mergers or centralization of company functions, treatment of electronic money, and treatment of the increased number of clearing houses.

[489] The SFD explicitly covered collateral and mandated that the laws of the country of the relevant account of the collateral taker apply. However, this did not cover the multiplicity of standards and additional guidance was felt necessary. A group of experts prepared a draft in early 2001 that was adopted in 2002 for application in national legal codes by yearend 2003 (actually implementation took longer). This very rapid schedule was encouraged by market participants who strongly supported common arrangements.

Collateral Directive

16.83. Efficient and reliable operation of a collateral system was considered very important for the operation of European financial markets.[490] Collateral provides a mechanism to guarantee completion of transactions and is especially important for cross-border transactions. Collateral reduces credit risk on the underlying transaction and frees credit lines for other uses.[491] Collateral reduces systemic risk in payment and settlement systems, supports a repurchase agreement market which had grown very rapidly, helps secure general bank lending, and is used for securities and government treasury transactions.

16.84. The Directive was intended for use by central banks, official entities, and financial institutions.[492] It permits collateral to be provided in two ways; either with full transfer of ownership to the collateral taker (like a repurchase agreement), or using a pledge or lien over assets that remain under the ownership of the collateral giver. A very broad range of financial instruments can be used for collateral, although there is a little used provision that allows exclusion of the collateral providers' own shares or shares of affiliates.

16.85. The Directive constituted a paradigm shift in Community legislation toward explicit harmonization of practice across the union by enacting specific rules. This replaced an earlier focus on minimum harmonization across countries or mutual recognition. These looser arrangements might be easier for new unions to adopt, but the experience in Europe favored more explicit common practices adopted through legislation applicable in all union countries.

Directive on Markets in Financial Instruments

16.86. This directive, effective in 2006, covered investment companies and activities. It replaced the principle of mutual recognition with a "single passport" that permits investment companies to operate across the union, but also applied a high level of protection for consumers. It also established a comprehensive regulatory framework covering investment transactions on exchange and trading systems. For example, it has rules mandating that investment companies have procedures for safekeeping of client's assets.

Winding up Directive for Credit Institutions

16.87. This directive applied the principle of application of single state laws to insolvency proceedings by mandating that the home-state rules apply. This means that branches outside the home country fall under the legal control of the home country. Subsidiaries, however, are handled by the host country.

Directive on Bank Recovery and Resolution

16.88. In 2014, the EU enacted a directive laying out procedures for smooth closing and resolution of failed banks, following FSB guidelines in *Key Attributes of Effective Resolution Regimes for Financial Institutions.* Among the many aspects of the Directive were establishing the legal framework for cross-

[490] Before the Directive, collateral arrangements within the EU were fragmented and covered by individual national laws. This increased costs and delays for cross-border transactions and often required separate legal decisions for each transaction. Multiple jurisdictions were involved because the residence of counterparties, the location of the collateral, and the location of the exchange and depository could be in different countries and thus determination of the relevant laws was difficult.

[491] Prior to the financial crisis, all ESCB lending against monetary policy operations was required to be collateralized with high-quality collateral. However, standards were eased during the crisis because (1) banks had shortages of high-quality collateral, and (2) urgent very large liquidity operations made collateral quality a secondary priority.

[492] Companies may also fall under provisions if the counterparty is one of the designated types of participants. However, national authorities can exclude application to companies to not create exceptions to general rules for organizations, but only Austria has used the exemption.

border cooperation in closing failed banks, including setting up Crisis Management Groups involving relevant authorities under a designated lead authority. One important feature was that each bank prepare a plan describing "bail-in steps" that guarantee owners pay costs of closing banks before public expenditures are involved.

Securities held by intermediaries

16.89. Several years prior to the start of the EMU, an EU Commission chaired by Alberto Giovannini outlined steps to remove impairments in clearing and settlement systems. Fifteen actions were specified as needed to bring about greater harmonization to permit efficient trading across borders. A schedule was established that called up public and private sector entities to take steps to resolve the problems.

16.90. A thorny aspect dealt with securities trading by depositing securities in a book-entry form with intermediaries, which was the prevailing practice in securities trading in Europe. This facilitates efficient and timely trading, helps maintain market liquidity, and is useful to operate repurchase agreement markets. However, the legal status of the securities held as book entries by intermediaries differed between EU countries. The Giovannini Report argued that a common substantive law should be applied to create harmonized arrangements to provide evidence of rights in the securities held by intermediaries. Five elements to establish unambiguous rights are (1) defining owner's rights, (2) providing protection from bankruptcy of the intermediary, (3) assuring tradability of the account and properly crediting the account holder, (4) determining competing interests in the account by the order they are recorded in the account, and (5) ensuring intermediaries have access to liquidity to cover demands on the account.

16.91. The Report proposed a working group of legal experts be established to aim for *sufficient* – not complete – harmonization to achieve the above aims. Three years was allotted for the task.

16.92. An important aspect of this exercise was that it demonstrated the legal challenges involved in attempting to bring about more harmonized practices between countries. A range of tasks must be addressed, multiple public and private entities are involved, activities must be coordinated and sequenced, and a thorny issue can take years of work by high level working groups to resolve. This is just for sufficient – not complete – harmonization.

16.93. This lesson applies both to currency unions and other regional integration schemes. Essentially the same process will be followed, although the process in an union might be somewhat more efficient. For purposes of planning an union, it is clear that an extended schedule is needed that can proceed somewhat independently of the union-building process. Work can begin before the union starts and perhaps continue into the union period.

Conclusions on the financial market directives

16.94. The EU directives described above show the importance of common practices in multiple key areas of financial infrastructure. Widespread use of common standards can greatly simplify cross-border transactions and make them cheaper, more secure, and timely. These conditions support growth of cross-border transactions and thus contribute to building of an union-wide market. The EU felt that introducing more common practices was justified and thus crafted the Directives to introduce common cross-border practices. This required carving out specific exceptions to national legal codes in order to introduce the common standards. The directives were major steps in moving from mutual recognition of national practices to application of supranational powers on the countries.[493]

[493] The EU already had many supranational powers and many of the secondary aspects of setting up an union were already legally mandated for adoption by the country members. These included for example the definition of regulated banks, accounting standards, many bank supervisory standards, etc.. If such standards had not already been in place more directives might have been needed to start up the EMU.

16.95. Outside the EU, it might not be politically possible to impose common standards, the best practices and the ultimate system might not be known, and during the early challenging days of creating an union it could be counterproductive to expend time and resources to devise and implement common systems except where they are absolutely critical for union operations. Also, creating a full common infrastructure for an union can be lengthy and could delay start-up of the union, which could be politically unacceptable. Thus, it would not be unlikely for many future unions to allow numerous cases where national practices and national legal frameworks could continue within the union. Subsequent pressures for greater harmonization can be expected especially if serious problems develop, and the European case argues for more rather than less harmonization (which requires greater legal control over national practices). But, like in Europe, some of the decisions and implementation can be delayed until the union is operating.

16.96. In conclusion, the Euroarea found mutual recognition increasingly unable to deal with cross-border situations and changes in market practices and innovations. Specific rules applicable to all jurisdictions were introduced with active support of market participants. Costs were reduced, delays were avoided, and cross-border transactions were easier to understand and do.

D. Currency unions as supranational bodies

Concept of primacy of ECB powers

16.97. In various contexts, questions have been raised about the degree and extent of the powers of the ECB; the degree of ECB control over management of foreign currency reserves held by NCBs, the authority for supervision of banks, and the ability of national authorities to sanction NCB governors. The extent of the union central bank's powers is especially important for future unions because potential member countries will want to know types of powers they will cede to the union central bank.

16.98. In a controversial argument, Zilioli and Selmayr (2001) hold that the legal principle of independence of the ECB as a supranational central bank is enshrined in Maastricht and leads to the conclusion that the "regulator of the ESCB is, first of all, the ECB and not the Council of the European Union." "As a matter of substance, the ECB is regulator whenever regulation is required within its field of competence, in particular within the field of monetary policy, but also in related fields such as statistics or payments systems."…"The ECB is also the Community regulator in the field of monetary policy, thus reflecting the exclusivity of the competencies transferred to the ECB by Member Countries through the EC Treaty and the Statute." (p. 39) *Thus, they argue that although the ECB is an entity within the EU framework, inside that framework the ECB is the primary actor within its specified field and has power to constrain the full community.*

16.99. Moreover, they argue that EU law requires Community institutions adopt secondary legislation in areas of the ECB competence. In a number of areas the EU Council does not act as a regulator of the ECB, but per Article 42 of the Statute is required to specify and make concrete powers already given to the ECB. (p. 40) They cite for example the need for the EU Council to define limits and conditions under which the ECB could impose fines or periodic penalty payments for failure to meet obligations under ECB Regulations and Decisions, so that the ECB can exercise its sanctioning regime. Similarly, ECB powers are especially embodied in the requirement that national authorities consult with the ECB in any draft legislation touching on the ECB's areas of competence.[494]

16.100. Similarly, in the field of monetary policy, the Council is obliged to consult with or take recommendations from the ECB before enacting rules, but "the decision-making bodies of the ECB may always

[494] This important power pushes member countries to implement union policies as intended and not introduce legal provisions that contradict union policy. The problem was that it was not mandatory that member countries implement proposals made by the ECB, which could threaten the union if that happened.

exercise their regulatory power without the need to formally involve the Community institutions" (p. 43)

16.101. Thus, per Zilioli and Selmayr, *direct provision of powers in the monetary field and related areas under Maastricht confirmed that "the ECB remains the primary regulator (as opposed to a complementary regulator) in the field of monetary policy."* (p. 43) Thus, they hold that the Council is obligated to act in a complementary role to specify and make concrete powers that were granted by Maastricht to the ECB. Similar requirements affect the member states, who are required to enact secondary legislation compatible with the ECB rules and procedures.

16.102. The Zilioli and Selmayr argument is not without criticism. For example, they cite a critic who argues that their argument could cause "irreparable damage to the Community and to the whole institutional order of the European Union (including of the ECB itself)." (p.1) Moreover, there are obligations on the ECB to regularly report to the public and to EU bodies. ECB matters can end up before the European Court of Justice. Thus, the ECB has a mix of powers and obligations and it might be exaggerated to simply describe it as the primary regulator – an unambiguously supranational entity – in its field of competence. Resolution of this disagreement is well beyond the scope of this study, but it is clear that the issue itself can have important implications that might be played out in future unions.[495]

> In part, this debate arises because of the role of central bank independence in contemporary monetary economics. Great importance was placed (*prior to the GFC*) on the independence of central banks as the best means of bringing about price stability and supporting economic growth. Independent central banks were seen as being able to make policy choices based on long-term economic benefits of the country without political interference. Conversely, political involvement was viewed as possibly resulting in poor policy choices. Such views helped entrench defense of ECB independence as a core belief of the Eurosystem.
>
> Second, monetary policies are important and politically sensitive. National authorities or groups within countries can be expected to advocate positions that benefit national or more specific interests. The ECB as a supranational organization is responsible for the union as a whole, and thus it can prefer to make legally binding decisions independently of national political influences.
>
> Third, diverse conditions might prevail between countries that could call for policies that differ from the common union policy. For example, a low union interest rate policy could clash with a need for higher rates in some member countries to prevent economic overheating.[496] National policy initiatives reflecting diverse national interests might need to be suppressed by a supranational entity to avoid compromising union-wide policy.
>
> Fourth, in order to carry out the common policy, the ECB regulates aspects of national policy and

[495] An important event in 2014 clarified questions of legal primacy. Crises in sovereign bonds for several members led the ECB to a policy of "Outright Monetary Transactions" in which the ECB purchased sovereign bonds in the secondary market to calm credit markets. The German Constitutional Court found that the program exceeded the ECB's mandate, but referred the issue to the European Court of Justice for final decision. This established a precedent that legal oversight of union-wide monetary policy had to be at a union-wide level. (Financial Times, February 7, 2014).

[496] In the extreme, an union central bank could apply a policy for the entire union that could be harmful to individual countries. This could create many legal problems – can the country appeal to the union's courts? Is compensation required? Can the country seek IMF assistance? Another thorny case is whether ECB surveillance powers can impose costly conditions on individual countries (in much the same way as Eurostat has gained new powers of surveillance over national budgets).

can require national legislation to be compatible with union requirements.

Finally, the policies of the larger political union that encompasses the union central bank might need to be constrained to create institutional arrangements that support the union central bank and to avoid situations where union policies compromise union monetary or exchange rate policy.

16.103. As a practical matter, EMU experience seems to be that the assertion of policy independence chafes politically and gives rise to tensions, but pressures have been ameliorated by the extraordinary number of steps taken by the ECB to report its activities to the European Council and European Parliament, legal oversight by the European Court of Justice, the inclusive governance structure, an extensive public information program, sharing of implementation powers with the NCBs, and effective recruitment of staff from throughout the region. Moreover, the Union itself has asserted that the monetary union is part of the EU. In such ways, a potent issue has been handled. This could be an important lesson for future unions.

16.104. For future unions, the degree of independence that Zilioli and Selmayr argue exists for the ECB could be a matter of serious concern. Future unions might wish to constrain union central bank powers in order to retain more national or union-level political prerogative over the policies of the union central bank or to be able to promote national interests. Or they might wish to create mechanisms that promote regular inputs from national authorities acting as a group[497] - indeed, creating such a mechanism could be politically necessary in order to create the union. Alternatively, some regions might choose to not create a full-fledged union to avoid creating supranational entities with powers unconstrained by national political and policy influence.

16.105. Unfortunately, the EMU experience offers limited guidance. This could be a tough issue for new unions to resolve. Their decisions must reflect the internal politics of the union, but will also need to be outward looking to provide the international community confidence that the new union will be based on economically sound decisions removed from potentially damaging political interference. Initially, many of the new unions could have limited credibility in markets and the success of dealing with issues of central bank independence over policy might be decisive in building that credibility.

Judicial Oversight

16.106. Article 35 "Judicial Control and Related Matters" covers control over the ECB and NCBs by courts. Article 35 describes a range of plausible situations for which future unions will probably need to develop rules.

16.107. Article 35.1 states that the acts or omissions of the ECB are open to review or interpretation by the European Court of Justice (ECJ) under conditions laid down in the Treaty. Conversely, the ECB can also initiate proceedings. The inclusion of the term "omissions" covers cases where the ECB failed to act as demanded by the treaty, but could leave the ECB open to challenges that certain actions should have been taken in the views of a plaintiff, but were not. If the court agrees, the mandate of the union could expand beyond what the ECB interprets.

16.108. Article 35.2 states that disputes between the ECB and creditors, debtors, "or any other person" should be decided by national courts, except in matters where the Court of Justice has been granted jurisdiction. That is, most disputes involving the ECB will be resolved in national courts according to national laws. By implication, similar cases might be resolved different ways by different courts and an action in one country does not necessarily set a precedent for other countries and rulings could be in conflict. Moreover,

[497] It is unacceptable in an union for individual country influences to directly affect union policy, and therefore decisions must be made by the group acting as a group.

because many situations involving the ECB will be new and are not explicitly covered in existing national laws, early rulings in specific types of cases could tend to set precedents.

16.109. Article 35.3 states that the ECB is liable as described by Article 288 or the Treaty, but NCBs are liable according to their respective national laws. Article 288 states;

a. The contractual liability of the Community shall be governed by the law applicable to the contract in question.

b. In the case of non-contractual liability, the Community shall, in accordance with the general principles common to the laws of the Member States, make good any damage caused by its institutions or by its servants in the performance of their duties.

c. The preceding paragraph shall apply under the same conditions to damage caused by the ECB or by its servants in the performance of their duties.

d. The personal liability of its servants towards the Community shall be governed by the provisions laid down in their Staff Regulations or in the Conditions of employment applicable to them.

16.110. This states (1) that the EC's and ECB's contracts are subject to the laws of the country of the contract, (2a) noncontractual obligations of the EC and ECB are covered by general principles that apply to laws of all the member states, which implies that EU-wide principles or laws are applicable, and (2b) the ECB and NCBs acting under ECB direction are under obligation to "make good any damage caused by its institutions or by its servants in performance of their duties", which implies that these supranational institutions are not granted blanket sovereign immunity for their actions, and (3) personal liability of EC or ECB employees is covered in their employment contracts and regulations, which is language that leaves open issues of privileges and exemptions of individual ECB staff.

16.111. Article 35.4 states the ECJ has jurisdiction relating to any arbitration clause in ECB contracts, whether under public or private law. Because employment disputes fall under this category and could potentially tie up the Court of Justice, a separate "Court of First Instance" was set up to hear such cases, as well as a number of other types of cases unlikely to have major union-wide impacts.

16.112. Article 35.5 states that the Governing Council makes decisions whether the ECB should take cases to the ECJ.

16.113. Article 35.6 says that the ECJ has jurisdiction in cases filed by the ECB over whether NCBs are fulfilling their Treaty obligations. The ECB must first provide a reasoned opinion why it feels that the member has not fulfilled an obligation, to which the member has an opportunity to respond. If the NCB does not comply within a period set by the ECB, the ECB can take the matter to the Court of Justice. (The text is silent if and under what conditions an NCB can bring a complaint against the ECB.)

16.114. Article 40 states that the "ECB shall enjoy in the territories of the Member States such privileges and immunities as are necessary for the performance of its tasks, under the conditions laid down in the *Protocol on the privileges and immunities of the European Communities.*" The Protocol established certain strong immunities for the ECB, reflecting its status as an EC organization, which include;

> The ECB's property, premises, assets, operations, and archives are inviolable and exempt from search or confiscation. The property and assets are not subject to administrative or legal constraints unless authorized by the Court of Justice.[498]

> Assets, revenues, and property are exempt from direct taxes. For indirect and sales taxes, such as value added taxes, the member governments should take appropriate steps to refund the amounts included in the prices of movable or

[498] An issue to address is how to deal with illicit operations conducted within the premises of the union. Do local authorities have authority to search the premises for evidence?

immovable property used for official purposes. However, this action is not to be used if there is a distorting effect on competition in the union. Also, there is no tax exemption for taxes and dues that constitute charges for public utilities services.

The Union is also exempt from customs duties and restrictions. Imported articles cannot be disposed, either for payment or gratis by the union, except under conditions approved by the host country.

Official communications and documents have the same privileges as for diplomatic missions. Official communications cannot be censored.

Union officials may receive laissez-passer entitling them to travel to any of the member states, and agreements can be made to permit travel to other countries.

Representatives of the member states, and advisers and technical experts, have privileges to travel to Union offices for official purposes.

Officials and employees of the union are immune from legal proceeding for actions, or spoken or written statements, done in their official capacity. This immunity continues after they have left office.

Officials and employees of the union and their families are not subject to immigration restrictions nor formal registrations for aliens.

They and families have certain rights to maintain their households, including currency and exchange regulations accorded to officials of international organizations, movement of furniture and possessions, and import and re-export of cars free of duty.

Union officials and employees are subject to a tax "for the benefit of the Union" on income paid to them by the Union. (That is, their official income is taxed by the EU and not by individual countries.) Conversely, this income is exempt from national taxes.

For various tax purposes, staff of union institutions can retain their residence in their home country, provided it is within the union.

The social security pension system for staff will be covered by European law, which will be derived after consultation with the institutions involved.

The local governments will be informed periodically of the names, grades, and residences of staff.

Privileges, immunities, and facilities are accorded "solely in the interests of the Union." Each institution is required to waive the immunity of officials or staff whenever the institution considers the waiver is not contrary to the interests of the union. (That is, immunities irrelevant to the interest of the Union should be discarded.)

The Union will cooperate with local authorities for application of the Protocol.

16.115. And finally, the Protocol has specific language indicating it applies to the ECB.

> "The Protocol shall also apply to the European Central Bank, to the members of its organs, and to its staff, without prejudice to the Protocol of the Statue of the European System of Central Bank and of the European Central Bank."

> "The ECB shall, in addition, be exempt from any form of taxation or imposition of a like nature on the occasion of any increase in its capital and from the various formalities which might be connected therewith in the State where the Bank has its seat. The activities of the Bank and of its organs carried on in accordance with the Statue of the ESCB and of the ECB shall not be subject to any turnover tax."

16.116. New unions will need to create a system of immunities and privileges of their currency union institutions and their staff in ways similar to the Protocol. Because the EU Protocol already existed for EU institutions, it was not needed in the Maastricht Treaty. The ECJ already existed with established procedures. New unions, however, will need to include privileges and immunities within the framework of their monetary union agreement. Tactically, describing privileges and immunities within a Protocol attached to the basic Agreement is a good strategy that facilitates future adaptations to changing conditions or as experience is gained. New unions will also need to clarify the judicial structure that applies.

Dispute resolution

16.117. An union must have methods to settle disputes and to make binding legal decisions on country members, on banks or other financial institutions, and on the public participating in actions initiated by the union. These powers will even extend over the union central bank and NCBs, and potentially over the member countries.

16.118. Disputes can arise over virtually any aspect of the operation of a union. Means must be available to provide the parties with a fair hearing and decisions based on the facts of the case and the applicable legal provisions. Once decided, sanctions might be needed to enforce the decision. An appeals process is also needed. A decision for future unions is whether appeals will be decided within the judicial system, or are ultimately referred to political bodies for decision.

16.119. A union begins with a situation of multiple legal codes, upon which new legal arrangements are imposed. There might also be laws or standards for regional bodies that might also apply. For example, what employment and pension laws pertain to staff from a country working for the union central bank located in a different country – home country, host country, or union rules? The EU rules and other relevant national rules can create situations of "choice of laws" and "conflicts of laws". They will inevitably occur because the essence of a union is that banks and other financial institutions have the freedom to operate throughout the union and to undertake transactions anywhere within the union. If different laws and procedures for resolving conflicts over laws exist within a union, cross-border operations could be inhibited and impair the effectiveness of the union.[499]

16.120. One method applied to resolve legal conflict situations is "mutual recognition". Mutual recognition states that if an authority in one country decides on a matter, such as granting a license to a bank, other countries must agree with that choice and permit the bank to operate as a bank in their countries. Granting mutual recognition privileges of course implies that each country makes its decisions in a fair and technically correct manner.

16.121. The application of the "subsidiarity" concept is important in choice of law situations. If an union agrees that NCBs and national governments retain substantial operational control or decision-making within the union, then many legal matters should be resolved within the national legal systems. For example, national laws might cover all employment rules at NCBs and national offices of the union (such as depositories or settlement offices). This can simplify legal arrangements for the union, because matters are handled locally and avoid problems because union employees have different rights than local employees.

16.122. Conflict of laws cover situations in which rules differ between countries. For example, countries might have different bankruptcy procedures to cover seizure of real estate collateral. Following the failure of a bank that operates throughout the union, how will the seizure be handled if countries differ on the value of the claim, procedures to file a claim, the court of jurisdiction, the mechanics of the seizure, and the tax rules?

16.123. Unions will begin without case law, which must be built up. There will be a natural tendency to look at what has been done in the EMU. This might

[499] This also applies in regional settings. For example, in Asia legal uncertainty about the ability to make claims in other Asian countries is said to limit cross-border securities investments within the region, and therefore investments are often made outside the region in international money market centers. This, of course, can seriously impair regional financial market development. One way this is being addressed is by mandating that all transactions at securities exchanges fall under the legal rules of the country of the exchange.

provide answers, but there must be clear recognition that conditions and institutions and the overall legal framework will differ in other unions. Using the EMU for guidance should be done very cautiously case-by-case. Early decisions can be especially important for the union itself because they can establish precedents – the union itself might want to monitor early decisions closely, even when it is not a direct party in the action, and should have the power to express its views as part of its oversight of matters relating to monetary, exchange, or reserves policy.

16.124. Some can be decided by national law under a subsidiarity concept. Such cases might include disputes over payment for services or breach of contract.

16.125. The ECB, although a supranational agency, was not granted blanket sovereign immunity for its actions, and legal actions can be brought against it, in national or EU courts. New unions will need to decide if there are areas of immunity for the union central bank or any of its arms.

Judicial structure of the union

16.126. For future unions, a judicial structure must be put in place that is likely to differ considerably from what exists in Europe.

16.127. If a regional grouping has an existing supreme, supranational court, it should become responsible for judicial oversight of the currency union and its organs. Language to this effect needs to be in the monetary agreement. The court might need some restructuring to handle new types of cases relating to a currency union.

16.128. If the region does not already have a supranational court system, some method to handle currency cases is needed or a new court should be created.

16.129. The least complex arrangement is to take cases through national court systems for preliminary review or judgments, then move a limited number of cases with systemic importance to a special judicial tribunal for resolution or appeal. For example, if a case arises regarding basic powers of control of international reserve assets, it might be referred by the highest court of a member state to a tribunal for decision. The tribunal would draw members from the highest court of each member country. Separate legal provisions will be needed to establish powers and procedures of the tribunal. Its decisions then have force throughout the entire union and set a precedent for all national legal systems.

16.130. Alternatively, a standing court system could be set up to cover operations of the currency union. This can provide for more established procedures and development of specialized procedures relating to the union and cross-border actions. Moreover, there is greater need for such a court arrangement to handle dispute resolution because of the development of cross-border and regionally integrated financial institutions and markets, and also because of the legalities of handling the many new international codes and standards affecting the financial sector – capital adequacy, accounting, anti-money laundering, and many more. Financial market integration is increasingly a component of currency union programs, and thus a common court arrangement for currency union and financial market cases makes sense. However, this might be an expensive alternative for smaller unions.

16.131. Both these options will deal with complex legal issues that might be better served by a specialized court system rather than regular civil or criminal courts.

16.132. Finally, creating an union involves creation of a new body of treaty, regulatory, and case law that will be complex. This body of law will exist within a context of different national laws and a wide range of international rules and best practices. The laws must be interpreted flexibly but robustly to deal with unforeseen situations and evolving market practices. Content of financial market transactions might be technically difficult. A core of qualified public and private lawyers and judges will need to be built up – building this expertise will be a challenge for all future unions.

Constitutional challenges

16.133. It can be expected that one or more major legal challenges will be made against the new union. In the case of the EMI, a group of distinguished German lawyers filed suit arguing that the Deutschmark was legally recognized in the Constitution of Germany, and thus it was constitutionally impossible replace it with the euro. This dispute came during the early days of the EMI and held up the planned move of the EMI staff from Basel, Switzerland to Frankfurt, Germany. Ultimately, a decision in favor of the euro was made, which cleared away a path for creation of the euro (and movement of the EMI to Frankfurt.)[500]

16.134. New unions can expect such existential challenges, and should prepare for them. In each case, the specifics of the legal infrastructure of each union will be important in deciding how to proceed, and perhaps ultimately whether the union will be able to proceed.

Emergency powers

16.135. Following the attacks on September 11, 2001, questions arose of how national authorities should respond to maintain operation of the financial system. In the Euroarea, Finland introduced legislation covering financial sector operations in emergencies, especially considering that much financial infrastructure is located outside Finland. As required, the legislation was sent for review to the ECB that responded that it affected core principles of EU law. It was found to conflict with rules on the free movement of capital and exercise of Euroarea monetary policy. Also, the ECB argued that it was the responsibility of the Eurosystem to deal with emergency situations.[501] The draft law was passed by the Finnish parliament despite the ECB objections.

> In 2018, Finland requested further review of its financial sector emergency preparedness situation, which prompted an ECB opinion covering monetary institutions, TARGET 2, and cyber resilience, among other topics. The opinion cited many preparedness features built into the Euroarea financial infrastructure and also the high costs of attempting to build an independent emergency system.

16.136. An analysis by Zilioli concluded that provisions in conflict with Maastricht are only permitted if specifically allowed by a Treaty provision, and that "Member states cannot take back competences transferred to the Community, particularly in the case of competences related to Community monetary policy, where the Treaty explicitly states that the move is irrevocable." Moreover, if emergency conditions arise, countries should first consult other members and take actions that least affect the common situation if Community institutions are unable to act. The competencies transferred to the Euroarea under treaty cannot be repatriated based on national initiative. (Zilioli 2005, p. 119-120; 132-133).

16.137. From this example, it is clear that unions need to make arrangements for emergency operations, including providing guidelines to cover cases where central control lapses over some aspect of union operations. In such a situation, a local branch of the central bank or other arm of the union (mint, settlement house, depository, etc.) might be in a position where it makes transactions, either on its own volition or at the direction of national authorities under emergency authority. The legal validity of such actions after the fact is uncertain. The union could provide some clarification for some cases by describing principles that could apply – it is unlikely that all types of problem situations can be anticipated and spelled out in a way that permits precise rules to be developed. Moreover, new unanticipated situations will arise. Thus, there will probably always be uncertainty in these situations.

E. Equivalent regional institutions

16.138. Kenen and Meade (2008, p.178) discuss the "institutional deficit" affecting initiatives at regional integration in Asia. Their conclusions are distinctly

[500] Later, the same group of lawyers resurrected their legal challenges during the Greek crisis.

[501] ECB (2002) and (2018).

pessimistic about prospects of building regional arrangements without the advantages of a supranational legal framework such as exists in Europe.

> "It might take much longer, however, to solve the fundamental problem – closing the institutional deficit that stands in the way of deeper economic integration, even among the ASEAN countries. It is not necessary to create supranational institutions resembling those of the EU .... Special-purpose entities might be created to take on the various tasks performed by the EU institutions during and after the transition to the EMU. It would be necessary, however, to grant them the authority they would need to perform those tasks, and this could take longer than Europe took to move from the Treaty of Rome to the start of the EMU. The institutional deficit is deeper in East Asia than it was in Europe fifty years ago. Asia has just begun to develop intergovernmental institutions. It has not even begun to contemplate supranational institutions. Indeed, the whole notion of supranationality is alien to Asian thought and history."

16.139. Their conclusion seems too pessimistic. Even without agreement that a new union will be put into place, it is possible for regional organizations to introduce piecemeal cooperative arrangements that can serve functions similar to what is done in unions. Advances in regional cooperation in East Asia are a good example.

> The CMIM organizes policy discussions amongst the ASEAN+3 countries to address regional problems and seek cooperative solutions. Its data gathering and analytical efforts are substantial. The CMIM has introduced mandatory elements into the regional currency swap arrangements, which begins to move it toward becoming like an Asian Monetary Fund.
>
> The ASEAN has a series of working groups covering many aspects of regional financial integration. This work could be done within an union, but ASEAN is showing that substantial legal integration can occur prior to creating an union.

16.140. Each of these piecemeal advances is likely to involve new laws or rules, or institutional changes. The legal issues faced in introducing a full union might be faced repeatedly on a much smaller scale. This work is advancing within the specific framework and institutions of each region, and it seems to be moving more rapidly than occurred in Europe. Regions can become more like unions relatively quickly, and plausibly regions can explicitly seek to be like unions without actually being one, and without the strong legal framework a true currency union requires.

16.141. Advantages of regional initiatives in Southeast Asia are well-educated professional staff in regional governments and relatively high income to support efforts; perhaps counterbalanced by some strong feelings that outsiders should not interfere in domestic political affairs.

F. Changing union tasks; Amending the Treaty

16.142. An important decision of new unions will whether to include in the Union Treaty or other founding document language authorizing the union to undertake new functions not specified in the treaty, or whether the Treaty itself should be amended.[502]

16.143. A currency union involves a large transfer of sovereignty to a supranational institution that countries will want carefully described and often with specific limits or prohibitions to preserve national prerogatives or prevent overreaching by the central bank. However, over time conditions change and new functions might be undertaken by the central bank. The question is whether the Treaty itself should be amended, which can be difficult, costly, and often

[502] Possible new functions could include expanding union membership; authorizing the central bank to collect taxes or assess penalties on financial institutions; expanding the central bank supervisory role; permitting the central bank to issue securities to the public, issuing CBDCs, or specifying unforeseen emergency functions of the central bank.

requiring unanimous support, or whether other amending procedures are specified.

16.144. This issue became very important during the GFC when the European Council introduced major changes into the EU supervisory system and assigned the ECB and ESCB important roles in support of the new system. This was done through an EC decision in line with the Maastricht ¶105(6) that states,

> "The Council may, acting unanimously on a proposal from the Commission and after consulting the ECB and after receiving the assent of the European Parliament, confer upon the ECB specific tasks concerning policies relating to the prudential supervision of credit institutions and other financial institutions with the exception of insurance undertakings."

16.145. This formulation made it unlikely that new supervisory functions would be adopted by the EMU except in cases of major need. However, the language is permissive without requiring use of the cumbersome, slow, and uncertain[503] process of changing the Treaty.

16.146. ¶105(6) is related to a general orientation of the union, in line with the broad mandate of the Treaty, that supervisory powers reside with national authorities, and not to specific practices of the ESCB. But if the Treaty had been very specific and had enumerated exactly which supervisory functions were to be performed at the union or national levels, then a simpler method of amending the treaty would be needed (perhaps even by simple majority vote of members) because there could often be specific needs to amend a function or change a rule without changing the fundamental nature of the Treaty.

16.147. To conclude, new unions might include language within the Treaty permitting new tasks to be undertaken within the Treaty framework, but with protections that changes are not too easy and clearly reflect a consensus among the member countries. However, given the severity of the GFC and the covid crisis, the argument has already been decided decisively that the legal frameworks of future unions must somehow encompass issues of financial stability and the fiscal costs of dealing with financial market turmoil. Global financial conditions have changed dramatically since the Maastricht Treaty was signed and have created legal complexities for new unions never foreseen when the Eurosystem was established.

G. Conclusions

16.148. Compared to the experience in Europe, new monetary unions will face large challenges in developing the legal frameworks for their unions.

16.149. The overarching EU legal framework promoted convergence in legal practice and introduction of comparable practices across the union. It also had flexibility to facilitate the introduction of new arrangements once the union is operating, to reflect changing international standards, new market practices, improve operations, and handle unexpected situations. Much needed to operate the union was already in place through EU treaties or legislation.

16.150. New unions might have a much more limited legal framework available than in Europe. For unions developing from preexisting trade or customs unions, a body of legal arrangements and practices and established decision-making experiences can be drawn on, although they might be very incomplete or remote from a monetary or financial perspective. A preexisting dispute settlement or adjudication method is quite helpful. Most planned unions are being built around some sort of preexisting arrangement.

16.151. However, new unions are likely to need to specify many more legal standards in their monetary treaty to cover matters already handled in Europe by the EU legal framework. For example, to define what constitutes a bank eligible to participate in monetary policy actions. Because of this the monetary treaties of new unions might be more complex than in the

[503] Opening up a treaty for amendments in one area creates the danger that there will be many changes proposed and that the fundamental nature of the treaty could be changed.

Maastricht Treaty, but if items are not spelled out conflicts could arise later that might imperil the union or make it less effective.

16.152. New unions will also need to design methods to make secondary or ancillary changes to make the union operate more smoothly and adapt over time. If an overarching legal framework does not exist, this might be done by several possible methods; (1) conclude a new treaty or provision, (2) agreement by qualified majority, (3) issue directives that tell countries to make changes to achieve some end in accordance with their national legal framework, (4) provide model legislation that countries can adopt with appropriate local modifications to fit into national codes, or (5) endow the union after specified consultations with powers to introduce legal changes within its operational sphere. Each has advantages and disadvantages.

Option one, conclude a new treaty or provision, is the most powerful in that it binds countries to the new provisions. Some important decisions might need to be ratified by members in this way. For example, expanding membership of a union and changing voting procedures and formulas for capital contributions might be reasons for a new treaty-like agreement. However, it can prove difficult or lengthy to come to agreement and ratification can take a long time. This requires unanimous approval for the change which can be difficult to obtain and therefore every country has veto power over the proposed change.

Option two, agreement by qualified majority, defines a voting process in which votes by something stronger than a simple majority are binding on the parties. Several Maastricht provisions call for decisions by a qualified majority. This method allows decisions to be made without unanimity, *which should be avoided whenever possible*, but recognizes that some decisions are extra important and should not be imposed on the union membership unless there is very strong agreement. There might be several criteria for a vote to be valid, for example, agreement by two-thirds of countries, or by voting shares, which gives extra power to large countries in the union.

Option three, to issue directives, is useful where wide differences exist between national legal codes and where technically flexibility is acceptable so long as the end result is achieved. A directive is based on firm legal powers by the union to make national authorities adopt the goals or provisions of the directive into the national legal codes. Therefore, the power to do so must be specified in the union treaty or other agreements. In the case of conflicts a judicial mechanism must be in place.

Option four, model legislation, has the advantage of allowing the union to be specific about the shape of national practices and thus permits greater harmonization. It can also guarantee that national practices are compatible with union-wide systems. This is also useful to introduce international best practices and codes into national codes, which is especially important now given the broad range of new international financial sector standards adopted during the GFC. It is possible to allow national flexibility in various provisions while retaining strict interpretations for some provisions. Model legislation has less force than a directive and thus there is no guarantee that all countries adopt the model code fully or exactly in the way it was intended, and provisions of the code might not easily mesh with some national practices. This could create *de facto* conflicts or gaps even when attempts are made to harmonize as much as possible.

Option five, to endow the union with legislative powers within its sphere of competence; for example, grant the union power to changes to settlements systems eligibility and procedures based on majority agreement of the union Governing Board.. This requires that the areas of union power and approval methods are specified by treaty and countries acquiesce to introduce the changes on the basis of this process.

16.153. Decisions on the degree of legal power of the union over national authorities defines the extent that member countries cede sovereignty to the union. Multiple methods could be used depending on the specific topic or the urgency of action, but the conditions permitting action must be clearly spelled out.

16.154. Once agreement is reached on the method or methods under which changes can be, many types of actions might not need to be specified in the union treaty, but can be introduced over time or as needed or as conditions change. Legal review of proposed national implementation of union standards is needed, as is an arbitration or judicial mechanism.

Timeline	
Preparatory period	Decision to create a monetary union. Negotiation of Monetary Union Treaty
Early actions (four years prior)	Ratify Monetary Union Treaty
Three years prior	Create Legal Committee Decision on union-level versus national level legal actions Draft legal framework on central bank Draft legal framework for common currency Begin review of national legal codes related to union activities Consult with topical committees on their legal needs First report on legal convergence Design of union judicial arrangements
24 months prior	Begin drafting common legal provisions National legal implementation begins
18 Months Prior	Drafting of legal provisions continues National legal implementation continues
Final 12 months	Final report on legal convergence Union judicial body created
Final 6 months	Publication of review of legal convergence; Agreement on introduction of final changes Conclude legislation on union and national central bank relationships Conclude legislation on central bank independence Complete changes to other national legislation Early launch of union central bank shifts legal powers
Run-up to union	Union-level judicial body in place
Union day	Widespread changes in legal arrangements
Early union period	Build case law Continuing evolution of legal arrangements Address legal challenges to union or to key elements

Chapter 17 – Communications

What are the roles of official and public communications in building and operating currency unions?

A. Introduction: Communications as drivers of union building

17.1. Communications play a different role in unions compared to national settings. An union has diverse communities with different legal and institutional settings, varying policy perspectives, and often different languages. The union must take special steps to be able to communicate its goals and policies throughout the region and to make clear that its actions are for the benefit of the region as a whole and not for particular countries or interests. The union will speak as a single voice in many matters for itself and its members, which must be done in a way that reflects commonly agreed governance and decision-making.

17.2. Likewise, the union will speak to the world as the voice of the union and in many matters as the voice of its member countries. The communications rights and responsibilities of the union will compete with the rights of member countries to speak on economic and financial issues, both domestically and to international audiences. Union member countries belong to international organizations and fora where they rightfully are expected to participate and express their views. Thus, communications policy must delineate when the union has paramount responsibility and when national prerogative prevails.

17.3. This chapter covers some of the key aspects of a major function of currency unions – communications to enhance policy effectiveness and to more efficiently operate the union. This is an area among so many others where work needs to begin early in the union-building process.

B. Euroarea communications policy

17.4. In the Euroarea, communications were seen as serving the goals of policy transparency and accountability. Special responsibilities stem from the independent, multi-country nature of a union central bank. The Euroarea stressed the importance of the independence of the central bank and its decision making, which is basically undemocratic. In response, and fully in line with the democratic foundations of the EU, the Eurosystem held that it had a special obligation to justify its decisions and communicate frequently and in-depth with its populations, world markets, and political entities. ECB practice far exceeds the formal minimum communications requirements. Communications are in multiple languages and multiple media. The Eurosystem communications process also goes from the periphery into the center – the ECB has multiple avenues to hear about the conditions and views in member countries and it seeks legitimacy by emphasizing its willingness to reflect these views in its deliberations.

17.5. The Eurosystem is exemplary in policy communications, which it describes as "democratic accountability" and a necessary obligation in a democratic society given the system's policy independence. Policy reporting obligations exist both to elected authorities and the general public. Transparency regarding policy is also viewed as bolstering to policy effectiveness by creating public support.

17.6. The foundations of the Eurosystem are democratically legitimate based on the agreement of the member countries to sign the Maastricht Treaty to form the union and later agreement in the Lisbon treaty. However, once the union was established, the policy process is independent of national control and the ECB has strongly defended its independence. The obligation to explain in detail union policy and the evidence upon which it is based followed from the system's independence.

17.7. Policy communications include press conferences by the ECB President and Vice President immediately after the monthly policy meeting of the Governing Council. Transcripts are published on the ECB website in several languages quickly after the press conference. A detailed statement of policy is presented in the *ECB Economic Bulletin*, along with multiple research articles, and extensive statistical tables.

17.8. The ECB regularly communicates with the EU political arms. This is to both communicate its goals, policies, and results, and engage in a dialog with other official institutions given the Eurosystem's status as an EU organization that must honor other goals of the EU.

> The ECB's President presents the ECB Annual Report to a plenary session of the European Parliament. The Parliament evaluates the report and drafts and adopts a resolution covering the ECB's activities and effectiveness.
>
> The ECB President appears quarterly before the Economic and Monetary Affairs Committee of Parliament. These sessions have become the principal venue for political oversight of the Eurosystem activities.
>
> Other members of the ECB Governing Council also testify before Parliamentary committees in their areas of competence.
>
> Committee meetings are open to the public and verbatim reports are available on the ECB website.
>
> Any Parliament member can submit written questions through the ECB's Economic and Monetary Affairs Committee. All questions and answers are published in the EU's Official Journal.

17.9. In all areas related to monetary policy, the ECB seeks to ensure that it controls the message and that communications from member countries are not in conflict. In this regard it has described itself as a "control freak" who make it clear that the ECB is the sole authority to speak on monetary policy and that other countries do not make contradictory statements. This includes for example regulations that preclude countries from releasing national statistical information prior to comparable series for the entire union.[504]

17.10. In the areas of exchange rates and the Euroarea's international representation, powers are shared between the ECB and the EU Council. This means that regular consultations on these matters must be held, but because of the ECB's policy independence the consultations are nonbinding.

17.11. The Eurogroup is comprised of the Euroarea finance ministers and the head of the Parliament's Economic and Monetary Affairs Committee and covers issues of common concern. The ECB is invited to all meetings, and thus it also participates in discussions of macroeconomic, fiscal, and external policy throughout the region.

17.12. At the top level, the European Commission acting through a specialized subgroup (ECOFIN) carries out regular policy dialog and coordinates the ECB's dealings with other arms of the union. These include areas such as statistics, payments systems, financial market integration, supervision of banks and other institutions, and convergence and expansion of the membership of the union. These interactions highlight that the Eurosystem is firmly embedded within the EU structure and that all parts of the union must mutually support each other. Transparency, open communications, and in-depth policy dialog are essential in this arrangement.

17.13. The President of the ECB and Members of the Governing Council regularly speak at public and professional events, and provide interviews to the press of member countries and the international media. Many of these presentations are published on the ECB website.

17.14. Finally, the ECB makes excellent use of its website, www.ecb.int, to provide a wide range of useful information about the economic conditions, policy, and operations of the union. There is much useful material provided on the page and thus users refer to it frequently as their first source of information about the union, which enhances prospects

---

[504] A case of disagreement at the level of the ECB Governing Council occurred in October 2010 when one member, Axel Weber, spoke in favor of ending the ECB's bond purchase program for European governments and banks. ECB President Trichet spoke out to state that Weber's statement did not represent the views of the Governing Council. (Bloomberg 2010b)

of policy success. It sets a high standard for other unions to follow.

17.15. The cover page provides the option to display it in English or any of twenty-three other languages.

17.16. At the top of the page are links to nine major topics related to the union. The topics pages highlight major stories of current interest, and also provide links to relevant legal documents, press releases, publications, topics, research, and web links to key projects.

17.17. The links to each project provide additional levels of detail to the extent that a heavy majority of users will not need to investigate further. In addition, key documents such as press releases, regulatory releases, reports to inform Parliament, etc. related to projects are available to be downloaded, which serves the purposes of many specialized users.

17.18. The site provides links to the *ECB Economic Bulletin* (which replaced the *ECB Monthly Bulletin* in 2014). The Bulletin is published 8 times a year to describe the basis for policy decisions by the Governing Council, with more comprehensive analysis in the quarter-end Bulletins.

C. Communications in future unions

17.19. Future unions must develop communications policy, infrastructure, and methods to serve the same goals as in Europe of policy transparency and accountability, but must also undertake the more ambitious task for communications of reaching all corners of the union and promoting the basic idea of the union and a unified economic region. Europe had numerous advantages including a long history of the development of the concept of the union, good communications infrastructure in the press and various media, developed national political and economic reporting in local languages, fully literate populations, and a relatively compact area. Some future unions lack one or more of these advantages and thus must work on building basic infrastructure in addition to communicating specific information about the union.

Introducing the currency union concept

17.20. An important communications task is to introduce the concept of the union to the public, financial institutions, and businesses in all potential union countries. Some future unions have incompletely communicated the purposes of the union, how businesses and the public will benefit, union plans, and the state of preparations. Unions will affect virtually every aspect of the economy of the member countries and costs will be incurred by everyone. The populations and businesses can provide support and contribute to the union or they can be wary or resistant and make the process more challenging. Potentially, lack of support and unwillingness to budget resources and incur the costs of the union could doom the project.

17.21. Also, it can be useful to communicate that a future currency union is the culmination of a long-term integration and development process. This helps establish legitimacy and allows the public to see the union in a broader context to which it might be easy to relate, such as a customs union, common visa and travel freedom within the union, cross-border financial integration, or shared infrastructure, etc.. In some unions, but not all, a common language and cultural history can help support a sense of union identity.

17.22. Often promotion of the concept of the union can be improved. First, there is a history to overcome. Some early attempts to create unions were overoptimistic about how quickly and easily the union could be built, leaving the public cynical due to failed or deferred attempts.

17.23. Often, government officials, analysts, IMF staff, and others have treated achieving macroeconomic convergence as the main task in creating an union. Without appreciation of the many challenges outlined in this volume, they might treat union-building as a two- or three-year convergence process that can be easily achieved. One goal of effective communications about the union-building process is to foster realistic expectations to allow good decision-making and avoid later disillusionment.

17.24. The length and costs of creating the union must be explained so that the proper effort can be made – the author has repeatedly heard from technical professionals that their budgets for staff and travel are too limited to carry out the work, which is something that will only be resolved when information on needed resources is communicated to politicians so that the funding can be appropriated.

17.25. Of course, willingness to incur the costs of building an union requires communicating a positive message about the advantages and/or necessity of the union. The public must understand that the union provides many benefits and thus is high on the agenda and something worth the costs.

Conveying technical information about the project, currency, and transition

17.26. As shown in this volume, a currency union has many facets that involve the public at large or specific industries or sectors. The public for example must understand the transition process to the new currency, the repricing mechanism, and the usability and security features of the currency. Banks must understand the features of the currency, cash handling mechanics, the currency retirement and circulation process, how monetary policy will be implemented, accounting and statistical processes of the union, and much more. Businesses must know the features of the new currency and introduce new processing procedures. New standards for ATMs will be introduced, and venders must recalibrate or replace many thousands of machines. All these changes require that specific technical information is conveyed to very broad audiences or very specific counterparts to union activities, *in multiple languages*. Each activity will often involve a unique schedule, audience, or media and thus will have its own communications strategy. Much of this information will be a part of the transition program, but the process could begin earlier than the formal transition period or involve a continuous exchange of information to develop and implement particular aspects of the union program.

17.27. Because of this project-by-project uniqueness, it is recommended that whenever possible communications strategies should be developed by union technical committees or working groups to fit the technical requirements and the audience. Work should be done in collaboration with an union central bank communications group that can advise on technical aspects of communications over various media and can provide common platforms for technical teams to use.

Policy communications, transparency, and accountability

17.28. Once the union is underway, the union must conduct its communications policy so that its messages are clear, quickly transmitted throughout the union and to those directly affected, and executed in ways that maximize chances of success. The practices in the Euroarea of in-depth reporting to the public and official arms of the EU as described above provide an excellent example for other unions.

Internet

17.29. Websites, which are now the first point of access to information on future unions, need to be significantly improved and kept up to date. From the earliest stages of planning, the public and international markets will seek out information about the union from the internet. It is important that users get a good first impression of the union and its prospects. Unfortunately, web sites for some future unions have not been supportive in general, but are now being significantly improved in several cases. Also, early establishment of a statistical bureau and easy access to data about the union and its members (including on macroeconomic convergence) contributes to the union program by drawing users regularly to the site.

Operational systems

17.30. Several key union systems will require dedicated communications systems to be able to operate union activities in all countries. Future unions often begin with less developed operational systems than existed in Europe, and thus face the expensive dual challenge of creating the basic system and adjusting operations to fit into evolving specifics of the union policy and institutional arrangements. In this regard, future unions might be vulnerable to delays in start-up if key operational systems are not in place when needed.

17.31. Among specialized communications systems could be those for;

Monetary policy or exchange market operations, including open-market operations throughout the union, transfer of collateral, and crediting or debiting the accounts of monetary policy counterparties.

Policy communications from consultations to final decisions are needed to be able to exchange information on economic conditions throughout the union, deliberate, make decisions, take implementing actions, and follow up on results. The EU had a system for secure communications between countries prior to the start of work on the union.

Payments and Settlements Systems will need to transfer securities, payments drafts, and payments throughout the union, including cross-border transactions.

Statistical communications are needed to format and transfer data and descriptions of data to the union statistical operations and also transfer statistics back to the countries. The Eurosystem created a new statistical messaging language for this purpose.[505]

17.32. Some of these systems need to be confidential and highly reliable in order to process transactions and sustain critical operations. These systems could be encoded and sent through dedicated wires, over the internet, or through satellite connections, depending on local conditions, but they must have a high degree of reliability and at least one level of back-up. The physical connections need to be backed up by an independent power system to run the system.

17.33. The degree of redundancy needed in developing regions will be greater than what existed in Europe, reflecting greater distances and less developed infrastructure in place. Recruiting and training of staff to operate the system will also be an expensive challenge.

17.34. Major operational communications systems are complex, and must be compatible with best international standards of efficiency, reliability, and security. International tenders for hardware, operating systems, installation, and training could be used to acquire systems.

17.35. These steps are expensive and perhaps prohibitive for lower income countries. It is possible that a centralized budget will be needed to install the communications systems in all countries. International development funding for technical infrastructure development also might be sought.

Languages

17.36. For most unions, communications will be primarily in the official languages of the union and English. This will be simple in the case of the GCC (Arabic) or EAC (Swahili), where only two major languages will be involved. In the extreme opposite case of the SADC, the language of communications could be a major problem – English, French, and Portuguese are official languages, but large populations speak indigenous languages (Zulu or Xhosa) or the introduced Afrikaans. This leaves a situation in which official legal documents and policy communications will be in a limited set of languages, but many communications for the effective operation of the union and to inform broad populations must also be in indigenous languages. A priori it is unclear how large a target group needs to be in order to justify use of a separate union language, in part because communication needs will vary by issue.

17.37. The EMU has a policy that official documents and much economic analysis should be available in all official languages of the union as well as

[505] Over time, the original ECB statistical communications platform transformed into a widely used international standard system, called SDMX. Future unions should expect to use SDMX.

for key languages of candidate countries. As of 2021, twenty-four different languages were supported to various degrees. Translation is a time consuming and expensive activity beyond the resources of the ECB itself. Therefore, the ECB concentrated on a few major working languages and left regular translation (of the *ECB Economic Bulletin*, for example) to the NCBs.[506]

17.38. During the transition to the physical currency, the ECB itself produced a range of promotional documents describing the advantages of the new currency and its security and usability features. This was done in multiple languages, including languages of several nonEU countries that were expected to informally use or ultimately adopt the euro.

17.39. Also, euro banknotes display the name 'euro' in Latin, Greek, and Cyrillic scripts, and as new countries entered the Euroarea the acronym for 'ECB' was depicted in additional national languages – now ten in total.

17.40. Future unions will need to design language policies to cover the initial launch of the union, ongoing operations and policy actions, and formal legal texts that apply common rules to national settings. Each of these activities requires high-quality translations so that meanings are correctly conveyed or laws and regulations are correctly implemented. Each of these types of actions require different language configurations (for example, legal translations should require that the union central bank review the accuracy of national translations).

17.41. An infrastructure needs to be built up to handle the language demands. For some union member countries, this might involve recruitment of new translators well qualified to handle translation to and from the union central bank's working language, English, and national languages. Language abilities in themselves are insufficient – the translators must build subject matter expertise to be able to understand the underlying message and convey it properly. Building the infrastructure and recruiting and training qualified translators could take two to four years work prior to the start of the union.

International audiences

17.42. Communications with parties outside the currency union are also important. This includes international organizations (IMF, World Bank, BIS, and many more), regional organizations, regulators and standards setters (Basel supervisory committees, accounting and auditing authorities, global financial markets, neighboring countries, and the international press and public at large).

17.43. These communications must begin well prior to the startup of the union to help build international confidence in the union and work out operational arrangements in areas such as international payments, exchange rate intervention, adherence to international standards, etc.. These communications will also include policy discussions such as how to coordinate exchange rate interventions, operational matters like exchange market intervention or cooperation on anticounterfeiting efforts, and general outreach about economic conditions and policy. Also, as shown in the financial crisis, unions need to be involved in regular consultations with the IMF in order to participate in coordinated fiscal stimulation and liquidity support.

17.44. Regular communications with the international press through press releases interviews, speeches, etc. can also build international support for the union and convey a sense of the solidity of the enterprise. This will be especially important in the period immediately running up to the start of the union to communicate issues related to the redenomination of the currency and to support the exchange rate of the new currency.

17.45. Finally, communication to the public about features of the new currency and the transition

[506] This solution avoided a situation characterized by a running joke at the EMI about where to find qualified Finnish-Greek translators.

procedures are critical to both smooth the process and protect the public from fraud.

It appears that introduction of CBDCs will often be accompanied by efforts to defraud the public who will be unfamiliar with the system – authorities should communicate well before the launch date about the official transition process and how to spot potential fraud.

Timeline

Preparatory period	
Early actions (four years prior)	• Set up currency union information website • Build operational communications systems • Establish regular schedule for communication to governing authorities on union preparations and policies • Begin regular communications with financial press
Three years prior	• Draft union communications policies • Begin recruitment of translation staff at union and country levels. • Design transition campaigns for radio, television, internet and other media • Begin building of operational communications infrastructure • Launch website
24 months prior	• Complete materials for transition for public, businesses, and special audiences. • Begin communications with international media about the union and the new currency • Begin translation of transition materials.
18 Months Prior	• Circulation of transition materials in multiple languages commenced.
Final 12 months	• Operational communications systems must be near completion.
Final 6 months	• Intense media campaign on union begins • Early set up of union central bank and its assumption of responsibility of policy communications. • Live testing of operational communications systems.
Run-up to union	• High intensity communications with public and international media
Union day	• Operational systems are fully active
Early union period	• Reports on experiences with union start up and currency changeover
Union steady state	

CHAPTER 18 – TRANSITION TO THE NEW CURRENCY

How will the old currency be retired and the new currency introduced? What will be done to educate the public and markets and to assist their transition to the new currency?

A. Introduction

18.1. This chapter covers the actual transition from national currencies into the new union currency. Many of the specific steps involved have been covered in earlier chapters, but this chapter attempts to pull the elements together into a description of the process.

18.2. The introduction of a new currency is a major economic event that affects all segments of the economy. All businesses, banks, the central bank, the public, the government and all public institutions will be affected. Moreover, many relationships with foreigners will be affected, and the introduction of a new currency alters the international financial relations and image of the country. Many changes will be introduced for which careful preparations must be made. Managing the transition involving many parties can be expensive and time consuming. *The transition process takes two to three years – after years of careful planning and preparation.*

> The changeover is a major event for all parties involved: banks, citizens of the member countries, financial markets, government, etc.
>
> All parties must be fully informed of the implications of the changeover in time to make preparations. Many parties must be consulted in order to ensure a smooth and undisturbed changeover.
>
> A changeover scenario must be defined (Big Bang; staggered; parallel circulation) for the union and each member country and implications will have to be elaborated.

18.3. In the EMU, the principles of decentralization and subsidiarity were applied to the transition. Each country was responsible for devising its own plans to recall the existing national currency and to introduce the euro, but general guidelines regarding the changeover existed and national plans were subject to review by the ECB. The national mechanisms and procedures for the changeover differed considerably, with each national plan presumably tailored to best address its market institutions and conditions. The ECB itself did not exchange any banknotes and coins.

B. Phase I – the euro as a virtual currency

18.4. The Euroarea was created on January 1, 1999. The euro was created as a virtual currency that existed as an accounting identity. Physical euros did not exist – the existing national currencies continued to circulate as "components of the euro". Each national currency had fixed exchange values against the euro.

18.5. Introducing the virtual euro involved many separate steps that were carefully planned prior to the start of the union. Implementation of some steps began well before the start of the union.

> Setting the conversion rate from national currencies into the euro currency. This was done about eight months before the start of the union. Once the initial membership of the union was set, "irrevocable conversion rates" between the national currencies and the euro as a weighted average value of the national currencies was calculated, as described in *Chapter 9 – Currency.*
>
> Irrevocable rates were specified to six significant digits for all countries so that all parties use the same values.
>
> Once the conversion rates were set, all national-currency values could be redenominated into euros. For example, a firm in Belgium selling an item for 100 francs applied the conversion rate (1 euro = 40.3399 francs) to get the new euro price of €2.48.
>
> Businesses used the conversion rates to reprice their goods and services into euros. Prices on signs and products were often displayed in both euros and the national currency. Dual pricing began months before the start up.
>
> On January 1, banks were required to denominate their accounts into euros. Deposits were made in national currency, but deposit balances were recorded in euros, and disbursements were made in

national currency. Published bank accounts were in both currencies. Extensive preparations had to be made to bank processing and accounting systems for this.

The TARGET euro payments system became operational. All transactions had to be in euros. Bank transactions with the ESCB, such as for required reserves transactions, had to go through TARGET, as did government transactions.

Government financial accounts were converted into euros.

Based on implementing legislation, all securities and financial contracts were converted into euros at the start of the union. This had to be done in ways that did not invalidate the financial flows and rights and obligations of the instruments.

Discussions and agreements with international markets were conducted in order to ensure acceptance of redenomination of contracts and securities into the euro.

Monetary policy operations in euros began using new standardized monetary policy instruments and standing facilities. Before this could happen, counterparties had to be defined and certified for participation in operations. Collateral for operations and TARGET participation had to be identified. Monetary policy instruments had to be designed and implemented; counterparties had to be informed about the characteristics of operations and instruments and adjust their systems. Extensive education campaigns for the public and markets explained the changes.

18.6. This is an extensive list of tasks. The EMI/ECB concentrated on setting the overall framework, drafting standards and model legislation, reviewing national transition plans, and monitoring progress toward implementation. Problems had to quickly come to the EMI/ECB's attention so that adjustments could be made. In contrast, NCBs had extensive implementation responsibilities: each NCB had responsibility to draft and implement a changeover plan, conduct training and public information campaigns, enact implementing legislation, implement actions, and enforce required changes.

18.7. The ECB and the NCB were each responsible for securing staffing and financial resources for these tasks. ECB efforts were intended to be financed from earning on its contributed capital, but these funds were insufficient and a special assessment was made on NCBs to cover the ECB cost overruns. NCBs incurred all costs of the transition in their countries.

18.8. Banks, firms, and households were expected to incur the costs of the transition on their own.

C. Phase II – Introduction of euro banknotes and coins

18.9. Physical euro banknotes and coins were introduced on January 1, 2002. The virtual euro had already existed for three years and was deeply integrated into banking, government finances, pricing of goods and services, denomination of financial instruments, and payments and clearing arrangements. Moreover, it was heavily traded in exchange markets, used for international trade, and widely accepted internationally. Thus, the introduction of physical currency in 2002 was only one aspect of the creation of the union, although probably the aspect that most directly affected most of the population.

18.10. Physical euros were issued in 2002, but before this currency stocks had been built up and working balances distributed to banks, businesses, and the public. On January 1, 2002 they were to be used for transactions. ATMs were adjusted to distribute physical euros.

18.11. On January 1, 2002 the process of withdrawal of the physical national currency began. In principle, national currencies were accepted at banks and businesses, balances were credited in euros, and withdrawals and change given in euros.

18.12. In Europe in 2002, the process of distributing the stock of currency was greatly facilitated by the widespread and highly automated formal banking system. Although some segments of the population remained fully or very heavily committed to using cash, many workers had their regular paychecks deposited into banks (where amounts were recorded in euros), had many recurring payments (health insurance, utilities, etc.) automatically debited from the bank and paid directly, and only made cash withdrawals as needed. Many depositors also had checking facilities or used debit cards. This automated formal system allowed the public to limit their total cash use; indeed, the ratio of cash use in total transactions had been declining for some time. ATMs were widely available and accounted for most of the distribution of banknotes to the public. Many vending machines also accepted bills and gave change in coins. These patterns greatly affected the distribution of the new currency in Europe;

A large portion of the population used noncash payments methods, thus limiting the total amount of euros banknotes and coins that had to be put into circulation.

Depositors' accounts were already denominated in euros, and therefore the process of introducing euros into accounts was invisible to depositors. Banks did not have to handle large inflows of physical euro banknotes from diverse sources.

Banks could receive physical shipments of euros in large volume shipments directly from their NCBs. This was efficient and secure.

ATMs were widely used, permitting the euros to be distributed without face-to-face transactions at banks. The cost of ATM transactions emitting euro banknotes was cheaper than going to a bank and converting physical national currency banknotes into physical euros.

National currencies were withdrawn from circulation by banks and business when received for deposits or transactions.

18.13. These were large advantages for issuing euro banknotes to the public. However, they did not cover the entire population and many diverse channels for distributing the currency had to be covered. No segment of the population could be ignored. In general, it can be assumed that the nonautomated issuance of euros was both more expensive and slower than using automated means.

18.14. Thus, the cash changeover system in Europe had many advantages that will be unavailable in other unions, or might only be available to portions of the population such as those living in principal cities. European populations were also highly literate and educated. Large portions of the populations in the planned African unions have not had access to formal banking facilities, and the new forms of basic banking being offered through cell phones and telecommunications companies are not well-suited for distributing large amounts of cash. The ability of informal Hawala money transfer systems to reliably and cheaply introduce a new currency is very uncertain. *The introduction of new currencies in future unions might be relatively more expensive and slower than in Europe, and greater difficulties will be faced in reaching all segments of the population.*

ESCB roles

18.15. The ECB and the NCBs played very different roles in the retirement of existing national currencies and the introduction of euro banknotes and coins. The ECB set some basic rules and schedules, reviewed national plans, monitored the process, and provided various types of public information. The NCBs were responsible for devising changeover plans for their countries and actually carrying out the exchanges. The process in fact went very smoothly in all Euroarea countries.

18.16. The ECB was not directly involved in providing the currency to the banks and withdrawing the national currencies. It did not exchange any banknotes and coins. It limited its activities to setting a limited number of common rules for NCBs to follow,[507] setting the schedule for the changeover, reviewing national plans to ensure that they offered complete and timely exchange of the currencies, and monitoring the process in order to coordinate rapid responses to problems that might arise. It also played important roles in publicizing the introduction process, making information about the new currency available, and conveying a positive image for the currency so that the public would want to hold it.

18.17. The NCBs in contrast had direct responsibility for the changeover. This respected the Maastricht concept of subsidiarity and allowed national plans to be customized (including by language) to differences in conditions and practices between member countries. Each NCB prepared national plans and submitted them for review by the ECB. Plans and implementation steps were required to be in place before the beginning of December 1998. *That is, full plans were required three full years before introduction of the physical euro.*

18.18. Logically, the costs of retiring the old national currency falls on the NCBs, which had issued the national currencies, earned seigniorage income on them, managed the stock of currency, and had responsibility to retire the bills when they become damaged and old. The arrangements for legal responsibility of future unions could be handled in different ways and perhaps giving the union central bank a larger role. Of course, if the union adopts a single central bank organization operating in all member countries, a completely different model from the EMU must be used.

18.19. The EMU arrangement went a step beyond this because the NCBs were given responsibility for arranging for introduction of the euro. One important consequence was that NCBs incurred substantial costs to introduce the euro, and the ECB avoided such costs. These costs have never been tallied, but were certainly substantial.

18.20. One of the first steps for the NCBs was to arrange for the needed amounts of euro currency. National presses and mints produced the currency, but each specialized in certain banknotes in order to provide guarantees of quality and achieve economies of scale. Each NCB was responsible for ordering the needed amount of each denomination banknote from other member countries.

18.21. Euroarea countries were permitted to place time limits on the period during which the national currency could be redeemed for euros, as shown below. The public had time to collect the old currency and redeem it, but time limits permitted authorities to close the books on the old currencies and remove the liability from their balance sheets. In countries that used limits, relatively short periods were provided for coins, with the expectation that the low value of coins would prevent any holders from experiencing large losses if redemptions were not made by the deadline. Also, since coins were usually recorded as liabilities of the government, this allowed the fiscal gain on unreturned coins to be recorded quickly in the government accounts. In contrast, at least ten years were provided to redeem banknotes. A special concern for banknotes was that notes of some countries, such as Germany or France, might have been extensively held outside the Euroarea and that an extended period might be needed to inform holders and have them arrange to exchange the banknotes. Also, the NCBs benefitted if large value banknotes were redeemed slowly or were never redeemed.

[507] For example, The ECB mandated that each country must have at least one location (the NCB was often selected) where the public could exchange the currencies of other union member countries in exchange for euros. Other rules were that the NCBs were permitted to limit the number of or total value of banknotes that could be exchanged at one time, and mandating that precirculation packets of euros with specified amounts of small banknotes and coins must be offered to the public just prior to the changeover date to the euro.

Time limits to exchange national banknotes and coins for euros

Country	Banknotes	Coins
Belgium	Unlimited	31 December 2004
Germany	Unlimited	Unlimited
Ireland	Unlimited	Unlimited
Greece	1 March 2012	1 March 2004
Spain	Unlimited	Unlimited
France	17 February 2012	17 February 2005
Italy	29 February 2012	29 February 2012
Cyprus	31 December 2017	31 December 2009
Luxembourg	Unlimited	31 December 2004
Malta	31 January 2018	1 February 2010
The Netherlands	1 January 2032	1 January 2007
Austria	Unlimited	Unlimited
Portugal	28 February 2022	31 December 2002
Slovenia	Unlimited	31 December 2016
Finland	29 February 2012	29 February 2012

Introducing the new currency to banks

18.22. In a "Big Bang" transition, a large stock of the new currency must be prepositioned prior to the introduction of a new currency so that it can quickly be introduced throughout the economy. Frontloading included putting euros into the banking system and into businesses so that they could transact in euros on its first day.

18.23. The EMU called this process "frontloading." Subsequent shipments of the euro to businesses and local distribution points was called "subfrontloading". In the EMU, from the first day of the introduction of the currency, transactions such as withdrawals from ATMs or use in vending machines were allowed only in the new currency, which required that large amounts of currency be in the hands of businesses and the public. Total frontloading of euro banknotes equaled €133 billion, and frontloaded coins equaled €12.4 billion.

Text box: Frontloading of currency[508]

Key events and dates for frontloading of euros to banks and businesses are described below.

August 3, 2000. First press release by the ECB about the cash changeover.[509] *(Seventeen months before circulation of euro.)*

September 1, 2001. Frontloading of euro banknotes and coins to credit institutions begins. Distribution was without collateral because banknotes and coins were still non-legal tender cash that was officially retained by the Eurosystem. However, the institutions receiving the euros were responsible for theft, loss, or destruction of the currency.

September 1, 2001. Credit institutions can begin distributing funds ("subfrontloading") to cash handlers (retailers, vending machine operators, etc.). Subfrontloading required delivery of collateral to the NCBs.

December 31, 2001. Frontloading continued until this date. Delivery of collateral by credit institutions to the Eurosystem was required by this date for frontloaded cash not yet debited.

January 1, 2002. Euro banknotes and coins officially put into circulation.

[508] See Solans 2000.

[509] ECB. "Financial modalities for credit institutions for the 2002 cash changeover" Press Release August 3, 2000.

18.24. Each NCB was responsible for distribution of euros to their banks. Banks incurred all the costs of transition, which included setting up their systems to receive and process the retired national currencies, distribute the new union currency, train staff, install new equipment, etc.

18.25. ATMs operated by banks were one of the most important channels to providing euro banknotes to the public. In Europe, most cash is distributed through machines – mostly €20 and €50 banknotes. It was important that banks received ample banknotes to be able to stock machines, and to have a good supply of other denomination banknotes and coins.

18.26. Bulk shipments from NCBs, under heavy guard, provided the stock of currency to the banking system. Coin shipments were particularly bulky and heavy. National implementation plans covered shipment of the currency under armed guard. Once delivered to banks, it was their responsibility to ensure safe delivery to their offices and distribution points. The process was reversed when national currencies were collected and returned to the NCBs. Large return shipments would occur, but probably on a more extended, more erratic schedule than for the new currency.

18.27. The large volume of currency that moved during a short period provided a tempting target for theft or violent attacks on money shipments. Shipments must be made on a secret schedule and with high security, possibly including military escorts.

18.28. Banks receiving the currency might be unable to make immediate payment for it or have sufficient unencumbered collateral available. For this reason, the EMU instituted a "linear debiting model" (described below) in which frontloaded cash remained property of the NCB until the legal issuance date when banks gradually began incurring the obligation to purchase the euros.

18.29. Preparations for banks to handle the new currency began several years before the changeover. They must set up a distribution system, accounting system, purchase and test new money handling equipment, train staff, arrange communications with client business, arrange information campaigns, design new processing forms, etc.. Training on currency security features and procedures to handle counterfeits was needed. All changes must reflect national and union standards, and systems to interact with other banks, payment systems, and financial institutions had to be in place. All these tasks were underway two full years prior to the changeover.

Introducing the new currency to businesses

18.30. Businesses must receive a stock of currency in order to carry out business at the start of the union. It is preferable for businesses to receive the old national currency in the course of their regular business, then provide change in the new union currency. They will then deposit the old currency in banks where it is removed from circulation.

18.31. However, there was a period of several weeks to three or six months during which the existing national currency would continue to circulate as legal tender. During this period, business might need to operate in both currencies until customers are familiar with the new union currency, to make change for national currency transactions, and to deal with temporary shortages of the union currency.

18.32. Businesses face many specific tasks in handling the new currency, including creating an accounting system, purchasing new registers and new money handling equipment, training staff, arranging information campaigns, designing new processing forms, changing signs, etc.. All changes must reflect procedures and guidelines of their banks to be in accord with national and union standards. For large, multisite businesses, these tasks must be underway about eighteen months prior to the changeover; small formal businesses must begin preparations at least 6 months in advance and earlier is better. Cash-based small farmers, small businesses, traders, etc. might possibly be treated like the general public – they might need only limited amounts of the new currency at the start of the union, but it is important that they be trained about the new currency and its security features.

18.33. All business staff handling currency with the public need to be trained about the security features of the new currency and procedures for handling suspected counterfeits.

18.34. The EMU permitted banks to begin distributing currency to businesses one month before the union date so that it could be distributed to all offices and sales points. "Starter kits" with a selection of currency were prepared for help businesses build their stock of currency, but they were not heavily used.

18.35. Businesses operated in both currencies during the changeover period, which is expensive for businesses. EMU businesses expressed strong preferences for rapid changeover to the new currency.

18.36. Banks supplying businesses should remain alert to the needs of their business customers and problems they experience. Problems should be quickly reported back to the NCB so that the situation can be actively monitored and adjustments made, as needed.

Introducing the new currency to the public

18.37. The new currency should be introduced to the general public in ways that encourage its smooth acceptance, avoid economic disruptions, and prevent the changeover being used for fraud or counterfeiting. In addition to presenting the currency to the general public, special efforts will be needed to introduce the currency to special subgroups, such as the blind, children, or elderly. In addition to making the public knowledgeable about the currency, effective means must be found to deliver the new currency to the public in all areas of the union. The ESCB promoted the new currency strongly to encourage rapid reception by the public. A formal campaign called "My Euro" was created to introduce the new currency. Numerous training materials were prepared in a wide range of languages and covering a range of special communities such as the blind. Public relations firms were hired to handle much of the information campaign.

18.38. To help the public obtain small bills and coins needed for everyday purchases at the start-up of the union, countries prepared plastic pouch "starter kits" with a selection of coins or banknotes. For example, Finland had a pack with one each new coin, for a value of €3.88. Other kits tended to range between €10 and €20. Kits were available beginning two weeks before the start of the union, but could not legally be used until January 1, 2002,

Introducing the euro outside the Euroarea

18.39. To smooth the introduction of the euro, it was decided that the euro should be distributed to banks outside the Euroarea.[510] Credit institution counterparties were allowed to distribute euros to their branches, parents, or subsidiaries outside the Euroarea, but were not permitted to distribute it further.

18.40. Central banks were also allowed to receive euros. Frontloading to central banks was permitted beginning December 1, 2001. Collateral was required immediately and payment was due on the first business day of 2002.

D. Phase III – Introduction of a digital currency

18.41. This is a section that remains to be written. Many central banks are investigating issuing CBDCs, which are official digital instruments that are direct liabilities of the central bank similar to cash. As of 2021, several countries and regions have launched CBDCs or initial experiments (China, Eastern Caribbean Currency Union, El Salvador, Nigeria) and more are expected.

18.42. *Chapter 9D – The Digital Euro* describes CBDCs and work under way to create an euro version. Future monetary unions should review that

[510] ECB. "Distribution of frontloaded euro banknotes outside the Euroarea" Press Release 14 December 2000.

chapter and also monitor the very rapid evolution of technology and policy under way.

18.43. As described in Chapter 9D, Europe is undertaking a careful multi-year long review of the advantages, costs, and risks of issuing a digital euro. The transition in Europe can be expected to be undertaken as carefully as those for the virtual and physical euros.

18.44. However, digital technology allows CDBCs to be issued very quickly – by pressing a button so-to-speak. Some countries' experiments have started very quickly,[511] but sometimes without any considered analysis of the monetary and financial sector impacts, balance of payments implications, and soundness and operational risks, nor consideration of how easily it appears that digital fraud can follow.

18.45. It can be hoped that when this section is filled in it will include a long list of smooth and successful transitions to a digital currency. But that will depend on the prudence and acumen of the central banks and politicians in charge of the efforts.

E. Fear of price increases and inflation

18.46. A common complaint regarding the introduction of the euro was that it was used by businesses to increase prices. Such increases have tended to show up in official statistics as only marginal increases, if any, but perceptions of increases have remained. There are several reasons for such perceptions, including some for which the changeover to the euro is innocent.

Prices must be rounded when translated from the old currency to the euro. Fractional prices in euro probably tended to be rounded up.

The public might use inexact math to translate new euro values into the old currency with which they are familiar. In some cases, this might bias perceptions upward.

Businesses use the changeover to raise prices, sometimes fraudulently.

Items that directly affect consumers were among the most affected. Even though they had little weight in the official price indices, they did have a strong impression on the public.

Once the changeover started, all subsequent inflation was blamed on the euro, even years after the changeover.

Structural changes in prices because of membership in the union are blamed on the euro. The process of joining a union, including the EU, integrates the financial system with the rest of the union, can cause capital inflows that raise assets prices such as real estate, and can increase demand for specific goods or services. These changes can have important redistributive effects, for example helping those who own real estate, but hurting renters. The euro might be blamed for negative effects, although it had no direct role in the structural changes in prices.

18.47. Whatever the causes for the perceptions, it appears to be a common problem that new unions should address, both to suppress actual price jumps do not actually occur, and to deal with public perceptions. Special price measurement efforts might be needed that go beyond the standard price indices. Some economies required extended periods in which both the national currency price and the euro price must be posted on products.

18.48. Despite the redenomination of currencies, it is possible that some segments of the population will continue to think in terms of the old national currency and will be reluctant to give it up. The elderly might have a hard time adjusting to the new currency. The

[511] Motivations to rapidly issue CBDCs include enhancing financial inclusion, modernizing financial systems, or staunching invasions of private unregulated cryptocurrencies.

author saw prices in Austria posted in schillings six years after the issuance of physical euro currency.

Reproduction of the image of the euro

18.49. The ECB took the view that the public and businesses needed access to high quality images of the currency for use in educational campaigns, anti-counterfeit programs, training of money handlers, etc. The ECB created rules for reproduction of the currency for legitimate training and educational programs. The rules, for example, state that images had to be smaller or larger than the genuine bill, use different color backgrounds, show only small portions of banknotes, etc..

18.50. It is important that the images be changed in some way that the public can understand the features being discussed, but not be tricked into accepting the image as real currency. This includes not using electronic images of the currency with high resolution above set limits.

F. Retiring the old currency

18.51. The existing national currencies must be retired and replaced with the new union currency. This process is as complex as putting out the new currency. The public will have physical currency in the form of banknotes and coins, and will often have bank accounts denominated in the old currency that are actively used for both depositing and withdrawing currency. The bank accounts must be transitioned into handling accounts denominated in the new currency and during the transition accept the old currency, but make payments only in the new currency.

18.52. The volume, spread, and conditions of the old currency can create practical problems.

18.53. In terms of volume, a large stock has been built up over an extended period, but might be taken out of circulation quickly. A sudden, large influx of old currency at banks might create significant problems, such as insufficient staff, shortage of vault space, limited cash handling machinery, strained security, etc.. Bottlenecks might occur at the level of first receipt of the currency from the public, or at the point at which the central bank receives the funds. The ability of banks and other cash handlers to handle the flow of old currency might depend on how quickly and easily the central banks can receive the old currency and credit the banks' accounts.

> The collection of large amounts of coins is potentially a big problem because they are heavy and bulky. The volume and total tonnage of coins could overwhelm cash handlers.
>
> Usually, the two lowest denomination banknotes in a country are the most heavily used and create the greatest processing burdens when retiring the old currency, although only constituting a minor part of the value of the total stock of currency.
>
> In Europe, the total amount of national currency to withdraw exceeded the amount of euros initially put into circulation. The national banknotes in circulation amounted to €234.3 billion equivalent as of January 4, 2002, or about €100 billion more than the frontloaded euro banknotes.

18.54. In terms of spread, the old currency will be spread throughout the economy, often in locales remote from cash handling centers. In issuing currencies there might be an established structure with a finite number of issuing points – banks, ATMs, government offices, etc., each handling a reasonably well-known volume of transactions. But once put into circulation, the currency spreads throughout the economy, will no longer be concentrated, and might reside in awkward or remote locations. Decisions on how to collect the old currency, the number of receiving points, and the speed of the collection should consider information on the spread of currencies and the manner in which it is held. (The situation in future unions could be very different from Europe, where multiple central banks already existed within relatively small or medium-sized areas endowed with good travel infrastructure.)

18.55. Changeover procedures for the euro were also developed for overseas territories, and for withdrawing stocks from the rest of the world. These situations are much less relevant for future unions and probably can be handled in a very abbreviated way by local embassies or through correspondent banks.

18.56. Some returned banknotes might be in poor condition. In tropical climates and in many lower income countries, banknotes often continue in circulation despite being in poor condition, such as dirty, faded, or partially torn or punctured. Rules can be set for the minimally acceptable condition of redeemed currency (which can be generous, but must insist that at least 51% of banknotes must be provided.) Poor condition of currency complicates the process of collecting the money because poor quality bills cannot readily be handled in cash handling machinery and must be collected, processed, examined, and bundled by hand.

18.57. Retirement of the old currency will also collect counterfeit notes in circulation, and might be an occasion in which attempts are made to pass additional counterfeits because of the pressing demands. Detection of counterfeits often can be done by cash handling machines if banknotes are in good condition, but requires hand processing otherwise. Procedures to screen for counterfeits need to be included in the changeover planning.[512]

18.58. In light of the factors listed above, the process of collecting the existing currency could be difficult and costly. Moreover, it is a one-time exercise that does not generate income. Each of the demands for retiring the old currency directly competes with resources for issuing the new currency. Because of the costs and resource demand, the process of retiring the old currency needs to be carefully planned. Consultations with money handlers early in the process are recommended to gather information on ways to gather the old currency efficiently and avoid problems.

18.59. In some cases, the costs and possible difficulties in retiring old currency might result in situations where it might be best to not set a formal deadline to cease using the old currency and there will be an extended period in which the old and new currencies circulate together. This could be the case for large rural populations or isolated populations (on islands, perhaps) that might be able to handle transactions in the old currency for an extended period of time. That is, treat the old national currency as if it was a cocirculating foreign currency as a second-best situation. This is obviously not desirable and should be avoided, but might prove necessary.[513] Over time, the existing currency will be gradually withdrawn or will wear out, and the new currency will eventually prevail.

18.60. Retiring the old currency will require consultations with cash handlers well in advance of the process. Banks, other cash handlers, and the central banks will incur additional costs that can be minimized by careful planning. In this environment, the flow of old currency should be carefully planned to provide for efficiency and proper support.

18.61. The old currency still has value and it must be secure from the moment of receipt until destroyed.[514]

18.62. The EMU applied the concept of subsidiarity and left the mechanics of the retirement mostly to the national authorities.

18.63. A decision is needed of when and how the value of the existing currencies will be extinguished. Typically, banknotes are liabilities on the central

[512] The author has been in a (nonEuropean) country where during a currency changeover the value of returned old currency exceeded the amount ever issued.

[513] One obvious problem is that the legal code created for the union currency might be specified in terms of only one currency.

[514] There have been cases when retiring currencies in which it has been suspected that old currency was recycled out of the receiving banks and redeemed more than once.

bank balance sheet, and coins are liabilities on the balance sheet of either the central bank or the government. The central bank is obligated to credit the accounts of persons who deposit physical currency; as a result of the transition, the nature of that liability will change. First, the existing national liability under the old currency will somehow change into a union-wide liability against the new, union currency. The commitment to credit persons depositing the old national currency might or might not be continued – some unions might declare the old currency worthless after a short period in order to force the public to quickly make the change; other unions could honor the old currencies indefinitely, which protects the public but slows the exchange and possibly increases costs.

18.64. Statistical monitoring of the retirement of currencies is needed. The union central bank needs to know how rapidly the old currency is being retired, and the patterns in terms of denomination and location. Not all segments of the public will retire currencies equally rapidly or enthusiastically, and some segments of the population could face obstacles in making the change. This information might force the central bank to adjust its strategy in midstream to prompt the public to exchange the currency. Some situations that could arise include;

Banknotes of all denominations are returned slowly. This could indicate public resistance to adopt the new currency, insufficient redemption centers, burdensome identification requirements, lack of sufficient stock of the new currency, poor planning, high costs of making the exchange, concerns about the security of the new currency, or at worst distrust of the union initiative.

Low denomination notes are returned, but large denomination bills are returned slowly. This might reflect a slower velocity of circulation of large value bills, the use of large bills in hoards for savings purposes, hesitation to reveal holdings because of concerns about tax or legal complications, the use of the large banknotes in underground transactions, holdings of bills outside the country.

The speed of redemptions varies by country.

Concern about tax or legal complications.

Poor information or statistical systems on the status of retirement

Destruction of the old currency

18.65. The old national currencies must be collected and destroyed.

Security

18.66. Security must be provided for the old currency to prevent theft and loss. Banknotes have value in markets during the transition period and are likely to be redeemable for years. Coins will also have the same usage potential, but also have intrinsic value because of their metal content. Banknotes and coins will have numismatic or sentimental value for collectors. And there are legitimate historical and archival reasons for obtaining specimens of the banknotes and coins. Such reasons provide motivations to steal the old currency during the collection process.

18.67. However, there might be a feeling that once the old currency is retired, it lacks value and thus does not need to be closely watched. (It gets put in a sack in the back room, instead of in the vault with the new currency.) This loss of value cannot be assumed – although the currency lacks public value, it is credited in internal accounting and banks and money handlers will incur losses if accounting entries are not matched against physical currency. The same type of situation can incur for the NCBs who need to ensure that the amounts redeemed from the public are fully accounted for until the currency is certified destroyed or otherwise dealt with.[515] Thus, tight security over the

[515] Cases have been reported where lax controls by central banks during currency changeovers allowed some redeemed currency to leak back into circulation for redemption a second time.

old currency is needed through the entire retirement process.

Accounting, Verification, and Audit

18.68. The counterpart to tight security over the retired old currency is thorough accounting for the receipt, transfer, and disposal of the currency. It is possible that redeemed currency will go through several sets of hands through private banks and money handlers, to local then regional offices of the central bank, etc. At each stage, the recipient of the currency will credit the provider of the currency. Lax accounting for receipts and payments will result in losses. Also, thorough accounting for the currency receipts is needed to ensure that officials receiving the old currency do not fraudulently overpay the currency provider.

18.69. The special nature of the cash changeover, and the high values involved, suggest that transactions should be double-checked by personnel on the spot, and that later audits be performed. *Prior to the changeover, it should be made clear to the front-line and back-office staffs that their transactions will be verified and later audited.*

Historical, archival and numismatic value

18.70. The central bank, the Treasury, museums, and miscellaneous others have reasons to hold specimens of the old currency, for display or research purposes. The changeover provides an opportunity to collect sets of banknotes and coins for such purposes. The NCBs should select who has legitimate reasons to receive specimens of the old currency. Sets should also be sent to the new union central bank and member NCBs.

18.71. The banknotes and coins also have value for collectors. The changeover will also temporarily increase interest in holding examples of the old currencies, and there might be additional interest by foreign collectors. The changeover provides an opportunity to collect sets of banknotes and coins for resale to collectors. The receipt of great numbers of coins allows scanning for coins of different years, which increases their potential value.

18.72. Collecting banknotes and coins for numismatic purposes should be done for commercial reasons only. It could be a profitable part of the changeover, but should be avoided if the costs of collecting banknotes and coins for numismatic purposes exceeds the income generated.

Intrinsic value

18.73. Coins have value because of their metal content and can be melted down and resold as metal. Because of the weight and bulk of coins, using local smelters might be cost efficient.

18.74. Banknotes have much less intrinsic value, and thus they might often simply be burned or ground up. In some cases, they have been ground up and pressed into logs for use for home fuel. Polymer banknotes can be melted down and recycled into plastic products.

G. Costs of changeover

18.75. In Europe, the ECB made clear that it would not cover costs of the changeover incurred by other parties. This included the NCBs, businesses, and the public. This paralleled the treatment when the euro was created as an accounting entity in January 1999, which entailed costs for accounting changes, retraining of staff, reprogramming of software, printing of new materials, etc. The ECB was however prepared to cover the costs to credit institutions due to the necessity of holding extra cash during the changeover period, as described below.

18.76. During frontloading operations, credit institutions in the EMU were required to hold large amounts of cash in excess of their transactions needs. This increased banks' costs and could create problems in collateralizing their liability for the holdings. The ECB agreed to compensate for these extra holdings, using what is called the "linear debiting model".[516] Under the model;

> Prior to the official date for distribution of euros to the public, euros frontloaded to credit institutions were treated as remaining legally in the possession of the ESCB and the banks were not charged for them.
>
> Once distribution to the public began on January 1, 2002, banks were debited for their holdings in three steps, one-third each on January 2, 23, and 30. On January 2, €42.4 billion was charged to the banks, recorded in liability item 2.1 – "current accounts – covering the minimum reserve system".
>
> The euros frontloaded but not yet paid for through the linear debiting model were treated as collateralized, non-remunerated loans to the credit institutions, which were classified as "other claims on Euroarea credit institutions, denominated in euro." On January 2, 2002, the loan account recorded €88.5 billion, an increase of €88.0 billion over the previous week, comprised of euros frontloaded to the banking system, but not yet charged to it.
>
> The completion of the linear debiting model on January 30 meant that all positions under the model were eliminated from banks' balance sheets by the time of their first monthly reports used for compilation on monetary statistics.

Costs for the public

18.77. A currency changeover can entail inconveniences and costs for the general public. For physical currency, much of the changeover can be done quickly and at relatively low cost by accepting the old national currencies for normal transactions and deposits, and distributing the new currency as wages and as withdrawals from bank accounts, including at ATMs. In Europe, the automatic deposit of wages and heavy withdrawal of cash from ATMs resulted in a quick changeover, but these practices might not be available in future unions. If the public must physically redeem national currencies for the union currency, costs will certainly be higher to cover transportation to the bank, processing, and security.

18.78. Policies on conversion fees for businesses and the public need to be developed. Banks might be expected to exchange the currencies at no cost for customers as a part of their on-going business, but nominal fees such as 1 percent of transactions could be charged. It is recommended that a fee schedule be legally set to avoid exploiting the public.

18.79. Converting the public's noncurrency stores of value could be more complex. For example, how should value embedded in postage stamps, gift cards, swipe cards, or cell phone e-money systems be handled? Separate solutions might be needed for each type of system or store of value. For fairness and more complete coverage, union-wide rules or legislation are probably preferable.

18.80. It might be possible to provide incentives to the public to encourage the changeover and compensate for its costs. For example, fees could be waived for exchanges made during the first month of the changeover, or a one-percent discount on income taxes could be made, etc. The publicity for incentive campaigns will help encourage public interest and could be a useful public relations technique. .

H. Transition for new members

18.81. New members joining the EMU also followed the "Big Bang" approach, under which the euro was introduced rapidly and the national currency withdrawn in a short period. All candidate countries were required to introduce all of the legal requirements of the union and meet the convergence criteria. Following these steps, and agreement to formally extend membership to a candidate country, the country

[516] ECB. "Financial modalities for credit institutions for the 2002 cash changeover" Press Release August 3, 2000.

must quickly withdraw the national currency and introduce the euro. This process is considerably easier because lessons learned and facilities created in the existing Euroarea countries can be applied, and the transition period can be shortened.

18.82. The experiences of three countries – Slovenia, Cyprus, and Malta - have been carefully documented. All are small countries that benefitted from familiarity with the euro, made careful preparations, and succeeded in smooth introduction of the euro, using the "Big Bang" approach. Their experiences are described briefly below.

Slovenia

18.83. The transition of Slovenia in 2007 was rapid and smooth. It is an important example for several reasons; Slovenia was one of ten new EU members welcomed in 2004 and the first to switch over to the euro, with simultaneous transition of accounting entries and introduction of the new currency. It was carefully studied by the European Commission, the Government of Slovenia, and the Central Bank, and in a report by Deloitte. All accounts found the transition went smoothly and was completed within a two-week period. Some upward price adjustment was found, but it was not a major problem. The exchange of currencies was more complete than for the Euroarea in 2002. The European Commission pronounced it and the "Big Bang" approach used as successes and suggested to other candidate states that a two-week transition period was sufficient and that a short period would minimize costs and burdens.

18.84. Six months prior to joining, the irrevocable rate of exchange for the Slovenia tolar to the euro was formally set at 239.640 tolars per euro, the central rate when Slovenia entered the Exchange Rate Mechanism II in 2004. The six-month period allowed time for banks to redenominate accounts, contracts to be rewritten, businesses to reprice, ATMs and cash handling machines to be adjusted, etc..

18.85. Slovenia allotted only two weeks for the transition, from January 1 to January 14, 2007. Euro kits were made available from mid-December 2006. ATMs were permitted to dispense only euros from January 1. Banks were required to exchange tolars for euros free of charge through February, and the Bank of Slovenia handled exchanges afterwards.

18.86. Because of numerous charges of abuse of repricing when the euro was introduced in 2002, in Slovenia retailers were required beginning in March 2006 (even before its membership was formally accepted) to list both euro and tolar prices to allow time for adjustment and prevent unwarranted price hikes. Double pricing was mandatory for 16 months until end-June 2007. Also, the Slovenian Consumer Association monitored the transition and published names of retailers creating problems.

The Deloitte Report on the Slovenian changeover

18.87. The Deloitte Company was retained to prepare a report (2007) on the changeover experience. The key theme of the Deloitte report was the importance of thorough preparations, with strong backing and exercise of authority at the highest levels of government. The report cites the prior familiarity of the Slovenian public with the euro as a strong contributor to success. It also cited the need for a high degree of legal certainty.

18.88. Deloitte credits familiarity with the euro as contributing to the successful transition. Slovenia began with big advantages - it is a popular vacation destination in which transactions in euros were common and businesses and the population already had working stocks of banknotes and coins – highly favorable conditions that will rarely be duplicated elsewhere. As a result, the formal campaign to introduce the euro involved enhancing the general state of knowledge about the euro, and could highlight particular features of interest.

18.89. Deloitte said that the public campaign was comprehensive but highlighted developing the new scale of values, security features of banknotes and coins, counterfeit detection, and rounding of values and fair pricing. This high degree of familiarity allowed the campaign to be limited mostly to the last four months of 2006 and first two weeks of 2007. *This 4½ month long public campaign should be considered as the absolute minimum, given the highly favorable conditions that prevailed in Slovenia.*

18.90. Deloitte argued that there must be balance between the need to communicate as much to the public as early as possible and waiting for official recognition of the entry date. Under the EMU subsidiarity framework, it is each country's duty to set up and execute a communications policy for the transition. In deciding on a plan, the public will benefit from early notification to be able to plan for the transition, but for the most part will not make preparations – which can be costly – until the legal changeover date is set.

18.91. Deloitte cited the need for legal certainty in the changeover, and careful reworking of contracts, redenomination of prices, changing pay and tax schedules, etc. All these aspects were successfully completed.

18.92. There were no difficulties reported in information technology aspects, but Deloitte noted that "compressing the changeover into a short period can increase systemic risk in some types of IT changeover, and this needs to be carefully considered by other 'pre-ins'." Unfortunately, the report did not describe the nature of any contingency plans if difficulties had occurred.

18.93. Deloitte found that "Retail kits were not important in this particular context, but the difficulty of planning for retailers' requirements raises more general questions marks about retail kits. Kits for the general public, on the other hand, did serve a useful purpose. They had psychological value and were probably useful in introducing coins into circulation despite the particular Slovene context."

18.94. Finally, Deloitte found significant problems in perceptions of possible inflation. Surveys found that the perceived hikes in prices were greater than measured increases. Price increases were mostly in services, but the public did not distinguish. Possibly some price increases happened to be in common everyday items, especially at food establishments, and these stuck in the public imagination. Deloitte suggests that perceptions of price increases will affect future changeovers.

Cyprus and Malta

18.95. The ECB Annual Report 2007 devotes a section to the changeover experience of Cyprus and Malta. Both adopted the euro on January 1, 2008.

Finances and monetary policy operations

18.96. Upon joining the Euroarea, Cyprus and Malta contributed capital to the ECB and international reserves according to the same formulas used for existing members. When the countries joined the EU in 2004, they had paid 7 percent of their capital share in the ECB as a contribution to the ECB's operational costs. The balance of 93% was paid when they joined the Euroarea. Similarly, the countries' foreign currency shares were paid, comprised 15% of gold and 85% of U.S. dollar denominated assets. The transfer of the foreign exchange created a central bank claim on the ECB. Following Slovenia's example, Cyprus and Malta arranged with Greece and Ireland for management of their share of the ECB's foreign currency assets.

18.97. In order to participate in the ESCB monetary policy operations, the countries identified assets usable as collateral.

18.98. The day before the countries joined the Euroarea, the ECB published the list of institutions obligated to contribute required reserves. Reserves were due the first business day of the new year, totaling €1.5 billion. Because the ESCB's monthly reserve maintenance period extends from mid-month to mid-month, a special calculation was needed to calculate the reserve base for each institution and to begin a reserve period on January 1.

18.99. Upon entering the union, the balance sheet of the entire ESCB changed. In the case of Cyprus and Malta, national liquidity absorbing operations had begun before January 1 then were reversed on January 4 when the countries ended their independent monetary policy operations. "The autonomous liquidity factors in the balance sheets of the two central banks reduced the liquidity needs of the entire Euroarea banking sector by, on average, €2.7 billion during January 1-15." (ECB 2008, p. 139) In conjunction with the €1.5 billion increase in the reserve requirement, total liquidity requirements of the Euroarea banking sector were reduced by €1.2 billion. That is, the two countries had absorbed liquidity from their economies and their entry into the ESCB balance sheet *reduced* the liquidity needs of the banking sector by an average €2.7 billion during January 1-15, 2008. (This situation can occur when – just prior to the start-up of the union – banks have large claims on the NCBs above required reserves and a relatively limited reserve base.)

Cash changeover in Cyprus and Malta

18.100. Both countries designed their changeover programs well in advance of the entry date. The changeover was based on the legal framework adopted by the ECB in 2006. Under that framework, once the countries are formally approved to enter the union, they became eligible to borrow banknotes to frontload the distribution. The countries arranged for delivery from three countries, Greece, Italy, and Portugal. For production of coins, which carry designs of the issuing country and for which production is a national responsibility, the countries put out public requests for bids, which resulted in Finland producing the coins for Cyprus, and France for Malta.

18.101. Frontloading of coins to banks began first, with Malta beginning in late September. Frontloading of banknotes began in late October in Malta and mid-November in Cyprus. Cyprus permitted distribution to retailers and vending machines operators at the same time, but Malta began only on the first of December. In both countries, ATMs were converted before or on January 1, and retailers only provided euros beginning January 1.

18.102. As done previously, the NCBs of other Euroarea countries exchanged the old currencies of Cyprus and Malta at par value at no cost for two months.

18.103. The information campaign was based on the ECB's original "€ Our money" theme used during the 2002 introduction. Based on the review of the experience of Slovenia and research undertaken in 2006, the human element was stressed in the changeover, with pictures identifiable as a local citizen engaged in using the euro. The campaign involved a number of specific steps;

Publications

Public relations programs

Press programs and events

Web pages

Academic conferences

A two-day seminar at the ECB in Frankfurt for journalists.

18.104. The ECB printed 1.8 million publications in Greek, Maltese, English, and Turkish. Every household in both countries received materials. Cypriots also received a euro calculator, preprogrammed with the translation rate, and cards with the images of the new currency. In Malta, cards were distributed with the image of the €20 note and a conversion table with common amounts.

18.105. Blind and visually impaired citizens received an "€ talking card" which included a chip with a prerecorded message describing the currency and the features of the changeover.

Lessons for other regions

18.106. Slovenia, Cyprus, and Malta were probably in the most favorable of all situations regarding their adoption of a new currency. They were small countries already familiar with the euro because of tourism. The banking and financial systems were small. Communications were good. In each case, the government initiated intense, positively-oriented, saturation campaigns to introduce the currency. The changeover was quick and successful. The experiences were reviewed after the event.

18.107. A key lesson for other countries is that even in the most favorable situations, the public changeover campaign needs to be both widespread and deep. The messages should be provided in a variety of forms using a range of media. Some messages should convey a personal tone, involving everyday situations.

18.108. Involvement of banks, other financial institutions, retailers, and vending machine operators was critical. In each case, parties were able to operate in the new currency on the first day of the changeover.

18.109. Concern about inflation of prices because of the changeover was high. A dual-pricing program begun well before the changeover helped, and additional oversight of common prices was thought necessary.

18.110. It was reported in each case that the speed of the changeover was appreciated by the public and businesses and minimized costs.

I. Price hikes during transition

18.111. The transition to a new union currency is likely to face a problem of unwarranted increases in prices and also public perception that the increases were caused by the new currency. There appears to be some reality behind this. This issue should be anticipated and dealt with.

18.112. In 2002, the European Consumers' Organization surveyed prices throughout the Euroarea to see if the introduction of the euro had affected consumer prices. It found that significant price increases had occurred, affecting the same sectors across the Euroarea. Price increases occurred most frequently at hairdressers, bakeries, restaurants, garages and parking places, and cinemas. Later, increases occurred for lotteries, vending machines, and newsstands. This configuration of price increases directly affected consumers and thereby increased public concerns and complaints about the impact of the euro.

18.113. The apparent price increases created a policy problem for the ECB which took the position that the introduction on the euro had not contributed to inflation or price hikes. This position lost credibility at the time that the ECB was trying to establish its reputation. By the end of 1999, ECB President Duisenberg said "We were reluctant to admit that the transition somewhat pushed up prices. We should have shown more honesty in this respect. Then we could have explained that the upward effect had remained minimal for the overall package of products and services. (Forest 2006, p. 7)

18.114. There is no single explanation for the increases. One possibility is that (with the sole exception of the Irish punt) one euro had a larger purchasing power per unit than any of the pre-union currencies. Thus, the number of units of currency held as euros fell compared to the national currency – a resident of Belgium for example might have felt cheated by exchanging 100 francs for €2.48 (which came in the form of small handful of 6 coins!). It is possible that prior to the union it was comparatively easy to price objects at convenient levels, but this was more difficult with a larger unit of value and prices were effectively rounded up. For example, it took about 1.96 German marks to equal one euro, using the official conversion rate. Something costing 5 marks, perhaps a glass of wine, would have an euro equivalent of €2.56. This could be rounded up conveniently to €2.60, a price increase of about 1.6 percent. But for cash-based retail businesses, such as restaurants, it might be easier for the server and the customer to use whole number values, such as using 3 one-euro coins to pay for the wine. Although this is convenient, raising the price of the glass of wine to €3 is the equivalent of a 17-percent price increase. Although this argument seems plausible, it is only speculative. But it does suggest that it appears to matter that the new currency units mesh well with retail habits and general business practices.[517]

J. Conclusions

18.115. The exchange of a new union currency for existing national currency is a major event. All

[517] This could be an argument for making the purchasing power of each unit of the new currency relatively small so that it can fit relatively easily into consumers everyday purchasing patterns. A small purchasing power per unit can also make it easier to incorporate low-income countries into the union.

monetary transactions and financial and real assets and liabilities must be legally redenominated and the new physical currency introduced. Careful planning is needed to ensure the success of the changeover for all parties involved, from the most sophisticated segments of the economy to isolated populations distant from formal banking, poorly educated populations, and those with special needs.

18.116. Careful planning and coordination of many activities are needed to smoothly carry out a changeover. The introduction of the euro was successful and smooth. Planning for the transition in Europe was completed three full years before the cash changeover, and interaction with business and the public began in earnest about two years before start up. *The transition in future unions should be expected to take up to three years – outreach to banks, businesses, and the public must begin two years before the start of the union, based on plans completed about a year earlier.*

18.117. Future unions might face challenges not experienced or insignificant in Europe, including large unmonetized or partly monetized sectors of the economy, lack of access to formal banking institutions, nomadic populations and heavily rural populations, poor communications systems, cocirculation of foreign currencies, poor distribution channels for the new currency, covert holdings, or sharp seasonal differences in currency use. Such special conditions mean that every changeover will be unique. Numerous targeted special programs might be needed, which can prove complex and burdensome despite being relevant to only niche situations. The transition will be tougher for future unions than in Europe, and new paths might need to be created.

18.118. Banks and other financial institutions outside the union need to be involved in order advise on acceptable practices, to make their own preparations, and to have stocks for tourist or other transactions.

18.119. If the existing currency is used extensively outside the union, plans should be made to introduce it outside the union.

18.120. A changeover scenario is needed to plan the types of changes needed and their sequencing. It must include strategies to reach all segments of the population and have consultations with each population prior to the changeover and communications strategies for each population. A key aspect of the changeover scenario is a decision whether to make a sudden "big bang" change or gradually introduce the currency.

18.121. The conversion rates at which national currencies convert into the single currency must be determined and announced prior to the start of the currency union. This must be done far enough in advance so that market participants can redenominate all financial positions, such as securities, in preparation for the changeover date, can reprice products, and exchange the old currency for the new.

18.122. There will be numerous legal implications that require actions so that rights and obligations under the existing currency pass into the new currency regime without gain or loss or unfair advantages for any party involved. These will include changing the names and amounts used in contracts, ensuring continuity of contracts, legally specifying the conversion and rounding rules. Common laws to deal with fraud, counterfeiting, and other abuses must be introduced.

Timelines

The changeover to a new currency has two parts: introduction of the currency as a legal instrument (which applies to the virtual currency case) and introduction of the physical currency. Two timelines are provided below – one for virtual currency and a second for physical currency. In cases where the legal and physical currencies are introduced at one time both timelines apply simultaneously.

Transition I: Introduction of a virtual currency as legal tender	
Preparatory period	Agreement on process and timing – Big Bang, Virtual and cash schedules
Early actions (four years prior)	Set up Transition Committee, with liaison with Legal and Currency Committees Compile information on national practices on currency use and counterfeiting.
Three years prior	Agreement on central and national responsibilities during changeover Draft union and country changeover implementation programs Consult on user needs, including special needs Draft legal framework for use of common currency Decisions on electronic currency; handheld and mobile phone currency Decisions on CBDC Design of anti-counterfeiting program *Finalization of changeover implementation program*
24 months prior	National legal implementation Prepare materials for cash handlers and businesses Order cash handling machines Translation of materials into working languages
18 Months Prior	Begin training of money handlers, businesses, and public Certification of machines through live runs Union press releases begin on changeover steps
Final 12 months	Consultations on legal acceptance in foreign markets Decision on e-money virtual currency
Final 6 months	Set conversion rate from national currencies to union currency Dual pricing regime begins Publication of final accounting standards for banks and businesses Statistical monitoring of repricing begins Information campaign for international markets
Run-up to union	Public relations campaign on changes for businesses and public Anti-fraud campaign
Union day	Monitor experiences Financial accounting officially changes to union currency Possible launch of e-money virtual currency or CBDC
Early union period	Monitor repricing effects
Union steady state	Prepare report on changeover experience

Transition II: Introduction of a physical currency as legal tender	
Preparatory period	Compile data on currency demand, by country, denomination, seasonality, purpose data on currency demand, by country, denomination, seasonality, purpose
Early actions (four years prior)	Set up Transition Committee, with liaison with bank, money handlers, business, and public currency user groups
Three years prior	Consultations on user needs, including special needs Agreement on central and national responsibilities during currency changeover Draft union and country changeover programs Consultations on money sorting and authentication machines, ATMs, and vending machines Draft standards for machines, ATMs, and vending Design of anti-counterfeiting program *Finalization of currency changeover implementation program*
24 months prior	Preparation of materials for cash handlers
18 Months Prior	Begin training of cash handlers Tests of cash machines through live runs
Final 12 months	Shipments begin to central banks and distribution points
Final 6 months	By 6-month point, central banks must have working stock on hand Statistical systems set up to monitor uptake and retirement
Run-up to union	Distribution begins to banks and cash handlers; government offices Distribution to external users Distribution to central banks or distribution centers outside of union Loading of ATMs 20% reserve in the field by startup date Activate "linear debiting model" about one month prior to start-up. Sales of "starter kits" for consumers and businesses Banks begin distribution to businesses Public relations campaigns Education on security features and counterfeiting protections.
Union day	Monitor experiences
Early union period	Evaluate performance of machines Priority oversight of possible counterfeits Measure uptake of currency, by country Measure retirement of national currencies Initiate currency handling procedures, and procedures for pulling currency out of circulation Prepare report on changeover experience
Union steady state	Examine turnover and condition of banknotes Regular report on authenticity

Chapter 19 – Conclusions

What are the principal lessons from the European Monetary Union for development of unions in other regions. What will be the place of new unions within the global financial system? What assistance or programs are appropriate to support these efforts?

A. Moving the process forward

19.1. Over the course of this investigation, the author's opinion strengthened that the rationale and urge of countries to create currency unions and other regional policy arrangements is strong and widespread. This is despite the problems in the Euroarea and disruptions from recurring financial crises. These events demonstrated the critical roles of fiscal sustainability and financial system stability in fostering macroeconomic growth, financial integration, support of monetary rescues, and development. Authorities working to build future currency unions and regional arrangements appear to have internalized many of these concerns and adjusted their programs to some degree. The motivation to create unions might actually have been strengthened in response to the recent turmoil as countries realize that they can better withstand economic stresses cooperatively than if they face the dangers alone.

19.2. However, the views of the union-builders and the public (both within regions and internationally) appear very divergent. Much of the public seems to believe that Europe's experience has little relevance to other regions, that regions elsewhere will never cooperate and converge economically. Such views are often expressed as a shorthand statement that dismisses prospects of unions outside of Europe.

19.3. This study concludes that the union-building movement is serious and must be accepted and nurtured as a key element of the evolving global financial and exchange rate system. The emergence of the G20 as major players in the global system is part of this same dynamic – the addition of new unions and regional policy arrangements will help complete the transition and make the system much more inclusive as clusters of smaller countries join together to create globally significant economic entities. Individual currencies will continue to exist for the foreseeable future for countries of all sizes, but the international financial system appears likely to shift toward a system dominated by a limited number of currencies representing groups of countries. Within each currency bloc, countries' financial systems will become increasingly integrated, economies will converge, and regional monetary and fiscal rules will become prevalent. And among the countries that might still retain their own currencies, some (perhaps many) can be expected to link their exchange rates with unions or other large economies, thus effectively importing the monetary policy of the countries to whom they are linked.

19.4. Also, the advent of cryptoassets and CBDCs and their possible deep penetration into small- or medium-sized economies might also further induce countries to defensively join into larger blocs.

19.5. Building the unions will not be simple. This study has looked at some of the major tasks involved. The tasks are many and require long periods and hard work to achieve. Given the state of preparedness now, I believe that about six years is the likely minimum time to set up new unions. The process could easily take longer if critical tasks lag (for example, an inadequate or inequitable policy development system, weak payments systems, poor statistics, lack of legal convergence, etc.). All component systems need to operate at high levels for the union system as a whole to operate – which could be a major delaying factor.

19.6. Similarly, if some countries in a region lag in union preparations, the other members must either exclude the country until ready or make other arrangements to compensate for the deficiencies. The latter course might be a good strategy if lagging countries are small, poor, and lack needed technical skills – a cooperative regional effort might be capable of (and perhaps be the only option for) pulling poor weak countries into a larger economic unit in which economic development can begin.

19.7. I have major concerns that the resources being focused on union building are inadequate – resources that are being further depleted by the covid crisis and inflationary pressures. Costs will be high to capitalize the union operations, build infrastructure, and support operations. A high-quality professional staff is needed to design, build, and operate the systems. Some expensive systems (payments systems, cash counting machinery, IT systems with double backups, financial communications networks, etc.) might need to be procured.

19.8. The number of people working on the union preparations need to be sharply increased, which is costly and cannot occur overnight. Finding the human and financial resources will be hard for unions developing in low-income areas. All existing resources need to be used – it should be expected the every department of every central bank in a future union will be brought into the effort. Full time work on union preparations will be needed while continuing current operations – this level of commitment was needed to build the Eurosystem, and future unions must expect they need to do the same.

19.9. This commitment will be transformative. Lax operations, delays, staff indifference, nepotism, weak financial controls cannot be permitted to flourish if the union is going to succeed as an effective, multi-country enterprise. The benefits and responsibilities will be joint and thus each member must contribute to the common enterprise and be subject to oversight and possible sanction by other members if common interests are jeopardized. This transformation will be disruptive and must be well-planned to avoid chaos or excess costs, but the hope is that better, more efficient systems will be put in place of existing practices. Because unions must operate as a well-run cooperative system, they might become among the best-operated organizations in the region – and thus contribute to better governance of economic and financial systems. In some regions, this could be an important contribution to economic and political development.

19.10. It is important to not underestimate costs. The costs of setting up the union itself will be substantial (recruiting and training high quality staff, renting buildings, purchasing and setting up operating systems, calling meetings, developing standards, making policy decisions, and monitoring implementation, etc.). The Europeans were able to draw on ample resources of national authorities to supplement central operations, but ultimately ended up charging the countries for extra expenses. Most future unions will not have this luxury – in some cases, extra assistance could be needed to bring national operations up to minimum levels needed to operate the union.

19.11. Banks, businesses, and the public also face substantial costs. Banks and financial institutions are monetary policy agents that must revise their operations to fit the new arrangements. They might also have duties to support the transition of their customers and the public. Businesses must reprice all their products and contracts and change accounting, retire the old currency from their businesses and switch to a new currency. Vending machine companies, for example, must completely change their machines. The general public will also face substantial costs to revise all monetary values, change financial accounting, and adopt the new currency. The transition must be well planned to avoid imposing unnecessary costs on the public.

19.12. All the above costs could be substantial. The union building effort must be adequately funded so that all critical operations receive needed support – failure to adequately fund all activities could compromise the entire program. More broadly, businesses and the public will also incur costs and could resist acceptance of the new currency if costs are too high.

19.13. Future unions must carefully plan how to overcome the high costs of union development, which will be exploratory, intensely interactive, and multifaceted. Technical communications throughout the future union will have to be constant to contribute to making of sound decisions, which will be expensive. Centralization of the information exchange process through topical secretariats can alleviate some costs, and fortunately, internet communications now permit rapid cheap communications. But many technical and decision-making meetings will be needed and these must be designed so that they are as convenient and inexpensive as possible. Technical and policy decisions must be decisively communicated to all affected parties. The wrong solution is to limit costs by scheduling too few meetings, which could seriously impair the process.

19.14. Setting the time schedule for setting up the union is critical. Strong political demands to quickly launch the union will conflict with the building of the technical requirements for the union (perhaps 6 years) and the time needed to prepare the public (about two years, simultaneous with union technical preparations). Also, there might be technical infrastructure features (settlement systems, IT support, etc.) that must be in place and could hold up completion of the union. Bringing all these aspects on line in the proper sequence and with a common completion point is a major challenge.

19.15. Throughout the process, there should be pressure of a firm deadline to spur timely action by all parties – the Europeans needed a deadline in order to complete their process. The schedule must be supported by frequent stocktaking exercises to ensure that all parties complete their actions according to the prescribed schedule – pressure (or assistance) could be appropriate to bring laggards up to the common standards.

19.16. Many future unions will need external technical assistance to upgrade the skills of union staff and acquire the techniques needed to operate the union. The unions now being built have a small core setting the agenda and organizing the process, but they must recruit a substantial new staff for headquarter operations and train staff in member countries in a wide range of new skills needed for the union. The new unions begin with far fewer staff resources than was the case in Europe and many staff must first gain familiarity with the policy, institutional, and legal environments in which they will operate before moving to more complex duties required to run the union, analyze regional economic and financial situations with an evolving international environment, and make and implement policies.

19.17. Union efforts could benefit from substantial technical assistance from the international community, covering basic skills, evolving international financial standards and best practices, and specific union tasks. A coordinated international program, aligned to the specific goals and priorities of each union, is desirable. Such programs will be costly and will require a firm commitment and financial backing by international assistance providers to support union development.[518] Such commitments have not yet been made and the prospective unions need to undertake extended outreach and educational efforts to bring the international community aboard and convince them that creating unions will increase economic and financial development and growth, address poverty, provide financial stability, improve fiscal governance, and improve the operation of the international financial system.

B. Reprise: Six Major Decisions

19.18. In Chapter 1, six major decisions are listed that future currency unions must make to design and build their unions. These decisions cannot be made from the outside. They are decisions to be made by the unions themselves compatible with their institutions, union goals, and schedules. The six decisions are;

> Should the new currency should be introduced all at once ("Big Bang"), or should it be gradually introduced, and should there be a period with a "virtual currency"?

[518] Logically, the IMF should take the coordinating role, can provide substantial expertise, and can contribute funding in some regards such as supporting technical assistance in fields contributing to economic and policy surveillance. The World Bank can support regional infrastructure projects, especially now that it has increased its support of financial sector development. The BIS will be involved in monetary and exchange relations. International and regional supervisory bodies, accounting and audit authorities, and payments systems organizations will have interest in bringing union systems into line with international standards and best practices. Regional development banks of course can provide funding and expertise, and act as international advocates for union efforts within their regions.

What will be the degree of centralization of the policy and operations of the union?

What monetary and exchange rate policy regimes will be chosen?

What degree of fiscal redistribution or support between countries will be allowed?

What will be the union role in financial soundness and supervision of banks and the financial system?

What will be the crisis resolution process in the union?

19.19. Each of the six decisions will shape the new unions, how they operate, and possibly prospects for success. Each decision will be embedded in union and national legal codes, create or change union and national institutions, change operating instruments and procedures, and affect the interactions between the union and the union's banking sector, businesses, and public.

19.20. The decisions are not independent – a decision in one area must be integrated with decisions in all other areas – in the hope that activities across all union functions will seamlessly interlink. Smooth interaction cannot be assumed and will be achieved only through hard work and selfless willingness of union and national participants to collaborate in the interests of the union as a whole. The author saw extraordinary cooperation in Europe to pull the union package together and it can be hoped that similar cooperation will exist in future unions.

19.21. Decisions regarding the first three points can directly draw upon the experience of the Euroarea as a possible model or other models can be chosen that future unions feel are better fitted to their circumstances and the changed international policy and governance environment. Extensive discussions provided in this text cover each of the three points, and in each case plausible strategies that differ from the Euroarea model can be envisioned.

19.22. Decisions regarding the last three points will draw on the Euroarea experience, but in each of these areas global financial crises raised critical new problems that demanded strong and innovative solutions. To deal with the problems and to protect the unity of the area and the euro itself, the Euroarea forged new institutions and procedures and increasingly centralized oversight that radically changed the letter and spirit of the Maastricht Treaty. Changes are still occurring and the dust has not fully settled, but future unions can draw many lessons from the nature of the crisis and the European responses. Clearly, future unions must deal with financial supervision more directly than did Maastricht, the importance of fiscal oversight is highlighted, fiscal assistance between countries or on an union level seems to be on the table, and the need for unified or cooperative crisis resolution mechanisms is evident. These are areas where there is still much to learn.

C. Specific issues for future unions

Membership

19.23. In most planned unions or regional arrangements, a regional organization is already in place with a defined membership that provides a good sense of the ultimate membership of the union. In some cases, future unions will be based on a core of states that are fully prepared to join in the union and additional states can join later when economic or political conditions align. Therefore, much as was done in the EMU, arrangements must be made to establish the rights and obligations of future states, the conditions they must meet in order to join the union, financial arrangements, the decision-making process for joining, and the transition process. These conditions could be set in the basic union agreement, so that potential members understand what they must do to join and the process. Moreover, it should be agreed what forms of assistance can be given to potential members to advance their joining, and what form of policy oversight or emergency assistance might be offered to potential members.

19.24. Much of the process of accepting new members will revolve about the degree of economic convergence of potential new members with the union, whether convergence is expected to accelerate once the union is formed, and the capability of countries on their own to achieve the desired convergence. In some cases, the core union might act as a "big brother" to bring weaker candidates aboard.

19.25. As discussed in this volume, the process of bringing in new members into a union will differ from the process of creating an union from scratch and appropriate rules will be needed, which might permit a bit more latitude than in creating a new union. This latitude must not become a license to freely allow membership by nonconvergent economies, and thus the rules must be prudent and effective.

Institutional framework

19.26. A critical question will be the degree of centralization of decision-making and operations. The EMU model has centralized decision-making and decentralized operations, but other unions could choose different models. For example, in three existing unions, decisions and operations are centralized with operations in individual countries executed by branch offices of the union central bank. This pattern might naturally follow from the post-colonial origins of these unions, or it might apply where the member economies are small, poor, lack financial and staff resources, or lack history of international central banking. In contrast, future unions might have greater autonomy for national offices because the preexisting central banks are unwilling to cede too much power – in Asia or Latin America, for example, potential member countries might be comparatively large and not easily swayed to cede powers.

19.27. This fundamental question is interlaced with political considerations. Countries will need a good sense of what is economically and politically feasible and union institutions will have to be constructed within those boundaries.

19.28. However, many union operations can be facilitated by centralization, which might occur as an incremental process once the union is set up. An amending process should be in place to permit changes to the union structure to move to new, more centralized arrangements when appropriate. The amending process must also allow for introduction of new practices as conditions change or new market practices or technologies emerge. The union should not attempt to anticipate its full future shape, but have a process in which discussions can be held and decisions made to modify the structure for purposes such as fixing serious problems, adding new member countries, changing operating procedures, incorporating to new financial instruments or technologies, or shifting policy frameworks and instruments. Changes might also be needed to reflect shifts in international regulations or technical standards.

19.29. Within all frameworks, including within evolving frameworks, clear rules need to spell out the rights and obligations of each member state. The rights and obligations need not be equal, and are unlikely to be equal for all countries because of the inherent differences in the economic and political strengths of the member countries. However, there must be governance and operating procedures that all member countries find acceptable. The long-term stability of the union could be affected if not done successfully.

19.30. Finally, extraordinary integration between the European economies engendered by the common currency and its supporting rules and institutions made leaving the EMU very expensive and unlikely.[519] Future unions should understand that

[519] In 2021, the consequences of Brexit are still unfolding. Islam (2021) has a good summary of some Brexit consequences, which although negative appear less severe than had been initially feared. The economic dislocations and unexpected costs from the breakup might carry lessons for future unions.

In contrast, while attending meetings at the EMI, the author came to the conclusion that monetary union involves such deep integration of financial systems that leaving the union would be very difficult and costly, if not impossible. At the time it was noted (including also by many EMI staff) that the U.K. did not join

(continued)

leaving might not be a practical option – aberrant members might be punished or suspended from voting – but are likely to continue to use the common currency and at least some union institutions. Conversely, the unions themselves could become like joint liability companies with continuing obligations between their members, such as when the Euroarea had to create a support package for Greece despite its misbehavior. Of course, nothing is impossible and countries could leave unions, but this must be seen as truly extraordinary and very costly – something every potential union country should realize.

Policy

19.31. Each union must set its policy framework. Once agreed, there are many operational decisions that follow and implications for the member states. The policy framework must be set early enough so that its policy instruments can be put into operation at the start of the union.

19.32. Among possible policy choices are nominal exchange rate targeting, real exchange rate fixing, monetary targeting, inflation targeting, and hybrid inflation targeting-macroprudential regimes.

19.33. In some cases, such as the GCC, extending its historic peg to a single external currency (U.S. dollar) is a natural *initial* choice for the union currency. However, the GCC peg should be temporary because the monetary and exchange policy conditions of the United States will necessarily diverge from regional conditions. A process to find a new policy regime should begin relatively quickly after the start of the union.

19.34. For other regions, a new policy regime must be found. This should involve a full research process which examines the policy regimes and tools of the member countries and evaluates various alternatives. This process must begin early in the planning process to gather relevant information, conduct analysis and make decisions, and implement actions.

19.35. The choice of the policy regime cannot be independent of the conditions and policy framework of the international financial system. The choice should also be forward looking to reflect the likely future shape of the global financial system and the role of unions within it. A view implicit in this volume is that union currencies and a handful of large country currencies will increasingly dominate the global financial system and that this requires each union to be fully capable of independently participating in the system.

19.36. The economic power of each future union will bear on its decisions over policy. Economically large unions such as might exist in Africa, Southeast Asia, the Gulf, or South America must have the ability to forge independent monetary and exchange policies reflecting their key roles in the global financial system; Conversely, small unions have an option to link to a single external currency or to follow the policy lead of a large neighbor. In the middle, a grey area might exist in which choices will be difficult, and also in which policy regimes can evolve as the union gains confidence and economic strength.

Currency

19.37. The union currency will become the symbol of the union – measured by its stability, appearance, security, usefulness, and name, etc. Therefore, the

enthusiastically into the monetary union preparations – a hint of attitudes that years later led the U.K. to leave the EU.

nature of the currency must be well thought out. Work to design, print, and introduce the currency will take around four to six years.

19.38. Confidence in the currency will be critical. This will depend on four factors – the difficulty in counterfeiting the currency, stability of the purchasing power based on good policy, international acceptance of the currency, and confidence in the sustainability of the union. Confidence based on these factors is needed to induce the public to adopt the currency, including in situations where other international or cocirculating currencies are readily available. Achieving the required degree of confidence will require sustained work in each of the four areas listed above.

19.39. The same considerations arise when unions introduce a CBDC, but increased levels of policy, operational, and soundness risks are likely involved.

19.40. The currency also must be usable to the general public, business, and specialized users. Features such as banknote and coin size, color, design, symbols, language, durability, political or national neutrality, and ease of use for transactions, etc. all need to be considered, which can be a lengthy and contentious process. Usability must also deal with the changes in the condition of the currency as it is being used and how it is being handled.

19.41. Production of the currency will be decisive in scheduling the start-up of the union. The currency in all denominations in sufficient quantity and fully distributed to all potential users must be available prior to the start-up. The production schedule might also affect the process for introducing the currency to the public – for example, the Big Bang option is only feasible where the full stock of currency can be produced prior to the change-over, which cannot be assumed.

19.42. Finally, electronic money in some form will play a role in the future. The ECB is investigating creating a 'digital euro'. Future unions must review options relating to e-money and digital money and how they fit into the union program. In some regions, the union itself might be the purveyor of the new e-currency as a service to the public and an incentive to move into the union currency.

Financial integration and clearing and settlement

19.43. The Europeans put financial integration at the very center of their union program. The goal was to integrate all parts of the financial economy in all countries into a single integrated market. A fully integrated market was viewed as necessary to harvest the full benefits of the common currency. Many initiatives were undertaken with strong legal underpinnings that often produced a high degree of integration within the relatively short period of a decade. This involves setting a grand integration plan, identifying key projects and implementing them in both the public and private sectors, harmonizing legal codes to support the initiatives, introducing common market practices, creating dispute settlement mechanisms, and attracting market players to the new system. A special program was put in to make the costs of cross-border financial transactions within the Euroarea no more expensive than domestic transactions.

19.44. The union regional program also provided the means to introduce improved financial practices and regulatory systems throughout the region. This was intended to make the entire system more competitive in world markets and lower costs for financial businesses and the entire economy. The ECB has estimated that financial integration initiatives significantly reduced costs throughout the union.

19.45. Potential unions seem to have accepted that financial integration should be part of the union program (and even that many aspects are valuable in themselves regardless of creating an union). Thus, it is a matter of execution rather than commitment. The process is multifaceted with many linked parts and thus careful planning is needed. Some changes could be expensive to introduce, which must be factored into each union's plans. Legal harmonization and dispute settlement are important elements that might not be easily achieved.

19.46. Financial integration might proceed on a somewhat different schedule than the union itself. Some systems can be introduced at least partially prior to start-up, and other systems can be implemented later. However, systems related to money policy operations (collateral for credit operations, settlement system in the new currency, standardization of money market instruments, etc.) must be in place by start-up.

19.47. Different unions might find that they are working on the same financial integration issues and perhaps coming to the same conclusions. There is potential for unions to work together in some areas, which can save resources, effectively use scarce expertise, and speed the process. However, each union will effectively define a separate integrated financial area because each will have different currencies, market practices, institutions, and rules and judicial methods.

Supervision

19.48. In the two decades since the Euroarea was created, a complete change has occurred in attitudes regarding the role of financial supervision within currency unions. The Maastricht Treaty left supervision to national authorities as something extraneous to the central monetary policy aspirations of the union. Subsequently, the view grew that soundness of the financial system is critical for the execution of monetary policy, which was accentuated by the financial crisis. Moreover, contemporary monetary policy now takes a macroprudential view that looks at the interactions between monetary policy and financial soundness.

19.49. As a result, all future unions are expected to include financial supervision as part of their union programs. This will require introducing new, more centralized arrangements for supervision, supported by harmonized legal arrangements.

19.50. This will be a challenging task for new unions who face many other priorities. Also, the field is rapidly changing largely due to major innovations in international supervisory and accounting standards. The unions thus have a moving target to deal with. Finding the needed expertise and staffing agencies will also be a challenge. The supervised financial institutions themselves will be under pressure as they deal with new regulatory and supervisory standards and practices while transitioning to the new union and probably absorbing additional costs related to the currency changeover.

Accounting and statistics

19.51. Financial accounting and statistical systems are part of the foundation of an union. Financial accounting needs to be harmonized across countries and sectors so that financial information conveys the same meaning through the union and can be aggregated into comparable accounts for financial institutions, government, and other sectors of the economy, which provides the basis for statistical aggregates at the sector, country, and union levels to assess general financial conditions and develop policy. There is also a need to develop a special set of *intra*union accounting and statistical standards to deal with positions and transactions with other union member entities and countries.

19.52. The accounting and statistical standards and the specific types of intraunion items needed have been discussed in the chapters. Here, the key aspect is that both of these foundation systems require long lead times to create and implement the standards and ensure they are effectively applied in all member countries and at the union level.

19.53. Beyond this, complete and accurate accounting records are needed to handle the financial aspects of the union. Income and payments of member countries and the union will be pooled and shared and thus clear rules and audits acceptable to all are needed. Also, statistical convergence criteria are needed that measure the performance of individual economies against common standards and policies and can perhaps penalize countries – obviously, accuracy and impartiality are critical.

Finances

19.54. The financial arrangements for creating and operating an union can greatly affect options available. Creating the EMU was expensive and the full costs have never been totaled up. The EMI had a large budget, but exceeded it and ultimately sent the bill to the NCBs. The NCBs themselves incurred substantial costs, as did banks as key players in the process. Corporations and the public also incurred costs. In almost all cases, costs of the transition were borne directly by businesses and the public without any compensation. The process worked, but perhaps in large part because the European countries were rich and could afford to make changes in expectation of later advantages of the union.

19.55. In other regions, the situation could be very different. Governments, many businesses, and the public might have little spare income to devote to additional expenses for the union. Union plans might need to be adjusted to deal with this reality. In addition to seeking ways to reduce burdens, some unions have cases where support or subsidies are needed – which could prove to be a contentious process.

19.56. Arrangements will need to be made to fund the official operations to set up the union and to support on-going operations. The union will generate income from seigniorage, fees for services, taxes, penalties, and investment income, etc.. Against this there are expenses for staff, operations, and borrowing costs etc. Rules for handling this income and expense need to be agreed and a very good accounting system put in place to make the system work. It is instructive that the EMU could not agree on the division of monetary income (net seigniorage income) until after the union started – philosophies might differ and the calculated income and expenses matter greatly for the parties involved.

Communications

19.57. Communications play a different role in unions compared to national settings. An union will have diverse communities with different legal and institutional settings, and often different languages. The union must take special steps to be able to communicate its goals and policies throughout the union and to make clear that its actions are done for the benefit of the region as a whole and not for particular countries or interests. The union will speak as a single voice in many matters for itself and its members, which must be done in a way that reflects commonly agreed governance and decision-making. Likewise, the union will speak to the rest of the world as the voice of the union.

19.58. The communications rights and responsibilities of the union will compete with the rights of member countries to speak on economic and financial issues, both domestically and to international audiences. Union member countries will be members of international organizations and fora where they rightfully are expected to participate fully and express their views. Thus, part of the communications policy must be to delineate where the union has paramount responsibility and where national prerogative prevails.

19.59. The Euroarea stressed the importance of the independence of the central bank and its decision making. To stress its adherence to democratic foundations, the Eurosystem concluded it had a special obligation to justify its decisions and communicate frequently and in-depth with its populations, world markets, and political entities. Communications are in multiple languages and multiple media. Formal rules on reporting exist, but the ECB practice far exceeds the minimum requirements. This practice is recommended for future unions. The communications process also goes from the periphery into the center with multiple avenues to hear about the conditions and views in member countries; the ECB seeks to bolster its legitimacy by emphasizing its willingness to reflect these views in its deliberations.

19.60. Thus far, although improving, future unions have largely failed to fully and effectively communicate the purposes of the union, how businesses and the public will benefit, union plans, and the state of preparations. There is much room for improvement. Web sites, which are now the first point of information on future unions, should to be significantly improved and kept up to date.

Legal

19.61. Ultimately, the operations of an union rests on its legal foundations. An union will join together diverse states with different views. The legal system will need to delineate rights and responsibilities of each member so that each believes it is treated fairly and that each contributes equitably to the common good.

19.62. A treaty or other core document will lay out the legal arrangements for the union. National legal systems will need to be modified to be compatible with the common rules, but a wide range of variation exists about how tightly the legal arrangements are made. The European experience showed that harmonization of legal systems will not occur naturally and will be difficult to achieve because the provisions related to the union will be embedded in highly diverse national systems. Without having recourse to common legal frameworks, each country might implement the union provisions differently (and sometimes on purpose), which means that there must be thorough union-level review of the national legal changes.

19.63. Because a currency union affects nearly every aspect of a country's financial system, there will be many areas where national legal codes must be changed. Moreover, each change has implications for other parts of the legal code. The process will be long and complex, complicated by the need to take some matters to the legislature, which might modify proposed changes or introduce extraneous matters.

Administrative and personnel matters

19.64. Building an union is a highly complex operation, based on an evolving plan developed by a central authority, covering many topics, and involving all future members or potential members. All major topics addressed in this volume must be covered, and each has numerous projects and subprojects. Ultimately, each individual component must function well, with activities integrated into the activities of other topical fields, in all countries simultaneously. This is obviously a very challenging task in which tasks are distributed and progress must be closely monitored to ensure the needed degree of accomplishment. The process must be carefully planned and managed. Some unions might choose to employ professional management consultants to handle administrative matters – however, expertise in building currency unions is scarce and thus management consultants probably should be employed as administrators and not key planners and designers. Implementation, of course, must be left to the national and regional authorities.

19.65. Future unions have roughly followed the path of the Euroarea to set up a small monetary council or institute comprised of topical professionals often seconded from NCBs or other offices to plan the union and to act as secretariats to the countries in each topical area. These institutes are likely to start small and be regularly expanded to handle the growing volume of work, which requires recruiting operations and an inclusive framework to deal with personnel matters. Recruited staff must be high quality to deal with the technical matters and evolving plans and stages of implementation. They also must be capable of dealing with the bureaucracy and counterparts in the countries, placing national perspectives aside and adopting and transmitting a union-wide view.

19.66. This volume stresses that strong professional interaction at the technical level is mandatory. Technical matters must be constantly discussed in both directions between union and national officials, so that the center understands local conditions and needs and the local offices understand the full program and how their efforts interact with the work of others. Regular contact helps insure that each country is aware of work elsewhere and strive to maintain the schedule and quality needed. This work is probably best done in dedicated committees, which should meet very frequently. Intermittent contacts between union and country officials and communications only through the top levels of organizations will delay and could ultimately doom the process.

19.67. Training will be a key part of the process. Unlike Europe where a high minimum level of familiarity with skills in each topic could be assumed, in many unions staff training on union institutions, legal underpinnings, and technical skills are needed at the same time they are being given important responsibilities to set up the union. This could be a key constraint and a possible reason for not pressing for rapid launch of the union.

19.68. Language is a key issue. A single working language is useful, but all major legal matters, policy announcements, and public relations releases must be in all the major languages of the community. Also, banks and business must have business operating procedures readily available in their daily language. This will require that a language policy be set up with sufficient staff and resources at hand to carry it out, which is expensive and which probably will require contributions from local authorities with their deep pool of language skills.

19.69. Finally, by the startup of the union a large workforce will be created, with a wide range of technical skills, and spread through the union. Administrative and personnel procedures at this point must of course be much more organized and bureaucratized than during the early days of the union planning process.

Transition

19.70. The final topic addressed here is the transition from use of national currencies to the new union currency. This is a major process because the old currency must be retired and the new currency introduced and all parts of the economy must redenominate all monetary values. Informing banks, businesses, the public, special needs groups, and the international community is a major task. Among major issues are full application of accounting rules, the allocation of costs of the transition, and security issues in issuing the new currency and retiring the old national currencies. In Europe, national authorities were given most of the tasks in the common plan involving informing businesses and the public in their own languages. Future unions will also need to heavily involve local officials.

19.71. Many different models for the transition are possible depending on matters such as if the currency will be introduced all at once or gradually, whether a virtual currency will proceed the physical currency, whether countries will join at once or gradually, language issues, the degree of centralization, etc. In Europe, redenomination of values mostly occurred when the union was set up in 1999, and the physical change in the currency occurred in 2001. This worked well and spread burdens and limited strains on authorities and businesses. This model might be suitable elsewhere but other options are certainly possible.

19.72. The transition will be the first contact with the union for many businesses and the public. It must be done effectively to start the union off on the correct foot. One such area that will certainly arise is public concern that adoption of the union currency will cause a spike in prices; this issue must be addressed directly, through information campaigns and rules requiring dual pricing for periods of three to six months prior to the changeover.

19.73. The transition is a complex process. A full plan is needed before it starts. Preparatory work needs to begin about six years prior to the union launch date; two years minimum should be budgeted for the rollout of the new currency in all its forms to the public.

D. Final Note

19.74. This volume has offered some lessons from the experience of the European Monetary Union for unions being planned elsewhere. As of 2022, five projects are underway and others are under consideration. Some union practices can also apply to other nonunion regional financial integration arrangements, such as ASEAN. The breadth of topics is wide and each has depths beyond what can be explored in one volume. However, it is hoped that future unions will gain useful perspectives on the whole process, how parts fit into the whole, and conquer the specifics of each topic.

19.75. Future unions must tackle the issues with full recognition of the tasks involved, the complexity, the costs, and length. But against these costs, future unions should be driven by the hopes of achieving something that will transform their region, integrate financial systems across countries, provide a stable useful currency, break barriers and create more efficient and inclusive markets, gain standing in international markets, and – not least by far – spur growth and development to help break the chains of poverty. Those goals more than justify the hard work ahead for union builders. I wish them well.

References

Abiad, A., Lee, J, and Kannan, P. (2009) Evaluating Historical CGER Assessments: How Well Have They Predicted Subsequent Exchange Rate Movements? IMF Working Paper 09/32 2009.

Agarwala, R. (2003) "Road to a Single Currency for South Asia" RIS Policy Brief No. 9 Dec. 2003. pp. 1-4.

Agence France Presse. (2010) "Europe vows to help banks failing stress test" July 12, 2010.

Alloway, T. (2010) "Show me the Drachmas" Foreignpolicy.com. January 29, 2010.

Al-Mansouri, A.K.L. and Dziobek, C. (2008) "Providing Official Statistics for the Common Market and Monetary Union in the Gulf Cooperation Council (GCC) Countries—A Case for Gulfstat". Asian Development Bank. Emerging Asian Regionalism. (Manila; ADB) (2008).

Amicorum, L and Garavelli, P.Z. (2005) Legal Aspects of the European System of Central Banks. (Frankfurt: ECB).

Artis, M. J. (1991) "One Market, One Money: An Evaluation of the Potential Benefits and Costs of Forming and Economic and Monetary Union" Open Economies Review 2, pp. 315-321.

Aspetsberger, A. (1996) "Open Market Operations in EU Countries" European Monetary Institute Staff Working Paper No. 3. (Frankfurt: European Monetary Institute)

Association of African Central Banks. (2013) Joint AUC-AACB Strategy on the Establishment of the African Central Bank. June 2013.

Athanassiou, P. (2006). The Application of Multilingualism in the European Union Context. ECB Legal Working Paper No. 2. March 2006.

______ (2006). Withdrawal and Expulsion from the EU and EMU: Some Reflections. ECB Legal Working Paper No. 10. December 2009.

Badinger, H. and Dutzler, B. (2004) "Economic and Legal Issues in Reducing the Eurosystem's Excess of International Reserves" Journal of Common Market Studies, Vol. 42, No. 3, pp. 453-471, September 2004.

Baliño, T., A. Bennett, E. Borensztein, and others. (2004) "Monetary Policy in Dollarized Economies" IMF Occasional Paper No. 171.

Bayoumi, T. and Eichengreen, B. (1994) *One Money or Many. Analyzing the Prospects for Monetary Unification in Various Parts of the World.* Princeton Studies of International Finance 78. (Princeton, N.J.: Princeton) 1994.

Bank for International Settlements. (BIS) (1990) *Report of the Committee on Interbank Netting Schemes of the Central Banks of the Group of Ten Countries (Lamfalussy Report).*

Bank of Botswana (2021). Statement on crypto assets – participation and regulation. Press Release. November 10, 2021.

Barber, G. (2019). "The Fed Chair Says Facebook's Libra Raises 'Serious Concerns'" wired.com. July 10, 2019.

Basel Committee Cross-border Bank Resolution Group (2010) Report and Recommendations of the Cross-Border Bank Resolution Group – Final Paper. Basel. March 2010.

BBC (2010). "New European banking watchdog to be based in London" BBC News. July 13, 2010.

Berg, A., and E. Borensztein. (2000) "The Pros and Cons of Full Dollarization" IMF Working Paper WP/00/50.

Bessec, M., (2003) "Mean-reversion vs. adjustment to PPP: the two regimes of exchange rate dynamics under the EMS, 1979-1998," *Economic Modelling*, vol. 20(1), pages 141-164, January, (Elsevier).

Bhattacharyay, B. (2010) *Infrastructure for Asian Connectivity*. (Edgar Elgar: Cheltenham, U.K.)

Bini-Smaghi, L. (2009a) "Going Forward: Regulation and Supervision after the Financial Turmoil" Speech at the 4th International Conference of Financial Regulation and Supervision "After the Big Bang: Reshaping Central Banking, Regulation and Supervision" Bocconi University, Milano, 19 June 2009.

_______ (2009b) Bini Smaghi, L. "Europe cannot ignore its financial trilemma" Financial Times. June 21, 2009.

Bitcoinke.io (2021a) "The East African Community States to Explore Potential for a CBDC in a Move to Upgrade the Shared East African Payments System. https://bitcoinke.io/2021/06/eac-states-exploring-cbdc/

_______ (2021b) "Loss of Trust in Government Reason behind DeFi and Crypto, Says Governor" https://bitcoinke.io/2021/09/cbk-governor-talks-defi/.

Bloomberg News. (2021) "China's Digital Yuan Expands to 10 Million Eligible Users" July 8, 2021.

_______ (2022a) "Ditch Bitcoin: IMF urges El Salvador to rethink crypto" January 25, 2022.

_______ (2022b) "El Salvador's companies barely bother with bitcoin" March 18, 2022.

Boar, C., and A. Wehrli. (2021) "Ready, steady, go? Results of the third BIS Survey on central bank digital currency." BIS Papers No. 114. January 2021.

Böwer, U. (2006) "Risk Sharing, Financial integration, and "Mundell II" in the Enlarged European Union," Institute of European Studies, Working Paper. University of California. Berkeley.

Buiter, W. (2010) "Does the Eurosystem have enough capital?" blogs.ft.com/maverecon. May 15, 2010.

Buldorini, L., S. Makrydakis, and C. Thimann. (2002) "The effective exchange rates of the euro." ECB Occasional Paper No. 2. 2002. /

Bull, P. (2004) The Development of Statistics for Economic and Monetary Union. (ECB: 2004).

Carswell, S. (2010) "The big gamble: The inside story of the bank guarantee" The Irish Times. September 25, 2010.

Castle, S. (2010) "I.M.F. More Likely to Lead Efforts for Greek Aid" New York Times March 22, 2010.

Center for European Policy Studies – CEPS (2007). "A New Role for Deposit Insurance in Europe" European Shadow Financial Regulatory Committee Statement No. 5. 2007.

Clementi, D. (1999) Speech at S.W.I.F.T. U.K Regional Conference, May 25, 1999.

CLS Bank. (2008) CLS Bank International Rules. (New York: CLS Bank) May 15, 2008.

CLS-Group. (2008) Web site for Continuous-Linked Settlement (CLS) system. www.cls-services.com.

CNBC.com (2021) "162 million up for grabs after bug in DeFi Protocol Compound" Oct. 3, 2021.

______ (2022a) "A $3.5 billion bet on bitcoin becoming a 'reserve currency' for crypto is being put to the test" May 9, 2022.

______ (2022b) "EU agrees to landmark legislation to clean up crypto 'Wild West'" June 30, 2022.

COG - Committee of Governors of the Central Banks of the Member States of the European Economic Community. (1992) Annual Report: July 1990 to December 1991. Basel: April 1992.

______ (1993) Annual Report: 1992. Basel: April 1993.

Committee on Payment and Settlement Systems (CPSS) (2001) *Core Principles for Systemically Important Payment Systems.* (Basel: Bank for International Settlements)

De Grauwe, P. (1997) The Economics of Monetary Integration. Oxford University Press, Oxford.

Decentralized.trading (2021) "Bitcoin adoption could damage El Salvador's credit rating: Fitch" August 17, 2021.

Deloitte (2007) Review of the Slovenian changeover to the euro: Final Report. August 27, 2007.

DiVanna, J. (2010) "Islamic Monetary Union: Feasibility, Viability, and Sustainability of a New Global Currency", in *Islamic Finance: Innovation and Authenticity*, Cambridge, Massachusetts: Harvard Law School, ILSP: Islamic Finance Project, 2010, 317p

Drazen, A., and P. R. Masson, (1994) "Credibility of Policies versus Credibility of Policymakers," *Quarterly Journal of Economics,* 109, 735-54, August.

Dutta, M. (2008) "Financial Integration in Asia" Distinguished Speaker lecture at Asian Development Bank Institute, Tokyo. February, 2008.

Ehemann M., M. Fratzscher, R. Gürkaynak, and E. Swanson. (2007) "Convergence and Anchoring of Yield Curves in the Euro Area". ECB Working Paper 817. October 2007.

Eichengreen, B. (2006) "The Parallel Currency Approach to Asian Monetary Integration" American Economic Review. Pp. 432-436.

European Anti-Fraud Office (2008) Annual Report. 2008.

European Central Bank (ECB)

______ (1998) "Report on electronic money" August 1998.

______ (1999) Annual Report 1998. (Frankfurt: ECB). (1999)

______ (1999b) "Opinion of the European Central Bank at the request of the Council of the European Union under Article 109(3) of the Treaty establishing the European Community on three recommendations for three Council Decisions concerning monetary relations with the Principality of Monaco, the Republic of San Marino, and the Vatican City." (1999/C 127/05).

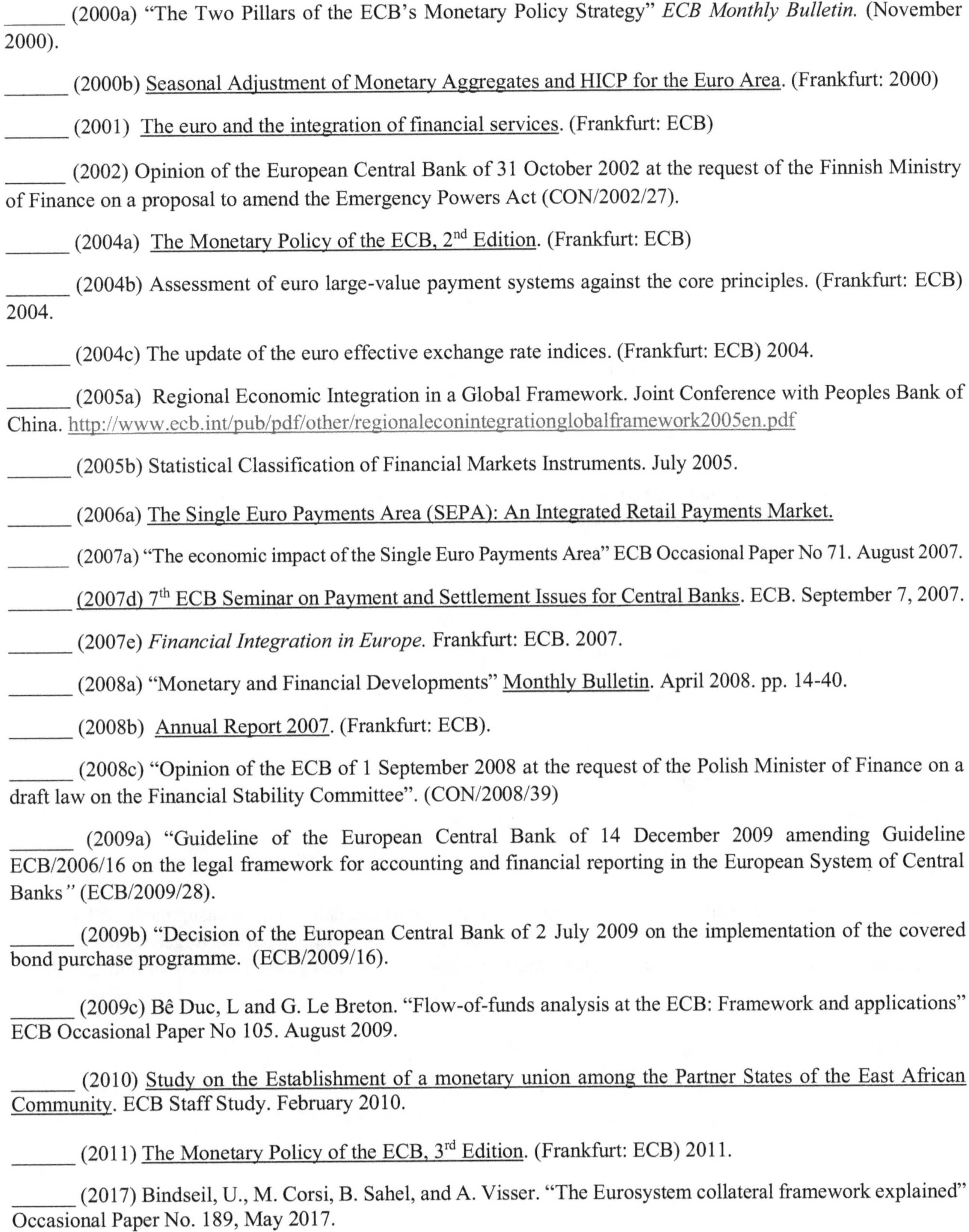

______ (2000a) "The Two Pillars of the ECB's Monetary Policy Strategy" *ECB Monthly Bulletin.* (November 2000).

______ (2000b) Seasonal Adjustment of Monetary Aggregates and HICP for the Euro Area. (Frankfurt: 2000)

______ (2001) The euro and the integration of financial services. (Frankfurt: ECB)

______ (2002) Opinion of the European Central Bank of 31 October 2002 at the request of the Finnish Ministry of Finance on a proposal to amend the Emergency Powers Act (CON/2002/27).

______ (2004a) The Monetary Policy of the ECB, 2nd Edition. (Frankfurt: ECB)

______ (2004b) Assessment of euro large-value payment systems against the core principles. (Frankfurt: ECB) 2004.

______ (2004c) The update of the euro effective exchange rate indices. (Frankfurt: ECB) 2004.

______ (2005a) Regional Economic Integration in a Global Framework. Joint Conference with Peoples Bank of China. http://www.ecb.int/pub/pdf/other/regionaleconintegrationglobalframework2005en.pdf

______ (2005b) Statistical Classification of Financial Markets Instruments. July 2005.

______ (2006a) The Single Euro Payments Area (SEPA): An Integrated Retail Payments Market.

______ (2007a) "The economic impact of the Single Euro Payments Area" ECB Occasional Paper No 71. August 2007.

______ (2007d) 7th ECB Seminar on Payment and Settlement Issues for Central Banks. ECB. September 7, 2007.

______ (2007e) *Financial Integration in Europe.* Frankfurt: ECB. 2007.

______ (2008a) "Monetary and Financial Developments" Monthly Bulletin. April 2008. pp. 14-40.

______ (2008b) Annual Report 2007. (Frankfurt: ECB).

______ (2008c) "Opinion of the ECB of 1 September 2008 at the request of the Polish Minister of Finance on a draft law on the Financial Stability Committee". (CON/2008/39)

______ (2009a) "Guideline of the European Central Bank of 14 December 2009 amending Guideline ECB/2006/16 on the legal framework for accounting and financial reporting in the European System of Central Banks" (ECB/2009/28).

______ (2009b) "Decision of the European Central Bank of 2 July 2009 on the implementation of the covered bond purchase programme. (ECB/2009/16).

______ (2009c) Bê Duc, L and G. Le Breton. "Flow-of-funds analysis at the ECB: Framework and applications" ECB Occasional Paper No 105. August 2009.

______ (2010) Study on the Establishment of a monetary union among the Partner States of the East African Community. ECB Staff Study. February 2010.

______ (2011) The Monetary Policy of the ECB, 3rd Edition. (Frankfurt: ECB) 2011.

______ (2017) Bindseil, U., M. Corsi, B. Sahel, and A. Visser. "The Eurosystem collateral framework explained" Occasional Paper No. 189, May 2017.

______ (2018) Opinion of the European Central Bank of 26 October 2018 on the review of Finnish law concerning preparedness obligations applicable in the financial sector (CON/2018/46).

______ (2020) Report on digital Euro. October 2020.

______ (2021a) "The ECB's monetary policy strategy statement" July 2021.

______ (2021b) Digital euro project. July 2021.

European Commission (EC) (1999) "Financial Services: Implementing the Framework for Financial Markets" 1999.

______ (2000) Directive 2000/46/EC of the European Parliament and of the Council "On the Taking up, Pursuit of and Prudential Supervision of the Business of Electronic Money Institutions".

______ (2015) The Five President's Report: Completing Europe's Economic and Monetary Union. 2015.

______ (2020) Communication from the Commission to the European Parliament, the Council, and the European Central Bank. November 18, 2020

European Monetary Institute (EMI) (1994) EMI Theme Selection Advisory Group "Interim Report on the Selection of a Theme for the European Banknote Series" 1994.

______ (1995) Annual Report: 1994. April, 1995.

______ (1996a) Annual Report: 1995. April, 1996.

______ (1996b) Progress towards Convergence.

______ (1996c) Payment Systems in the European Union. April 1996.

______ (1997) Annual Report: 1996. April, 1997

______ (1998a) Annual Report: 1997. April, 1998

______ (1998b) Convergence Report. March 1998.

ESRB – European Systemic Risk Board. (2020) Report on Systemic Cyber Risk. 2020.

Enoch, C. and Krueger, R. (2009) "Currency unions: key variables, definitions, measurement, and statistical improvements" Proceedings of the SARB/IFC seminar on "Economic and financial convergence en route to regional economic integration: experience, prospects, and statistical issues amidst global financial turmoil", Durban, South Africa, 14 August 2009.

European Commission. (EC) (2001) *"Enlargement Argumentaire*" Enlargement Papers No. 5.

______ (2002) "Financial Collateral Arrangements" Presentation on the Financial Collateral Directive. Available at http://ec.europa.eu/internal_market/financial-markets/collateral/index_en.htm.

_______ (2020a) European Commission. "Proposal for a regulation … on Markets in Crypto-assets" September 2020.

_______ (2020b) "Proposal for a regulation on a pilot regime for market infrastructures based on distributed ledger technology" September 2020.

European Communities (1984) The ECU.

Eurosystem. (2000a) The Euro: Integrating Financial Services. (Frankfurt: ECB).

______ (2008) A Single Currency – An Integrated Market Infrastructure. (Frankfurt: ECB).

Federal Reserve Board. (2022) "Money and Payments: The U.S. dollar in the Age of Digital Transformation" January 20, 2022.

Forest, D. (2006) "Practical information on the introduction of the euro for Business and Consumers" Presentation to Conference on Experience with and Preparations for the Euro. Linz, Austria May 11, 2006.

FT.com (2010a) "Berlin shifts stance on IMF role in Greece" March 18, 2010.

______ (2010b) "World leaders are choosing recession" March 20, 2010.

______ (2010c) "IMF finance role embarrassing for ECB" March 25, 2010.

______ (2010d) "Bini-Smaghi: ECB to stay independent after Greece deal" March 26, 2010.

Gerlach, S. (2007) "Interest Rate Setting by the ECB, 1999-2006: Words and Deeds" International Journal of Central Banking. September, 2007.

Giovannini Group. (2001) Cross-Border Clearing and Settlement Arrangements in the European Union. Brussels, November 2001.

Girardin, E. and Steinherr, A. (2008) "Regional Monetary Units for East Asia: Lessons from Europe" Asian Development Bank Institute Discussion Paper No. 116 (Tokyo: ADBI) September 2008.

Goodhart, C.A.E. (Ed.). (2000) *Which Lender of Last Resort for Europe?* (London: Central Banking Publications).

Goodfriend, M. (2000) "The role of regional banks in a system of central banks," FRB of Richmond Economic Quarterly. Winter 2000.

Gonzalez, M. (2021) "The surprising history of distributed ledger technology" medium.com. August 25, 2021.

Group of Central Banks. (2020) "Central bank digital currencies: foundational principles and core features", Joint Report, no 1, October 2020.

Gulde, A-M., D. Hoelscher, A. Ize, D. Marston, and G. De Nicolo. (2004) "Financial Stability in Dollarized Economies" IMF Occasional Paper No. 230.

Hartsink, G. (2007) Conversation with author. Dubai, December 5, 2007.

Hassan, T. A. (2009) Country size, currency unions, and international asset returns. Working papers, Booth School of Business. 2009.

Hong Kong. (2021) Government of the Hong Kong Special Administrative Region. "Joint statement on Multiple Central Bank Digital Currency (m-CBDC) Bridge Project" Press Release. February 23, 2021.

Horvath, R. and Komarek, L. (2006) "Equilibrium Exchange Rates in EU New Members: Applicable for Setting the ERM II Central Parity" MPRA Paper 1180, (University Library of Munich).

ICP – International Comparison Project. (1975) Kravis, I, Heston, A, and R. Summers. International comparisons of real product and purchasing power. United Nations Statistical Office and World Bank. 1975.

IFC – Irving Fisher Committee (2010) *Economic and financial convergence en route to regional economic integration: experience, prospects, and statistical issues amidst global financial turmoil.* IFC Bulletin No. 32. January 2010.

IFSB (2019) – Islamic Financial Standards Board. *Compilation Guide on Prudential and Structural Indicators for Islamic Financial Institutions (PSIFIs).* 2019.

Imbs, J. (2006). "The real effects of financial integration" Journal of International Economics, vol. 68(2), pp. 296-324.

IMF - International Monetary Fund. (1996) Financial Stability and Macroeconomic Policy. (Washington: IMF).

______ (2005) Real Estate Indicators and Financial Stability (2005).

______ (2016) Monetary and Financial Statistics Manual and Compilation Guide. (Washington: IMF).

______ (2020) Consumer Price Index Manual: Concepts and Methods | 2020.

______ (2021) Staff Report: Republic of San Marino 2021 Article IV Consultation (21/249). P. 7.

Islam, F. (2021) "Brexit: One year on, the economic impact is starting to show" BBC.com. Dec. 21, 2021.

Issing, O. (2008) The Birth of the Euro. Cambridge University Press.

Jensen (2005) "Inside EU, Outside EMU: Institutional and Legal Aspects of the Exchange Rate Mechanism II" in Amicorum and Garavelli (2005) pp. 135-146.

Kamar, B. and Ben Naceur, S. (2007) "GCC Monetary Union and the Degree of Macroeconomic Policy Coordination." IMF Working Paper WP/07/249. October 2007.

Kamin, S. and N. Ericsson. (1993) "Dollarization in Argentina" U.S. Federal Reserve Board International Finance Discussion Paper No. 460.

Kaminska, I. "Brexit, the Target2 angle." FT.com. July 19, 2016.

Karuhanga, J. (2008) "Stockholders meet over EAC Common Market negotiations" The New Times. October 29, 2008.

Kawai, H. and Wignaraja, G. (2008) EAFTA or CEPEA: Which Way Forward? (Tokyo: Asian Development Bank Institute) July 28, 2008.

Kenen, P., and Meade, E. (2008) Regional Monetary Integration. (Cambridge: Cambridge University Press).

Kim. S., Lee, J.W., and Park, C-Y. (2008) "Emerging Asia: Decoupling or Recoupling?" Paper presented at ADBI Conference on International Linkages. (Tokyo: Asian Development Bank Institute) October 2-3, 2008.

Krueger, R. (2012) "On a Blank Slate: Cash and Cash Requirements for Future Currency Unions" Bundesbank International Conference – The usage, costs, and benefits of cash: Theory and evidence from macro and micro data. Eltville, Germany February 27-29, 2012.

______ (2019) "Islamic Finance and GCC Economic Integration" Working Papers 1381, Economic Research

Forum of Egypt. Dec 2019.

Krueger, R., and Ha, J. (1995) "Measurement of the Cocirculation of Currencies." IMF Working Paper 95/34.

KKC. (Krueger, R., Kamar, B., and Carlotti, J-E.) (2009) "Establishing Conversion Values for New Currency Unions: Method and Application to the planned Gulf Cooperation Council (GCC) Currency Union" IMF WP 2009/184.

Krueger, R, and Kovarich, E. (2006) "Some Principles for the Development of Statistics of the Gulf Cooperation Council Currency Union". IMF Working Paper 06/141.

Levitov, M. and P. Abelsky (2010) "Russia may scrap Ruble for new customs union currency" www.bloomberg.com. March 5, 2010.

Lhoneux (2005) "The Eurosystem" in Amicorum and Garavelli (2005) pp. 161-178.

Löber, K. (2006) "The Developing EU Legal Framework for Clearing and Settlement of Financial Instruments" ECB Legal Working Paper Series No. 1.

Louis, J-V. (1995) Banking Supervision in the European Community: Institutional Aspects. Editions de l'Université de Bruxelles (Brussels).

______ (2005) "Monetary Policy and Central Banking in the Constitution" in Amicorum and Garavelli (2005) pp. 27-42.

Ma, D. (2021) "Laos central bank to partner with Soramitsu on CBDC study" www.centralbanking.com. October 7, 2021.

Maastricht (1991) Treaty Establishing the European Community. (Maastricht Treaty).

Maltzer, M.; Cappiello, L; De Santis, R.; and Manganelli, S. (2008) Measuring Financial Integration in New EU Member States. ECB Occasional Paper No. 81. March 2008.

Manninen, K. "Experimental Aggregate GCC Consumer Price Change Estimates" GCC-Stat. May 2015.

Martin, K.; Sherwood, J. (2009) Article on drop in Lithuania GDP for Dow Jones News Service. 2009.

Meyer, T. (2009) "Einen eigenen Währungsfonds für Europa" Frankfurter Rundschau. February 24, 2009.

Mauro, P. (2001) "Currency Unions". IMF Research Bulletin. December 2001. pp. 1,5-7.

McKinnon, R. (1963) "Optimum Currency Areas" The American Economic Review, (Sep., 1963), pp. 717-725.

McKinnon, R. (2000) "Mundell, the Euro, and Optimum Currency Areas" Stanford University http://www-siepr.stanford.edu/workp/swp00009.pdf. 2000.

MAS (Monetary Authority of Singapore) (2021) www.mas.gov.sg/news /media-releases/2021/mas-announces-15-finalists-for-for-the-global-cbdc-challenge.

Mongelli, F.P. (2002) "New" Views on the Optimum Currency Area Theory: What is the EMU telling us? ECB Working Paper No. 138. April 2002.

Mori, J; Kinukawa, M; Nukaya, H; and Hashimoto, M. (2002) "Integration of East Asian Economies and a Step-by-Step Approach towards a Currency Basket Regime," IIMA Research Report No. 2. November 2002.

Mundell, R. (1961) "A Theory of Optimum Currency Areas" American Economic Review. Vol 51. pp. 657-665.

Munster, B. (2019) "France vows to block Facebook's Libra in Europe" decrypt.co, Sept. 12, 2019.

Organization for Economic Cooperation and Development (OECD), Eurostat, International Monetary Fund, World Bank. International Transactions in Remittances: Guide for Compilers and Users. 2009.

Padoa-Schioppa, T. (2004) "East Asian Monetary Arrangements: A European Perspective," International Finance 7, pp 311-23.

Papadia, F. (2020) Presentation at "Lessons from the Global Financial Crisis in the Age of COVID-19" Virtual Conference organized by IMF and University of Tokyo. November 23, 2020.

Pymnts.com. (2021) "El Salvador Pours Bitcoin Profits into Health and Education Amid Ongoing Chivo Wallet Fraud Furor" Pymnts.com. November 5, 2021.

Reuters.com. (2022) "Russia proposes ban on use and mining of cryptocurrencies" Reuters.com. January 21, 2022.

RGEMonitor. (2009) "Credit easing on the Way in EMU? Who is the ECB's Recapitalizer of Last Resort?" RGE-Monitor.com. March 30.2009.

Roger, S. (1993) "The Management of Foreign Exchange Reserves" BIS Economic Papers No. 38. July 1993.

Rowley, A. (2010) "One of Asia's foremost experts on monetary matters offers a guide" Business Times (Singapore). June 4, 2010.

RTE (2007) "Agreement reached on cross-border banking" www.RTE.ie 27 March 27, 2007.

Saddam, R.S. (2019) Is the East African Community Ready for a Another Chequered Member? https://horninstitute.org/ December 16, 2019.

Saltmarsh, M. (2010) "IMF Chief calls for 'Fire Brigade' to aid European Banks" Financial Times. March 19, 2010.

Statute (1991) Protocol on the Statute of the European System of Central Banks and of the European Central Bank. (Annex to the Maastricht Treaty).

Sánchez, M. (2005) "Is Time Ripe for a Currency Union in Emerging East Asia? The Role of Monetary Stabilization" ECB Working Paper 567, December 2005.

Schäuble, W. (2010) "Why Europe's monetary union faces its biggest crisis" Financial Times. March 11, 2010.

Scheller, H. (2006) The European Central Bank: History, Role, and Functions 2nd Edition. European Central Bank.

Scheller, H. (2007) Discussions with author about the European Monetary Institute. Basel. November 30, 2007.

Schmiedel, H. (2007) "The Economic Impact of the Single Euro Payments Area" ECB Occasional Papers No. 71. August 2007.

Schnabel, E. (2020) "Going negative: the ECB's experience" Speech at 35th Congress of the European Economic Association Frankfurt am Main, 26 August 2020.

Smits, R. (2005) "The Role of the ESCB in Banking Supervision" in Amicorum and Garavelli (2005) pp. 199-212.

Solans, E. D. (2000) "Preparing the next steps until 2002: Introduction of the euro banknotes and coins" Speech to European Financial Markets Association seminar "2002: the euro in circulation". Dec. 11, 2000. www.ecb.int/press/key/date/2000/html/sp001211.en.html.

Subramanian, M., Taghizadeh-Hesary, F., and Kim, C.J. (2020) "Creation and Evolution of European Economic and Monetary Union: Lessons for Asian Economic Integration" ADBI Working Paper No. 1126. April 2020.

Takemiya, M. (2021) "Cambodia's digital currency can show other central banks the way" Paymentsjournal.com. August 30, 2021.

Tavlas, G. S. (1993) "The 'New' Theory of Optimum Currency Areas" The World Economy, pp. 663-685.

Tumusiime-Mutebile, E. (2010) "The Road to monetary union in East Africa" Keynote address at validation workshop of the draft final report of the monetary union study. Kampala, Uganda. BIS Review. 12/2010.

U.S. President's Working Group on Financial Markets (2021) Report on Stablecoins. November 2021.

van den Berg, C. (2005) The Making of the Statute of the European System of Central Banks: An Application of Checks and Balances. Dutch University Press. 2005.

Venner, K.D. (2007). *The Experience of the ECCU and its Relevance to the Gulf Cooperation Council Case.* Presentation at Dubai Council for Economic Analysis. November 2007.

Vergote, O., W. Studener, I. Efthymiadis, N. Merriman. (2010) "Main Drivers of the ECB Financial Accounts and ECB Financial Strength over the first 11 Years" ECB Occasional Paper No. 111.

Winkler, A., F. Mazzaferro, C. Nerlich, and C. Thimann. (2004) "Official Dollarisation/Euroisation: Motives, Features, and Policy Implications of Current Cases." ECB Occasional Paper No 11.

World Economic Forum. (2020) Central Bank Digital Currency Policy-Maker Toolkit. January 2020.

Wredenborg, S (2010) "Macroprudential oversight in the EU and related information needs" Presentation at the Joint Africa Institute, Tunis, March 19, 2010.

Wolf, M. (2010). "The eurozone crisis is now a nightmare for Germany" Financial Times. March 10, 2010. p. A15.

Zerohedge (2010) "Titlos SPV – Back in the Spotlight" Zerohedge.com. February 21, 2010.

Zilioli, C. (2005) "National Emergency Powers and Exclusive Community Competences – A Crack in the Dam?" in Amicorum and Garavelli (2005) p. 115-133.

Zilioli, C. and Selmayr, M. (2001) The Law of the European Central Bank. (Oxford: Hart Publishing).

Author

Russell Krueger has a Ph.D. in international economics from American University, Washington, D.C., USA. He has worked at the U.S. Department of Commerce, U.S. Federal Reserve Board, and the IMF where he was part of an IMF team dealing with statistical preparations for the European Monetary Union. Upon retirement, he worked as statistical consultant to the Islamic Financial Services Board in Kuala Lumpur, Malaysia.

Much of the material in this volume was investigated during a year-long sabbatical to study currency union preparations at the European Central Bank and Asian Development Bank Institute in Tokyo.

www.ingramcontent.com/pod-product-compliance
Lightning Source LLC
Chambersburg PA
CBHW082120210326
41599CB00031B/5819

* 9 7 8 0 5 7 8 2 6 6 8 6 2 *